A WORD GEOGRAPHY *of* ENGLAND

HAROLD ORTON and NATHALIA WRIGHT

A WORD GEOGRAPHY *of* ENGLAND

1974

SEMINAR PRESS *LONDON · NEW YORK · SAN FRANCISCO*
A SUBSIDIARY OF HARCOURT BRACE JOVANOVICH, PUBLISHERS

G
1816
.E3
.07

SEMINAR PRESS LIMITED
24/28 Oval Road,
London, NW1 7DX

United States Edition published by

SEMINAR PRESS INC
111 Fifth Avenue
New York, New York 10003

Copyright © 1974 by H. Orton and N. Wright

All Rights Reserved

No part of this book may be reproduced in any form, by photostat, microfilm, or any other means, without written permission from the publishers

Library of Congress Catalog Card No: 74–10331
ISBN: 0–12–785608–0

Printed in Great Britain
by The Whitefriars Press Ltd, London and Tonbridge.

PREFACE

The word maps appearing in this volume are based upon the material contained in the *Survey of English Dialects* (for bibliographical particulars of which see Book List, p. 32). For permission to use this material, which is the copyright of the University of Leeds, we are greatly indebted to the University and to Mr. Stewart F. Sanderson, Director of the Institute of Dialect and Folk Life Studies, where the manuscripts of all the field-recordings concerned are now housed.

The book is intended for the use of students of the English language and of English culture, and particularly for those in universities and teacher-training colleges. If it should in any way succeed in promoting the study of our mother-tongue, especially in the British Isles, the United States, Canada, Australia, and New Zealand, we should indeed be content.

To the various friends who have encouraged us to produce this book, we are grateful, especially to Mr. Sanderson, who granted us the full use of the amenities of his Institute. We have also received much typing assistance from Mrs. Lynn Kidd, secretary in the English Department of the University of Tennessee, and from Miss Jane Elmore, Mrs. Jean Graham, Mrs. Ann Smith, and Mrs. Debra Wagner, graduate students in the same Department. Mr. Hew Dobson, lately cartographer in the above-mentioned Institute, drew the map on the dust-jacket. We also wish to thank our publishers for their interested support and especially Mr. R. G. Thixton, for his invaluable cooperation, and Mr. R. Hollidge the cartographer, for his skilful preparation of our maps.

For the record it is perhaps important to state that Harold Orton wrote the whole of the Introduction and that Nathalia Wright drew the draft maps.

July, 1974

H. O.
N. W.

03290

TO
JOAN

Table of Contents

Abbreviations

a	*ante* before
adj	adjective
AF	Anglo-French
AN	Anglo-Norman
Angl	Anglian
app	apparently
Bd	Bedfordshire
Bk	Buckinghamshire
Brk	Berkshire
c[1]	central, *circa* about (acc context)
cf	*confer* compare
Ch	Cheshire
Co	Cornwall
conn w	connected with
Cu	Cumberland
D	Devon
Da	Danish
Db	Derbyshire
Do	Dorsetshire
Du	Dutch
Du (in county names)	Durham
e	east
EAngl	East Anglia(n)
Edd	editors
EM	East Midland(s)
EME	Early Middle English
EScand	East Scandinavian
Ess	Essex
f	formed from
F	French
Fl	Flemish
Gael	Gaelic
g	gesticulate
Gl	Gloucestershire
Ha	Hampshire
He	Herefordshire
Hu	Huntingdonshire
i	indicate, imitate
Icel	Icelandic
imit orig	imitative origin
Ind orig	Indian origin
inf	infinitive
Ir	Irish
K	Kent
L	Lincolnshire
La	Lancashire
LANE	*The Linguistic Atlas of New England*
Lat	Latin
Lei	Leicestershire
LG	Low German
LME	Late Middle English
loc f ns	local field names
loc pl ns	local place names
LOE	Late Old English
M	Map
Man	Isle of Man
MDu	Middle Dutch
ME	Middle English
Midl	Midland(s)
MLG	Middle Low German
Mon	Monmouthshire
MSw	Modern Swedish
MxL	Middlesex and London
n	north
Nb	Northumberland
nc	north-central
nd	not defined
ndg	not defined grammatically
ne	north-east

[1] This letter, as well as e, nc, ne, nw, s, se and sw, is attached to the county abbreviations to form composites as needed.

nf	not found
Nf	Norfolk
Norw	Norwegian
Nt	Nottinghamshire
Nth	Northamptonshire
nu	not used
nw	north-west
OCorn	Old Cornish
OE	Old English
OED	*Oxford English Dictionary*
OF	Old French
OI	Old Icelandic
ON	Old Norse
On	C. T. Onions, *The Oxford Dictionary of English Etymology*
ONF	Old Norman French
onomat orig	onomatopoeic origin
orig	origin
orig obsc	origin obscure
orig unkn	origin unknown
Oxf	Oxfordshire
p	point to
perh	perhaps
pl	plural
poss	possibly
pp	past participle
pres	presumably
prob	probably
prsg	present singular
pt	past tense
ptpl	past tense plural
R	Rutland
ref	referring to
repr	represent(s)
s	south
Sa	Shropshire
sb	substantive
Scand	Scandinavian
Scot orig	Scots origin
se	south-east
SED	*Survey of English Dialects*
Sf	Suffolk
sg	singular
So	Somerset
Sr	Surrey
St	Staffordshire
St E	Standard English
sv	*sub verbo* under the word
sw	south-west
Sx	Sussex
v	verb
var	variant
vbl n	verbal noun
w	west
W	Wiltshire
Wa	Warwickshire
We	Westmorland
WM	West Midland(s)
Wo	Worcestershire
Y	Yorkshire
YER	Yorkshire East Riding
YNR	Yorkshire North Riding
YWR	Yorkshire West Riding

Symbols and Conventions

□	show a picture
superior *	hypothetical etymological form
superior *	(before a date) first recording of compound concerned
superior +	additional response

MED encloses dates of composition of texts in round brackets. OED encloses certain dates of occurrence of words in square brackets for "subsidiary purposes." We follow these practices in the legends and footnotes.

Words in capital letters are keywords in SED.

Map of Numbered Localities in the Network

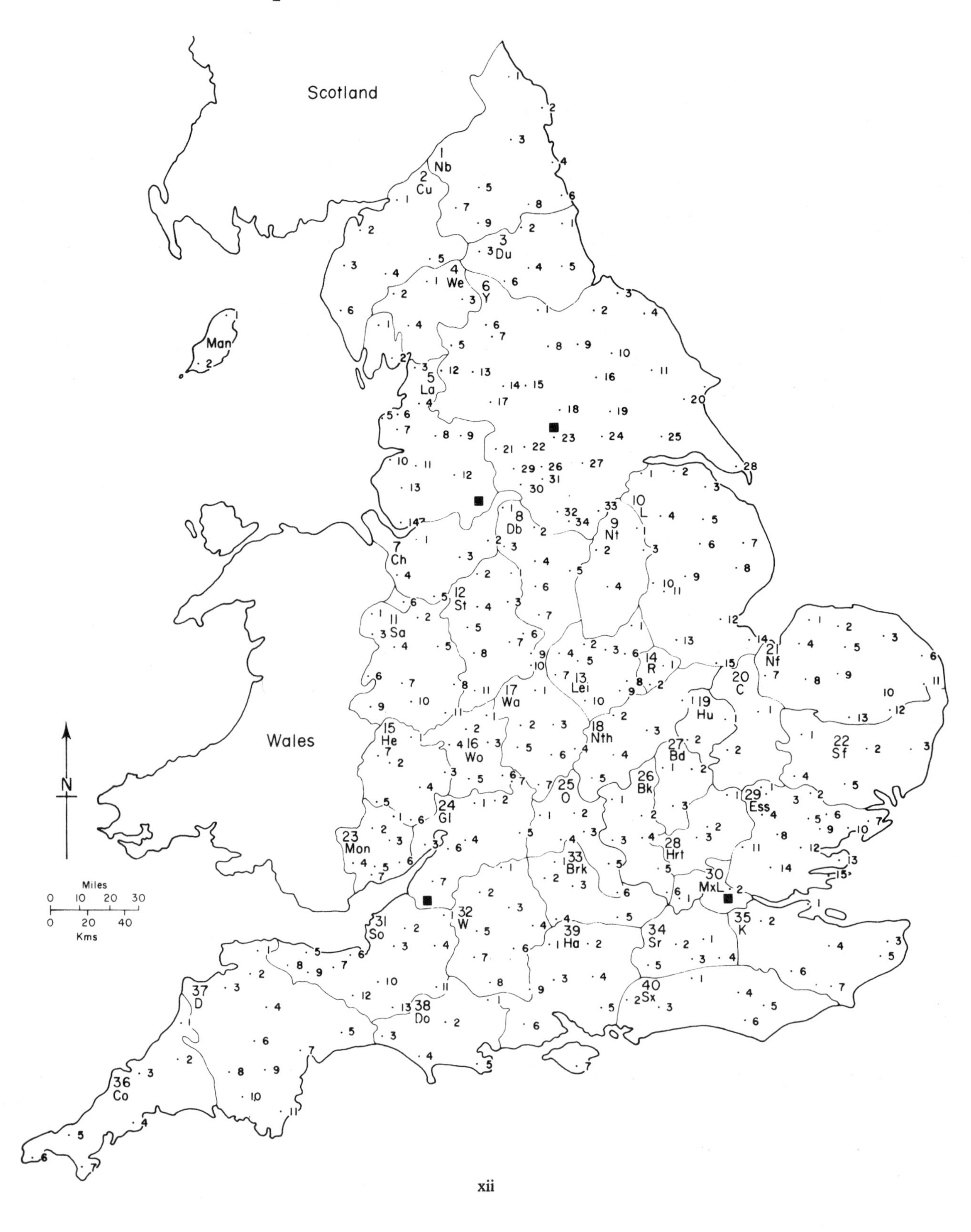

List of Localities in the Network

1 Nb
- 1 Lowick
- 2 Embleton
- 3 Thropton
- 4 Ellington
- 5 Wark
- 6 Earsdon
- 7 Haltwhistle
- 8 Heddon-on-the-Wall
- 9 Allendale

2 Cu
- 1 Longtown
- 2 Abbey Town
- 3 Brigham
- 4 Threlkeld
- 5 Hunsonby
- 6 Gosforth

3 Du
- 1 Washington
- 2 Ebchester
- 3 Wearhead
- 4 Witton-le-Wear
- 5 Bishop Middleham
- 6 Eggleston

4 We
- 1 Great Strickland
- 2 Patterdale
- 3 Soulby
- 4 Staveley-in-Kendal

5 La
- 1 Coniston
- 2 Cartmel
- 3 Yealand
- 4 Dolphinholme
- 5 Fleetwood
- 6 Pilling
- 7 Thistleton
- 8 Ribchester
- 9 Read
- 10 Marshside
- 11 Eccleston
- 12 Harwood
- 13 Bickerstaffe
- 14 Halewood

6 Y
- 1 Melsonby
- 2 Stokesley
- 3 Skelton
- 4 Egton
- 5 Dent
- 6 Muker
- 7 Askrigg
- 8 Bedale
- 9 Borrowby
- 10 Helmsley
- 11 Rillington
- 12 Burton-in-Lonsdale
- 13 Horton-in-Ribbles-dale
- 14 Grassington
- 15 Pateley Bridge
- 16 Easingwold
- 17 Gargrave
- 18 Spofforth
- 19 York
- 20 Nafferton
- 21 Heptonstall
- 22 Wibsey
- 23 Leeds
- 24 Cawood
- 25 Newbald
- 26 Thornhill
- 27 Carleton
- 28 Welwick
- 29 Golcar
- 30 Holmbridge
- 31 Skelmanthorpe
- 32 Ecclesfield
- 33 Tickhill
- 34 Sheffield

6a Man
- 1 Andreas
- 2 Ronague

7 Ch
- 1 Kingsley
- 2 Rainow
- 3 Swettenham
- 4 Farndon
- 5 Audlem
- 6 Hanmer (Flintshire)

8 Db
- 1 Charlesworth
- 2 Bamford
- 3 Burbage
- 4 Youlgreave
- 5 Stonebroom
- 6 Kniveton
- 7 Sutton-on-the-Hill

9 Nt
- 1 North Wheatley
- 2 Cuckney
- 3 South Clifton
- 4 Oxton

10 L
- 1 Eastoft
- 2 Saxby
- 3 Keelby

4 Willoughton
5 Tealby
6 Wragby
7 Swaby
8 Old Bolingbroke
9 Scopwick
10 Beckingham
11 Fulbeck
12 Sutterton
13 Swinstead
14 Lutton
15 Crowland

11 Sa
1 Weston Rhyn
2 Prees
3 Llanymynech
4 Montford
5 Kinnersley
6 Chirbury
7 All Stretton
8 Hilton
9 Clun
10 Diddlebury
11 Kinlet

12 St
1 Warslow
2 Mow Cop
3 Alton
4 Barlaston
5 Ellenhall
6 Hoar Cross
7 Mavesyn Ridware
8 Lapley
9 Edingale
10 Wigginton
11 Himley

13 Lei
1 Harby
2 Hathern
3 Seagrave
4 Packington
5 Markfield
6 Great Dalby
7 Sheepy Magna
8 Goadby
9 Carlton Curlieu
10 Ullesthorpe

14 R
1 Empingham
2 Lyddington

15 He
1 Brimfield
2 Weobley
3 Cradley
4 Checkley
5 Longtown
6 Whitchurch
7 Lyonshall

16 Wo
1 Romsley
2 Hartlebury
3 Hanbury
4 Clifton on Teme
5 Earls Croome
6 Offenham
7 Bretforton

17 Wa
1 Nether Whitacre
2 Hockley Heath
3 Stoneleigh
4 Napton-on-the-Hill
5 Aston Cantlow
6 Lighthorne
7 Shipston-on-Stour

18 Nth
1 Warmington
2 Welford
3 Little Harrowden
4 Kislingbury
5 Sulgrave

19 Hu
1 Warboys
2 Kimbolton

20 C
1 Little Downham
2 Elsworth

21 Nf
1 Docking
2 Great Snoring
3 Blickling
4 Grimston
5 North Elmham
6 Ludham
7 Outwell
8 Gooderstone
9 Shipdham
10 Ashwellthorpe
11 Reedham
12 Pulham St. Mary
13 Garboldisham

22 Sf
1 Tuddenham
2 Mendlesham
3 Yoxford
4 Kedington
5 Kersey

23 Mon
1 Skenfrith
2 Llanellen
3 Raglan
4 Crosskeys
5 Llanfrechfa
6 Shirenewton
7 Newport

24 Gl
1 Deerhurst
2 Gretton
3 Bream
4 Whiteshill
5 Sherborne
6 Slimbridge
7 Latteridge

25 Oxf
1 Kingham
2 Steeple Aston

3 Islip
4 Eynsham
5 Cuxham
6 Binfield Heath

26 Bk
1 Tingewick
2 Stewkley
3 Long Crendon
4 Buckland
5 Coleshill
6 Horton

27 Bd
1 Turvey
2 Great Barford
3 Harlington

28 Hrt
1 Therfield
2 Codicote
3 Wheathampstead

29 Ess
1 Great Chesterford
2 Belchamp Walter
3 Cornish Hall End
4 Henham
5 Stisted
6 West Bergholt
7 Little Bentley
8 High Easter
9 Tiptree
10 East Mersea
11 Netteswell
12 Little Baddow
13 Tillingham
14 Doddinghurst
15 Canewdon

30 MxL
1 Harmondsworth
2 Hackney

31 So
1 Weston
2 Blagdon
3 Wedmore
4 Coleford
5 Wootton Courtenay
6 Stogursey
7 Stogumber
8 Withypool
9 Brompton Regis
10 Stoke St Gregory
11 Horsington
12 Pitminster
13 Merriott

32 W
1 Ashton Keynes
2 Sutton Benger
3 Avebury
4 Burbage
5 Steeple Ashton
6 Netheravon
7 Sutton Veny
8 Fovant
9 Whiteparish

33 Brk
1 Buckland
2 Uffington
3 West Ilsley
4 Inkpen
5 Swallowfield

34 Sr
1 Walton-on-the-Hill
2 East Clandon
3 Coldharbour
4 Outwood
5 Thursley

35 K
1 Stoke
2 Farningham
3 Staple
4 Warren Street
5 Denton
6 Goudhurst
7 Appledore

36 Co
1 Kilkhampton
2 Altarnun
3 Egloshayle
4 St Ewe
5 Gwinear
6 St Buryan
7 Mullion

37 D
1 Parracombe
2 Swimbridge
3 Weare Giffard
4 Chawleigh
5 Gittisham
6 South Zeal
7 Kennford
8 Peter Tavy
9 Widecombe in-the-Moor
10 Cornwood
11 Blackawton

38 Do
1 Handley
2 Ansty
3 Whitchurch Canonicorum
4 Portesham
5 Kingston

39 Ha
1 Hatherden
2 Oakley
3 King's Somborne
4 New Alresford
5 Hambledon
6 Burley
7 Whitwell

40 Sx
1 Warnham
2 East Harting
3 Sutton
4 Fletching
5 Horam
6 Firle

INTRODUCTION

I. Editorial Methods and Mapping Procedures

The words mapped in this book result from an investigation into English dialects carried out from the Department of English Language and Medieval English Literature at the University of Leeds during the eleven years between 1950 and 1961. A reasonably full account of this project, including its publication programme, was given in H. O.'s *Introduction* (1962) to the SED. A summary description follows.

The English Dialect Survey—a convenient title for the investigation—was planned by Eugen Dieth, at the time Professor of English Language at the Swiss University of Zurich, and H. O., working in close collaboration. Its ultimate aim was the compilation of a comprehensive atlas of dialectal English as spoken by the older generation. This involved a concentrated investigation of the speech usages of the farmer and of his household and acquaintances. The investigations were restricted in this way because the initiators of the Survey had long been convinced that the agricultural communities best preserve the most conservative kind of vernacular speech.

With this objective in mind, a questionnaire of over 1300 virtual questions was specially drawn up, and, after extensive testing in various parts of the country, was applied by nine trained fieldworkers to carefully selected, elderly, dialect-speaking informants in 313 communities distributed all over England. The *Questionnaire* was organized in nine books or sections, the themes of which, in order, were: The Farm; Farming; Animals; Nature; The House and Housekeeping; The Human Body; Numbers, Time and Weather; Social Activities; States, Actions, Relations. All the questions were drawn up in full and the fieldworkers were directed to ask each question in the form set out in the *Questionnaire*. In this way strictly comparable responses would be more likely to emerge during the interviews with the informants. Formal questions could obviously produce more or less conditioned responses. Hence in order to avoid this as much as possible, the fieldworker always endeavoured to establish a friendly "pupil-and-master" relationship with his informant, who naturally played the role of master.

The informants' responses to the various questions were transcribed impressionistically in the phonetic alphabet of the International Phonetic Association by nine trained fieldworkers. Further, during the interviews they noted down any snippets from the informants' conversation that might bear upon the linguistic problems implicit in the *Questionnaire*. Unfortunately the interviews were not tape-recorded. Indeed, it was not until 1952 that a tape-recorder—the instrument had only recently been invented—first became available to the Survey; even then lack of money prevented the acquisition of all the needed apparatus. However, on completing the interviews the fieldworkers either tape-recorded their most suitable informant at once or did so subsequently. In order to obtain uninhibited examples of dialectal English, the fieldworkers encouraged the informant to talk with the utmost freedom about matters of general or personal interest, e.g. about how people and things were not what they used to be, about matters of special local interest, or about some aspect or other of the informant's occupation like ploughing, hedging, stacking. But at all times his free, natural speech was the target. The primary interest was not the substance of what he said, but rather how he said it. It is the intention, sooner or later, to publish representative specimens of these tape-recordings, together with orthographical and phonetic transcriptions.

All the words mapped below are to be found in the above-mentioned SED, which, in twelve books of "Basic Material", contains all the responses and relevant illustrative material collected during the fieldwork of the Survey. All this material is arranged in lists, which include well over 400,000 items of information. This abundant array of linguistic facts has, nevertheless, presented certain mapping problems, which are mentioned below.

In the first place, it has been no easy task to limit the notions[1] mapped to 207. The 251 word-maps actually included here have been selected from some 750. Our preferences have in general been influenced or determined by several factors, including the intrinsic interest of the notion to philologists (e.g. AXLE M178, COW-HOUSE M2, 2A, 2B, 2C, DIG M29, GORSE M33, RIVULET M39, 39A, SHARE M40, STACKS M41, each of which was expressed by two different words in Pre-Conquest times), its familiarity to the general public (e.g. BILBERRIES M181, CHAPS M137, DONKEY M7, FLEAS M70, HAWS M11, 11A, 11B, 11C, LITTER M157, SHREW-MOUSE M165, 165A, SWEETS M196), its wealth of expressions (e.g. EARWIGS M143, 143A, PIGSTY M22, SCARECROW M80, SNACK M115, WEAKLING [piglet] M206), its importance as a link with the speech of the U.S.A. (e.g. AFTERMATH M97, 97A, COME IN [call to cows, horses, pigs] M3, 3A, 4, 4A, 5, 81, 81A, COW-HOUSE M2, 2A, 2B, FUNNEL M10, GUTTER M123, 123A, PET-LAMB M126, SPRING ONIONS M105, 105A, 105B, WHINNY M129), and its successful elicitation of significant expressions derived from foreign sources (e.g. HEN-HOUSE M151, LEFT-HANDED M119, 119A, POLE-CAT M108, RAT M104, SLEDGE M112, STACKS M41, UDDER M50, 50A, WAGON M118).

In the second place, having chosen the notions for inclusion, we had to decide which of the emergent expressions deserved to be mapped. It soon became clear that it was both impracticable and imprudent to try to display all the responses and incidental material elicited by one question on a single map. The attempt usually produced clutter and obscurity. For example, 88 words were recorded for LEFT-HANDED, 72 for WEAKLING (piglet), 46 for each of SCRAPS and HAWS, 33 for COW-HOUSE, to mention but a few. Accordingly, with the intention of exhibiting the material to the greatest possible advantage, it was decided not to put all the responses for a particular notion on one map, but to present only a few words at a time for contrastive display, and to select these for valid reasons. For example, much depended upon whether the words originated from the same source language, on the closeness of the recorded dates of occurrence in documents, on whether a particular word was a borrowing that had obviously replaced an indigenous word, or whether the words, being compounds, had a particular element in common. (The question of variation in pronunciation did not arise because this atlas is concerned primarily with lexicon, not phonology.)

In considering how best to display the expressions on maps, several factors needed attention. First, the books of Basic Material are factual: they reproduce the responses and

[1] As represented by "keywords" in the Questionnaire (see *Survey of English Dialects*, pp. 44, 46-47).

ancillary information in phonetic transcription. In this respect, therefore, SED corresponds to all those national linguistic atlases that simply register the responses and offer no interpretations. Second, our maps were to be interpretative and show areas of distribution with sufficient clarity. This could be accomplished either by shading or by symbols. But shading can result in considerable obscurity; and it also tends to conceal outlying occurrences. Further, symbols are expensive to insert on a map; and, moreover, may not immediately reveal the distributional areas clearly enough. Third, maps may be multicoloured, or two-coloured, e.g. black on white, or grey, or even both on white. Fourth, linguistic boundaries are easily and simply indicated by lines, whether isoglossic or heteroglossic. Accordingly, after giving due consideration to all these points, it was decided to make maps that were simple, interpretative and isoglossic, as well as two-coloured, viz. black on white.

The base map itself requires little explanation. It shows an outline of England and, merely for "decorative" purposes, Wales and Southern Scotland. The positions of several cities are shown in order to facilitate the reader's orientation. County boundaries are included and the counties themselves are numbered consecutively from north to south and from west to east concurrently. The Isle of Man is listed separately and follows 6Y, i.e. Yorkshire. County abbreviations, as used by the English Place-Name Society[1], are also inserted. Dots represent each of the 313 places investigated. These are numbered within the individual counties from north to south, as well as from west to east. Distances are shown on a scale in both miles and kilometres.

To assist the reader in appreciating the possible linguistic influences of geographical features and centres of dense population, a pull-out map is provided following the word maps. It shows the main rivers, high ground over 300 feet variously shaded to indicate significant contour levels, and several of the chief towns and cities as included on the base map. But the county boundaries are excluded because they appear on the base map.

Our map shows areas of lexical distribution, i.e. regions characterized by the employment of an individual word. They do so by means of isoglosses, which enclose areas throughout which a particular expression is found. Thus the isogloss is a boundary line marking off clearly on the map one distributional area from an adjoining area in which the expression under consideration is either not recorded or else occurs only exceptionally. When two adjacent localities use different words, the isogloss in question is drawn approximately midway between them. Thus isoglosses do not in fact mark off separate divisions precisely, but are only rough boundaries between one feature and another.

The chief novelty in our mapping procedures concerns the method of indicating in the labelled areas of distribution the occurrence of words listed in the map legend. The practice in this case differs from that followed in non-labelled areas, where distributions are not under consideration. In these labelled areas, the locality dot has been given the additional function of representing an occurrence of the labelled form, but not so in non-labelled areas, where it always retains its primary function of representing one locality in the network of places investigated. Our mapping procedures may be specified in detail.

1. The locality dot in a labelled area of distribution has a twofold function. It represents not only the locality concerned, but also an occurrence of the labelled lexical feature.

[1] Except "O", which is expanded to "Oxf", thus avoiding confusion with the numeral.

2. Distributional areas are given arabic numerals, which are explained in the legend.

3. When, as often happens, the labelled item has not been recorded at a particular locality, the dot concerned is replaced by a small St. Andrew's Cross and completely obscured by the point of intersection of the two slants. Thus the cross indicates not only the locality, but also that the particular feature was not recorded by the fieldworker during his interview with the informant, though admittedly there is no certainty that the feature was not in fact used in the locality.

4. When a locality has been found using, not the labelled form, but some other item listed in the legend, the dot in question is again replaced by the cross, which is then enclosed by the symbol representing the intrusive element: thus ⩓, ⊓.

5. When a second item in the legend occurs collaterally with the labelled item, the locality dot is enclosed by the symbol chosen to represent it: thus ∧, ⊓.

6. If in addition, however, a third item listed in the legend occurs alongside the labelled item, the symbol representing it is here placed on the left of the composite symbol involved: thus ⊓ , ∧ .

7. If, again, two items in the legend are used to the exclusion of the labelled item, the locality dot is replaced, as usual, by the cross enclosed by the symbol for one of the intruders, the symbol for the other being inserted on the left of the composite: thus ⊓∧, ○∧.

8. Further, if because of its remoteness a particular item cannot be included in the distributional area to which it properly belongs, but instead occurs in a non-labelled area, the symbol for this outlier is then placed so that its top centre entirely covers the dot marking the locality: thus ∧, ⊓, ○.

9. When it has seemed desirable to map items that show no characteristic distribution but occur sporadically over the network of localities, they are represented by symbols placed so as to obscure the dots concerned, as described in 8 above. This has been done only rarely.

10. Where a cancellation would naturally occur between two isoglosses, it is usually indicated by placing the cross, the cancellation symbol, in the larger area.

11. When it is necessary to indicate precisely the area set off by the isogloss, the line in question has been provided with small pointers or barbs placed near each end and turned in the appropriate direction: thus ⊥⊥ . When, however, an isogloss separates adjoining areas of distribution, the barbs are not needed and are therefore omitted. Isoglosses are normally continued beyond coast lines and national borders.

On referring to the books of Basic Material it will be observed that some of the responses, though not many, are preceded by "s.w.", others by "n.f.", and still others by "n.u.". These abbreviations stand for respectively "suggested word", "not found", and "not used". (An additional abbreviation "s.f." representing "suggested form" also occurs; it signifies that the form of the cited word was in fact suggested to the informant by the fieldworker and accepted by him as being relevant. Since, however, it concerns a question of phonology, such forms do not enter into consideration here.) The abbreviations used in SED are explained in the *Introduction*, p. 25. Expressions preceded by "s.w." were approved by the informants and have accordingly been included in the maps without special mention in the footnotes except when it seemed necessary (see FLEAS M70). Further, "n.f." signifies that the expression was actually both known and used by the informant but that the informant believed that the object in question was "not found" in the locality. These words, too, have been duly considered when making our maps, and pointed out in the footnotes (see, e.g., *stackyard* M193, 4We.4, 6Y.13 and *sledge* M112, 40Sx. 2). Then there is the abbreviation "n.u.", which means unequivocally that the expression it precedes was in fact "not used" by the informant. In this case the word has been disregarded on the maps, though it is mentioned in the footnotes (see, e.g., *aftermath* M97, M97A, 6Y.20, *wagon* M118, 6Y.13). On the other hand, very many of the individual items reproduced in the Basic Material include expressions marked by a prefixed, superior, unfilled circle. Such forms have been adduced from the incidental material, which the fieldworker actually noted down from the informant's conversation during the interview. We regard them as collateral evidence of the highest importance; in our view, they have equal validity with the responses. We have therefore had no hestitation whatsoever in making use of them on our maps. Finally, in this connexion it has often happened that the fieldworkers have recorded the response in its plural form instead of the required singular; and, vice versa, the singular for the plural. Our feeling here is that the actual occurrence of the word is significant, not its grammatical number, and that the discrepancy might, therefore, be justifiably ignored on the maps. In the footnotes, however, the distinction has been mentioned when necessary.

All the words displayed on the maps are listed alphabetically in the map legends (on which see below). Many of these are simplexes, i.e. have no prefix or suffix or other components. They present no mapping problems. Other expressions are "solid compounds": they include an attribute that is essential to the compound and clinches the reference; strictly speaking they are semantically indivisible. See, e.g., *belly-band* M180, *cow-house* M2B, *dove-cote* M86, *farm-yard* M94, *mould-board* M114A. These, again, ordinarily offer no difficulty. But occasionally they drop the attribute and thus require special consideration, as described below. On the other hand, certain simplexes often emerge in combination with a prefixed attribute that enables speedier identification of the reference. See, e.g., *collar* (for horses) M92, (*plough-*) *handles* M187, *stall* M166, *stile* M74. Their treatment on the maps raises certain complications and these have been dealt with as indicated below.

Simplexes are also found alternating collaterally with compounds including the simplex itself to which is attached an attributive to make the meaning more precise. Such sporadic compounds may be represented by the formula (X-)A/B/C. . . , the X symbolizing the optional attribute. See, e.g., in addition to those mentioned above like *collar* and *stile*, (*cart-*)*axle* M178, *dregs* M87, (*scythe-*)*handles* M110, *pond* M38, *gate-posts* M75, and *stile* M74. In these cases, the simplex alone is listed in the legend and mapped as such. In the occasional compounds, however, the attributes have only subsidiary importance. They can therefore be conveniently mapped as simplexes, provided that, in the interests of accuracy, the compounds themselves, together with their locality reference, are not ignored on the maps. This is why we have considered it essential to enumerate these forms in the footnotes (see, e.g., the maps cited above).

This procedure offers a clue to the treatment of the afore-mentioned solid compounds, from which informants occasionally drop the initial attributive element as being unessential. See, e.g., *cart-shed* M199A, where the compounds *cart-linhay/lodge/shed* sometimes emerge without the attribute *cart*, which might ordinarily be regarded as essential to precise meaning. In this case the compound is structurally "solid" and of the type X-A/B/C. . . , with occasional alternating simplexes A/B/C etc. Since, however, the apparently essential attribute is dropped comparatively rarely, we have preferred to regard the expressions as compounds of the type X-A/B/C. . . , which sometimes emerge as the simplexes A/B/C. . . . Thus we put the common form, i.e. the compound, both in the legend and on the map, and cite the exception, i.e. the simplex, in the footnote.

A special type of alternative usage is observable at VI.7.13 LEFT-HANDED M119, 119A, where we sometimes find *cack*, *keggy* and *coochy* instead of compounds containing these words in combination with second elements. Note also *shaft* and *thill* for SHAFT-HORSE M120 at, respectively, 3Du.2 and 39Ha.2. The feature in question, however, is rare.

Each map includes a legend containing the notion mapped and its reference number in the Dieth-Orton *Questionnaire*, as well as a list of the terms mapped, their etymologies when known, the date, if available, of their first documentary record in the meaning concerned, and, when necessary, footnotes. The etymologies are cited from the *Oxford English Dictionary*, the (incomplete) *Middle English Dictionary*, and Onions' *Oxford Dictionary of English Etymology*, the etymologies from the last named being accorded special attention. Dates of occurrence, except for those words recorded in Old English, are reproduced from the *OED* unless an earlier date is mentioned by *MED*. Dates of compounds, again with the exception of those words recorded in Old English, are of interest and importance and are therefore cited and marked with the prefixed superior symbol "*".

In general, the footnotes mention, with locality references, variants of the mapped words, additional compounds containing the legend items, and any other matters of relevance. These variants may be grammatical alternatives of the mapped words, except that differences in grammatical number have been ignored on the maps. Much more often, however, they are legend items compounded with a restricting attribute. See, for example, M38, where *dew-pond* and *horse-pit* are very occasional alternatives to, respectively, *pond* and *pit* and have the function of narrowing the meaning. They are treated here as acceptable variants of the simplexes and fully entitled to consideration on the map. Accordingly, such variants have been consistently taken into account when mapping the simplexes. But they have always been enumerated in the footnotes, too. Nevertheless, the actual occurrences require two different kinds of treatment, as outlined below.

The word *stile* M74 may be taken as a good example. At locality 6Y.12 *stee-hole* alone is the response form, not *stee*, one of the words being mapped. At locality 6Y.17, however, *stee-hole* is found in addition to *stee*. In the first case, *stee-hole* has actually been represented on the map just as if it had been a genuine example of *stee*, for it clearly establishes that *stee*, rather than *stile*, is the term in local use. Yet to prevent any misunderstanding upon the point, *stee(-hole)*, with appropriate reference, is specifically mentioned in the footnote. On the other hand, in the second case, where *stee-hole* occurs collaterally with *stee*, the compound form is merely reproduced in the footnote, but to indicate beyond doubt that it is indeed additional, the locality number in the reference is marked with a superior plus sign. (See, also, *hedge-sides* M6, 12St.$^{+}$2/$^{+}$3.)

The footnotes also deal with compounds like *hedge-backs* M6, the map itself being concerned with the distribution of *hedge* versus *dike*, when the latter expression refers not to stones, but to bushes. All the compounds with initial *hedge-* enumerated in the footnote in question no doubt demonstrate that *hedge* at these localities refers to bushes and accordingly must receive attention on the map. Similarly, the compounds with initial *dike-* cited in the same footnote equally prove that the word at the localities concerned denotes *hedge*, not *wall*, and therefore deserves notice here. Additional examples are to be found on M33, where *furze-bush*, *gorse-bush* and *whin-bush/buss* certainly evidence that at the localities under consideration the terms *furze*, *gorse* and *whin* are both used and differentiated. Other examples abound.

The footnotes also include comments, some of which relate to grammar, about the material mapped.

Lastly, dialect expressions in the footnotes have, when possible, been etymologized.

II. Brief History of the Vocabulary of English

English was brought to the British Isles by the Anglo-Saxons who began to settle in Britain at latest by the middle of the 5th century. According to the Venerable Bede's *Ecclesiastical History* (731), they comprised Angles, Saxons and Jutes. But there were Frisians too. All of them belonged to pagan Germanic tribes who had previously been domiciled in the northern parts of Belgium, the Netherlands and present-day West Germany, i.e. the region stretching roughly from the estuary of the Rhine to the southern end of the Jutland Peninsula in eastern Denmark.

On coming here the Anglo-Saxons, as they are usually called today, found England or at least the south-eastern part of it inhabited by romanized Celts, who only a generation or so earlier had been enjoying the privileges of membership of the Roman Empire. They had been part of this for some 400 years beginning in A.D. 43, at which time their Celtic forefathers, the Britons, had been successfully invaded and conquered by Roman legions. But, even before their inclusion in the Empire, Celtic tribes had inhabited Britain during several centuries. However, in A.D. 410, the Romans under threat of attacks, chiefly by Goths and Vandals, on their homeland in Italy, withdrew from Britain and left the defenceless Britons to their own destiny. During the Roman period, government officials from other sections of the Empire and educated Britons were accustomed to speaking Latin as their first or second language, but the bulk of the native population used their mother-tongue, namely British, the ancestor of Modern Welsh.

When the Roman legions withdrew from this country the Britons continued to be harassed from the north by the Picts, who, originally speakers of a non-Celtic language—indeed it was not even Indo-European—had settled in pre-Celtic times beyond the Firth of Forth in eastern Scotland and had then become to some extent celticized; and, further, they were assailed from the West by the Scots who were Irish-speaking Celts from Northern Ireland. They therefore called in the help of Anglo-Saxon tribes who, after carrying out over a long period piratical raids upon the south-eastern and southern shores of England, had been established on these shores to guard against attacks of the same kind. The mercenaries soon rebelled against the new and weaker government of the Britons and made common cause with their marauding relatives from across the North Sea. Thus began the Anglo-Saxon invasion of this country, but it was a slow, though continuous migration lasting at least a century, by which time they had secured a firm grip on the greater part of southern central and eastern England, as well as on south-eastern Scotland as far north as the Firth of Forth. During this time some of the Britons were driven into the South-West of England (some crossed the English Channel and settled in Brittany where their language continues to flourish as Breton), as well as into Wales and north-western England. Yet many must have survived alongside or subject to the Anglo-Saxons, as is implied by the survival to a much later period of Celtic patterns of settlement, customary rights, and place-names.

The language, or, preferably, group of closely connected dialects, brought to this country by the Anglo-Saxons is today normally called Old English, a term which is applied to the period between the earliest settlements and about 1100, by which date the linguistic effects of the Norman Conquest of 1066 had become manifest. This accords with the names given to the two later (arbitrary) stages of the language, namely Middle English, which covers the period 1100 to 1450, and Modern English (from 1450 onwards).

Old English belongs to the West Germanic branch of the Germanic family of languages formerly spoken in northern Europe. Its affinities were closest with Frisian used in the Frisian Islands lying off the coast of the Netherlands; and they were rather less close with the West Germanic languages to the east and north. There was a fairly close connexion with Old Saxon, the ancestor of the Modern Low German dialects, Old Low Franconian, from which descends Dutch and Flemish, and further to the south, a remoter relationship with Old High German, chiefly today represented by Standard German. To the north of the West Germanic group were the North Germanic languages spoken in Scandinavia. These fall into two divisions, namely Old West Scandinavian, the forerunner of Norwegian and its derivatives Icelandic and Faroese (still spoken in the Faroe Islands), and East Scandinavian, the source of both Swedish and Danish. It was not until about 1000 or so, the end of the Viking Age, that differences between the older forms of Norwegian, Danish and Swedish begin to appear in runic inscriptions. It is noteworthy that the term Scandinavian at first probably referred to the regions surrounding the southern Baltic, namely southern Sweden, the Danish Islands and Jutland, as well as to the region about the mouth of the River Elbe. Further, when the Angles vacated their homeland in southern Jutland to emigrate to northern England, it was taken over by Danes (viz. in the 5th and 6th centuries).

We may now turn to the details of the Anglo-Saxon invasions of England. The Jutes were the first of the tribes to arrive. They did not emigrate from Jutland itself, but were descended from Jutes who had moved down into north-western Germany. They settled in Kent, as well as further west in the Isle of Wight and on the opposing coast of Hampshire. The Saxons, who inhabited Holstein in northern West Germany, colonized Essex (i.e. *East Saxons*), Sussex (i.e. *South Saxons*), and Middlesex (i.e. *Middle Saxons*), as well as the region north of the upper Thames stretching as far as South Warwickshire. They also soon overwhelmed the Jutish colonies, both in the Isle of Wight and in Hampshire. The Angles, from the Angeln district of northern Schleswig, also in present-day West Germany, spread through our Midland Counties and north-eastwards as far as the Firth of Forth in Lowland Scotland.

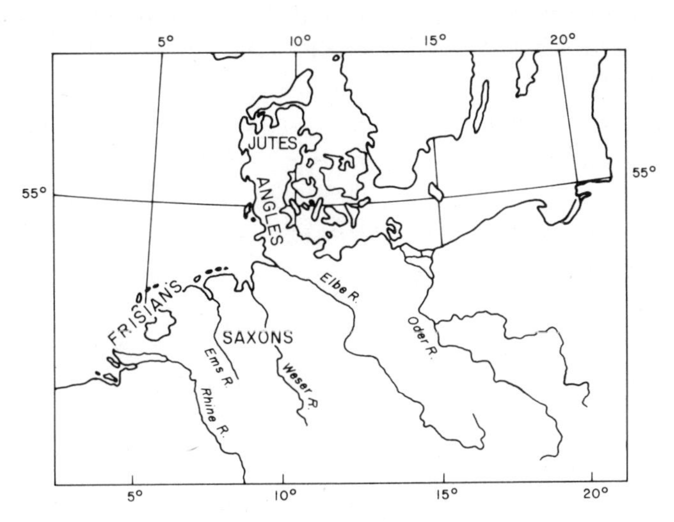

The Continental Homes of the English
(Adapted from A. C. Baugh, *A History of the English Language*, p. 55)
© 1957. By permission of Prentice Hall Inc., Englewood Cliffs, New Jersey

Old English is first recorded about A.D. 700. The language of its writings is comparatively uniform. At first sight it seems unintelligible, especially its 30,000 lines of traditional, highly sophisticated poetry covering three centuries. Its prose, of which there is a great deal including translations (from Latin), sermons, saints' lives, charters, grants (of land), and wills and even a Latin grammar, is in general, but not unexpectedly, much later than the poetry; its literary prose virtually begins late in the 9th century. Old English was a synthetic language, i.e. it used chiefly inflexional syllables rather than auxiliary words like prepositions to express grammatical relationships. Its orthography, based on the contemporary pronunciation of Latin, bore a consistent relationship to pronunciation, the vowels having "continental" values, i.e. the vowel letters, especially those representing long sounds, had about the same qualities as those of present-day European languages, not as in Standard English today. Words were stressed on the root syllable or as close to it as possible. The vowels of the other syllables consequently became more and more weakly stressed and in time lost their original quality. Inflexional syllables in nouns, adjectives and verbs were numerous. Nouns had grammatical gender, not natural, as now; and there were several (complicated) declensions. Adjectives, too, might have different case-endings chiefly according to the syntax of the phrase in which they occurred, as well as to the gender of the noun that they qualified. Verbs had a two-tense system, namely, present and past, which was beginning to be supplemented by constructions with auxiliary verbs. They fell into two categories, now termed "Strong" and "Weak". The Strong Verbs were primary (i.e. non-derived) and were conjugated by change in the quality of the stem vowel as well as by adding inflexions for person and number. The Weak Verbs were derived from other parts of speech (mainly nouns and adjectives) by the addition of suffixes and exhibited characteristic suffixes in the past tense and past participle. Since OE times, the Strong Verbs have been reduced from some 380 to about 90, whereas the

The Anglo-Saxon Settlements in England
(Adapted from H. Alexander, *The Story of Our Language*, p. 36)
Reproduced by courtesy of Thomas Nelson Limited

Weak Verbs have enormously increased in number. Indeed almost without exception (note *strive* and *thrive*) new verbs in English are conjugated weak, a term now appropriately replaced by "Regular" and the corresponding "strong" by "Irregular". The order of words in the sentence was relatively free, unlike today, when it is pretty rigid.

Dialects of some sort must surely have existed at the time of the Anglo-Saxon settlements in Britain during the 5th and 6th centuries. Yet even in the late Old English period (900–1100), when literary documents appear in relative abundance in Wessex and linguistic peculiarities begin to emerge with some regularity, the boundaries between one dialect and another are still vague and difficult to determine from the evidence available. All the same it is pretty generally agreed that there were three main Old English dialects, corresponding to the three Germanic tribes mentioned by Bede as taking part in the emigrations, namely the Angles, Saxons and Jutes. The Angles settled between the Thames and, on the eastern side of Britain, the Firth of Forth in Scotland. Their dialect is termed Anglian. But it is usually divided into two main groups: the more southerly, spoken between the Thames and the Humber-Mersey line (extending from the East Yorkshire coast to West Lancashire), is called Mercian, a term which does not cover the dialect of East Anglia, about which nothing is known; and the northern branch is customarily designated Northumbrian. The dialect of the Saxons settled south of the Thames, more particularly in Wessex, is spoken of as West Saxon. The remaining

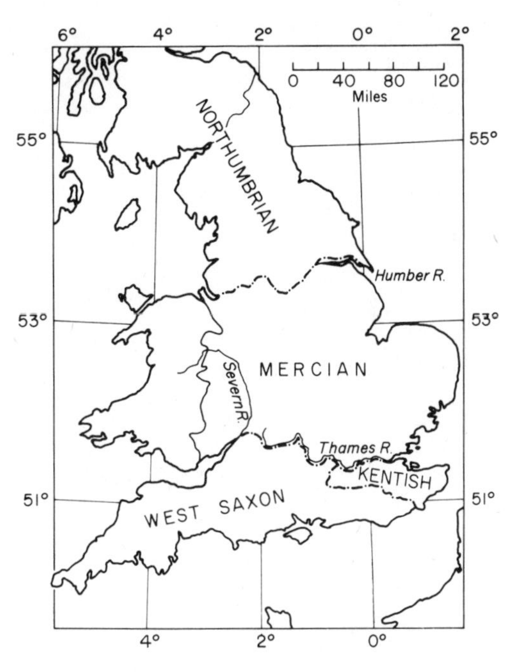

The Dialects of Old English
(Adapted from A. C. Baugh, *A History of the English Language*, p. 63)
© 1957. By permission of Prentice Hall Inc., Englewood Cliffs, New Jersey.

dialect was used by the Jutish colonists of Kent and is accordingly called Kentish. Thus our classification comprises Northumbrian, Mercian, West Saxon and Kentish.

During the Middle English period (1100–1450), the distribution of the principal dialects emerges more and more clearly. Roughly it resembles the Old English pattern. The delineation of the actual boundaries, though precise limits between adjacent dialects cannot reasonably be expected, presents serious problems, but they need not be taken into account here.

The main Middle English dialects correspond to those of Old English, but their names are conventionally changed. Northumbrian now becomes Northern. Mercian is designated Midland, with two sub-divisions called West Midland and East Midland, West Saxon is now Southern (or South Western), but Kentish retains its earlier appellation. It should be noted that whereas in the Old English period, West Saxon, centred upon the capital of Wessex, namely Winchester in Hampshire, was the most important of the Old English dialects, it was the dialect of London, where William the Conqueror at once established his capital, that was to give rise to Standard English. London English originated as a South-East Midland dialect, although, especially in its earlier stages, it contained certain Southern features. It was the dialect in which Chaucer wrote. Authors in the Middle English period always wrote in their own regional dialect. When, however, their manuscripts were copied for circulation, i.e. "published", the medieval scribes were accustomed to revise the language of the exemplar in order to make the text so copied more intelligible to their readers. In the process the

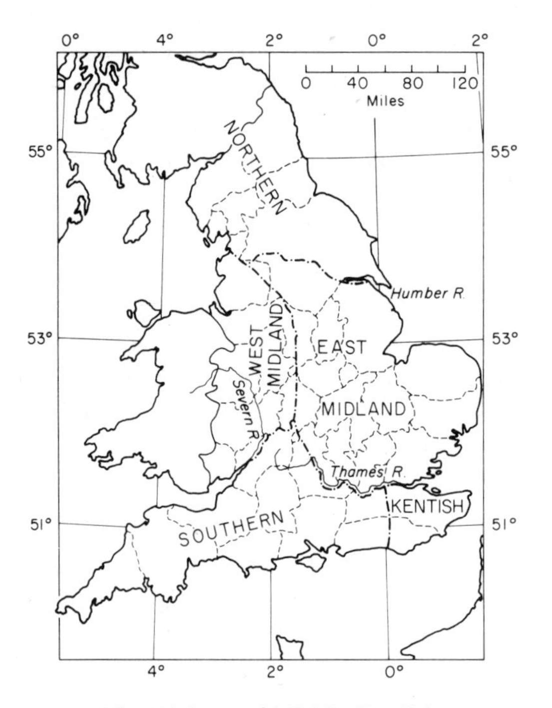

The Dialects of Middle English
(Adapted from A. C. Baugh, *A History of the English Language*, p. 235)
© 1957. By permission of Prentice Hall Inc., Englewood Cliffs, New Jersey.

regional features were removed and replaced by their equivalents in the copyist's own vernacular. But all this was changed when Caxton started printing manuscripts in the late 15th century. Under his example, spelling practices became stabilized and a standard form of the literary language came into being.

We now turn to a consideration of our vocabulary, the immediate concern of this book. Accounts of the growth of the number and sources of the words we use invariably emphasize the enormous size of the vocabulary. The thirteen volumes of the famous *Oxford English Dictionary* contain altogether well over 400,000 words, though not surprisingly in a historical dictionary, many of them are now obsolete. Nevertheless, its derivative, the *Concise Oxford Dictionary*, includes more than 45,000 words in its 1579 pages, all current in Standard English today. Whether so large a stock of words is advantageous to its users, native or foreign, is debatable; the decision seems to depend upon one's personal competence in handling the language. In treating the growth of our vocabulary, we shall do little more than examine briefly the genuinely native element and then pass on to outline the circumstances in which we acquired so many words from foreign languages.

The vocabulary of Old English is specially notable for four main features. These are the richness and high quality of the poetic diction in its surviving 30,000 lines of verse, although this was perhaps becoming archaic even in the earliest times; its effectiveness as a medium of prose as manifested in the late West Saxon period (not unnaturally the earliest prose was halting and inchoate); its facility for forming compound words from its own resources both by joining two words to express a third in terms of a double image—a characteristic feature of the poetry—and by attaching affixes to simple words; and lastly its ability to borrow wanted words from those foreign languages with which it came into contact. (We may note here that though Modern English has certainly not lost its power of forming new words by joining two words in a grammatical relationship to form a new word, it has abundantly developed the tendency to borrow needed words from foreign sources.)

It is time to consider the chief foreign elements in the English vocabulary and to explain their nature and the reasons for their incorporation. In citing samples of foreign loan words, special prominence will be given to those current in vernacular English.

As a result of the contact of the Germanic tribes with the Roman Empire on the Continent, the Anglo-Saxons brought a few Latin words with them to Britain. These include such essential words as *butter*, *cheese*, *church*, *kitchen*, *mile*, *mill*, *Saturday*, *street*, *wall* and *wine*. Again, about one hundred words must have been adopted in Old English between 450 and 650 consequent upon the close association of our ancestors with the Britons, who must obviously have been accustomed to using the expressions in question. They include the place-name element *-chester* (with its alternatives *-caster* and, via the Anglo-Normans, *-cester*) and such commonplace words as *anchor*, *chest*, *cup*, *fork*, *pail*, *pot* and *trout*. Further, following upon the introduction of Christianity into Britain by Roman missionaries beginning in 596 and by Celtic ones a little later, as well as through the later influence of Latin learning and civilization, a certain number of Latin words emerge in Anglo-Saxon writings. But very few of them gained a permanent footing, probably because they did not infiltrate into speech.

In passing it is worth mentioning that very few ordinary Celtic words were borrowed from the Britons, and of these only a mere handful established themselves in English. Among them are *brat*, *bannock*, *brock*, perhaps *ass* (ultimately from Latin—but the word is obsolescent in both dialectal and Standard English). Most of our major rivers and some of our chief cities, however, bear names of Celtic origin.

Additional Latin words were acquired direct in the Middle English period. They were technical terms belonging to religion, medicine, the law and learning. Some of them are well known to dialect speakers today, e.g. *admit*, *discuss*, *extravagant*, *interrupt*, *moderate adj.*, *necessary*, *picture*, *polite*.

The 14th century saw a great European revival of interest in classical thought and language. This Renaissance, as it is called, began in Italy and then spread in the 15th and 16th centuries across the Alps to western European countries. Latin language and culture rather than Greek formed the major interest. Latin words now began to stream into English literature, for Latin was widely used both in writings and as a spoken language in England during the 16th and 17th centuries. Moreover, translations of the masterpieces of Latin literature were in great demand. English scholars became wholly dissatisfied with the alleged unsuitability of their mother-tongue for learned works in prose and so introduced Latin words freely into their writings both as a stylistic embellishment and as an aid to greater precision in meaning. (This attitude was utterly rejected by certain "patriotic" Englishmen who zealously insisted on the high potential of their native language as a medium of literary expression: their aim was to keep the language "pure".) The Latin loanwords of the period under consideration were accordingly literary words, yet some of them have established a footing in vernacular English, e.g. *alphabet*, *area*, *circus*, *crisis*, *elastic*, *exit*, *hesitate*, *museum*, *pendulum*, *minimum*, *scheme*, *skeleton*, *system; enormous*, *pathetic; exist.*

The following 18th century loans are quite familiar to dialect speakers: *bonus*, *camera*, *extra*, *maximum*.

A vast number of words of Greek origin also found their way into English, especially so following upon the Renaissance. But most of these are indirect adoptions. In the Anglo-Saxon period, many were introduced through Latin learning. Middle English acquired an abundance from French, which had earlier taken them from Latin. In Modern English, most Greek borrowings, apart from the hybrids referred to below, are learned words that were assimilated from Latin and French literature, and particularly from scientific writings. Any number of these indirect Greek loanwords have become part of our everyday language, but since they were transmitted through French and Latin, they need not be dealt with here. The following are direct borrowings from Greek: *adenoids*, *cosmos*, *criterion*, *kinetic*, *kudos*, *nous*, *osteopath*, *topic*.

Large numbers of compound words emanating from Greek never had any actual independent existence in that language, but were coined in the 19th and 20th centuries from separate verbal elements, namely stems and affixes, in order to designate new notions in science. Among well-known hybrids are *creosote*, *dynamite*, *eucalyptus*, *kerosene* (U.S.A.), *panorama*, *photograph*. Especially noteworthy is *telly*, a clipped form of *television* (*set*), which is now fully established in vernacular English.

We must now turn back in time to deal with the very large number of loanwords borrowed from the Scandinavian languages as early as the Old English period. Thousands of words were absorbed into English, and more strikingly into the dialects of the North and East, following upon the Viking plundering-raids that began midway through the second half of the 8th century. These attacks, mostly by Danes and Norwegians, were disastrous for early English civilization, for most of the monasteries—the centres of learning—in northern and central and eastern England were pillaged and destroyed. Nevertheless, though the Vikings originally came, like the Anglo-Saxons before them, as pirates in search of booty, a hundred years later, i.e. in the second half of the 9th century, many of them began to settle here permanently; and during the 11th century became completely integrated "Englishmen" who defended their new homeland against foreign aggressors.

The Viking attacks belong to three main periods. During the first, namely 787–850, the raids were on a small scale and carried out by roving bands. The main objective was the treasure of the religious houses. During the second period, namely 850–990, large forces arrived, both to plunder and to settle. York, for example, was occupied in 876, and the Danish leader, King Halfdan, apportioned land in the neighbourhood among his followers. The main, indeed the sole, resistance came from King Alfred, who succeeded in defeating the Danes led by King Guthrum in Wiltshire and then made peace with him in 878 by the highly significant Treaty of Wedmore. Under its terms, the two kings agreed, amongst other things, upon the partition of England and the sovereignty over the whole of the region north and east of the old (Roman) Watling Street, stretching from London to Chester, was assigned to Guthrum. Though sporadic fighting continued, the Danes settled down peacefully. However, the Vikings from overseas between 990 and 1016—the third period—renewed their attacks with still greater ferocity and in consequence England's king, Ethelred the Unready, was in 1013 deposed and succeeded by King Svein of Denmark. But he died in 1016 and his son Canute mounted the throne. Canute was also monarch of Denmark and Norway but preferred to reside in England. With a Scandinavian king in such a key position, Scandinavian attacks on this country came to an end.

The Scandinavians approached the British Isles along two main routes. Danes, accompanied by some Swedes, sailed straight across the North Sea to Yorkshire and the East Midlands. Norwegians arrived via the North of Scotland and became settlers in Shetland, Orkney, the Western Isles, the North of Ireland and the Isle of Man, from where they established permanent colonies in North-West England, especially in Cumberland, Westmorland and North Lancashire. Naturally the question arises about the extent of the influence of these Scandinavians on English vernacular speech. Since the Middle English literary monuments from the regions concerned contain very many Scandinavian words, it is reasonable to assume that still more infiltrated into spoken English but found no place in literature.

Despite three periods of Viking military and political pressure on England before the Norman Conquest, and despite intermarriages between the two peoples as well as their fusion during the 11th century, only some eighty loanwords from Scandinavian emerge in writings prior to 1150. However, very few documents written during the 10th, 11th and 12th centuries in the North of England and the East Midlands, the regions of greatest Scandinavian influence, have come down to the present day. The loans in question are mainly technical and concern the sea, the lower social ranks, and the land. About thirty of them survive, including the following sample (the references are to the relevant articles in SED): *call*, *die* III.7.2, *egg v.*, *husband* VIII.1.25, *hustings*, *knife* I.7.18, *law*, *outlaw*, *root* IV.12.1, *take* IX.3.7 and *wrong* IX.7.1(a).

Hundreds of Scandinavian loanwords appear for the first time in writings of the 13th century, a sure indication that they had been adopted in spoken English in Anglo-Saxon times. Most occur in Northern and East Midland writings, though some are recorded in West Midland and Southern texts. The borrowings are chiefly commonplace words. Evidently the cultural levels of the two peoples were the same. The pronouns *they*, *their* and *them*, which are of Scandinavian origin, in time replaced the native counterparts, presupposing the most intimate contact between the two races, amongst whom some degree of bilinguality must have existed until Scandinavian ceased to be spoken in this country. Very many of the words concerned have found their way into Standard English. (It is noteworthy that some 1400 place-names of Scandinavian origin, over 600 of them ending in *-by*, occur in England alone.) Some of these ordinary, everyday words from Scandinavian sources have

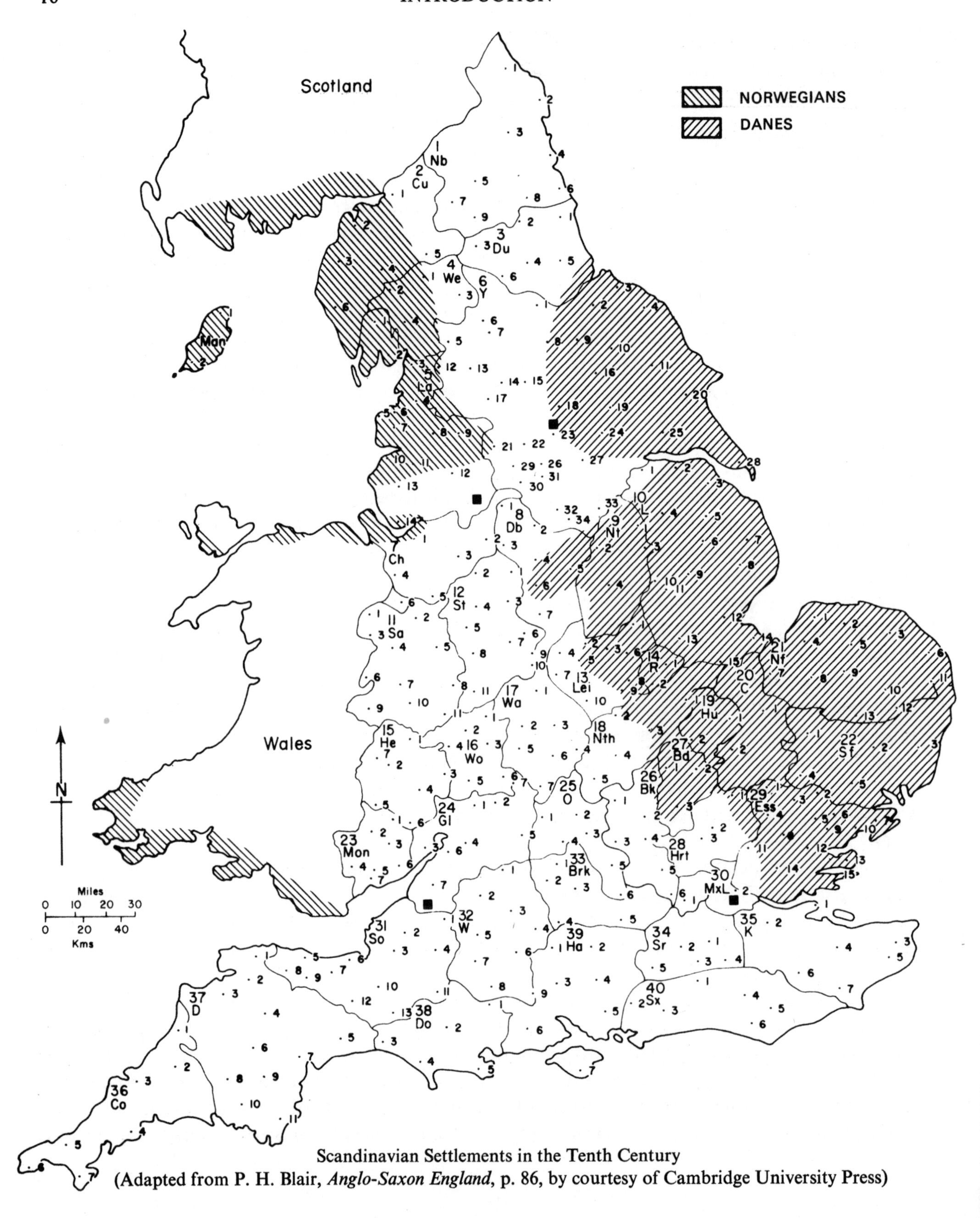

Scandinavian Settlements in the Tenth Century
(Adapted from P. H. Blair, *Anglo-Saxon England*, p. 86, by courtesy of Cambridge University Press)

become an indispensable part of Standard English and many more have an established place in dialects. The following are in regular use in both Standard and vernacular English and those treated in SED are appropriately referenced here: *band* ("bond"), *bank* ("slope"), *bull* III.1.14, *dirt*, *girth* I.5.8, *leg*, *seat*, *wing; awkward*, *ill* VI.13.1, *low*, *odd*, *sly; cast*, *crawl* IX.1.9, *droop*, *flit*, *gape* VI.3.7, *hit*, *lift*, *thrive*, *want; both* VII.2.11, *fro* VIII.2.11, *same*, *till* IX.2.2, M170, and *though*.

Many Middle English words of Scandinavian origin are found only in Northern and East Midland texts. It is not always possible to say with certainty whether a particular word is originally Scandinavian or Old English, because the vocabularies of both had many words in common, though with different inflexions. In some cases phonological criteria help to decide. Yet existing geographical distributions must also be taken into account. For example—the references are to SED—*bink*, *brig* IV.1.2, *kirk* VIII.5.1, *kirn* V.5.5, *kist*, and *rig* II.3.2, II.7.2, V.1.2(a) are doubtless Scandinavian words that replaced the native *bench*, *bridge*, *church*, *churn*, *chest* and *ridge* respectively. Not surprisingly, several thousands of Scandinavian loans are found in the present-day dialects of the North and East Midlands. All the words listed here are examples and all of them have been recorded in SED at the references specified and, if mapped here, with map numbers indicated:

Addled ("earned") VIII.1.26, M42, *axle(-teeth)* ("molars") VI.5.7, M179, *beal v.* ("bellow") III.10.2, M78, *blae-berries* ("bil-") IV.11.3, M181, *cush* (call to cows) III.10.1(b), M4A, *dess* ("cutting of hay") II.9.15, *drucken* ("drunken") VI.13.11, M62, *ewer* ("udder") III.2.5, M50A, *feal v.* ("hide") III.11.7, *femmer* ("brittle") IX.1.4, *gain* ("near") IX.2.10, *garth* ("yard") I.1.10, M63, *gaum(-less)* ("stupid") VI.1.5, *gilt* ("young sow") III.8.5, M54, *gimmer* III.6.5, *giss* (call to pigs) III.10.1(c), M81, *gowpen* ("double handful") VII.8.10, *grain* ("branch") IV.12.3, *keck v.* ("tip") I.11.5, M89, *ket* ("rubbish") V.1.15, M67, *lait v.* ("seek") III.13.18, M68, *lake v.* ("play") VIII.6.4, M45, *lea* ("scythe") II.9.6, M69, *lisk* ("groin") VI.9.4, M83, *lops* ("fleas") IV.8.4, M70, *loup v.* ("jump") IV.2.10, M57, *lowse v.* ("finish") VIII.6.2, *mun* ("mouth") VI.5.1, M190, *oast* ("curds") V.5.8, *pis-mire/mowr* ("dandelion") II.2.10, *rawk* ("mist") VII.6.8, *rean* ("furrow") II.3.1, *rout v.* ("bellow") III.10.2, *sark* ("shirt") VI.14.8, *saur* ("urine") I.3.10, M73, *skell(-boose)* ("partition") I.3.2, M191, *slape* ("slippery") VII.6.14, M25, *stack-garth* ("-yard") I.1.4, M194.

The following, with references to SED, are probable borrowings from Scandinavian: *gesling* ("gos-") IV.6.17, M16, *heft v.* ("stock up") III.3.6, *hime* ("hoar-frost") VII.6.6, M188, *kitling* ("kitten") III.13.11, M20, *laughter* ("brood") IV.6.12, M183, *mawks* ("maggots") IV.8.6, M189, *midden* V.1.14, M177, *neive* ("fist") VI.7.4, M59, *quey* ("heifer") III.1.5, M72, *reckling* ("weakling piglet") III.8.4, M206, *stee* ("ladder") I.7.14, M47, *steg* ("gander") IV.6.16, M194, *teem v.* ("pour") V.8.8, M48, *theak v.* ("thatch") II.7.5.

Lastly in this connexion many of the borrowings are characterized by the *sk*-sound initially, the native equivalent being *sh*-, except sometimes before an *r*. The following, commonplace examples have penetrated into Standard English (the references are to the relevant SED articles): *scab*, *scale* ("pan"), *scalp*, *scant*, *scare*, *score* ("twenty"), *scrap* ("piece") III.12.10, *scrape*, *skep* ("bee-hive") IV.8.8, M61, *skin*, *skirt* and *sky* VII.6.1.

The Norman Conquest of 1066 affected the English language fundamentally. Upon our vocabulary its influence was revolutionary and can hardly be exaggerated. However, its effect upon the inflexional system and consequently upon grammatical concord and word order was most probably only indirect and amounted to no more than reinforcing tendencies already in play. In point of word-stock, it has been estimated that, by 1500, over 10,000 French words had been adopted in Middle English. Since then the processes of borrowing have continued, though not on the same extensive scale. Today, English is permeated with loanwords from French. Indeed it is sometimes remarked, though jestingly, that English is really only French pronounced in a rather peculiar fashion.

The Normans originated from Scandinavia. They arrived in Northern France as pirates, just as their fellow-countrymen did in England. Yet after being granted domicile in (present-day) Normandy in 912, when at the same time Rollo, their leader, became the first Duke of Normandy, the Vikings within five generations had settled down as Frenchmen and had abandoned their mother-tongue in favour of French. In addition, they assimilated some of the most important elements of French civilization, namely a knowledge of warfaring and of the law and administration, as well as of Christianity. By the middle of the 11th century the Normans had become one of the most cultivated peoples in Europe.

The Norman Conquest of England was total and its effects were enduring. The native aristocracy were mostly eliminated and replaced by a new, Norman nobility with large estates and an abundance of retainers. At the same time, however, the Normans retained their lands on the Continent, and traffic across the English Channel was accordingly continuous. The Normans, who obtained all the responsible positions in Church and State, made no attempt to learn the language of their subjects, and the use of English was confined to the lower classes. For over 150 years, indeed not till the Anglo-Normans severed their ties with their kinsmen in Normandy and France in consequence of King John's loss of Normandy in 1204 and later on of his French possessions, did the English language begin to acquire status. Nevertheless, during the 12th century Anglo-Norman literature had prospered. Histories, romances and religious works were produced. Anglo-Norman was prestigious, but when the connexion with Continental French was broken, it began to fall into desuetude, because it was no longer useful. In the 13th century, French speakers on the Continent began to ridicule Anglo-Norman as being inferior and uncouth in comparison with Central French as used in Paris. This latter dialect had become fashionable amongst the cultivated. Accordingly the Anglo-Norman upper classes now began to learn and use Central French, while their subjects retained their English. Before long the two races became fused; and in the 14th century, English was used universally. In the 15th century, French more or less disappeared as the language of ordinary communication.

Anglo-Norman language and culture affected most aspects of English life. This is evidenced by the incorporation into English of loanwords concerned with government, both national and local, with the Church, the Law Courts, and social ranks and positions. They were essential words and had to be understood, and acquired, by the lower classes from their Norman masters. By the 13th century, French had replaced English as the second language in the Law Courts, Latin being the first; and it was not finally abolished from them until 1731. In Parliament, proceedings were opened in English for the first time in 1362, though, in general, French continued in use until 1483. In the schools, the language of instruction was French, but it was superseded by English by the end of the 14th century. Between 1350 and 1400, Medieval English literature had attained the summit of its achievement and authors had made great use of French loanwords in order to meet the requirements of verse, metre and alliteration. A wealth of synonyms thus accrued to the language and French words often replaced English expressions for the same notion. In addition the practice of employing pairs of words, one French and formal, the other English and accordingly emotive, developed out of the desire to achieve stylistic effect, as well as greater clarity.

Words were borrowed from French in two stages. Down to 1250 they were adopted by the lower classes, the English, from their Anglo-Norman masters; and they were mainly essential, organizational words. In the later period, i.e. after 1250, they were transmitted from Central French by the nobility in speaking English with their servants. They now included elevated words relating to fashion, food and social life, as well as to art, learning and medicine.

In the limited space available here, it is impossible to cite an adequate selection of French loanwords in Middle English. They form, however, an essential part of the literary vocabulary. They also constitute an important and, indeed, indispensable element in vernacular English, which is our chief concern here. The following examples, because well known to dialect speakers, are worth mention. Some are contained in the Dieth-Orton _Questionnaire_ and so are here marked with a small, superior x; and those that are included in the _Questionnaire_ because they evidence the development of certain vowel sounds in the Middle English phonological system—thus pointing to early integration into the vocabulary of English—here carry a superior * (as in the _Questionnaire_ itself).

1. ADMINISTRATION, LAW: _crown, parliament, reign, royal, state; city, council, court, evidence, fine, fraud, gaol, prison_

2. DRESS: ^{x}_apron_*, ^{x}_bonnet_, ^{x}_boot_*, _brooch_, ^{x}_chain_*, _collar, jacket, jewel_, ^{x}_(boot)lace, ornament, petticoat_

3. FAMILY: ^{x}_aunt_*, ^{x}_cousin_*, ^{x}_nephew_*, ^{x}_niece_*, ^{x}_uncle_*

4. FOOD, MEALS, FRUITS: ^{x}_bacon_*, _beef, mutton_, ^{x}_partridge_*, ^{x}_pheasant_*, ^{x}_pigeon, pork, poultry, sausage, tripe, veal; dinner, feast_, ^{x}_sugar_*, _supper; date, fig, grape, lemon, orange, raisin_

5. HOME, HOUSEHOLD, FURNITURE: _chamber_, ^{x}_pantry_, ^{x}_parlour, scullery, blanket, coverlet curtain_, ^{x}_cushion_*, ^{x}_quilt_*, _towel_, ^{x}_chair_*, _dresser, wardrobe_

6. MILITARY: _army, battle, guard, navy, peace, soldier, spy._ (Note also military ranks.)

7. RANKS: _clerk, duke_, ^{x}_farmer_*, _master_*, ^{x}_mistress_*, _prince, servant, sir_

8. RELIGION: _abbey, convent, lesson, mercy, parson, pity, prayer, preacher, saint, sermon_, ^{x}_sexton_*, _vicar_

9. MISCELLANEOUS: ^{x}_dozen_*, ^{x}_flour_*, ^{x}_flower_*, ^{x}_(cart-)grease_*, ^{x}_hour_*, ^{x}_litter_, ^{x}_mange_*, ^{x}_money_ ^{x}_oil_*, ^{x}_ounce_*, ^{x}_pasture_*, ^{x}_people_, ^{x}_person_, ^{x}_pocket_, ^{x}_quarry_*, ^{x}_quart_*, ^{x}_quarter_*, ^{x}_rein_, ^{x}_second,_* ^{x}_squirrel_*, ^{x}_stallion_, ^{x}_stranger, tailor_, ^{x}_tune_*

The rate of absorption of French words into English decreased in the 15th century, and still more so in the centuries immediately following. After 1500 or so, the borrowings were consistently cultivated words which were transmitted through literature and polite society. In the 17th century in particular, English writers were prone to imitate their French counterparts and late in the century it became fashionable, consequent upon the re-establishment of a royal court and with it a renewal of French cultural influences, for the upper classes to lard their conversation with French expressions.

Among the words that have filtered through to the vernacular, the following deserve to be mentioned. They are classified by centuries.

15th century: *serge*, *serviette*
16th century: *cartridge*, *colonel*, *scene*, *sirrah* (obsolescent), *trophy*, *vase*
17th century: *gauze*, *invalid*, *moustache*, *portmanteau*, *spa*
18th century: *attic*, *blancmange*, *bureau*, *canteen*, *crayon*, *debut*, *depot*, *envelope*, *fete*, *picnic*, *souvenir*, *tureen*, *valse*
19th century: *acrobat*, *barrage*, *blouse*, *cafe*, *char-a-banc* (obsolescent), *glycerine*, *restaurant*
20th century: *garage*

Contact between speakers of English and of Low German dialects (viz. Dutch, Flemish and Old Saxon and its derivatives) has been maintained since before the Norman Conquest. In Middle English times it was specially close. Dutch and Flemish craftsmen, especially weavers, and merchants and refugees often emigrated to England and settled in all parts of the country. Hence the loanwords as a whole are in no way restricted to any one part of the country. Further, the resemblances between Old English and Middle English on the one hand, and Low German dialects on the other are so close that the origin of some words first appearing in the 14th century cannot be attributed with certainty to either source. Accordingly, no bundles of isoglosses are to be expected. Yet several individual words have emerged with restricted geographical distributions. See, e.g., *elder* ("udder") M50A, *hames* M109, *fitchew* ("pole-cat") M108, *mate* VIII.4.2, *pad* ("path") M111, *pushes* ("boils") M107, *tackle v.* ("gear") M51, *wagon* M118, *wagoner*.

Italian provides the fourth largest contribution of foreign words to English. Many of them arrived through French. These were the earliest. Many others, though pretty well established in English, still look foreign. The earliest loans were commercial and military terms. Those adopted during the last three centuries are mainly cultivated words, chiefly derived from art, music and literature. Unlike the Scandinavian and doubtless very many of the French borrowings, the Italian expressions penetrated into vernacular English via the Standard language and are therefore indirect loans. In the circumstances they need no detailed treatment here. Despite, in some instances, their foreign character, a few of them have made themselves thoroughly at home in vernacular use, e.g. *balloon*, *duet*, *firm*, *manage*, *piano*, *solo*, *umbrella*. The following may reasonably be considered to belong to the vocabulary of dialect, but again they arrived here circuitously, this time via Standard English and French: *alarm*, *attack*, *concert*, *disgrace*, *florin* (now obsolescent), *gala*, *million*, *model*, *muslin*, *pedal*, *post* (*office*), *traffic*.

Spanish has contributed a fair number of words to English, but the borrowing occurred latish, namely from the 16th century onwards. Some of the words were acquired from Spaniards in Europe, while others were absorbed by English sailors either in hostile contact with Spanish mariners on the high seas, or else with Spanish-speaking settlers on the coasts of North and South America. The following loans are well known to dialect speakers; they no doubt derive indirectly through Standard English: *banana*, *booby*, *cannibal*, *cigar*, *cocoa*, *coconut*, *Negro*, *potato*, *tobacco*.

The source languages dealt with above are not the only ones to enrich the vocabulary of English, both Standard and dialectal. Many words, for example, have reached us from Arabic, Hebrew, and Russian, as well as languages indigenous to India. More recently American English has exercised considerable pressure upon our native varieties of speech through the indirect medium of print, the film industry and the *wireless* (? obsolescent for "radio", normal in American English). Some of the more recent examples of this pressure are *cafeteria*, *freight* ("goods") *train*, *right now*, *rocks* ("stones"), *truck* ("lorry") and *ya* ("yes"). But the possibility of direct borrowing of Americanisms by speakers of regional and dialectal English in this country may well require investigation in due course. Perhaps the idea is not too far-fetched in view of the fact that many American military units were stationed here during World War II, and also for long periods afterwards; and some even remain today.

III. Analysis of the Maps

A primary aim of linguistic geography is to reveal the occurrence and distribution of speech usages, especially those characteristic of particular regions. Their diffusion can be mapped clearly and simply. Close study of the resultant maps permits significant deductions to be drawn about the movements of those usages: whether, for example, they are spreading or contracting, or whether, indeed, they have been partly supplanted by other features. As a rule speech changes almost imperceptibly, but sometimes it changes with great rapidity. The latter is especially true today of English dialects, which are known to have long been disturbed by the pressure of St E, by general education and by the printed word, and, further, in more recent decades by wireless programmes and by the conscription, in two universal wars, of both men and women into the military and industrial labour forces. Nevertheless, SED abundantly demonstrates that the older generation of natural dialect speakers in rural districts have undoubtedly preserved much of their traditional vernacular. It also reveals interesting and at times surprising facts about the distributions of many vernacular usages. For example, dialects in eY[1] have been strongly affected by external pressure from more southerly varieties of English and have already lost, or are losing, characteristic features; Nb has been penetrated by usages from the North-East, presumably from Scotland, and, as might be expected, St E elements are everywhere ousting distinctly regional traits.

Linguistic geography also endeavours to determine the causes of existing distributions. This involves etymological and historical considerations. Thus many expressions mapped

[1]This is a composite abbreviation, e denoting east and Y, Yorkshire; and similarly nY, wY and sY. See List of Abbreviations.

below prove to be derived from two or more words found in OE. Here are distinct historical problems for which solutions are required. Again, other expressions emanate from foreign sources. As we have seen, the Vikings made numerous contributions to the English vocabulary and our maps often show remarkably clearly the wide range of their settlements in this country. Still other words were introduced to our ancestors by the Norman conquerors and their descendants. Despite the absorption of several thousands of these terms, the patterns of distribution revealed by our maps are inconsistent. Many of them seem to confirm the general belief that French words are more extensively used in the South than in the North. Nevertheless, certain French loanwords emerge in the North but not in the South. Moreover, the borrowings from the Low German languages are equally inconsistent in their distribution, though the Dutch ones in particular presuppose no extensive emigrant settlements.

The space at our disposal here makes it impossible for us to discuss all our maps in detail. So we call attention only to maps that seem to us specially noteworthy.

A few matters of general interest may be mentioned first. The North and the South are clearly divided about the name of the blackberry, the fruit of the bramble in our hedgerows. Map 1 shows that, in the South, *blackberries* is firmly established; whereas L and the North, excluding La, favours *brambles*, though it is obviously fast receding in L. The expressions for *cow-house* (SED I.1.8, M2, 2A, 2B, 2C) are of much interest both here and in the U.S.A. and demonstrate in a striking way the value of linguistic geography. Two of these expressions, *byre* (M2) and *shippon*, were expressed in OE times by two independent words, the essential meaning of which was "shed". Today *byre* is northern, whereas *shippen* emerges in two western enclaves widely separated by counties extending from Ch to So inclusive. *Cow-stable* (M2A), occurring in nL and recorded too, somewhat astonishingly, in the Isle of Wight, is a curious usage, for *stable* is normally associated with horses. In *LANE*[1] it is the keyword for "cow-shed" and is found sporadically in various parts of the U.S.A. *Cow-house* (M2B), a compound recorded in literature rather late and widespread today in the Midlands and the North-East, looks as if it had overwhelmed earlier native words. But it is itself being rapidly displaced by *cow-shed* (M2C), a compound recorded for the first time as late as 1886, when it appears in an Act of Parliament. Quite likely, therefore, it has been spread by government literature and officials. At any rate it has already made deep incursions into the EM and at the considerable expense of the earlier, apparently non-traditional expression *cow-house*. To call in horses from the field, *cup* (M3) ranges widely and surrounds certain enclaves where the same call is employed to bring in cows (M4). That the call, presumably representing *come-up*, should have different applications is understandable, but the overlap (M5)—it occurs only in the sWM[2]—is not extensive.[3] *Dike* (M6) undoubtedly means "hedge" in a wide belt running from Cu to Nb. DONKEY (SED III.13.16) has thrown up some striking terms. *Donkey* (M7) is a pet form of a Christian name, namely *Duncan*. So are the vernacular names *dicky*, from

[1] *Linguistic Atlas of New England*, ed. H. Kurath *et al.* 3 vols in 6. Providence, R. I., 1939–1943. Reprinted, with a new introduction by Raven I. MacDavid Jr., 1971.

[2] On the use of s here and of other directional abbreviations, see p. 21, footnote 1.

[3] For additional calls to horses, see M3A, and to cows, see M4A.

Richard, *neddy*, from *Edward*, and *cuddy*, from *Cuthbert*. The last-mentioned is widely used in the North-East where, incidentally, many churches are dedicated to St. Cuthbert (b. c634), the hermit of the Farne Islands, off the Northumbrian coast, and previously Bishop of Lindisfarne. *Cuddy*, too, is also found as an expression, or part of a compound expression, for *left-handed*, where it is presumably deprecatory.[1] *Evening* (M8) is not a Northern usage. Neither is it used deep down in the cMidl or to the south-east in MxL. Further, it is not found in a narrow spur extending from MxL into Ess and Sf; nor, again, in sDo. *Flick* (M9), which is the name in So, sGl, W and Do, as well as in the adjacent parts of the neighbouring counties, for the inner layer of pig's kidney-fat, apparently originates from the same OE word as *flitch* (not mapped below), which in the sense of "side of bacon" proves to be commonly used in the North, and in the cMidl, though rarely (SED III.12.3). FUNNEL (SED V.9.3) reveals a very definite cleavage between, on the one hand, *funnel* (M10) used extensively in the North, the EM, EAngl, and south-east England, as far west as W, and, on the other, *tundish*, which is widespread in the WM and southwards in So, Do, and eD. But both *funnel*, a word of French origin, and *tundish*, a compound derived from two OE words, have a strong competitor on their northern borders in the North of England in *tunnel*, another loan from French. The latter also remains well established in Sf and Ess, but to a much less extent in W.[2] As shown by the samples included below, the expressions for HAWS (SED IV.11.6) clearly merit investigation in detail. *Haigs* (M11), phonologically difficult to explain, probably derives from a Scandinavian source. *Hag-haws* (M11A) is repetitious and seemingly reflects two OE words; and *hag-hawses*, like *hawses*, is a double plural. The type *haggle* (M11) appears to produce several variants ending in *-el* (see SED IV.11.6) that result from folk-etymologies.[3] *Ram* (M12), from OE, and the synonymous *tup*, a word of obscure origin apparently unrecorded until 1844, are distinctively contrasted, the former being southern, and the latter characteristic of the Midl and North. The north of EAngl, well known for raising sheep in medieval times, seems to be an area in which *ram* has been replaced by *tup*. The harvesting terms *shocking* (M13) and *stooking* (M13A), for "setting up corn-sheaves for drying", reveal well-marked regional distributions. *Shocking*, from OE sources, emerges strongly in the Home Counties and EAngl, while *stooking*, borrowed from Dutch, is northern. The latter has a by-form in *stowking*, solidly established in L and just inside the counties to the south. *While* (M14) meaning "till" often produces misunderstanding amongst the uninitiated. It is diffused on a large scale in Y and less extensively in the EM.

English dialects have long been affected by St E pressures and have consequently lost many traditional usages that have been replaced by equivalent St E expressions. Several instances were noticed above. The present section contains numerous additional illustrations.

Anvil (M15) provides an excellent example. In the North the current synonym is the Scandinavian loanword *stithy*, which is still widespread. Yet in almost every locality in which it is found, it is in fierce competition with St E *anvil* and obviously cannot survive much longer. *Gosling* (M16), too, is advancing against its Scandinavian counterpart, *gesling*, in the North,

[1]For maps showing LEFT-HANDED, see M119, 119A

[2]For additional expressions for FUNNEL, see M10A.

[3]For additional terms for HAWS, see M11B and 11C.

where this was once doubtless characteristic, and has overwhelmed it completely in eY. *Hedgehog* (M17), moving up from the South, has eroded into the extensive area in the North and the WM where *urchin*, adopted from French, was widely current. *Know* (M18) is swiftly gaining ground on *ken*, now an obvious weakling that survives, apart from in a small strip just south of the Scottish Border, only in a narrow belt extending from nY to the Cu coast. *Kitten sb.* and *v.* (M19, 19A, 20) is obviously driving out *kitling*, the synonymous Scandinavian loanword, and the derived *kittle* in the North, and again it is eY that has succumbed most. Note also *nostrils* (M21), a word of native origin, occurring extensively in the cMidl, EAngl and the South, as well as in the extreme North. Yet in the rest of the North and far down in the Midl, *noseholes*, a late compound of indigenous elements, was no doubt the prevailing vernacular expression; but the map now shows much infiltration of the St E term. *Pigsty* (M22) has almost swept the country, but certain distinctive dialect words still hold on firmly in the North and West, though in wSo and just across the border in D the foothold is rather tenuous. *Nothing* (M23), first recorded as a Post-Conquest compound and now securely in possession of EAngl, contrasts with *naught*, which is perhaps well known as a typical Northern usage. The latter is, however, a native word that was in common use in OE times. So that one is not surprised to find it struggling in a narrow ribbon from the cMidl right down into K on the east and into D, So and Co on the west. But the map clearly demonstrates that *naught* is here being swiftly replaced by its current St E equivalent, *nothing*. The latter has roughly the same distribution as its antonym *somewhat* (M24), which is found consistently in Northern England, except for the *something*-area in Nb. *Somewhat* also characterizes the Midl and the South-West. But here its position is obviously being undermined by the expansion of *something*. *Slippery* (M25), a St E usage of native origin, is seen to be speedily advancing upon *slippy*, a very popular word in the cMidl, where it was probably introduced from a Low German dialect. Not surprisingly, *slippery* is also eroding the spread of *slape*, a Scandinavian word still widely current in the North. Similarly the native *son* (M26) is obliterating *lad* in the North, which is thus losing yet another word that may have been acquired from Scandinavian sources. Finally it is noteworthy that St E *yeast* (M27) is swamping *barm*, which derives from an OE etymon that must formerly have been distributed throughout the country, but is now pretty well restricted to the western counties from La down to Co.

In two instances mentioned above, namely *byre* (M2) and *shippon*, representing COW-HOUSE (SED I.1.8), and *awns* (M28) and its synonym *ails*, the expressions are based upon independent words in OE. This implies that in these cases clear-cut distributional areas existed as early as the OE period. A few additional examples may now be cited.

Delve (M29) and *grave* are synonymous terms for DIG (SED I.7.8) in the North-West. Besides deriving from OE sources, they have the additional interest of adjacent distributions, *grave* being interposed between two *delve*-areas. Further, the map suggests that *grave* formerly enjoyed a wider distribution in Y and also that *delve* earlier extended into the cMidl. *Giddy* (M30) is now widespread in the South, the WM and much of the cMidl. The corresponding Northern word is *dizzy*, though it also makes sporadic appearances right down the centre of England as far as Ha. Both originate from OE words. *Eaves* (M31), referring to a stack, is extensively employed in the EM, cMidl, and sWM, as well as in the South excluding the

South-West. Otherwise, the most widely used expression is *easing*, a Northern word that reaches down into the nWM. Alternative synonyms are *oaves*, current in the South-West, and *ousing*, found in a small enclave in sLa. *Eaves* and *easings* both descend from OE words; and *oaves* and *ousings* are here presumed to derive from OE etymons. *Flails* (M32) with all its variety of forms is the expression most frequently recorded for this antiquated agricultural implement. It occurs regularly in the North, the cMidl and EM, EAngl and the South. The map, however, reveals a vigorous competitor, *threshel*, which once dominated the South-West and even stretched northwards into the WM. Yet *flails* has already infiltrated into the South-West. The latter certainly goes back to an OE source, and the former probably does so too. But no doubt with the disappearance of the implement in question, both words cannot long survive. *Gorse* (M33), a native word, is solidly established throughout the Midl, excluding the South-East portion, and is seen to be making inroads in the South, where *furze*, also of native origin, is regularly employed. The North relies upon *whin*, a borrowing from Scandinavian. But here again *gorse* from St E has begun its penetrations. Another striking example of the presumptive employment of two expressions for a single notion in OE times is provided by *newt* (and derivatives) (M37) and *ask* (and derivatives). The former dominates in the eMidl, EAngl and the South, whereas *ask* is strongly favoured in western counties, excluding those in the South-West. *Pond* (M38), also in St E, is the most extensively used term for a small body of (confined) water on a farm. *Pit* was apparently preferred the whole way across the nMidl and Nf, as well as in La. But *pond* has cut through the centre of this extensive distributional area and is now obviously attacking the flanks. In the central portion of the WM, *pool* is still holding on pretty firmly. All three words derive from OE expressions. *Ricks* (M41) once dominated almost the whole of the WM and cMidl, and most of the South, but not the South-West, where *mows* is well established. Both expressions are from OE. But *stacks*, a word of Scandinavian origin, has swept far southwards, in fact right down into the South-East, doubtless because it is the preferred name in St E. The notion RIVULET (SED IV.1.1) is now almost consistently represented by *brook* (M39, 39A) in the greater part of the Midl, much less widely by *burn* in the extreme North of England, and by *stream* in the South, where it is under great pressure from *brook*, and also in isolated enclaves in the Midl. All three derive from OE sources. Incidentally the Scandinavian parts of England still retain *beck*, a well-known Scandinavian borrowing.

SHAFT (SED I.7.7, I.7.12, II.9.7) and its synonyms are worth a special note. When referring to part of a spade, *shaft* (M34), a native word, is widely current in the North, apart from a much smaller area in the far North, where another native word, *shank*, is favoured. An alternative expression, *handle*, again from a native source, is well entrenched in the cSMidl, the South, and EAngl. But *stick*, too, descended from a fourth OE word, is found in nD and part of So, as well as a little to the north in He, sWo and nGl. When referring to a hayfork, *shaft* (M35), *handle* and *stick* have, perhaps not unexpectedly, almost the same distributions as when they apply to a spade, though *stick* is occasionally found in the sEMidl, too. However, *shaft* (M36)[1] and *handle* show a much different spread when referring to a scythe. *Shaft* begins as far north as L, and sweeps still further north into Y and eDu, and also

[1]For other terms for (scythe-)*shaft*, see M36A.

northwest into We and Cu. *Handle*, however, is now very much restricted and prevails only in a small strip extending from the upper Thames to the district surrounding Bristol. *Stick* is understandably much more frequent and dominates EAngl, Hu and Nt. Nevertheless, yet another synonym, *pole*, from an OE etymon and much more appropriate to the implement, is widely used in Ch and the north-western counties but excluding Cu and nWe.

Finally, (*plough-*)*share* (M40) and *sock*, both of which were found in OE, are seen to be in competition, *share*, as might be expected, now being much the commoner. *Sock* is Northern and North-Western, but Y is abandoning its traditional usage.

Many of the words we have elected to map below derive from Scandinavian sources. Some of them are still widely distributed and mark off clearly those parts of England, more particularly in the North and L, which the Vikings colonized after abandoning their piratical activities (*supra*, p. 14). The counties specially concerned here are Cu, We, La, Y and L. Three words, *beck* (M39), *slape* (M25) and *stithy* (M15), which are good examples of the extensive distribution of the Scandinavian borrowings, have already been dealt with above (pp. 24–5). Several others, similarly widespread, are briefly discussed in the next section.

Addled (M42) meaning "earned" is still well evidenced in the region, but has been eroded in nCu by St E *earned*, a native word, and may now be seen to be giving way in eY and L too. Note its twofold occurrence in eSt. *Clipping* (M43) is widely diffused and competes with the Southern and Midl expression *shearing* from OE. Since, however, *clipping* stretches as far south as MxL and K, as well as into Co in the South-West, it may well have increased its spread because it is customary in St E. *Gimmer*(-lamb) (M44) persists vigorously *vis-à-vis ewe*, except in L, where it was not recorded. Similarly the verb *lake* (M45) was once securely established in the region except in nY and L. It is obviously being squeezed out in eY and sDu by St E *play*. *Sile* (M46), an important notion in the farmer's vocabulary, is a first-rate example of Scandinavian influence. It has held its ground—and indeed even thrust into the far North-East—against the native *sieve* (M46A) and *sie*, as well as against the widespread *strain*, a French loanword and a St E usage. *Stee* (M47), typical of the Scandinavian element in Northern English, occurs almost consistently alongside the alternative *ladder*, which is also the St E term and of native origin. It will therefore soon be crushed out. Equally significant in respect of its expansive currency is *teem* (M48), which is, however, evidently being crowded out, especially in eY and nY, by *pour*, an expression of uncertain origin that dominates the whole of the South and all the Midl except L, Db and the North-East. *Throng* (M49), still favoured in the North, now competes with the native *busy*, which is already sapping the distribution of the Scandinavian loan in Y and the far North.

Many words of Scandinavian origin have undoubtedly extended their original boundaries, some northwards, some southwards, and others both north and south. The reasons for this expansion need to be determined, though when the words themselves also occur in St E there is perhaps no necessity to look for any other explanation. Scandinavian loans like *bag* (M50) meaning "udder", the verb *gear* (M51), (*hay-*)*loft* (M52) presumably spread because they were also current in St E. Other examples are *awns* (M28), *stacks* (M41), and *teem* (M48), all of them discussed above. The undermentioned also merit notice here.

Bing (M53), referring to the gangway in a cowhouse, though not found in the North, is prevalent in the nWM. *Ewer* (M50A), meaning "udder", clearly spread northwards but has receded in nL and YWR. It has, however, firmly maintained its position in eY. *Gilt* (M54), a farmer's word for a young sow, certainly penetrated northwards. But it has also become widely diffused, to the exclusion of *yelt* and its variants, in the nMidl and cMidl, as well as in the South-East and South-West. *Grain* (M55), referring to the prong of an agricultural fork, shows a distinctly curious distribution. First, it is not found, as one might reasonably expect, in cY and eY, but it has spread northwards into Du, southwards into the WM, and problematically into So, Do and D. Its most vigorous competitor is *tine*, which stretches from the cMidl, eMidl and EAngl right up to eY. In Nb, *graip* (M56) means "muck-fork" and descends from a Scandinavian loanword. But it is not evidenced further south in the Scandinavian North, from which it is excluded by *gripe*, a native word. The far South-West favours *evil*. The verb *loup* (M57), which contrasts with *jump*, an echoic word in origin, derives from a Scandinavian word. Like *graip* above, it, too, crossed into Nb, but at the other extreme in L, it is giving way under the assaults of *jump* from the South. *Mun* (M58) "must" was undoubtedly firmly entrenched in the region and even extended its range down into Db and parts of Ch and Sa. Yet *must*, the St E expression deriving from an OE etymon, is vigorously encroaching upon its territory and will doubtless soon predominate everywhere. *Neive* (M59) similarly spread northwards into Nb, but retreated in nY and eY before the advance of *fist*. On the other hand, *seg* (M60), referring to a callosity on the hand and now found in the westerly parts of the North, seems to have made its way as far as Sa in the WM. *Skep* (M61), the name of the old-fashioned straw bee-hive, has travelled extensively from its habitat in the North and has swallowed up much of the WM, and the whole of EAngl and south-east England. Yet the native *hive* occurs in an EM enclave and makes sporadic appearances elsewhere. It also occurs on the southern border of *skep* in the North, namely in La, Ch, parts of Db, cY and L. *Whin* (M33), which contrasts with *gorse* and *furze*, both from OE sources, is still clearly popular in Northern England and has infiltrated into Nb. It also occurs in Nf. But St E *gorse* is now penetrating its habitat, and Y will no doubt soon succumb to it.

Certain borrowings from Scandinavian tend to show, or actually do show, that their original distributional areas have undergone various degrees of contraction under external pressure, mostly from St E. The adjective *drucken* (M62) cannot much longer survive the competition of *drunken*, which is general throughout almost the whole of England. The latter has apparently already displaced the Scandinavian word in nLa and has penetrated eastwards as far as seNb. *Garth* (M63) designates a small field for sick animals on the farm.[1] Although found in swNb, its grip on sY has been lost, as well as on nLa. *Gaumless* (M64) has yielded to the native *daft*, except in a strip stretching from nDu into the extreme north of Y and then into the western borders of Y. *Gowk* (M65), applying to an April Fool, is confined to the west of the Scandinavianized regions, though it still persists in nwY. *Kale* (M66), denoting "charlock",[2] is now limited to a narrow band beginning in Cu and stretching across nWe into nwY. Similarly *ket* (M67) meaning "rubbish" maintains its hold merely in a narrow band running across small parts of Cu, We, nY and Du. *Kitling* (M20) has penetrated southwards

[1]For St E *paddock*, see M63A.
[2]For other expressions for *charlock*, see M66A.

as far as Ch and nDb and northwards into Nb, but it has lost much ground in eY, where it is replaced by St E *kitten*. *Lait* (M68), which expresses the notion LOOK FOR (SED III.13.18), is now squeezed into roughly the same restricted area as the above-mentioned *ket*, namely parts of Cu, Wm, nY and Du. *Lea* (M69) has abandoned almost the whole of YWR to the St E expression *scythe* and is, moreover, giving way in YER, nLa, and We. *Lops* (M70) is not found on the west in La, Wm and Cu, but is dominant in nL, wY, Du and seNb. It is certainly popular in the North-East. Since, however, the keyword here is FLEAS (SED IV.8.4), which the fieldworker was required to obtain for its phonological significance, *fleas* would not perhaps have appeared so consistently in the Northern recordings as indeed it does. Thus the currency of *fleas vis-à-vis lops* may well have been exaggerated. *Nay* (M71) reveals a most irregular distribution and is clearly now, as it must have been earlier, under much pressure from the collateral St E *no*. Its present focus is YWR, with spurs running north, south, east and west. It is noteworthy that a small enclave of *nay*, with subsidiary *no*, is found in Lei and just across the border in the neighbouring Wa. *Quey* (M72) has been split in two by St E *heifer* coming in from the north and east, and by *stirk* from the west, as well as by *heifer* from the south. Hence *quey* is now found scantily in Cu, where it competes with the vigorous *heifer*, now forcing its way into eY. Its chances of enduring much longer seem remote. All that is left of the area of *saur* (M73), a distinctly farming term denoting "urine" draining from the cow-house, is a small area in Y bordering upon La. *Stee* (M74) has been eroded by St E *stile* in eY, as well as in nLa from the south and in nCu from the north. This occasions no surprise since *stile* dominates all the rest of the country. *Stoops* (M75), designating "gate-posts", predominates in most of the eastern half of the Scandinavian regions and has even travelled north-east into wNb. But it has been undermined by *(gate-)posts*, which, apart from being general throughout the Midlands and South, has broken deeply into the flank of *stoops* in eY. Lastly *stower* (M76) in the sense of *rung*[1] (of a ladder) survives only in nY.

Some maps seem to confirm presumed derivation from Scandinavian sources. The words concerned include the following: *bairn* (M77), firmly established in the North (excluding sLa) and L; *beal* (M78) and *bellow*, surviving only in a narrow ribbon in Cu, Wm and nLa; *brant* (M79) "steep", which stretches from Cu across We, Du and right to the nY coast; *cush* (M4A), a call to cows, wide-spread from Cu to sL; *flay(-crow)* (M80), the first element of a word denoting "scare-crow"; *giss* (M81), a call to pigs,[2] which persists strongly in the North as far south as a line roughly drawn from nLa to nY; *haigs* (M11) "haws", which characterizes sLei, swY and nDb; *lad* (M82), strongly entrenched in the Northern counties (except Nb, which prefers the derivative *laddie*), but obviously giving way to St E *boys* on the southern borders of its area of distribution in the nMidl; *lisk* (M83) "groin", though it has presumably been replaced by the St E expression in nLa and sY; *lugs* (M84) denoting "ears", which is widespread in the North, but weakening in L and Nf; and lastly *sile v.* "strain" referring to milk (M46), a farming word with an extensive coverage in the North and L.

On the other hand, certain words cast doubt upon the assumption of direct descent from Scandinavian etymons in their present habitat. They include: *athwart* (M85), meaning

[1]See M76A.
[2]For additional calls to pigs, see M81A.

"diagonally", recorded only in So and Do; *dove* in *dove-cote* (M86), prevalent in the EM; *dregs* (M87),[1] which reaches out from Sa in the west right across to the coast of L, as well as into the sWM; *durn* (M88) "doorpost",[2] found in the south-western counties consistently, in sL with a spur running out in Nf, and, additionally, in a small enclave in So; and, finally, *keel* (M89) "overturn" occurring in So.

Many words of French origin appear on our maps. How French words in general came to be borrowed into English has been explained above (p. 18). Understandably the Southern dialects employ more French words than those in the North, presumably because their geographical position exposed them more deeply to the influence of Anglo-Norman and French. In the following section we cite examples of French words that appear on our maps mainly in the South and not in the North.

Beak (M90) is preferred almost all over the Midl and in the South except in a narrow band lying roughly south of the Thames, where *bill*, a native word, is now found though apparently less widely distributed than hitherto. *Neb*, also native, is the corresponding name in the extreme North, but is now evidently under French pressure from both *beak* and *bill. Braces* (M91) and *bracers*, both French loans, occupy almost the whole country south of a line drawn from the Mersey to just south of the Humber. This is almost the old North North-Midland boundary. The North is characterized by *gallows* (usually in the double-plural form *gallowses*), which derives from Scandinavian. *Braces* is now seen to be infiltrating into this area, too. *Collar* (M92), a French borrowing, competes with the native *bargham* as the name of a most important piece of the horse's harness. It is found everywhere except in the northern regions. *Cave* (M93)[3] in the extreme South-West designates a heap in which potatoes are stored in a field over winter. Further west in Sx the equivalent term is *pie*, also from French. Nevertheless, this is also current all the way from sDu down through Y as far as Nt and L. *Corn* (M60) is a Southern word for a callosity on the hands. In small enclaves in W and So, *court* (M94) means "farmyard". *Gutter* (M95) appears to designate a cow-house drain in the South-West, as well as in spurs running north-east into the cMidl and EM, as well as eastwards as far as K and Ess. *Harness* (M51) competes in popularity with *gear* (from Scandinavian) as the name of the various leather belts and straps placed on a cart-horse. It is used throughout the South, the sMidl and EAngl. Further, it has penetrated into Y, and from the opposite direction is also moving southwards (? from Scotland) from Nb into Du and nY. *Pick* (M96) denoting "strip", with reference to removing the feathers of a dead chicken, is still vigorous in the South-West, as well as in the Home Counties, but is here retreating before the advance of *pluck*, a native word that has come down to St E. *Rowan* (M97)[4] seems to be a relic expression for "second crop" in the South-East. *Round* (M76A) designates the rung of a ladder in an extensive area in the sMidl, reaching down through Brk and Ha to the south coast. Perhaps in W it has already been replaced by St E *rung*, a native word. Finally *strain* (M46A) is the term preferred for the dairying process of "passing milk through a sieve" in the

[1]For other expressions for DREGS, see M87A.
[2]For additional terms for JAMBS, see M88A.
[3]For synonyms, see M93A.
[4]For synonyms, see AFTERMATH M97A.

whole of the South and the cMidl and EM. Because it is a St E word it will doubtless in time overwhelm *sie* and *sieve*, both native words, as well as *sile*, a Scandinavian loan, all three of these current further north than *strain*.

So far the French borrowings discussed above are found in the South of England. The following paragraph deals with words originating from French that are current in the North, but not recorded by SED in the South.

Bobbin (M98), a late French loan, is now used instead of the native *reel* with reference to cotton-thread in two small enclaves in neY and in sCh and Sa. To the south-east of the latter area—and again it is small—another very late French loan, *spool*, competes with both *bobbin* and *reel*. *Car* (M99) denotes a farmcart in Cu and just across the border in We. The verb *clear* (M100), meaning "remove" (viz. cups, saucers, plates, etc. from the table after a meal), prevails not only in the South and Midl, but also in the North-East. The native *side* is used extensively elsewhere in the North but is now giving way here and there to *clear*. *Closes* (M101) is preferred to *fields* (not mapped) in large parts of Y and nL, as well as to the south in a small part of Bd and its eastern neighbour, C. (*Cow-*)*stable* is to be noted in this connexion, see p. 22 and M2A. *Howlet* (M102), under intense pressure from its native synonym *owl*, was obviously characteristic of the Northern dialects. It also reached down into Sa. But evidently it cannot survive much longer in either region. *Poke* (M103), a very early French loanword denoting a large sack, was apparently extensively used in the extreme North, but is being ousted by the St E term. *Poke* is widely used in the U.S.A. as the name for bags of various sizes. Similarly, *ratten* (M104) was clearly well established in the traditional Northern dialects, but has recently ceded much of its earlier hold in the east and south of the region. *Saim* (M9), meaning "pig's fat", is now confined to the extreme north, the native word being *leaf*, which is strongly entrenched further south within a short distance of the Thames valley. *Saim*, too, is, or has been, known in the U.S.A. *Scallions* (M105), a very early borrowing from Norman-French, is the preferred term in the North (excluding seY) for "spring onions".[1] It is also found (rather as a relic) in the EM and Ess. It is known, too, in this sense among others in the U.S.A. *Stanchions* (M88) is sparsely recorded today, though it persists in eDu and the adjacent portions of Nb and Y. Its strongest competitors are the native *cheeks* on the west and the widely spread *jambs*, from French, to the south.

Loanwords have also been acquired from Dutch and Low German. Some of them, mainly non-St E, have been mapped below. As pointed out earlier (see p. 20), however, unlike the Scandinavian borrowings in general, they are not confined to a particular region, but occur in separate enclaves variously distributed. If frequent anywhere, it is, perhaps, in the cMidl.

Blinkers (M106), referring to the eye-pieces of the horse's headgear, is pretty general over the whole country except in the eastern half of the North-country, where *blinders* occurs, and in three enclaves in the WM, the EM, and K, where *winkers* is current. Both *blinkers* and *winkers* are native in origin. *Pushes* (M107) denotes "boils" in EAngl, C and Hrt, but its position is being challenged by St E *boils*, which, though it looks foreign, is actually indigenous. Of the several expressions for a storage-place for potatoes in a field, *clamp* (M93A) is a Dutch loan. It still occurs, though irregularly, in EAngl and the Home Counties,

[1]For additional terms, see M105A, 105B.

excluding, however, most of Sx. *Elder* (M50A), designating the udder of a cow, is wide-spread in the WM and northwards in La, as well as in the east in L. The two areas are separated by *bag*, probably from Scandinavian, and to some extent by the encroachment of *udder*, which is of native stock and characteristic of the South, though, being St E too, it is moving northwards. *Fitch* (M108) "polecat" has only a very limited distribution, being confined to Co and swD. To the north of this area, the synonymous French word *fitchen* is still in secure possession. It is very curious that *hames* (M109), referring to the curved piece of metal round the horse-collar and supposedly a Dutch word, should be so firmly entrenched over the whole country, except in EAngl, where the synonymous *sails* and *seals* are in jeopardy and apparently disappearing. *Nibs* (M110), denoting "scythe-handles", appears in two extensive distributional areas. One begins in nY stretching westwards into the adjacent parts of La and southwards down into L. The other enclave lies in the central sMidl, with a spur running southwards into Ha and then westwards into Do. In both regions, *nibs* is still pretty vigorous, though under challenge from the St E and indigenous *handles*. *Pad* (M111), referring to a path through a field, is derived from either Dutch or Low German. Used extensively in La and the contiguous parts of Ch and of nwY, as well as in the east in L, Nt, Ru and nNth, it shows no signs of being replaced by its St E cognate *path*. *Ploat* (M96), one of the several words for stripping the feathers of a dead bird prior to cooking it, is a Low German borrowing characteristic of neEngland excluding, however, large tracts of cY and sY. In the South, *pick*, from French, is usual west of the Isle of Wight (see above p. 29). *Slead* (M112) meaning "sledge", a vehicle for carrying heavy loads in winter, is found in two small eastern enclaves, one in nL, the other in wSf with a spur running into cEss. A synonymous variant *sled*, though now competing with St E *sledge*, is certainly dominant in the North-West. *Slip* (M113) as the name for a horse's halter is restricted to three small enclaves, one in nNf, a second in nL, and a third in sSt. *Slipe* (M114), from Low German, is used in the sense of "mould-board"[1] in a rather small area in seY. *Slippy* (M25), meaning "slippery", is widespread. Probably Low German in origin, it occurs with great frequency in the nwMidl and cMidl, as well as in an area stretching from Bk through Hrt and in a narrow strip in cEss. It is also found in the extreme North-East. All in all, the various expressions for this notion reveal distinctive distributional areas, including one word adopted from Scandinavian (see p. 24 above). In the heart of the ncMidl the Low German loanword *snap* (M115) is extant for the "mid-morning snack". It is also used, though sparingly, in nEss. To the west and south of this enclave we find the striking expression, *bever*, from French. *Snout* (M116), which, despite its prevalence in a large part of Scandinavian England, is to be regarded as a borrowing from Low German. It is, however, everywhere under acute pressure from its St E counterpart *nose*, a native word, which is the normal expression everywhere else. By far the commonest expressions for a "small, thin piece of wood that has been broken off and pierced the skin" are *splint* (M117) and *splinter*,[2] both being of Dutch origin. The former, emergent in the nWM, has much the smaller distribution. The latter is dominant in the cMidl (but not in L, Nf and Sf), the sMidl, and the south of England. *Tackle* (M51), meaning "put the cart-

[1]For additional expressions, see M114A.
[2]For additional terms, see M117A, 117B.

horse's harness on", originates from Low German. It is usual in the ncMidl. *Wagon* (M118) has become the expression most used for a four-wheeled flat-topped vehicle. Apart from in the North-West, there is scarcely any serious rival.

Only three words of undoubted Celtic origin have been mapped below. One is *tallet* (M52), denoting "hay-loft". This is prevalent in a large area bordering Wales, as well as extending southwards down through sGl and into nCo. Further, it reaches out eastward from So as far as sHa. The other two words are the combining elements *car-* (M119) and *clicky-*.[1] *Car-* is compounded with *handed* and *pawed*, and *clicky-* with *handed* to mean "left-handed". *Car-* is current in Nb, into which it probably infiltrated from Scotland, but *clicky-* is found at the other extreme in Co and wD.

To conclude this part of the Introduction, we may call attention to the following maps containing vernacular words that also occur in the English of the U.S.A. No doubt there will be others that have this same interest, but we must leave the reader to detect them for himself: AFTERMATH (M97A), COME IN! (to horses) (M3, 3A), COME IN! (to cows) (M4, 4A), DIAGONALLY (M85), FALL OF THE LEAF/YEAR (M121), GRANDDAD (M122), GUTTER (M123), HAY-COCKS (M124), HAY-LOFT (M52), HAY-STACKS (M125), MOO (M126), PADDOCK (M63A), PET-LAMB (M127), POKE (M103), POLE-CAT (M108), POND (M38), RAM (M12), RIVULET (M39, 39A), SACK (M103), SCALLIONS (M105), SITTING-ROOM (M128, 128A), SLED (M112), SNACK (M115), WHINNY (M129), WISH-BONE (M130).

Book List

The undermentioned books will be of much help to those who wish to explore in general the linguistic and cultural background of the words mapped in this volume. In preparing our Introduction we have leant heavily on the authoritative and complementary treatments of the vocabulary by Mary Serjeantson and J. A. Sheard.

Alexander, H. *The Story of our Language.* Toronto, 1940.
Baugh, A. C. *A History of the English Language.* New York, 1957.
Blair, P. H. *Anglo-Saxon England.* Cambridge University Press, 1956.
Brook, G. L. *History of the English Language.* London, 1958.
Clark, J. *Early English: A Study of Old and Middle English.* London, 1957.
Jespersen, O. *Growth and Structure of the English Language.* Oxford, 1948.
Kurath, H., *et al. Linguistic Atlas of New England.* Providence, 1939–43. 3 vols. in 6.
McKnight, G. H. *English Words and their Background.* New York, 1923.
Pyles, T. *The Origin and Development of the English Language.* New York, 1964.
Robertson, S., and Cassidy, F. G. *Development of Modern English.* Rev. ed. New York, 1954.
Serjeantson, Mary S. *A History of Foreign Words in English.* London, 1961.
Sheard, J. A. *The Words We Use.* London, 1954.
Thorson, P. *Anglo-Norse Studies. An Inquiry into the Scandinavian Element in the Modern English Dialects. Part I.* Amsterdam, 1936.
Wrenn, C. L. *The English Language.* London, 1949.

[1]For other expressions, see M119A.

The undermentioned dictionaries should be readily available for consultation.

Bense, J. F. *A Dictionary of the Low Dutch Element in the English Vocabulary*. 's-Gravenhage, 1939.
Kurath, H., and Kuhn, S. M., eds. *Middle English Dictionary*. Ann Arbor, 1954– (A–L published).
Onions, C. T. *The Oxford Dictionary of English Etymology*. Clarendon Press, Oxford, 1966.
Oxford English Dictionary, ed. J. A. H. Murray, *et al.* Clarendon Press, 1933.
Partridge, E. *A Dictionary of Slang and Unconventional English*. New York, 1961.
Wright, J., ed. *The English Dialect Dictionary*. 6 vols. London, 1898–1905, etc.

The maps in this volume are interpretations of the material contained in the undermentioned books.

Survey of English Dialects, ed. H. Orton and (†) E. Dieth. (A) *Introduction* by H. Orton, 1962. (B) *The Basic Material:* Vol. 1, ed. H. Orton and W. J. Halliday, 1962–63; Vol. 2, ed. H. Orton and M. V. Barry, 1969–71; Vol. 3, ed. H. Orton and P. M. Tilling, 1969–71; Vol. 4, ed. H. Orton and M. F. Wakelin, 1967–68.

The Maps

This section contains the word-maps (M1–130) that have been discussed in Part III of the Introduction. They have been arranged in the order in which they have been reviewed above. Following them are over a hundred maps that merited the same detailed consideration but could not receive it here through lack of space. This second series is ordered as follows: Old English words (M131–176), Scandinavian words (M177–194), French words (M195–205), miscellaneous words (M206, 207). Within these groups they are arranged alphabetically according to the word or words the distribution of which the map concerned is intended to emphasize. A map of rivers, contours of 300 and 600 feet and chief cities, will be found at the end of the book.

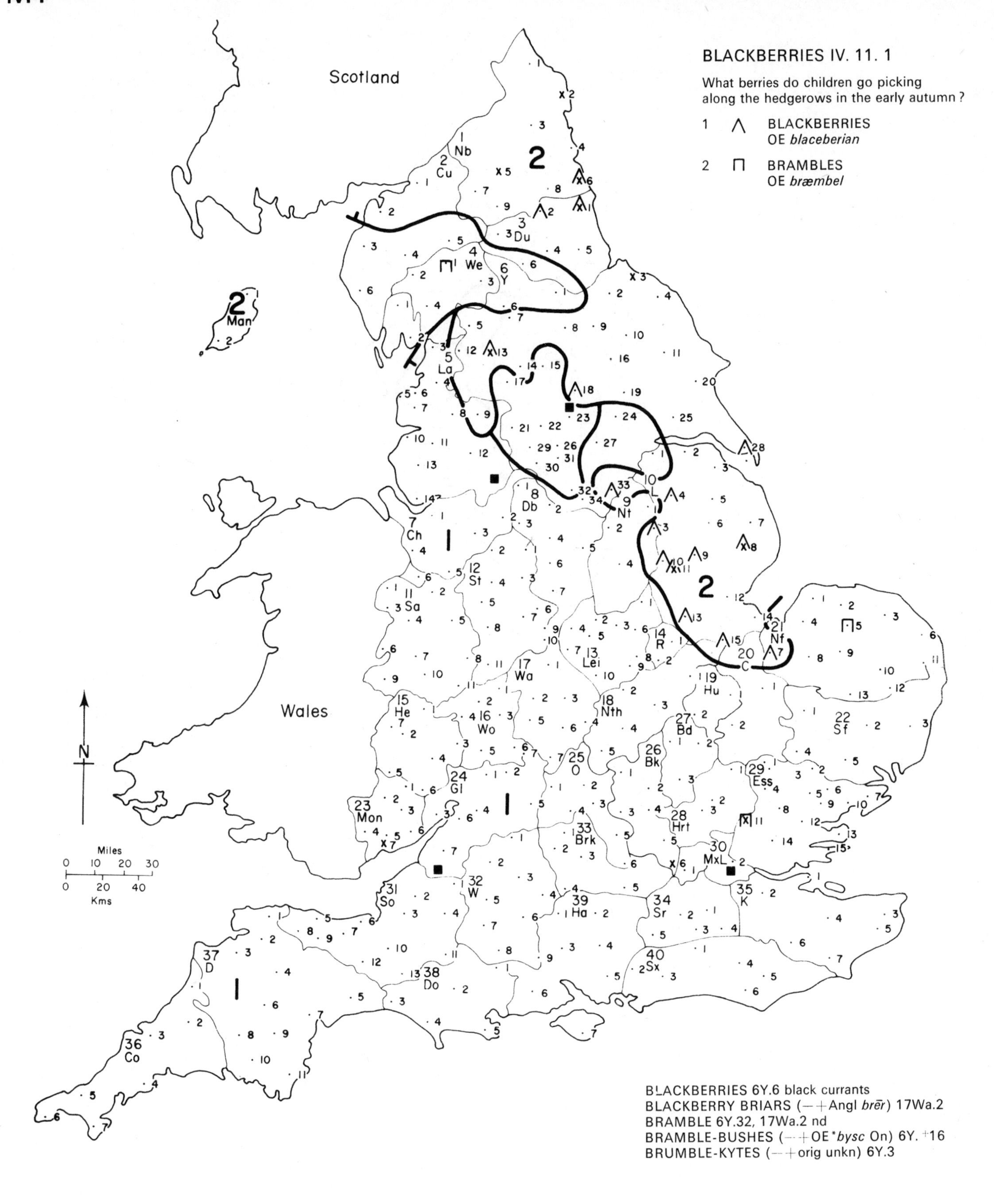
BLACKBERRIES IV. 11. 1
What berries do children go picking along the hedgerows in the early autumn?
1 Λ BLACKBERRIES
OE blaceberian
2 ⊓ BRAMBLES
OE bræmbel
Scotland
Wales
Man
Miles
0 10 20 30
0 20 40
Kms
N
BLACKBERRIES 6Y.6 black currants
BLACKBERRY BRIARS (—+Angl brēr) 17Wa.2
BRAMBLE 6Y.32, 17Wa.2 nd
BRAMBLE-BUSHES (—+OE *bysc On) 6Y. +16
BRUMBLE-KYTES (—+orig unkn) 6Y.3

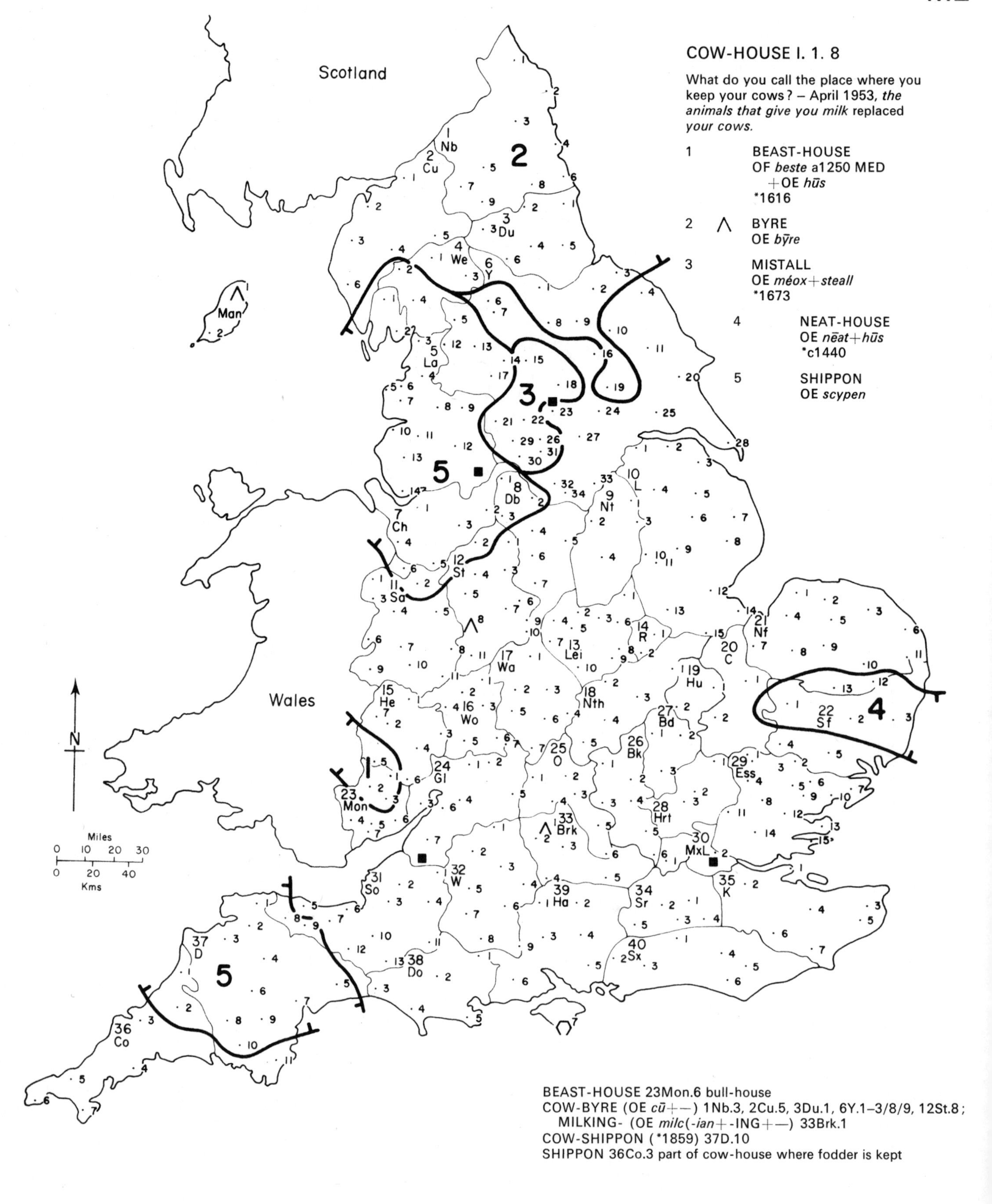

COW-HOUSE I. 1. 8

What do you call the place where you keep your cows? – April 1953, *the animals that give you milk* replaced *your cows.*

1 BEAST-HOUSE
OF *beste* a1250 MED
+OE *hūs*
*1616

2 ⋀ BYRE
OE *bȳre*

3 MISTALL
OE *méox*+*steall*
*1673

4 NEAT-HOUSE
OE *nēat*+*hūs*
*c1440

5 SHIPPON
OE *scypen*

BEAST-HOUSE 23Mon.6 bull-house
COW-BYRE (OE *cū*+—) 1Nb.3, 2Cu.5, 3Du.1, 6Y.1–3/8/9, 12St.8;
MILKING- (OE *milc*(*-ian*+-ING+—) 33Brk.1
COW-SHIPPON (*1859) 37D.10
SHIPPON 36Co.3 part of cow-house where fodder is kept

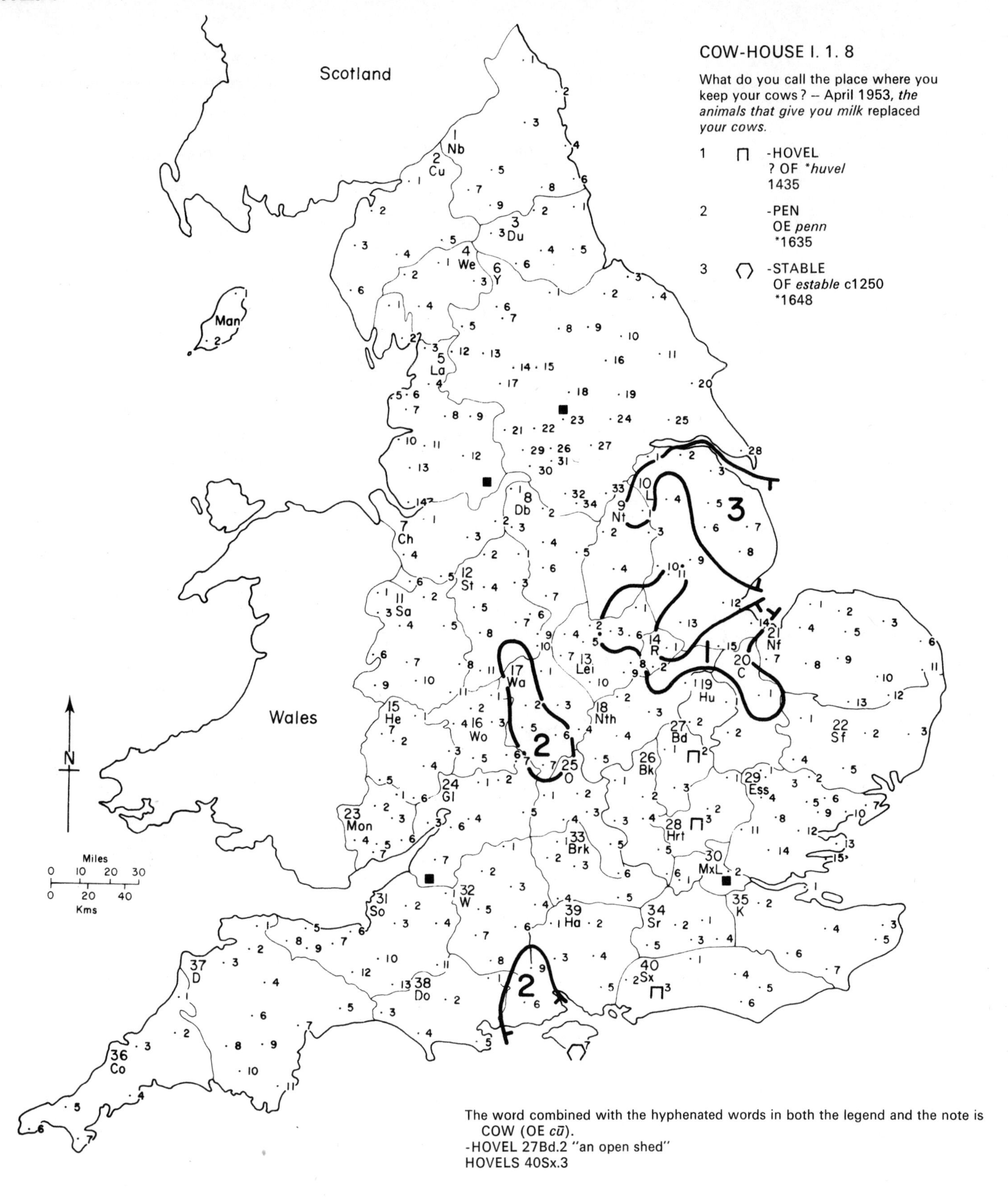

The word combined with the hyphenated words in both the legend and the note is COW (OE *cū*).
-HOVEL 27Bd.2 "an open shed"
HOVELS 40Sx.3

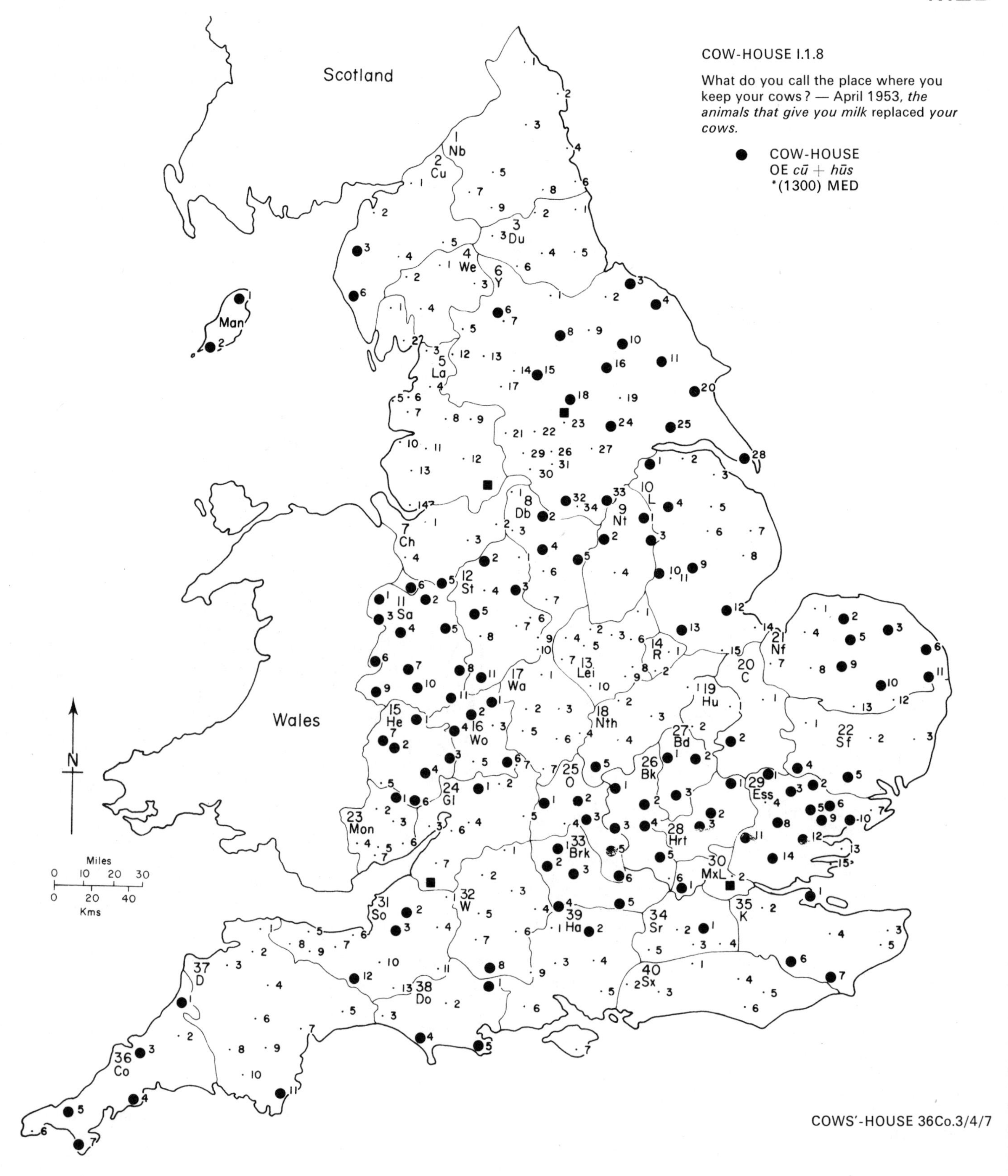
COW-HOUSE I.1.8
What do you call the place where you keep your cows? — April 1953, *the animals that give you milk* replaced *your cows.*
● COW-HOUSE
OE *cū* + *hūs*
*(1300) MED
Scotland
Wales
Man
N
Miles
0 10 20 30
0 20 40
Kms
COWS'-HOUSE 36Co.3/4/7

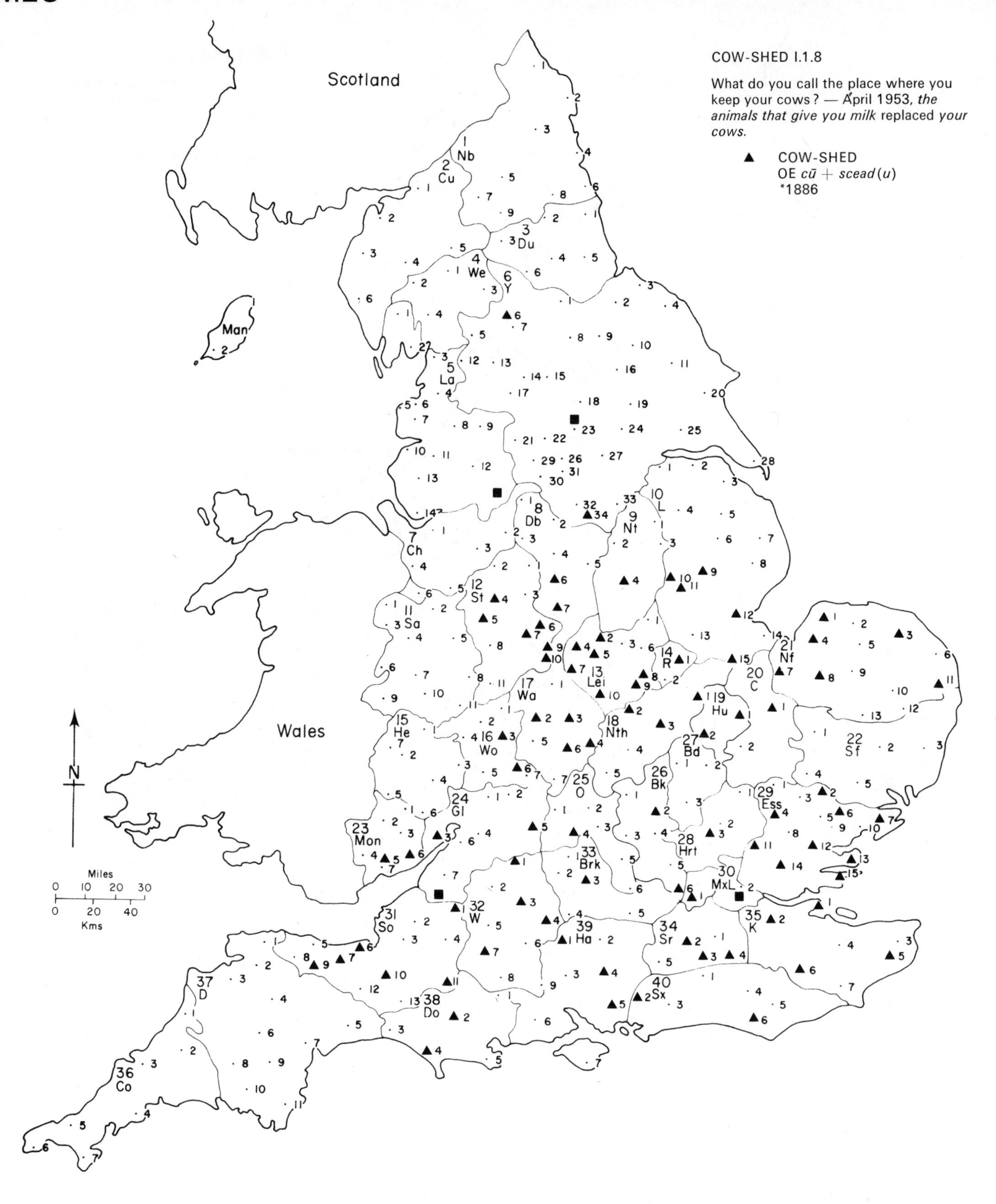
COW-SHED I.1.8
What do you call the place where you keep your cows? — April 1953, *the animals that give you milk* replaced *your cows*.
▲ COW-SHED
OE *cū* + *scead*(*u*)
*1886
Scotland
Wales
Man
N
Miles
0 10 20 30
0 20 40
Kms

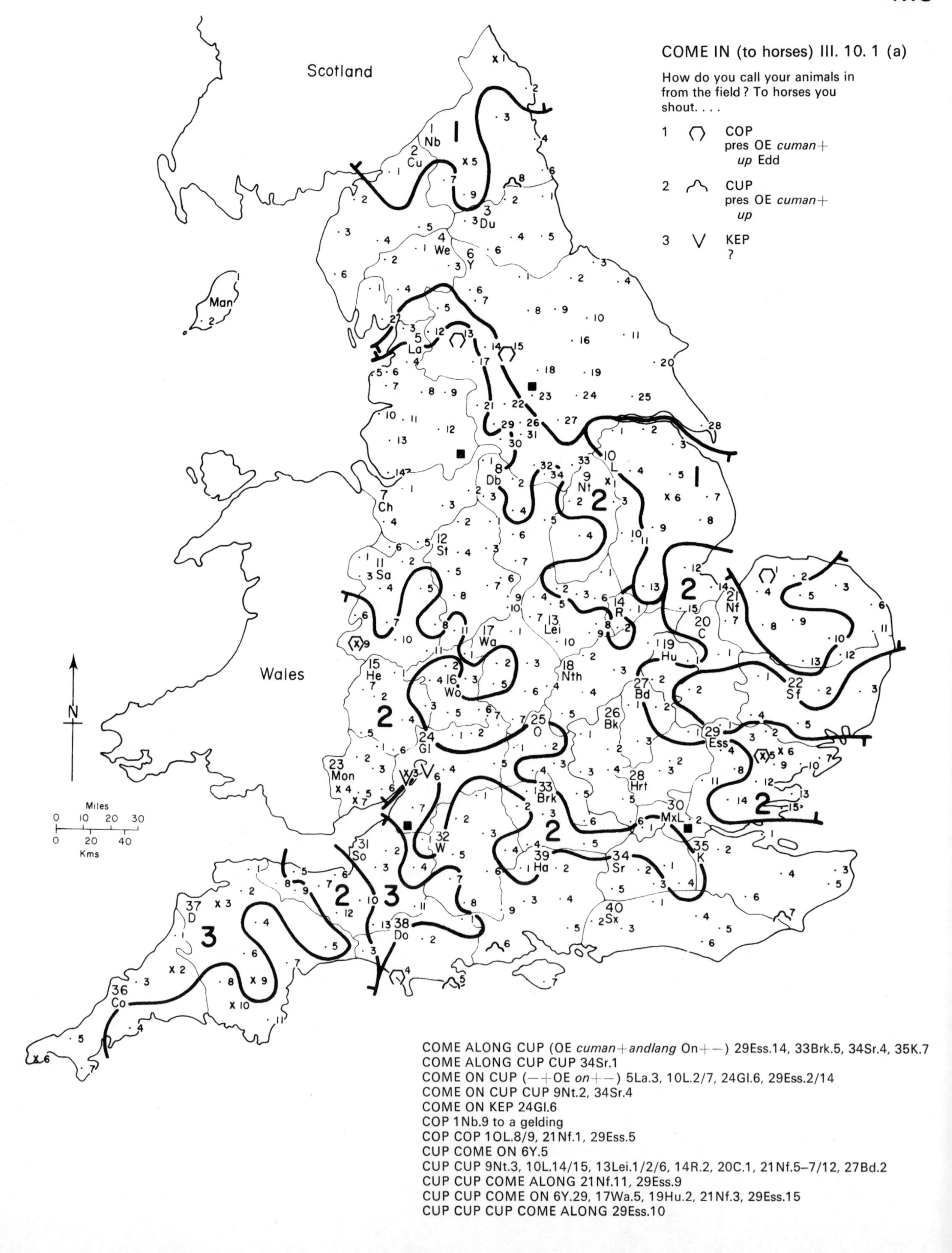

COME ALONG CUP (OE *cuman*+*andlang* On+−) 29Ess.14, 33Brk.5, 34Sr.4, 35K.7
COME ALONG CUP CUP 34Sr.1
COME ON CUP (−+OE *on*+−) 5La.3, 10L.2/7, 24Gl.6, 29Ess.2/14
COME ON CUP CUP 9Nt.2, 34Sr.4
COME ON KEP 24Gl.6
COP 1Nb.9 to a gelding
COP COP 10L.8/9, 21Nf.1, 29Ess.5
CUP COME ON 6Y.5
CUP CUP 9Nt.3, 10L.14/15, 13Lei.1/2/6, 14R.2, 20C.1, 21Nf.5–7/12, 27Bd.2
CUP CUP COME ALONG 21Nf.11, 29Ess.9
CUP CUP COME ON 6Y.29, 17Wa.5, 19Hu.2, 21Nf.3, 29Ess.15
CUP CUP CUP COME ALONG 29Ess.10

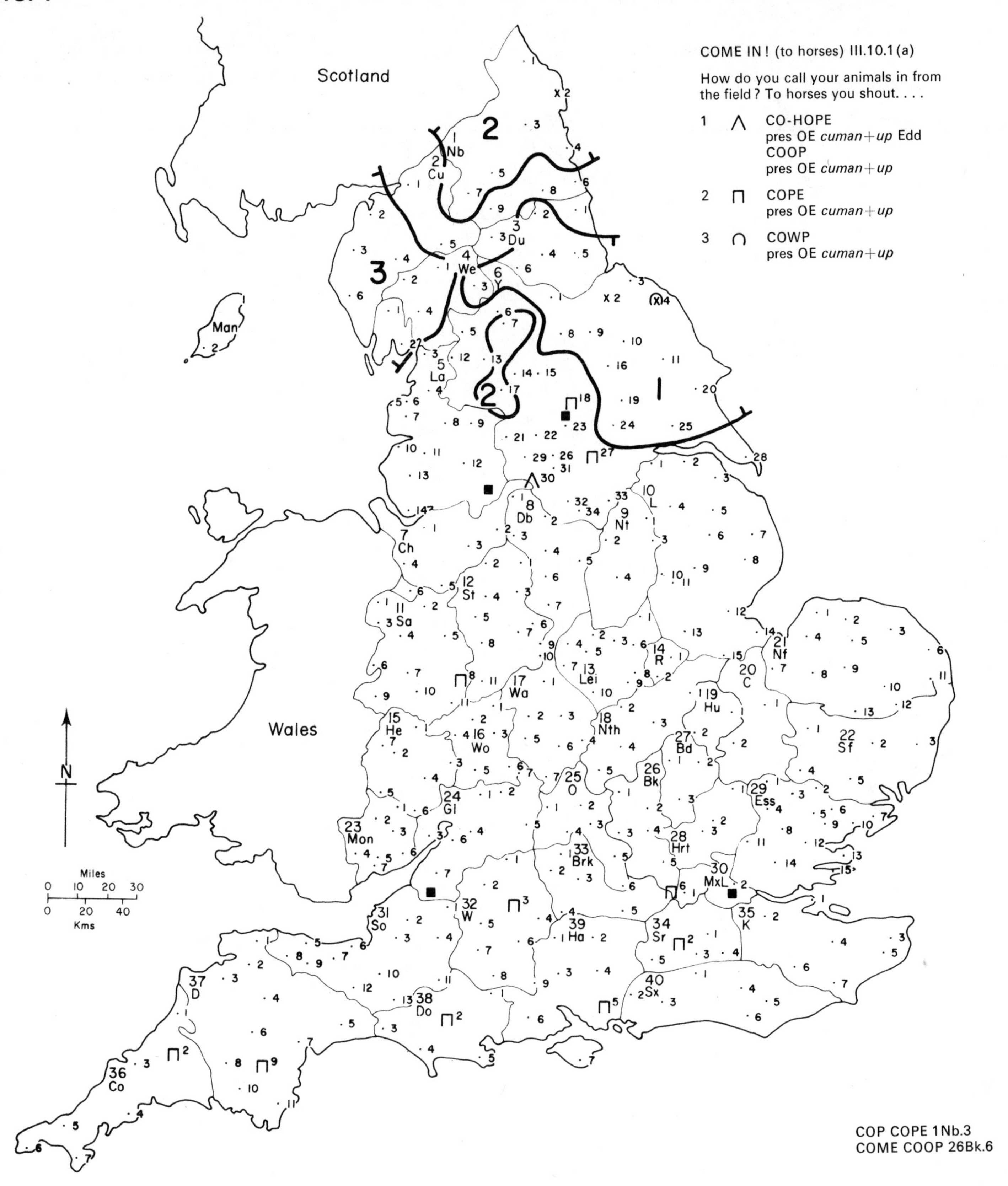
COME IN! (to horses) III.10.1 (a)
How do you call your animals in from the field? To horses you shout. . . .
1 Λ CO-HOPE
pres OE cuman+up Edd
COOP
pres OE cuman+up
2 ⊓ COPE
pres OE cuman+up
3 ∩ COWP
pres OE cuman+up
Scotland
Wales
Man
N
Miles
0 10 20 30
0 20 40
Kms
COP COPE 1Nb.3
COME COOP 26Bk.6

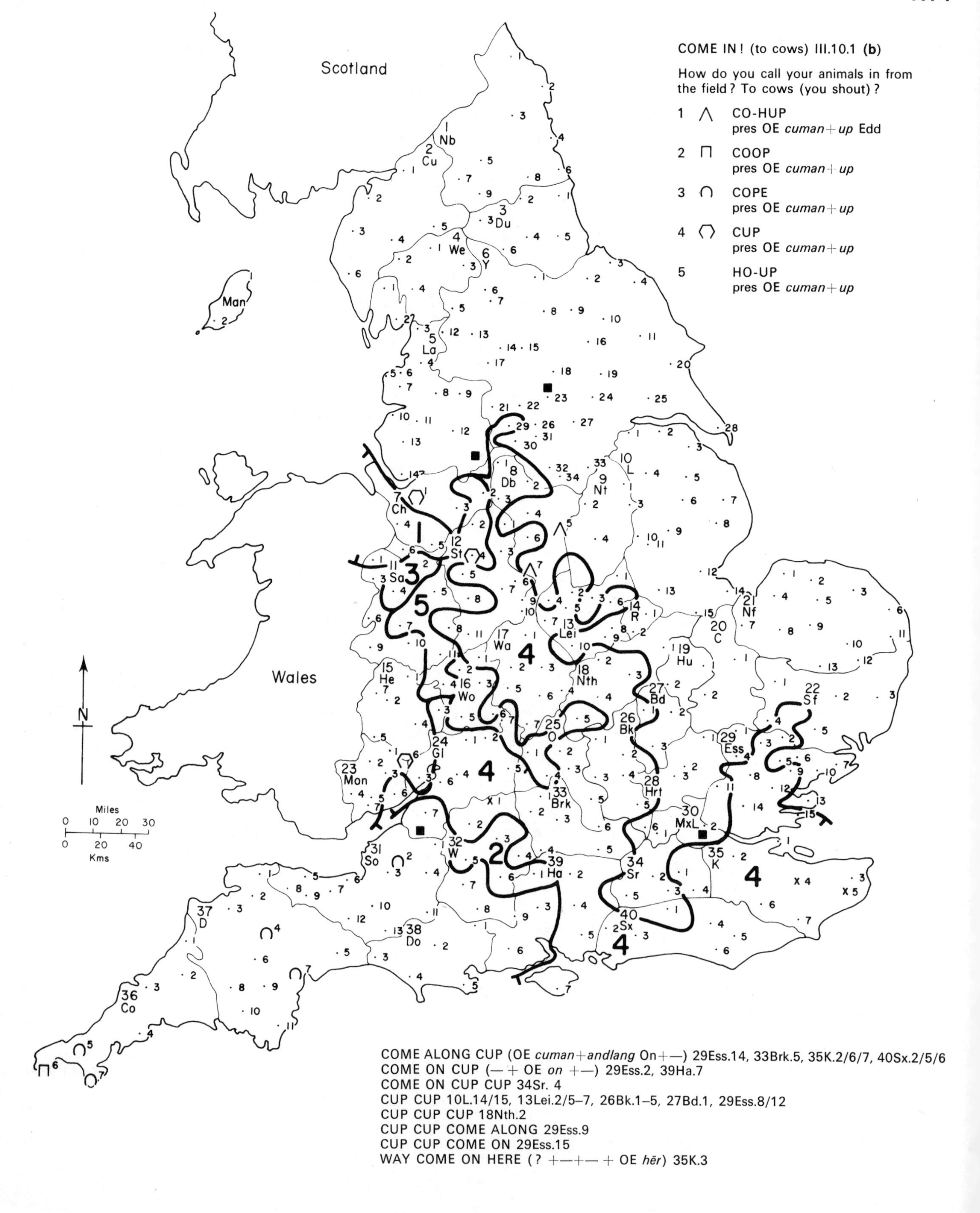
COME IN! (to cows) III.10.1 (b)
How do you call your animals in from the field? To cows (you shout)?
1 CO-HUP pres OE cuman + up Edd
2 COOP pres OE cuman + up
3 COPE pres OE cuman + up
4 CUP pres OE cuman + up
5 HO-UP pres OE cuman + up
Scotland
Wales
Man
Miles 0 10 20 30
0 20 40 Kms
COME ALONG CUP (OE cuman+andlang On+—) 29Ess.14, 33Brk.5, 35K.2/6/7, 40Sx.2/5/6
COME ON CUP (— + OE on +—) 29Ess.2, 39Ha.7
COME ON CUP CUP 34Sr. 4
CUP CUP 10L.14/15, 13Lei.2/5–7, 26Bk.1–5, 27Bd.1, 29Ess.8/12
CUP CUP CUP 18Nth.2
CUP CUP COME ALONG 29Ess.9
CUP CUP COME ON 29Ess.15
WAY COME ON HERE (? +—+— + OE hēr) 35K.3

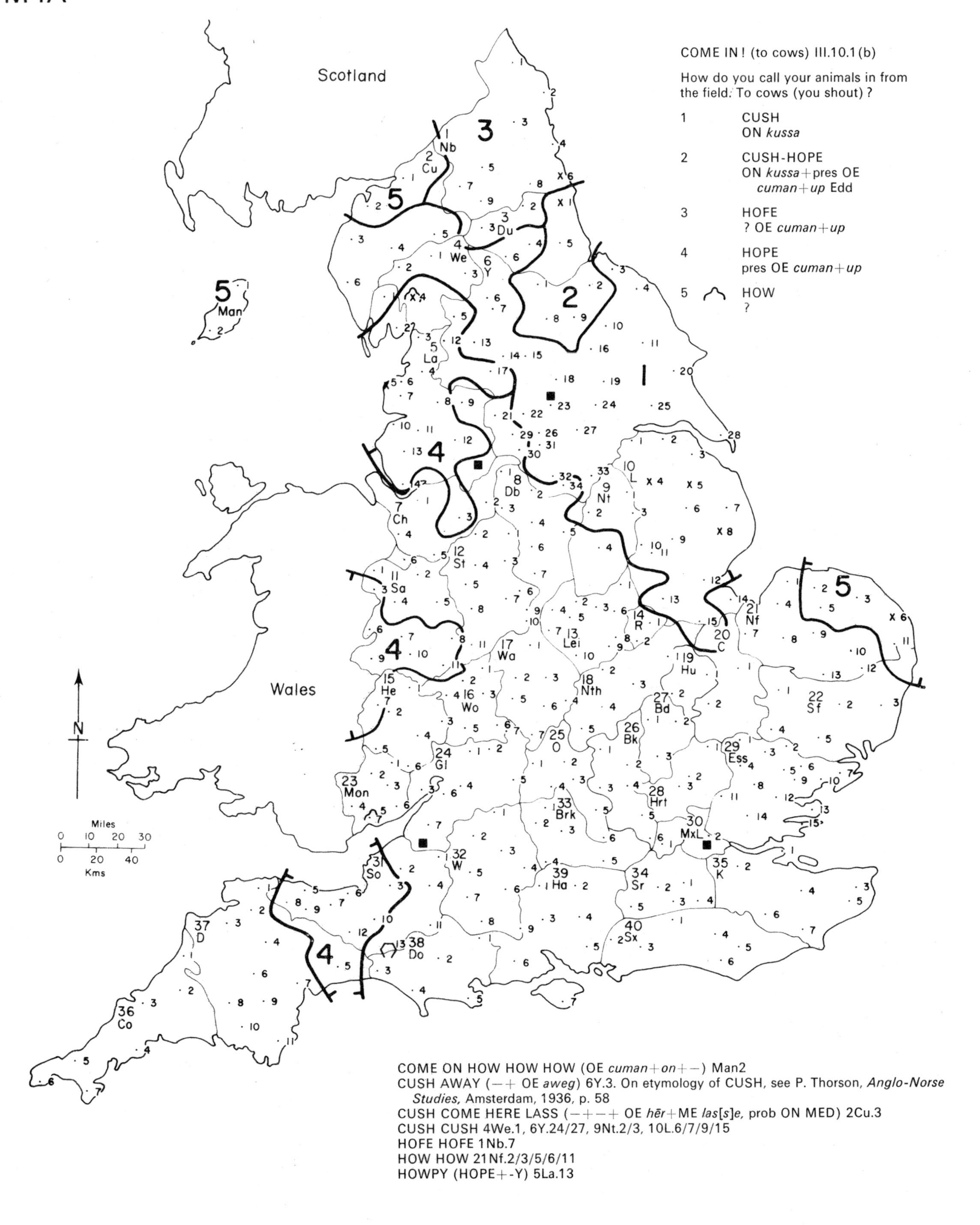

COME IN! (to cows) III.10.1(b)
How do you call your animals in from the field: To cows (you shout)?
1 CUSH
ON kussa
2 CUSH-HOPE
ON kussa + pres OE cuman + up Edd
3 HOFE
? OE cuman + up
4 HOPE
pres OE cuman + up
5 HOW
?
Scotland
Wales
Man
Nb
Cu
Du
We
Y
La
Ch
Db
Nt
L
St
Sa
Lei
R
Nf
Wa
C
He
Wo
Nth
Hu
Bd
Sf
O
Bk
Gl
Ess
Mon
Hrt
Brk
MxL
So
W
K
Ha
Sr
D
Do
Sx
Co
Miles
0 10 20 30
0 20 40
Kms
N
COME ON HOW HOW HOW (OE cuman + on + —) Man2
CUSH AWAY (— + OE aweg) 6Y.3. On etymology of CUSH, see P. Thorson, Anglo-Norse Studies, Amsterdam, 1936, p. 58
CUSH COME HERE LASS (— + — + OE hēr + ME las[s]e, prob ON MED) 2Cu.3
CUSH CUSH 4We.1, 6Y.24/27, 9Nt.2/3, 10L.6/7/9/15
HOFE HOFE 1Nb.7
HOW HOW 21Nf.2/3/5/6/11
HOWPY (HOPE + -Y) 5La.13

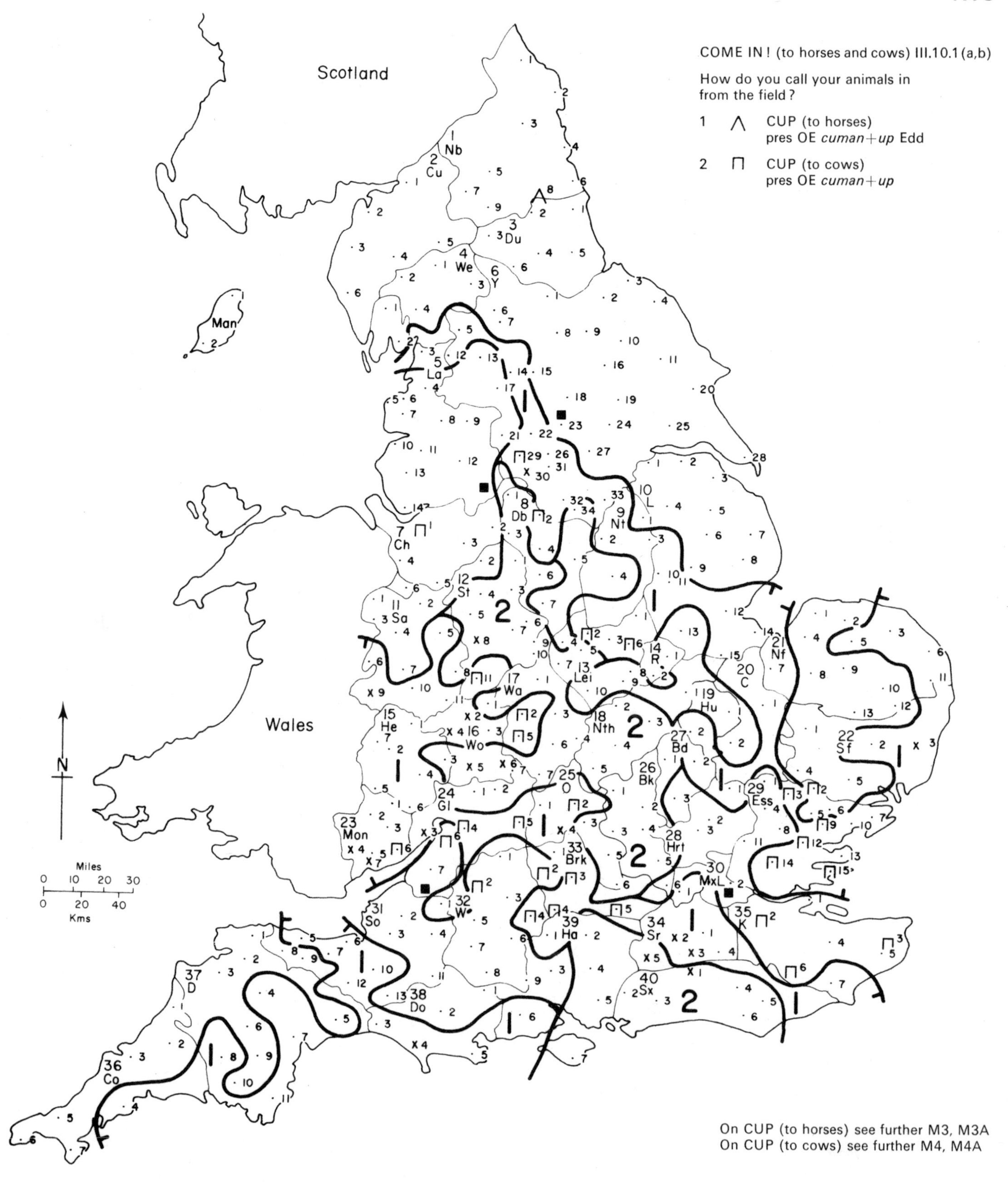
COME IN! (to horses and cows) III.10.1 (a,b)
How do you call your animals in from the field?
1 ⋀ CUP (to horses) pres OE cuman+up Edd
2 ⊓ CUP (to cows) pres OE cuman+up
On CUP (to horses) see further M3, M3A
On CUP (to cows) see further M4, M4A
Scotland
Wales
Man
N
Miles
0 10 20 30
0 20 40
Kms

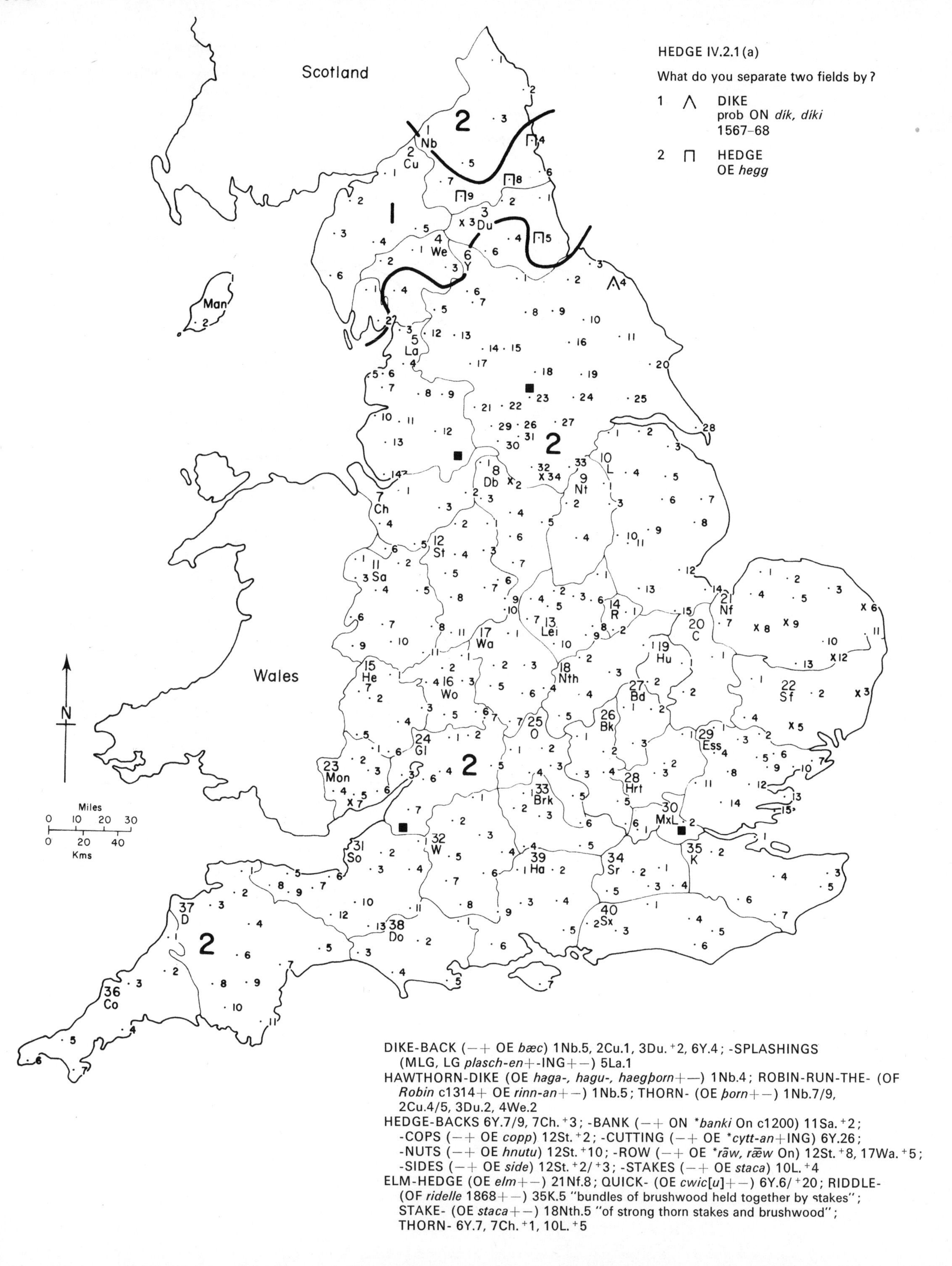

DIKE-BACK (—+ OE *bæc*) 1Nb.5, 2Cu.1, 3Du.+2, 6Y.4; -SPLASHINGS (MLG, LG *plasch-en*+-ING+—) 5La.1

HAWTHORN-DIKE (OE *haga-, hagu-, haegþorn*+—) 1Nb.4; ROBIN-RUN-THE- (OF *Robin* c1314+ OE *rinn-an*+—) 1Nb.5; THORN- (OE *þorn*+—) 1Nb.7/9, 2Cu.4/5, 3Du.2, 4We.2

HEDGE-BACKS 6Y.7/9, 7Ch.+3; -BANK (—+ ON **banki* On c1200) 11Sa.+2; -COPS (—+ OE *copp*) 12St.+2; -CUTTING (—+ OE **cytt-an*+ING) 6Y.26; -NUTS (—+ OE *hnutu*) 12St.+10; -ROW (—+ OE **rāw, rǣw* On) 12St.+8, 17Wa.+5; -SIDES (—+ OE *side*) 12St.+2/+3; -STAKES (—+ OE *staca*) 10L.+4

ELM-HEDGE (OE *elm*+—) 21Nf.8; QUICK- (OE *cwic[u]*+—) 6Y.6/+20; RIDDLE- (OF *ridelle* 1868+—) 35K.5 "bundles of brushwood held together by stakes"; STAKE- (OE *staca*+—) 18Nth.5 "of strong thorn stakes and brushwood"; THORN- 6Y.7, 7Ch.+1, 10L.+5

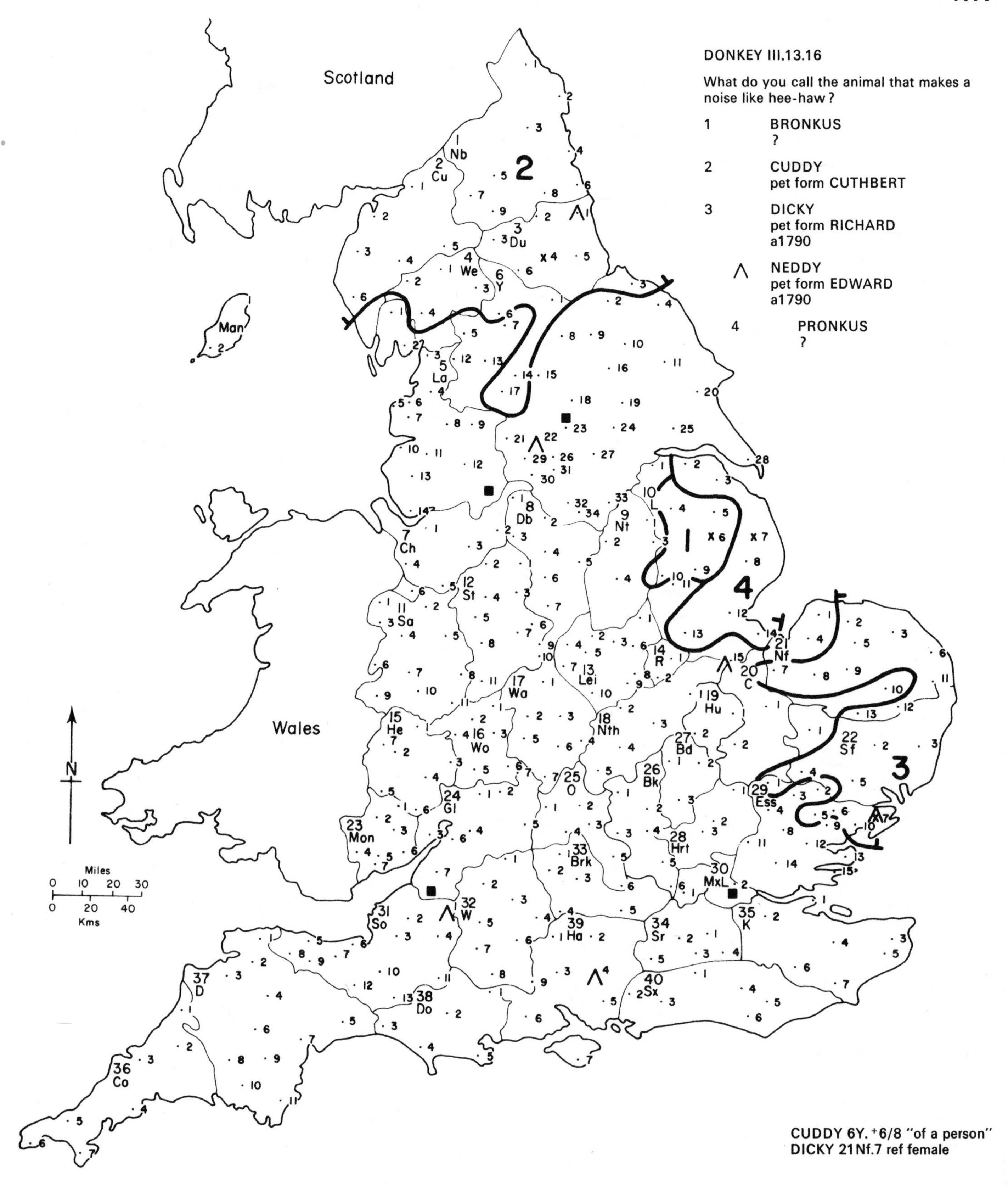

CUDDY 6Y. +6/8 "of a person"
DICKY 21Nf.7 ref female

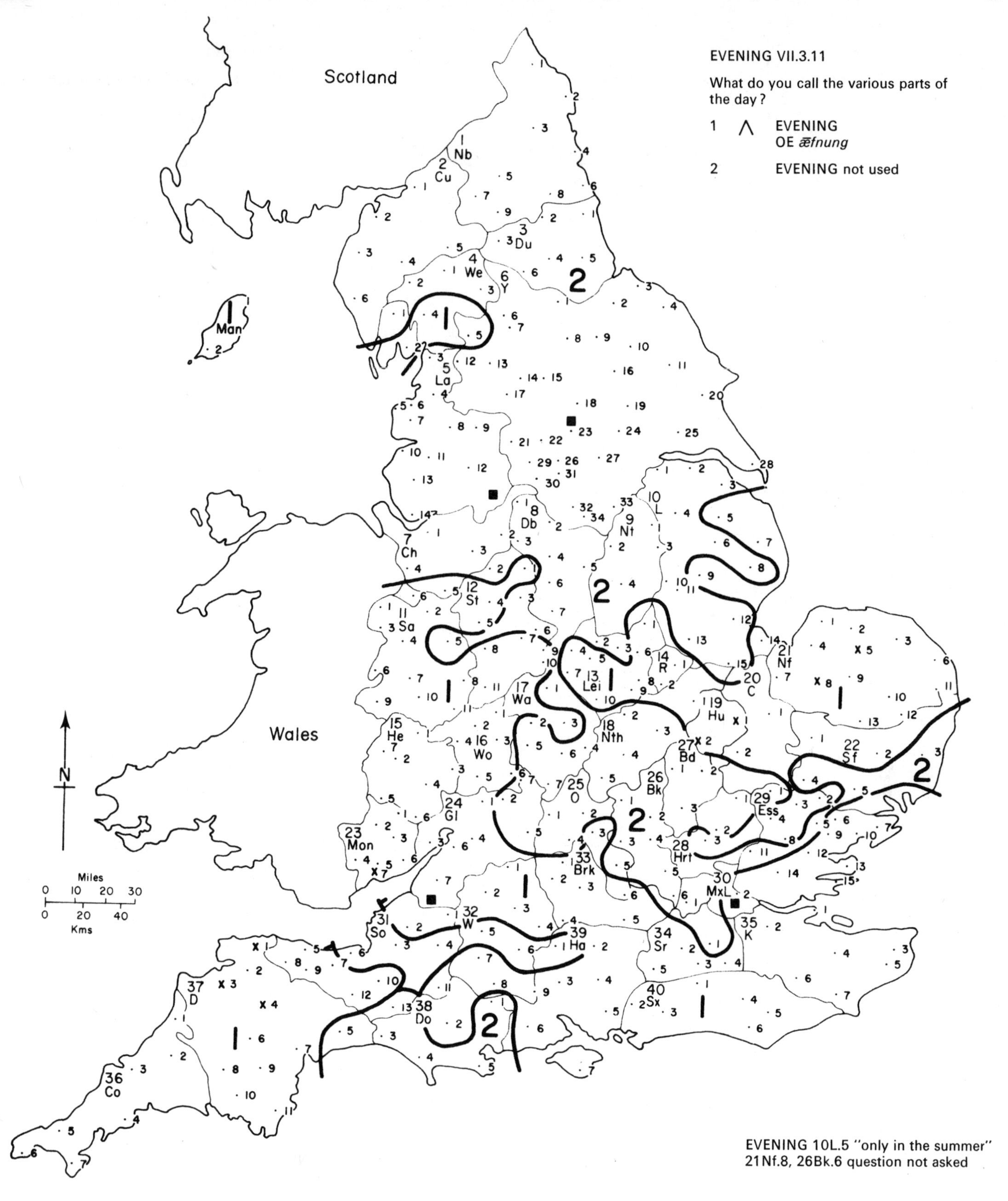

EVENING 10L.5 "only in the summer"
21Nf.8, 26Bk.6 question not asked

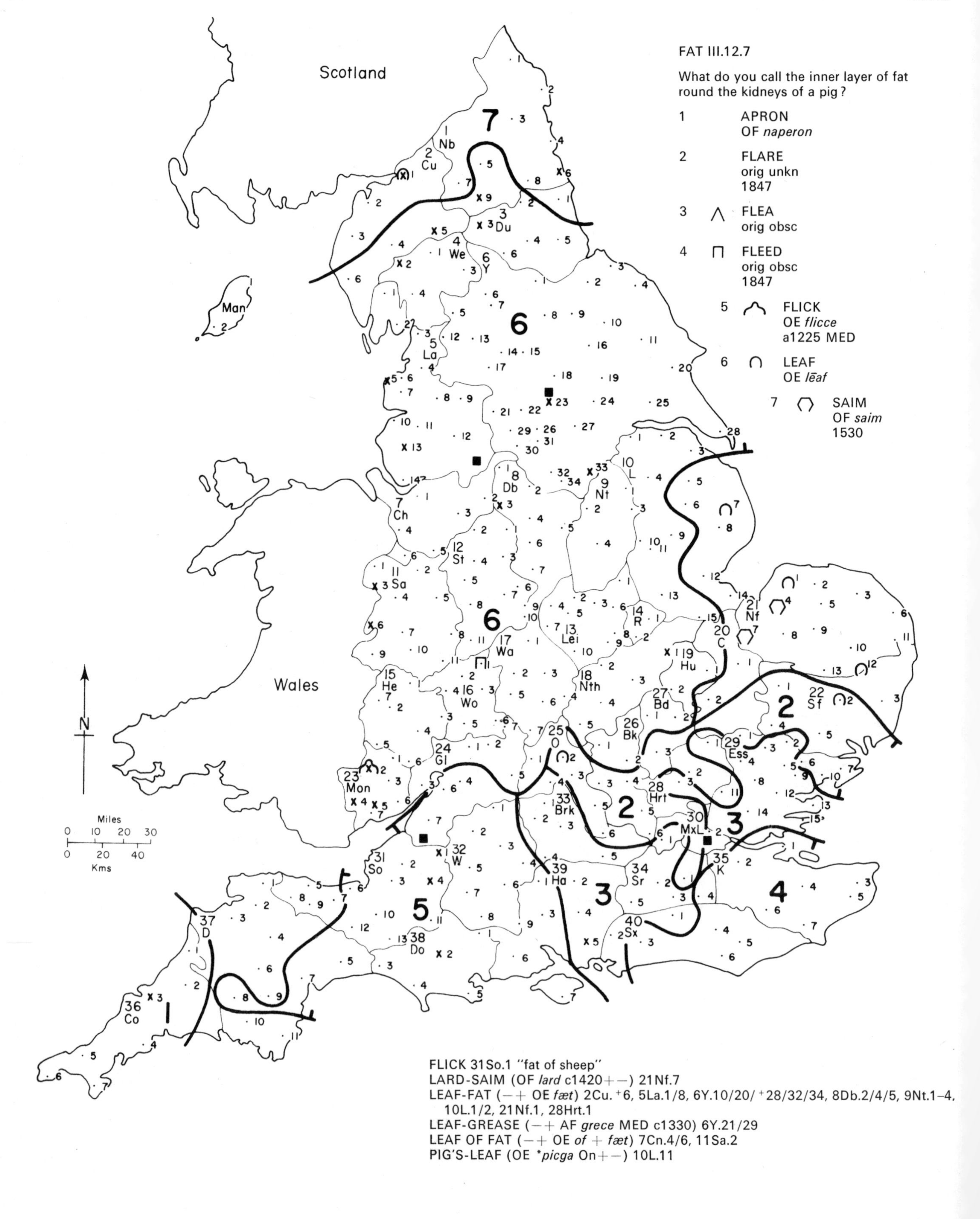
Scotland
Wales
Man
FAT III.12.7
What do you call the inner layer of fat round the kidneys of a pig?
1 APRON
OF *naperon*
2 FLARE
orig unkn
1847
3 FLEA
orig obsc
4 FLEED
orig obsc
1847
5 FLICK
OE *flicce*
a1225 MED
6 LEAF
OE *lēaf*
7 SAIM
OF *saim*
1530
Miles
0 10 20 30
0 20 40
Kms
N
Nb
Cu
Du
We
Y
La
Ch
Db
Nt
L
Sa
St
Lei
R
Nf
Wa
Hu
C
He
Wo
Nth
Bd
Sf
Gl
O
Bk
Ess
Mon
Hrt
Brk
MxL
So
W
Ha
Sr
K
Sx
D
Do
Co
FLICK 31So.1 "fat of sheep"
LARD-SAIM (OF *lard* c1420+—) 21Nf.7
LEAF-FAT (—+ OE *fæt*) 2Cu.+6, 5La.1/8, 6Y.10/20/+28/32/34, 8Db.2/4/5, 9Nt.1–4, 10L.1/2, 21Nf.1, 28Hrt.1
LEAF-GREASE (—+ AF *grece* MED c1330) 6Y.21/29
LEAF OF FAT (—+ OE *of* + *fæt*) 7Cn.4/6, 11Sa.2
PIG'S-LEAF (OE *picga* On+—) 10L.11

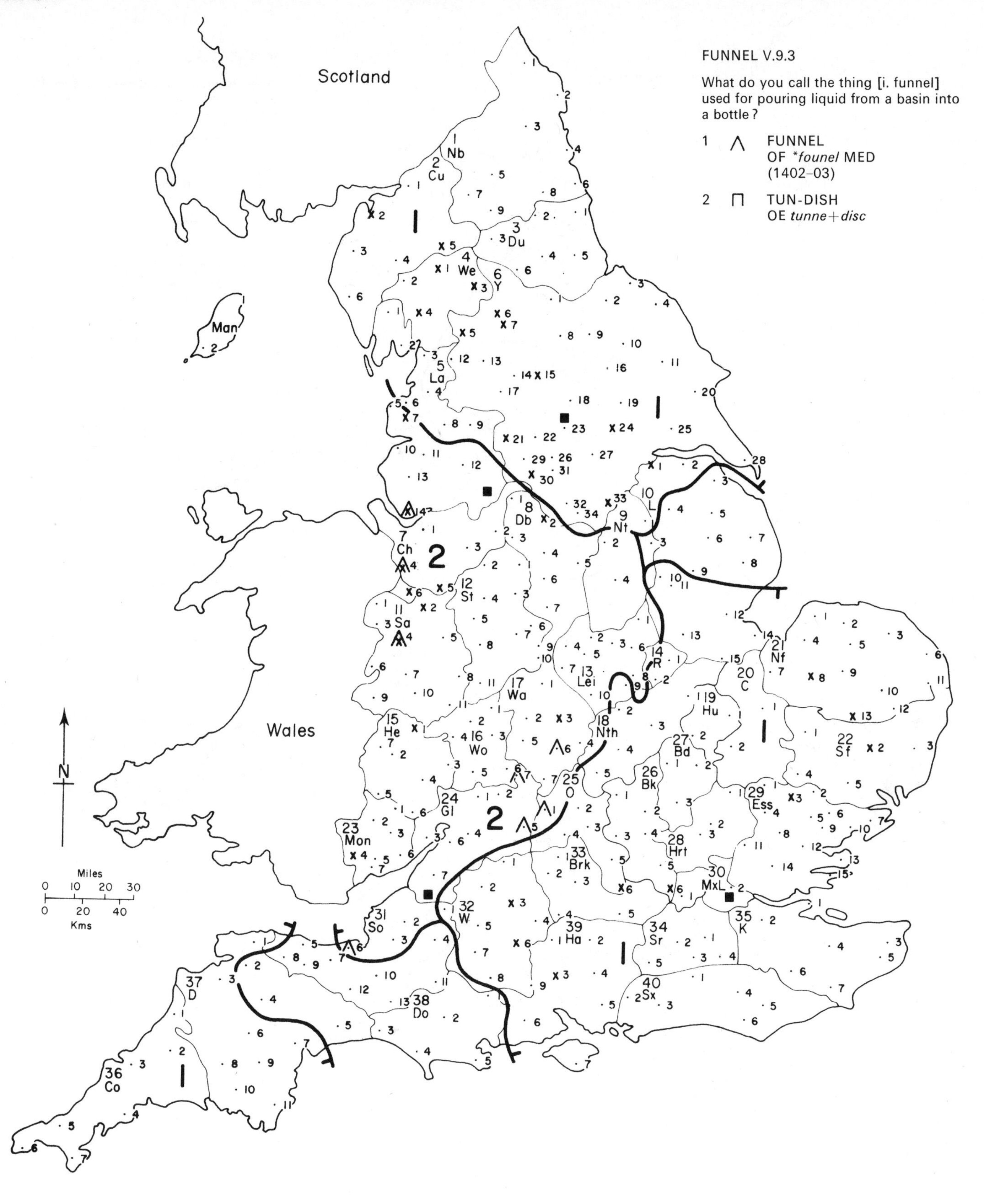
FUNNEL V.9.3
What do you call the thing [i. funnel] used for pouring liquid from a basin into a bottle?
1 Λ FUNNEL
OF *founel MED (1402–03)
2 ⊓ TUN-DISH
OE tunne+disc
Scotland
Wales
Man
N
Miles
0 10 20 30
0 20 40
Kms

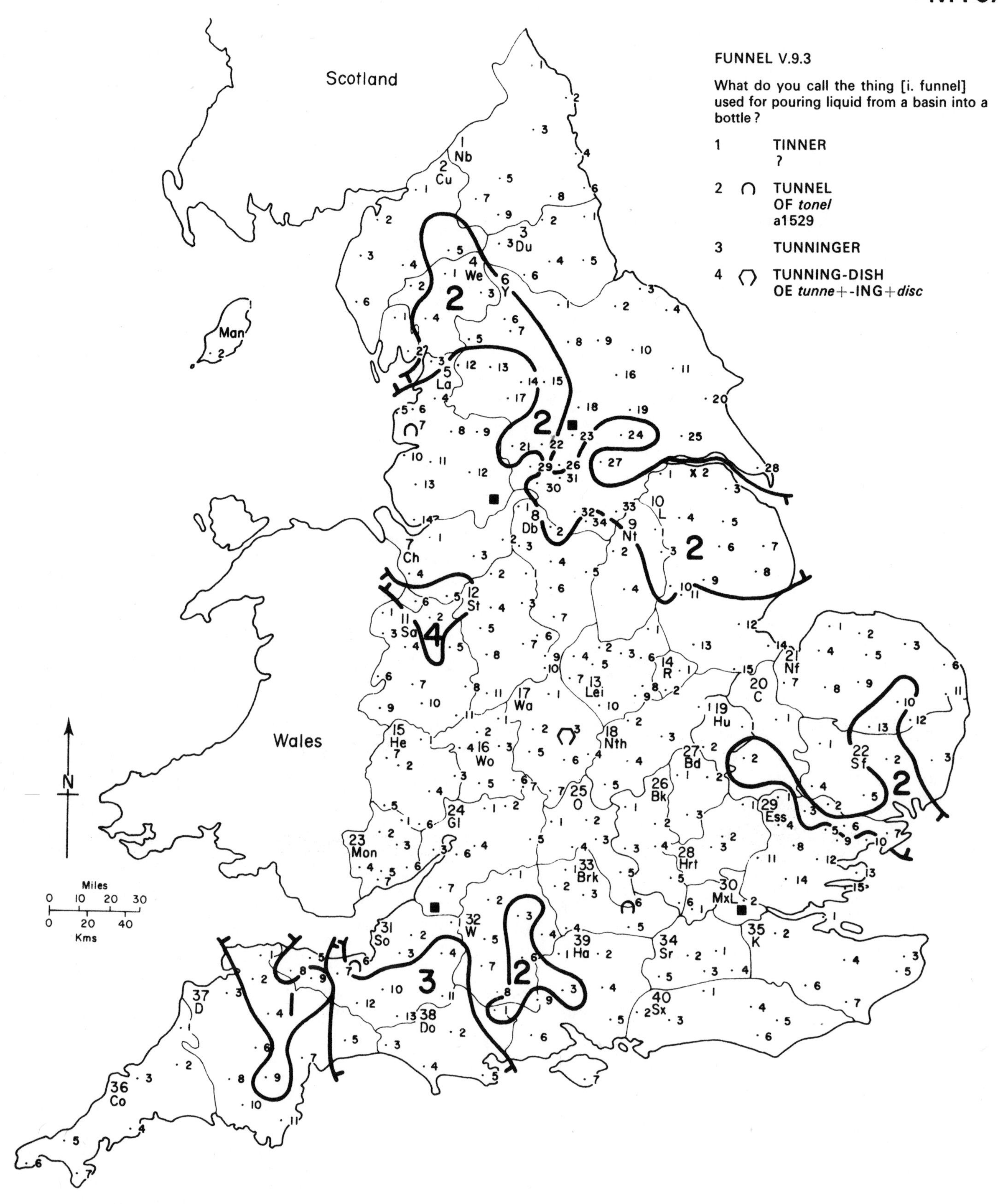
FUNNEL V.9.3
What do you call the thing [i. funnel] used for pouring liquid from a basin into a bottle?
1 TINNER
?
2 TUNNEL
OF *tonel*
a1529
3 TUNNINGER
4 TUNNING-DISH
OE *tunne*+-ING+*disc*
Scotland
Wales
Man
N
Miles
0 10 20 30
0 20 40
Kms
Nb
Cu
Du
We
Y
La
L
Db
Nt
Ch
St
Sa
Nf
R
Lei
C
Wa
Hu
He
Wo
Nth
Bd
Sf
Bk
O
Gl
Ess
Mon
Hrt
Brk
MxL
So
W
K
Ha
Sr
D
Do
Sx
Co

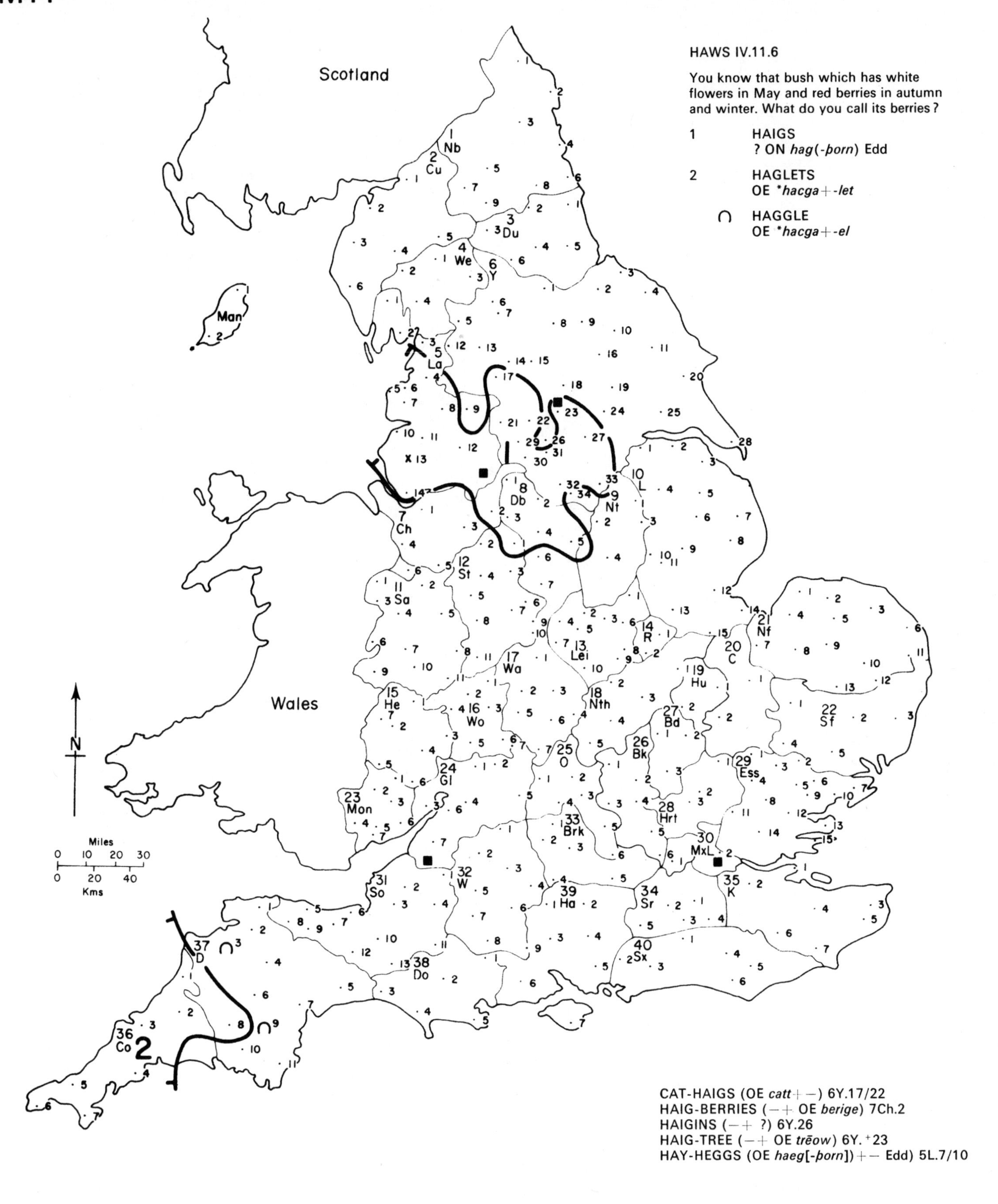
HAWS IV.11.6
You know that bush which has white flowers in May and red berries in autumn and winter. What do you call its berries?
1 HAIGS
? ON hag(-þorn) Edd
2 HAGLETS
OE *hacga+-let
∩ HAGGLE
OE *hacga+-el
Scotland
Wales
Man
N
Miles
Kms
CAT-HAIGS (OE catt+—) 6Y.17/22
HAIG-BERRIES (—+ OE berige) 7Ch.2
HAIGINS (—+ ?) 6Y.26
HAIG-TREE (—+ OE trēow) 6Y.+23
HAY-HEGGS (OE haeg[-þorn])+— Edd) 5L.7/10

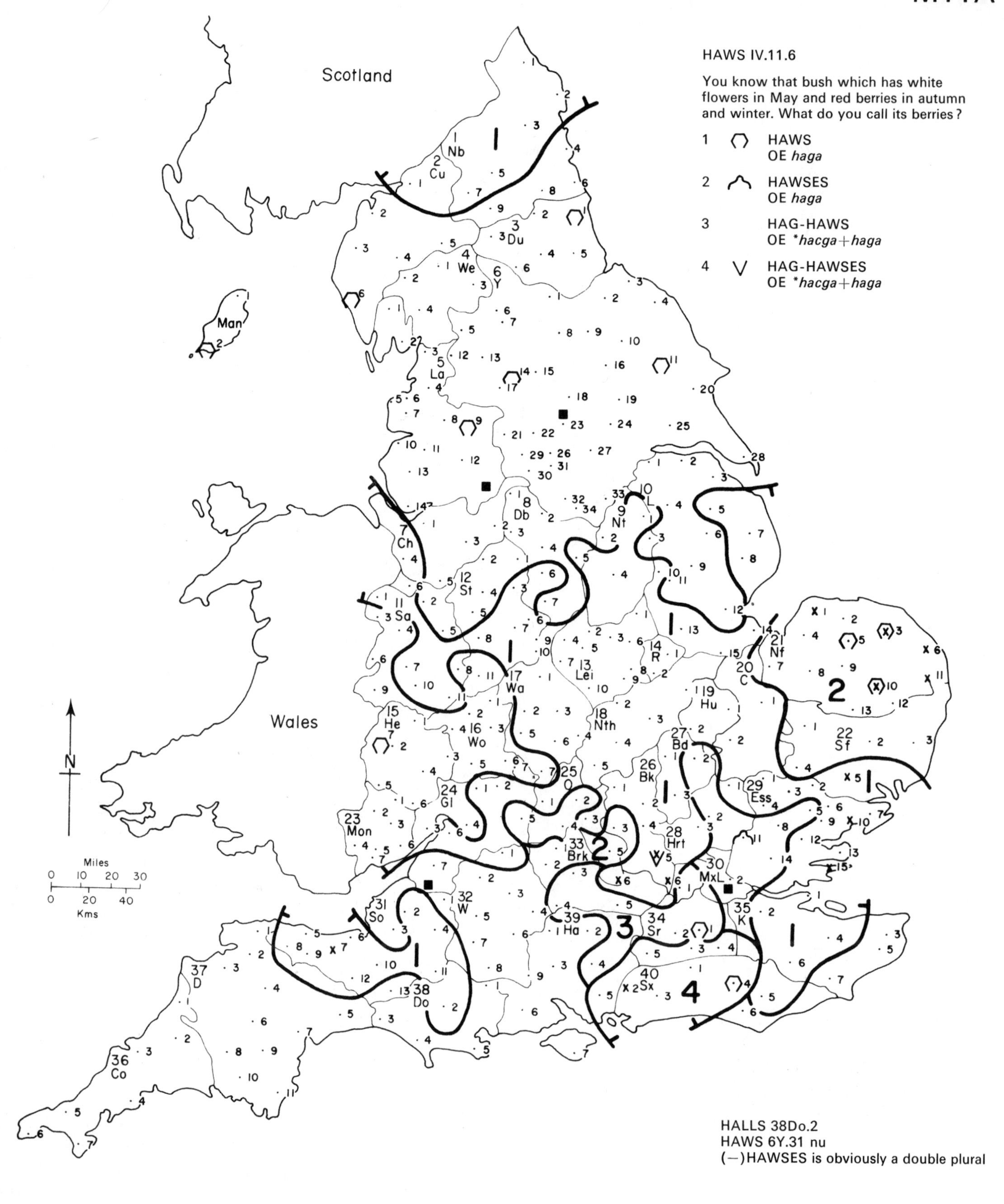

HALLS 38Do.2
HAWS 6Y.31 nu
(—)HAWSES is obviously a double plural

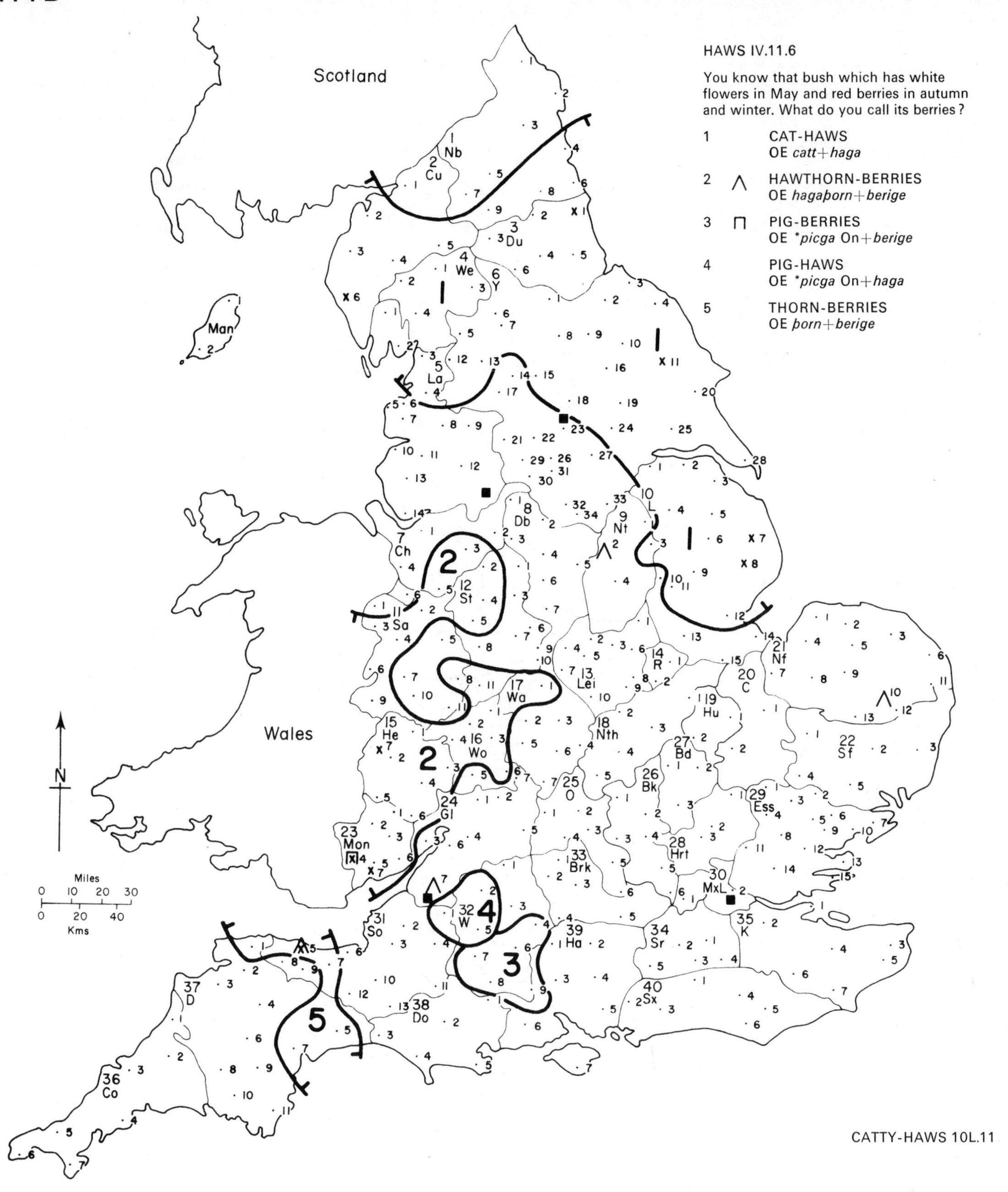
HAWS IV.11.6
You know that bush which has white flowers in May and red berries in autumn and winter. What do you call its berries?
1 CAT-HAWS
OE catt+haga
2 ⋀ HAWTHORN-BERRIES
OE hagaþorn+berige
3 ⊓ PIG-BERRIES
OE *picga On+berige
4 PIG-HAWS
OE *picga On+haga
5 THORN-BERRIES
OE þorn+berige
Scotland
Wales
Man
Nb
Cu
Du
We
Y
La
L
Db
Nt
Ch
St
Sa
Lei
R
Nf
C
Wa
Hu
He
Wo
Nth
Sf
Bd
Bk
Ess
Gl
O
Mon
Hrt
Brk
MxL
W
So
Ha
Sr
K
Sx
D
Do
Co
N
Miles
0 10 20 30
0 20 40
Kms
CATTY-HAWS 10L.11

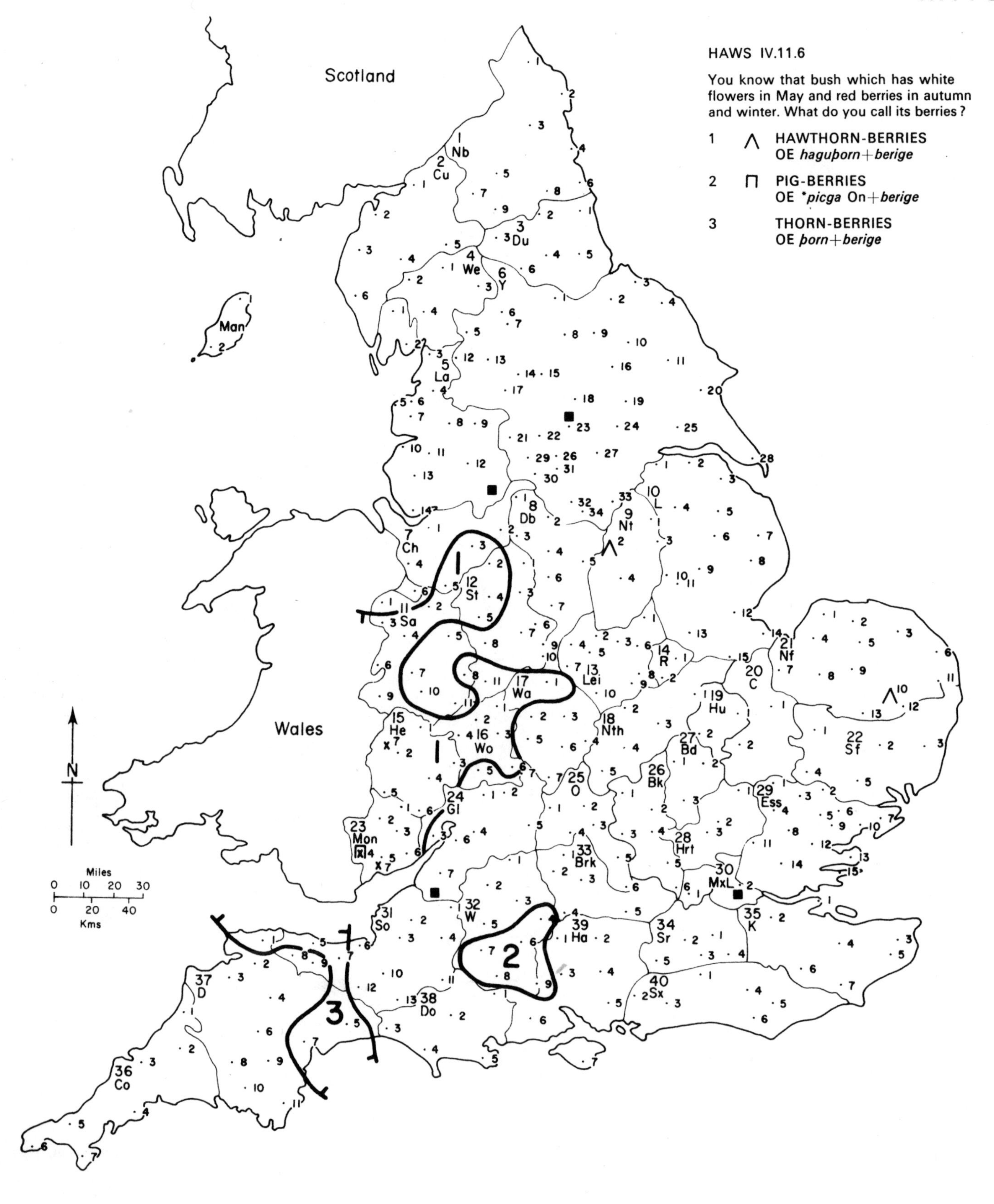
HAWS IV.11.6
You know that bush which has white flowers in May and red berries in autumn and winter. What do you call its berries?
1 Λ HAWTHORN-BERRIES
OE *haguþorn+berige*
2 ⊓ PIG-BERRIES
OE **picga* On+*berige*
3 THORN-BERRIES
OE *þorn+berige*
Scotland
Wales
Man
Nb
Cu
Du
We
Y
La
Ch
Db
Nt
L
St
Sa
Lei
R
Nf
Wa
C
Hu
He
Wo
Nth
Bd
Sf
O
Bk
Gl
Ess
Mon
Hrt
Brk
MxL
So
W
Ha
Sr
K
D
Do
Sx
Co
N
Miles
0 10 20 30
0 20 40
Kms

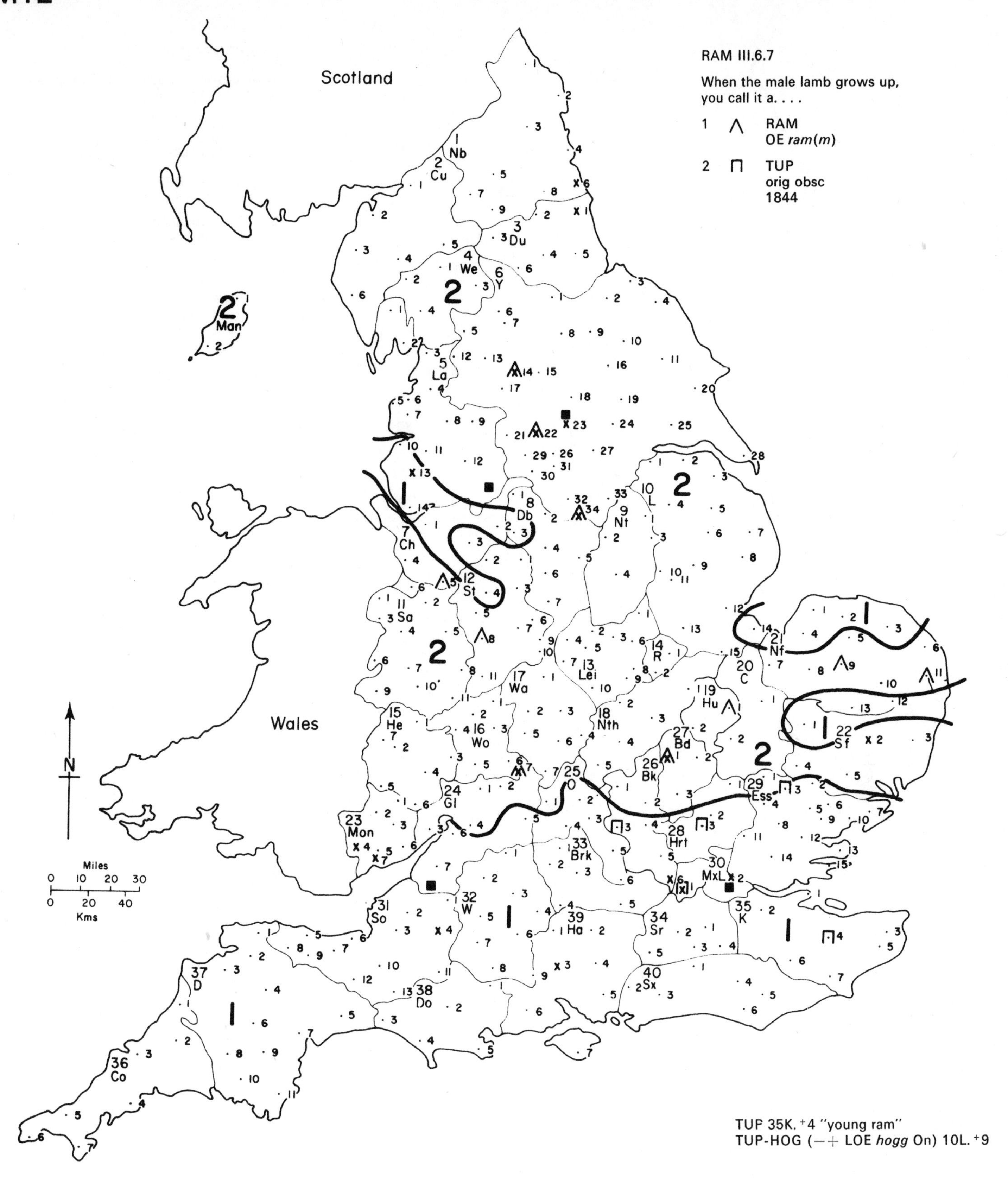
RAM III.6.7
When the male lamb grows up, you call it a. . . .
1 Λ RAM
OE *ram(m)*
2 ⊓ TUP
orig obsc
1844
Scotland
Wales
Man
N
Miles
0 10 20 30
0 20 40
Kms
TUP 35K. +4 "young ram"
TUP-HOG (—+ LOE *hogg* On) 10L. +9

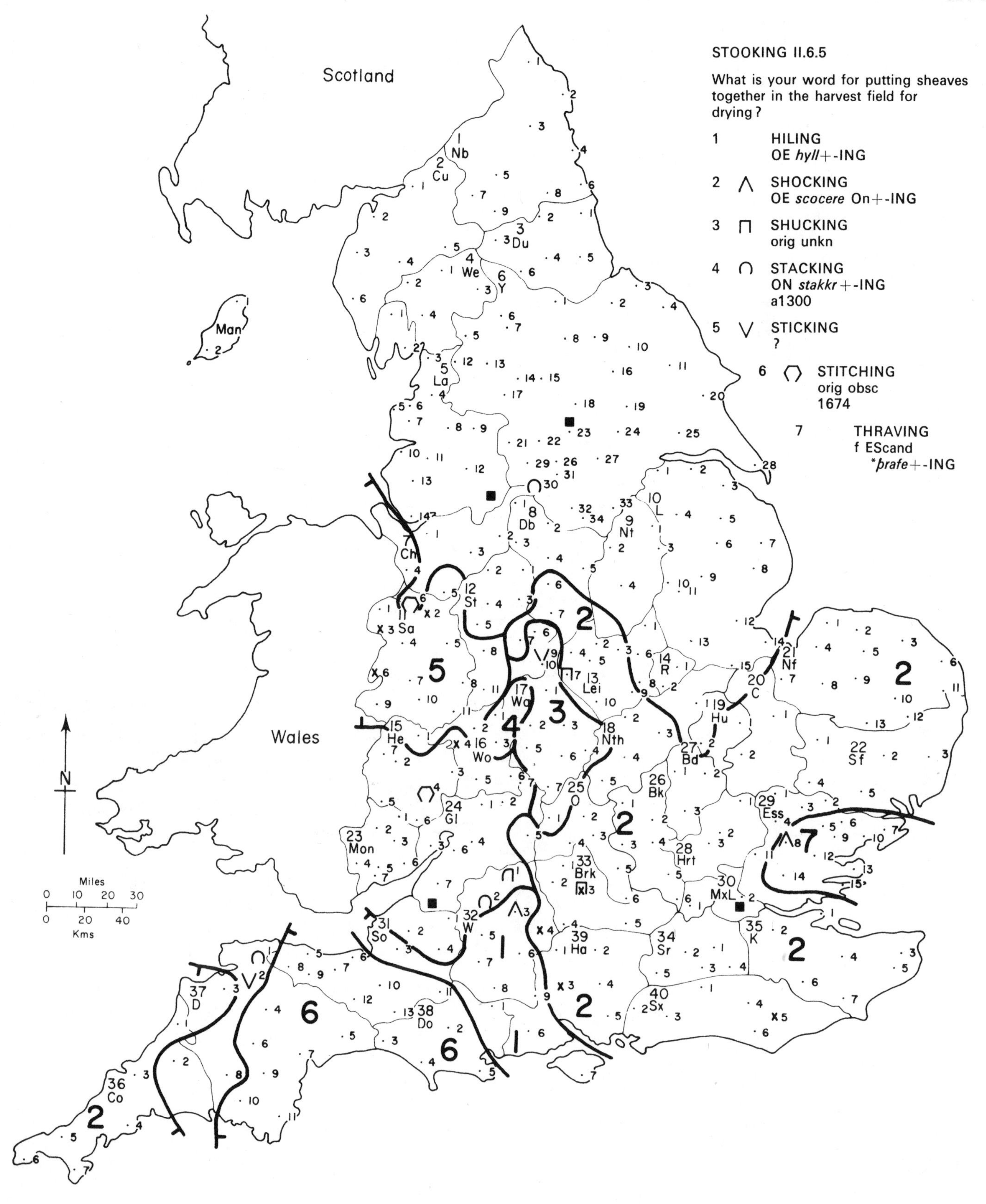

STOOKING II.6.5
What is your word for putting sheaves together in the harvest field for drying?
1 HILING
OE *hyll*+-ING
2 Λ SHOCKING
OE *scocere* On+-ING
3 ⊓ SHUCKING
orig unkn
4 ∩ STACKING
ON *stakkr*+-ING
a1300
5 V STICKING
?
6 STITCHING
orig obsc
1674
7 THRAVING
f EScand
*þrafe+-ING
Scotland
Wales
Man
Nb
Cu
Du
We
Y
La
Ch
Db
Nt
L
St
Sa
Lei
R
Nf
C
Wa
He
Wo
Nth
Hu
Bd
Sf
Gl
O
Bk
Ess
Mon
Brk
Hrt
MxL
So
W
Ha
Sr
K
D
Do
Sx
Co
Miles
0 10 20 30
0 20 40
Kms
N

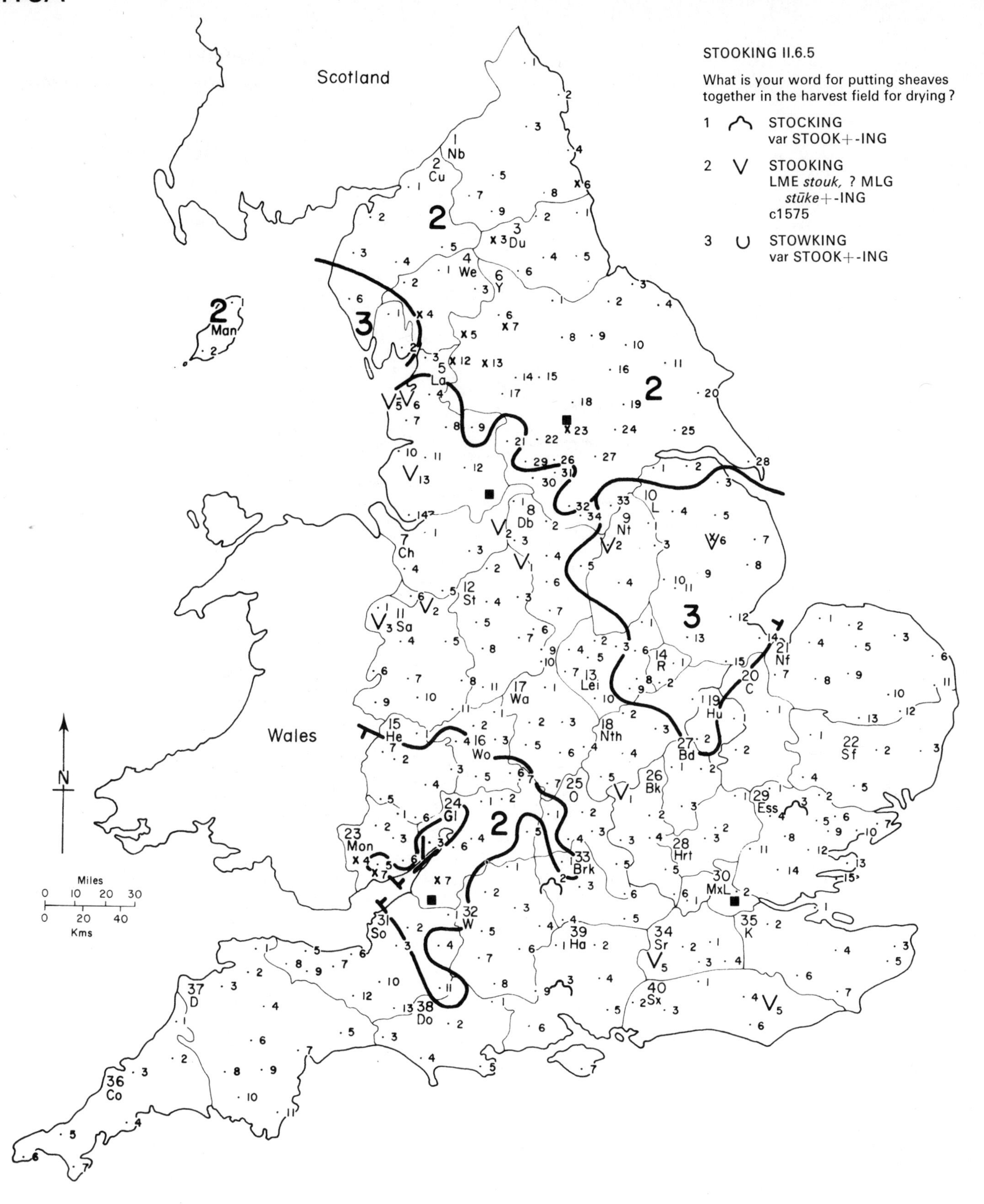
STOOKING II.6.5
What is your word for putting sheaves together in the harvest field for drying?
1 STOCKING
var STOOK+-ING
2 STOOKING
LME *stouk*, ? MLG
stūke+-ING
c1575
3 STOWKING
var STOOK+-ING
Scotland
Wales
Man
N
Miles
0 10 20 30
0 20 40
Kms

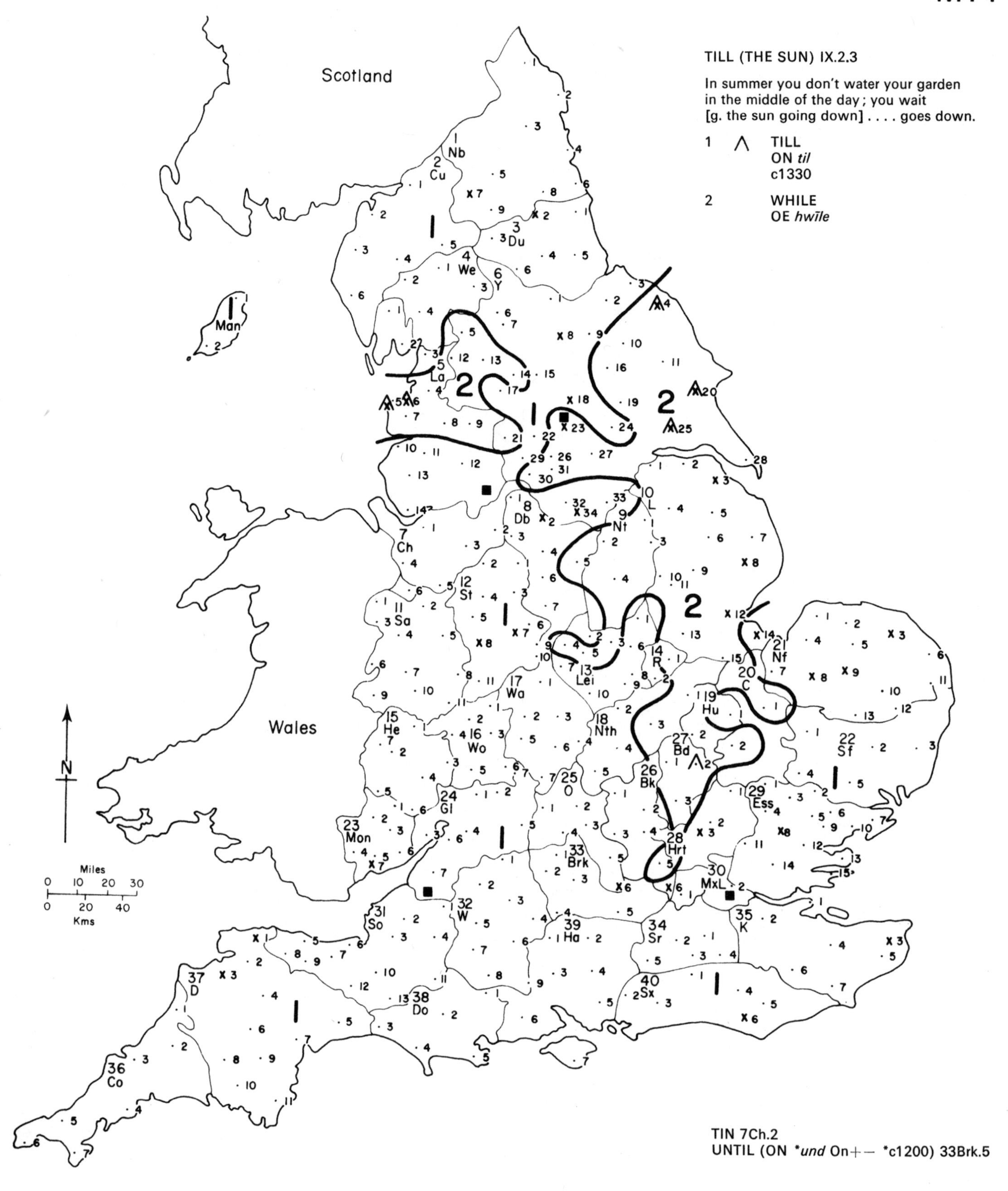
TILL (THE SUN) IX.2.3
In summer you don't water your garden in the middle of the day; you wait [g. the sun going down] . . . . goes down.
1 Λ TILL
ON *til*
c1330
2 WHILE
OE *hwīle*
Scotland
Wales
Man
N
Miles
0 10 20 30
0 20 40
Kms
TIN 7Ch.2
UNTIL (ON *und* On+— *c1200) 33Brk.5

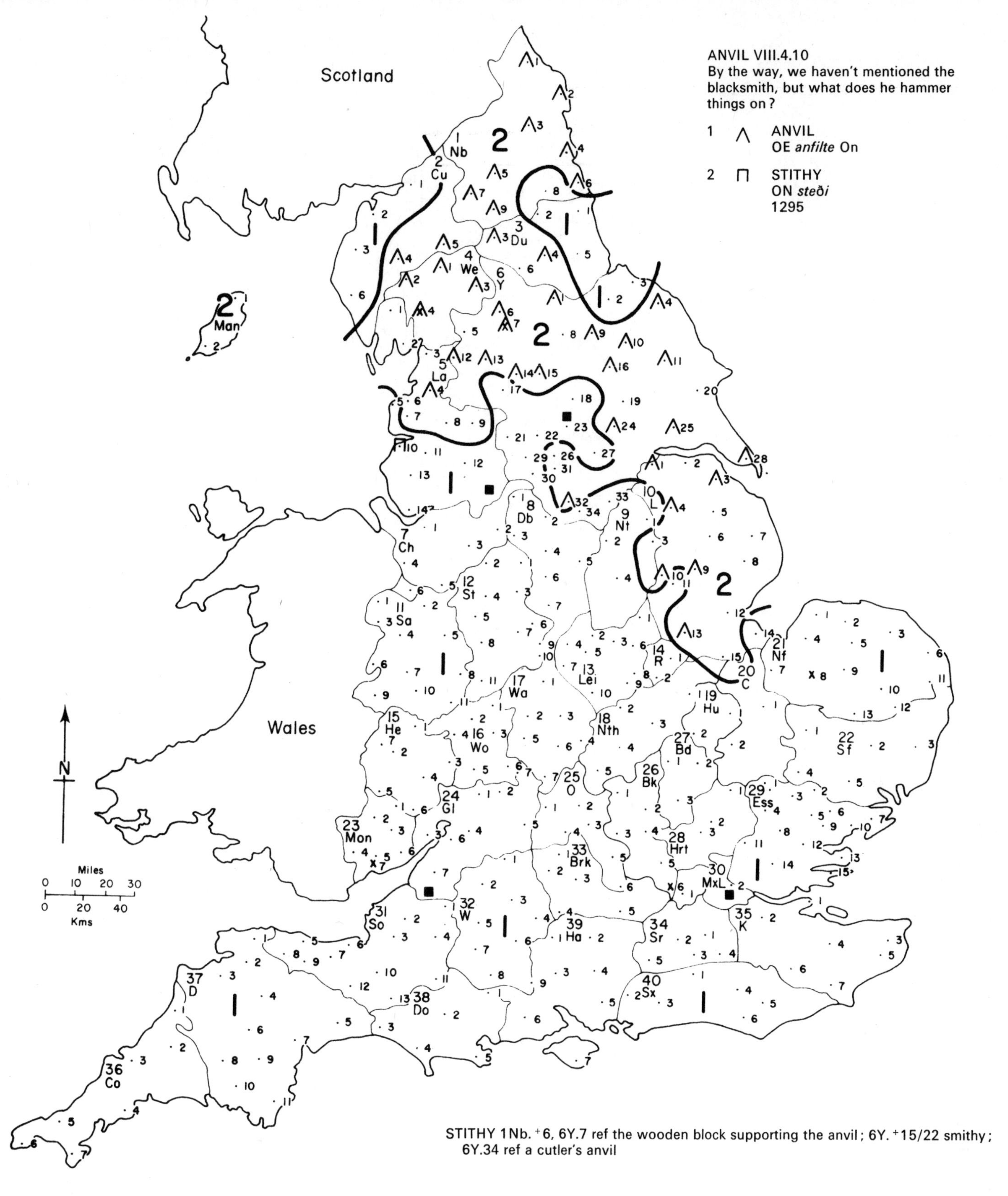

STITHY 1Nb. +6, 6Y.7 ref the wooden block supporting the anvil; 6Y. +15/22 smithy; 6Y.34 ref a cutler's anvil

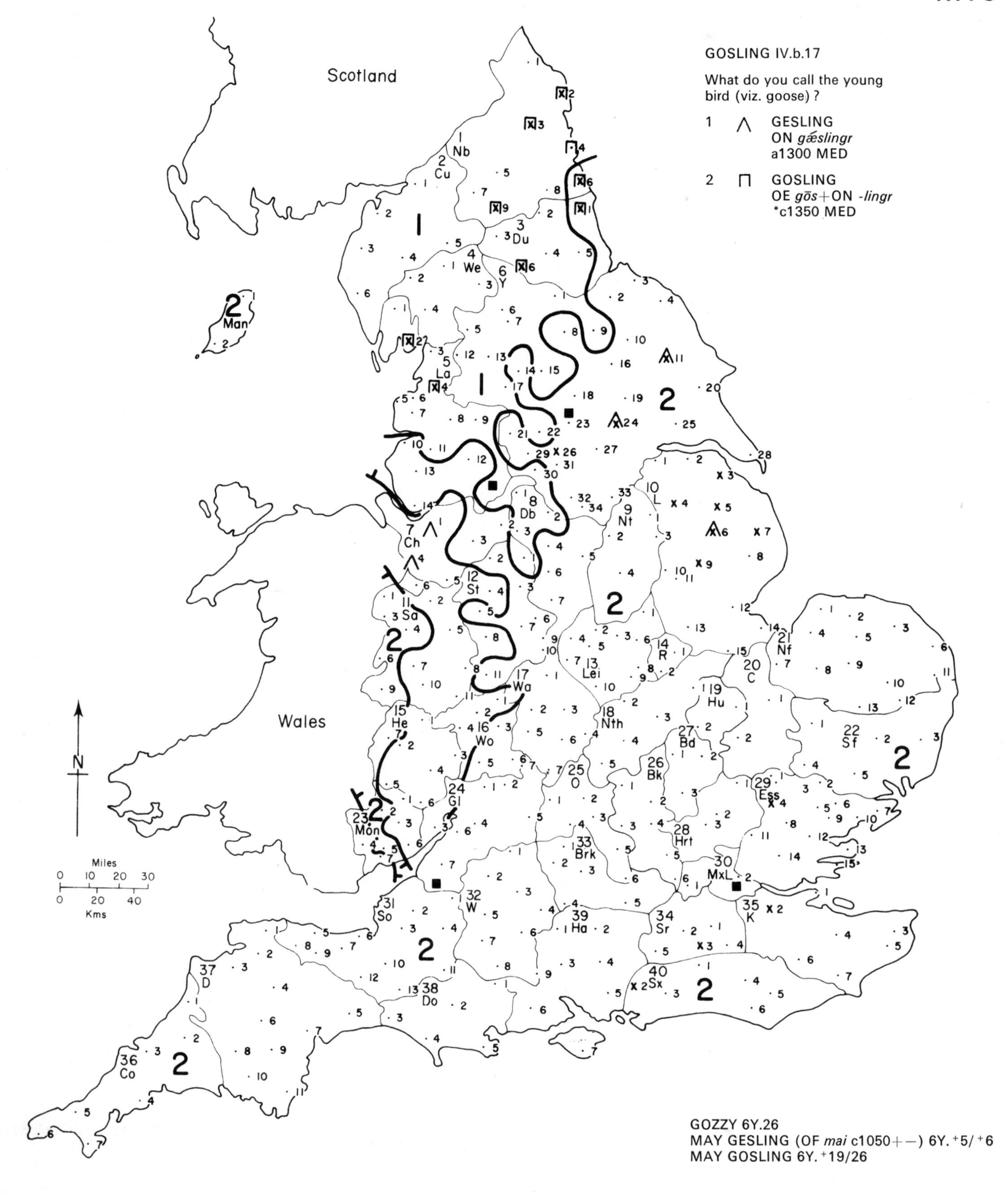
GOSLING IV.b.17
What do you call the young bird (viz. goose)?
1 GESLING ON *gǽslingr* a1300 MED
2 GOSLING OE *gōs*+ON *-lingr* *c1350 MED
Scotland
Wales
Miles 0 10 20 30
0 20 40 Kms
N
GOZZY 6Y.26
MAY GESLING (OF *mai* c1050+—) 6Y.+5/+6
MAY GOSLING 6Y.+19/26

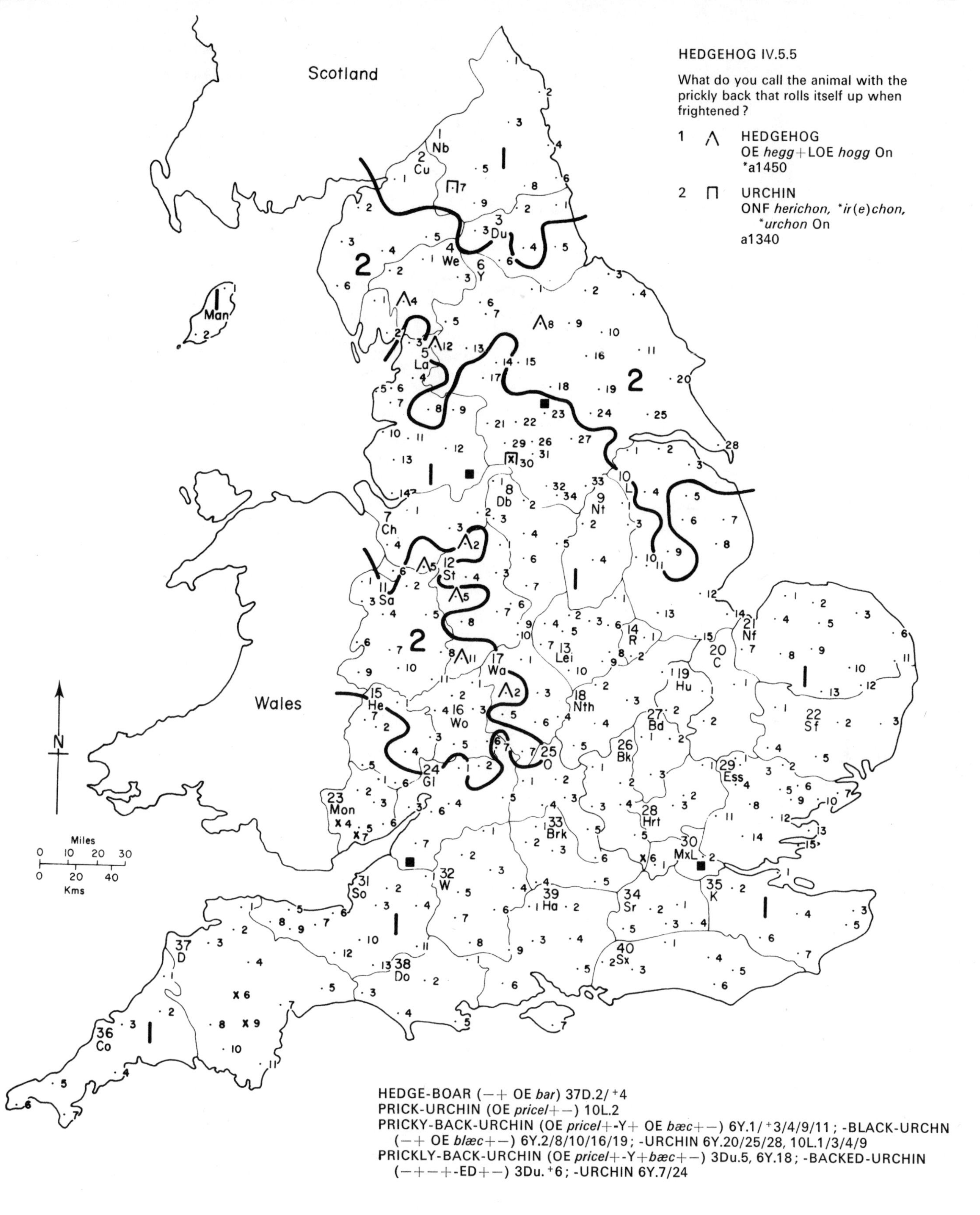

Scotland
Wales
Man
HEDGEHOG IV.5.5
What do you call the animal with the prickly back that rolls itself up when frightened?
1 /\ HEDGEHOG
OE *hegg*+LOE *hogg* On *a1450
2 ⊓ URCHIN
ONF *herichon*, **ir(e)chon*, **urchon* On a1340
Miles 0 10 20 30
0 20 40 Kms
N
1 Nb
2 Cu
3 Du
4 We
6 Y
5 La
7 Ch
8 Db
9 Nt
10 L
11 Sa
12 St
13 Lei
14 R
15 He
16 Wo
17 Wa
18 Nth
19 Hu
20 C
21 Nf
22 Sf
23 Mon
24 Gl
25 O
26 Bk
27 Bd
28 Hrt
29 Ess
30 MxL
31 So
32 W
33 Brk
34 Sr
35 K
36 Co
37 D
38 Do
39 Ha
40 Sx
HEDGE-BOAR (—+ OE *bar*) 37D.2/ +4
PRICK-URCHIN (OE *pricel*+—) 10L.2
PRICKY-BACK-URCHIN (OE *pricel*+-Y+ OE *bæc*+—) 6Y.1/ +3/4/9/11 ; -BLACK-URCHN (—+ OE *blæc*+—) 6Y.2/8/10/16/19 ; -URCHIN 6Y.20/25/28, 10L.1/3/4/9
PRICKLY-BACK-URCHIN (OE *pricel*+-Y+*bæc*+—) 3Du.5, 6Y.18 ; -BACKED-URCHIN (—+—+-ED+—) 3Du. +6 ; -URCHIN 6Y.7/24

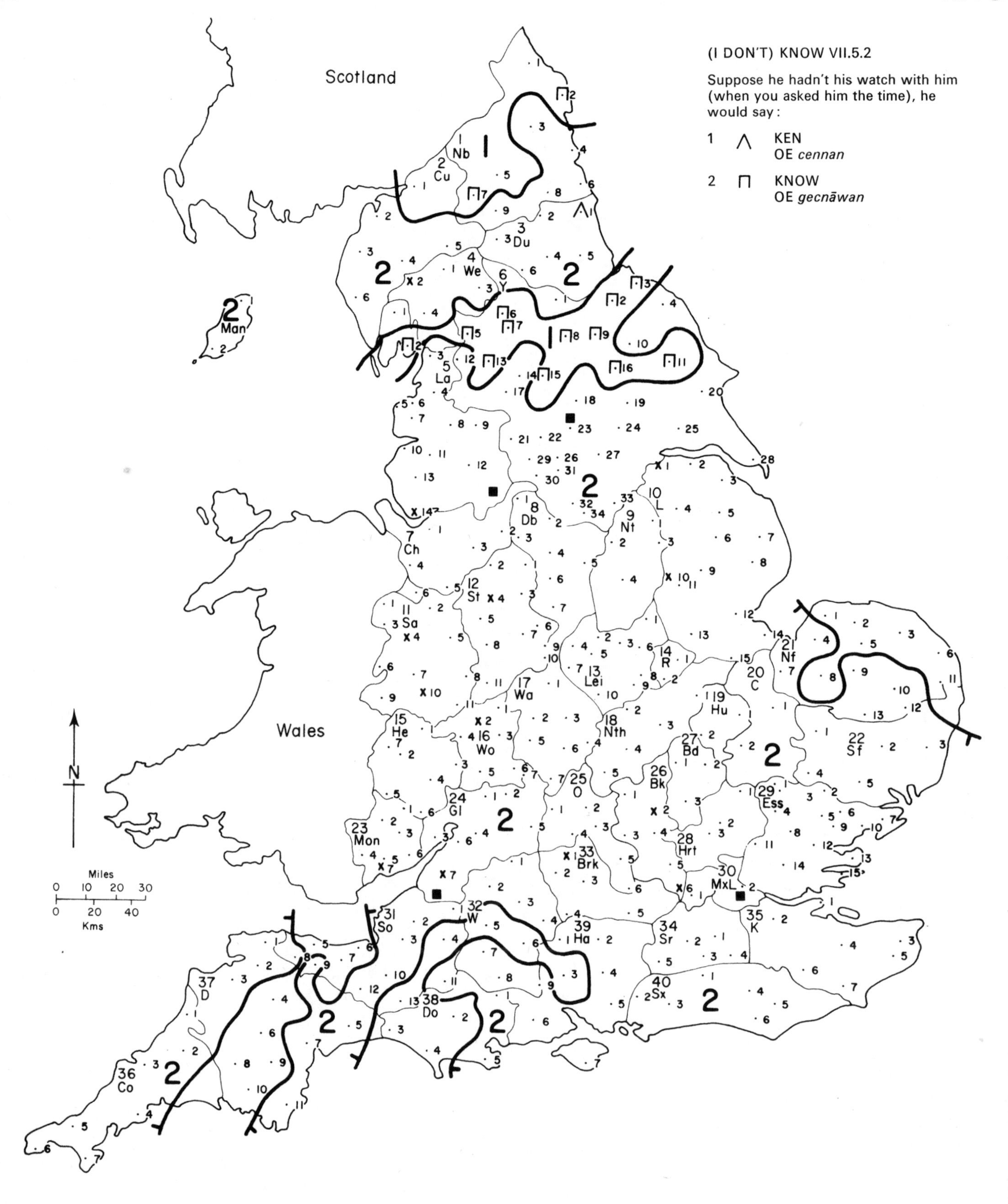
(I DON'T) KNOW VII.5.2
Suppose he hadn't his watch with him (when you asked him the time), he would say:
1 KEN OE *cennan*
2 KNOW OE *gecnāwan*
Scotland
Wales
Man
N
Miles
0 10 20 30
0 20 40
Kms
Nb
Cu
Du
We
Y
La
Ch
Db
Nt
L
St
Sa
Lei
R
Nf
Wa
C
Hu
He
Wo
Nth
Bd
Sf
O
Bk
Gl
Ess
Mon
Hrt
Brk
MxL
So
W
Ha
Sr
K
D
Do
Sx
Co

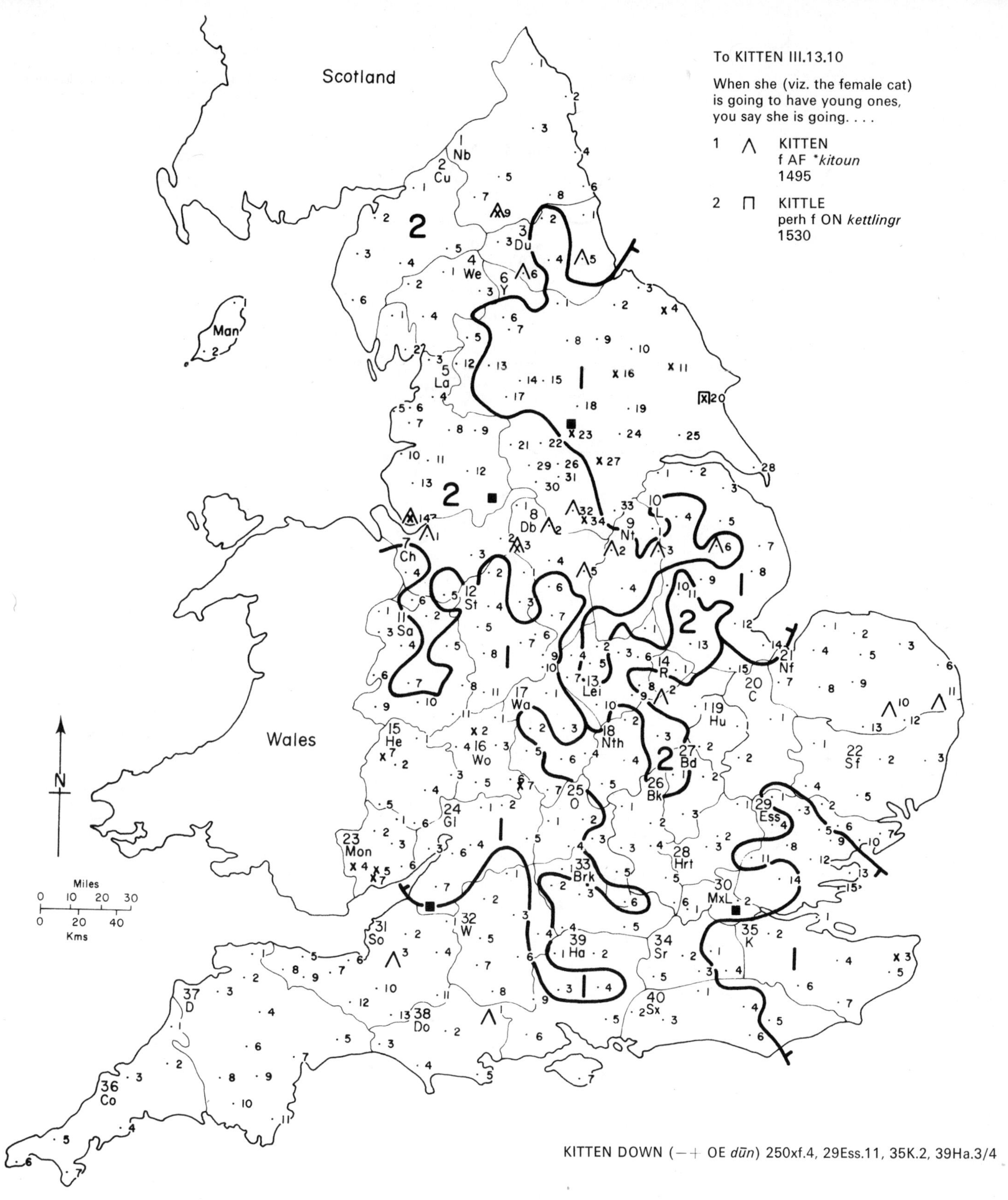

To KITTEN III.13.10
When she (viz. the female cat) is going to have young ones, you say she is going. . . .
1 ⋀ KITTEN f AF *kitoun 1495
2 ⊓ KITTLE perh f ON kettlingr 1530
Scotland
Wales
Man
Nb
Cu
Du
We
Y
La
Ch
Db
Nt
L
St
Sa
Lei
R
Nf
Wa
He
Wo
Nth
Hu
C
Bd
Sf
Gl
O
Bk
Ess
Mon
Hrt
Brk
MxL
So
W
Ha
Sr
K
Sx
D
Do
Co
N
Miles
0 10 20 30
0 20 40
Kms
KITTEN DOWN (—+ OE dūn) 25Oxf.4, 29Ess.11, 35K.2, 39Ha.3/4

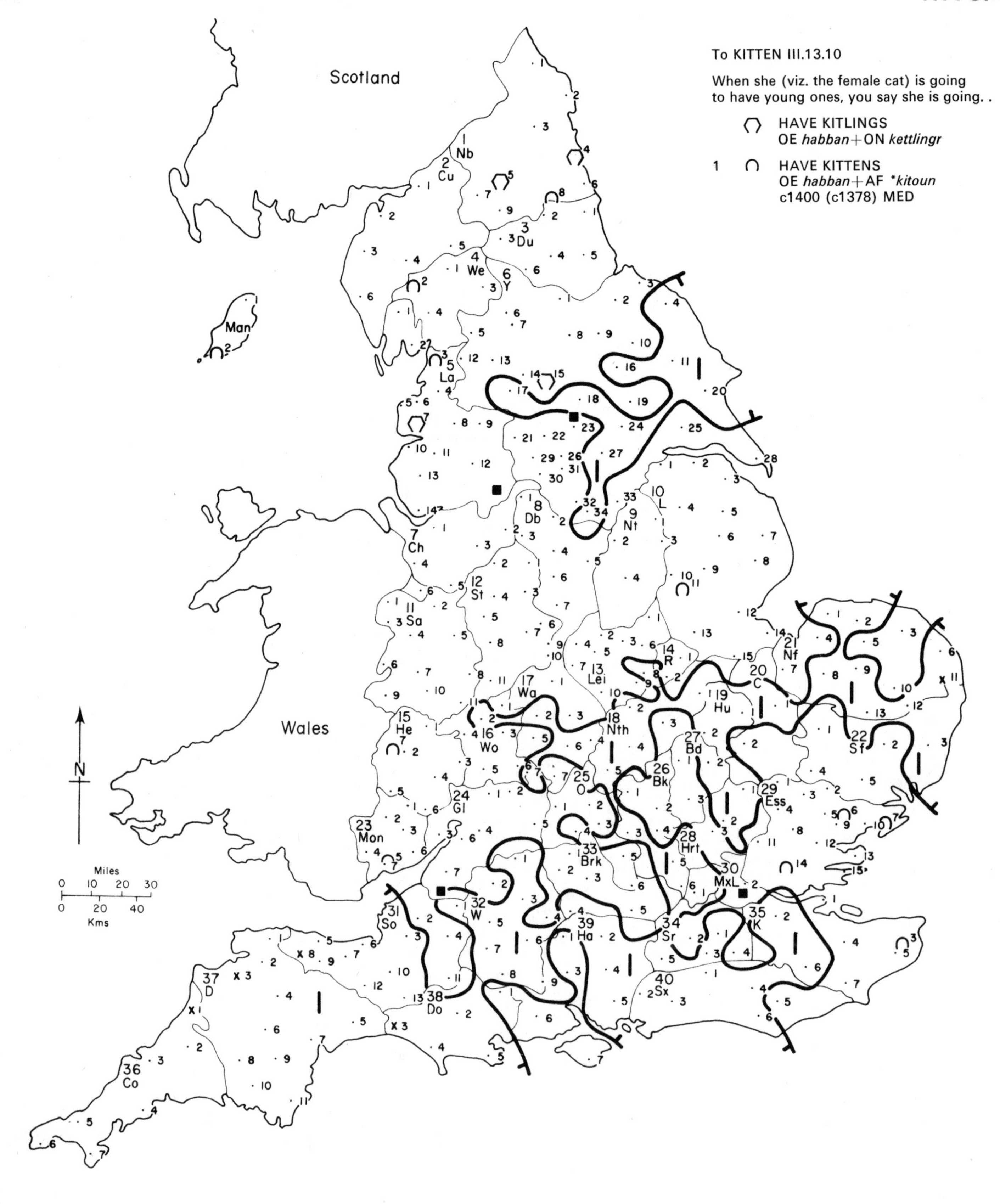

To KITTEN III.13.10

When she (viz. the female cat) is going to have young ones, you say she is going. .

- HAVE KITLINGS
  OE *habban*+ON *kettlingr*
- 1 HAVE KITTENS
  OE *habban*+AF **kitoun*
  c1400 (c1378) MED

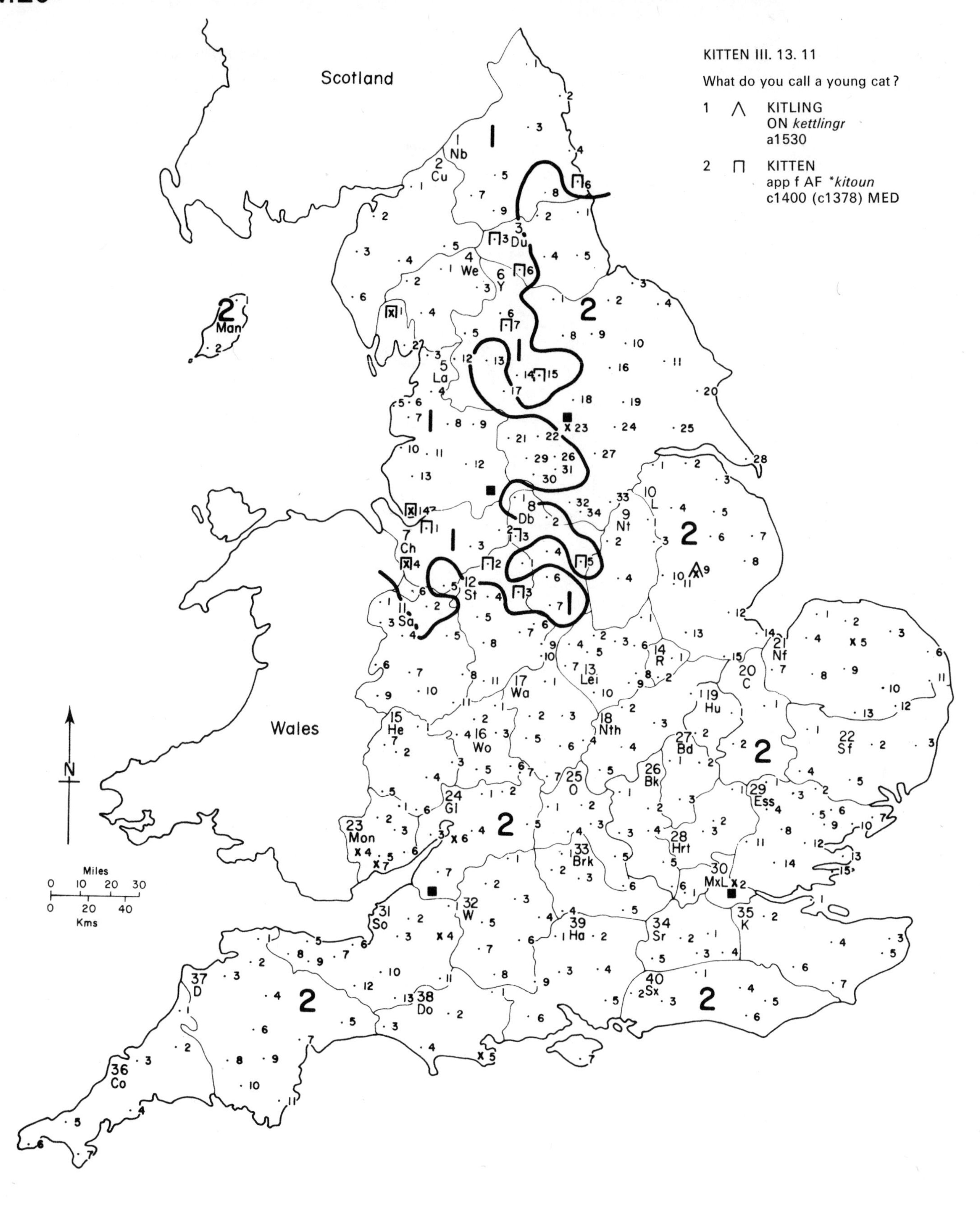
KITTEN III. 13. 11
What do you call a young cat?
1 ⋀ KITLING
ON *kettlingr*
a1530
2 ⊓ KITTEN
app f AF *kitoun
c1400 (c1378) MED
Scotland
Wales
Miles
Kms

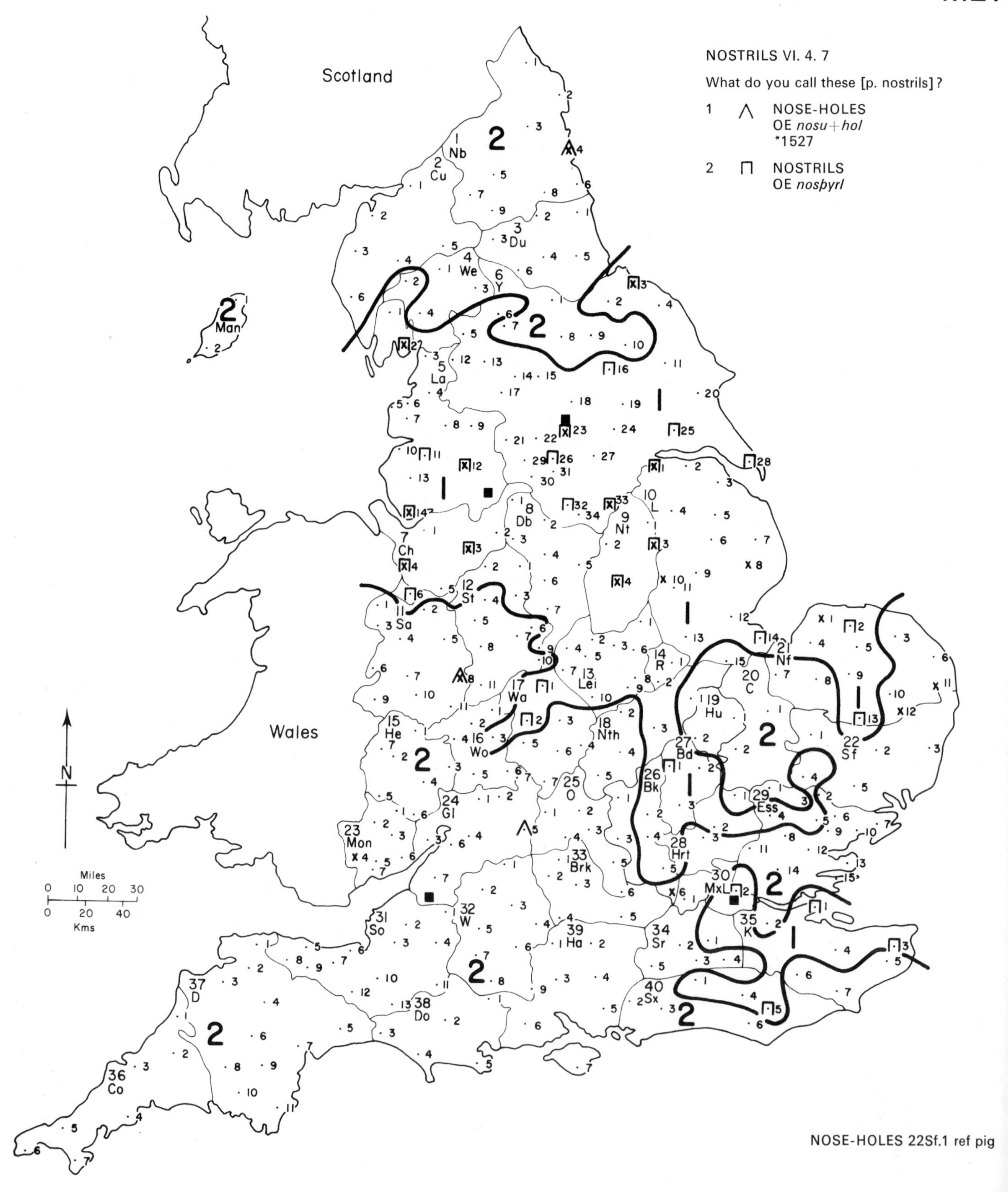

NOSE-HOLES 22Sf.1 ref pig

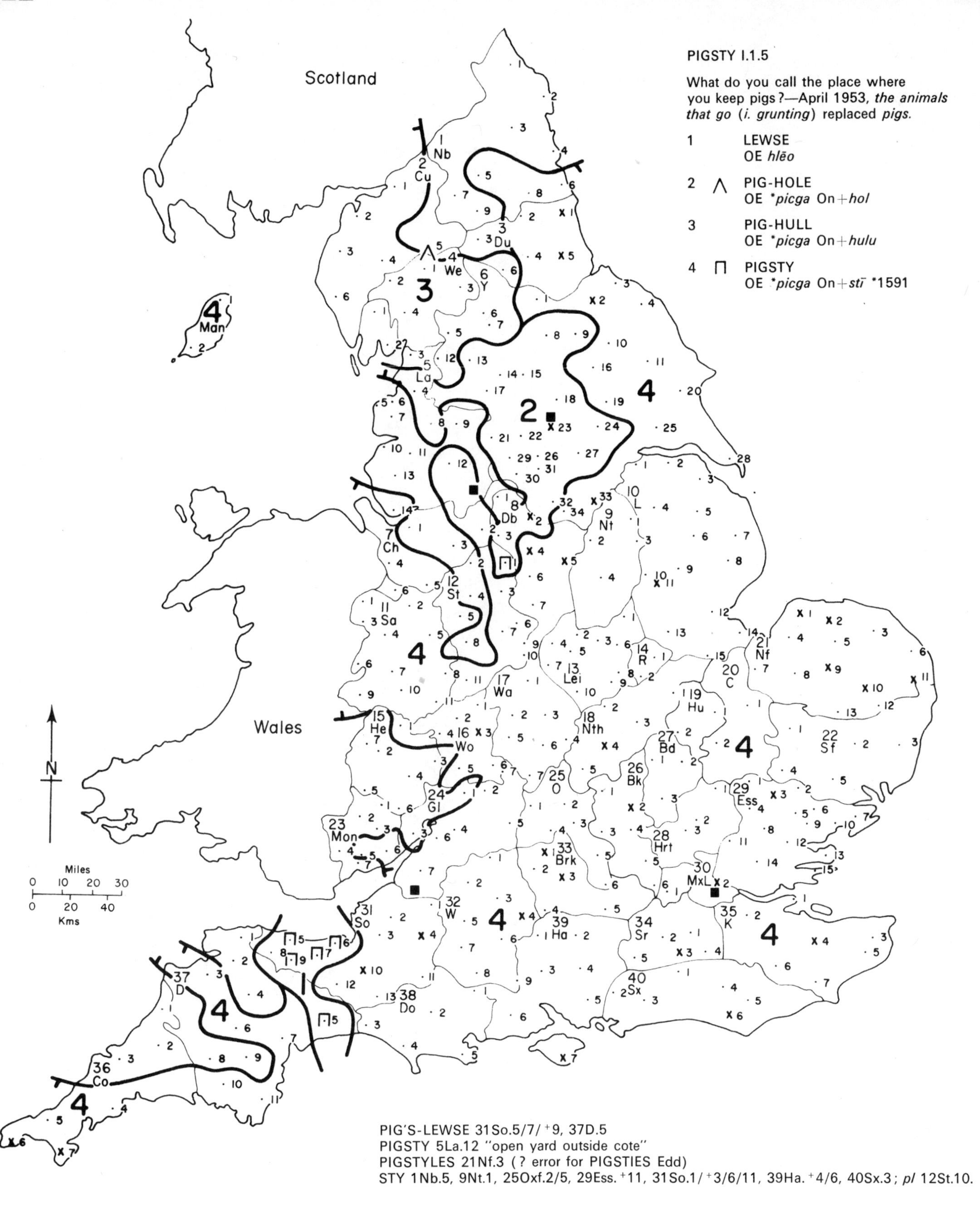

PIG'S-LEWSE 31So.5/7/⁺9, 37D.5
PIGSTY 5La.12 "open yard outside cote"
PIGSTYLES 21Nf.3 (? error for PIGSTIES Edd)
STY 1Nb.5, 9Nt.1, 25Oxf.2/5, 29Ess.⁺11, 31So.1/⁺3/6/11, 39Ha.⁺4/6, 40Sx.3; *pl* 12St.10.

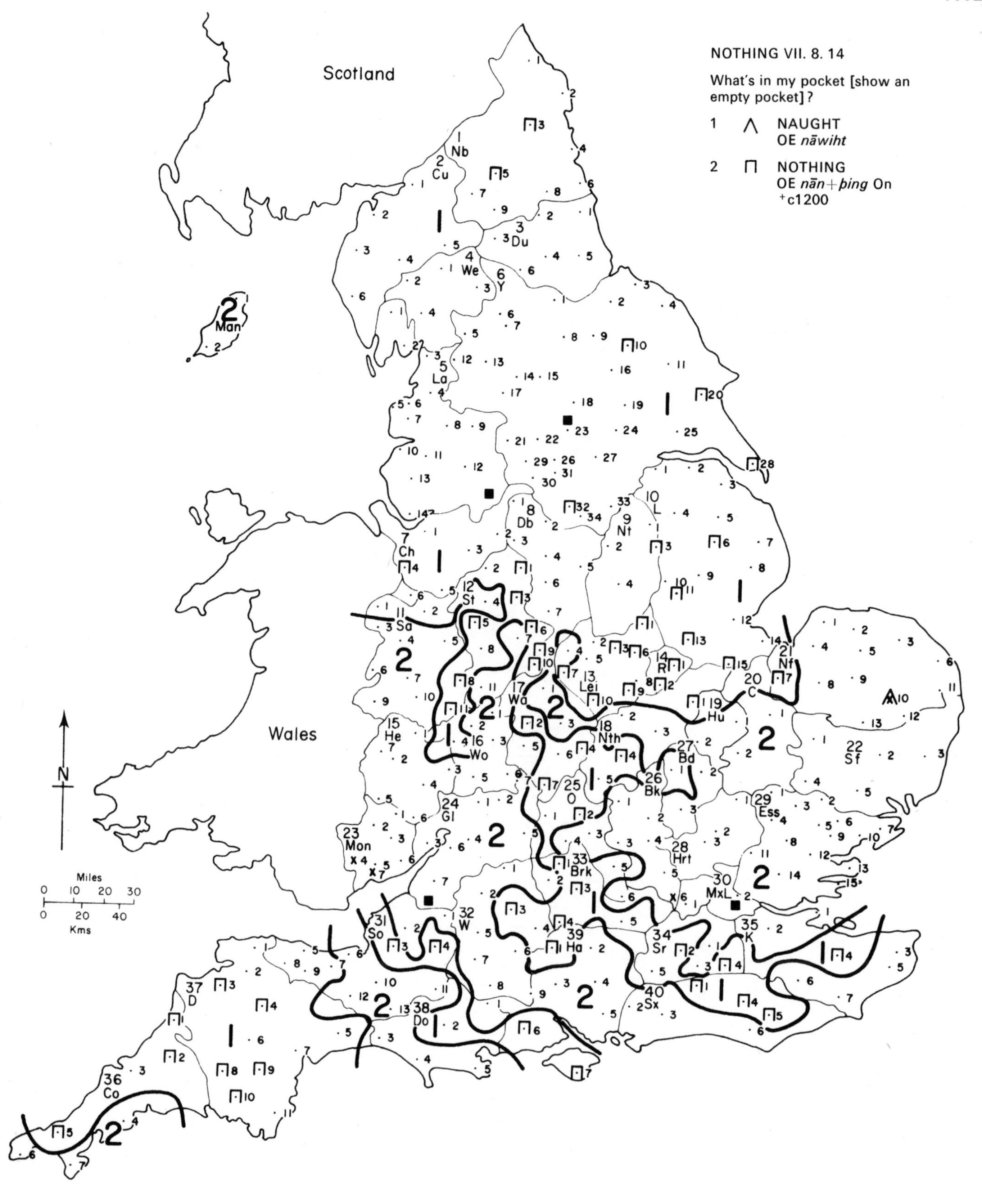
NOTHING VII. 8. 14
What's in my pocket [show an empty pocket]?
1 Λ NAUGHT OE *nāwiht*
2 ⊓ NOTHING OE *nān+þing* On +c1200
Scotland
Wales
Miles
Kms

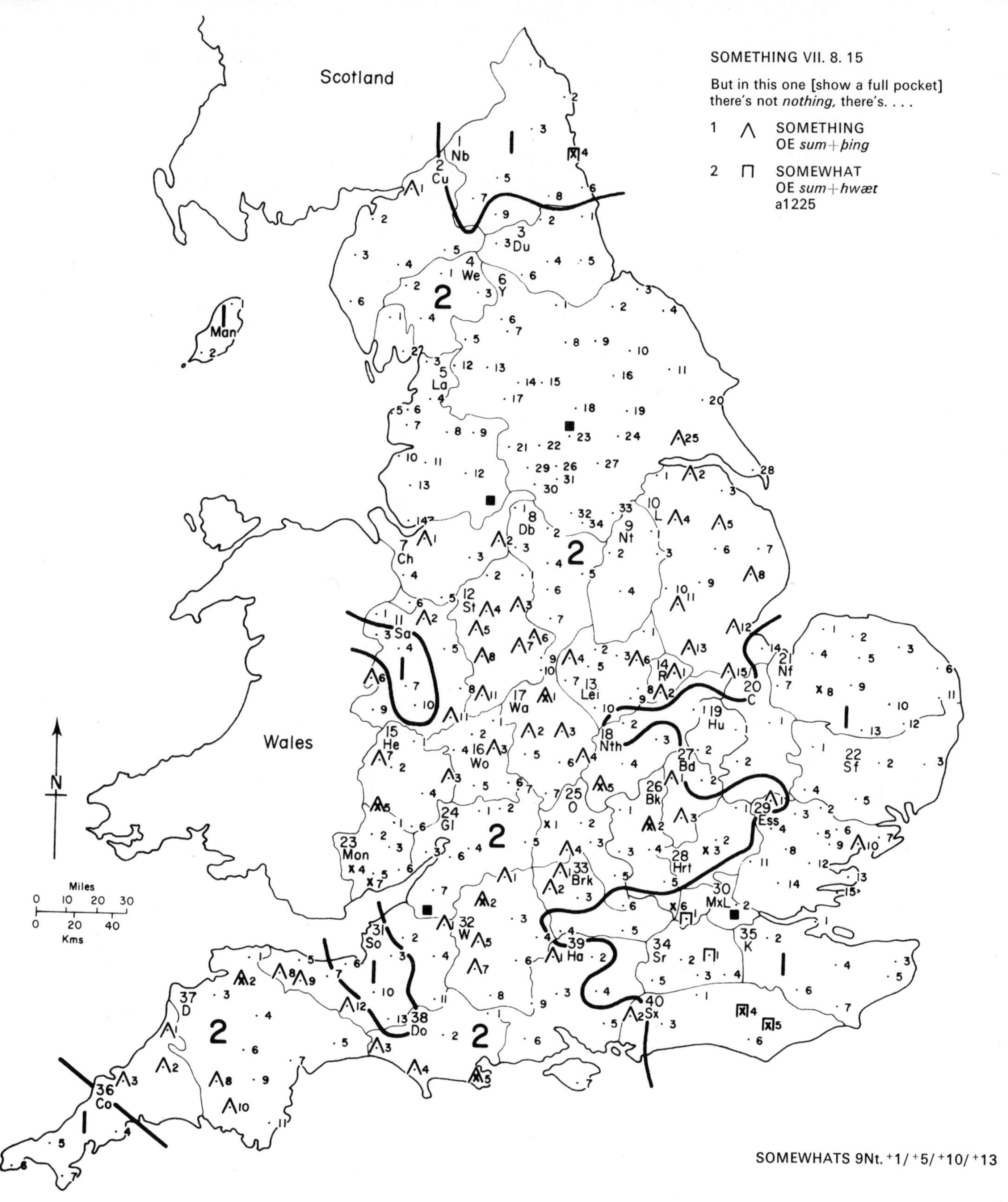
Scotland
Wales
SOMETHING VII. 8. 15
But in this one [show a full pocket] there's not *nothing,* there's. . . .
1 ⋀ SOMETHING
OE *sum+þing*
2 ⊓ SOMEWHAT
OE *sum+hwæt*
a1225
Miles
0 10 20 30
0 20 40
Kms
N
SOMEWHATS 9Nt. +1/ +5/ +10/ +13

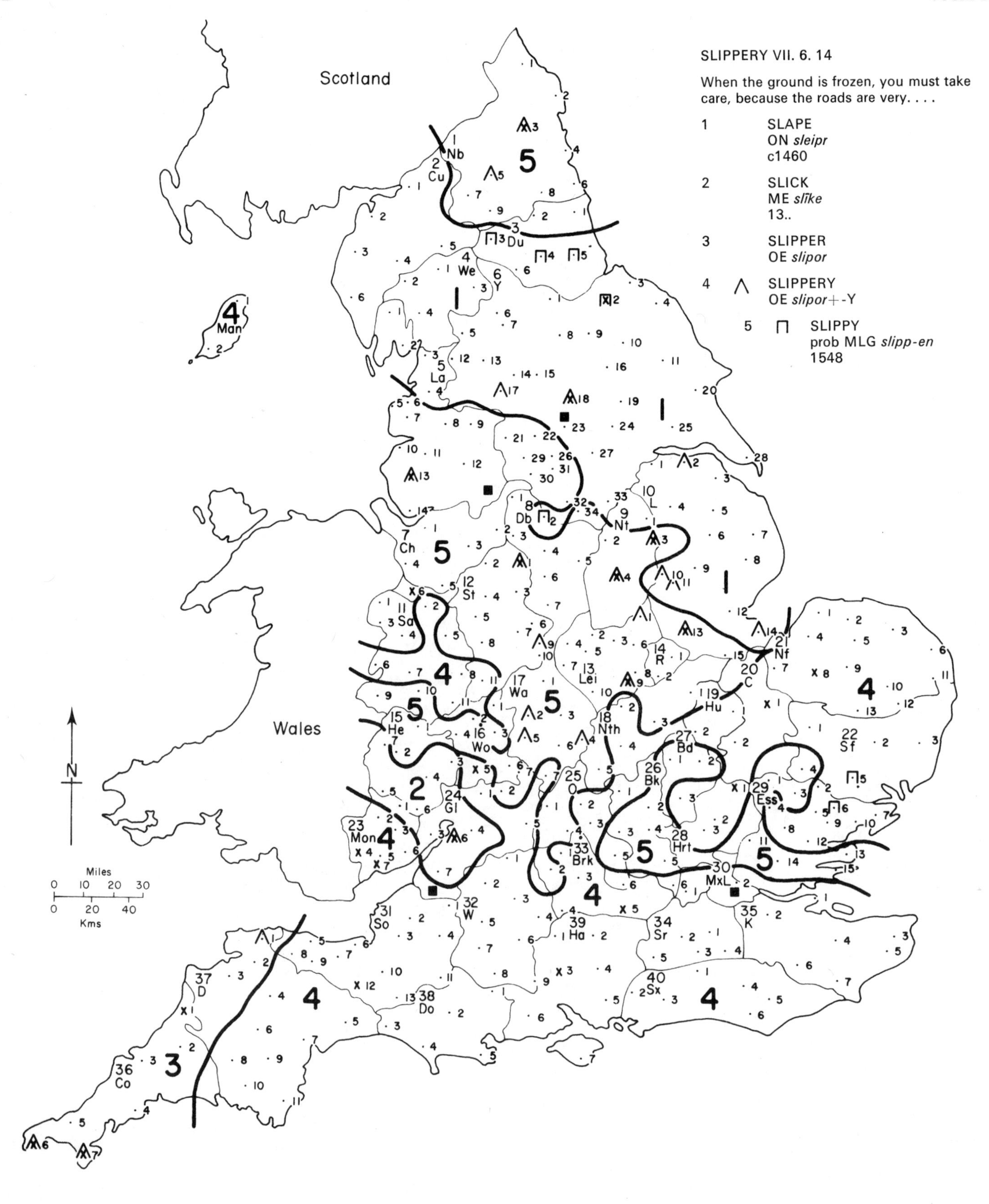
SLIPPERY VII. 6. 14
When the ground is frozen, you must take care, because the roads are very. . . .
1 SLAPE
ON *sleipr*
c1460
2 SLICK
ME *slīke*
13..
3 SLIPPER
OE *slipor*
4 Λ SLIPPERY
OE *slipor*+-Y
5 ⊓ SLIPPY
prob MLG *slipp-en*
1548
Scotland
Wales

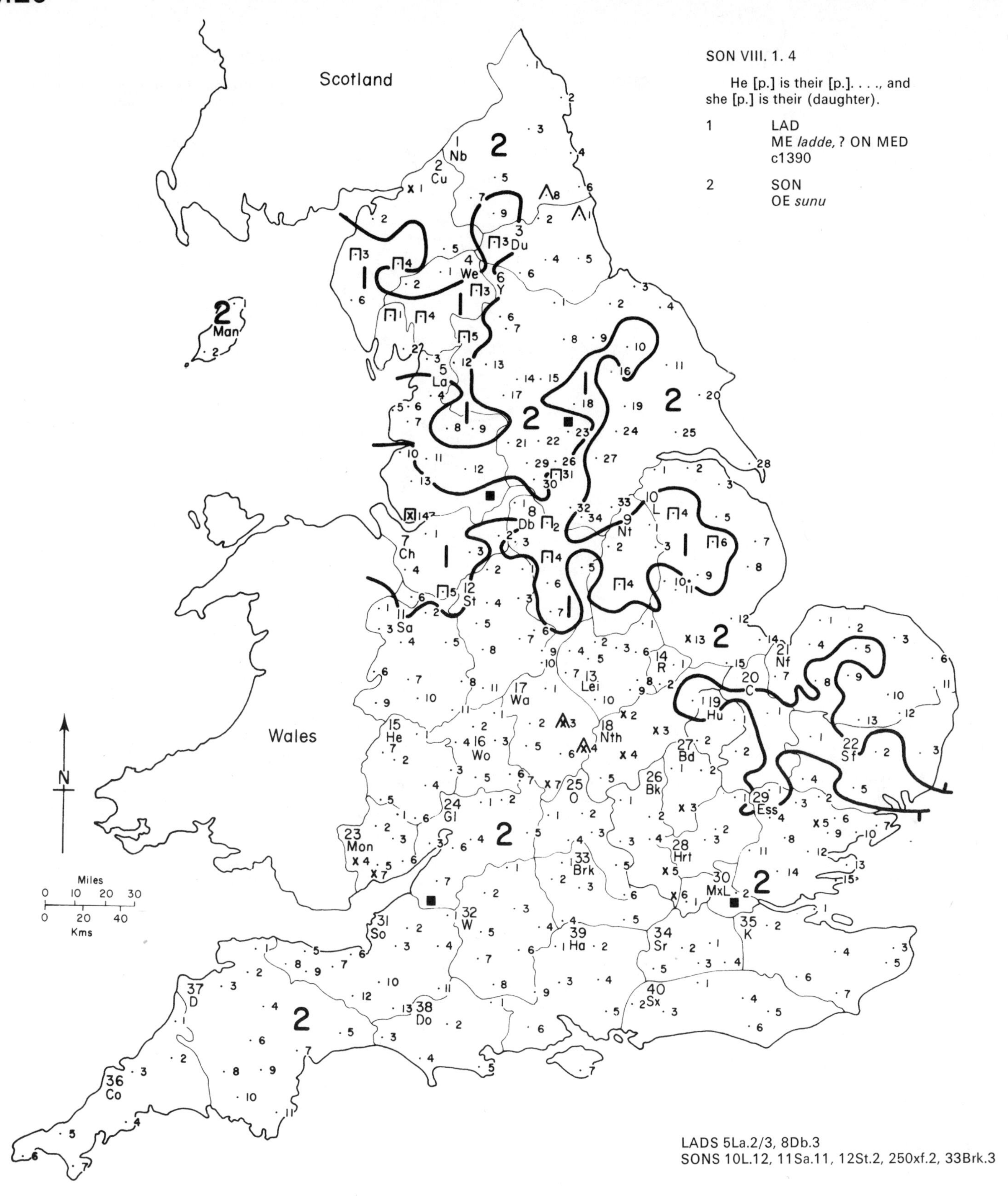
SON VIII. 1. 4
He [p.] is their [p.]. . . ., and she [p.] is their (daughter).
1 LAD
ME *ladde*, ? ON MED c1390
2 SON
OE *sunu*
Scotland
Wales
Man
Miles
Kms
LADS 5La.2/3, 8Db.3
SONS 10L.12, 11Sa.11, 12St.2, 25Oxf.2, 33Brk.3

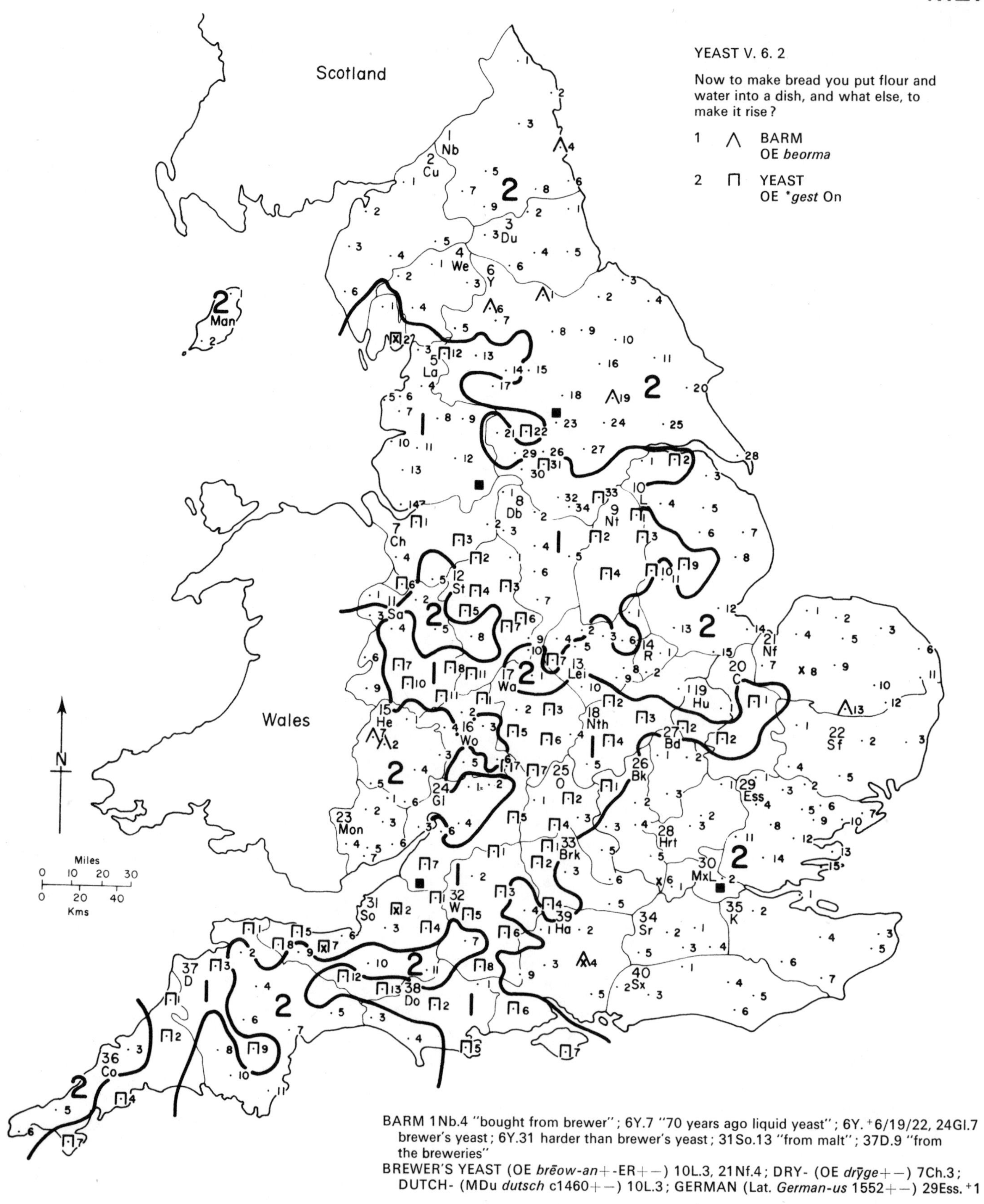

YEAST V. 6. 2

Now to make bread you put flour and water into a dish, and what else, to make it rise?

1 ⋀ BARM
OE *beorma*

2 ⊓ YEAST
OE **gest* On

BARM 1Nb.4 "bought from brewer"; 6Y.7 "70 years ago liquid yeast"; 6Y.⁺6/19/22, 24Gl.7 brewer's yeast; 6Y.31 harder than brewer's yeast; 31So.13 "from malt"; 37D.9 "from the breweries"

BREWER'S YEAST (OE *brēow-an*+-ER+—) 10L.3, 21Nf.4; DRY- (OE *drȳge*+—) 7Ch.3; DUTCH- (MDu *dutsch* c1460+—) 10L.3; GERMAN (Lat. *German-us* 1552+—) 29Ess.⁺1

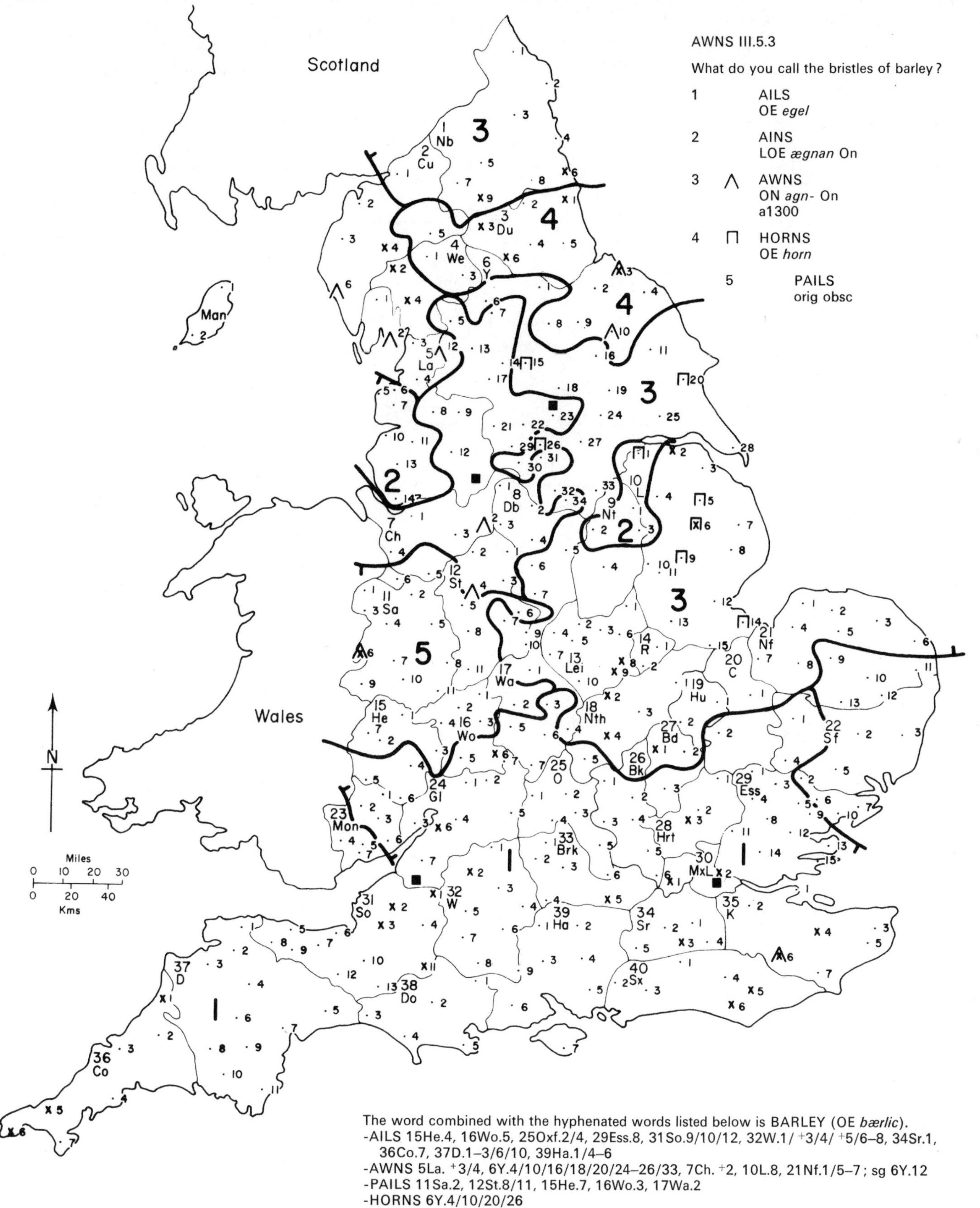

The word combined with the hyphenated words listed below is BARLEY (OE *bærlic*).
-AILS 15He.4, 16Wo.5, 25Oxf.2/4, 29Ess.8, 31So.9/10/12, 32W.1/ +3/4/ +5/6–8, 34Sr.1, 36Co.7, 37D.1–3/6/10, 39Ha.1/4–6
-AWNS 5La. +3/4, 6Y.4/10/16/18/20/24–26/33, 7Ch. +2, 10L.8, 21Nf.1/5–7; sg 6Y.12
-PAILS 11Sa.2, 12St.8/11, 15He.7, 16Wo.3, 17Wa.2
-HORNS 6Y.4/10/20/26
HANGS at 2Cu.3, 5La.1/3/4 though it may prove to be a form of AWNS has been ignored here.
The responses in the HORN area may prove to be forms of AWNS.

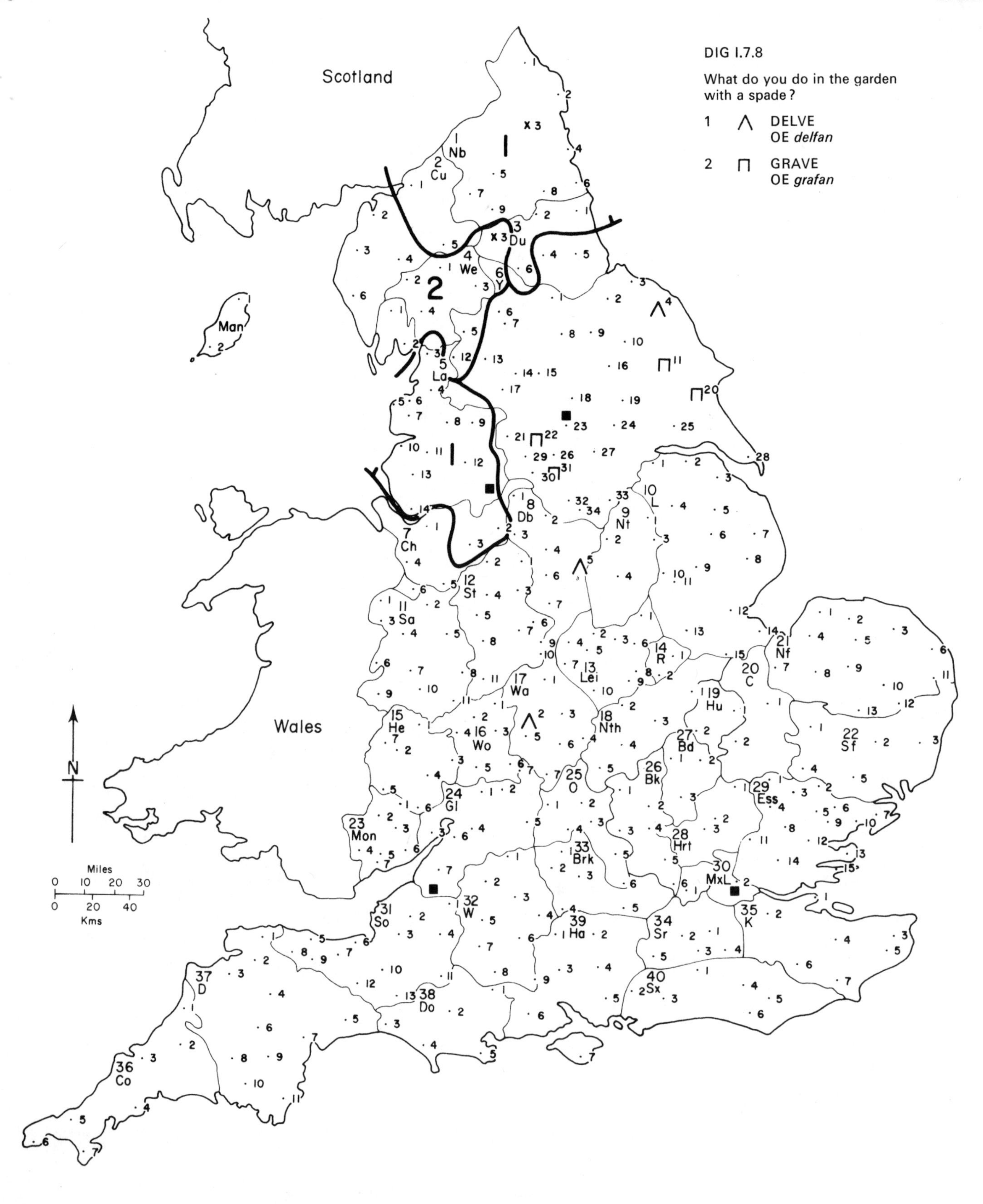
DIG I.7.8
What do you do in the garden with a spade?
1 DELVE
OE *delfan*
2 GRAVE
OE *grafan*
Scotland
Wales
Man
Miles
Kms

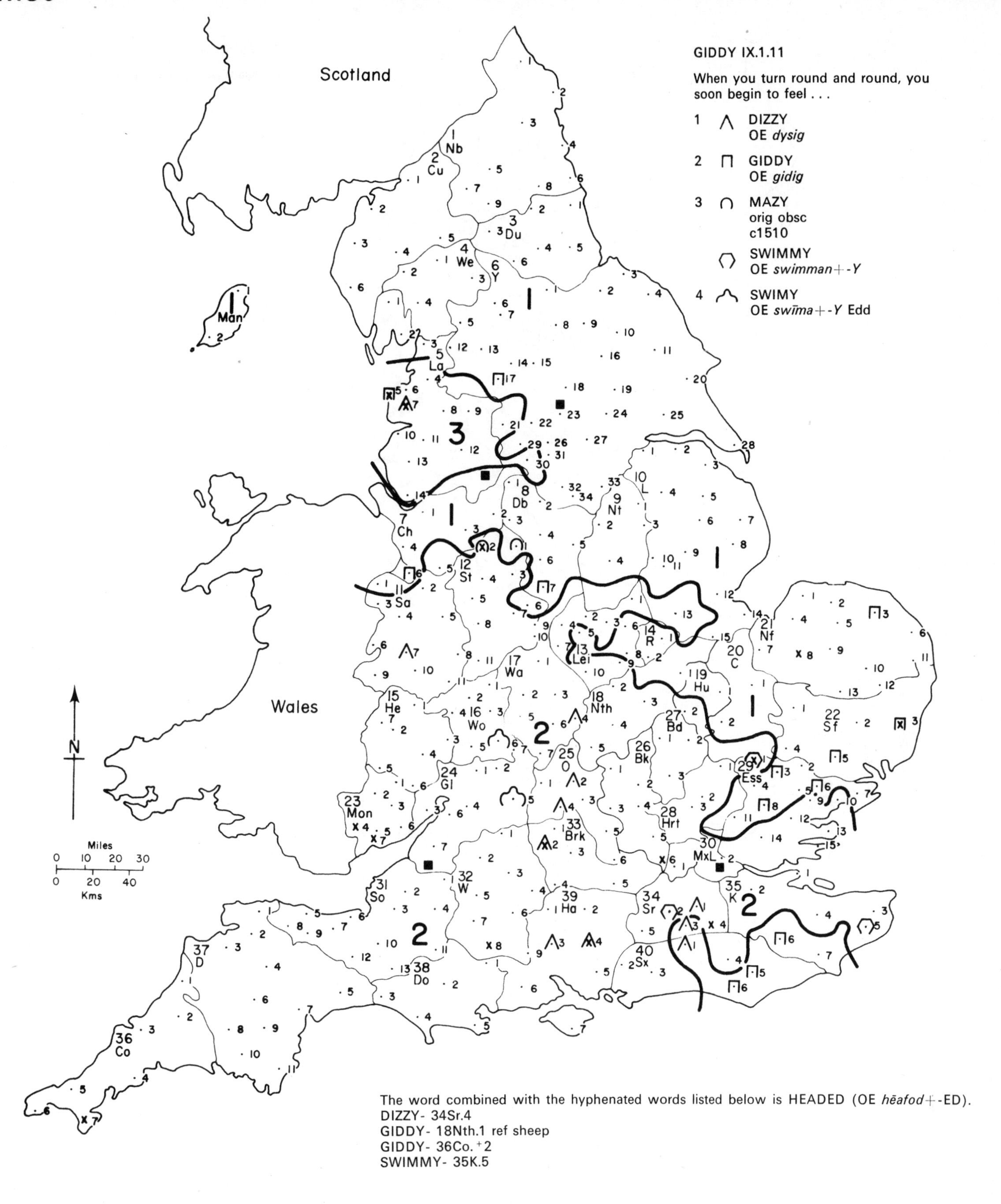
GIDDY IX.1.11
When you turn round and round, you soon begin to feel . . .
1 DIZZY OE *dysig*
2 GIDDY OE *gidig*
3 MAZY orig obsc c1510
SWIMMY OE *swimman*+-*Y*
4 SWIMY OE *swīma*+-*Y* Edd
Scotland
Wales
Miles
Kms
The word combined with the hyphenated words listed below is HEADED (OE *hēafod*+-ED).
DIZZY- 34Sr.4
GIDDY- 18Nth.1 ref sheep
GIDDY- 36Co.+2
SWIMMY- 35K.5

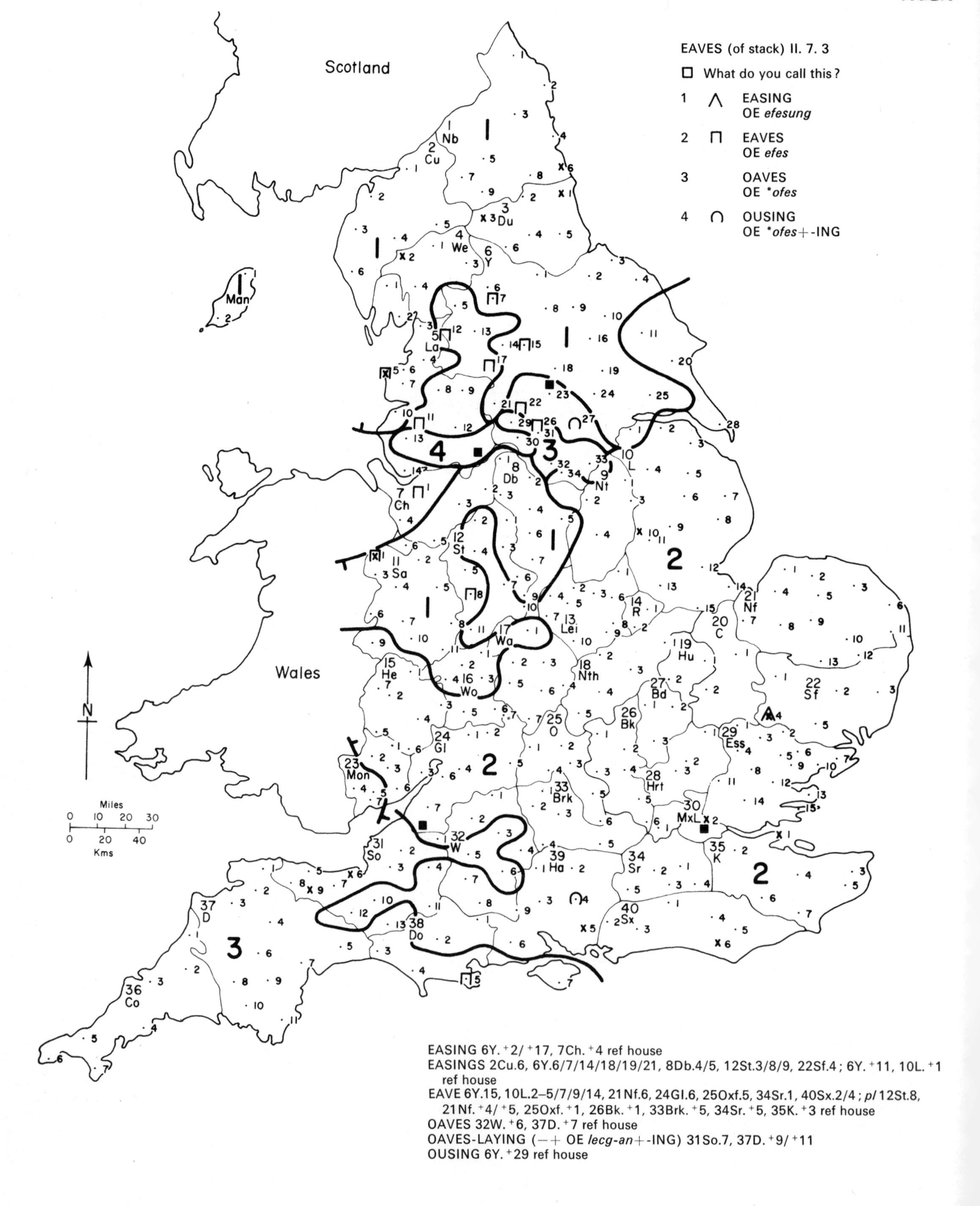

EASING 6Y.+2/+17, 7Ch.+4 ref house
EASINGS 2Cu.6, 6Y.6/7/14/18/19/21, 8Db.4/5, 12St.3/8/9, 22Sf.4; 6Y.+11, 10L.+1 ref house
EAVE 6Y.15, 10L.2–5/7/9/14, 21Nf.6, 24Gl.6, 25Oxf.5, 34Sr.1, 40Sx.2/4; *pl* 12St.8, 21Nf.+4/+5, 25Oxf.+1, 26Bk.+1, 33Brk.+5, 34Sr.+5, 35K.+3 ref house
OAVES 32W.+6, 37D.+7 ref house
OAVES-LAYING (—+ OE *lecg-an*+-ING) 31So.7, 37D.+9/+11
OUSING 6Y.+29 ref house

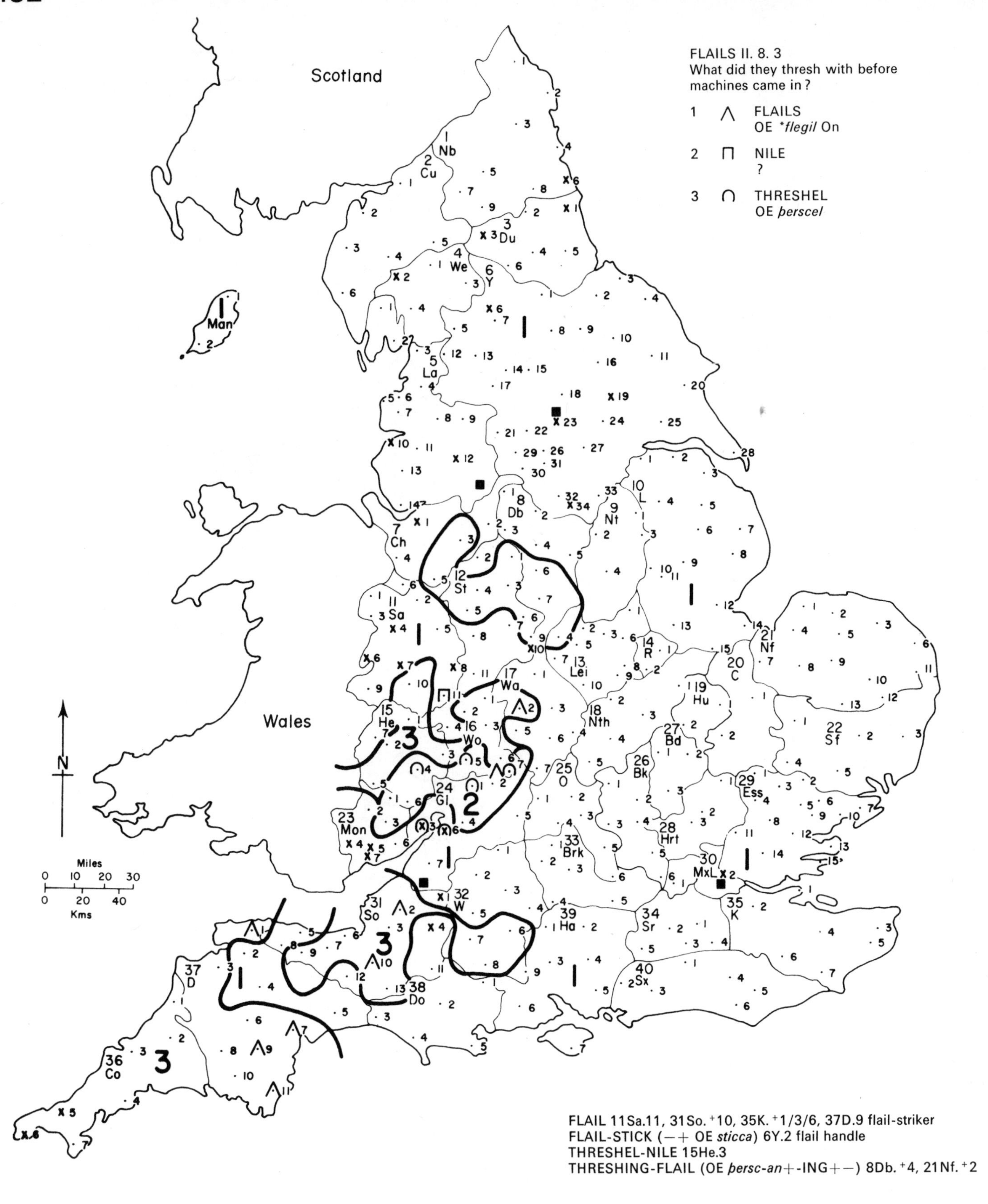

FLAIL 11Sa.11, 31So. +10, 35K. +1/3/6, 37D.9 flail-striker
FLAIL-STICK (—+ OE *sticca*) 6Y.2 flail handle
THRESHEL-NILE 15He.3
THRESHING-FLAIL (OE *þersc-an*+-ING+—) 8Db. +4, 21Nf. +2

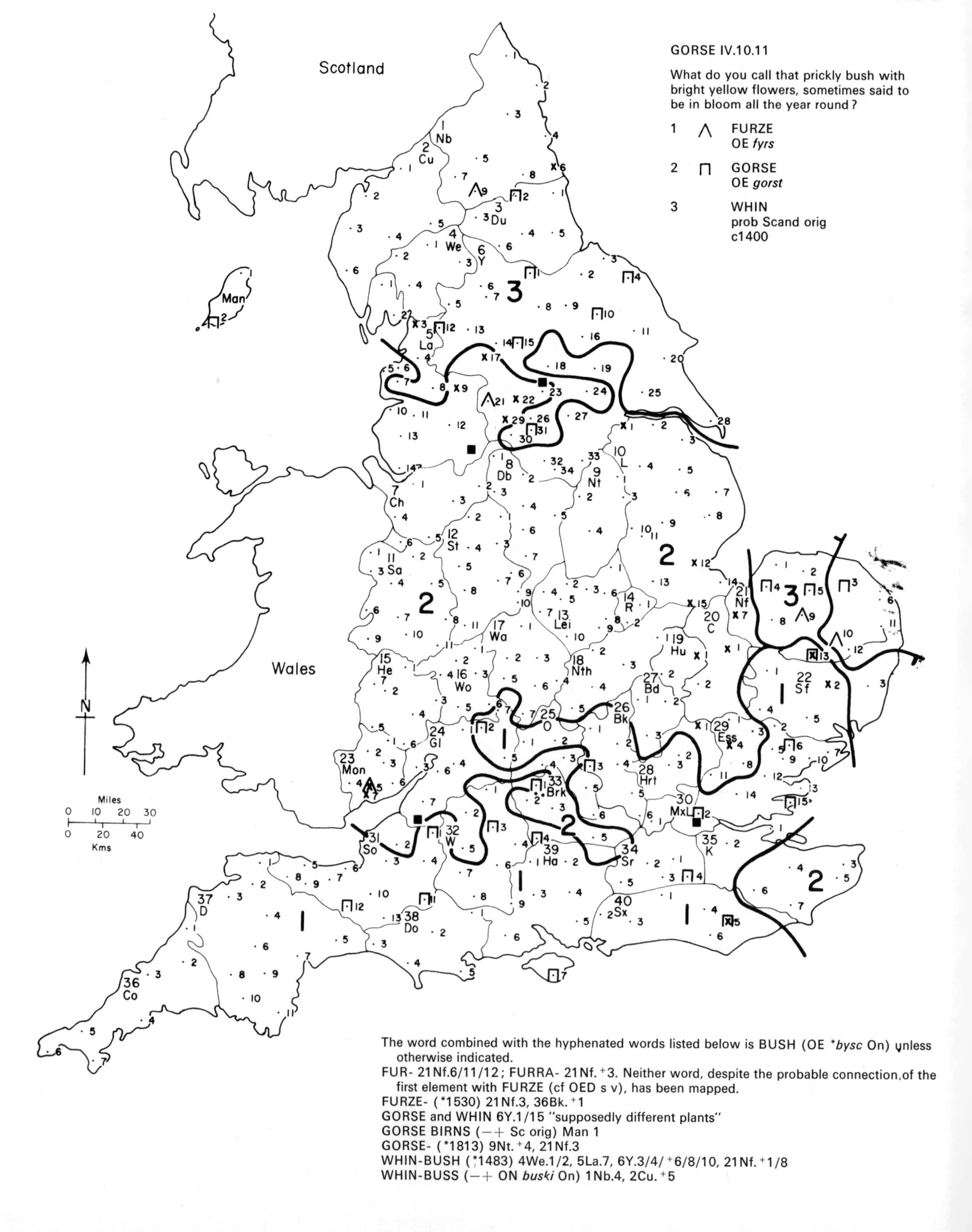

The word combined with the hyphenated words listed below is BUSH (OE *bysc On) unless otherwise indicated.

FUR- 21Nf.6/11/12; FURRA- 21Nf. +3. Neither word, despite the probable connection, of the first element with FURZE (cf OED s v), has been mapped.

FURZE- (*1530) 21Nf.3, 36Bk. +1

GORSE and WHIN 6Y.1/15 "supposedly different plants"

GORSE BIRNS (—+ Sc orig) Man 1

GORSE- (*1813) 9Nt. +4, 21Nf.3

WHIN-BUSH (*1483) 4We.1/2, 5La.7, 6Y.3/4/ +6/8/10, 21Nf. +1/8

WHIN-BUSS (—+ ON *buski* On) 1Nb.4, 2Cu. +5

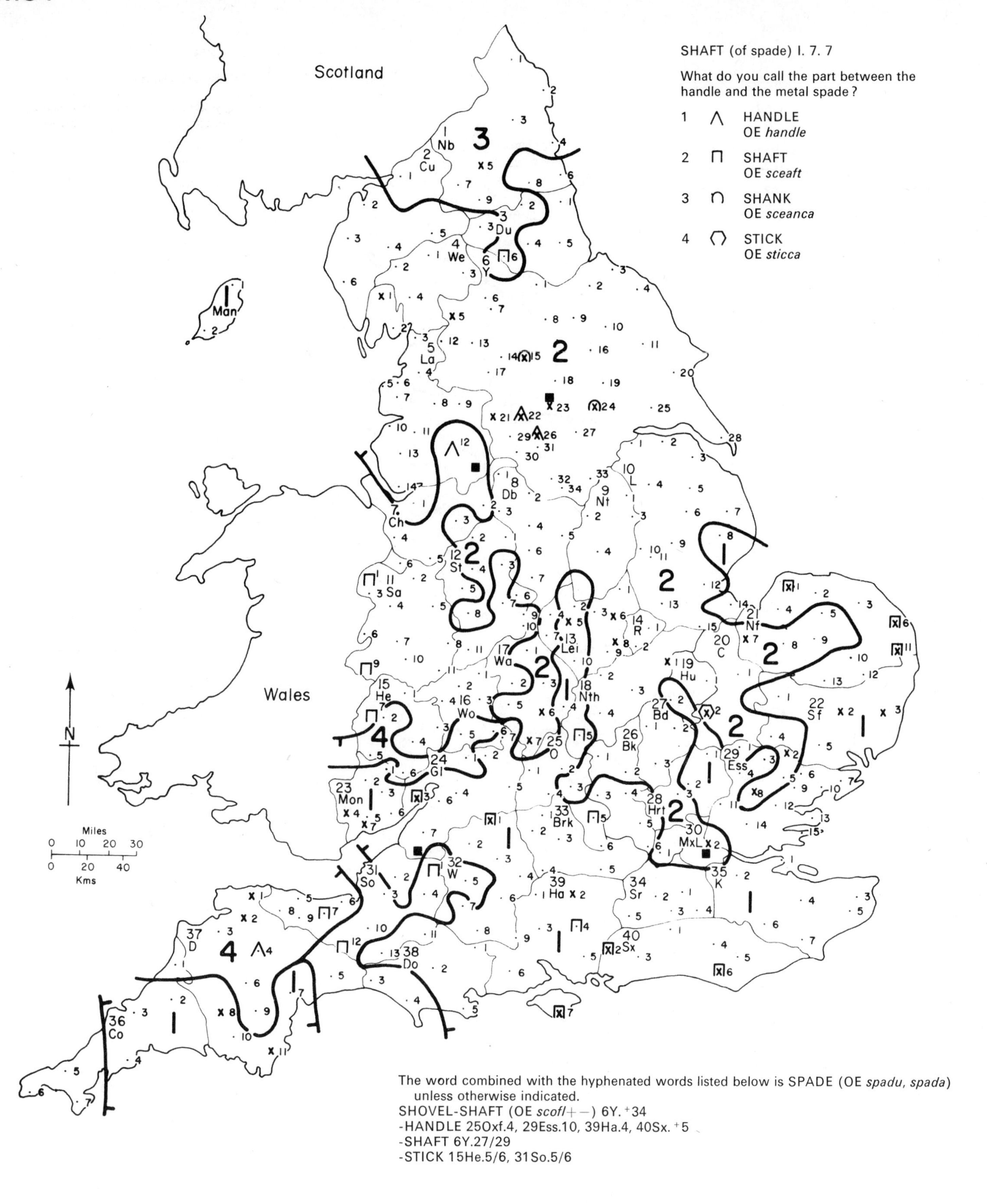

The word combined with the hyphenated words listed below is SPADE (OE *spadu, spada*) unless otherwise indicated.
SHOVEL-SHAFT (OE *scofl*+—) 6Y. +34
-HANDLE 25Oxf.4, 29Ess.10, 39Ha.4, 40Sx. +5
-SHAFT 6Y.27/29
-STICK 15He.5/6, 31So.5/6

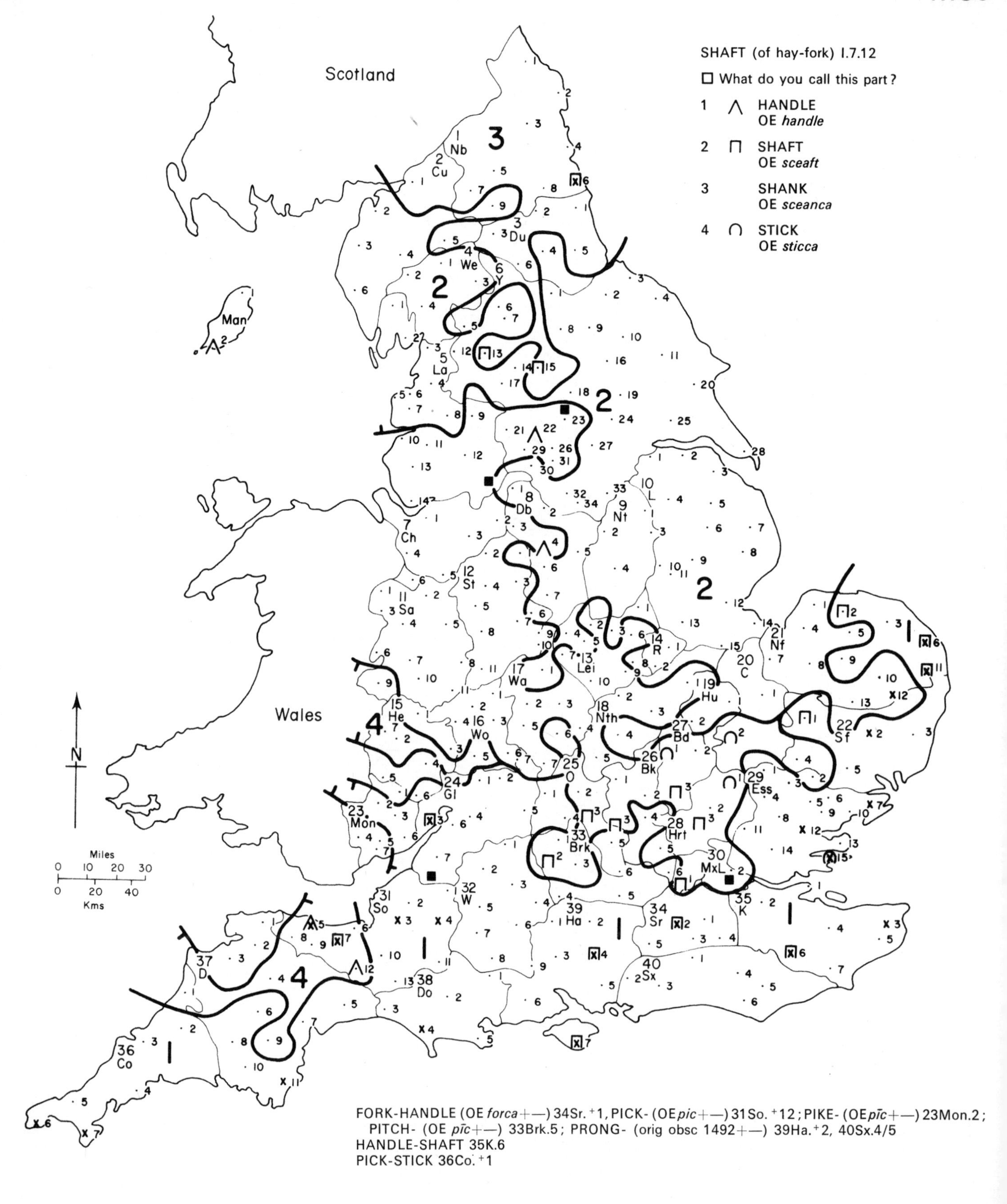

FORK-HANDLE (OE *forca*+—) 34Sr.⁺1, PICK- (OE *pic*+—) 31So.⁺12; PIKE- (OE *pīc*+—) 23Mon.2; PITCH- (OE *pīc*+—) 33Brk.5; PRONG- (orig obsc 1492+—) 39Ha.⁺2, 40Sx.4/5
HANDLE-SHAFT 35K.6
PICK-STICK 36Co.⁺1

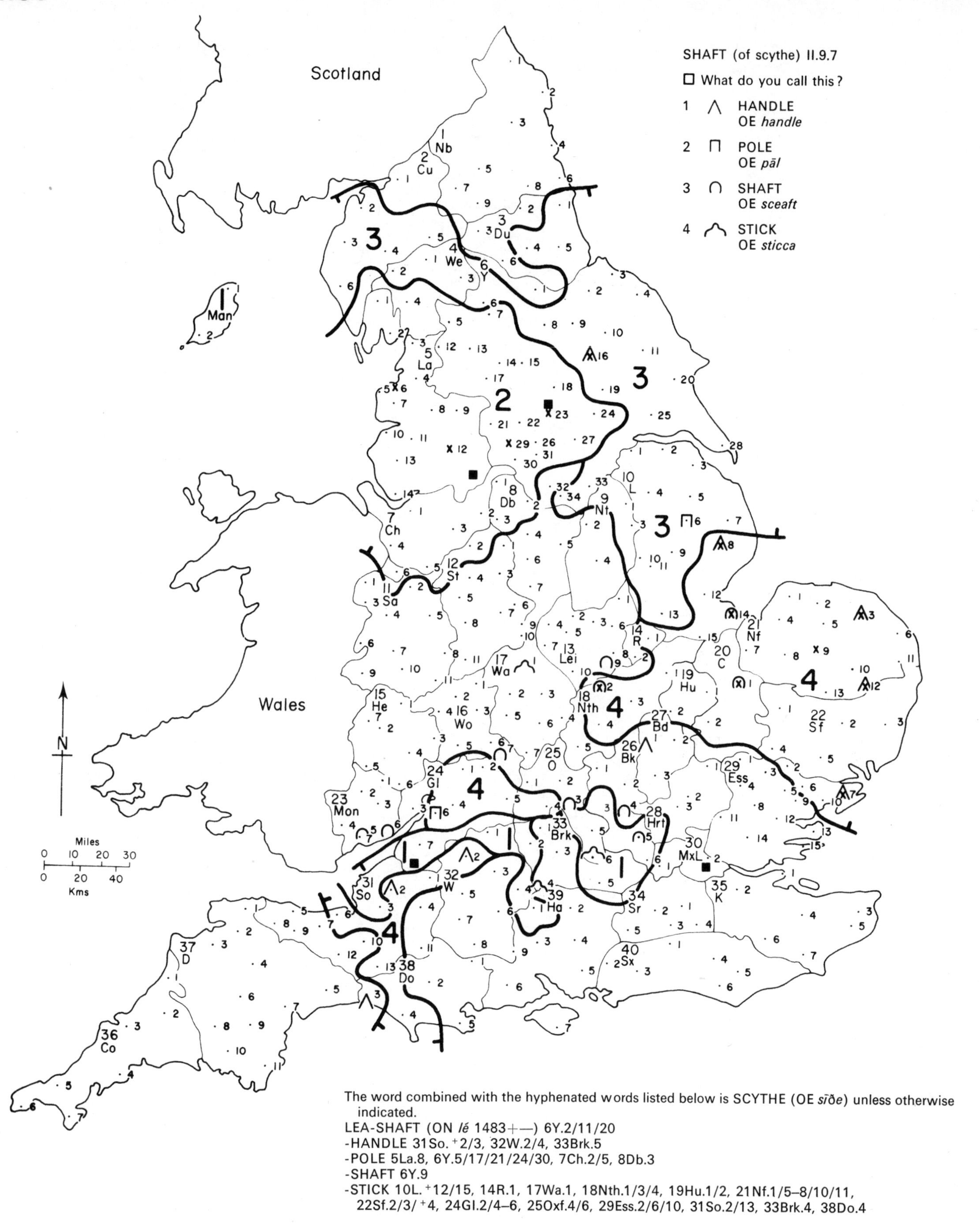

The word combined with the hyphenated words listed below is SCYTHE (OE *sīðe*) unless otherwise indicated.

LEA-SHAFT (ON *lé* 1483+—) 6Y.2/11/20
-HANDLE 31So.+2/3, 32W.2/4, 33Brk.5
-POLE 5La.8, 6Y.5/17/21/24/30, 7Ch.2/5, 8Db.3
-SHAFT 6Y.9
-STICK 10L.+12/15, 14R.1, 17Wa.1, 18Nth.1/3/4, 19Hu.1/2, 21Nf.1/5–8/10/11, 22Sf.2/3/+4, 24Gl.2/4–6, 25Oxf.4/6, 29Ess.2/6/10, 31So.2/13, 33Brk.4, 38Do.4

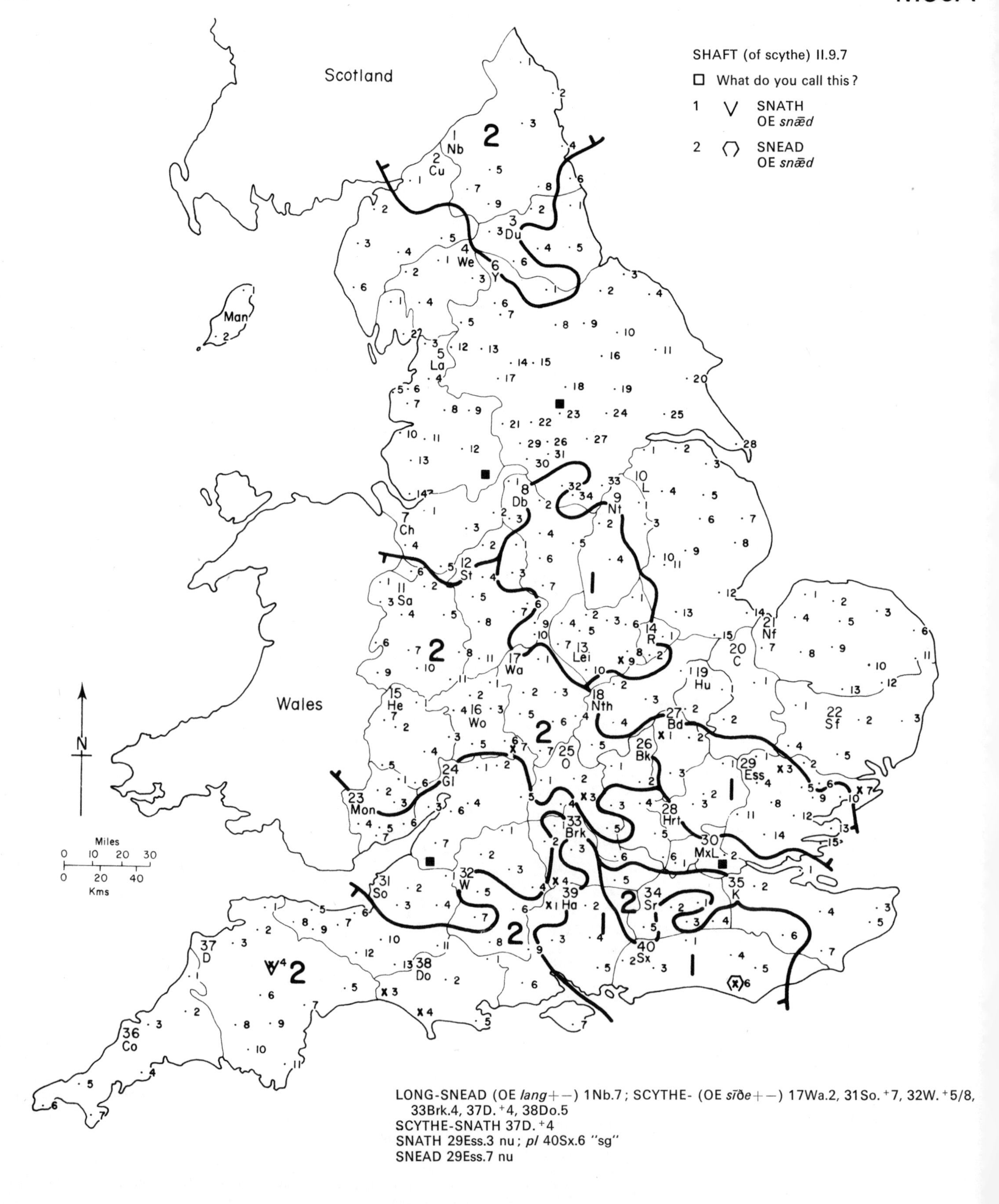

LONG-SNEAD (OE *lang*+—) 1Nb.7; SCYTHE- (OE *sīðe*+—) 17Wa.2, 31So.⁺7, 32W.⁺5/8, 33Brk.4, 37D.⁺4, 38Do.5
SCYTHE-SNATH 37D.⁺4
SNATH 29Ess.3 nu; *pl* 40Sx.6 "sg"
SNEAD 29Ess.7 nu

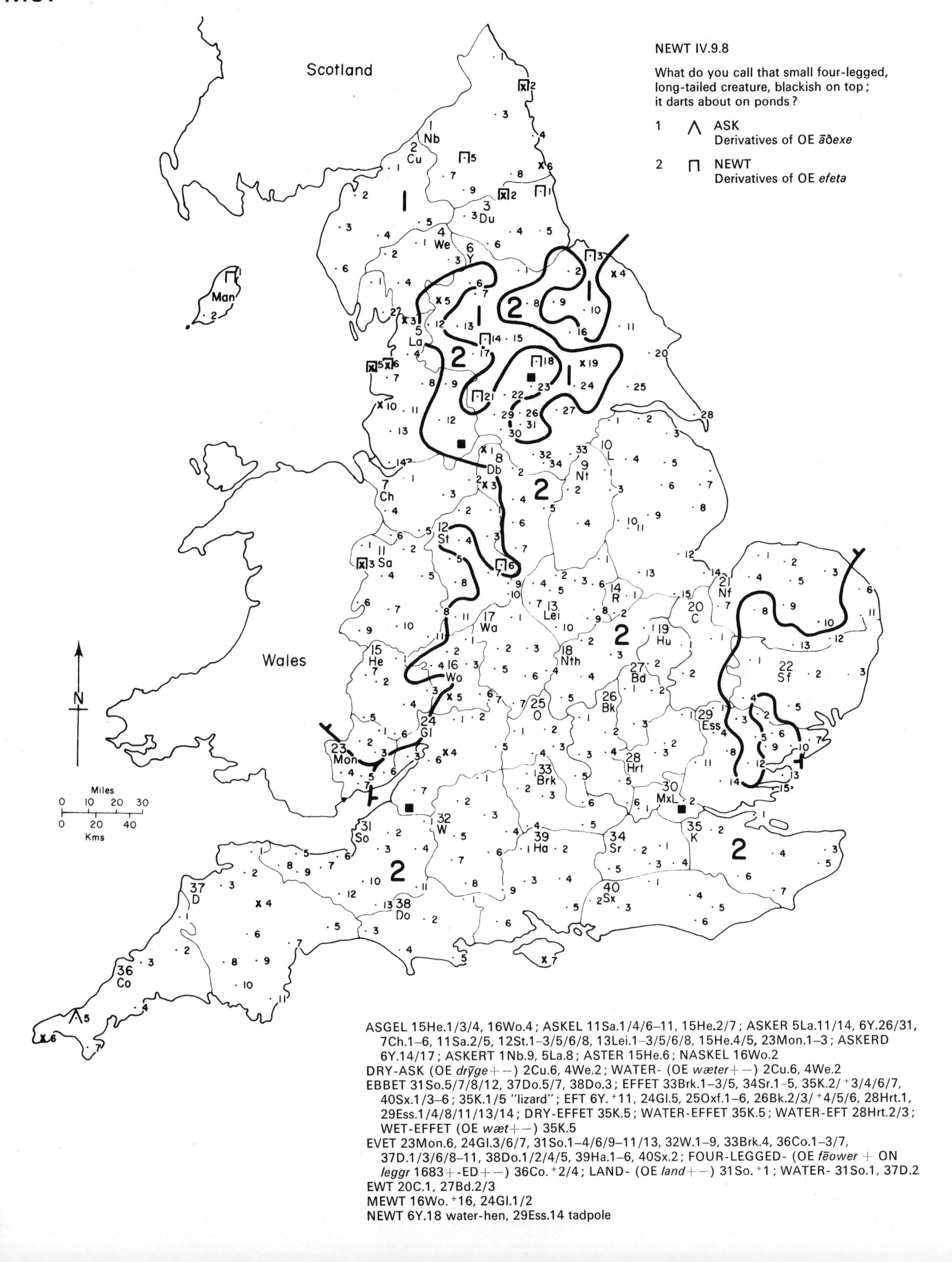

ASGEL 15He.1/3/4, 16Wo.4; ASKEL 11Sa.1/4/6–11, 15He.2/7; ASKER 5La.11/14, 6Y.26/31, 7Ch.1–6, 11Sa.2/5, 12St.1–3/5/6/8, 13Lei.1–3/5/6/8, 15He.4/5, 23Mon.1–3; ASKERD 6Y.14/17; ASKERT 1Nb.9, 5La.8; ASTER 15He.6; NASKEL 16Wo.2

DRY-ASK (OE *drȳge*+–) 2Cu.6, 4We.2; WATER- (OE *wæter*+–) 2Cu.6, 4We.2

EBBET 31So.5/7/8/12, 37Do.5/7, 38Do.3; EFFET 33Brk.1–3/5, 34Sr.1–5, 35K.2/+3/4/6/7, 40Sx.1/3–6; 35K.1/5 "lizard"; EFT 6Y.+11, 24Gl.5, 25Oxf.1–6, 26Bk.2/3/+4/5/6, 28Hrt.1, 29Ess.1/4/8/11/13/14; DRY-EFFET 35K.5; WATER-EFFET 35K.5; WATER-EFT 28Hrt.2/3; WET-EFFET (OE *wæt*+–) 35K.5

EVET 23Mon.6, 24Gl.3/6/7, 31So.1–4/6/9–11/13, 32W.1–9, 33Brk.4, 36Co.1–3/7, 37D.1/3/6/8–11, 38Do.1/2/4/5, 39Ha.1–6, 40Sx.2; FOUR-LEGGED- (OE *fēower* + ON *leggr* 1683+-ED+–) 36Co.+2/4; LAND- (OE *land*+–) 31So.+1; WATER- 31So.1, 37D.2

EWT 20C.1, 27Bd.2/3

MEWT 16Wo.+16, 24Gl.1/2

NEWT 6Y.18 water-hen, 29Ess.14 tadpole

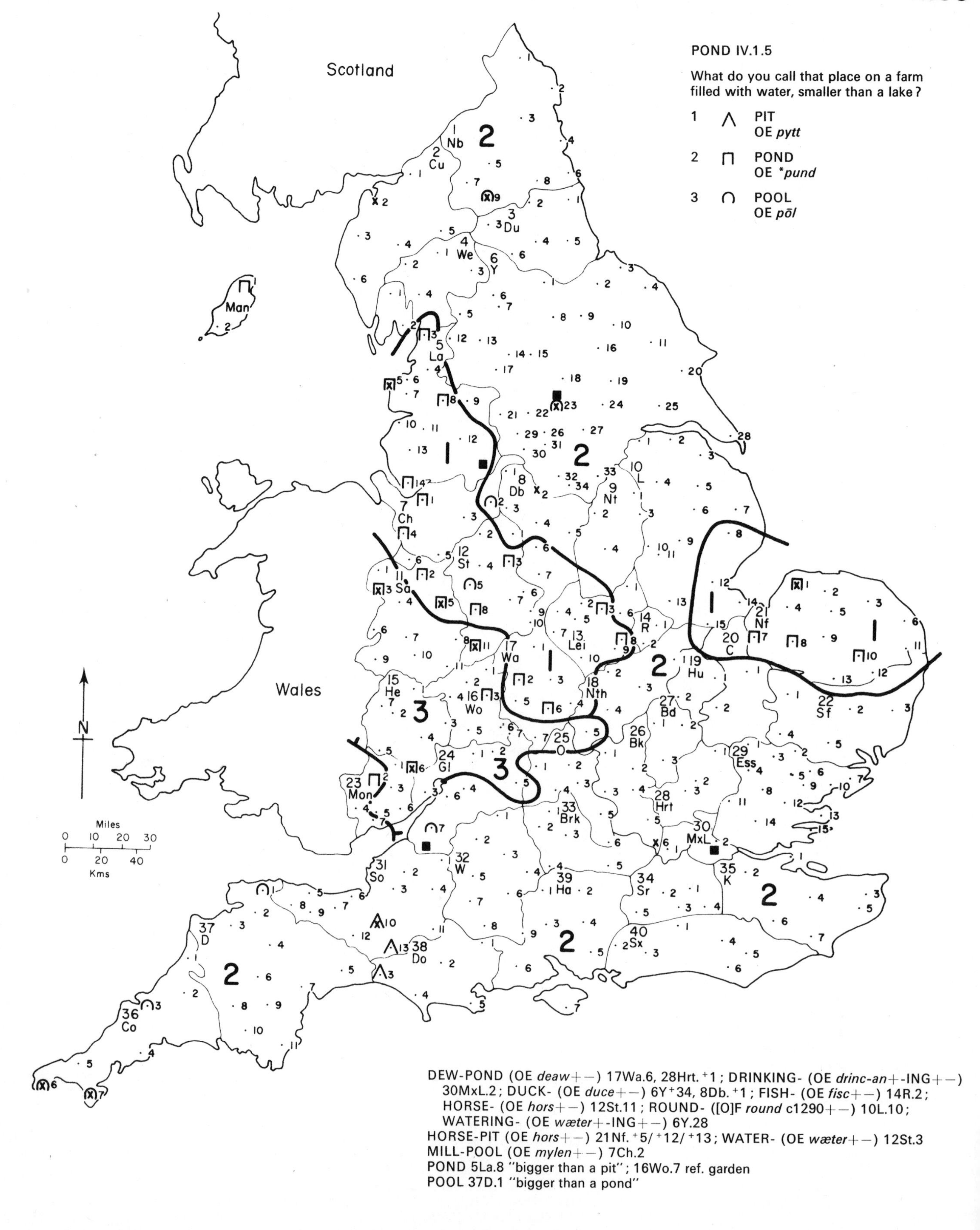

DEW-POND (OE *deaw*+—) 17Wa.6, 28Hrt.+1; DRINKING- (OE *drinc-an*+-ING+—) 30MxL.2; DUCK- (OE *duce*+—) 6Y+34, 8Db.+1; FISH- (OE *fisc*+—) 14R.2; HORSE- (OE *hors*+—) 12St.11; ROUND- ([O]F *round* c1290+—) 10L.10; WATERING- (OE *wæter*+-ING+—) 6Y.28
HORSE-PIT (OE *hors*+—) 21Nf.+5/+12/+13; WATER- (OE *wæter*+—) 12St.3
MILL-POOL (OE *mylen*+—) 7Ch.2
POND 5La.8 "bigger than a pit"; 16Wo.7 ref. garden
POOL 37D.1 "bigger than a pond"

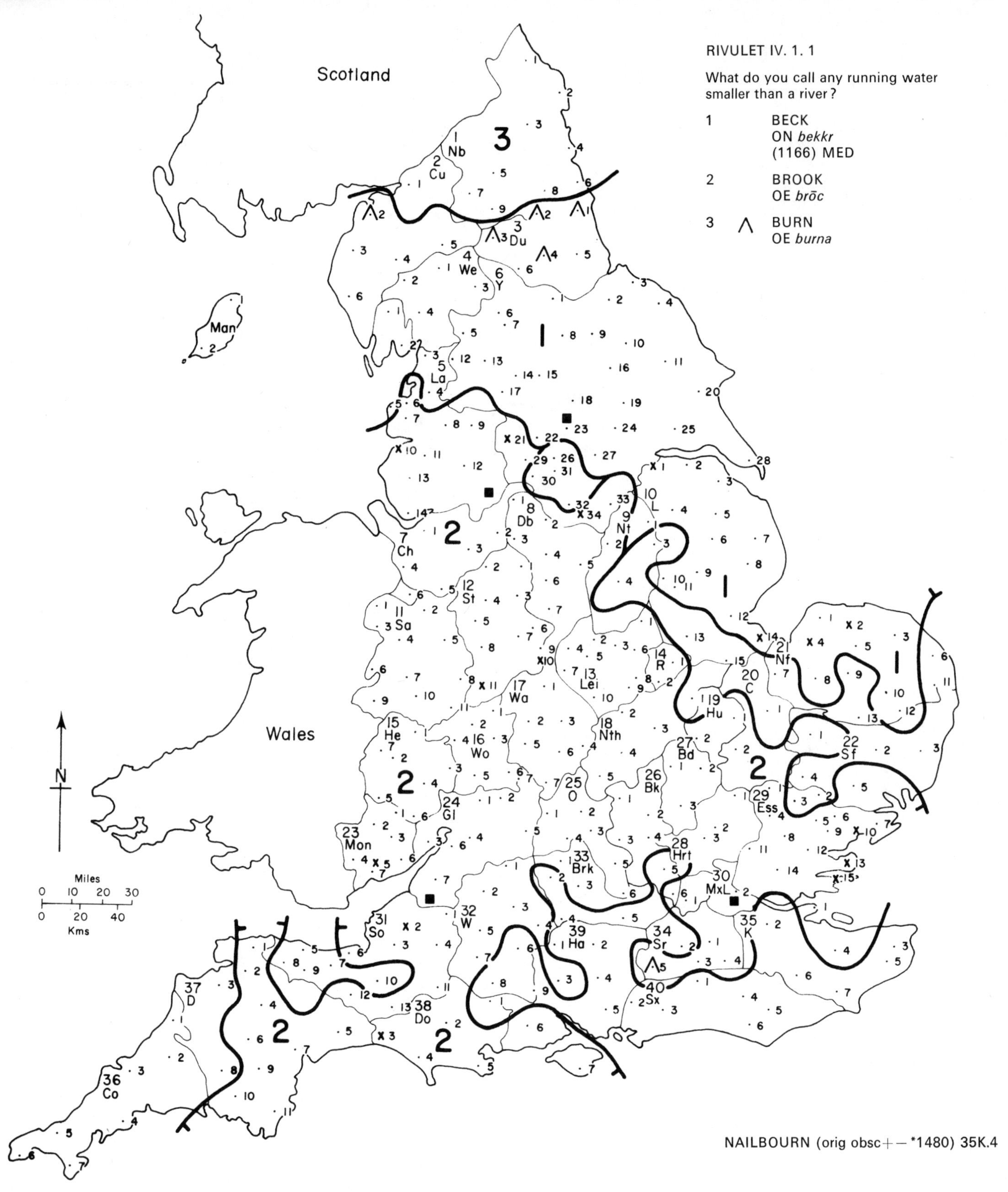

NAILBOURN (orig obsc+—*1480) 35K.4

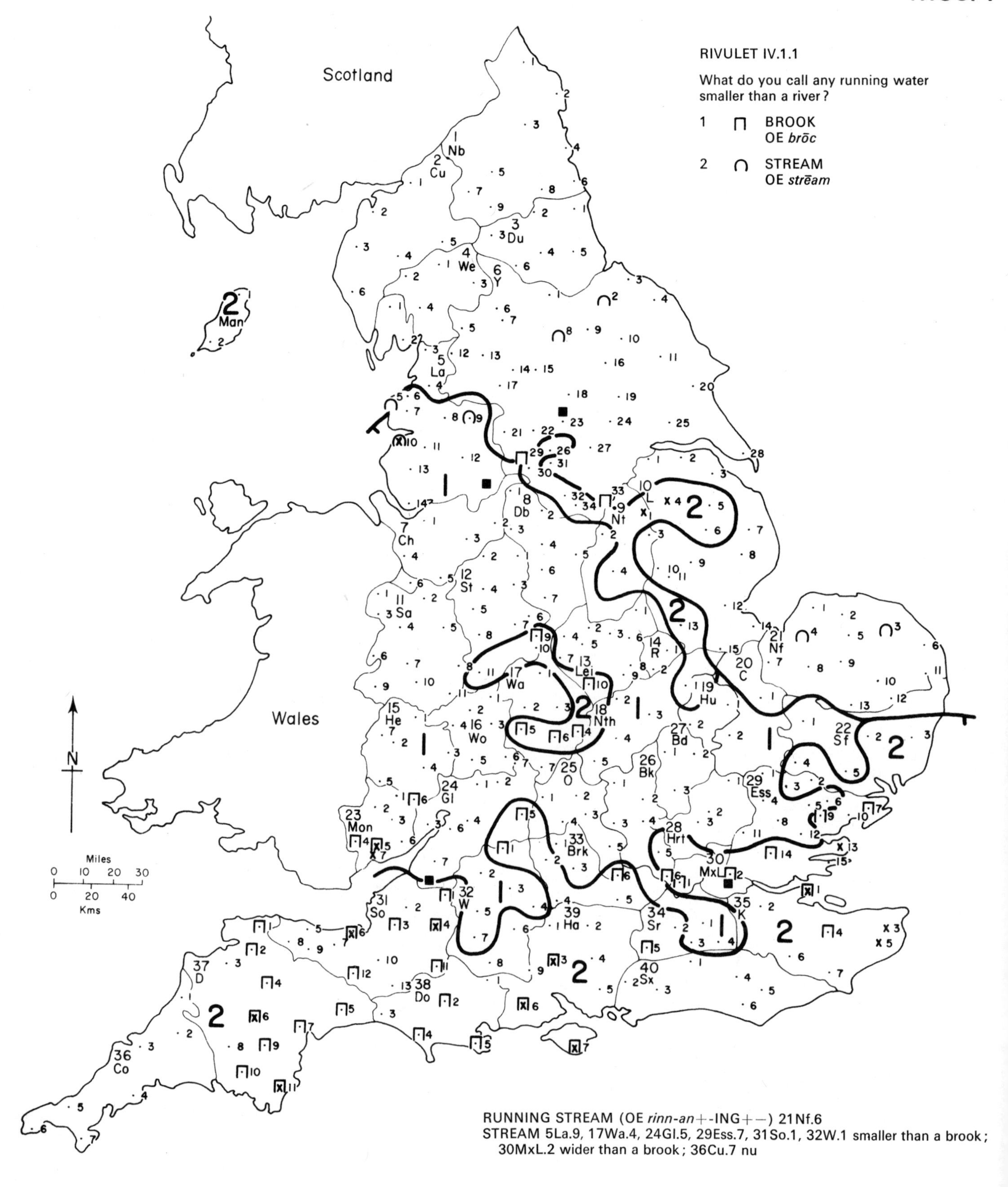

RUNNING STREAM (OE *rinn-an*+-ING+—) 21Nf.6
STREAM 5La.9, 17Wa.4, 24Gl.5, 29Ess.7, 31So.1, 32W.1 smaller than a brook; 30MxL.2 wider than a brook; 36Cu.7 nu

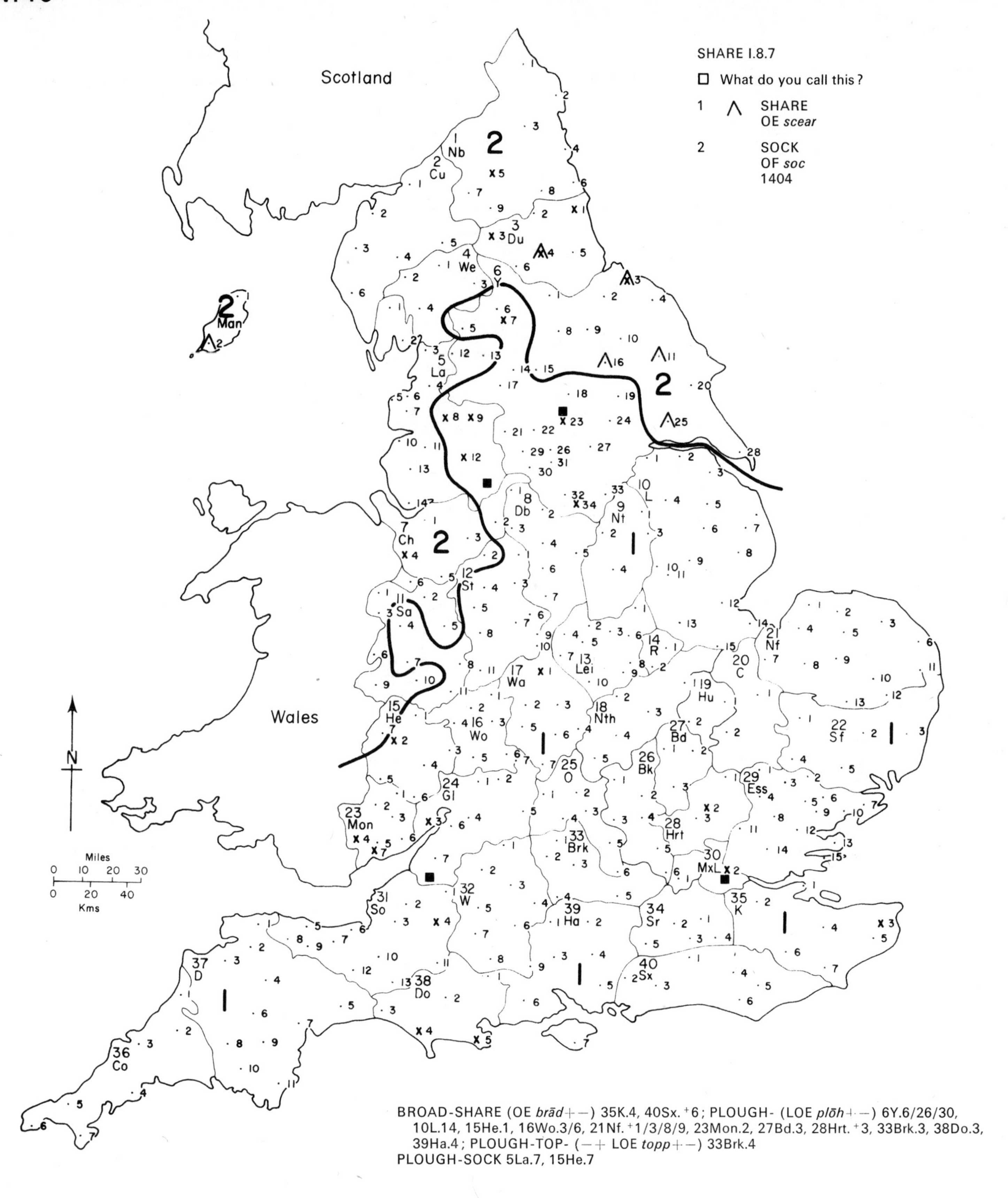

BROAD-SHARE (OE *brād*+−) 35K.4, 40Sx.+6; PLOUGH- (LOE *plōh*+−) 6Y.6/26/30, 10L.14, 15He.1, 16Wo.3/6, 21Nf.+1/3/8/9, 23Mon.2, 27Bd.3, 28Hrt.+3, 33Brk.3, 38Do.3, 39Ha.4; PLOUGH-TOP- (−+ LOE *topp*+−) 33Brk.4
PLOUGH-SOCK 5La.7, 15He.7

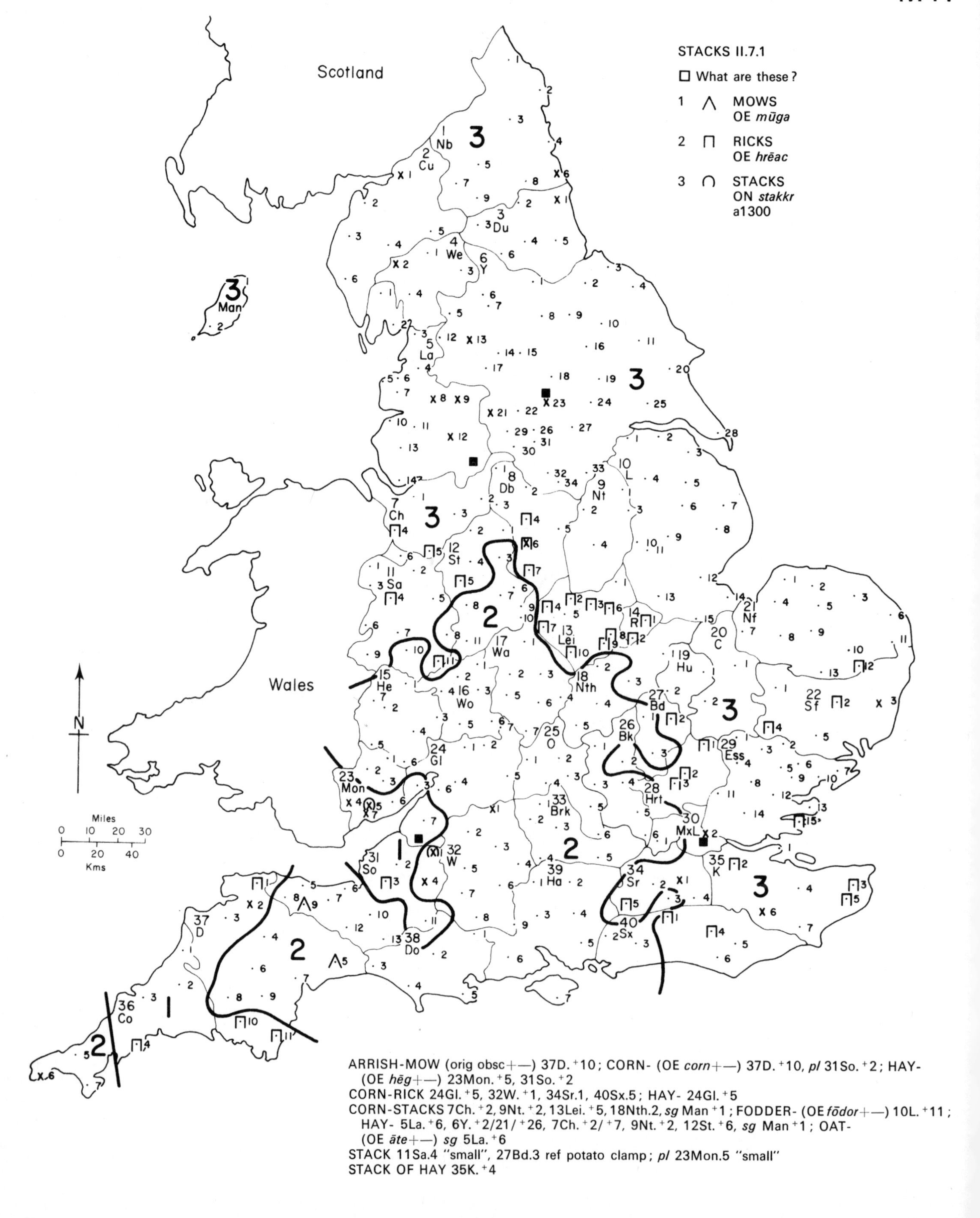

ARRISH-MOW (orig obsc+—) 37D.+10; CORN- (OE *corn*+—) 37D.+10, *pl* 31So.+2; HAY- (OE *hēg*+—) 23Mon.+5, 31So.+2

CORN-RICK 24Gl.+5, 32W.+1, 34Sr.1, 40Sx.5; HAY- 24Gl.+5

CORN-STACKS 7Ch.+2, 9Nt.+2, 13Lei.+5, 18Nth.2, *sg* Man+1; FODDER- (OE *fōdor*+—) 10L.+11; HAY- 5La.+6, 6Y.+2/21/+26, 7Ch.+2/+7, 9Nt.+2, 12St.+6, *sg* Man+1; OAT- (OE *āte*+—) *sg* 5La.+6

STACK 11Sa.4 "small", 27Bd.3 ref potato clamp; *pl* 23Mon.5 "small"

STACK OF HAY 35K.+4

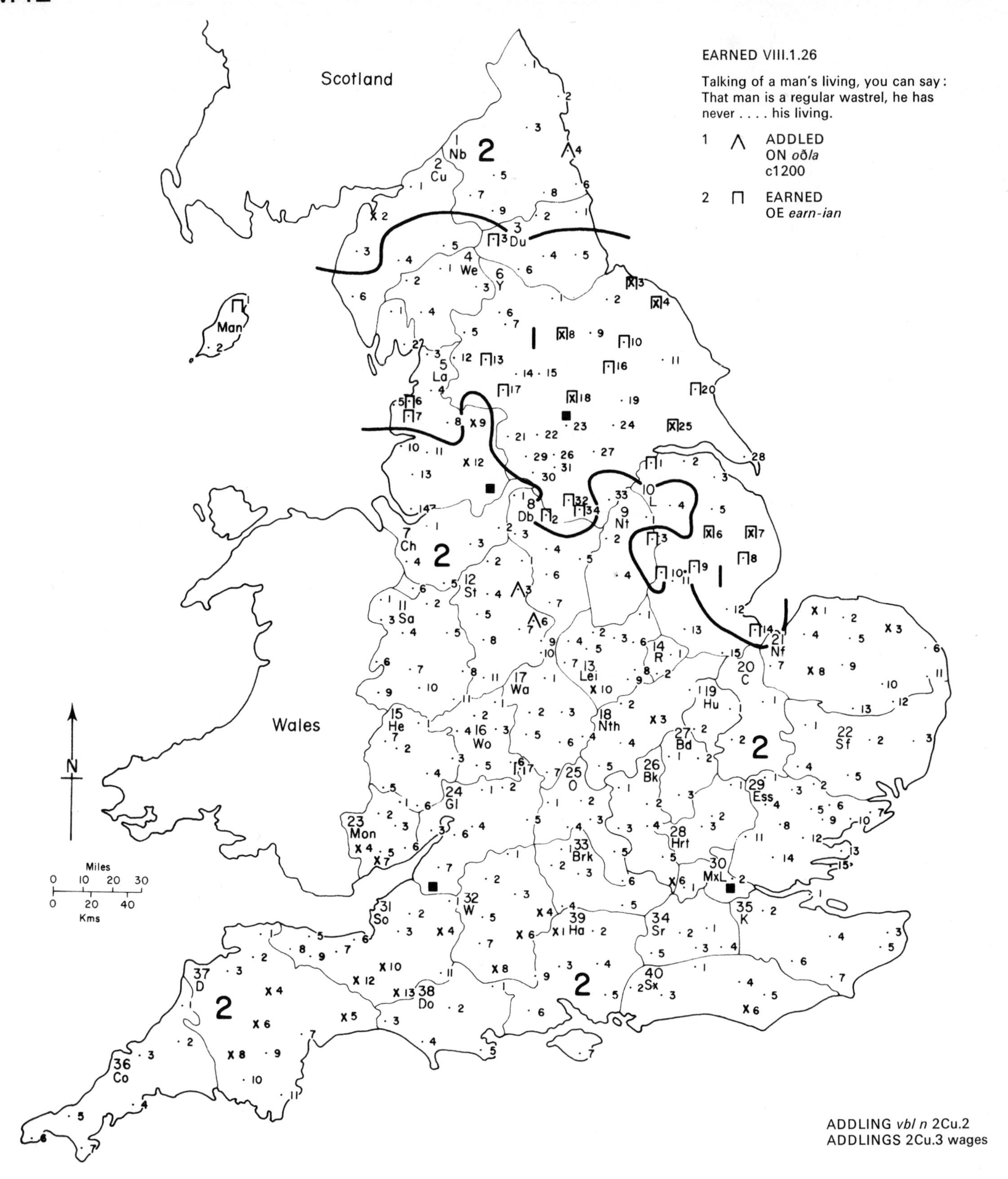
EARNED VIII.1.26
Talking of a man's living, you can say: That man is a regular wastrel, he has never . . . . his living.
1 ADDLED ON *oðla* c1200
2 EARNED OE *earn-ian*
Scotland
Wales
Man
N
Miles
0 10 20 30
0 20 40
Kms
ADDLING *vbl n* 2Cu.2
ADDLINGS 2Cu.3 wages

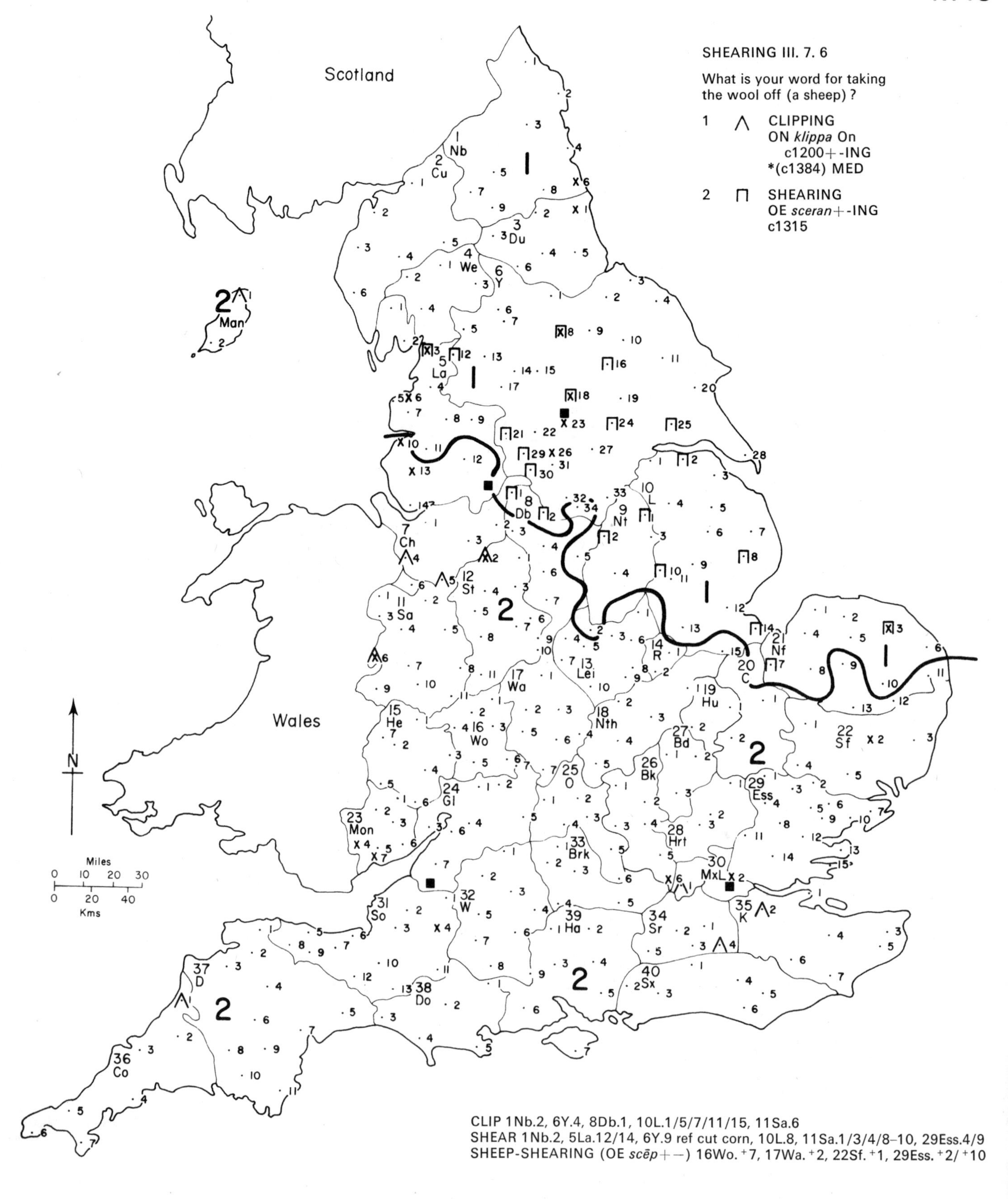
SHEARING III. 7. 6
What is your word for taking the wool off (a sheep)?
1 Λ CLIPPING
ON *klippa* On
c1200+-ING
*(c1384) MED
2 ⊓ SHEARING
OE *sceran*+-ING
c1315
Scotland
Wales
Miles
Kms
CLIP 1Nb.2, 6Y.4, 8Db.1, 10L.1/5/7/11/15, 11Sa.6
SHEAR 1Nb.2, 5La.12/14, 6Y.9 ref cut corn, 10L.8, 11Sa.1/3/4/8–10, 29Ess.4/9
SHEEP-SHEARING (OE *scēp*+–) 16Wo.+7, 17Wa.+2, 22Sf.+1, 29Ess.+2/+10

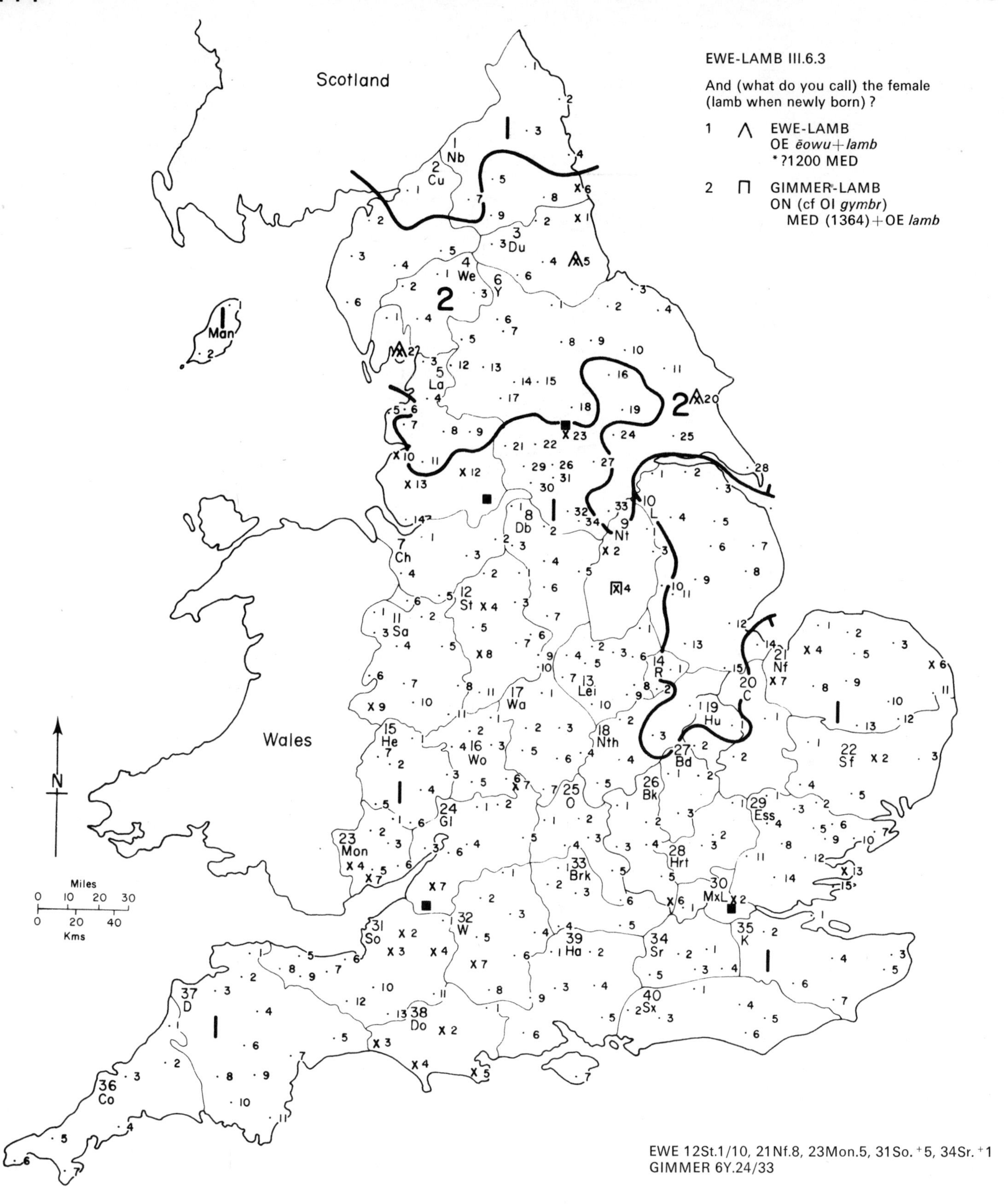
EWE-LAMB III.6.3
And (what do you call) the female (lamb when newly born)?
1 Λ EWE-LAMB
OE ēowu+lamb
*?1200 MED
2 ⊓ GIMMER-LAMB
ON (cf OI gymbr)
MED (1364)+OE lamb
Scotland
Wales
N
Miles
0 10 20 30
0 20 40
Kms
EWE 12St.1/10, 21Nf.8, 23Mon.5, 31So.+5, 34Sr.+1
GIMMER 6Y.24/33

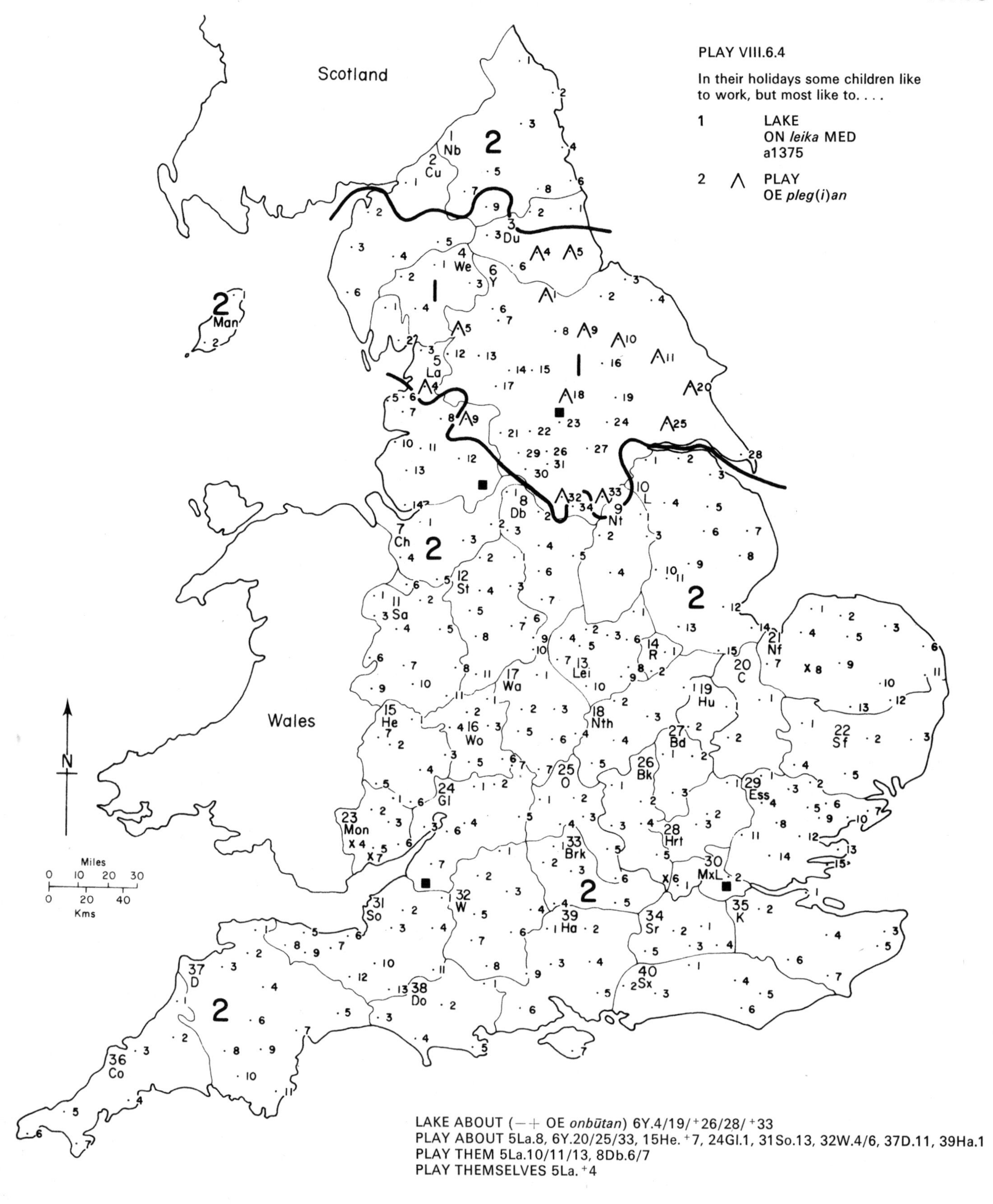

LAKE ABOUT (— + OE *onbūtan*) 6Y.4/19/+26/28/+33
PLAY ABOUT 5La.8, 6Y.20/25/33, 15He.+7, 24Gl.1, 31So.13, 32W.4/6, 37D.11, 39Ha.1
PLAY THEM 5La.10/11/13, 8Db.6/7
PLAY THEMSELVES 5La.+4

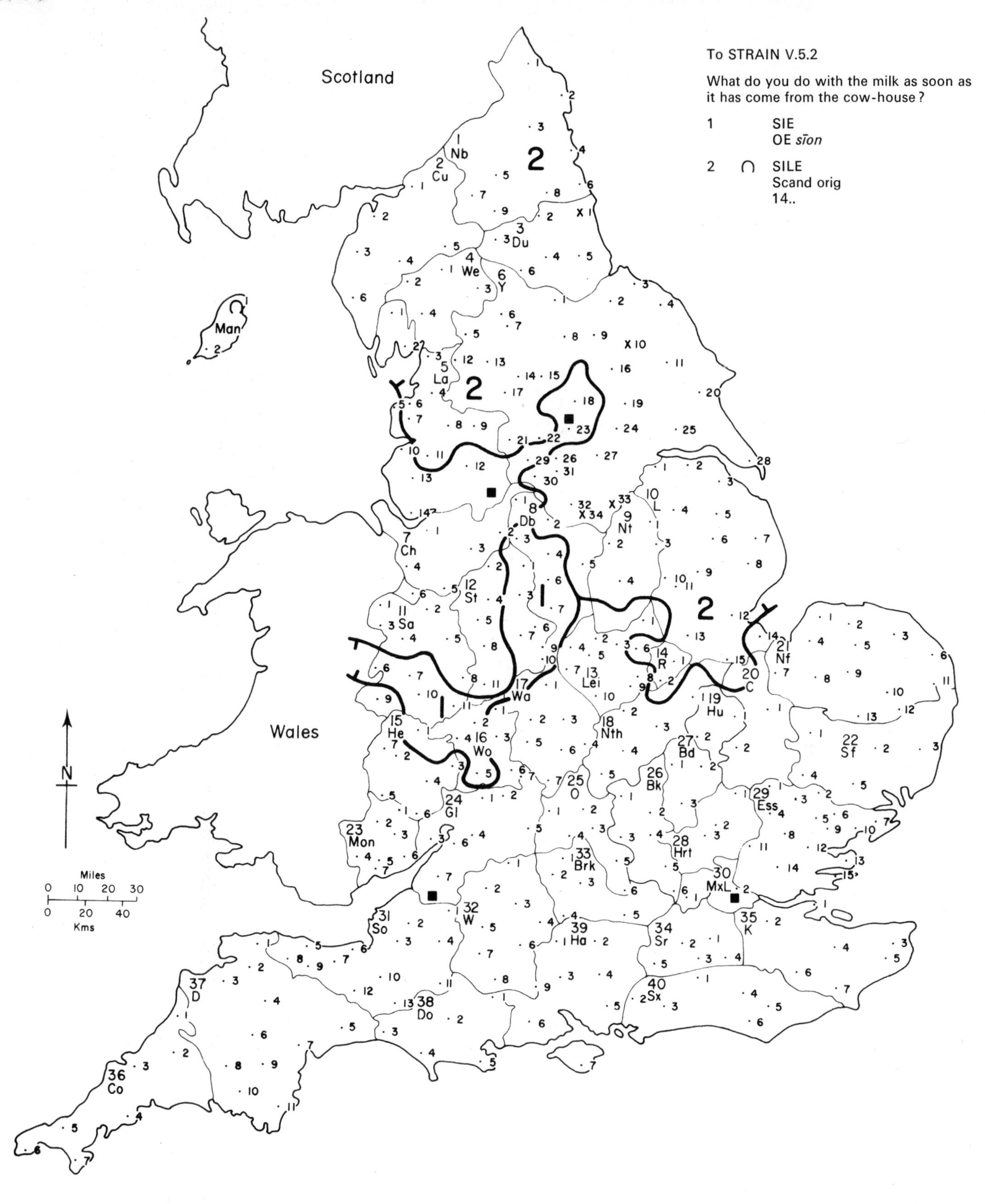
To STRAIN V.5.2
What do you do with the milk as soon as it has come from the cow-house?
1 SIE
OE sīon
2 ∩ SILE
Scand orig
14..
Scotland
Wales
Man
Nb
Cu
Du
We
Y
La
Ch
Db
Nt
L
St
Sa
Lei
R
Nf
He
Wa
Wo
Nth
Hu
C
Bd
Sf
Gl
O
Bk
Ess
Mon
Hrt
Brk
MxL
So
W
Ha
Sr
K
D
Do
Sx
Co
N
Miles
0 10 20 30
0 20 40
Kms

To STRAIN V.5.2

What do you do with the milk as soon as it has come from the cow-house?

1 Λ SIEVE
OE *sife*

2 ⊓ STRAIN
OF *estreindre* On c1386

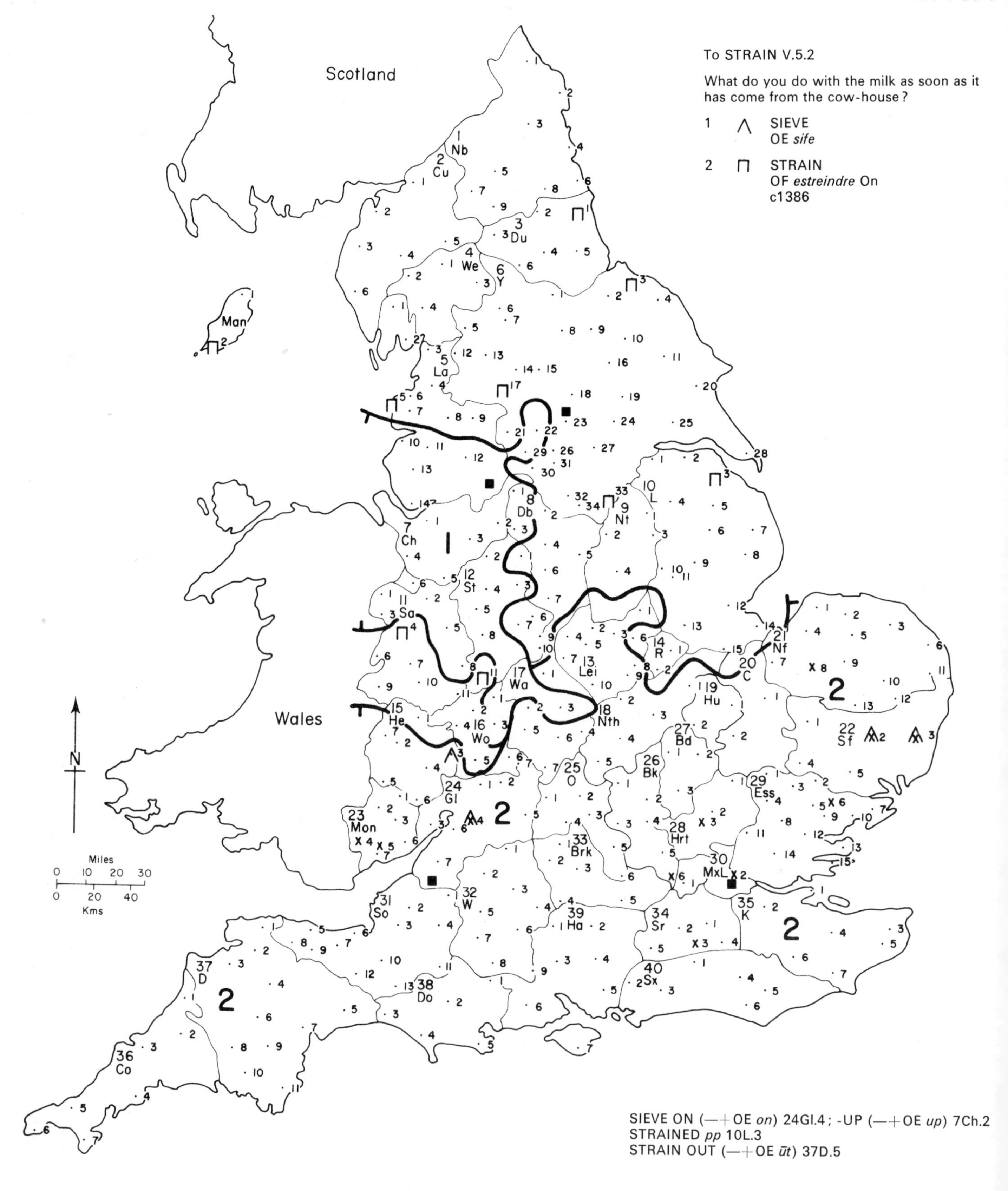

SIEVE ON (—+OE *on*) 24Gl.4; -UP (—+OE *up*) 7Ch.2
STRAINED *pp* 10L.3
STRAIN OUT (—+OE *ūt*) 37D.5

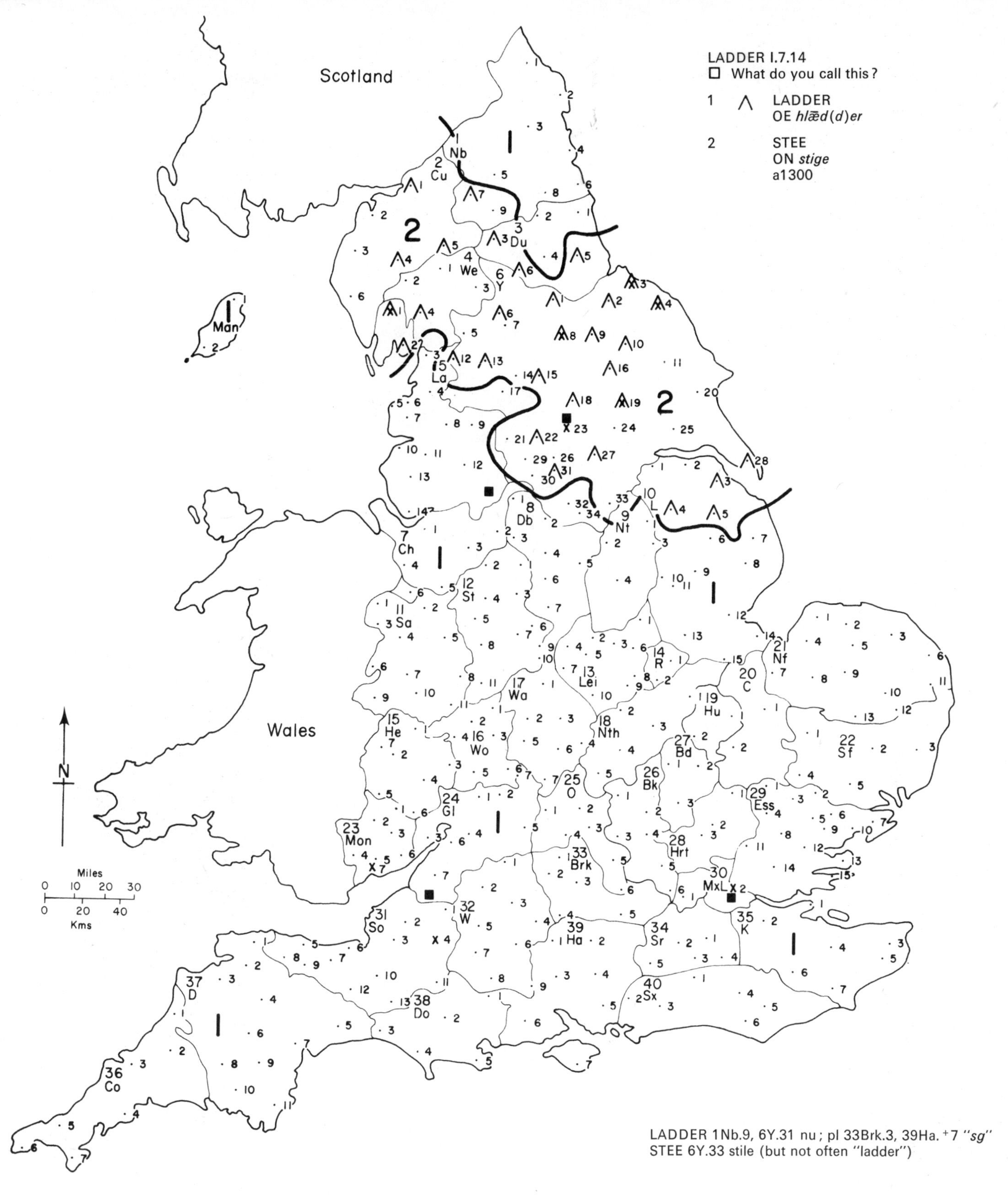

LADDER 1Nb.9, 6Y.31 nu; pl 33Brk.3, 39Ha.+7 *"sg"*
STEE 6Y.33 stile (but not often "ladder")

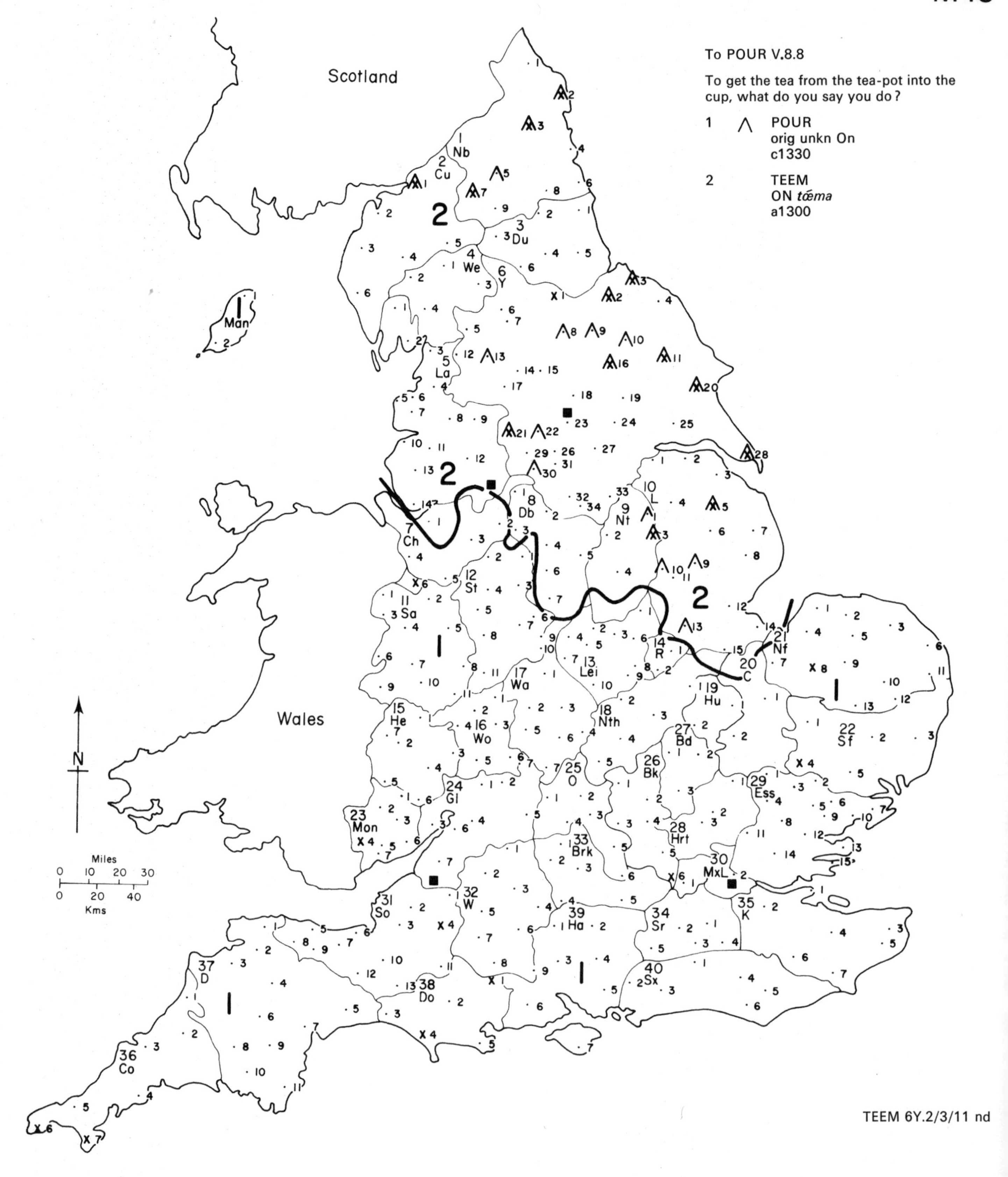
To POUR V.8.8
To get the tea from the tea-pot into the cup, what do you say you do?
1 ∧ POUR
orig unkn On
c1330
2 TEEM
ON *tœ́ma*
a1300
Scotland
Wales
Man
Nb
Cu
Du
We
Y
La
Ch
Db
Nt
L
St
Sa
Lei
R
Nf
C
Wa
He
Wo
Hu
Nth
Bd
Sf
Gl
O
Bk
Ess
Mon
Brk
Hrt
MxL
So
W
Ha
Sr
K
D
Do
Sx
Co
Miles
0 10 20 30
0 20 40
Kms
N
TEEM 6Y.2/3/11 nd

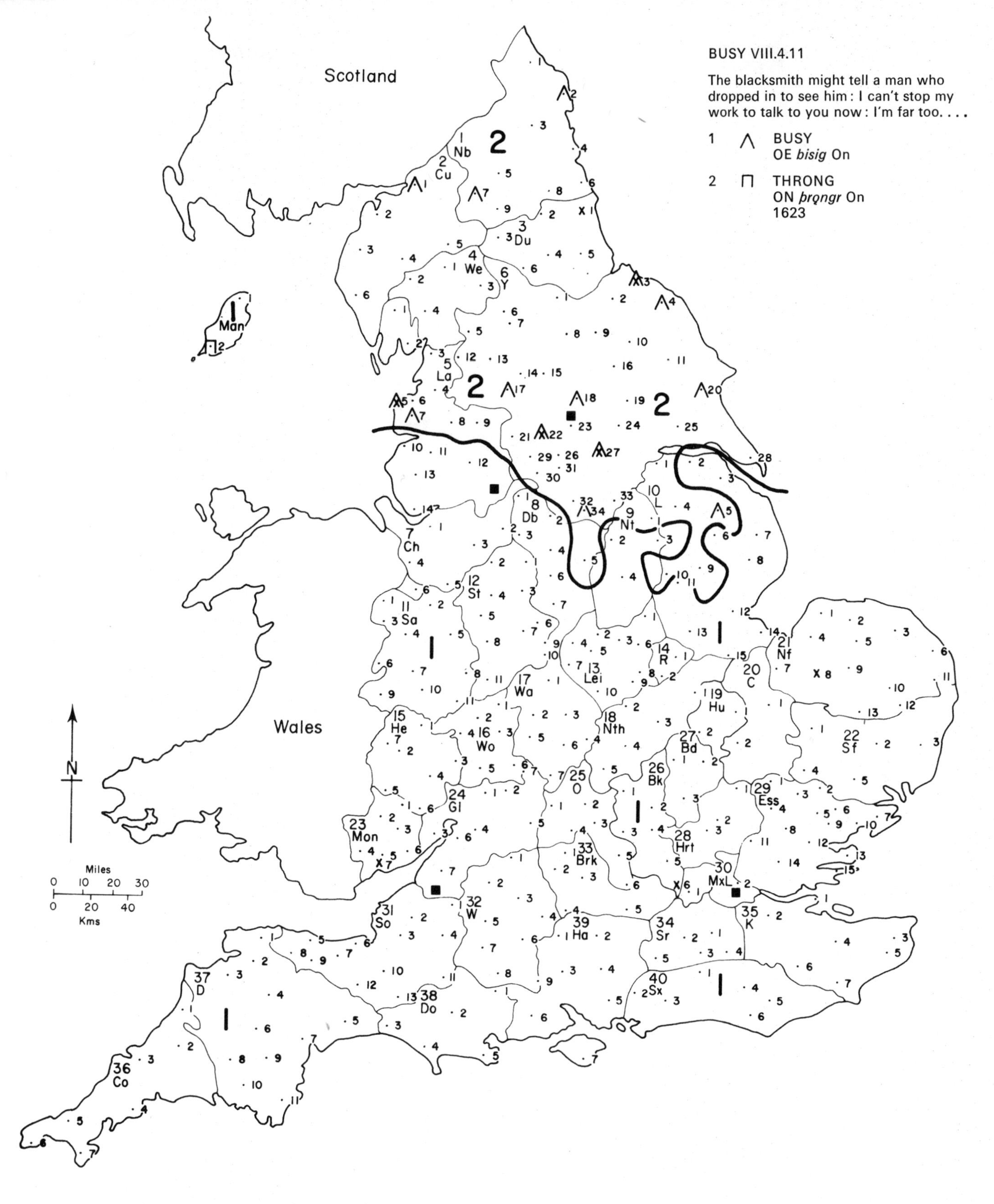
BUSY VIII.4.11
The blacksmith might tell a man who dropped in to see him: I can't stop my work to talk to you now: I'm far too. . . .
1 ∧ BUSY
OE *bisig* On
2 ⊓ THRONG
ON *þrǫngr* On
1623
Scotland
Wales
N
Miles
0 10 20 30
0 20 40
Kms

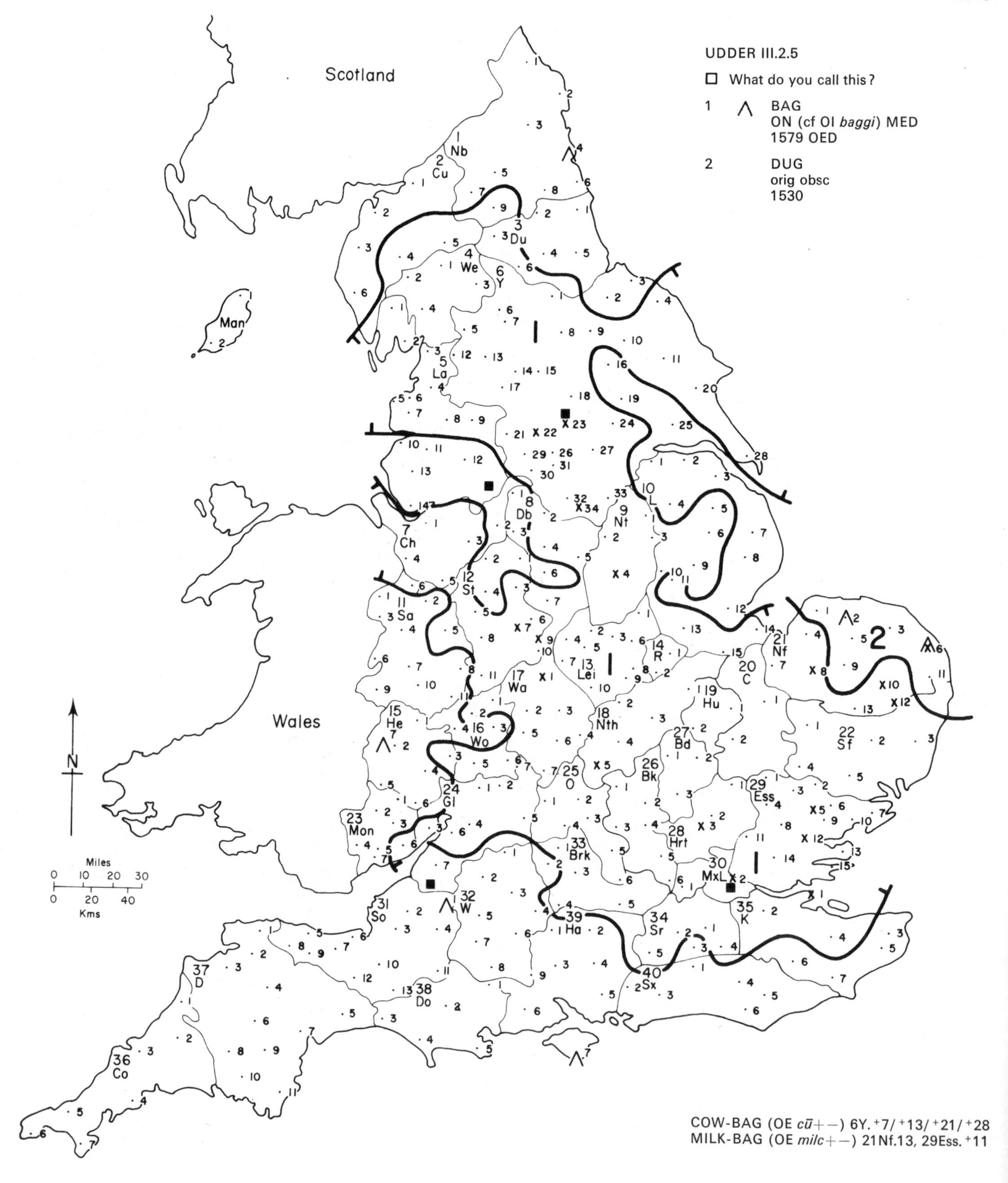

COW-BAG (OE *cū*+—) 6Y.+7/+13/+21/+28
MILK-BAG (OE *milc*+—) 21Nf.13, 29Ess.+11

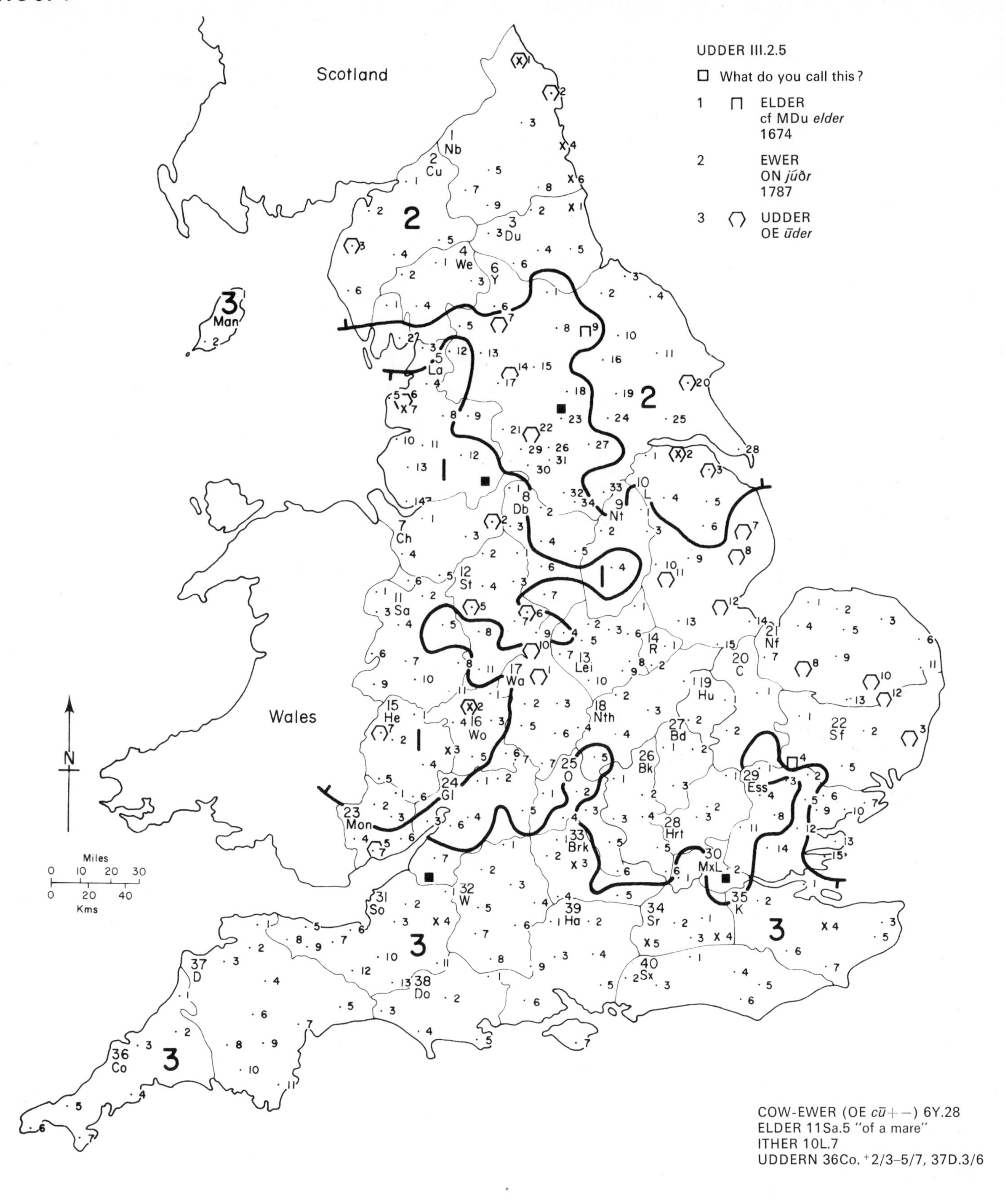
UDDER III.2.5
☐ What do you call this?
1 ⊓ ELDER
cf MDu *elder*
1674
2 EWER
ON *jūðr*
1787
3 ⬡ UDDER
OE *ūder*
Scotland
Wales
Man
N
Miles
0 10 20 30
0 20 40
Kms
COW-EWER (OE *cū*+—) 6Y.28
ELDER 11Sa.5 "of a mare"
ITHER 10L.7
UDDERN 36Co.⁺2/3–5/7, 37D.3/6

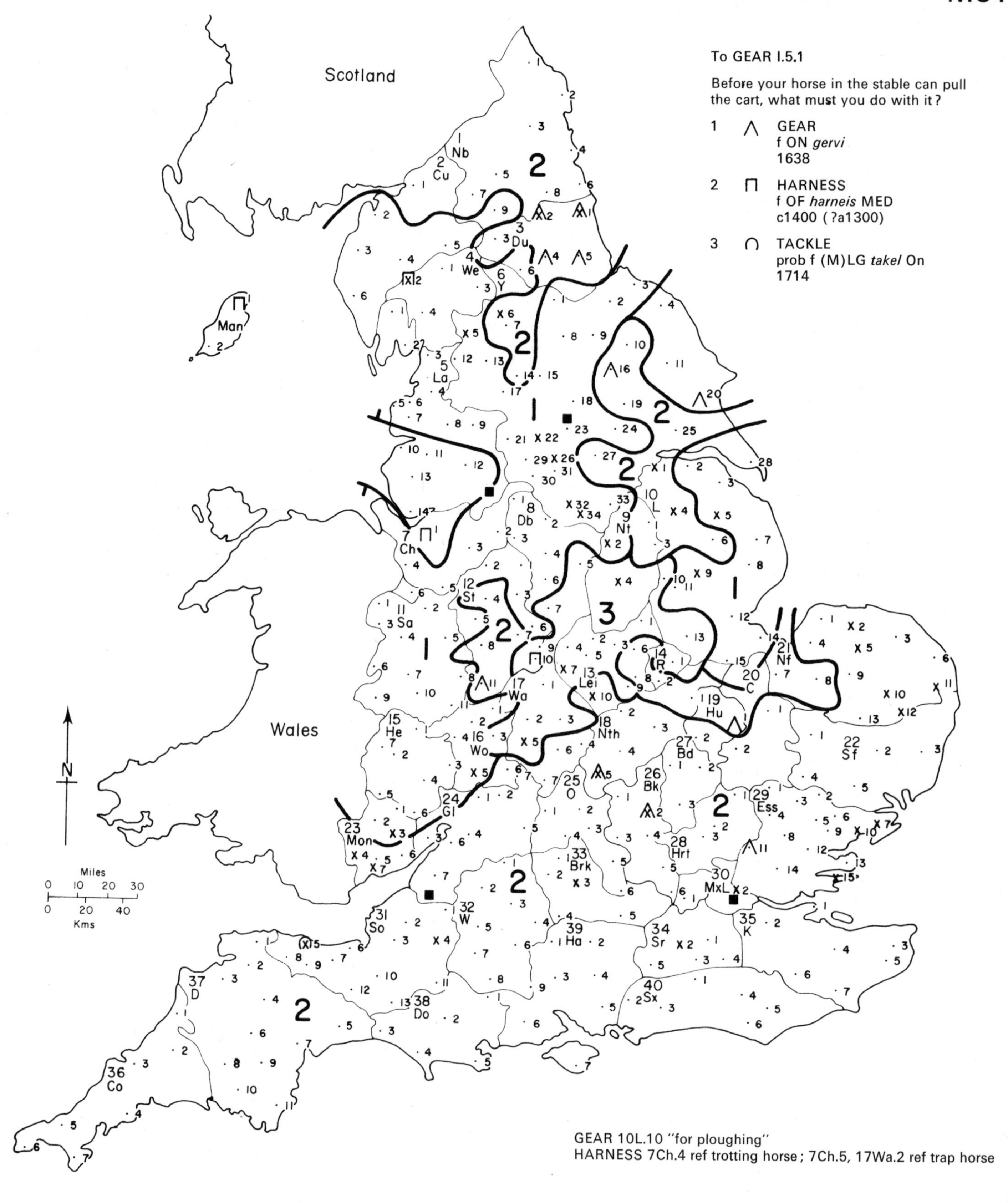

GEAR 10L.10 "for ploughing"
HARNESS 7Ch.4 ref trotting horse; 7Ch.5, 17Wa.2 ref trap horse

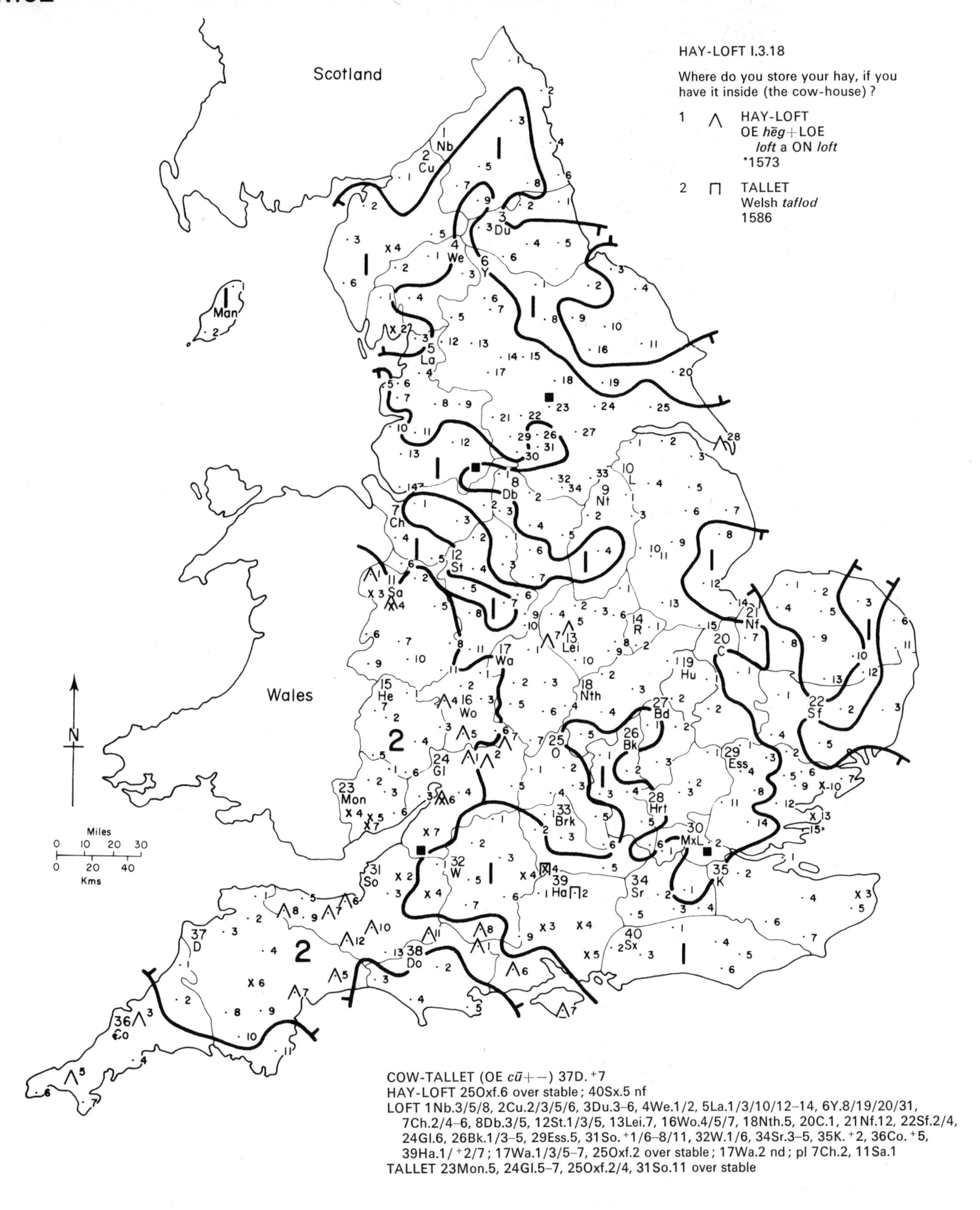

COW-TALLET (OE *cū*+—) 37D.+7
HAY-LOFT 25Oxf.6 over stable; 40Sx.5 nf
LOFT 1Nb.3/5/8, 2Cu.2/3/5/6, 3Du.3–6, 4We.1/2, 5La.1/3/10/12–14, 6Y.8/19/20/31, 7Ch.2/4–6, 8Db.3/5, 12St.1/3/5, 13Lei.7, 16Wo.4/5/7, 18Nth.5, 20C.1, 21Nf.12, 22Sf.2/4, 24Gl.6, 26Bk.1/3–5, 29Ess.5, 31So.+1/6–8/11, 32W.1/6, 34Sr.3–5, 35K.+2, 36Co.+5, 39Ha.1/+2/7; 17Wa.1/3/5–7, 25Oxf.2 over stable; 17Wa.2 nd; pl 7Ch.2, 11Sa.1
TALLET 23Mon.5, 24Gl.5–7, 25Oxf.2/4, 31So.11 over stable

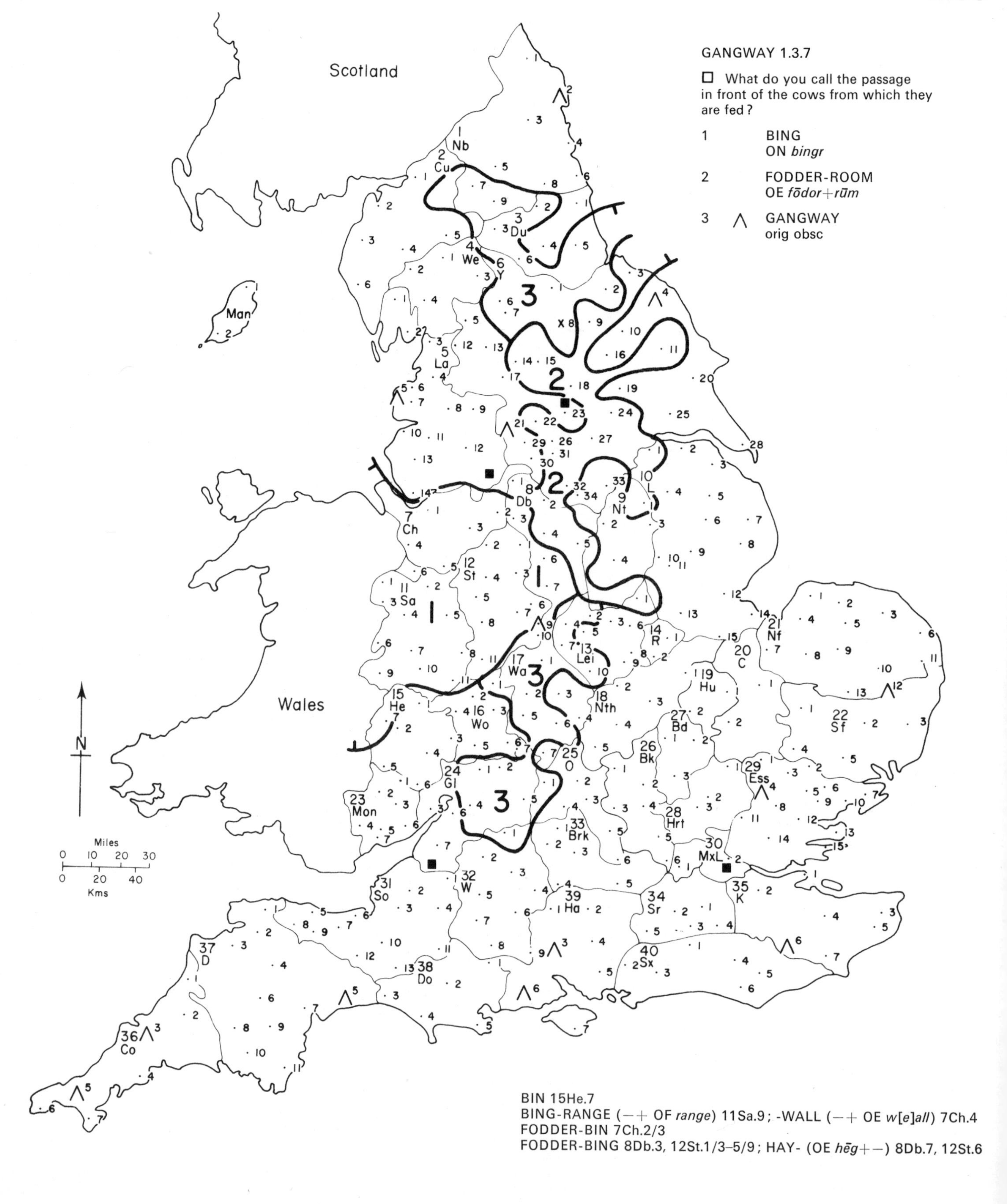

GANGWAY 1.3.7

□ What do you call the passage in front of the cows from which they are fed?

1		BING ON *bingr*
2		FODDER-ROOM OE *fōdor+rūm*
3	Λ	GANGWAY orig obsc

BIN 15He.7
BING-RANGE (—+ OF *range*) 11Sa.9; -WALL (—+ OE *w[e]all*) 7Ch.4
FODDER-BIN 7Ch.2/3
FODDER-BING 8Db.3, 12St.1/3–5/9; HAY- (OE *hēg*+—) 8Db.7, 12St.6

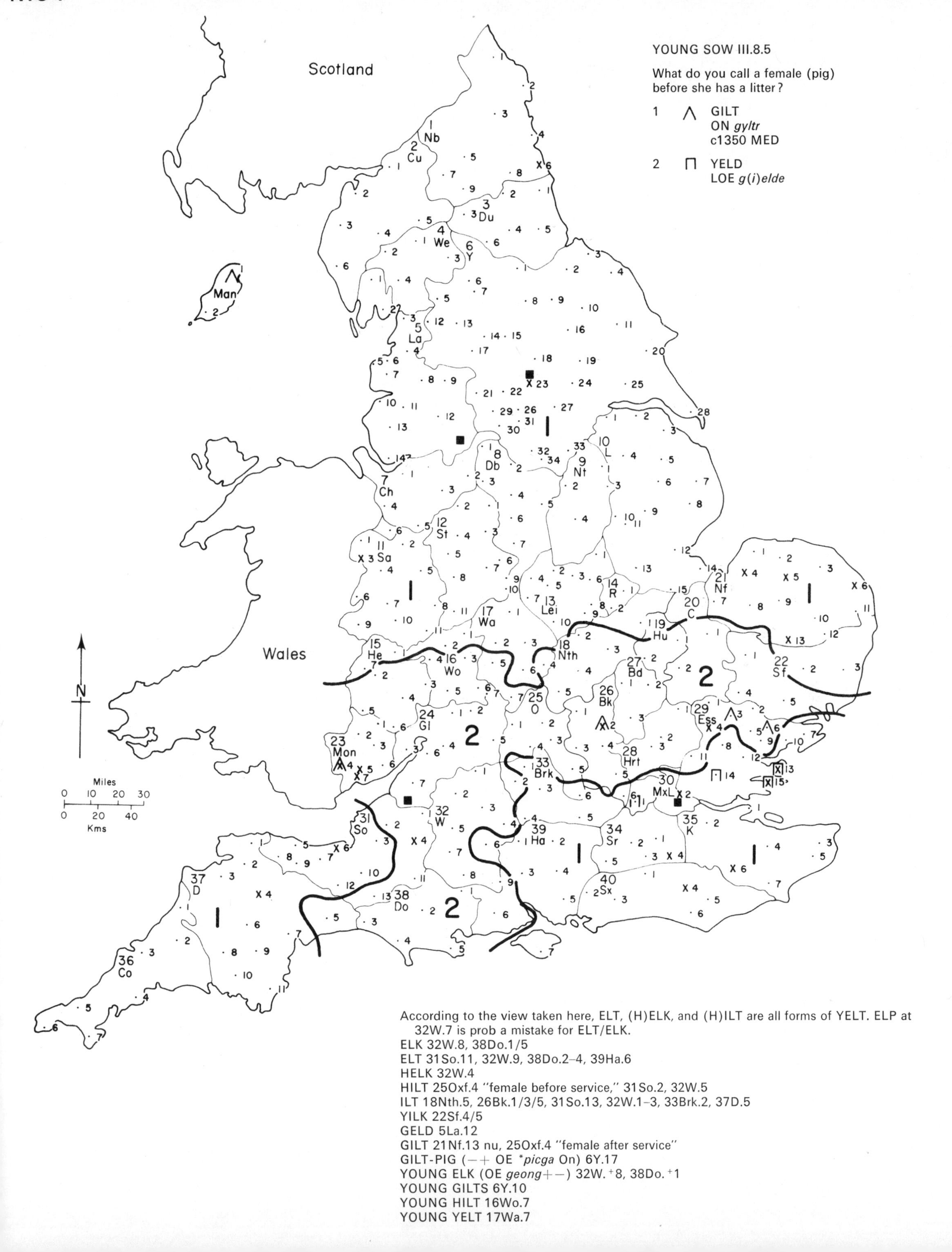

According to the view taken here, ELT, (H)ELK, and (H)ILT are all forms of YELT. ELP at 32W.7 is prob a mistake for ELT/ELK.
ELK 32W.8, 38Do.1/5
ELT 31So.11, 32W.9, 38Do.2–4, 39Ha.6
HELK 32W.4
HILT 25Oxf.4 "female before service," 31So.2, 32W.5
ILT 18Nth.5, 26Bk.1/3/5, 31So.13, 32W.1–3, 33Brk.2, 37D.5
YILK 22Sf.4/5
GELD 5La.12
GILT 21Nf.13 nu, 25Oxf.4 "female after service"
GILT-PIG (—+ OE **picga* On) 6Y.17
YOUNG ELK (OE *geong*+—) 32W.⁺8, 38Do.⁺1
YOUNG GILTS 6Y.10
YOUNG HILT 16Wo.7
YOUNG YELT 17Wa.7

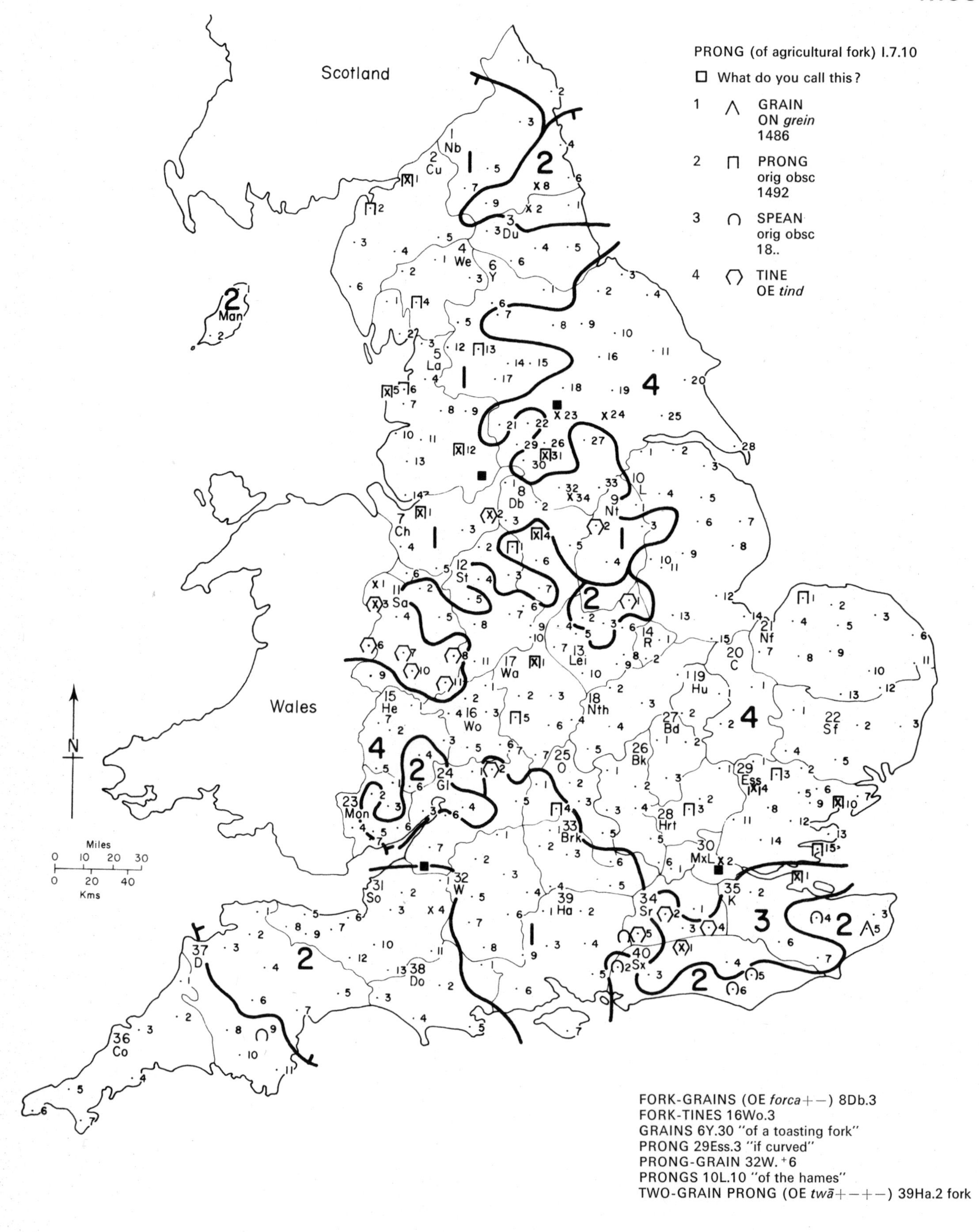
PRONG (of agricultural fork) I.7.10
☐ What do you call this?
1 ∧ GRAIN ON *grein* 1486
2 ⊓ PRONG orig obsc 1492
3 ∩ SPEAN orig obsc 18..
4 ⬡ TINE OE *tind*
Scotland
Wales
Man
Miles 0 10 20 30
0 20 40 Kms
N
FORK-GRAINS (OE *forca*+−) 8Db.3
FORK-TINES 16Wo.3
GRAINS 6Y.30 "of a toasting fork"
PRONG 29Ess.3 "if curved"
PRONG-GRAIN 32W. +6
PRONGS 10L.10 "of the hames"
TWO-GRAIN PRONG (OE *twā*+−+−) 39Ha.2 fork

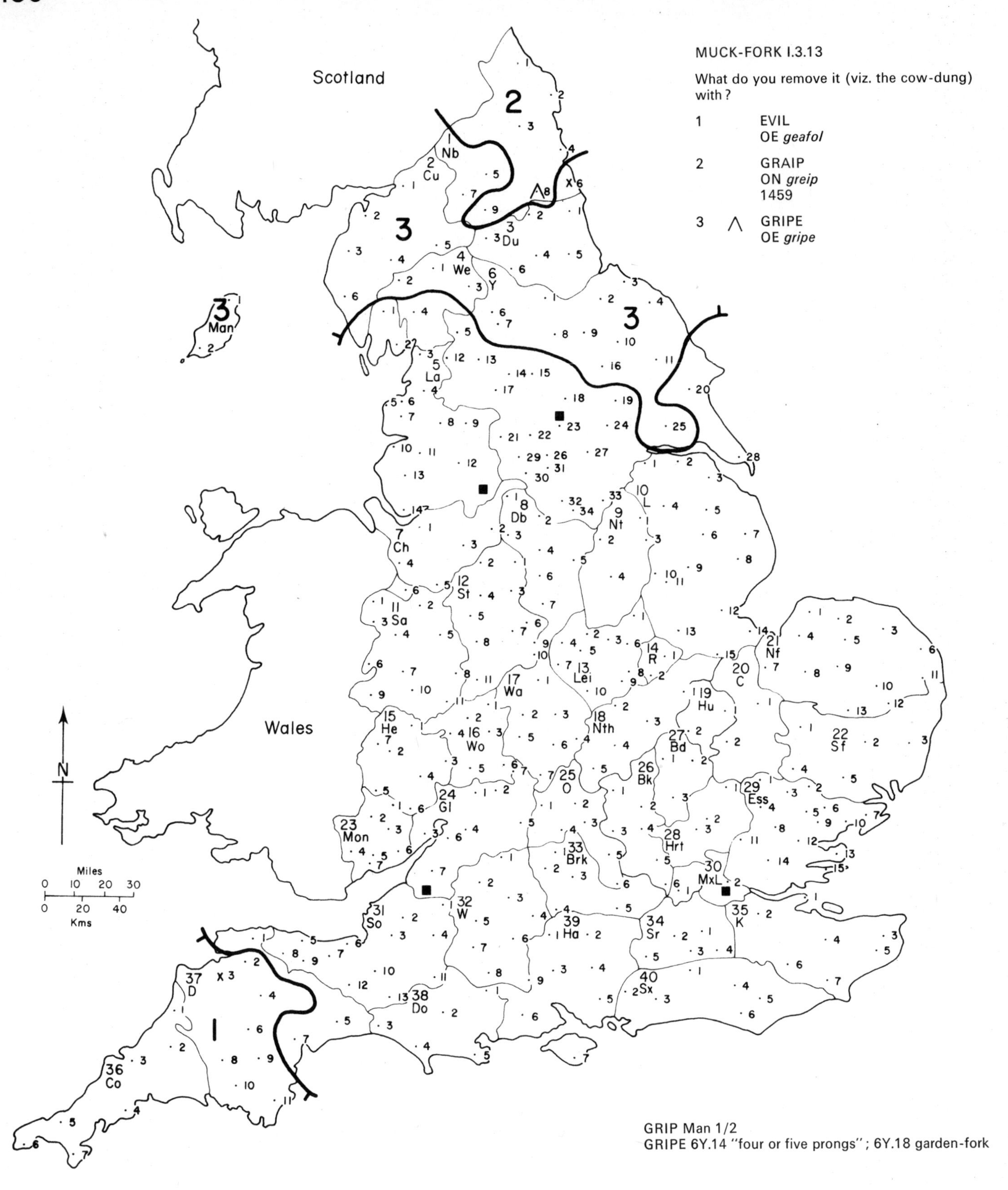
MUCK-FORK I.3.13
What do you remove it (viz. the cow-dung) with?
1 EVIL
OE *geafol*
2 GRAIP
ON *greip*
1459
3 Λ GRIPE
OE *gripe*
Scotland
Wales
N
Miles
0 10 20 30
0 20 40
Kms
GRIP Man 1/2
GRIPE 6Y.14 "four or five prongs"; 6Y.18 garden-fork

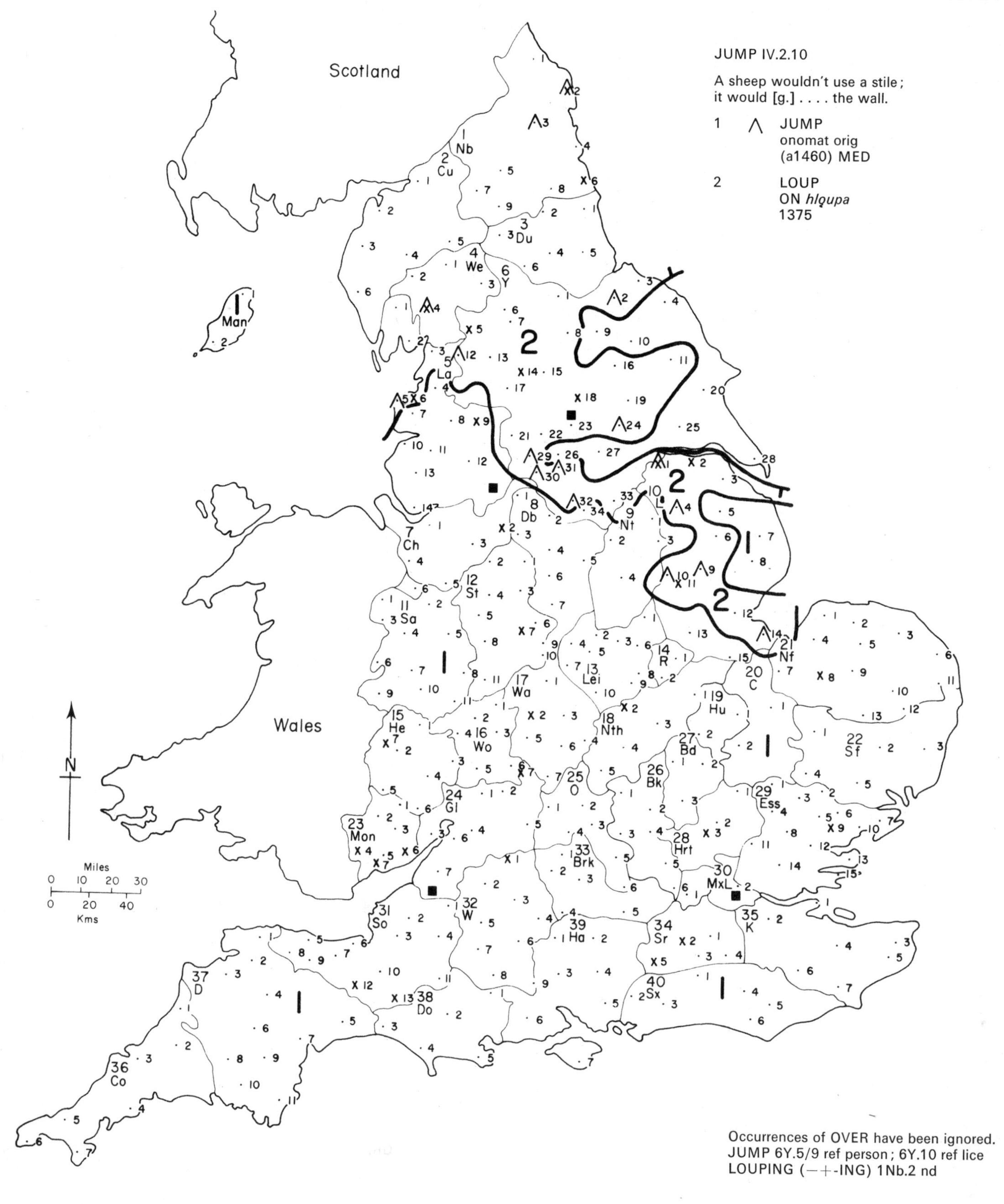
JUMP IV.2.10
A sheep wouldn't use a stile; it would [g.] . . . . the wall.
1 /\ JUMP
onomat orig
(a1460) MED
2 LOUP
ON *hlǫupa*
1375
Scotland
Wales
Man
N
Miles
0 10 20 30
0 20 40
Kms
Occurrences of OVER have been ignored.
JUMP 6Y.5/9 ref person; 6Y.10 ref lice
LOUPING (—+-ING) 1Nb.2 nd

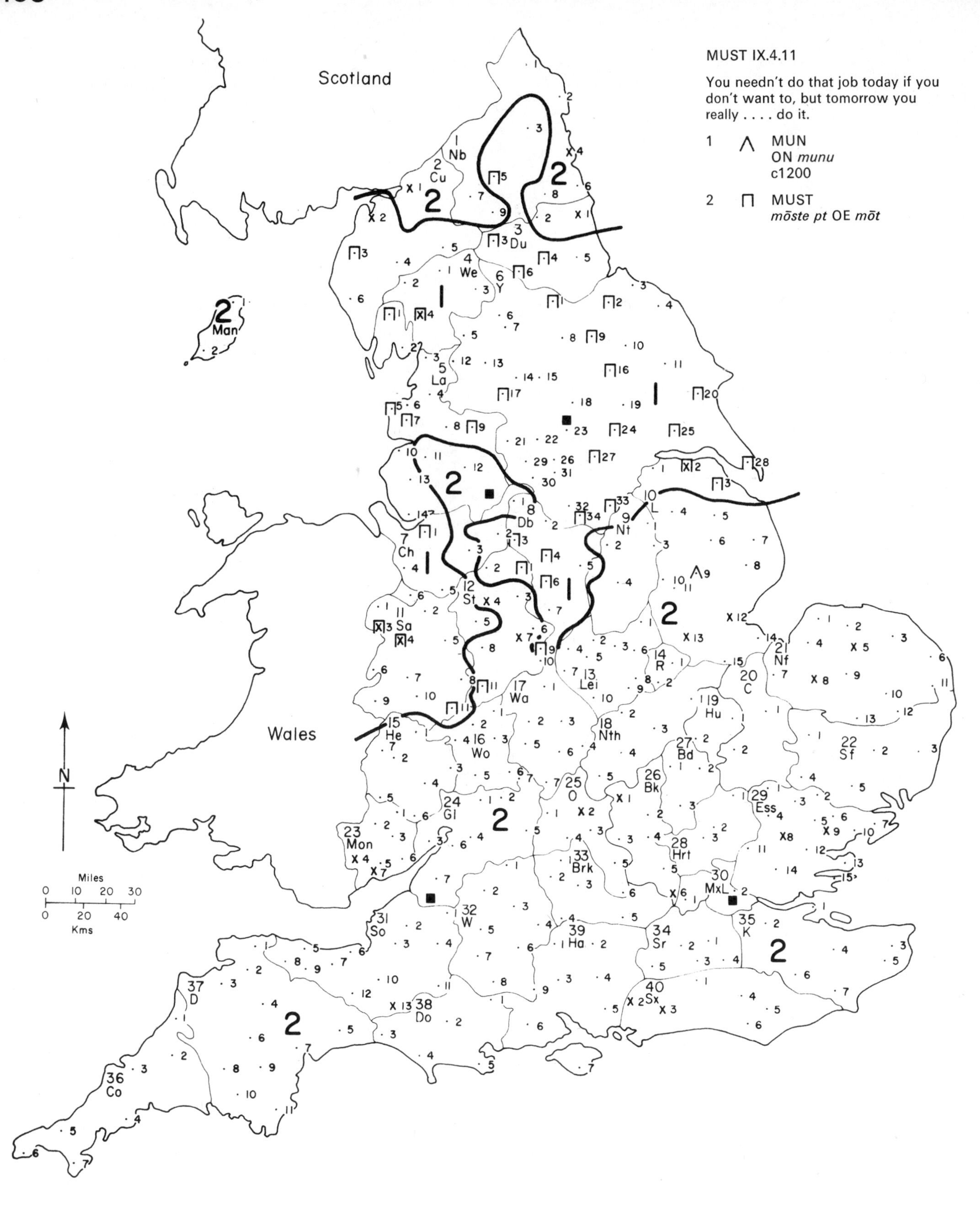
Scotland
Wales
MUST IX.4.11
You needn't do that job today if you don't want to, but tomorrow you really . . . . do it.
1 Λ MUN
ON *munu*
c1200
2 ⊓ MUST
mōste pt OE *mōt*
Miles
0 10 20 30
0 20 40
Kms
N
Nb
Cu
Du
We
Y
Man
La
Ch
Db
Nt
L
St
Sa
R
Lei
Nf
C
Wa
Hu
He
Nth
Wo
Bd
Sf
Bk
O
Gl
Ess
Mon
Hrt
Brk
MxL
So
W
K
Ha
Sr
Sx
D
Do
Co

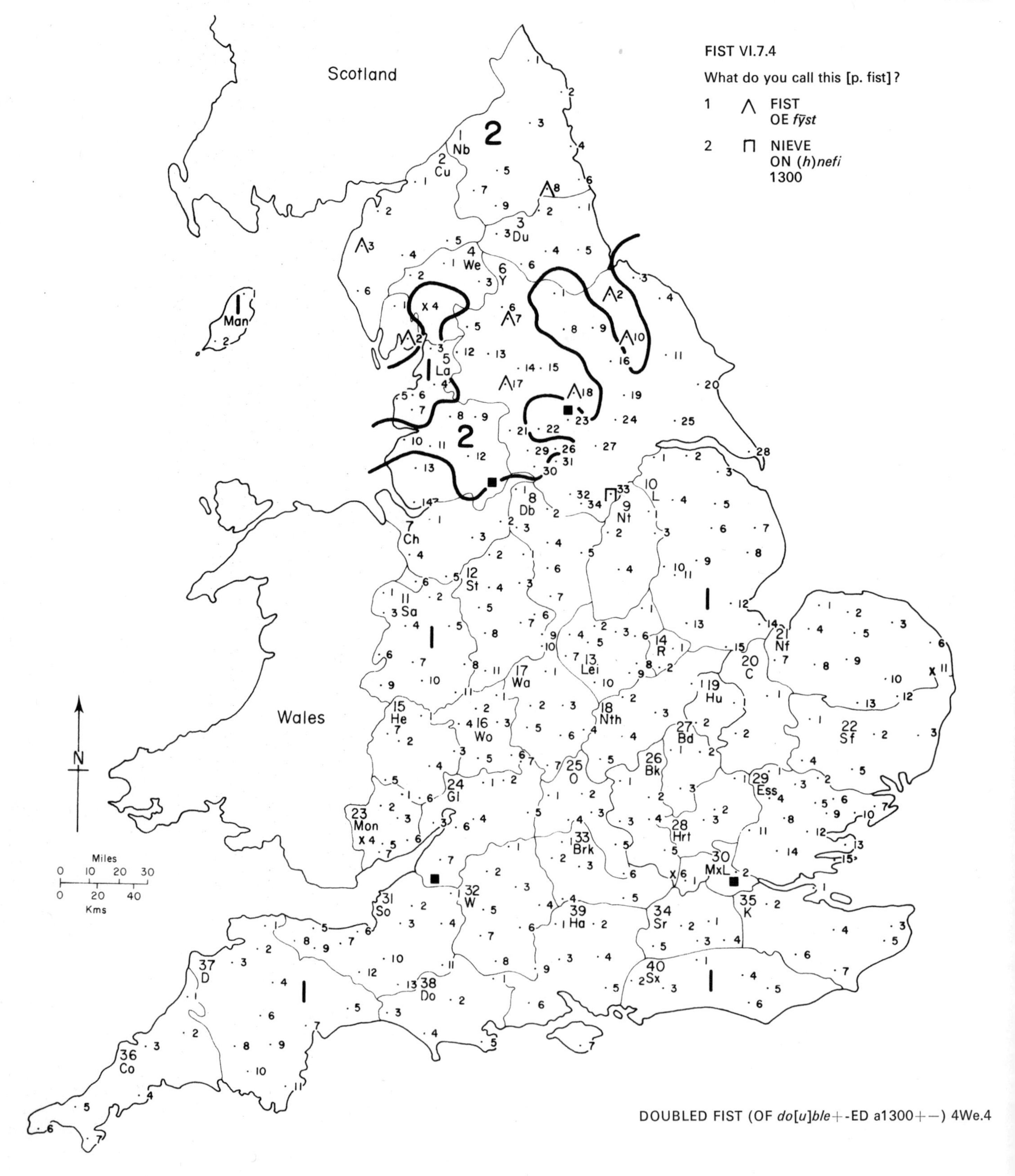
FIST VI.7.4
What do you call this [p. fist]?
1 ∧ FIST
OE *fȳst*
2 ⊓ NIEVE
ON (*h*)*nefi*
1300
Scotland
Wales
Man
N
Miles
0 10 20 30
0 20 40
Kms
DOUBLED FIST (OF *do*[*u*]*ble*+-ED a1300+—) 4We.4

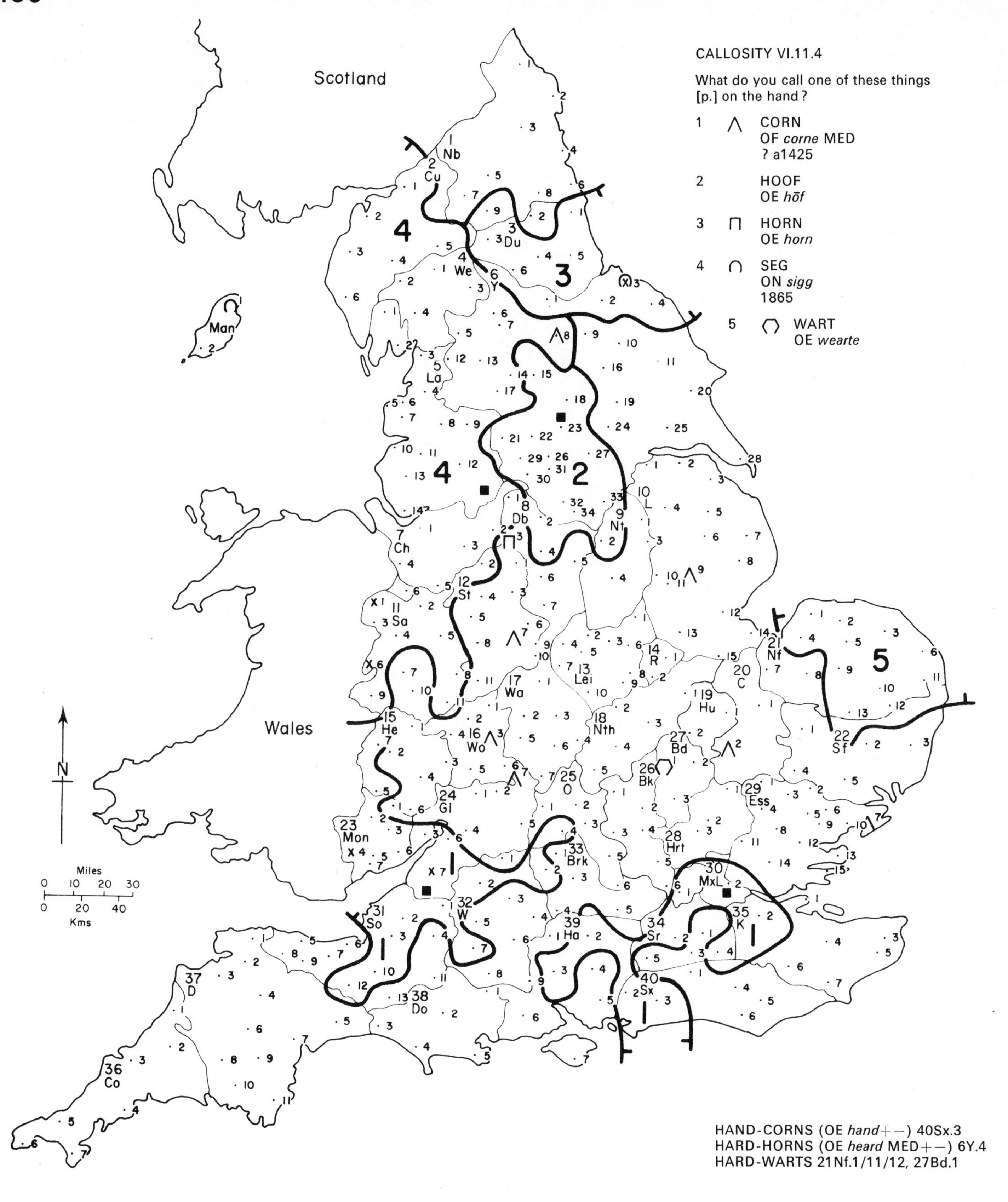
CALLOSITY VI.11.4
What do you call one of these things [p.] on the hand?
1 CORN OF *corne* MED ? a1425
2 HOOF OE *hōf*
3 HORN OE *horn*
4 SEG ON *sigg* 1865
5 WART OE *wearte*
Scotland
Wales
Man
N
Miles
0 10 20 30
0 20 40
Kms
HAND-CORNS (OE *hand*+—) 40Sx.3
HARD-HORNS (OE *heard* MED+—) 6Y.4
HARD-WARTS 21Nf.1/11/12, 27Bd.1

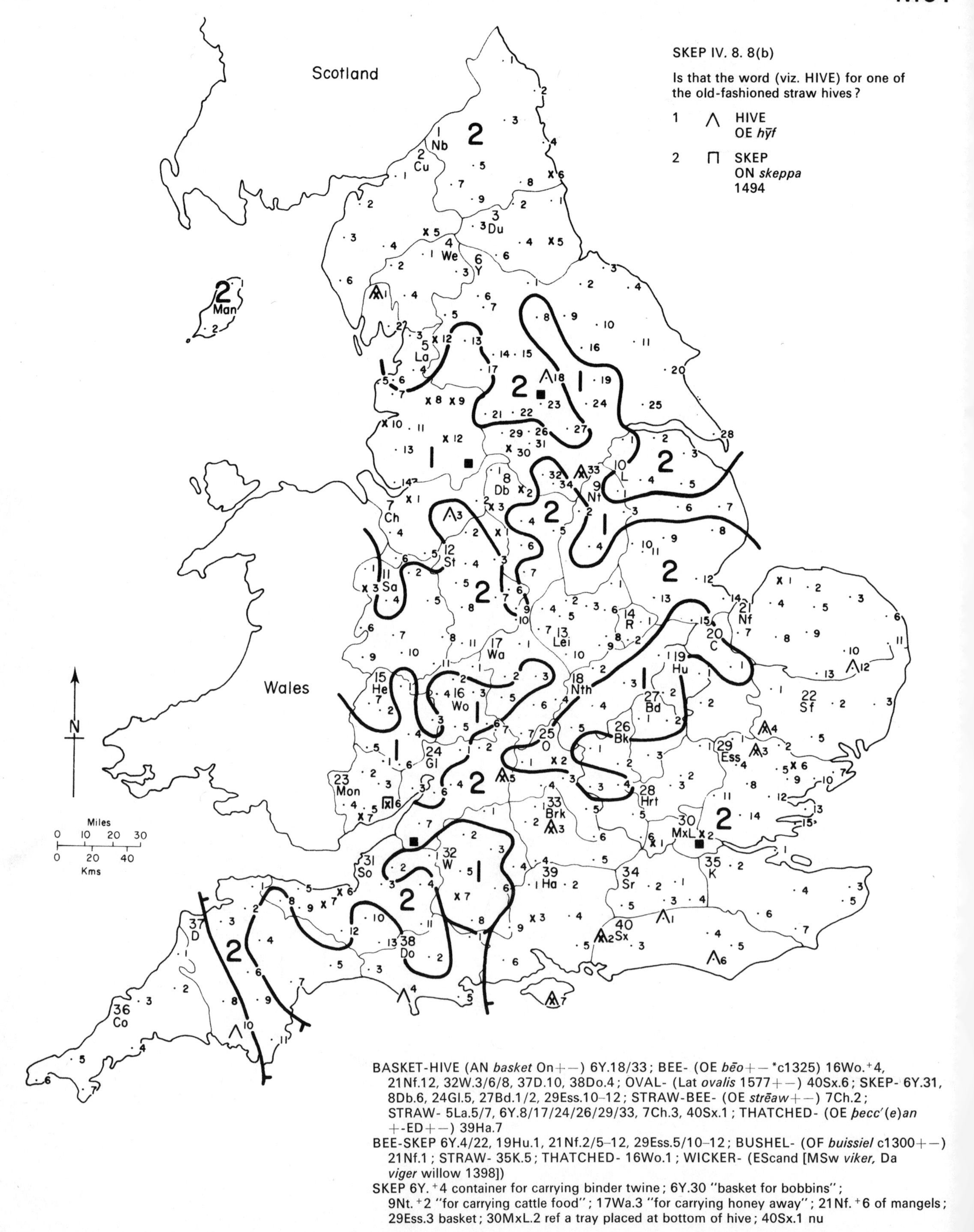

BASKET-HIVE (AN *basket* On+−) 6Y.18/33; BEE- (OE *bēo*+− *c1325) 16Wo.+4, 21Nf.12, 32W.3/6/8, 37D.10, 38Do.4; OVAL- (Lat *ovalis* 1577+−) 40Sx.6; SKEP- 6Y.31, 8Db.6, 24Gl.5, 27Bd.1/2, 29Ess.10–12; STRAW-BEE- (OE *strēaw*+−) 7Ch.2; STRAW- 5La.5/7, 6Y.8/17/24/26/29/33, 7Ch.3, 40Sx.1; THATCHED- (OE *þecc'(e)an* +-ED+−) 39Ha.7

BEE-SKEP 6Y.4/22, 19Hu.1, 21Nf.2/5–12, 29Ess.5/10–12; BUSHEL- (OF *buissiel* c1300+−) 21Nf.1; STRAW- 35K.5; THATCHED- 16Wo.1; WICKER- (EScand [MSw *viker*, Da *viger* willow 1398])

SKEP 6Y.+4 container for carrying binder twine; 6Y.30 "basket for bobbins"; 9Nt.+2 "for carrying cattle food"; 17Wa.3 "for carrying honey away"; 21Nf.+6 of mangels; 29Ess.3 basket; 30MxL.2 ref a tray placed at bottom of hive; 40Sx.1 nu

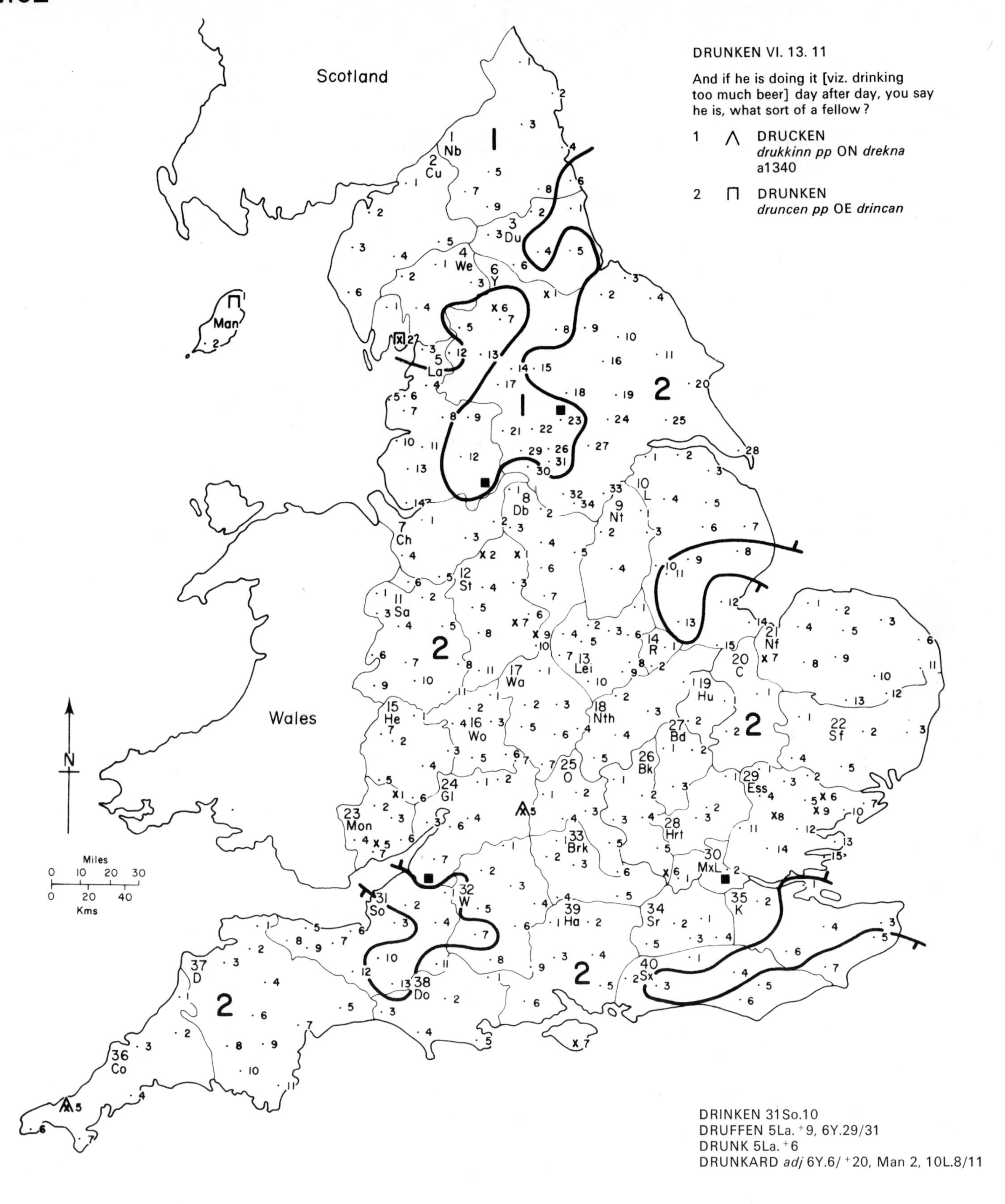
DRUNKEN VI. 13. 11
And if he is doing it [viz. drinking too much beer] day after day, you say he is, what sort of a fellow?
1 Λ DRUCKEN
drukkinn pp ON drekna
a1340
2 Π DRUNKEN
druncen pp OE drincan
Scotland
Wales
Man
N
Miles
0 10 20 30
0 20 40
Kms
DRINKEN 31So.10
DRUFFEN 5La. +9, 6Y.29/31
DRUNK 5La. +6
DRUNKARD adj 6Y.6/ +20, Man 2, 10L.8/11

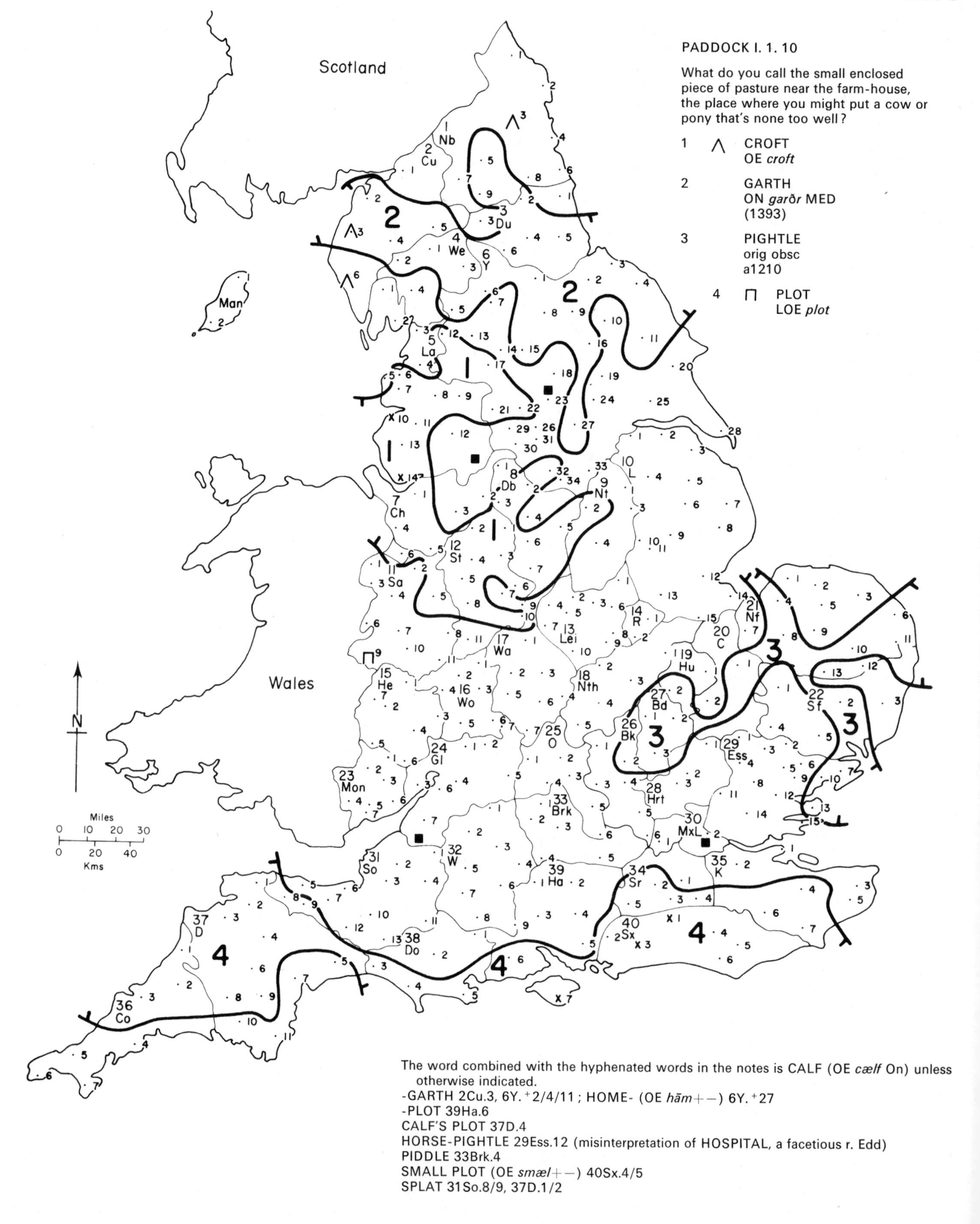

PADDOCK I. 1. 10

What do you call the small enclosed piece of pasture near the farm-house, the place where you might put a cow or pony that's none too well?

1 Λ CROFT
OE *croft*

2 GARTH
ON *garðr* MED (1393)

3 PIGHTLE
orig obsc
a1210

4 ⊓ PLOT
LOE *plot*

The word combined with the hyphenated words in the notes is CALF (OE *cælf* On) unless otherwise indicated.

-GARTH 2Cu.3, 6Y.+2/4/11; HOME- (OE *hām*+ —) 6Y.+27
-PLOT 39Ha.6
CALF'S PLOT 37D.4
HORSE-PIGHTLE 29Ess.12 (misinterpretation of HOSPITAL, a facetious r. Edd)
PIDDLE 33Brk.4
SMALL PLOT (OE *smæl*+ —) 40Sx.4/5
SPLAT 31So.8/9, 37D.1/2

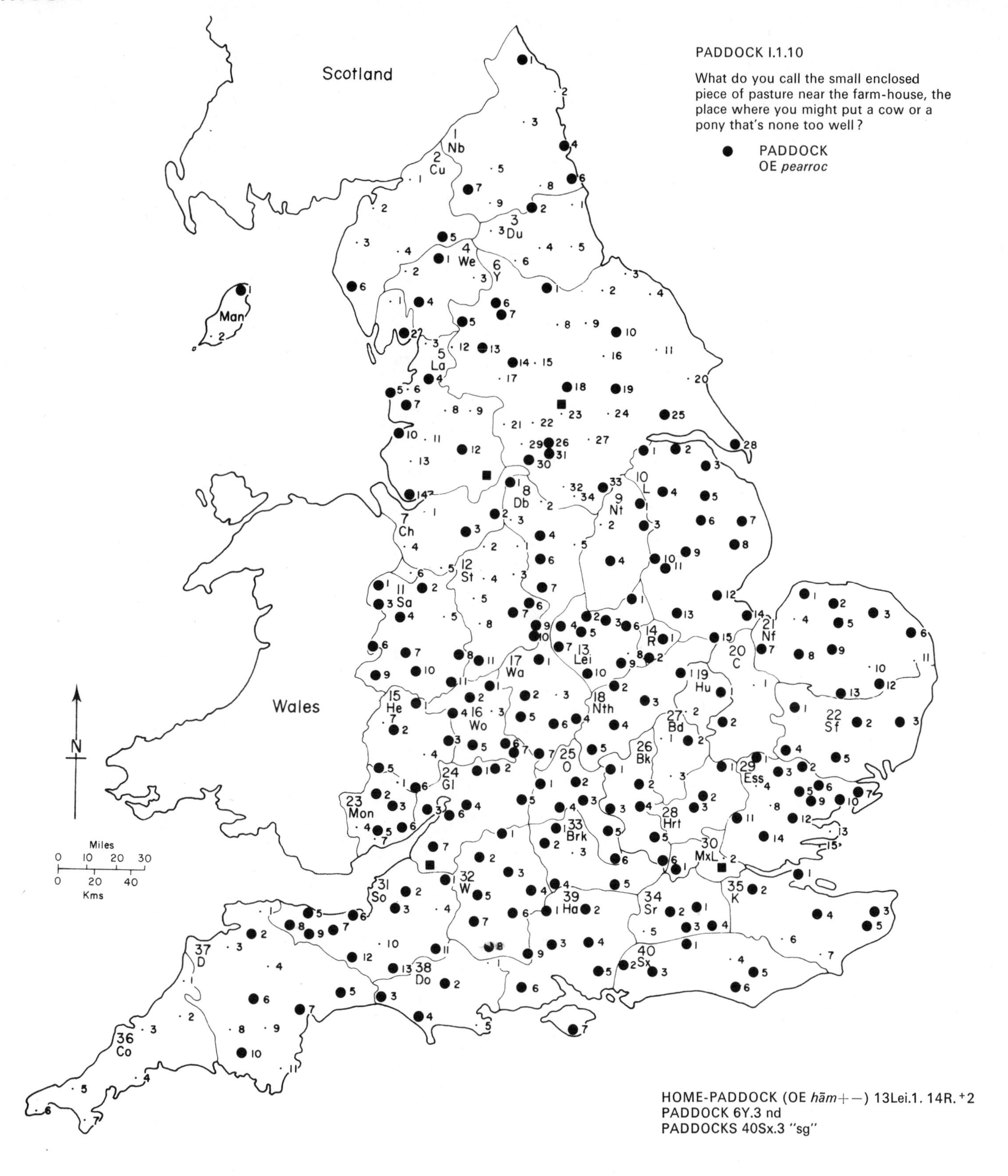
PADDOCK I.1.10
What do you call the small enclosed piece of pasture near the farm-house, the place where you might put a cow or a pony that's none too well?
● PADDOCK
OE *pearroc*
Scotland
Wales
Man
N
Miles
0 10 20 30
0 20 40
Kms
HOME-PADDOCK (OE *hām*+—) 13Lei.1. 14R.+2
PADDOCK 6Y.3 nd
PADDOCKS 40Sx.3 "sg"

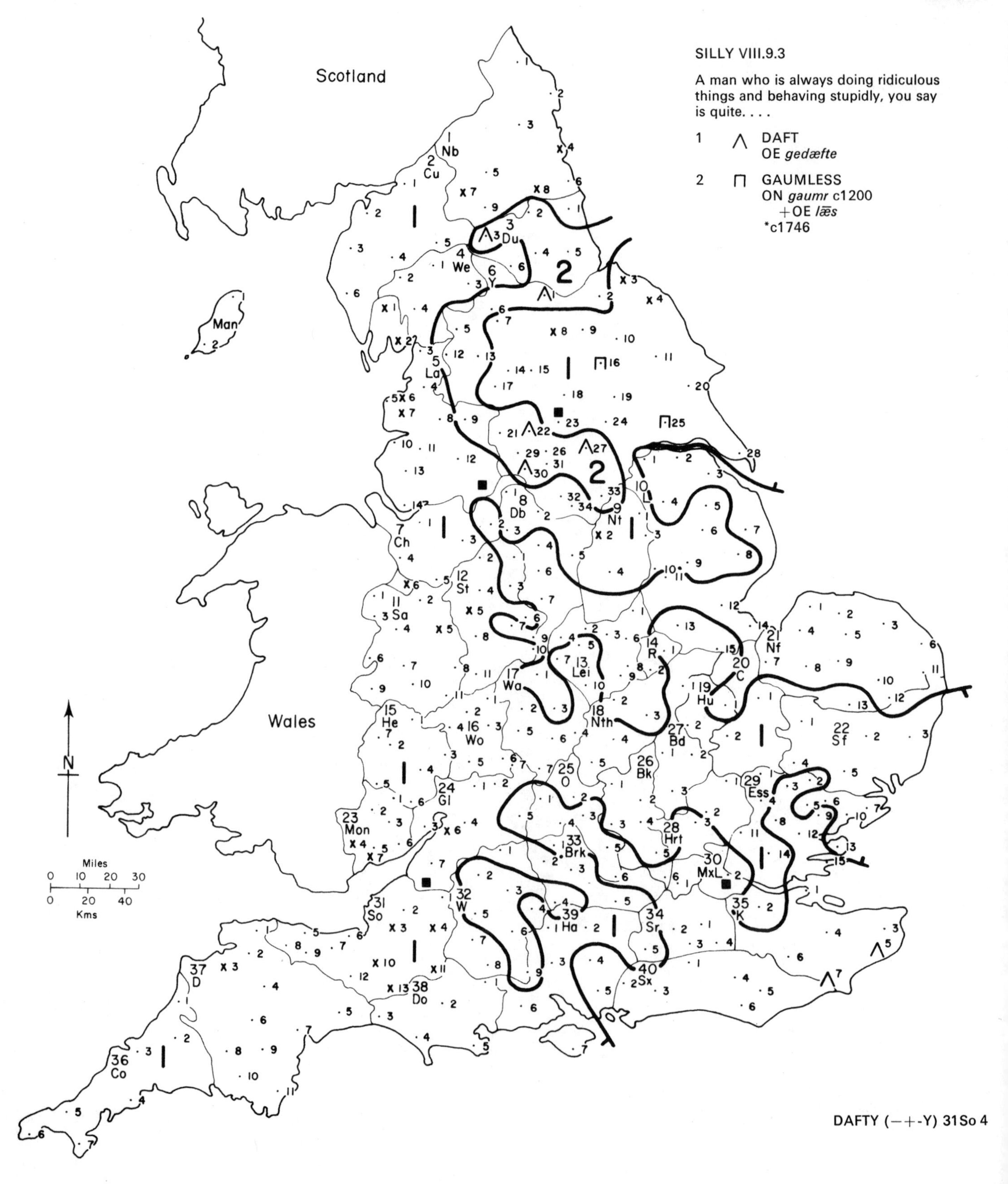
SILLY VIII.9.3
A man who is always doing ridiculous things and behaving stupidly, you say is quite. . . .
1 Λ DAFT
OE *gedæfte*
2 ⊓ GAUMLESS
ON *gaumr* c1200
+OE *lǣs*
*c1746
Scotland
Wales
Man
Miles
0 10 20 30
0 20 40
Kms
N
DAFTY (—+-Y) 31So 4

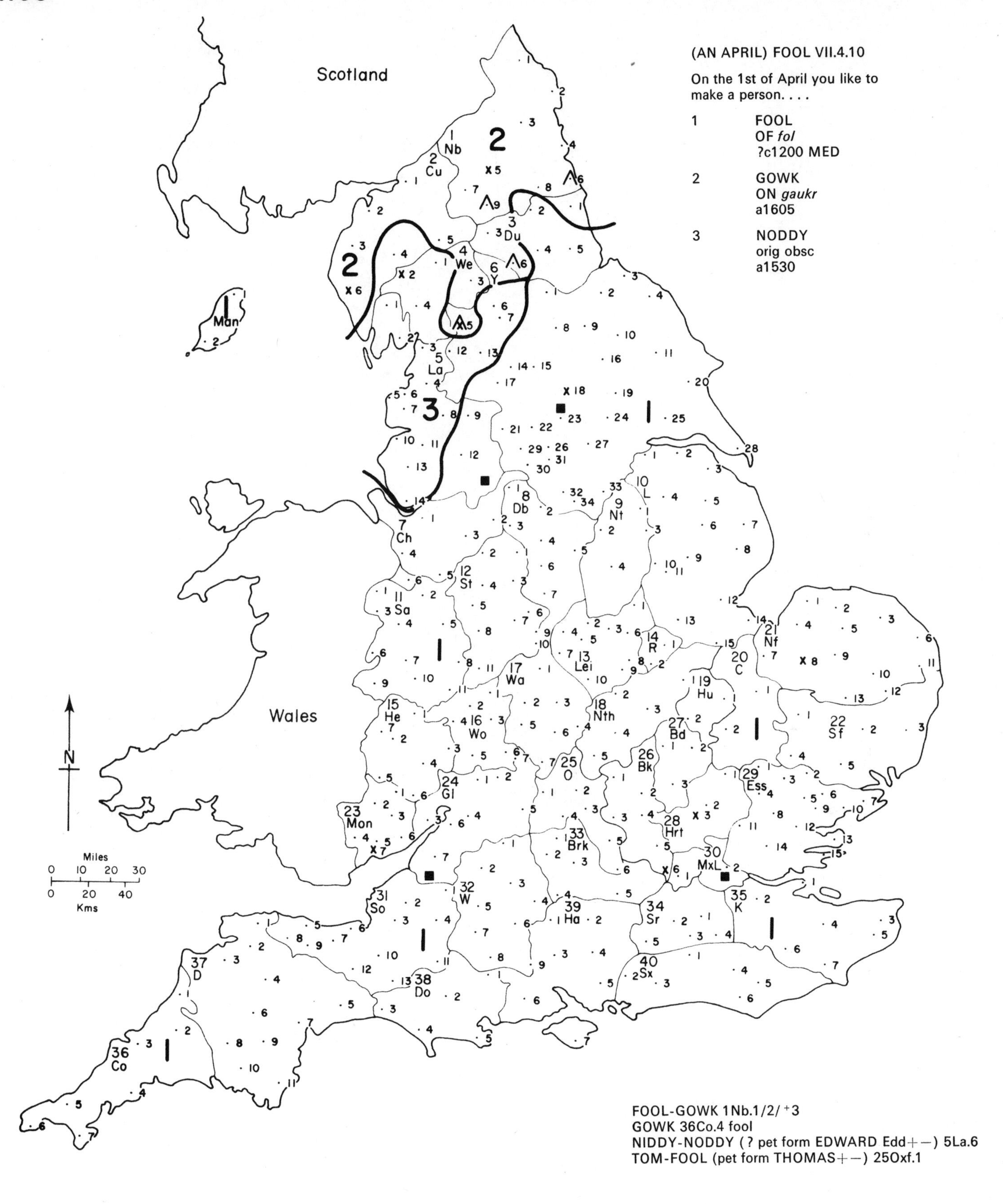
(AN APRIL) FOOL VII.4.10
On the 1st of April you like to make a person. . . .
1 FOOL
OF *fol*
?c1200 MED
2 GOWK
ON *gaukr*
a1605
3 NODDY
orig obsc
a1530
Scotland
Wales
N
Miles
0 10 20 30
0 20 40
Kms
FOOL-GOWK 1Nb.1/2/+3
GOWK 36Co.4 fool
NIDDY-NODDY (? pet form EDWARD Edd+−) 5La.6
TOM-FOOL (pet form THOMAS+−) 25Oxf.1

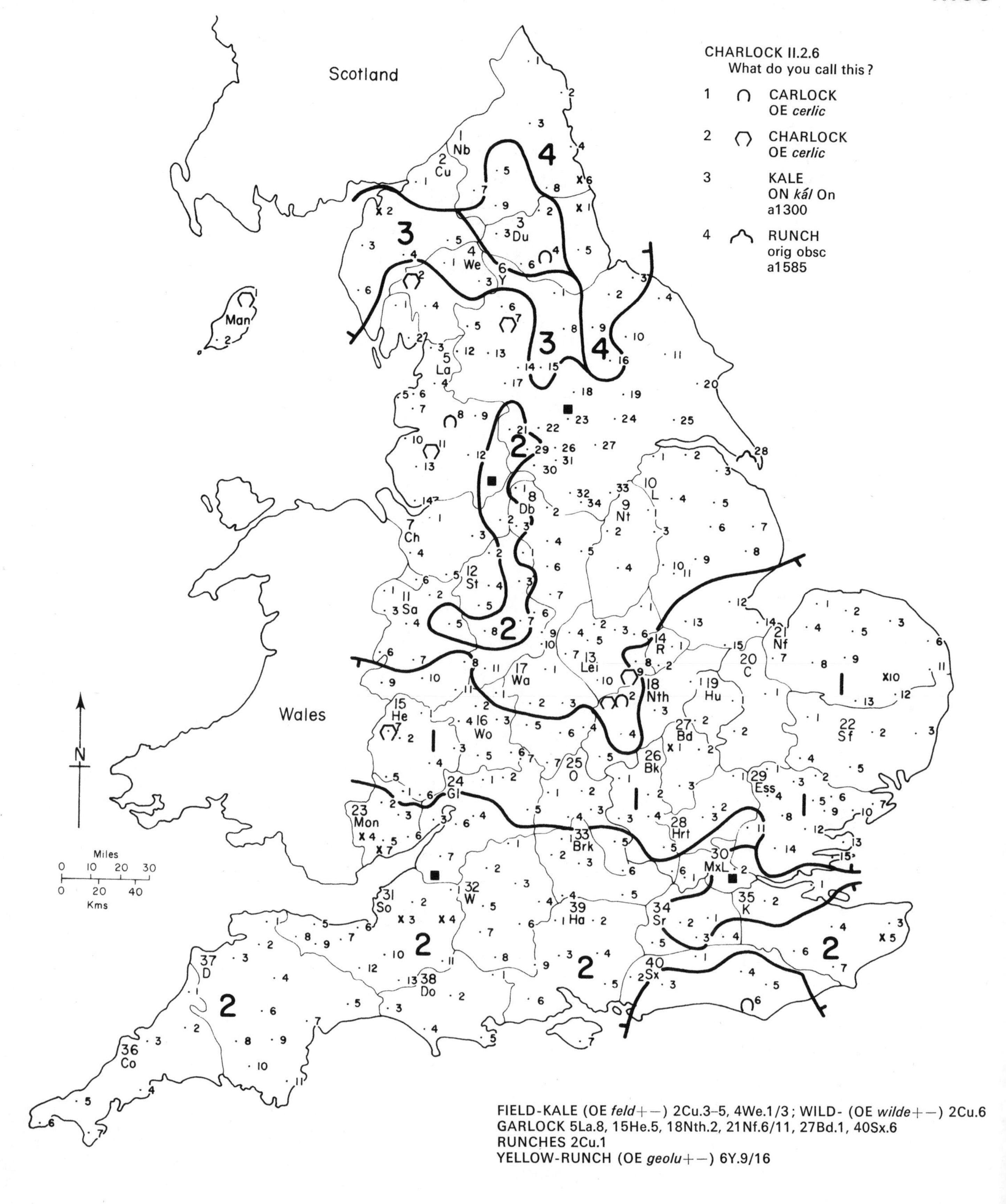

FIELD-KALE (OE *feld*+—) 2Cu.3–5, 4We.1/3; WILD- (OE *wilde*+—) 2Cu.6
GARLOCK 5La.8, 15He.5, 18Nth.2, 21Nf.6/11, 27Bd.1, 40Sx.6
RUNCHES 2Cu.1
YELLOW-RUNCH (OE *geolu*+—) 6Y.9/16

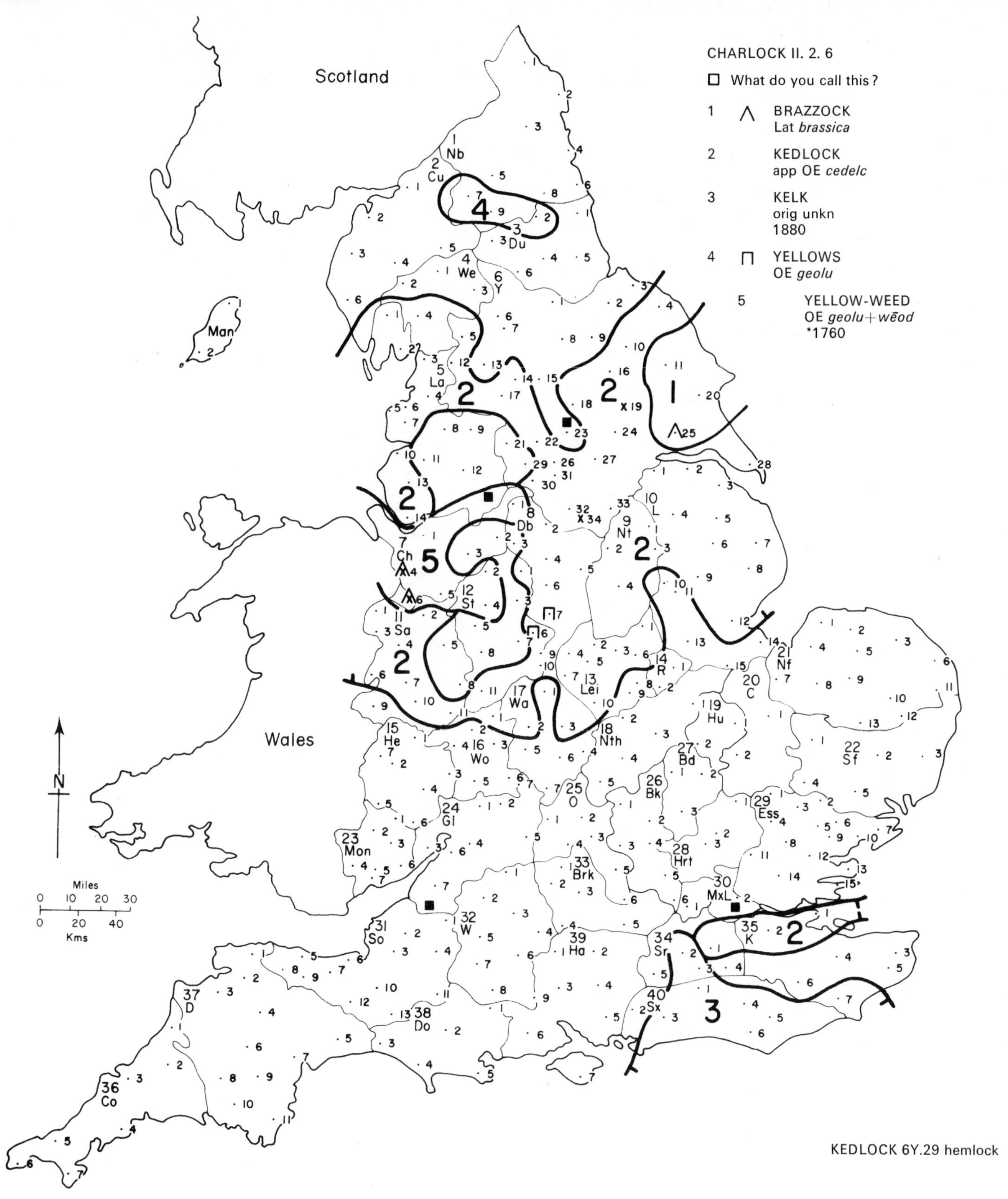
CHARLOCK II. 2. 6
☐ What do you call this?
1 ⋀ BRAZZOCK
Lat *brassica*
2 KEDLOCK
app OE *cedelc*
3 KELK
orig unkn
1880
4 ⊓ YELLOWS
OE *geolu*
5 YELLOW-WEED
OE *geolu*+*wēod*
*1760
Scotland
Wales
Man
Miles
0 10 20 30
0 20 40
Kms
N
KEDLOCK 6Y.29 hemlock

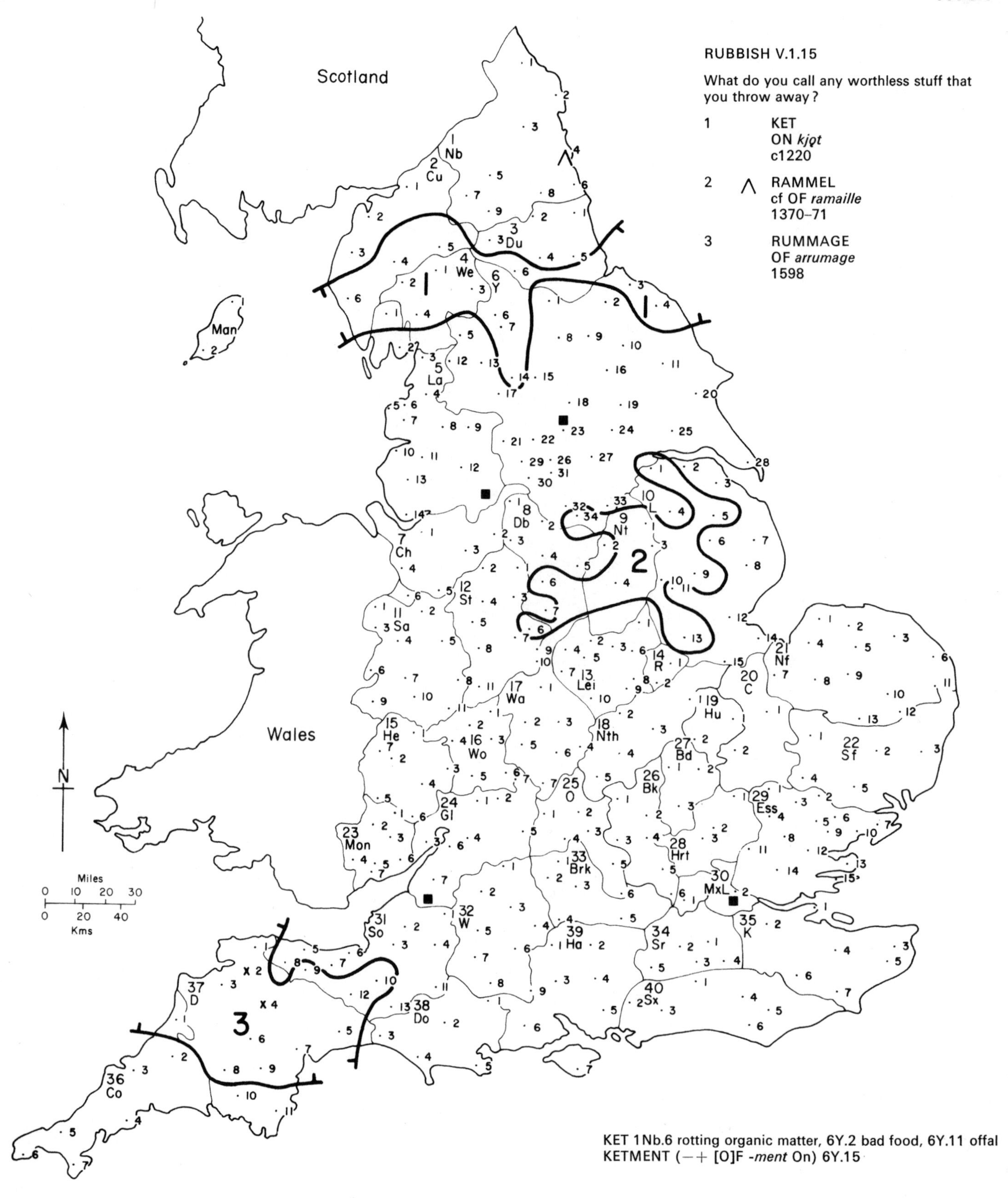

RUBBISH V.1.15

What do you call any worthless stuff that you throw away?

1 KET
ON *kjǫt*
c1220

2 ∧ RAMMEL
cf OF *ramaille*
1370–71

3 RUMMAGE
OF *arrumage*
1598

KET 1Nb.6 rotting organic matter, 6Y.2 bad food, 6Y.11 offal
KETMENT (—+ [O]F *-ment* On) 6Y.15

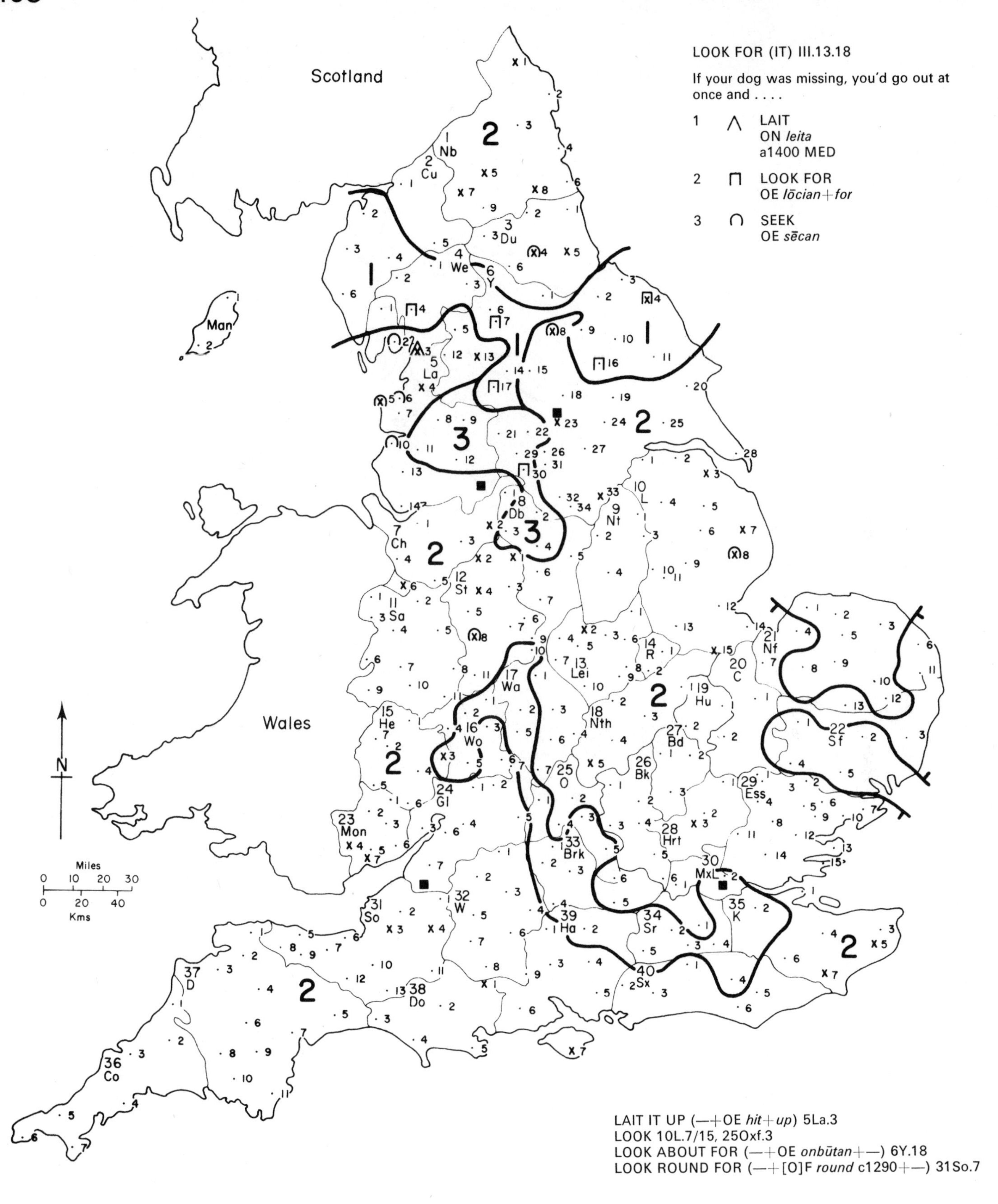
LOOK FOR (IT) III.13.18
If your dog was missing, you'd go out at once and . . . .
1 Λ LAIT
ON *leita*
a1400 MED
2 ⊓ LOOK FOR
OE *lōcian+for*
3 ∩ SEEK
OE *sēcan*
Scotland
Wales
Man
N
Miles
0 10 20 30
0 20 40
Kms
LAIT IT UP (—+OE *hit+up*) 5La.3
LOOK 10L.7/15, 25Oxf.3
LOOK ABOUT FOR (—+OE *onbūtan+*—) 6Y.18
LOOK ROUND FOR (—+[O]F *round* c1290+—) 31So.7

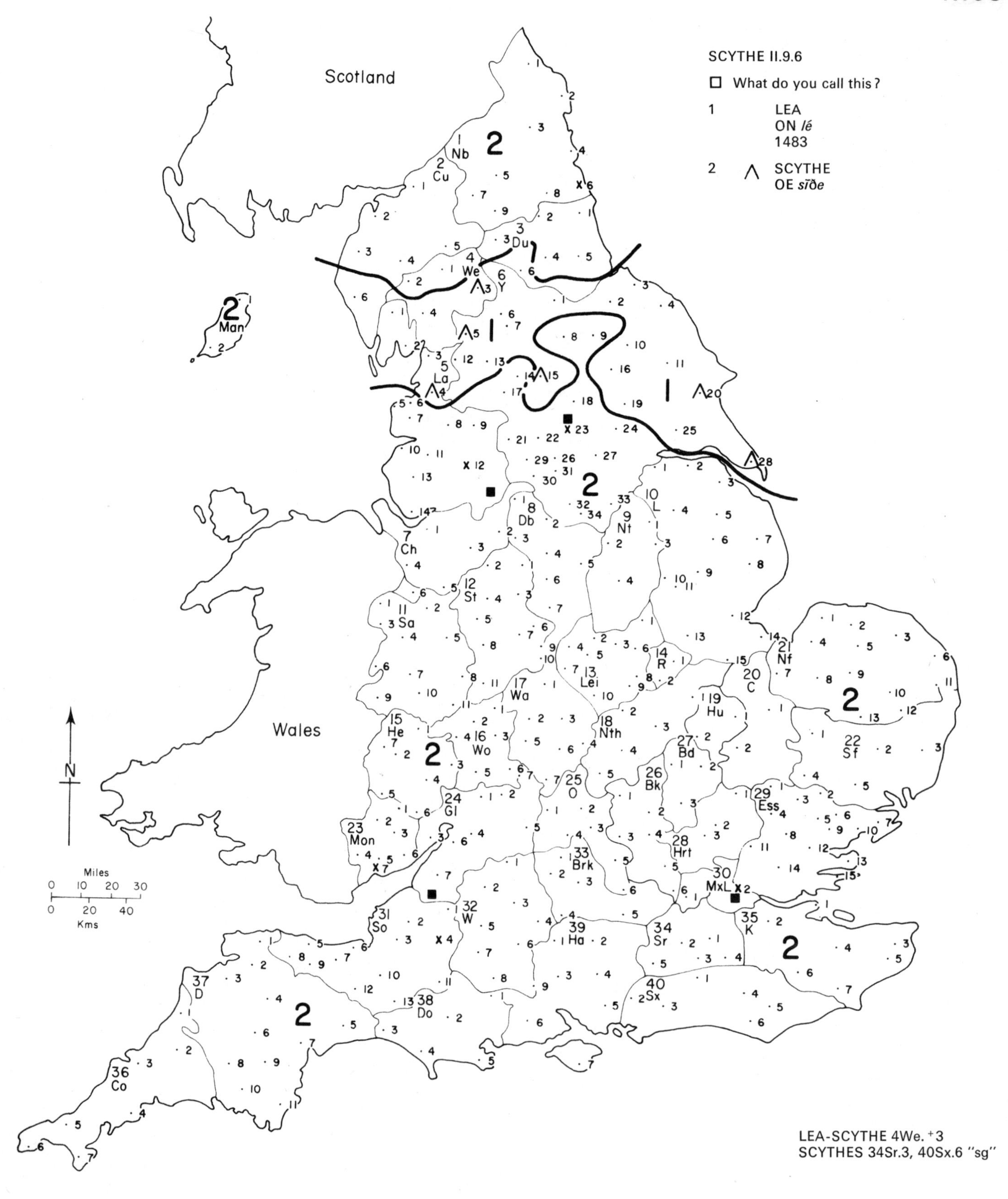

LEA-SCYTHE 4We. +3
SCYTHES 34Sr.3, 40Sx.6 "sg"

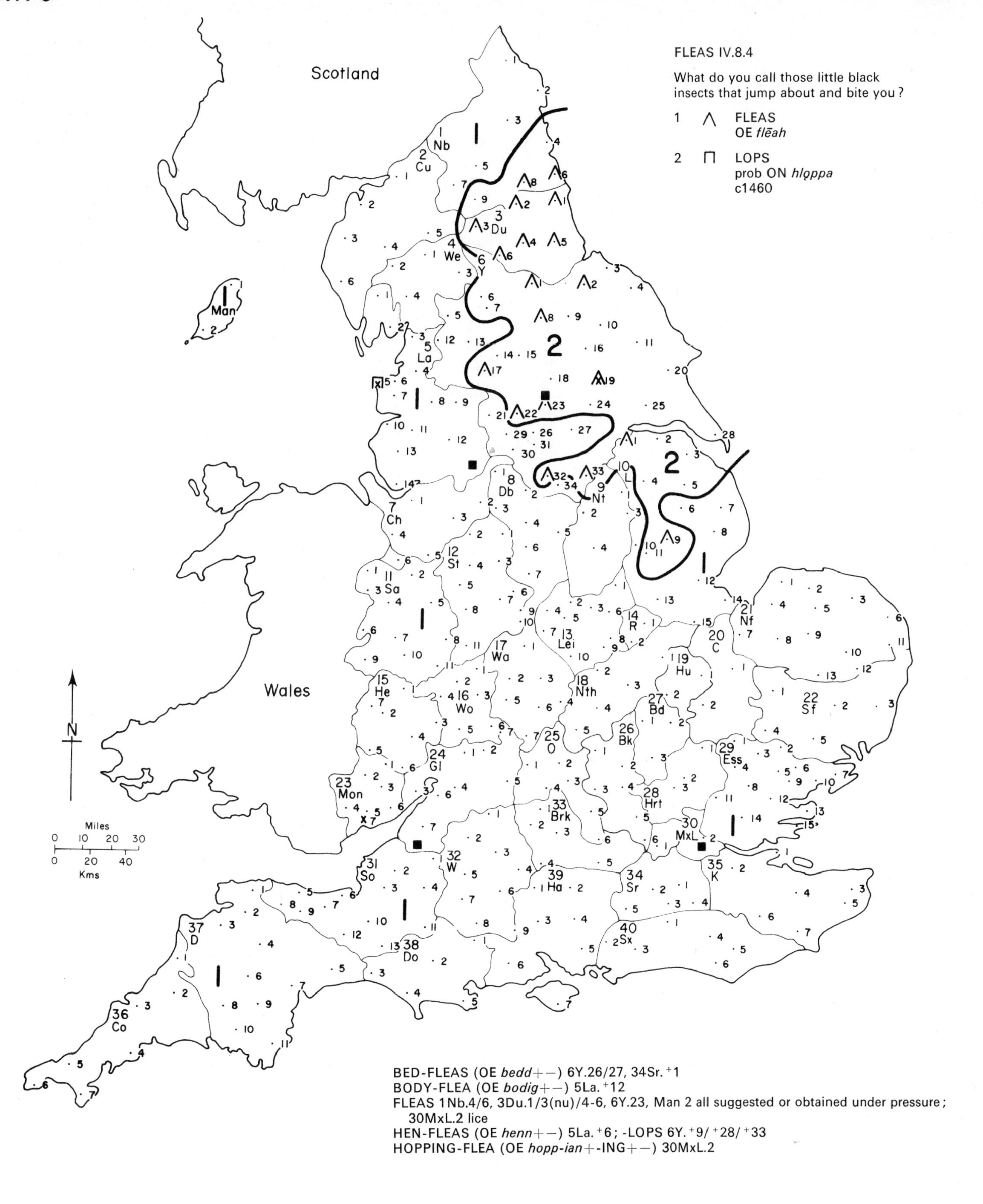

BED-FLEAS (OE *bedd*+—) 6Y.26/27, 34Sr. +1
BODY-FLEA (OE *bodig*+—) 5La. +12
FLEAS 1Nb.4/6, 3Du.1/3(nu)/4-6, 6Y.23, Man 2 all suggested or obtained under pressure; 30MxL.2 lice
HEN-FLEAS (OE *henn*+—) 5La. +6; -LOPS 6Y. +9/ +28/ +33
HOPPING-FLEA (OE *hopp-ian*+-ING+—) 30MxL.2

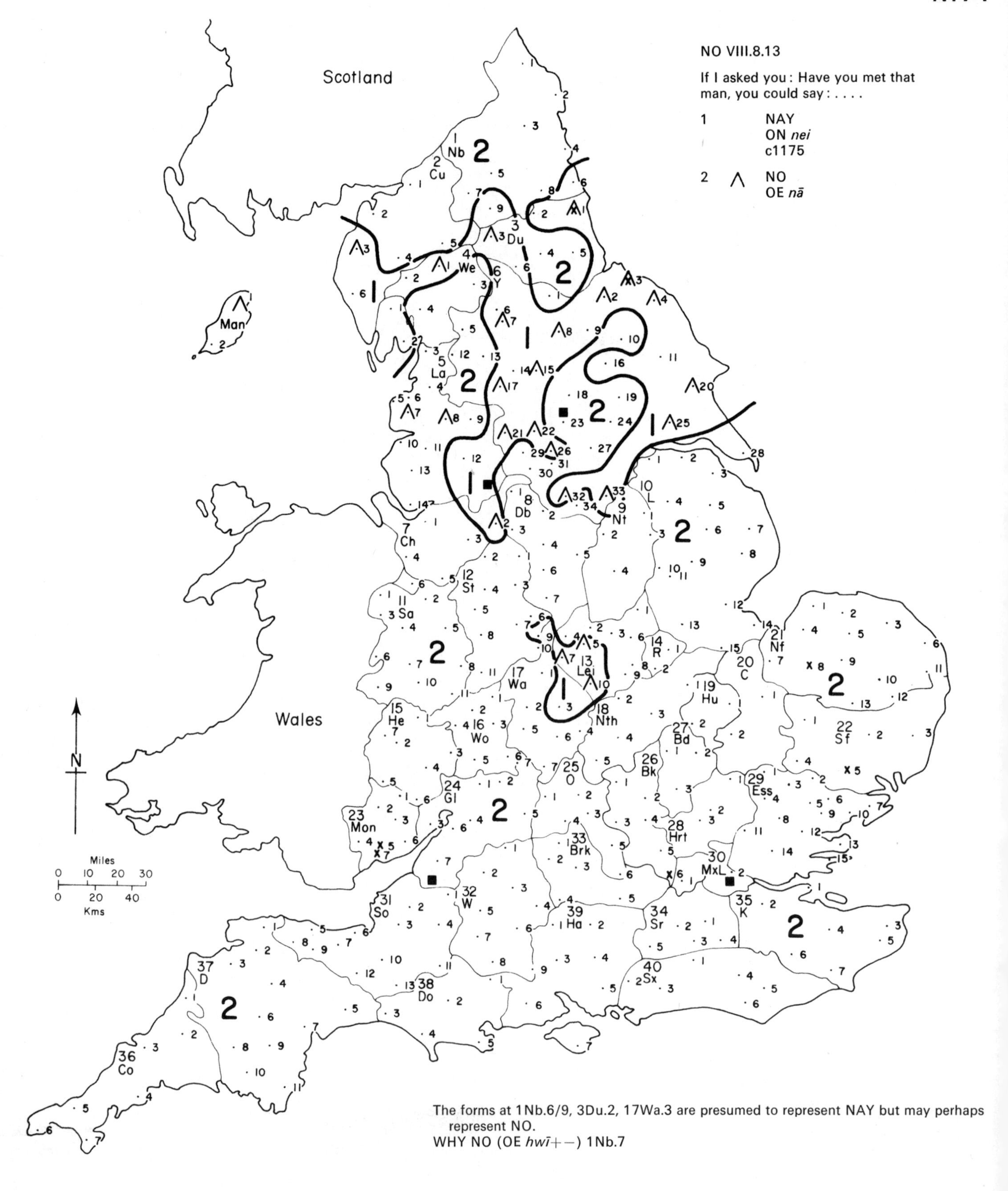

The forms at 1Nb.6/9, 3Du.2, 17Wa.3 are presumed to represent NAY but may perhaps represent NO.

WHY NO (OE *hwī*+ –) 1Nb.7

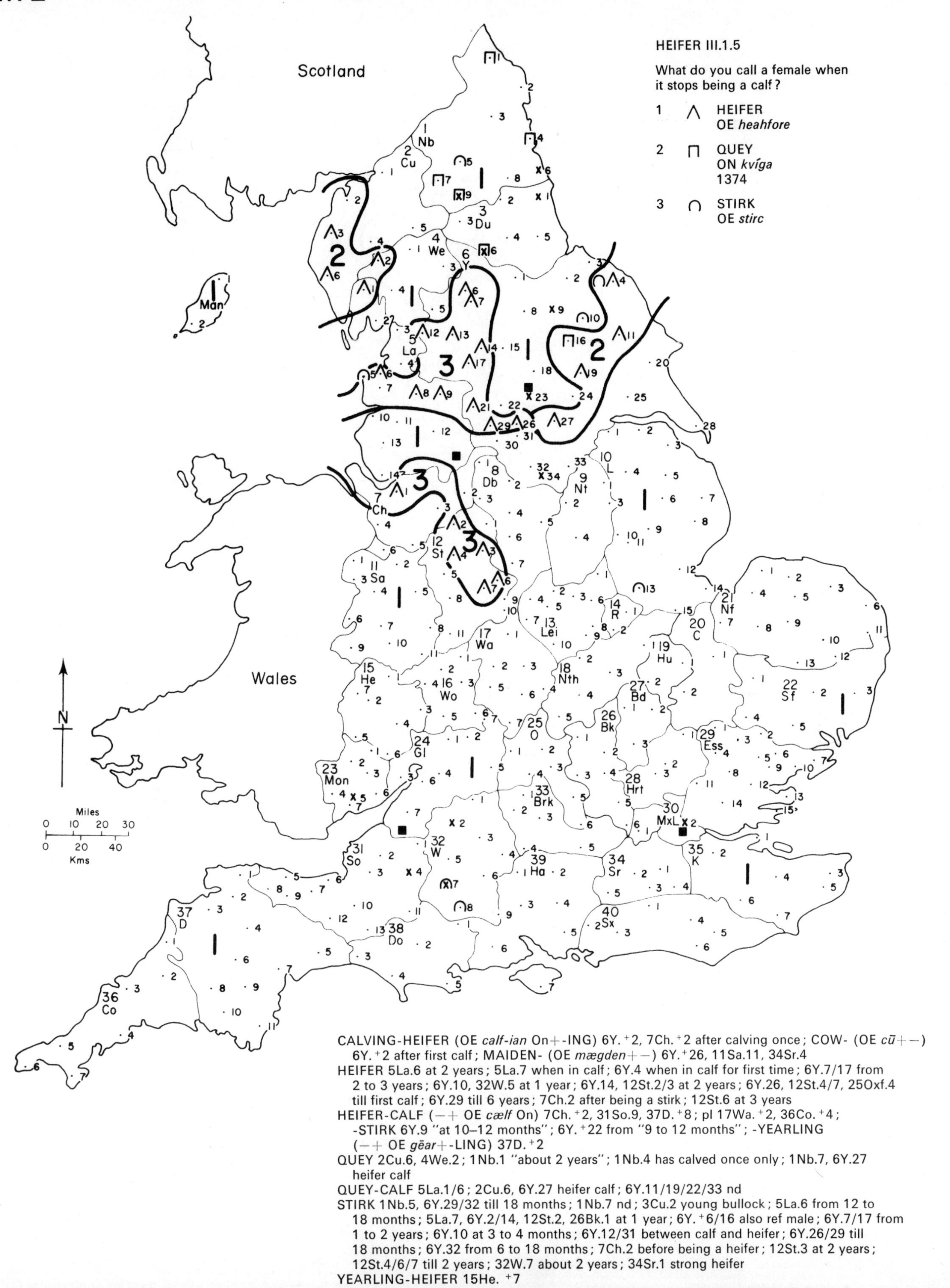

CALVING-HEIFER (OE *calf-ian* On+-ING) 6Y.+2, 7Ch.+2 after calving once; COW- (OE *cū*+—) 6Y.+2 after first calf; MAIDEN- (OE *mægden*+—) 6Y.+26, 11Sa.11, 34Sr.4

HEIFER 5La.6 at 2 years; 5La.7 when in calf; 6Y.4 when in calf for first time; 6Y.7/17 from 2 to 3 years; 6Y.10, 32W.5 at 1 year; 6Y.14, 12St.2/3 at 2 years; 6Y.26, 12St.4/7, 25Oxf.4 till first calf; 6Y.29 till 6 years; 7Ch.2 after being a stirk; 12St.6 at 3 years

HEIFER-CALF (—+ OE *cælf* On) 7Ch.+2, 31So.9, 37D.+8; pl 17Wa.+2, 36Co.+4; -STIRK 6Y.9 "at 10–12 months"; 6Y.+22 from "9 to 12 months"; -YEARLING (—+ OE *gēar*+-LING) 37D.+2

QUEY 2Cu.6, 4We.2; 1Nb.1 "about 2 years"; 1Nb.4 has calved once only; 1Nb.7, 6Y.27 heifer calf

QUEY-CALF 5La.1/6; 2Cu.6, 6Y.27 heifer calf; 6Y.11/19/22/33 nd

STIRK 1Nb.5, 6Y.29/32 till 18 months; 1Nb.7 nd; 3Cu.2 young bullock; 5La.6 from 12 to 18 months; 5La.7, 6Y.2/14, 12St.2, 26Bk.1 at 1 year; 6Y.+6/16 also ref male; 6Y.7/17 from 1 to 2 years; 6Y.10 at 3 to 4 months; 6Y.12/31 between calf and heifer; 6Y.26/29 till 18 months; 6Y.32 from 6 to 18 months; 7Ch.2 before being a heifer; 12St.3 at 2 years; 12St.4/6/7 till 2 years; 32W.7 about 2 years; 34Sr.1 strong heifer

YEARLING-HEIFER 15He.+7

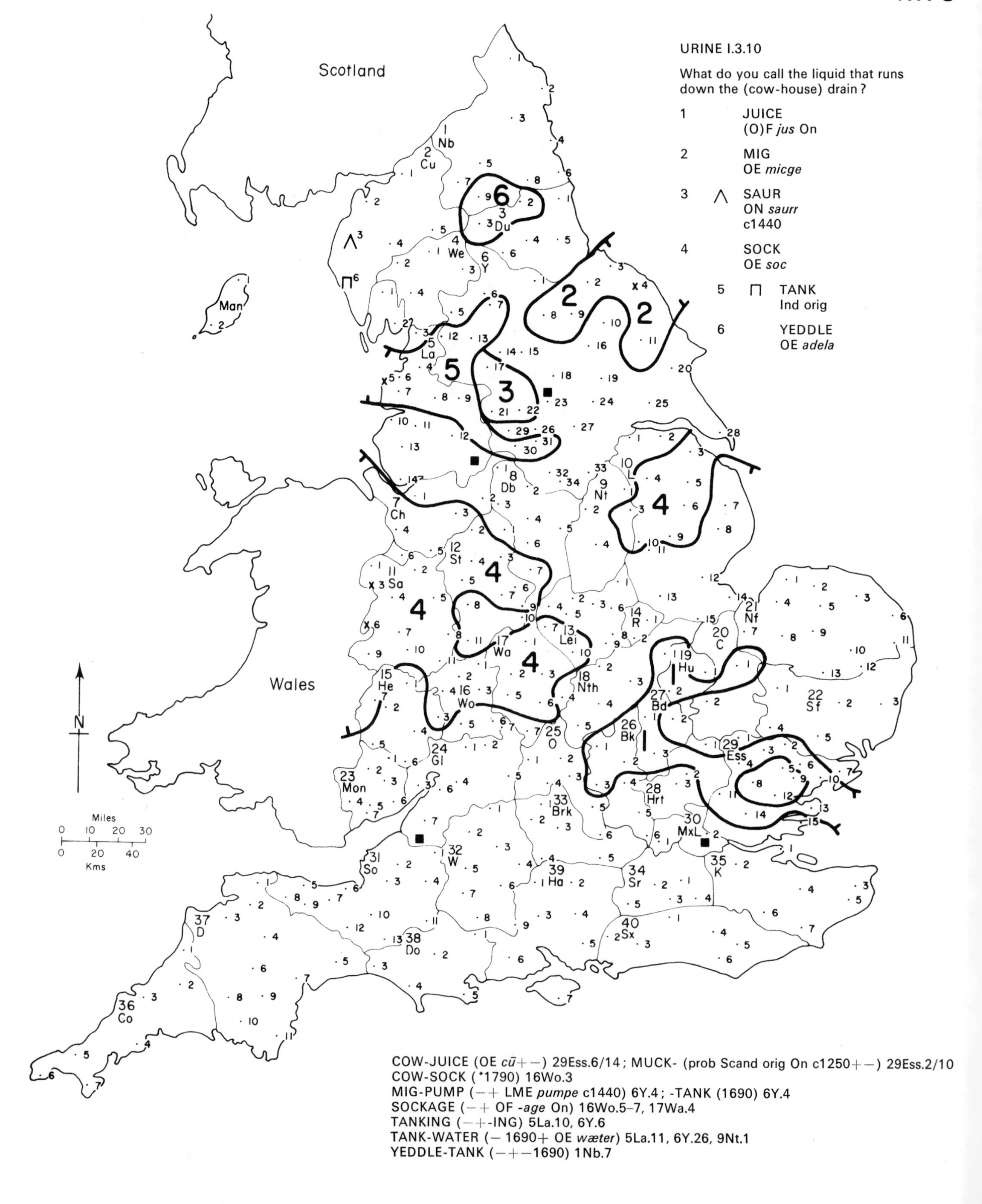

COW-JUICE (OE *cū*+ —) 29Ess.6/14; MUCK- (prob Scand orig On c1250+ —) 29Ess.2/10
COW-SOCK (*1790) 16Wo.3
MIG-PUMP (— + LME *pumpe* c1440) 6Y.4; -TANK (1690) 6Y.4
SOCKAGE (— + OF *-age* On) 16Wo.5–7, 17Wa.4
TANKING (— + -ING) 5La.10, 6Y.6
TANK-WATER (— 1690+ OE *wæter*) 5La.11, 6Y.26, 9Nt.1
YEDDLE-TANK (— + — 1690) 1Nb.7

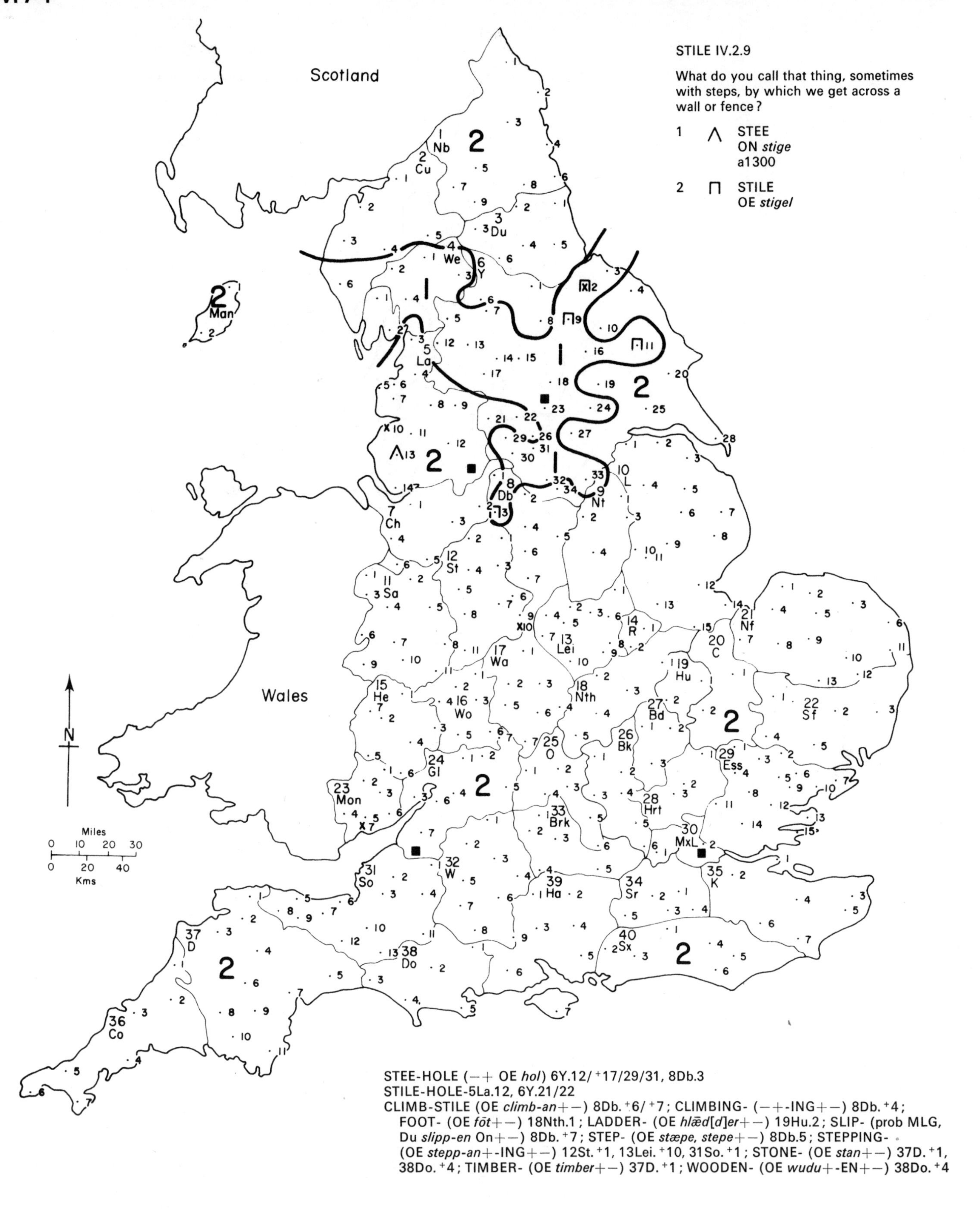

STEE-HOLE (—+ OE *hol*) 6Y.12/$^{+}$17/29/31, 8Db.3
STILE-HOLE-5La.12, 6Y.21/22
CLIMB-STILE (OE *climb-an*+—) 8Db.$^{+}$6/$^{+}$7; CLIMBING- (—+-ING+—) 8Db.$^{+}$4; FOOT- (OE *fōt*+—) 18Nth.1; LADDER- (OE *hlǣd*[*d*]*er*+—) 19Hu.2; SLIP- (prob MLG, Du *slipp-en* On+—) 8Db.$^{+}$7; STEP- (OE *stæpe, stepe*+—) 8Db.5; STEPPING- (OE *stepp-an*+-ING+—) 12St.$^{+}$1, 13Lei.$^{+}$10, 31So.$^{+}$1; STONE- (OE *stan*+—) 37D.$^{+}$1, 38Do.$^{+}$4; TIMBER- (OE *timber*+—) 37D.$^{+}$1; WOODEN- (OE *wudu*+-EN+—) 38Do.$^{+}$4

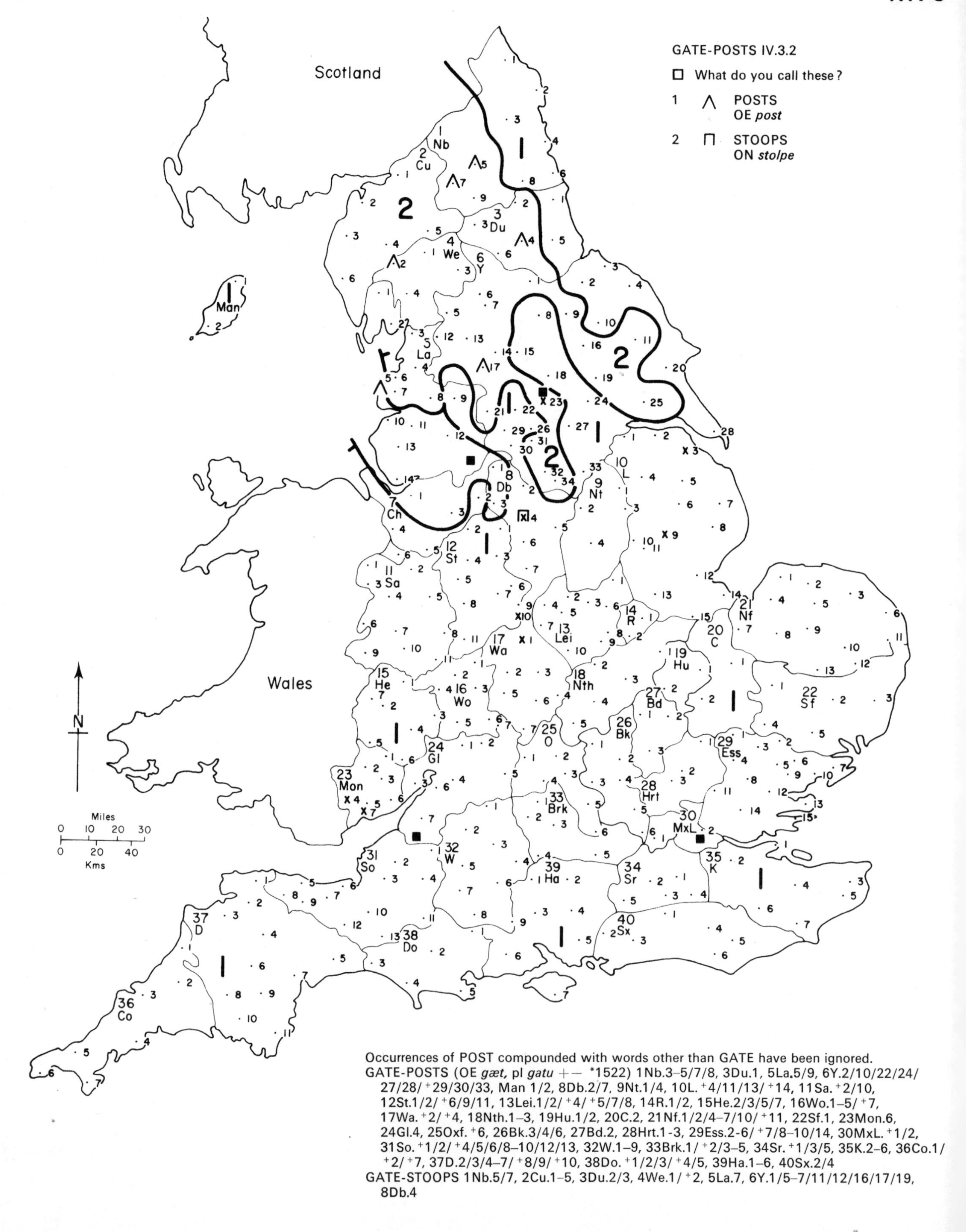

Occurrences of POST compounded with words other than GATE have been ignored.

GATE-POSTS (OE *gæt,* pl *gatu* +— *1522) 1Nb.3–5/7/8, 3Du.1, 5La.5/9, 6Y.2/10/22/24/27/28/+29/30/33, Man 1/2, 8Db.2/7, 9Nt.1/4, 10L. +4/11/13/+14, 11Sa. +2/10, 12St.1/2/+6/9/11, 13Lei.1/2/+4/+5/7/8, 14R.1/2, 15He.2/3/5/7, 16Wo.1–5/+7, 17Wa. +2/+4, 18Nth.1–3, 19Hu.1/2, 20C.2, 21Nf.1/2/4–7/10/+11, 22Sf.1, 23Mon.6, 24Gl.4, 25Oxf. +6, 26Bk.3/4/6, 27Bd.2, 28Hrt.1-3, 29Ess.2-6/+7/8–10/14, 30MxL. +1/2, 31So. +1/2/+4/5/6/8–10/12/13, 32W.1–9, 33Brk.1/+2/3–5, 34Sr. +1/3/5, 35K.2–6, 36Co.1/+2/+7, 37D.2/3/4–7/+8/9/+10, 38Do. +1/2/3/+4/5, 39Ha.1–6, 40Sx.2/4

GATE-STOOPS 1Nb.5/7, 2Cu.1–5, 3Du.2/3, 4We.1/+2, 5La.7, 6Y.1/5–7/11/12/16/17/19, 8Db.4

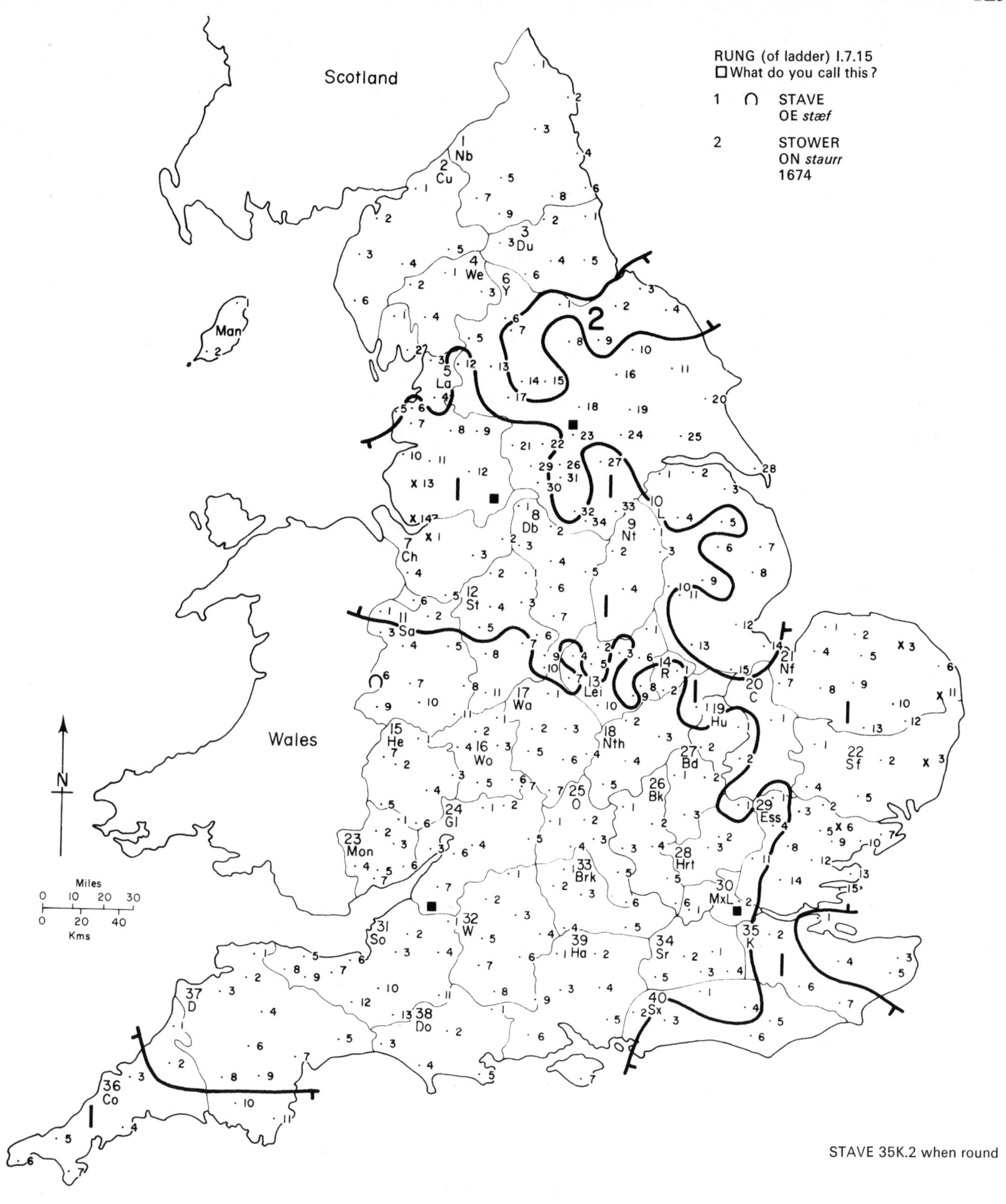

STAVE 35K.2 when round

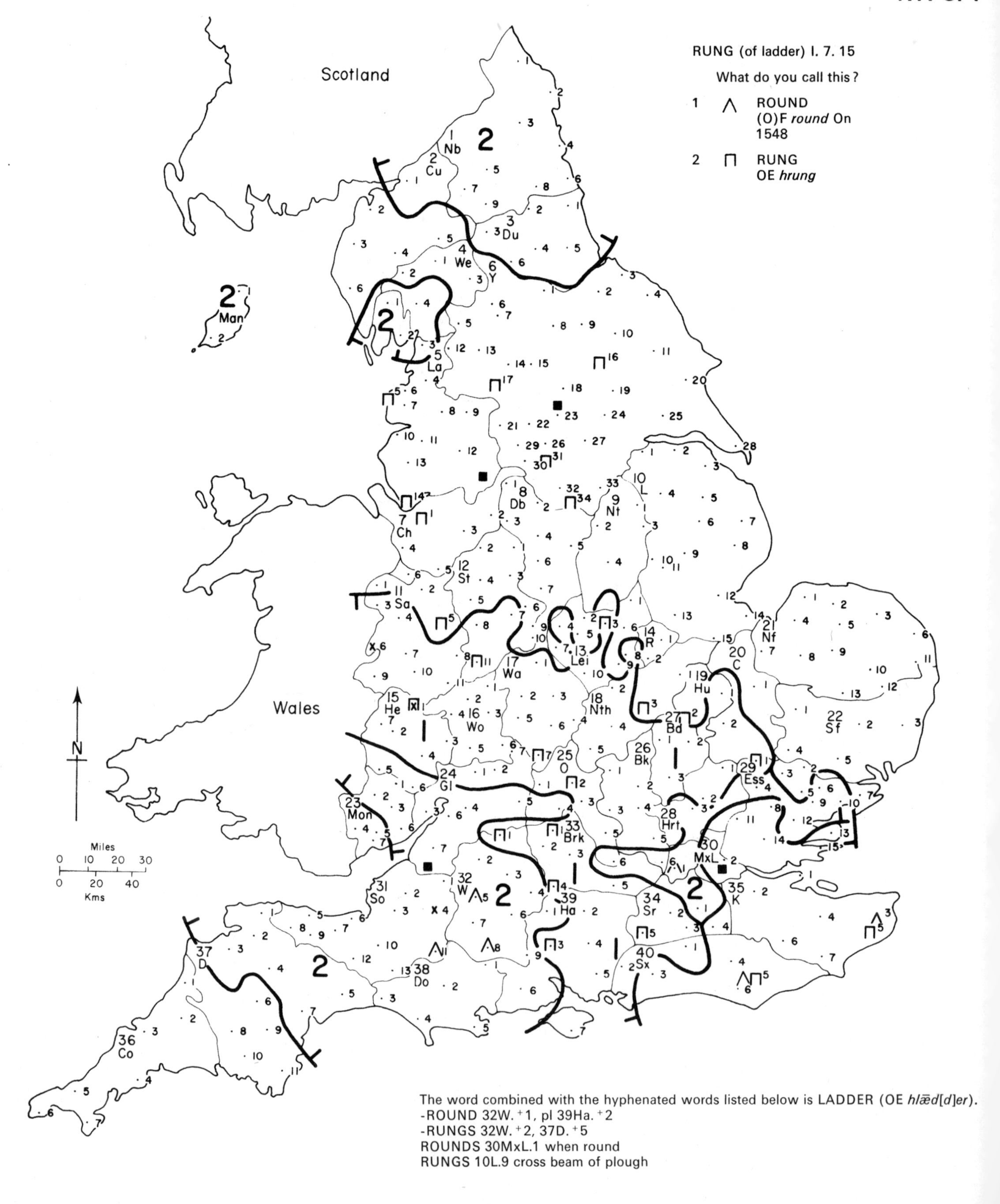

The word combined with the hyphenated words listed below is LADDER (OE *hlǣd[d]er*).
-ROUND 32W. +1, pl 39Ha. +2
-RUNGS 32W. +2, 37D. +5
ROUNDS 30MxL.1 when round
RUNGS 10L.9 cross beam of plough

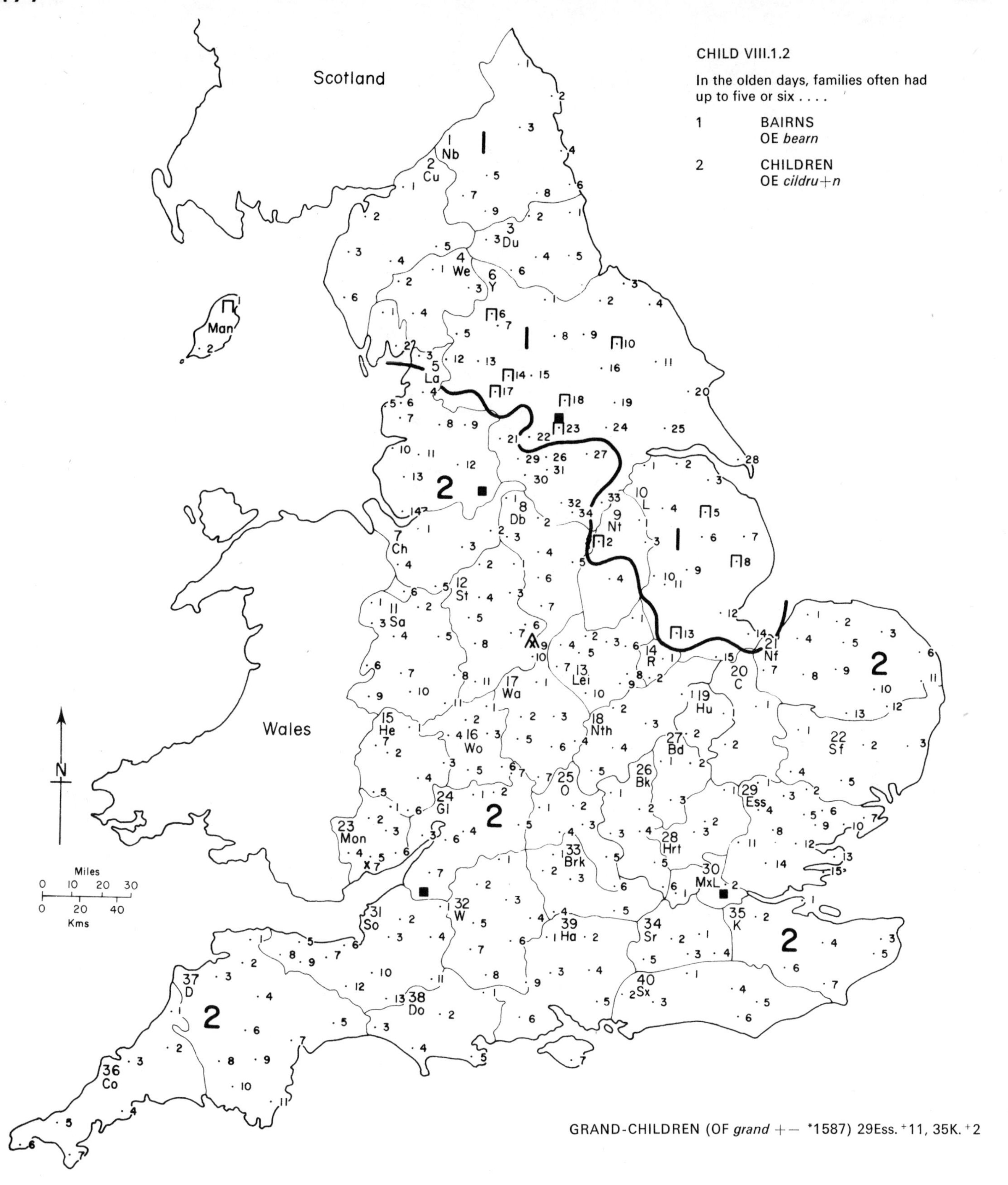

GRAND-CHILDREN (OF *grand* +— *1587) 29Ess. +11, 35K. +2

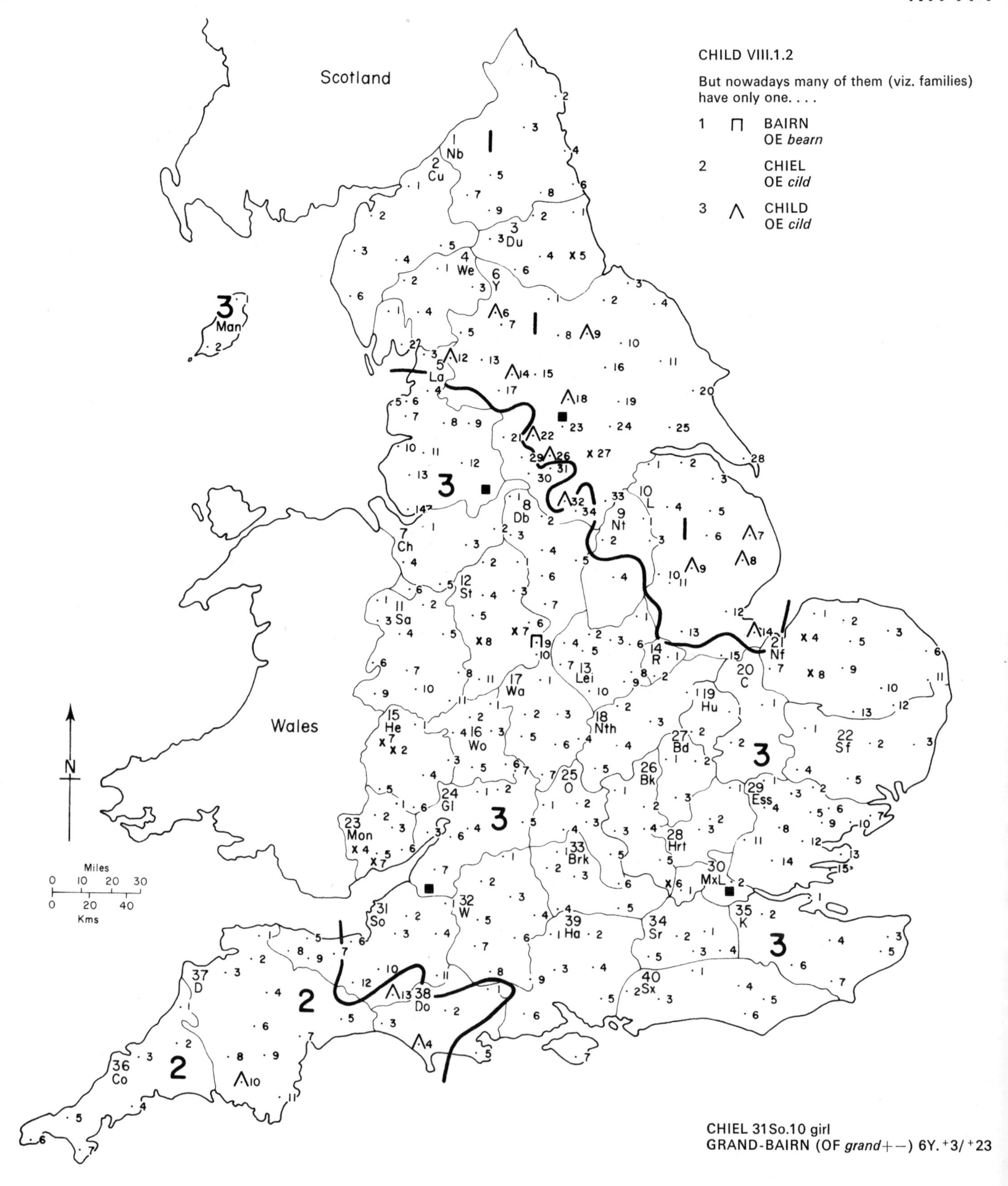
Scotland
Wales
CHILD VIII.1.2
But nowadays many of them (viz. families) have only one. . . .
1 ⊓ BAIRN OE *bearn*
2 CHIEL OE *cild*
3 ∧ CHILD OE *cild*
Miles 0 10 20 30
0 20 40 Kms
N
Nb
Cu
Du
We
Y
Man
La
Ch
Db
Nt
L
St
Sa
Lei
R
Nf
C
Wa
He
Wo
Nth
Hu
Bd
Sf
Bk
O
Gl
Ess
Mon
Hrt
Brk
MxL
W
So
K
Ha
Sr
D
Do
Sx
Co
CHIEL 31So.10 girl
GRAND-BAIRN (OF *grand*+—) 6Y.+3/+23

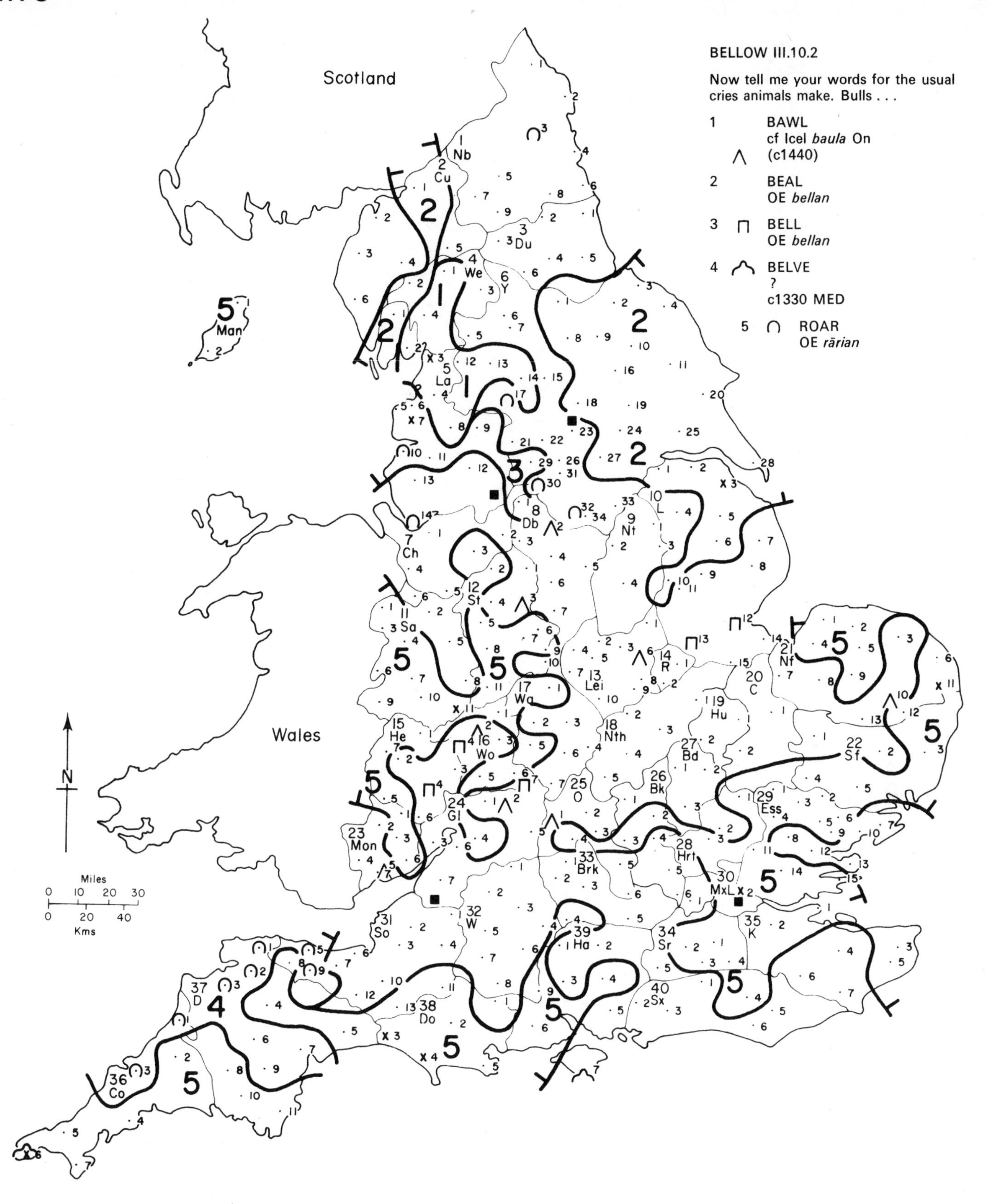
BELLOW III.10.2
Now tell me your words for the usual cries animals make. Bulls . . .
1 BAWL cf Icel *baula* On (c1440)
2 BEAL OE *bellan*
3 BELL OE *bellan*
4 BELVE ? c1330 MED
5 ROAR OE *rārian*
Scotland
Wales
Man
N
Miles 0 10 20 30
0 20 40 Kms
Nb Cu Du We Y La Ch Db Nt L St Sa R Lei Nf He Wo Wa Nth Hu C Sf Gl O Bd Bk Ess Hrt Mon Brk MxL So W Ha Sr K D Do Sx Co

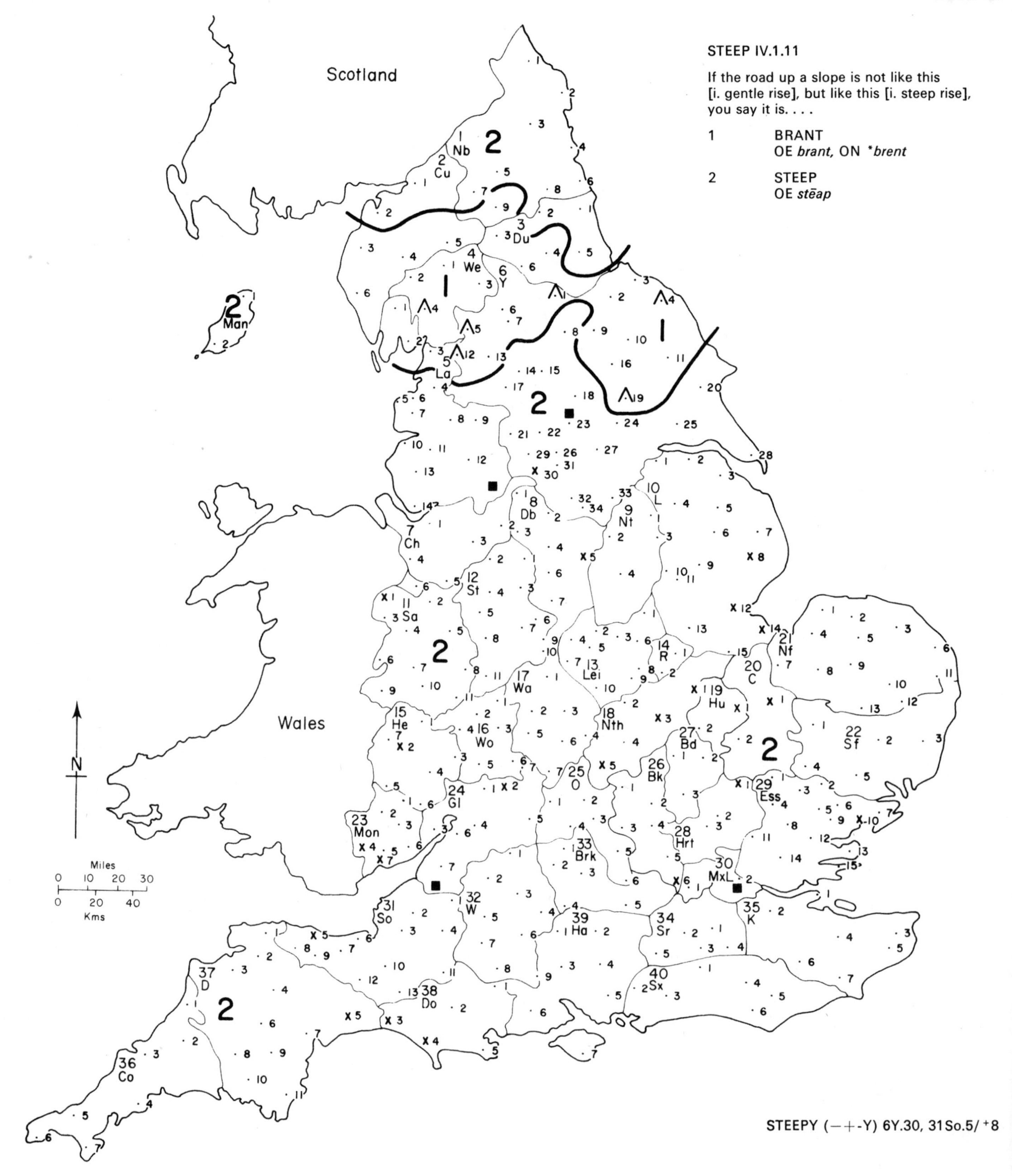

STEEP IV.1.11

If the road up a slope is not like this [i. gentle rise], but like this [i. steep rise], you say it is. . . .

1 BRANT
OE *brant*, ON **brent*

2 STEEP
OE *stēap*

STEEPY (—+-Y) 6Y.30, 31So.5/⁺8

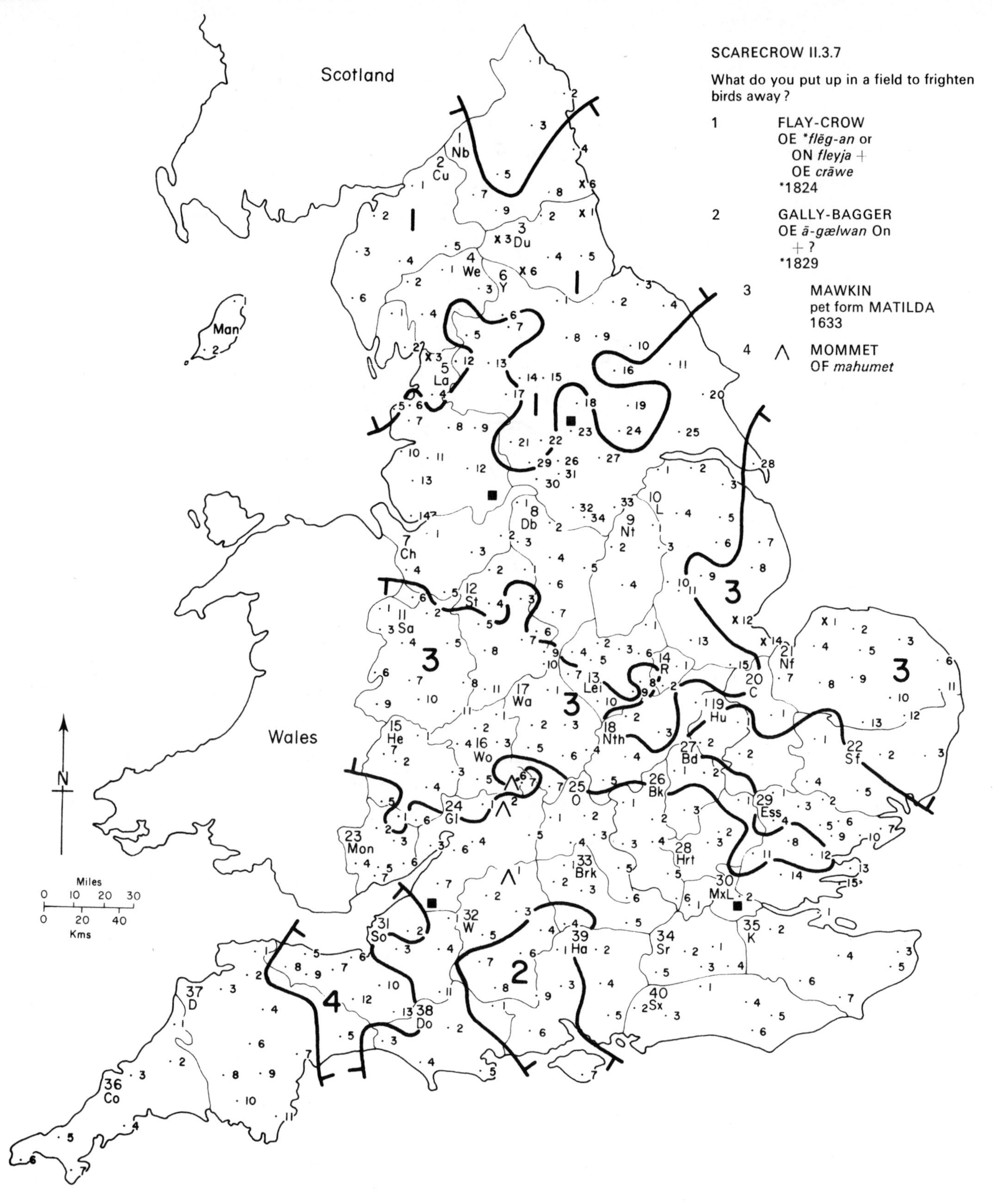
SCARECROW II.3.7
What do you put up in a field to frighten birds away?
1 FLAY-CROW
OE *flēg-an or
ON fleyja +
OE crāwe
*1824
2 GALLY-BAGGER
OE ā-gælwan On
+?
*1829
3 MAWKIN
pet form MATILDA
1633
4 Λ MOMMET
OF mahumet
Scotland
Wales
Man
N
Miles
0 10 20 30
0 20 40
Kms

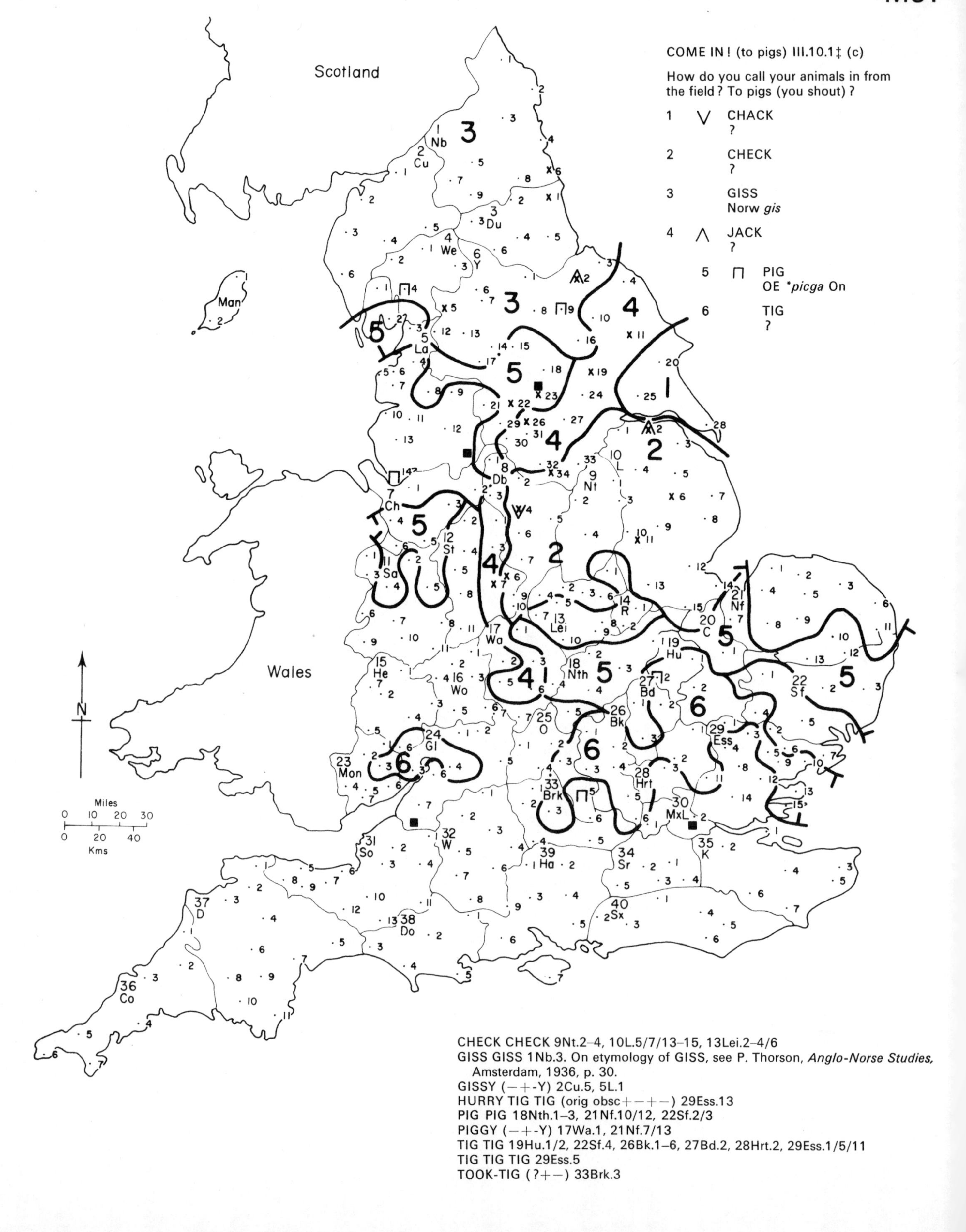

CHECK CHECK 9Nt.2–4, 10L.5/7/13–15, 13Lei.2–4/6
GISS GISS 1Nb.3. On etymology of GISS, see P. Thorson, *Anglo-Norse Studies,* Amsterdam, 1936, p. 30.
GISSY (—+-Y) 2Cu.5, 5L.1
HURRY TIG TIG (orig obsc+—+—) 29Ess.13
PIG PIG 18Nth.1–3, 21Nf.10/12, 22Sf.2/3
PIGGY (—+-Y) 17Wa.1, 21Nf.7/13
TIG TIG 19Hu.1/2, 22Sf.4, 26Bk.1–6, 27Bd.2, 28Hrt.2, 29Ess.1/5/11
TIG TIG TIG 29Ess.5
TOOK-TIG (?+—) 33Brk.3

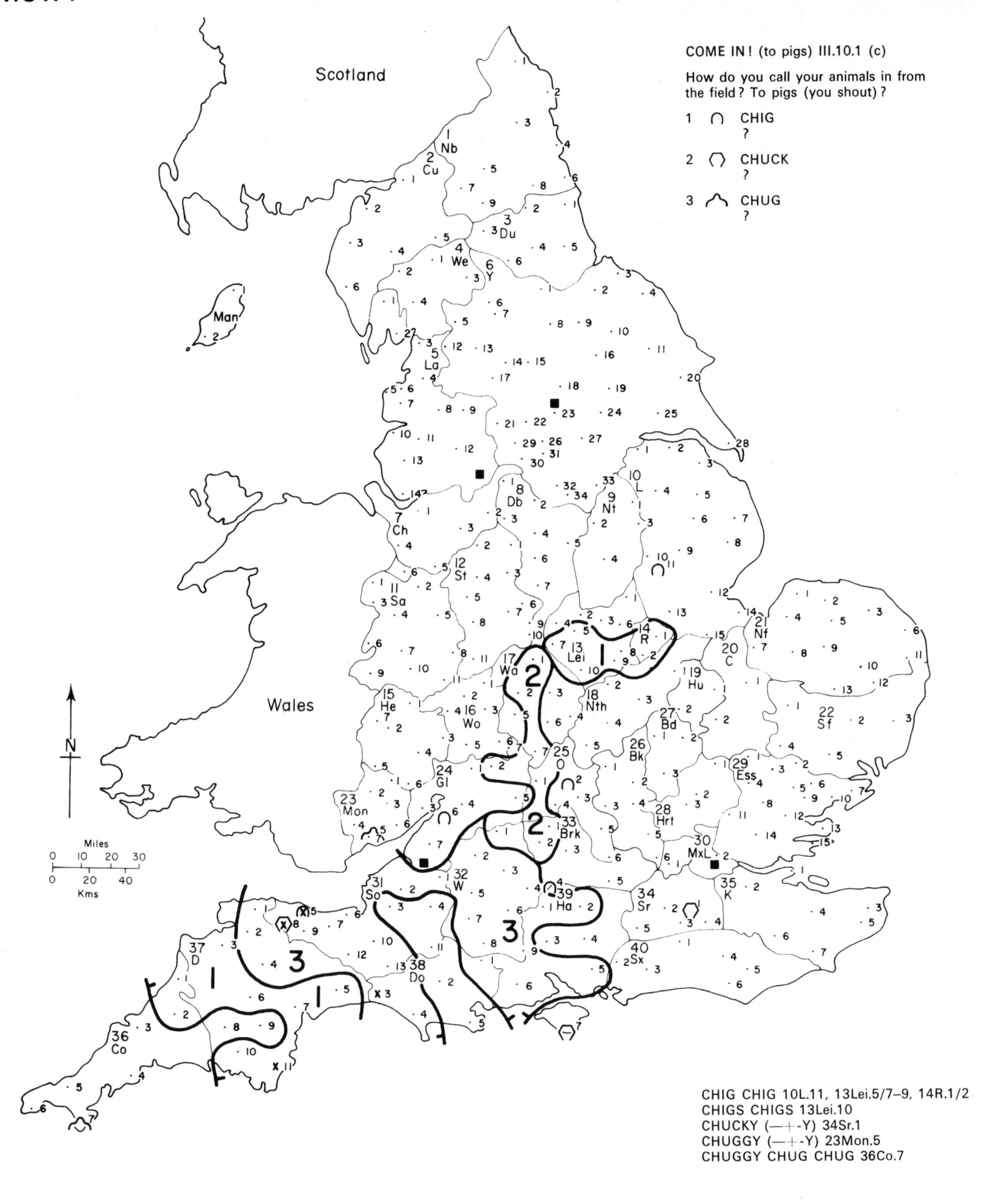
COME IN! (to pigs) III.10.1 (c)
How do you call your animals in from the field? To pigs (you shout)?
1 ∩ CHIG ?
2 ⬡ CHUCK ?
3 ⌒ CHUG ?
Scotland
Wales
Man
N
Miles
0 10 20 30
0 20 40
Kms
CHIG CHIG 10L.11, 13Lei.5/7–9, 14R.1/2
CHIGS CHIGS 13Lei.10
CHUCKY (—+-Y) 34Sr.1
CHUGGY (—+-Y) 23Mon.5
CHUGGY CHUG CHUG 36Co.7

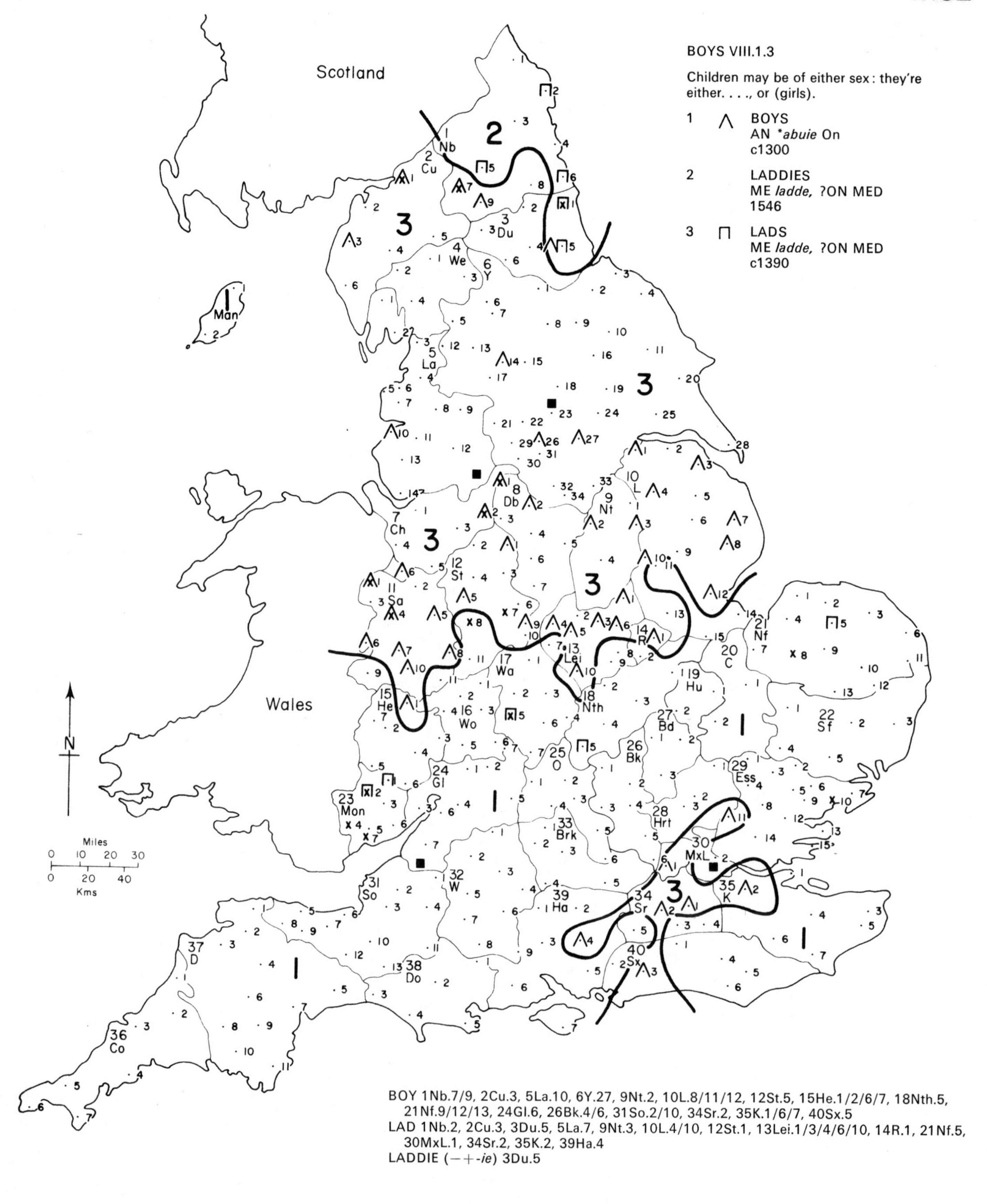

BOYS VIII.1.3

Children may be of either sex: they're either. . . ., or (girls).

1 ⋀ BOYS
AN *abuie On
c1300

2 LADDIES
ME *ladde*, ?ON MED
1546

3 ⊓ LADS
ME *ladde*, ?ON MED
c1390

BOY 1Nb.7/9, 2Cu.3, 5La.10, 6Y.27, 9Nt.2, 10L.8/11/12, 12St.5, 15He.1/2/6/7, 18Nth.5, 21Nf.9/12/13, 24Gl.6, 26Bk.4/6, 31So.2/10, 34Sr.2, 35K.1/6/7, 40Sx.5

LAD 1Nb.2, 2Cu.3, 3Du.5, 5La.7, 9Nt.3, 10L.4/10, 12St.1, 13Lei.1/3/4/6/10, 14R.1, 21Nf.5, 30MxL.1, 34Sr.2, 35K.2, 39Ha.4

LADDIE (—+-*ie*) 3Du.5

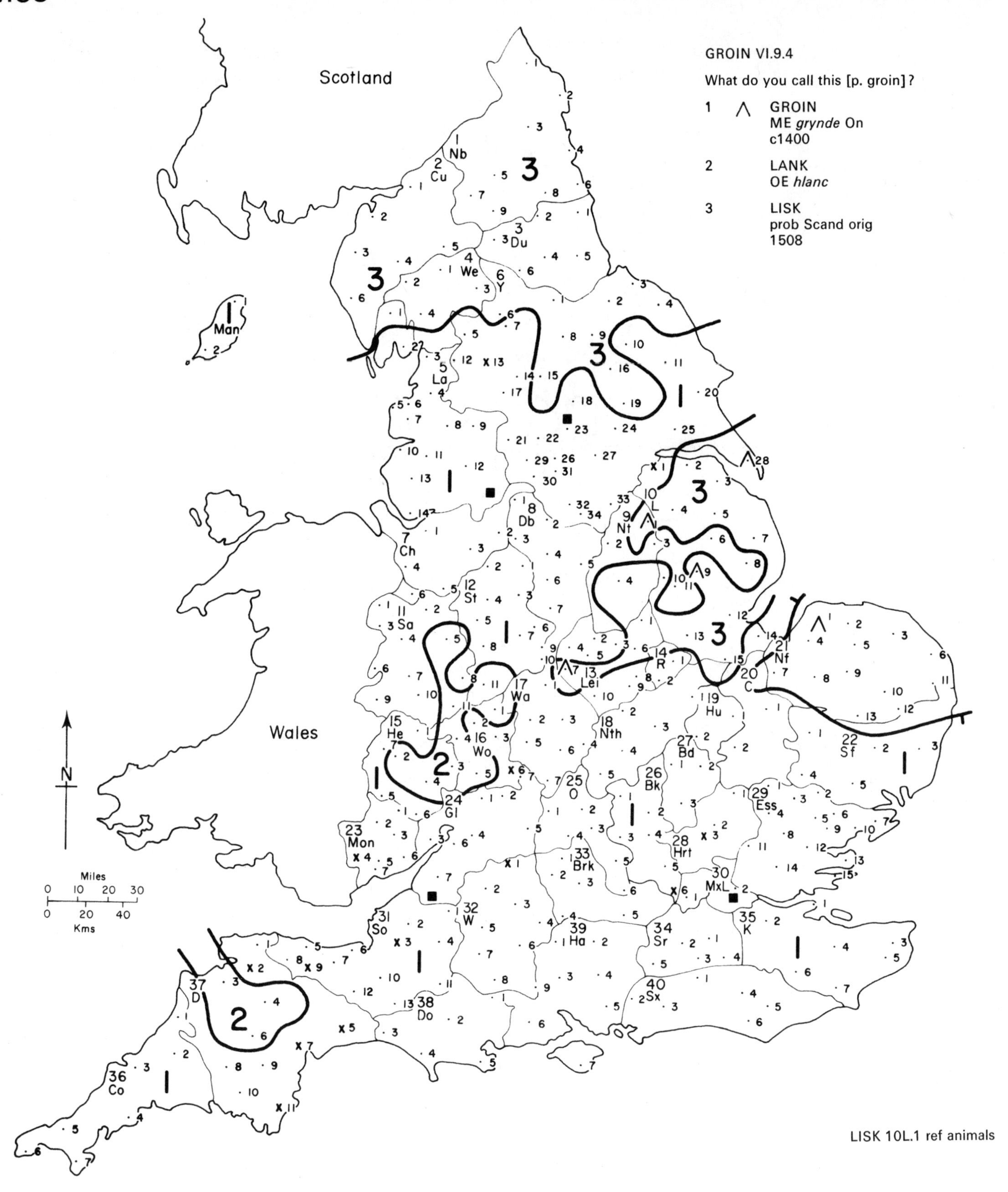
GROIN VI.9.4
What do you call this [p. groin]?
1 Λ GROIN
ME grynde On
c1400
2 LANK
OE hlanc
3 LISK
prob Scand orig
1508
Scotland
Wales
Man
N
Miles
0 10 20 30
0 20 40
Kms
LISK 10L.1 ref animals

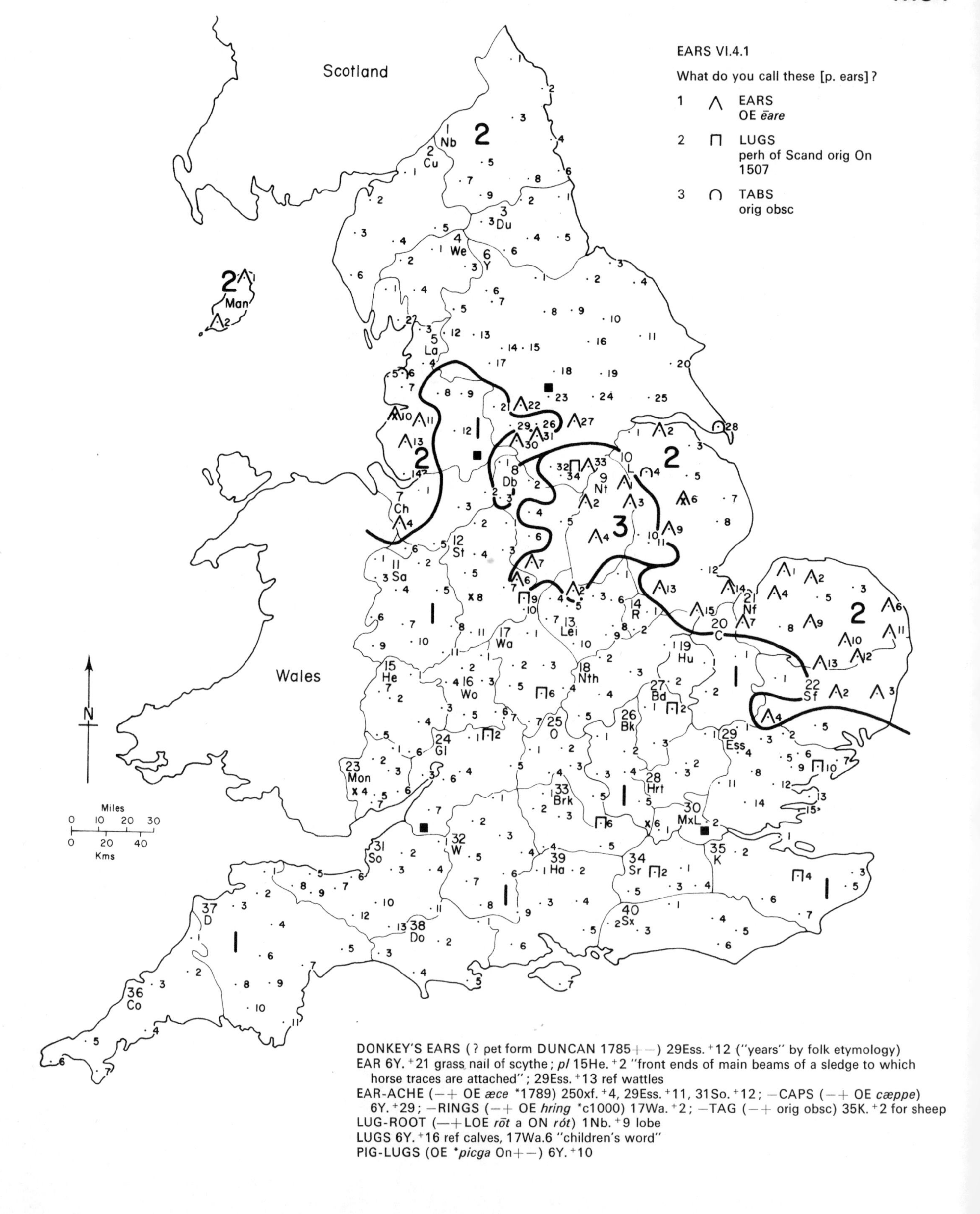

DONKEY'S EARS (? pet form DUNCAN 1785+—) 29Ess.+12 ("years" by folk etymology)
EAR 6Y.+21 grass nail of scythe; *pl* 15He.+2 "front ends of main beams of a sledge to which horse traces are attached"; 29Ess.+13 ref wattles
EAR-ACHE (—+ OE *æce* *1789) 250xf.+4, 29Ess.+11, 31So.+12; —CAPS (—+ OE *cæppe*) 6Y.+29; —RINGS (—+ OE *hring* *c1000) 17Wa.+2; —TAG (—+ orig obsc) 35K.+2 for sheep
LUG-ROOT (—+LOE *rōt* a ON *rót*) 1Nb.+9 lobe
LUGS 6Y.+16 ref calves, 17Wa.6 "children's word"
PIG-LUGS (OE *picga* On+—) 6Y.+10

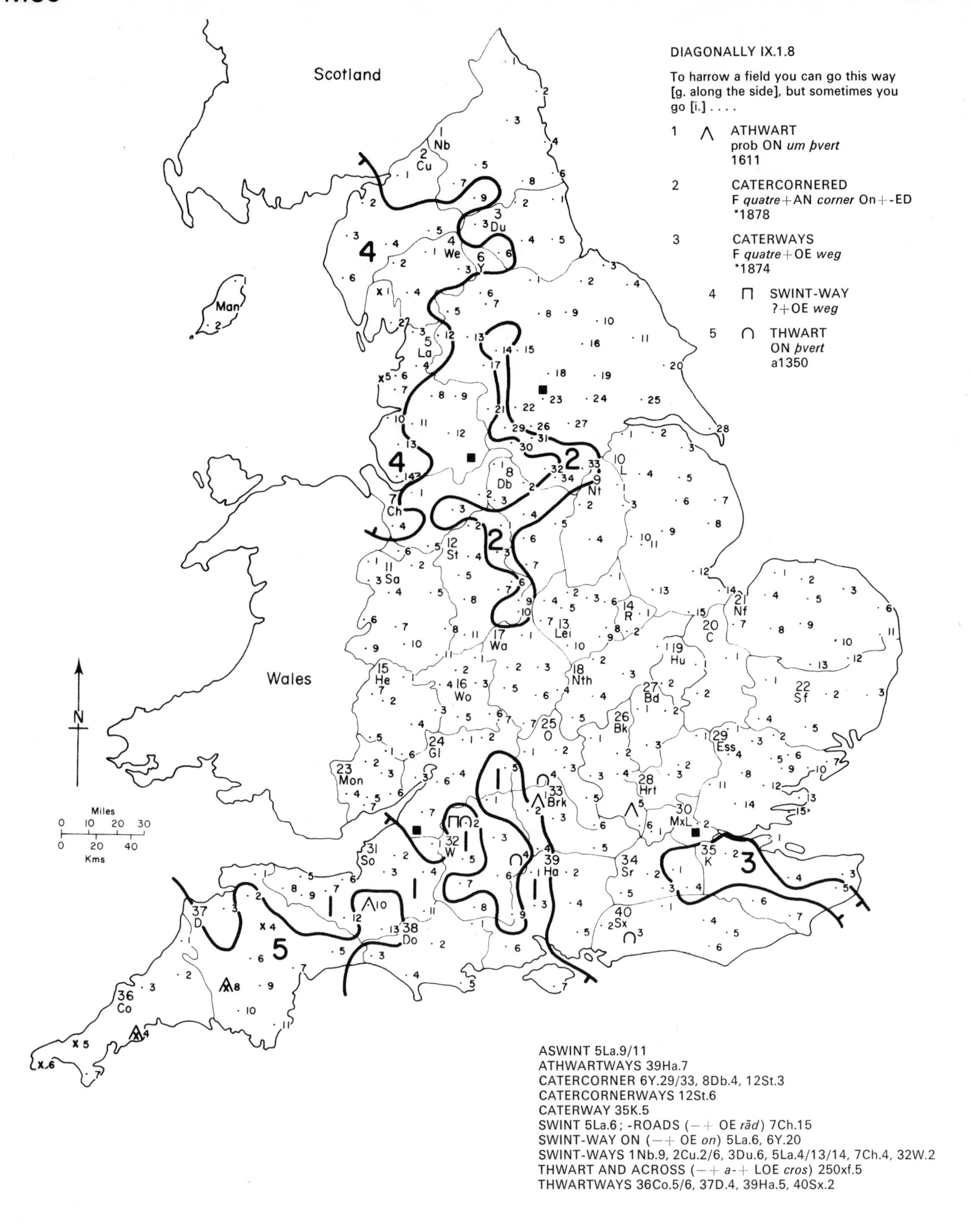
Scotland
Wales
Man
DIAGONALLY IX.1.8
To harrow a field you can go this way [g. along the side], but sometimes you go [i.] . . . .
1 ATHWART prob ON um þvert 1611
2 CATERCORNERED F quatre+AN corner On+-ED *1878
3 CATERWAYS F quatre+OE weg *1874
4 SWINT-WAY ?+OE weg
5 THWART ON þvert a1350
Miles 0 10 20 30
Kms 0 20 40
N
ASWINT 5La.9/11
ATHWARTWAYS 39Ha.7
CATERCORNER 6Y.29/33, 8Db.4, 12St.3
CATERCORNERWAYS 12St.6
CATERWAY 35K.5
SWINT 5La.6; -ROADS (—+ OE rād) 7Ch.15
SWINT-WAY ON (—+ OE on) 5La.6, 6Y.20
SWINT-WAYS 1Nb.9, 2Cu.2/6, 3Du.6, 5La.4/13/14, 7Ch.4, 32W.2
THWART AND ACROSS (—+ a-+ LOE cros) 25Oxf.5
THWARTWAYS 36Co.5/6, 37D.4, 39Ha.5, 40Sx.2

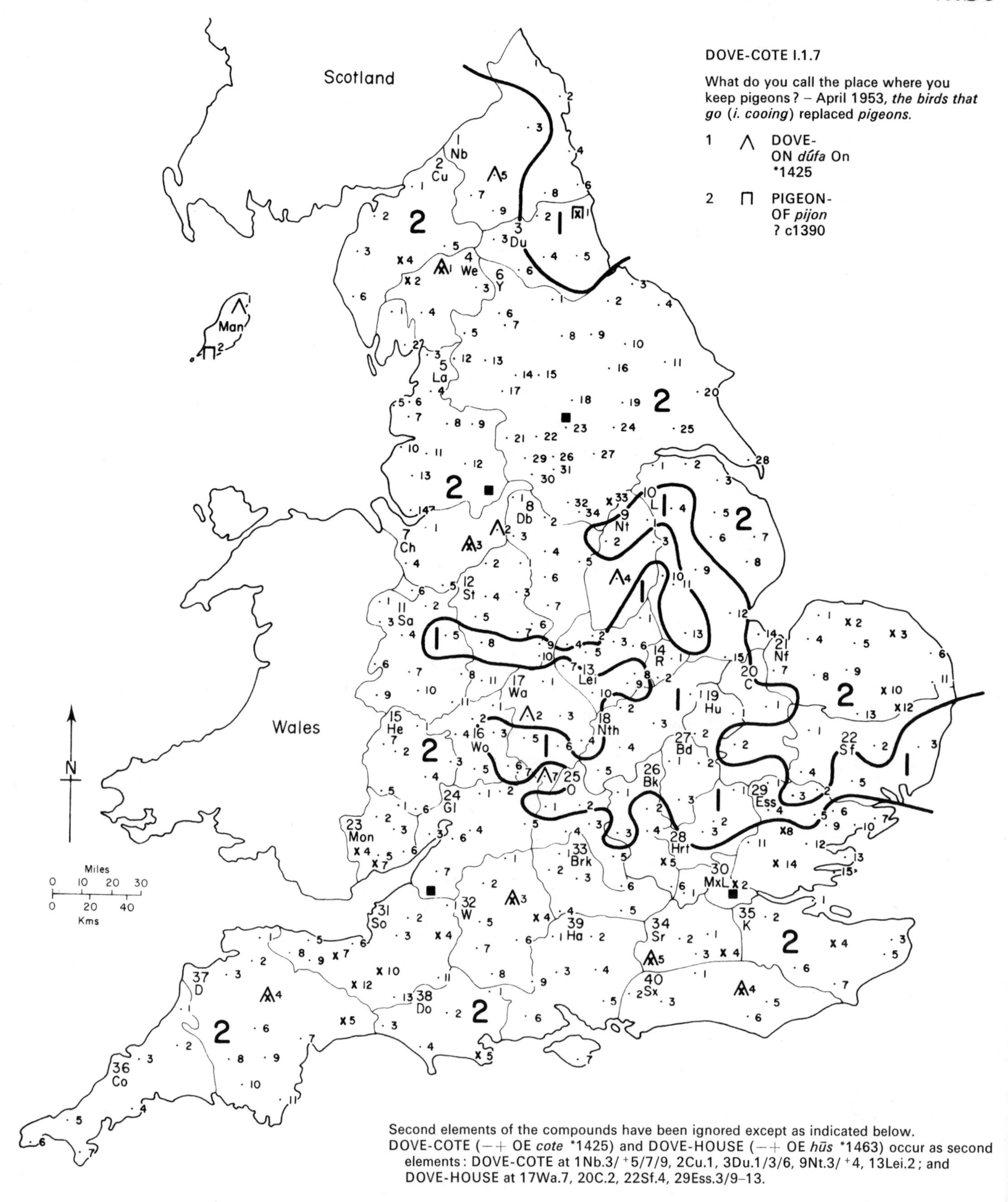

Second elements of the compounds have been ignored except as indicated below.
DOVE-COTE (—+ OE *cote* *1425) and DOVE-HOUSE (—+ OE *hūs* *1463) occur as second elements: DOVE-COTE at 1Nb.3/ +5/7/9, 2Cu.1, 3Du.1/3/6, 9Nt.3/ +4, 13Lei.2; and DOVE-HOUSE at 17Wa.7, 20C.2, 22Sf.4, 29Ess.3/9–13.

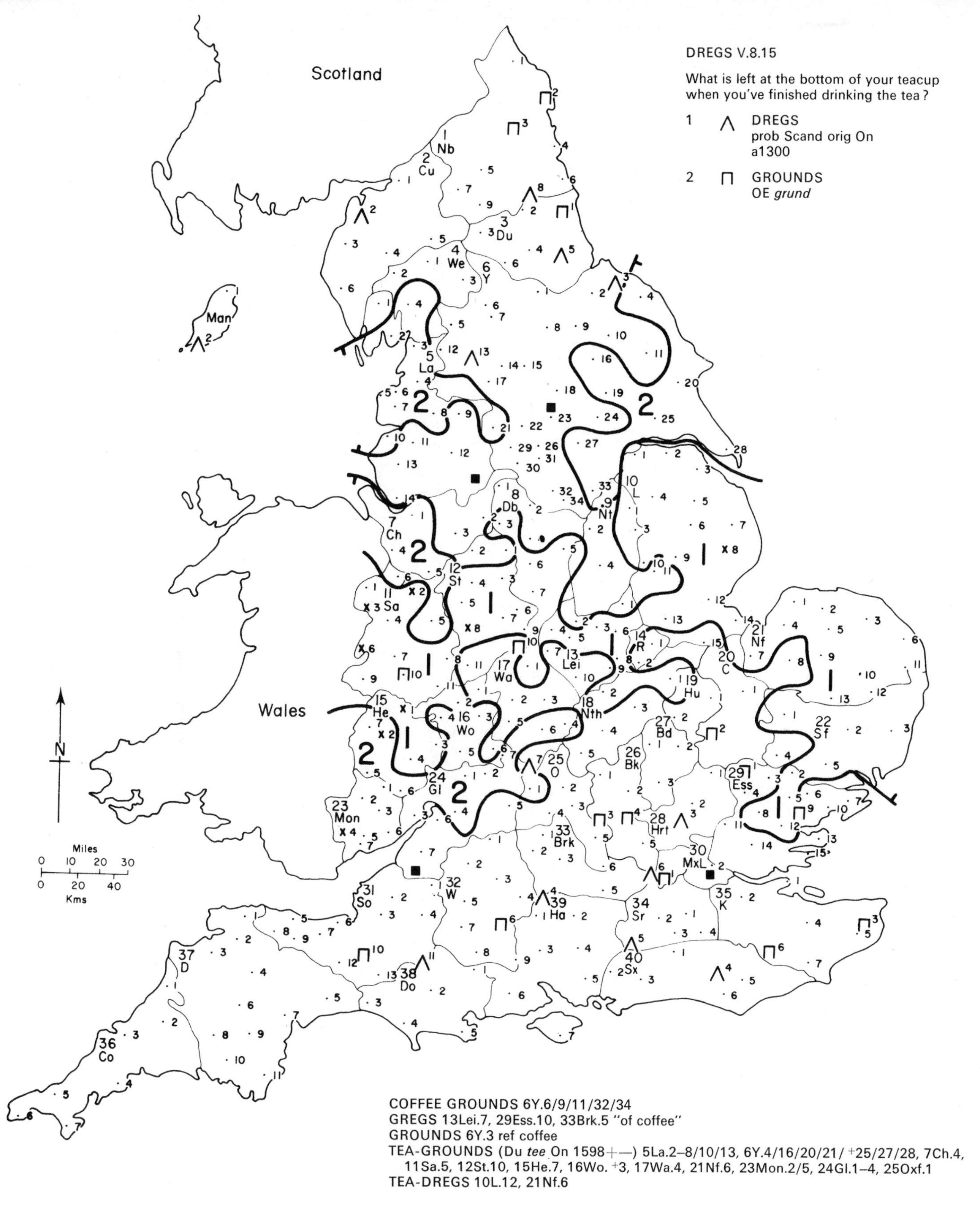

COFFEE GROUNDS 6Y.6/9/11/32/34
GREGS 13Lei.7, 29Ess.10, 33Brk.5 "of coffee"
GROUNDS 6Y.3 ref coffee
TEA-GROUNDS (Du *tee* On 1598+—) 5La.2–8/10/13, 6Y.4/16/20/21/ +25/27/28, 7Ch.4, 11Sa.5, 12St.10, 15He.7, 16Wo. +3, 17Wa.4, 21Nf.6, 23Mon.2/5, 24Gl.1–4, 25Oxf.1
TEA-DREGS 10L.12, 21Nf.6

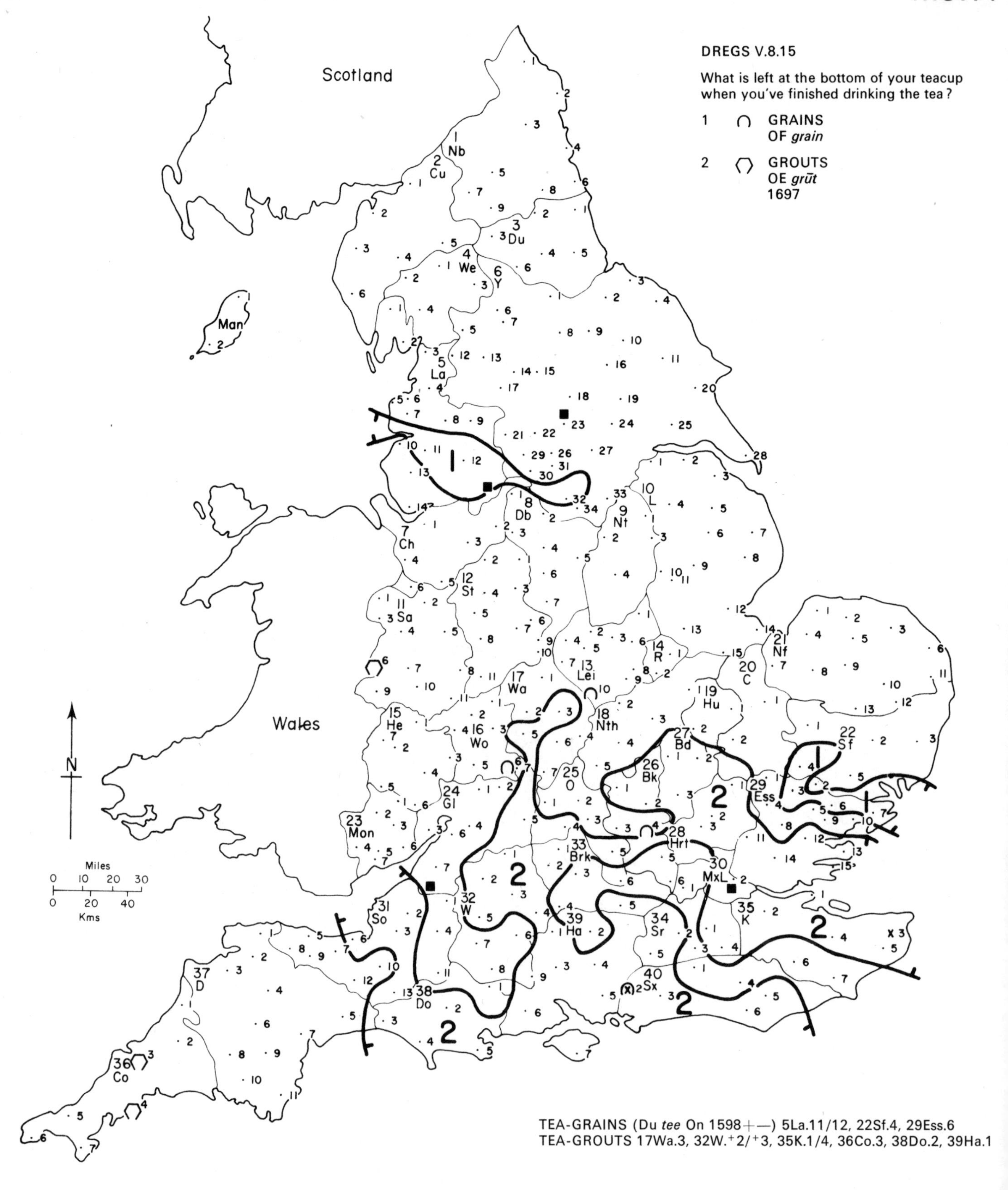

TEA-GRAINS (Du *tee* On 1598+—) 5La.11/12, 22Sf.4, 29Ess.6
TEA-GROUTS 17Wa.3, 32W.+2/+3, 35K.1/4, 36Co.3, 38Do.2, 39Ha.1

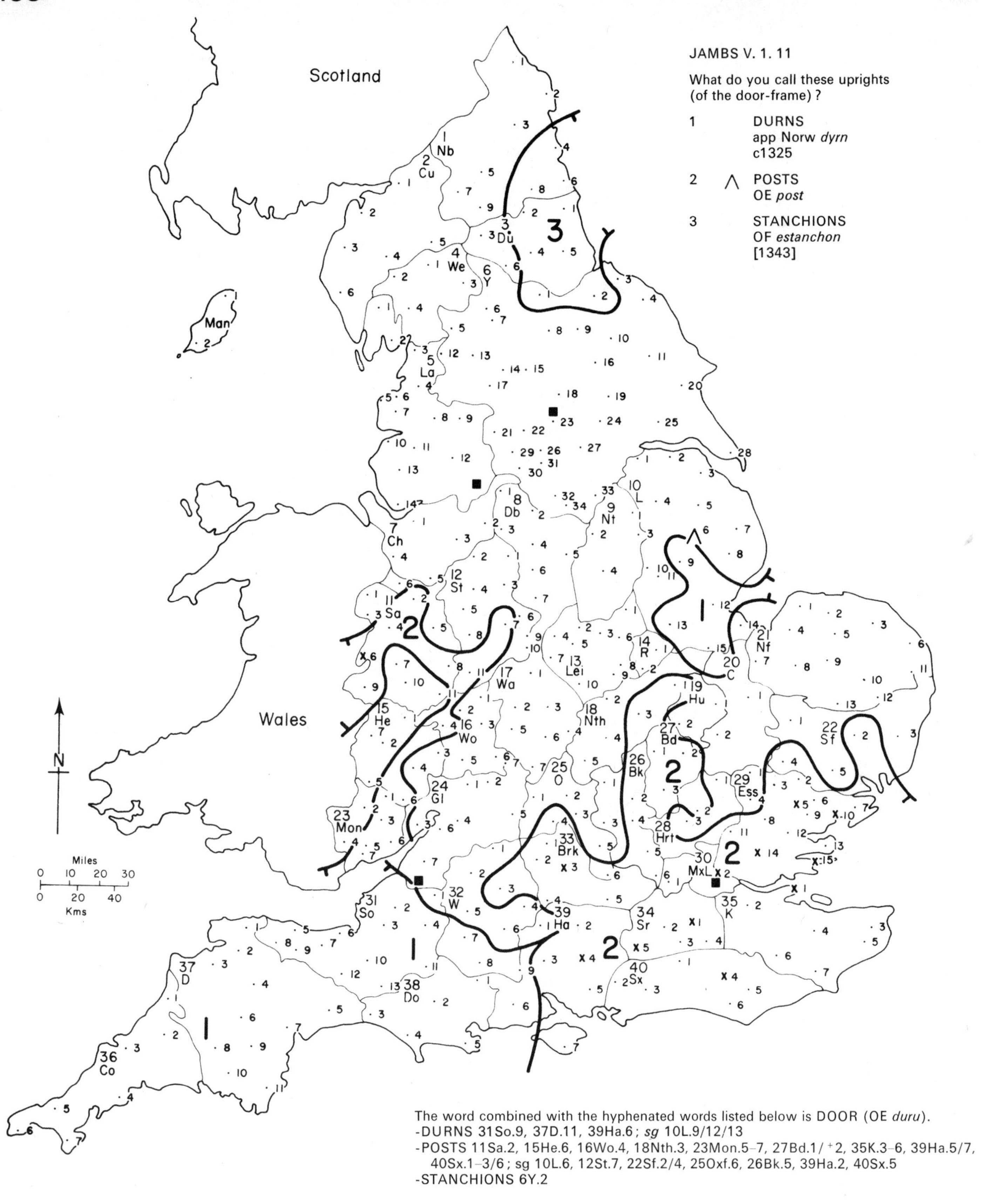

The word combined with the hyphenated words listed below is DOOR (OE *duru*).
-DURNS 31So.9, 37D.11, 39Ha.6; *sg* 10L.9/12/13
-POSTS 11Sa.2, 15He.6, 16Wo.4, 18Nth.3, 23Mon.5–7, 27Bd.1/ +2, 35K.3–6, 39Ha.5/7, 40Sx.1–3/6; sg 10L.6, 12St.7, 22Sf.2/4, 25Oxf.6, 26Bk.5, 39Ha.2, 40Sx.5
-STANCHIONS 6Y.2

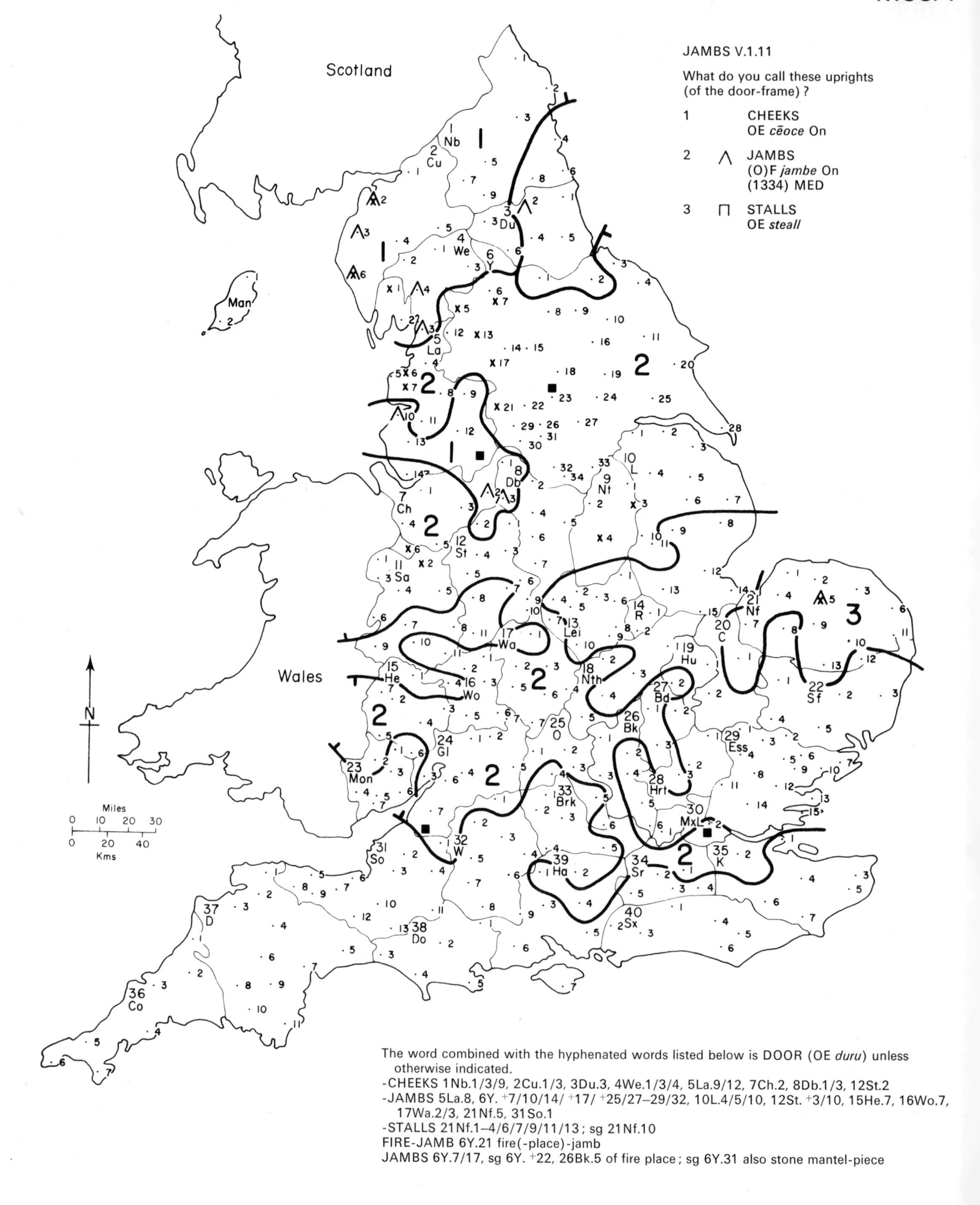

The word combined with the hyphenated words listed below is DOOR (OE *duru*) unless otherwise indicated.

-CHEEKS 1Nb.1/3/9, 2Cu.1/3, 3Du.3, 4We.1/3/4, 5La.9/12, 7Ch.2, 8Db.1/3, 12St.2

-JAMBS 5La.8, 6Y. +7/10/14/ +17/ +25/27–29/32, 10L.4/5/10, 12St. +3/10, 15He.7, 16Wo.7, 17Wa.2/3, 21Nf.5, 31So.1

-STALLS 21Nf.1–4/6/7/9/11/13; sg 21Nf.10

FIRE-JAMB 6Y.21 fire(-place)-jamb

JAMBS 6Y.7/17, sg 6Y. +22, 26Bk.5 of fire place; sg 6Y.31 also stone mantel-piece

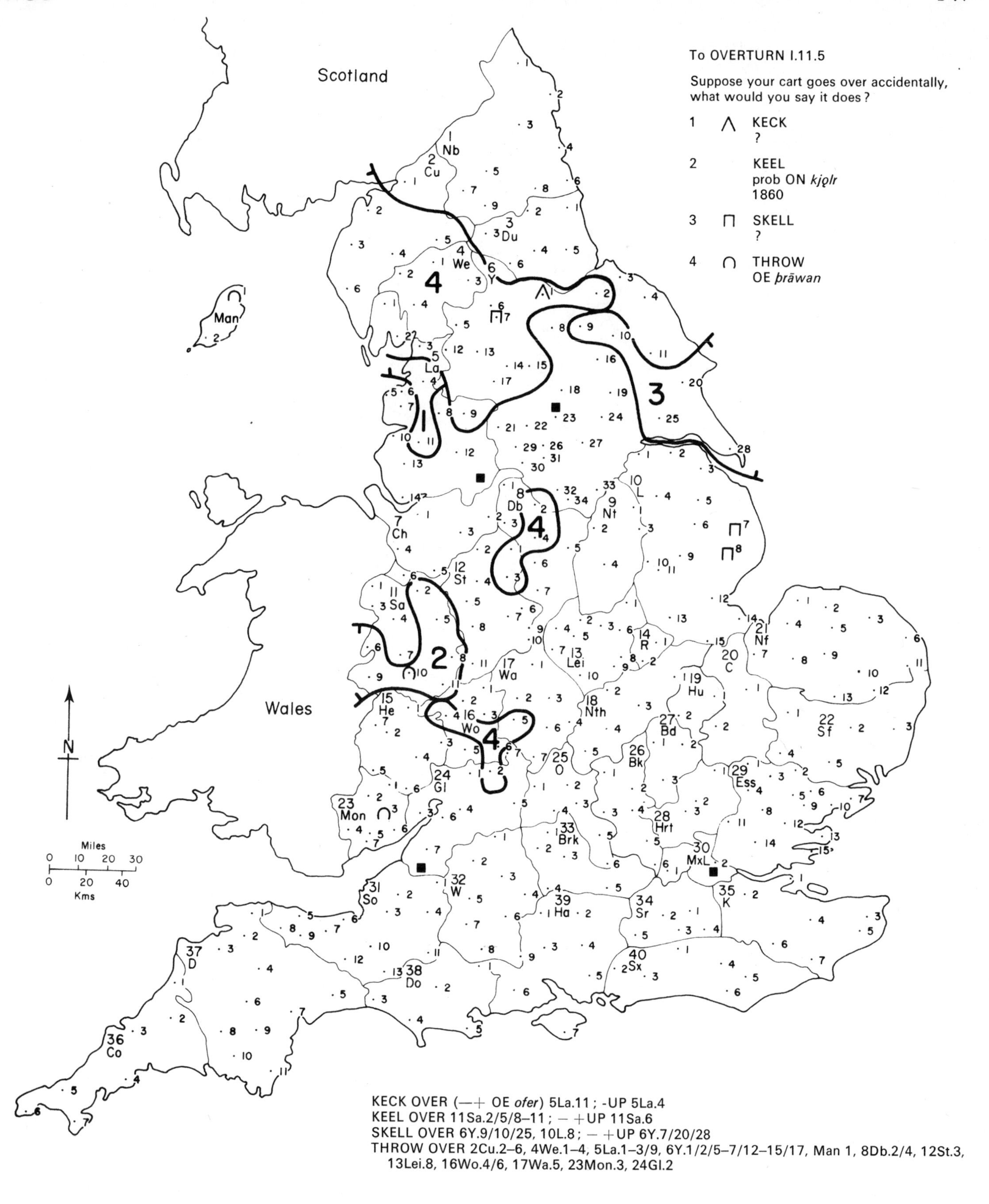
Scotland
Wales
Man
To OVERTURN I.11.5
Suppose your cart goes over accidentally, what would you say it does?
1 KECK ?
2 KEEL prob ON *kjǫlr* 1860
3 SKELL ?
4 THROW OE *þrāwan*
Miles 0 10 20 30
0 20 40 Kms
N
KECK OVER (—+ OE *ofer*) 5La.11; -UP 5La.4
KEEL OVER 11Sa.2/5/8–11; — +UP 11Sa.6
SKELL OVER 6Y.9/10/25, 10L.8; — +UP 6Y.7/20/28
THROW OVER 2Cu.2–6, 4We.1–4, 5La.1–3/9, 6Y.1/2/5–7/12–15/17, Man 1, 8Db.2/4, 12St.3, 13Lei.8, 16Wo.4/6, 17Wa.5, 23Mon.3, 24Gl.2

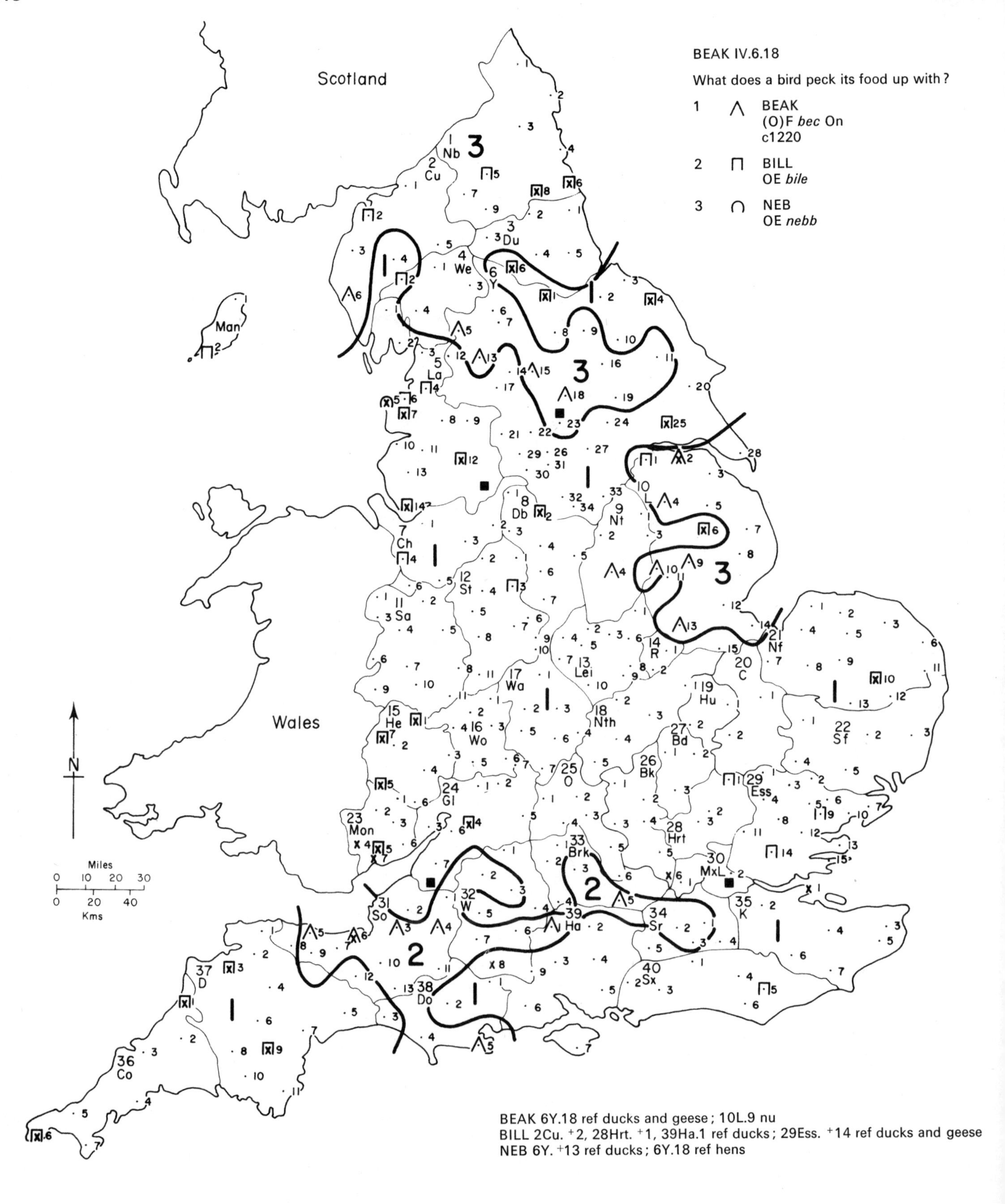
BEAK IV.6.18
What does a bird peck its food up with?
1 BEAK (O)F *bec* On c1220
2 BILL OE *bile*
3 NEB OE *nebb*
Scotland
Wales
Man
N
Miles
0 10 20 30
0 20 40
Kms
BEAK 6Y.18 ref ducks and geese; 10L.9 nu
BILL 2Cu. +2, 28Hrt. +1, 39Ha.1 ref ducks; 29Ess. +14 ref ducks and geese
NEB 6Y. +13 ref ducks; 6Y.18 ref hens

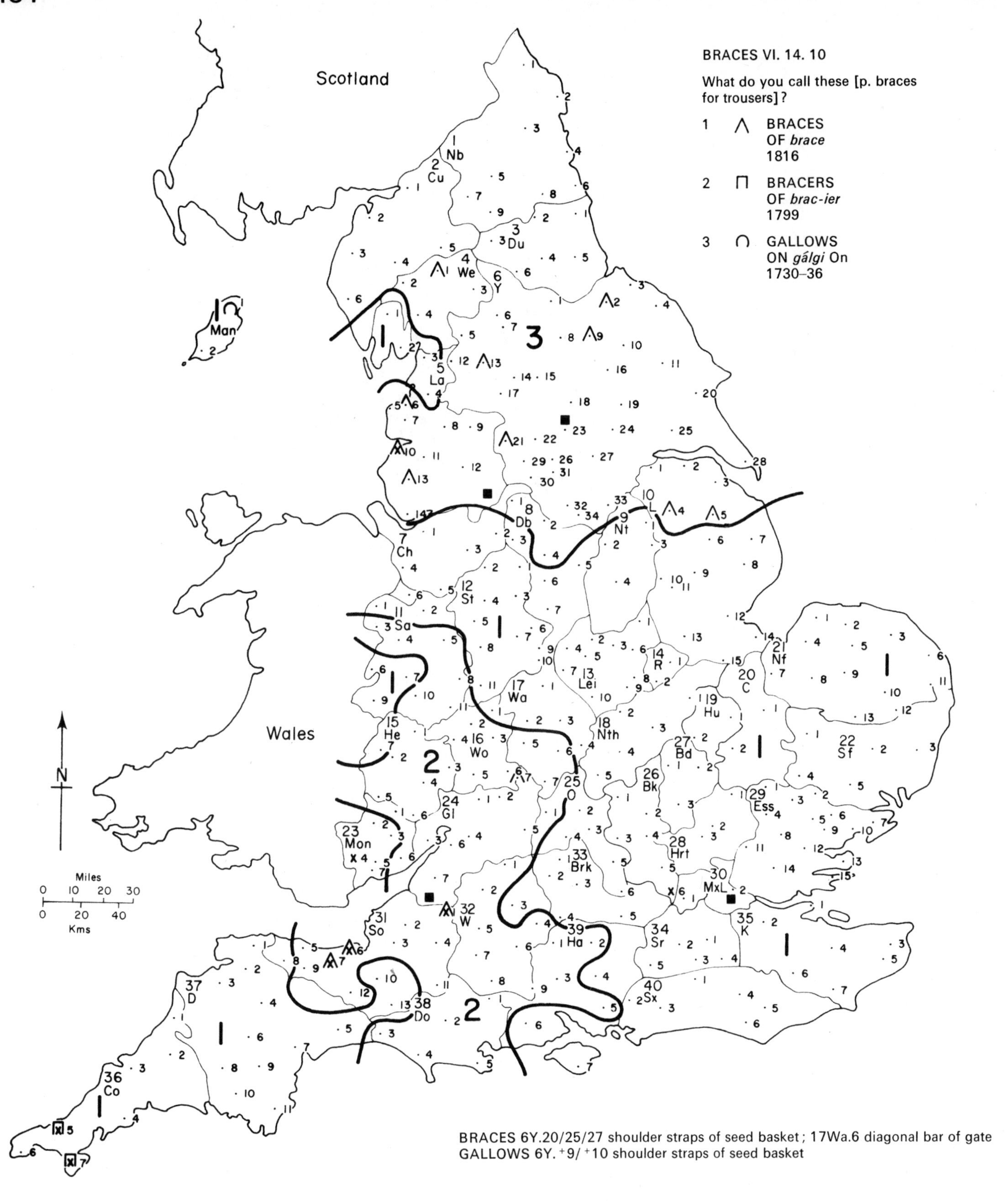
BRACES VI. 14. 10
What do you call these [p. braces for trousers]?
1 ⋀ BRACES
OF *brace*
1816
2 ⊓ BRACERS
OF *brac-ier*
1799
3 ∩ GALLOWS
ON *gálgi* On
1730–36
Scotland
Wales
Man
N
Miles
0 10 20 30
0 20 40
Kms
BRACES 6Y.20/25/27 shoulder straps of seed basket; 17Wa.6 diagonal bar of gate
GALLOWS 6Y.+9/+10 shoulder straps of seed basket

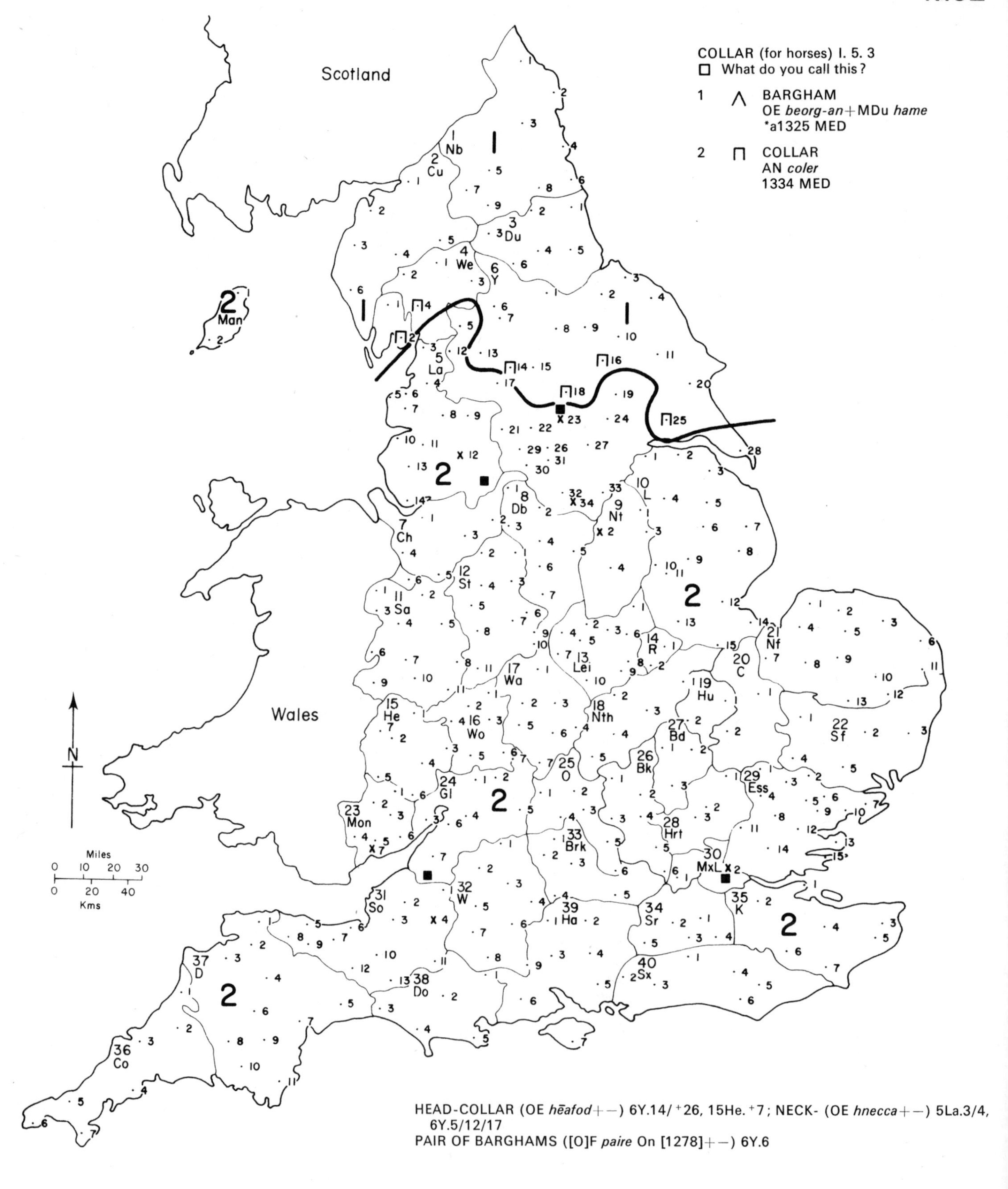

HEAD-COLLAR (OE *hēafod*+–) 6Y.14/ +26, 15He. +7; NECK- (OE *hnecca*+–) 5La.3/4, 6Y.5/12/17
PAIR OF BARGHAMS ([O]F *paire* On [1278]+–) 6Y.6

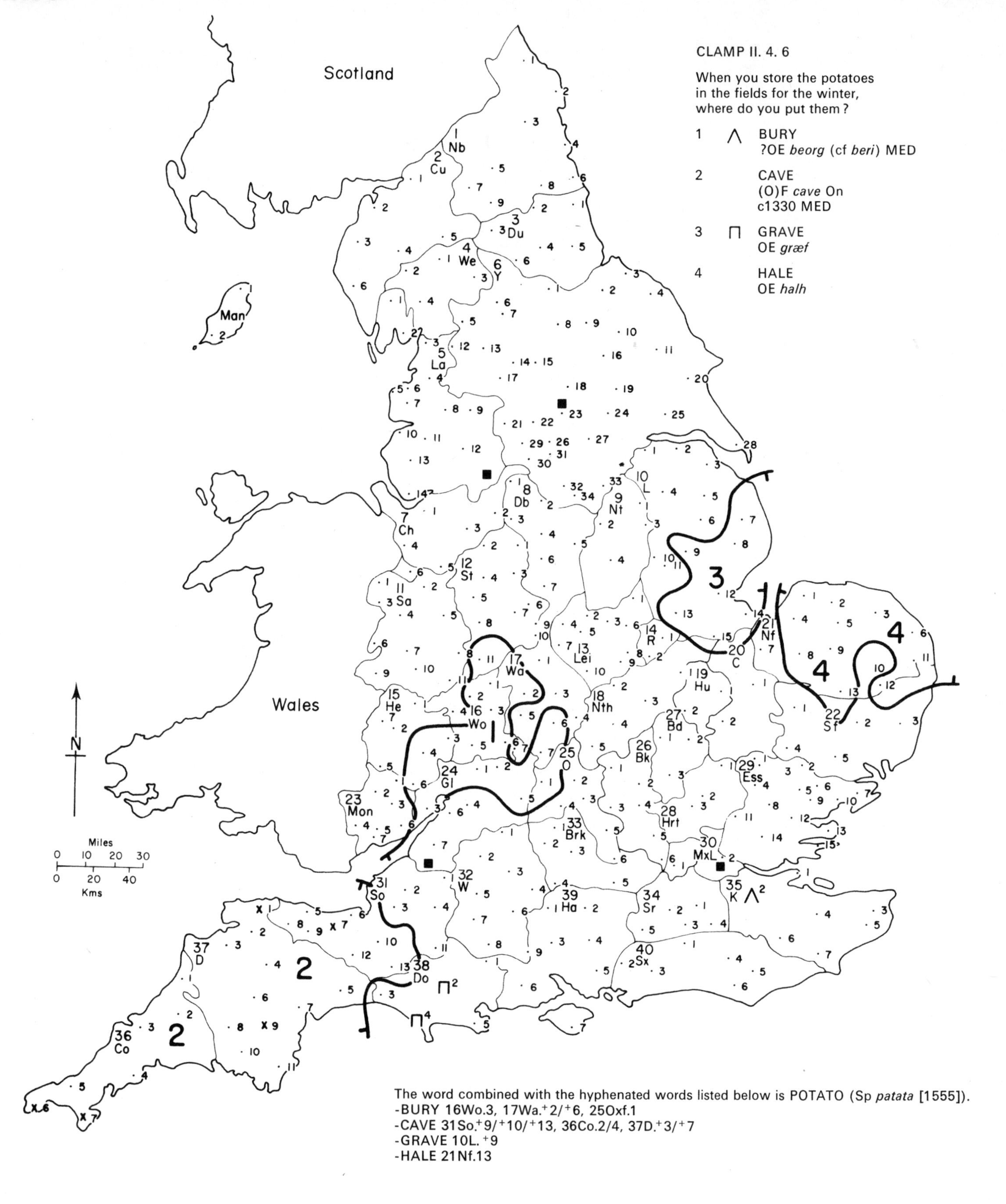
CLAMP II. 4. 6
When you store the potatoes
in the fields for the winter,
where do you put them?
1 ⋀ BURY
?OE *beorg* (cf *beri*) MED
2 CAVE
(O)F *cave* On
c1330 MED
3 ⊓ GRAVE
OE *græf*
4 HALE
OE *halh*
Scotland
Wales
Man
N
Miles
0 10 20 30
0 20 40
Kms
The word combined with the hyphenated words listed below is POTATO (Sp *patata* [1555]).
-BURY 16Wo.3, 17Wa.+2/+6, 25Oxf.1
-CAVE 31So.+9/+10/+13, 36Co.2/4, 37D.+3/+7
-GRAVE 10L.+9
-HALE 21Nf.13

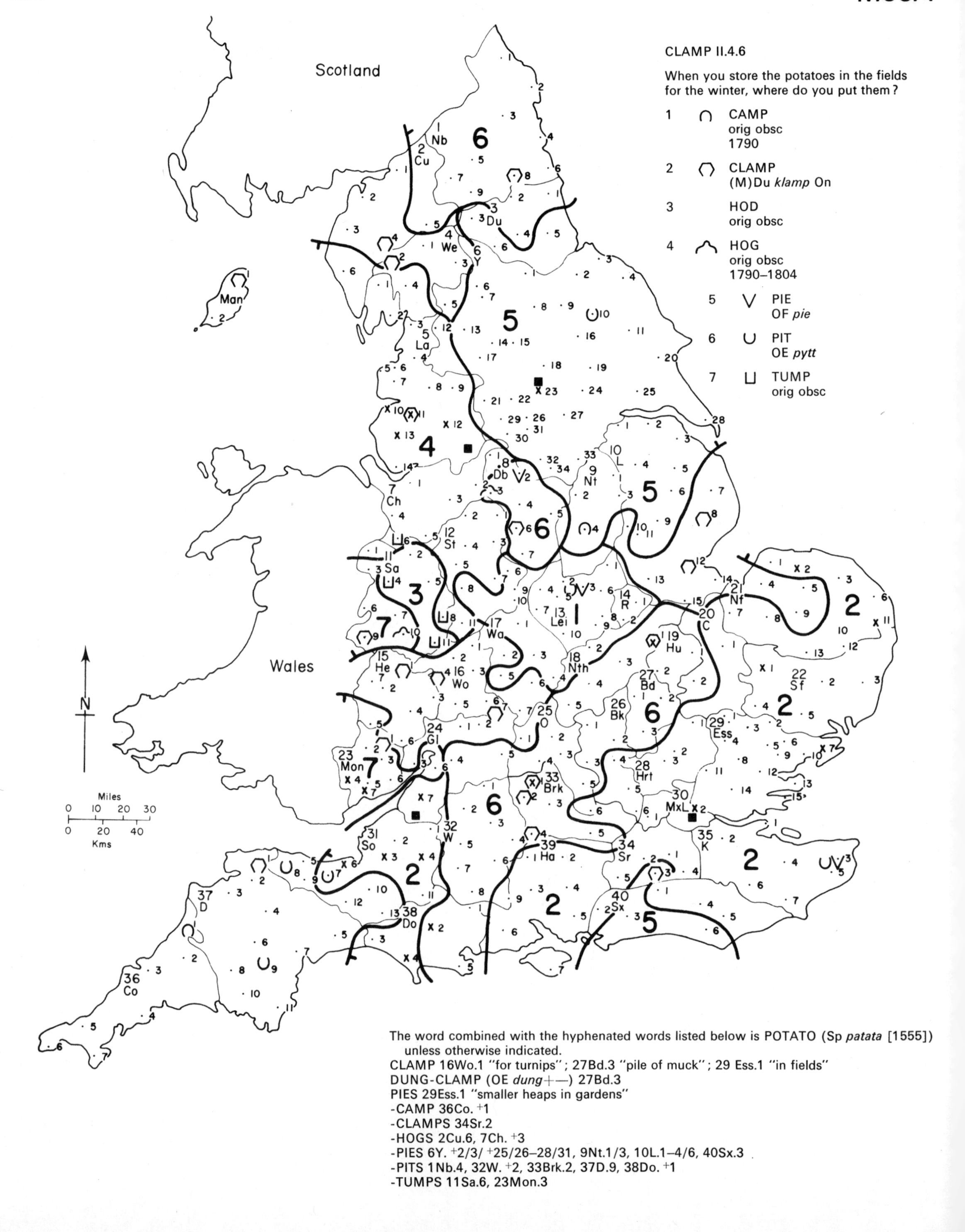

The word combined with the hyphenated words listed below is POTATO (Sp *patata* [1555]) unless otherwise indicated.
CLAMP 16Wo.1 "for turnips"; 27Bd.3 "pile of muck"; 29 Ess.1 "in fields"
DUNG-CLAMP (OE *dung*+—) 27Bd.3
PIES 29Ess.1 "smaller heaps in gardens"
-CAMP 36Co. +1
-CLAMPS 34Sr.2
-HOGS 2Cu.6, 7Ch. +3
-PIES 6Y. +2/3/ +25/26–28/31, 9Nt.1/3, 10L.1–4/6, 40Sx.3
-PITS 1Nb.4, 32W. +2, 33Brk.2, 37D.9, 38Do. +1
-TUMPS 11Sa.6, 23Mon.3

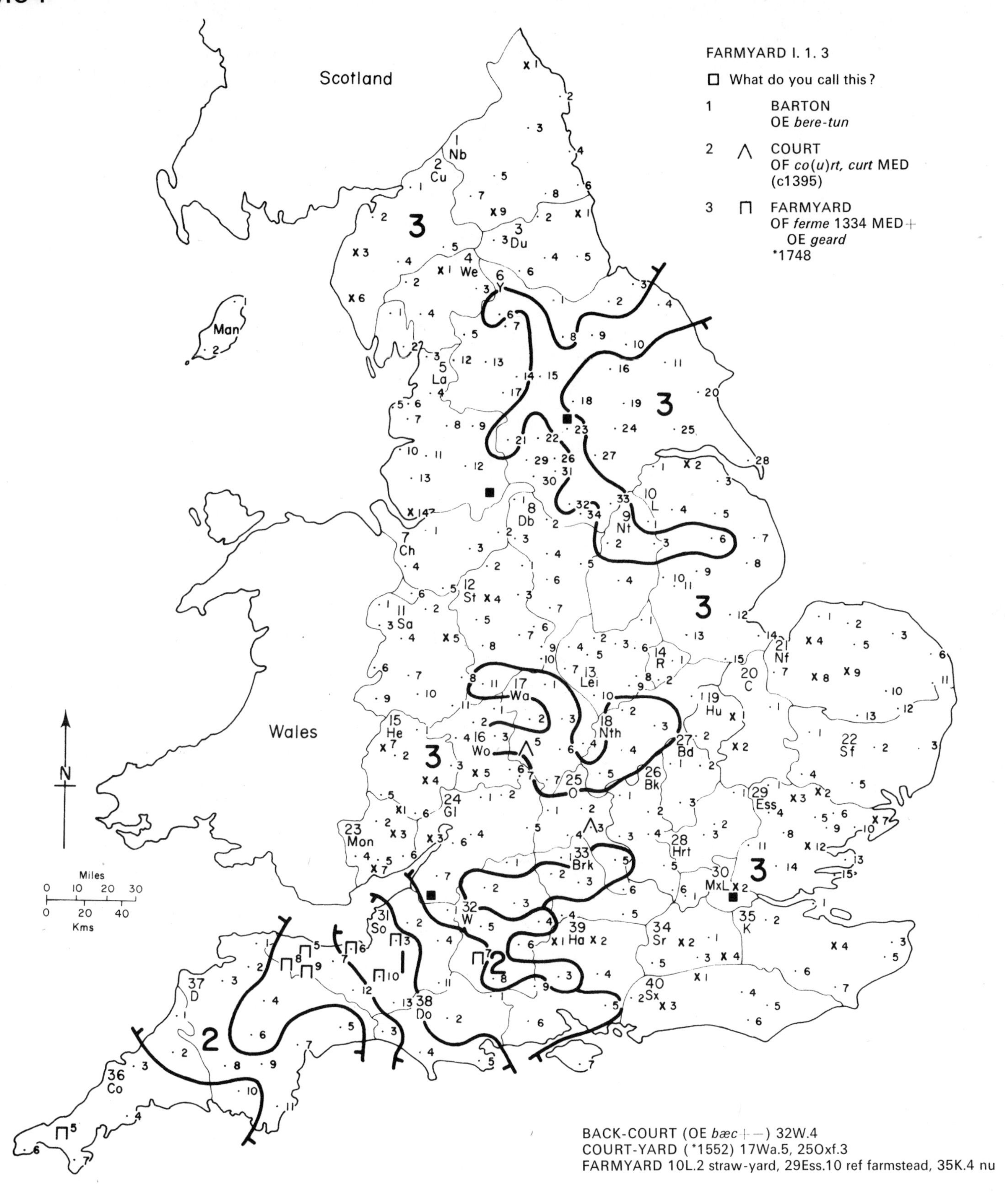

BACK-COURT (OE *bæc* + —) 32W.4
COURT-YARD (*1552) 17Wa.5, 25Oxf.3
FARMYARD 10L.2 straw-yard, 29Ess.10 ref farmstead, 35K.4 nu

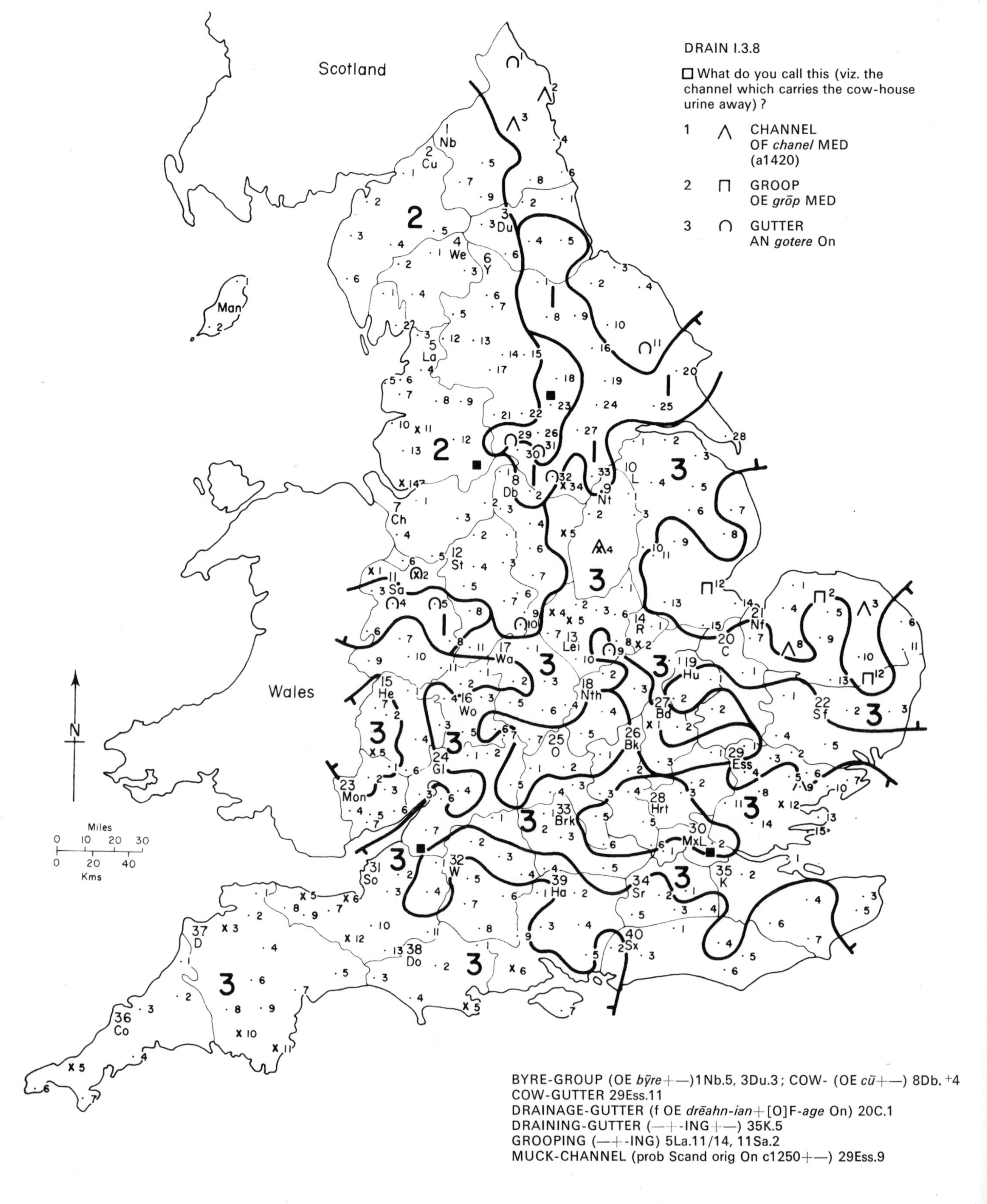

BYRE-GROUP (OE *bȳre*+—)1Nb.5, 3Du.3; COW- (OE *cū*+—) 8Db. +4
COW-GUTTER 29Ess.11
DRAINAGE-GUTTER (f OE *drēahn-ian*+[O]F-*age* On) 20C.1
DRAINING-GUTTER (—+-ING+—) 35K.5
GROOPING (—+-ING) 5La.11/14, 11Sa.2
MUCK-CHANNEL (prob Scand orig On c1250+—) 29Ess.9

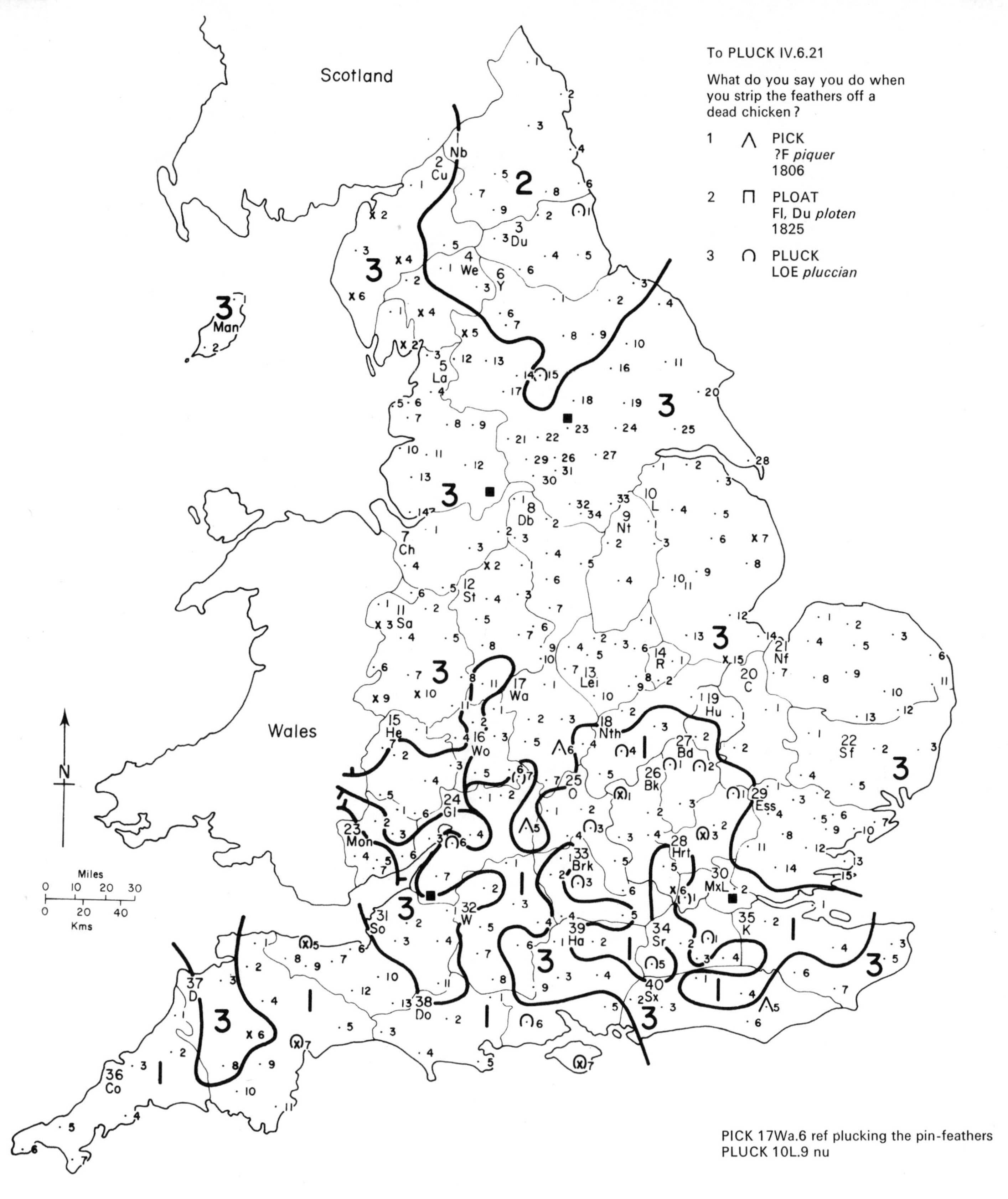

To PLUCK IV.6.21
What do you say you do when you strip the feathers off a dead chicken?
1 Λ PICK ?F *piquer* 1806
2 ⊓ PLOAT Fl, Du *ploten* 1825
3 ∩ PLUCK LOE *pluccian*
Scotland
Wales
Miles 0 10 20 30
Kms 0 20 40
N
PICK 17Wa.6 ref plucking the pin-feathers
PLUCK 10L.9 nu

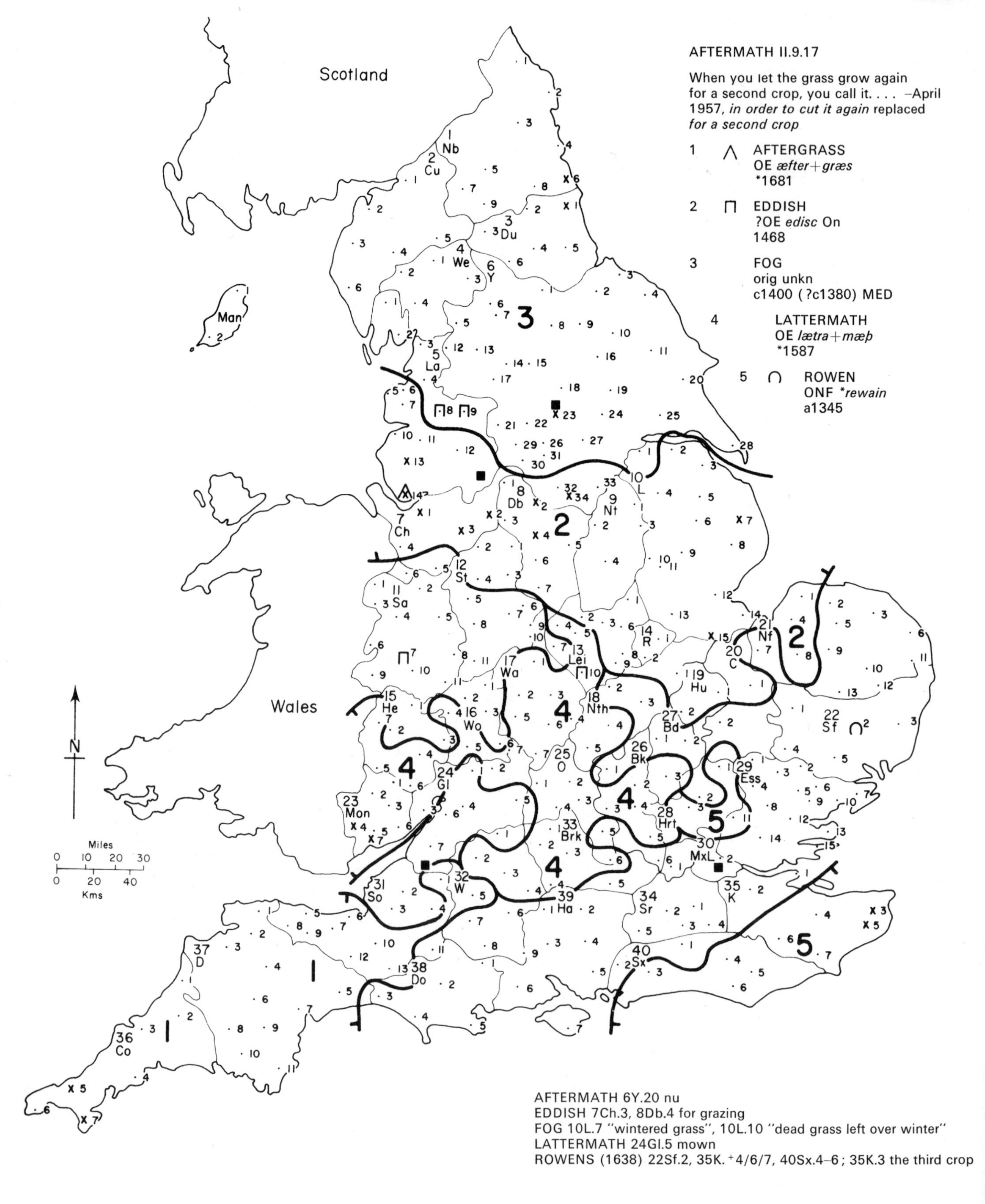
AFTERMATH II.9.17
When you let the grass grow again for a second crop, you call it. . . . –April 1957, *in order to cut it again* replaced *for a second crop*
1 ∧ AFTERGRASS
OE *æfter+græs*
*1681
2 ⊓ EDDISH
?OE *edisc* On
1468
3 FOG
orig unkn
c1400 (?c1380) MED
4 LATTERMATH
OE *lætra+mæþ*
*1587
5 ∩ ROWEN
ONF **rewain*
a1345
Scotland
Wales
Man
Miles
0 10 20 30
0 20 40
Kms
N
AFTERMATH 6Y.20 nu
EDDISH 7Ch.3, 8Db.4 for grazing
FOG 10L.7 "wintered grass", 10L.10 "dead grass left over winter"
LATTERMATH 24Gl.5 mown
ROWENS (1638) 22Sf.2, 35K.+4/6/7, 40Sx.4–6; 35K.3 the third crop

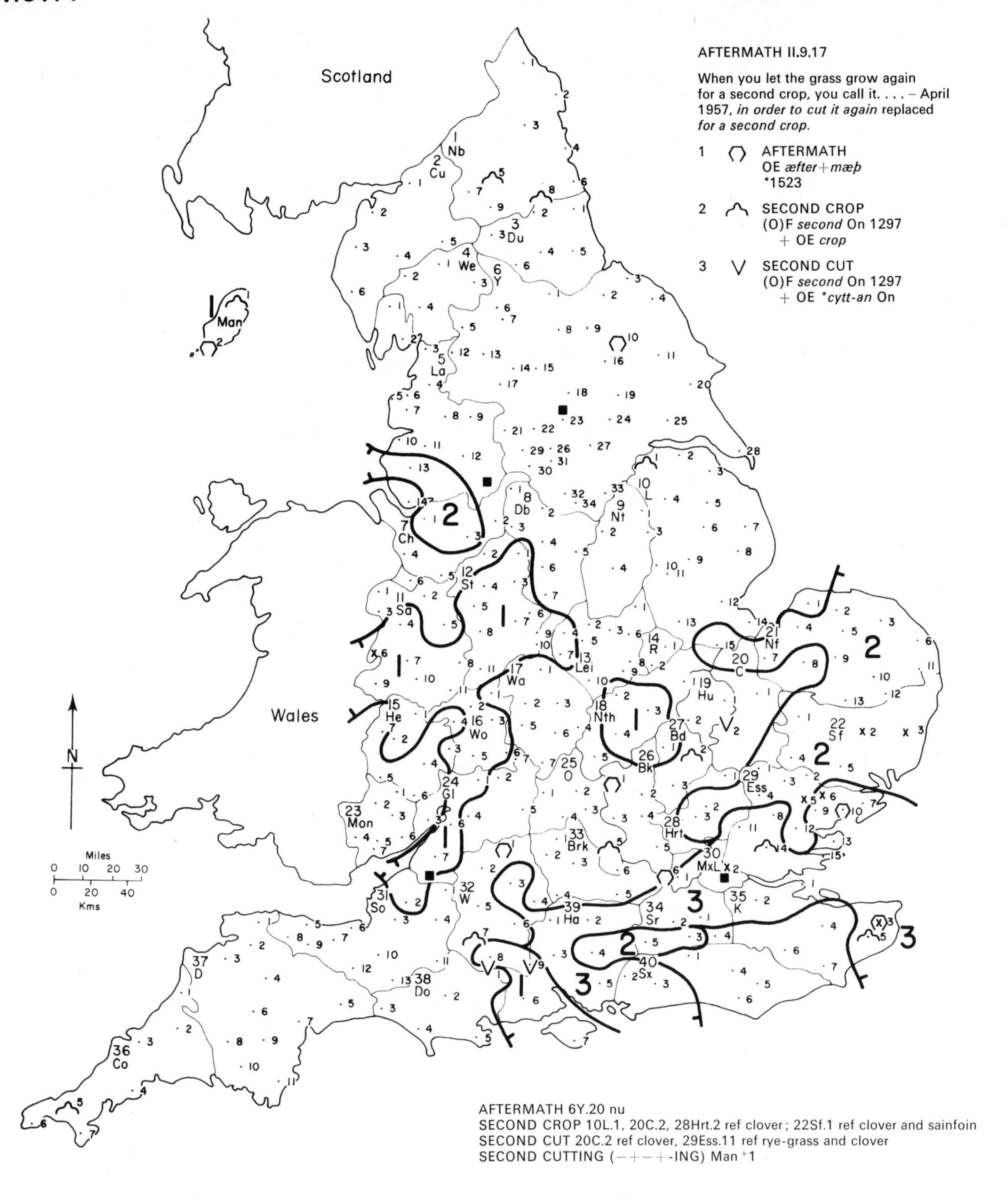
AFTERMATH II.9.17
When you let the grass grow again for a second crop, you call it. . . . – April 1957, *in order to cut it again* replaced *for a second crop.*
1 AFTERMATH
OE *æfter*+*mæþ*
*1523
2 SECOND CROP
(O)F *second* On 1297
+ OE *crop*
3 V SECOND CUT
(O)F *second* On 1297
+ OE **cytt-an* On
Scotland
Wales
Man
Miles
0 10 20 30
0 20 40
Kms
N
AFTERMATH 6Y.20 nu
SECOND CROP 10L.1, 20C.2, 28Hrt.2 ref clover; 22Sf.1 ref clover and sainfoin
SECOND CUT 20C.2 ref clover, 29Ess.11 ref rye-grass and clover
SECOND CUTTING (—+—+-ING) Man [+]1

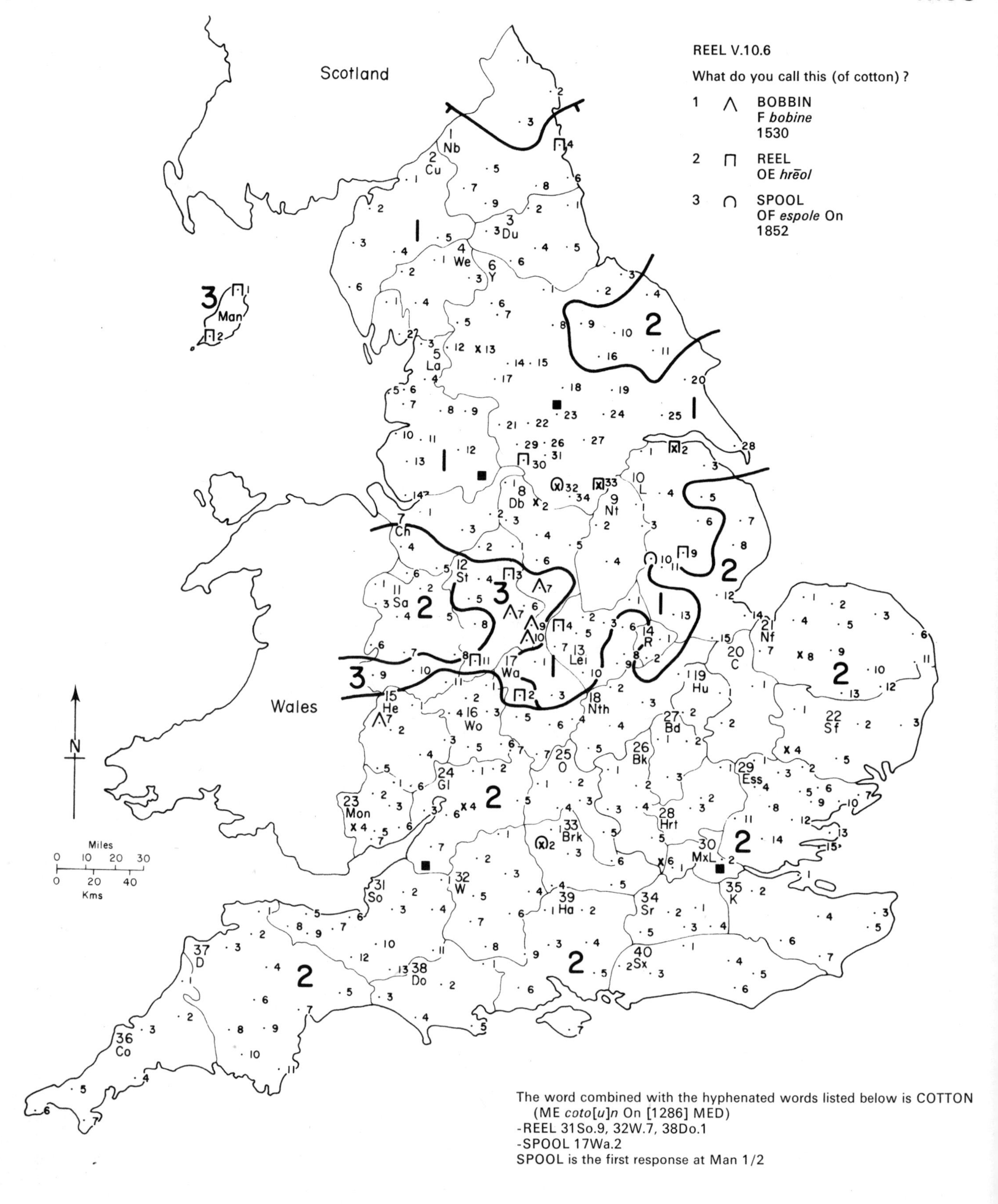

The word combined with the hyphenated words listed below is COTTON (ME *coto[u]n* On [1286] MED)
-REEL 31So.9, 32W.7, 38Do.1
-SPOOL 17Wa.2
SPOOL is the first response at Man 1/2

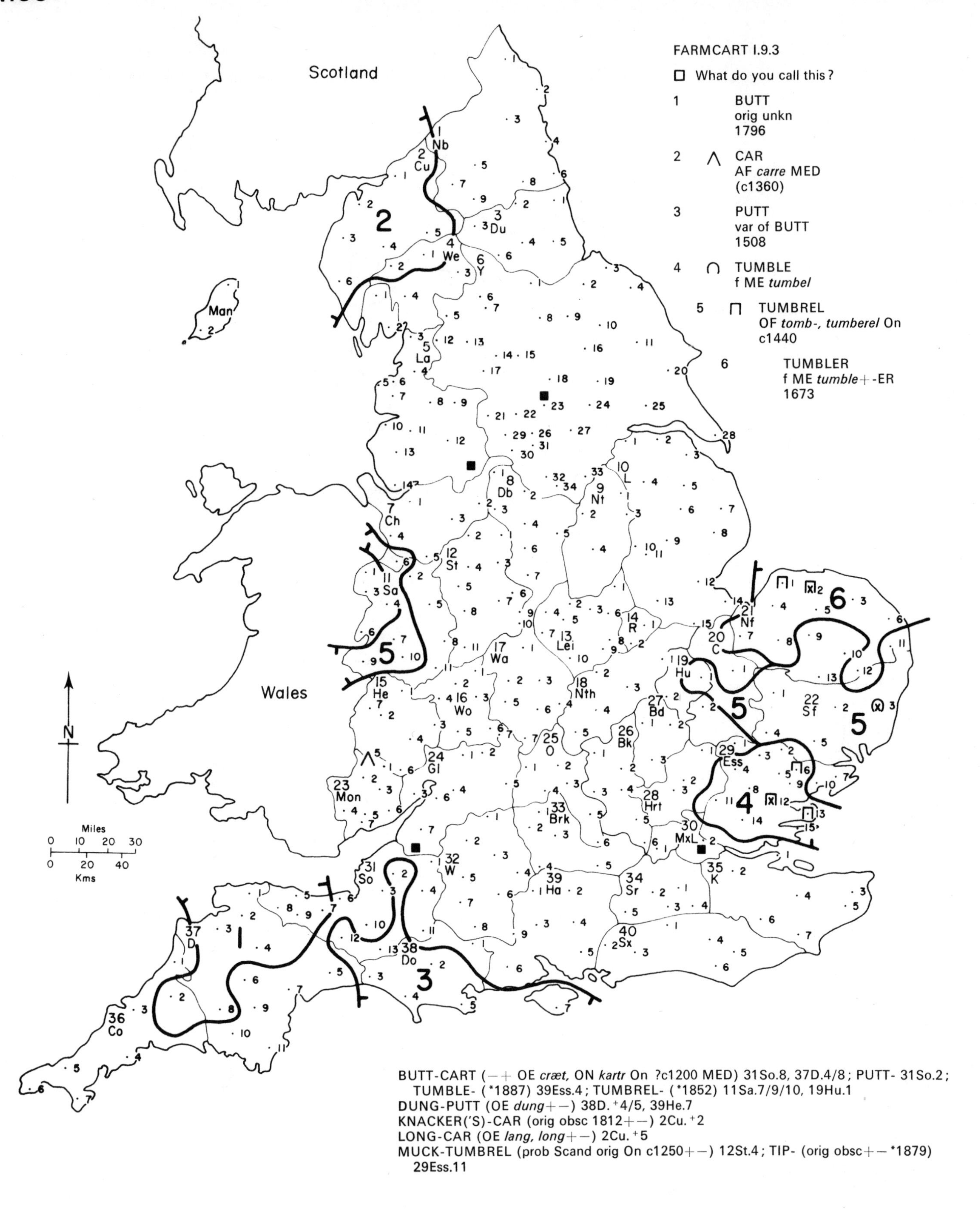

BUTT-CART (—+ OE *cræt*, ON *kartr* On ?c1200 MED) 31So.8, 37D.4/8; PUTT- 31So.2; TUMBLE- (*1887) 39Ess.4; TUMBREL- (*1852) 11Sa.7/9/10, 19Hu.1
DUNG-PUTT (OE *dung*+—) 38D.+4/5, 39He.7
KNACKER('S)-CAR (orig obsc 1812+—) 2Cu.+2
LONG-CAR (OE *lang, long*+—) 2Cu.+5
MUCK-TUMBREL (prob Scand orig On c1250+—) 12St.4; TIP- (orig obsc+—*1879) 29Ess.11

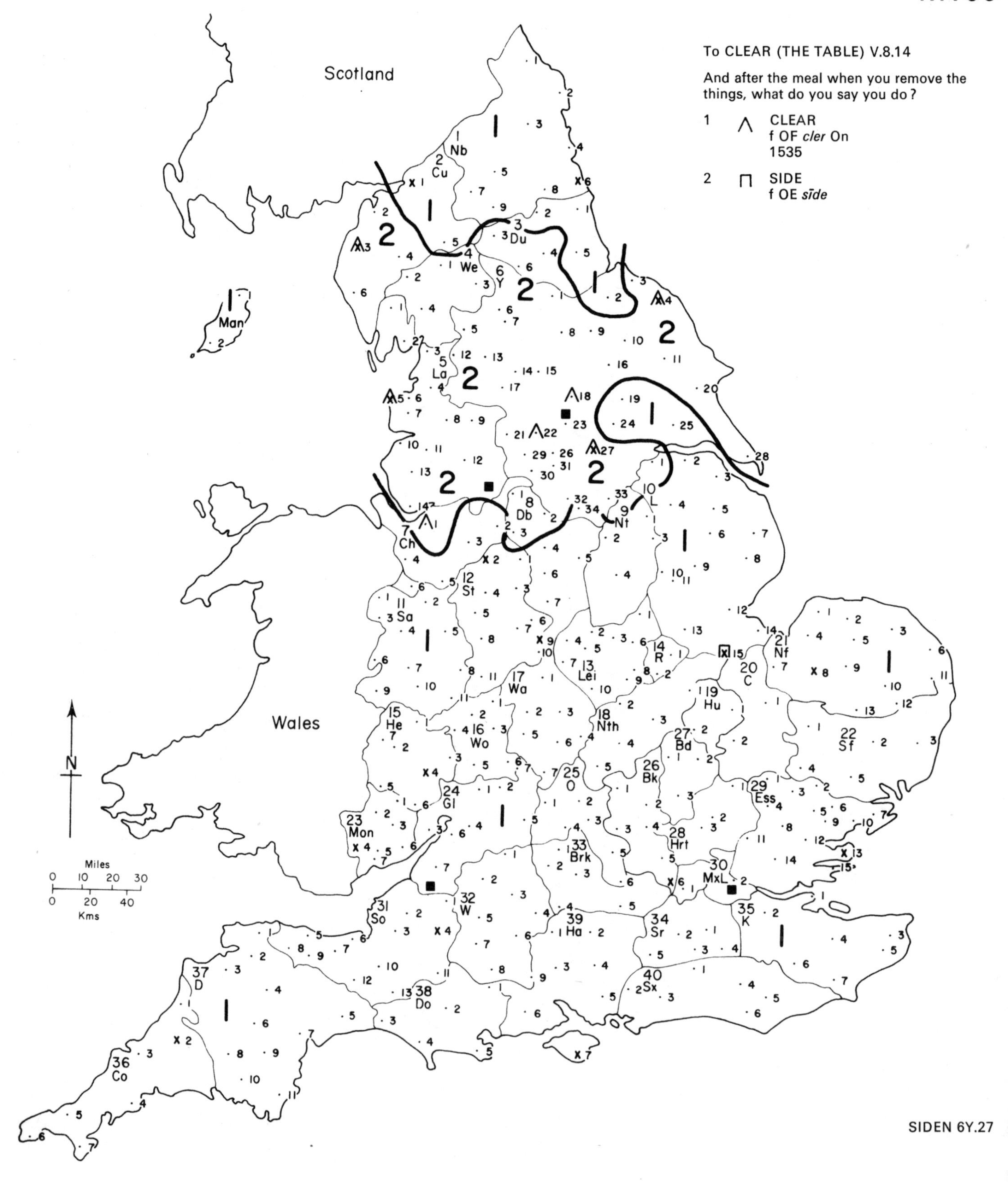
To CLEAR (THE TABLE) V.8.14
And after the meal when you remove the things, what do you say you do?
1 Λ CLEAR
f OF *cler* On
1535
2 ⊓ SIDE
f OE *sīde*
Scotland
Wales
Man
N
Miles
0 10 20 30
0 20 40
Kms
SIDEN 6Y.27

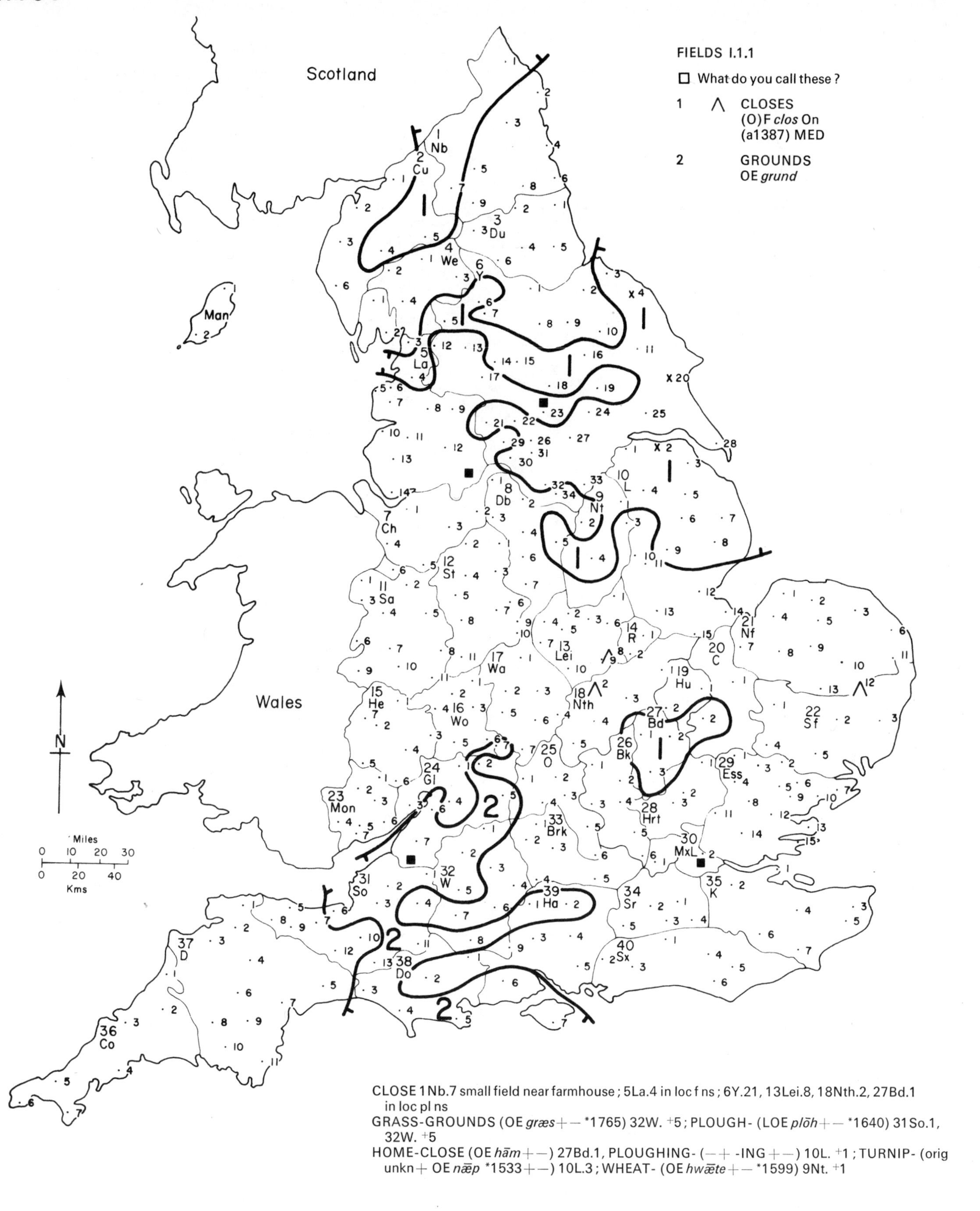

CLOSE 1Nb.7 small field near farmhouse; 5La.4 in loc f ns; 6Y.21, 13Lei.8, 18Nth.2, 27Bd.1 in loc pl ns

GRASS-GROUNDS (OE *græs*+— *1765) 32W. +5; PLOUGH- (LOE *plōh*+— *1640) 31So.1, 32W. +5

HOME-CLOSE (OE *hām*+—) 27Bd.1, PLOUGHING- (—+ -ING+—) 10L. +1; TURNIP- (orig unkn+ OE *nǣp* *1533+—) 10L.3; WHEAT- (OE *hwǣte*+— *1599) 9Nt. +1

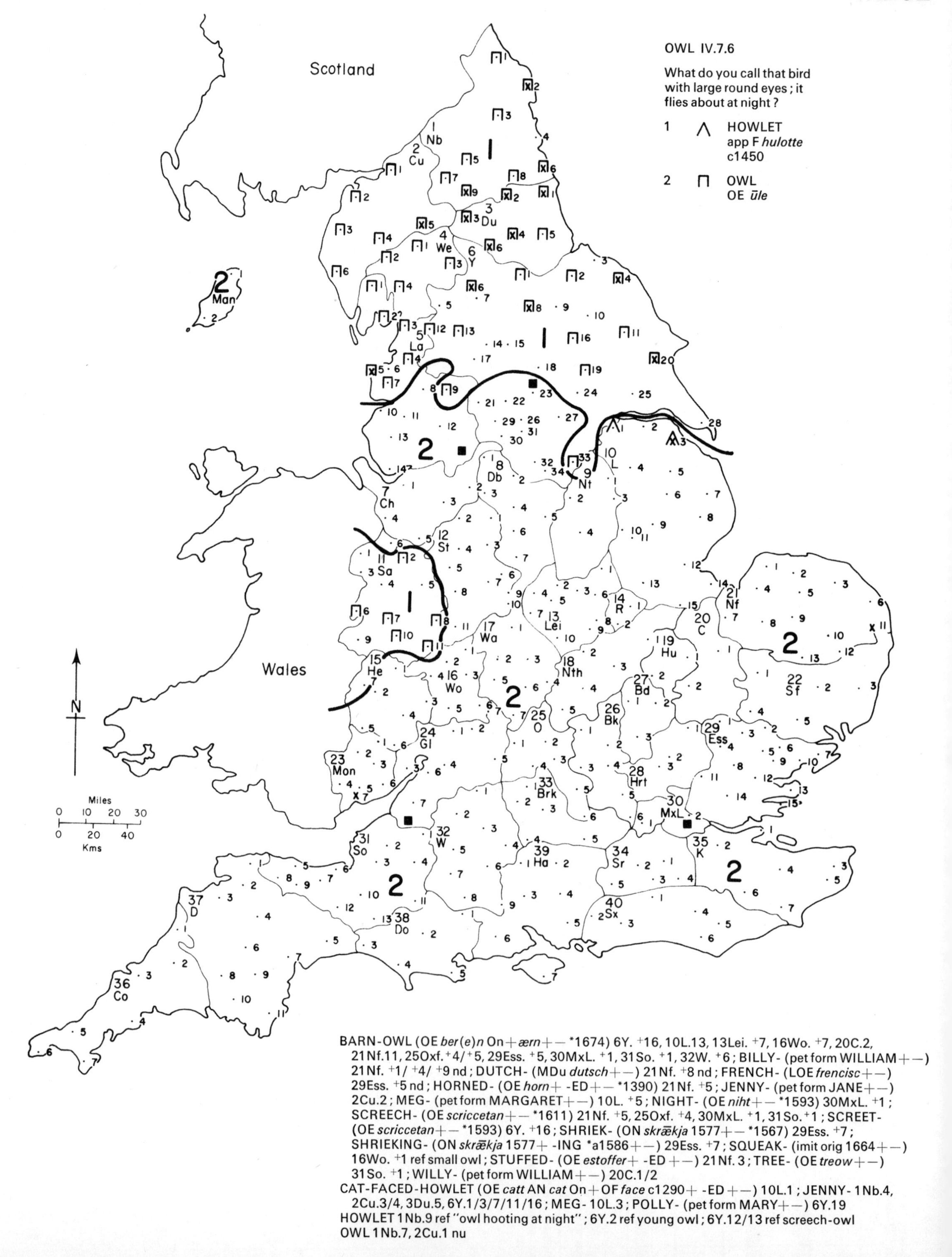

BARN-OWL (OE *ber(e)n* On+*ærn*+— *1674) 6Y. +16, 10L.13, 13Lei. +7, 16Wo. +7, 20C.2, 21Nf.11, 25Oxf. +4/+5, 29Ess. +5, 30MxL. +1, 31So. +1, 32W. +6; BILLY- (pet form WILLIAM+—) 21Nf. +1/ +4/ +9 nd; DUTCH- (MDu *dutsch*+—) 21Nf. +8 nd; FRENCH- (LOE *frencisc*+—) 29Ess. +5 nd; HORNED- (OE *horn*+ -ED+— *1390) 21Nf. +5; JENNY- (pet form JANE+—) 2Cu.2; MEG- (pet form MARGARET+—) 10L. +5; NIGHT- (OE *niht*+— *1593) 30MxL. +1; SCREECH- (OE *scriccetan*+— *1611) 21Nf. +5, 25Oxf. +4, 30MxL. +1, 31So. +1; SCREET- (OE *scriccetan*+— *1593) 6Y. +16; SHRIEK- (ON *skrǣkja* 1577+— *1567) 29Ess. +7; SHRIEKING- (ON *skrǣkja* 1577+ -ING *a1586+—) 29Ess. +7; SQUEAK- (imit orig 1664+—) 16Wo. +1 ref small owl; STUFFED- (OE *estoffer*+ -ED+—) 21Nf. 3; TREE- (OE *treow*+—) 31So. +1; WILLY- (pet form WILLIAM+—) 20C.1/2

CAT-FACED-HOWLET (OE *catt* AN *cat* On+OF *face* c1290+ -ED+—) 10L.1; JENNY- 1Nb.4, 2Cu.3/4, 3Du.5, 6Y.1/3/7/11/16; MEG- 10L.3; POLLY- (pet form MARY+—) 6Y.19

HOWLET 1Nb.9 ref "owl hooting at night"; 6Y.2 ref young owl; 6Y.12/13 ref screech-owl

OWL 1Nb.7, 2Cu.1 nu

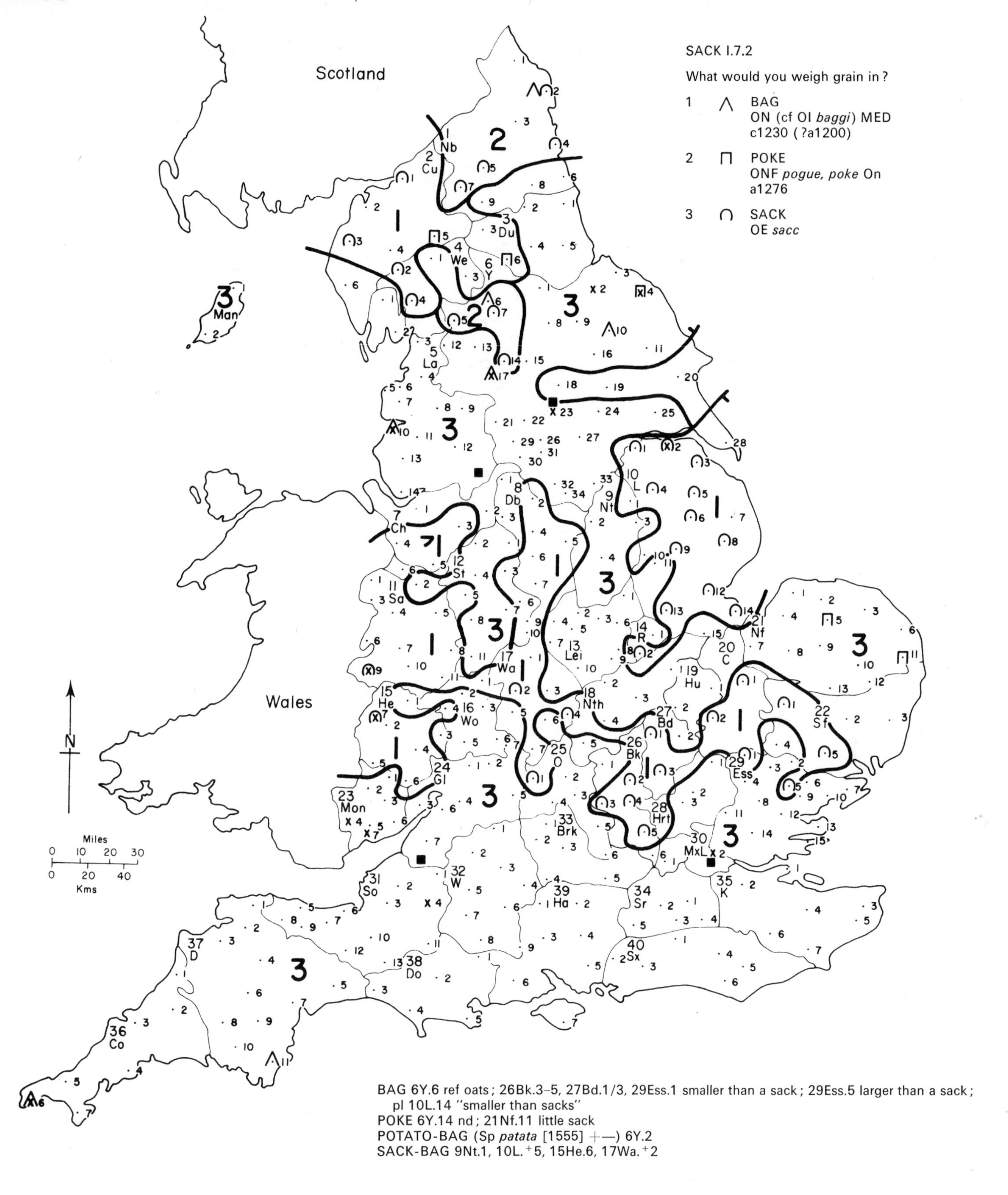

BAG 6Y.6 ref oats; 26Bk.3–5, 27Bd.1/3, 29Ess.1 smaller than a sack; 29Ess.5 larger than a sack; pl 10L.14 "smaller than sacks"
POKE 6Y.14 nd; 21Nf.11 little sack
POTATO-BAG (Sp *patata* [1555] +—) 6Y.2
SACK-BAG 9Nt.1, 10L.+5, 15He.6, 17Wa.+2

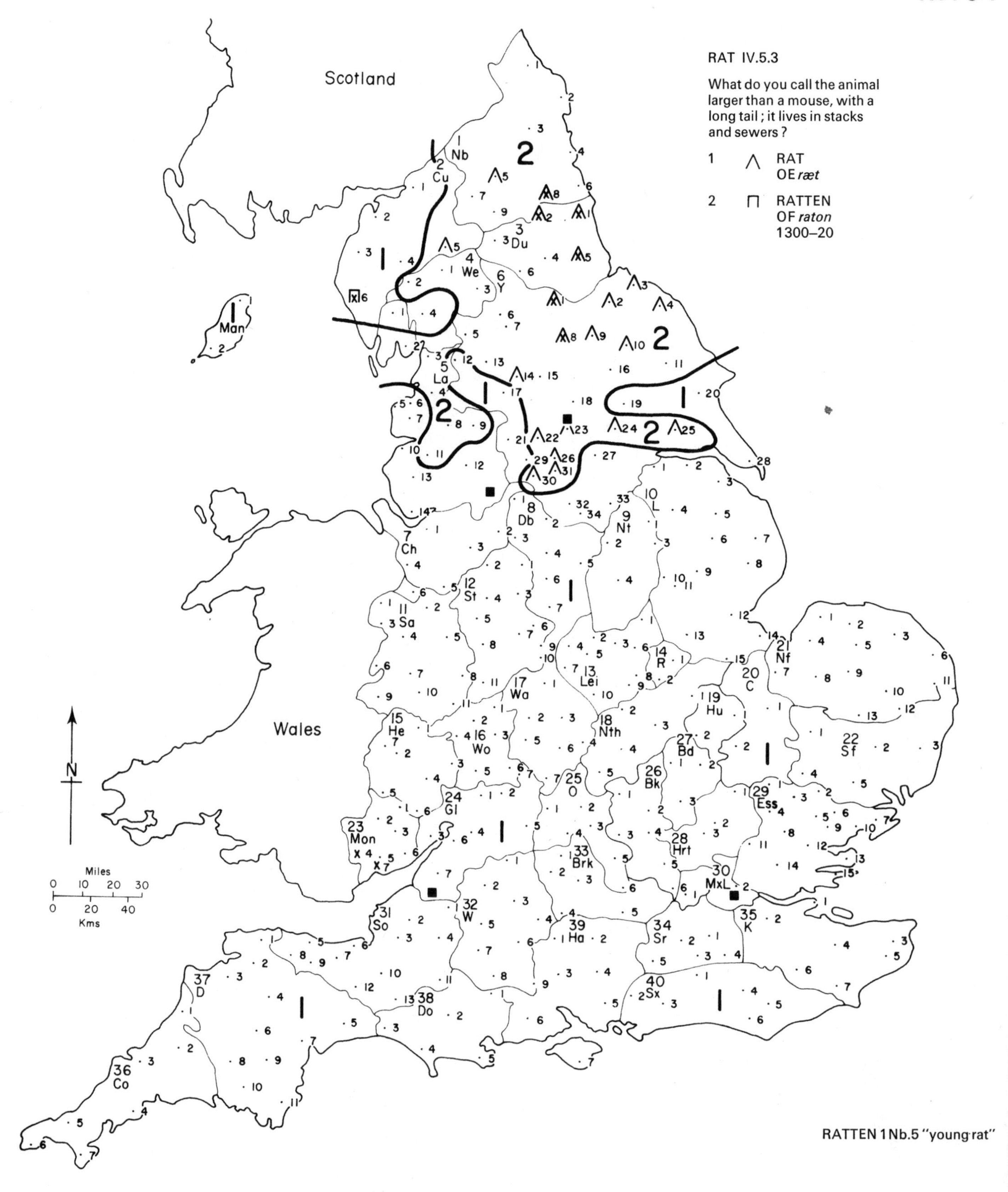

RATTEN 1 Nb.5 "young rat"

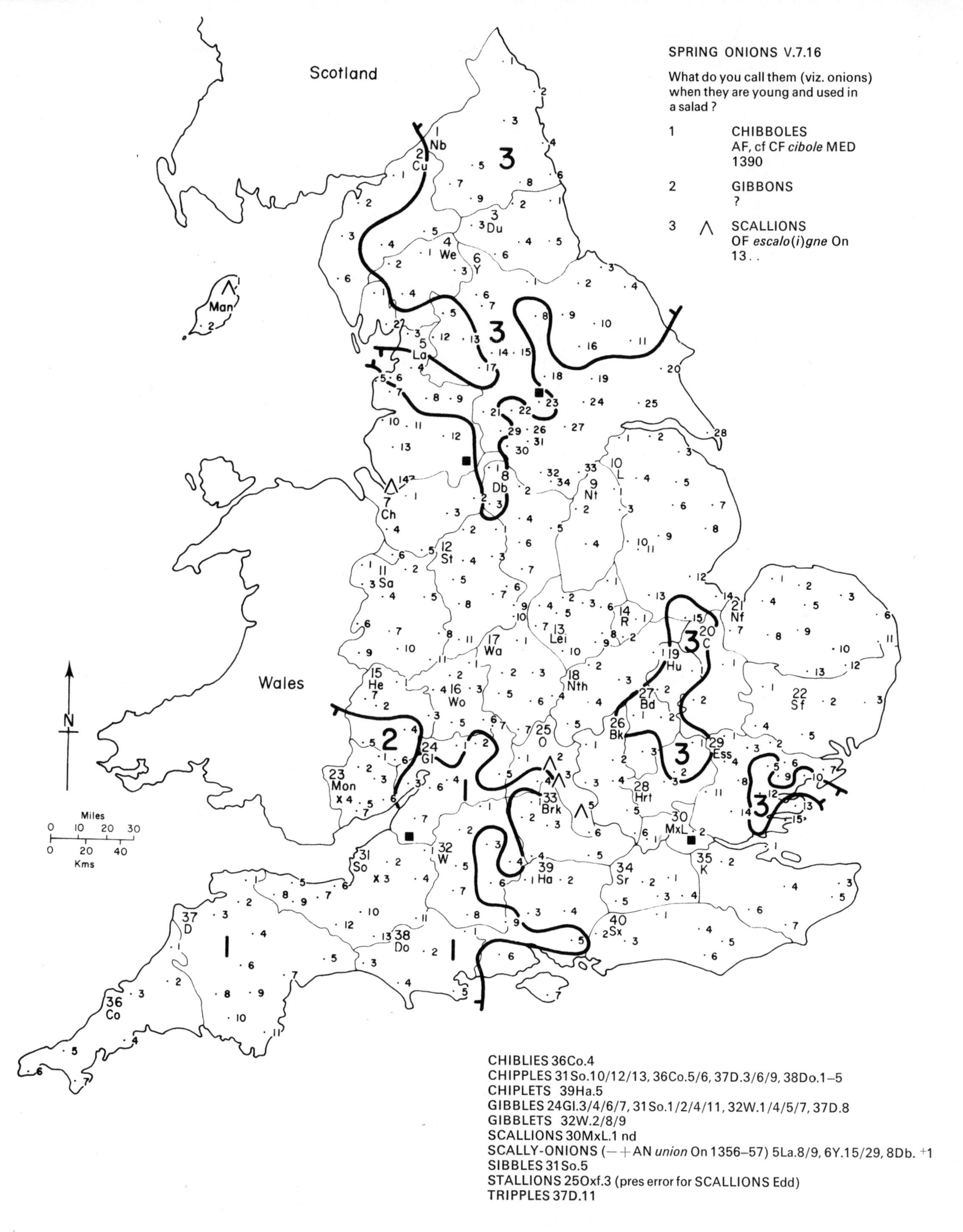

SPRING ONIONS V.7.16
What do you call them (viz. onions) when they are young and used in a salad ?
1 CHIBBOLES AF, cf CF *cibole* MED 1390
2 GIBBONS ?
3 ⋀ SCALLIONS OF *escalo(i)gne* On 13. .
Scotland
Wales
Man
Miles 0 10 20 30
0 20 40 Kms
N
CHIBLIES 36Co.4
CHIPPLES 31So.10/12/13, 36Co.5/6, 37D.3/6/9, 38Do.1–5
CHIPLETS 39Ha.5
GIBBLES 24Gl.3/4/6/7, 31So.1/2/4/11, 32W.1/4/5/7, 37D.8
GIBBLETS 32W.2/8/9
SCALLIONS 30MxL.1 nd
SCALLY-ONIONS (— + AN *union* On 1356–57) 5La.8/9, 6Y.15/29, 8Db. +1
SIBBLES 31So.5
STALLIONS 25Oxf.3 (pres error for SCALLIONS Edd)
TRIPPLES 37D.11

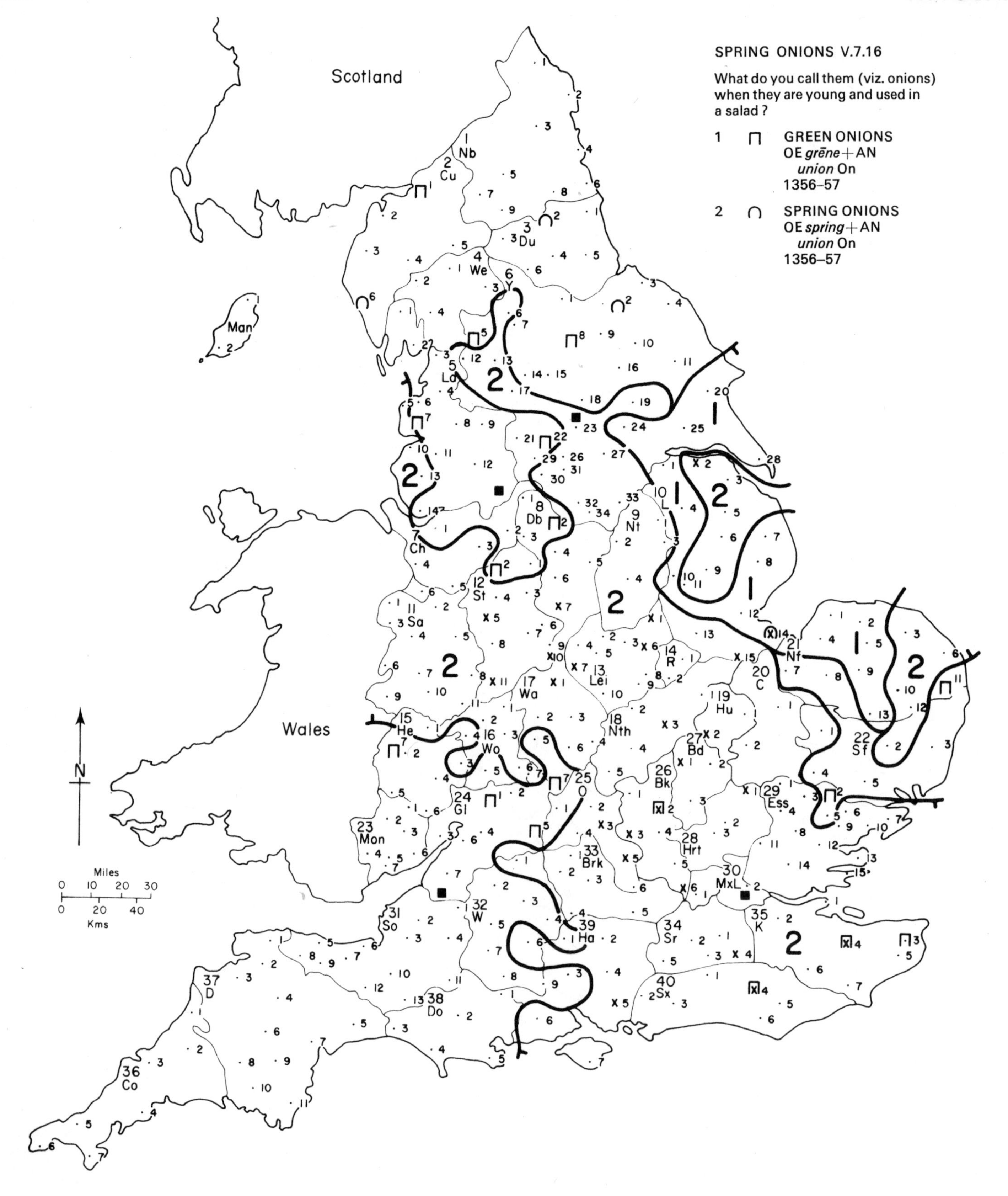
SPRING ONIONS V.7.16
What do you call them (viz. onions) when they are young and used in a salad ?
1 ⊓ GREEN ONIONS
OE grēne + AN union On 1356–57
2 ∩ SPRING ONIONS
OE spring + AN union On 1356–57
Scotland
Wales
Man
Nb
Cu
Du
We
Y
La
Ch
Db
Nt
L
St
Sa
R
Lei
Nf
Wa
Hu
C
He
Wo
Nth
Sf
Bd
Gl
O
Bk
Ess
Mon
Hrt
Brk
MxL
So
W
Ha
Sr
K
D
Do
Sx
Co
N
Miles
0 10 20 30
0 20 40
Kms

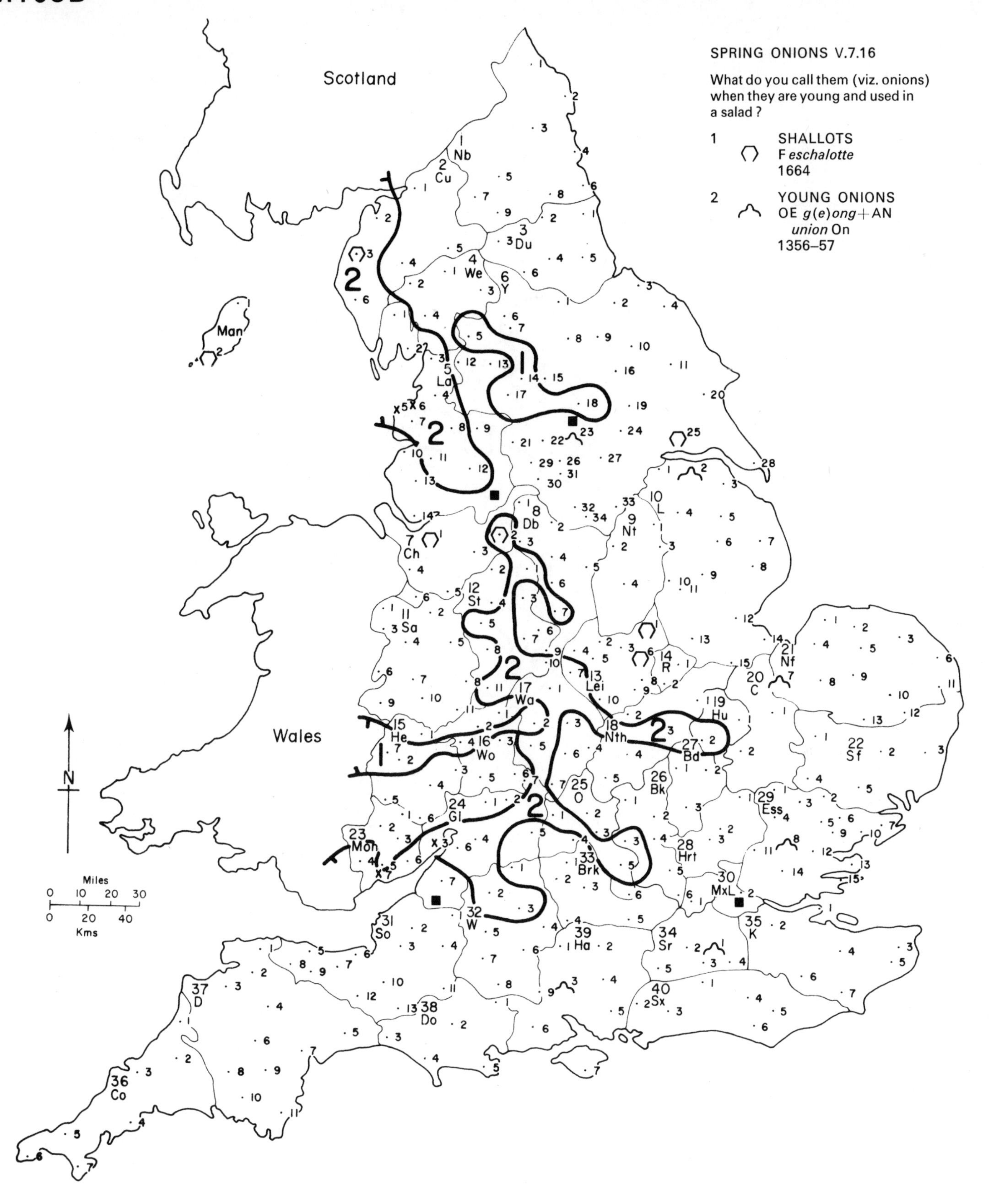

SPRING ONIONS V.7.16

What do you call them (viz. onions) when they are young and used in a salad?

1 SHALLOTS
F *eschalotte*
1664

2 YOUNG ONIONS
OE *g(e)ong* + AN *union* On
1356–57

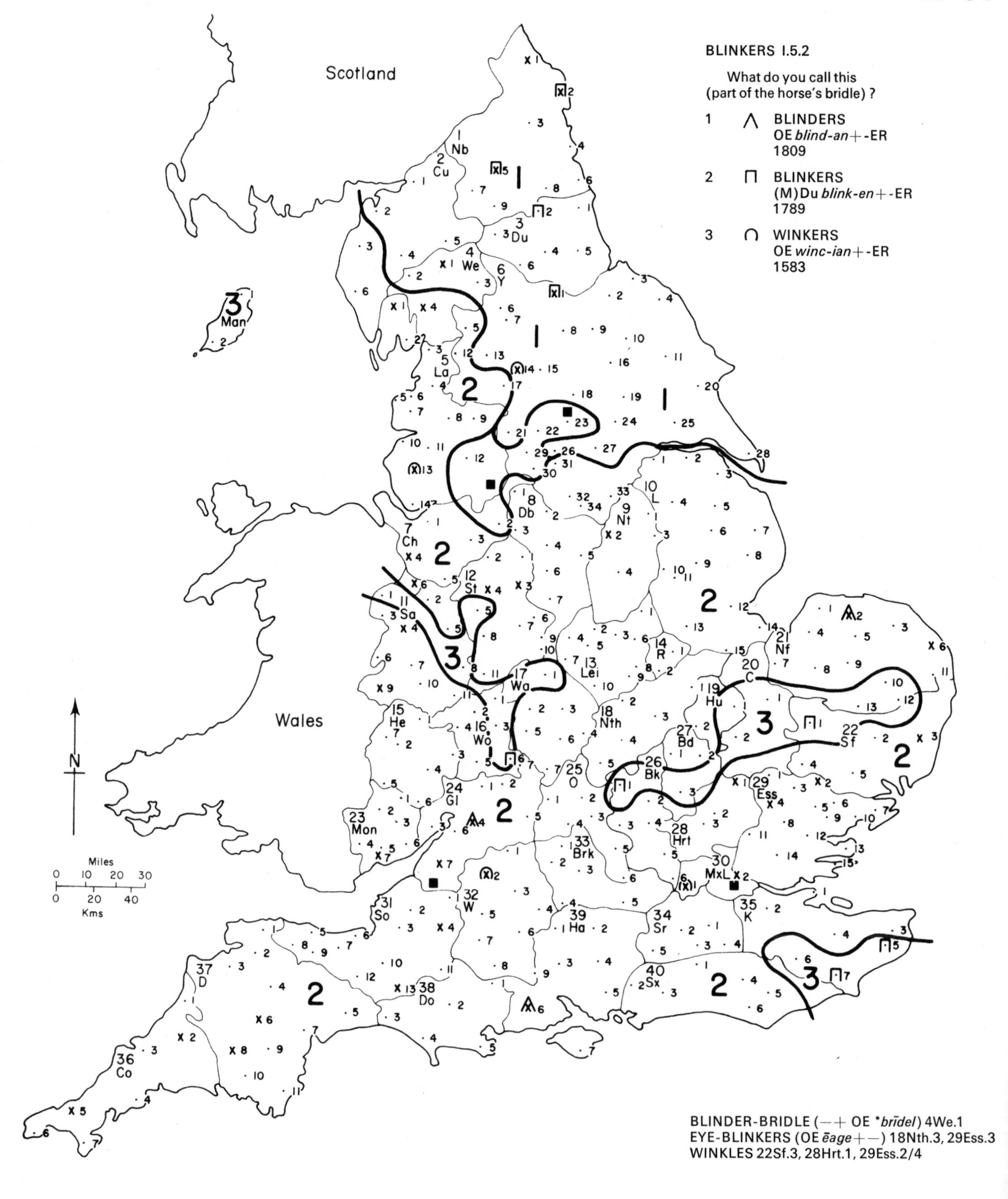
BLINKERS I.5.2
What do you call this
(part of the horse's bridle) ?
1 Λ BLINDERS
OE *blind-an*+-ER
1809
2 ⊓ BLINKERS
(M)Du *blink-en*+-ER
1789
3 ∩ WINKERS
OE *winc-ian*+-ER
1583
Scotland
Wales
Man
N
Miles
0 10 20 30
0 20 40
Kms
BLINDER-BRIDLE (—+ OE **brīdel*) 4We.1
EYE-BLINKERS (OE *ēage*+—) 18Nth.3, 29Ess.3
WINKLES 22Sf.3, 28Hrt.1, 29Ess.2/4

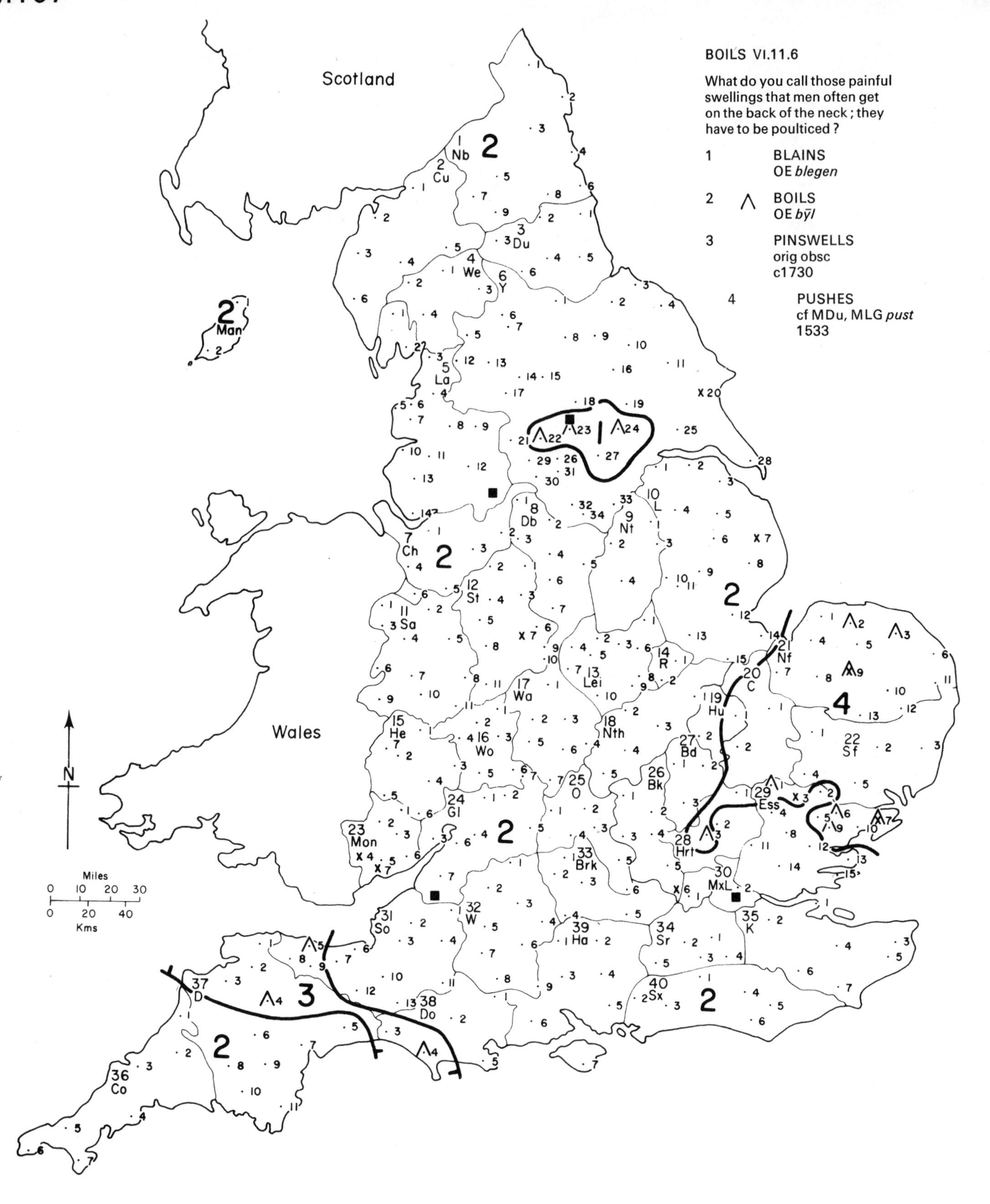
BOILS VI.11.6
What do you call those painful swellings that men often get on the back of the neck; they have to be poulticed?
1 BLAINS
OE *blegen*
2 ʌ BOILS
OE *bȳl*
3 PINSWELLS
orig obsc
c1730
4 PUSHES
cf MDu, MLG *pust*
1533
Scotland
Wales
Man
N
Miles
0 10 20 30
0 20 40
Kms
Nb
Cu
Du
We
Y
La
Ch
Db
Nt
L
St
Sa
Lei
R
Nf
C
Hu
Wa
He
Wo
Nth
Bd
Sf
Bk
O
Gl
Mon
Ess
Hrt
Brk
MxL
So
W
Ha
Sr
K
D
Do
Sx
Co

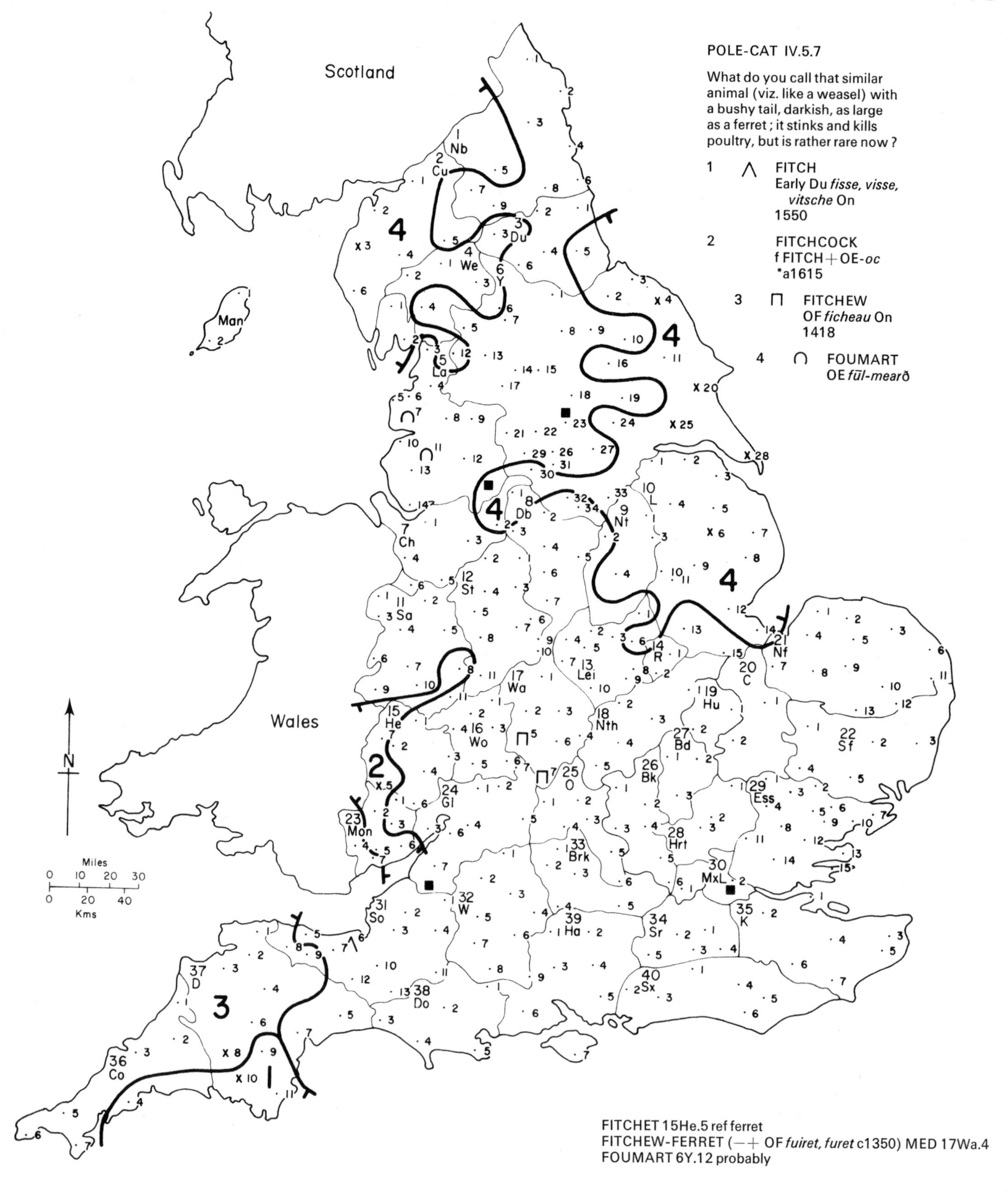
POLE-CAT IV.5.7
What do you call that similar animal (viz. like a weasel) with a bushy tail, darkish, as large as a ferret; it stinks and kills poultry, but is rather rare now?
1 FITCH
Early Du *fisse, visse, vitsche* On 1550
2 FITCHCOCK
f FITCH + OE-*oc* *a1615
3 FITCHEW
OF *ficheau* On 1418
4 FOUMART
OE *fūl-mearð*
Scotland
Wales
Man
N
Miles
0 10 20 30
0 20 40
Kms
FITCHET 15He.5 ref ferret
FITCHEW-FERRET (— + OF *fuiret, furet* c1350) MED 17Wa.4
FOUMART 6Y.12 probably

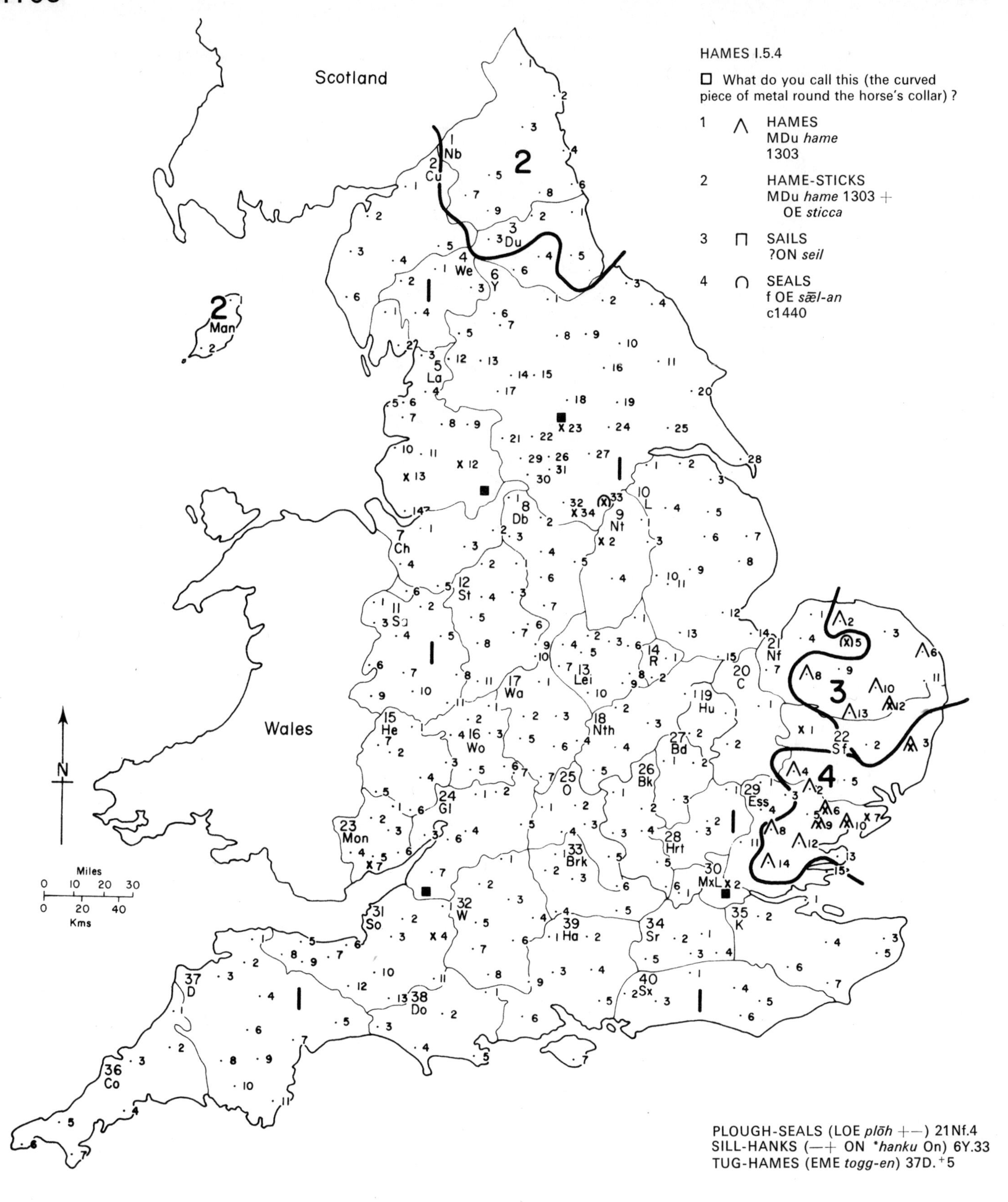
Scotland
Wales
HAMES I.5.4
□ What do you call this (the curved piece of metal round the horse's collar) ?
1 Λ HAMES
MDu *hame*
1303
2 HAME-STICKS
MDu *hame* 1303 +
OE *sticca*
3 ⊓ SAILS
?ON *seil*
4 ∩ SEALS
f OE *sǣl-an*
c1440
N
Miles
0 10 20 30
0 20 40
Kms
PLOUGH-SEALS (LOE *plōh* +—) 21Nf.4
SILL-HANKS (—+ ON **hanku* On) 6Y.33
TUG-HAMES (EME *togg-en*) 37D.+5

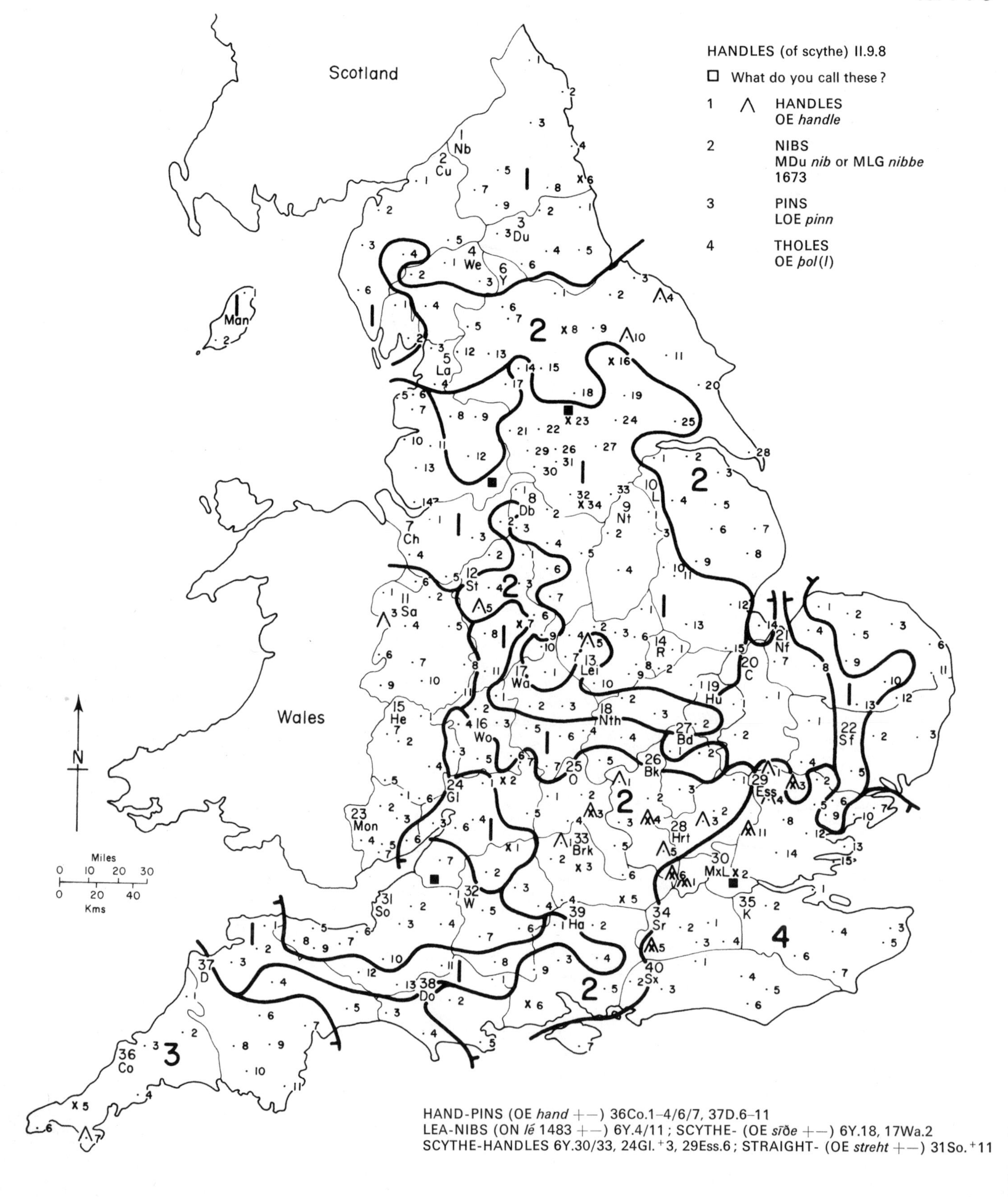
HANDLES (of scythe) II.9.8
☐ What do you call these?
1 Λ HANDLES
OE *handle*
2 NIBS
MDu *nib* or MLG *nibbe*
1673
3 PINS
LOE *pinn*
4 THOLES
OE *þol(l)*
Scotland
Wales
N
Miles
0 10 20 30
0 20 40
Kms
HAND-PINS (OE *hand* +—) 36Co.1–4/6/7, 37D.6–11
LEA-NIBS (ON *lé* 1483 +—) 6Y.4/11; SCYTHE- (OE *sīðe* +—) 6Y.18, 17Wa.2
SCYTHE-HANDLES 6Y.30/33, 24Gl.+3, 29Ess.6; STRAIGHT- (OE *streht* +—) 31So.+11

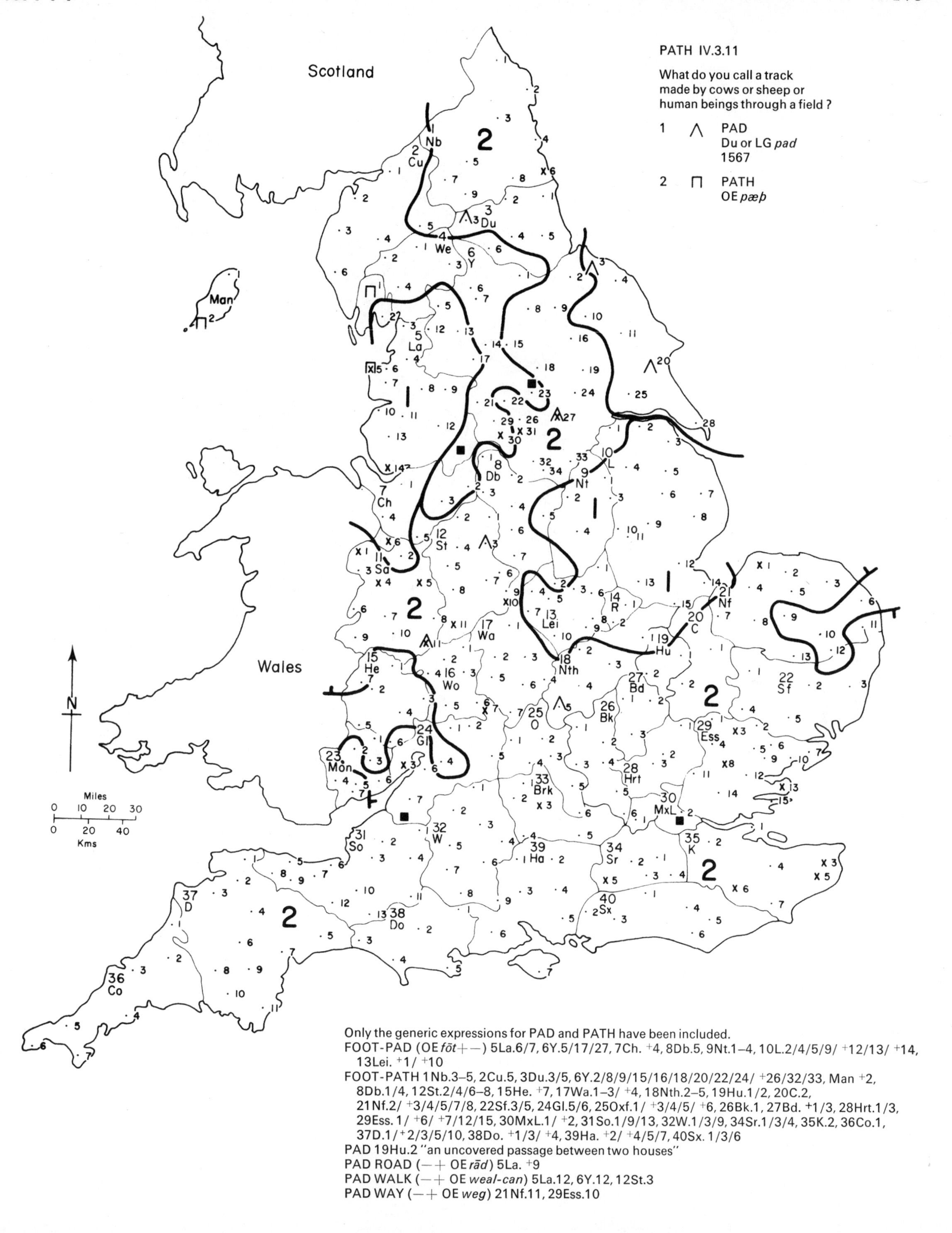

Only the generic expressions for PAD and PATH have been included.

FOOT-PAD (OE *fōt*+—) 5La.6/7, 6Y.5/17/27, 7Ch. +4, 8Db.5, 9Nt.1–4, 10L.2/4/5/9/ +12/13/ +14, 13Lei. +1/ +10

FOOT-PATH 1Nb.3–5, 2Cu.5, 3Du.3/5, 6Y.2/8/9/15/16/18/20/22/24/ +26/32/33, Man +2, 8Db.1/4, 12St.2/4/6–8, 15He. +7, 17Wa.1–3/ +4, 18Nth.2–5, 19Hu.1/2, 20C.2, 21Nf.2/ +3/4/5/7/8, 22Sf.3/5, 24Gl.5/6, 25Oxf.1/ +3/4/5/ +6, 26Bk.1, 27Bd. +1/3, 28Hrt.1/3, 29Ess.1/ +6/ +7/12/15, 30MxL.1/ +2, 31So.1/9/13, 32W.1/3/9, 34Sr.1/3/4, 35K.2, 36Co.1, 37D.1/+2/3/5/10, 38Do. +1/3/ +4, 39Ha. +2/ +4/5/7, 40Sx.1/3/6

PAD 19Hu.2 "an uncovered passage between two houses"

PAD ROAD (—+ OE *rād*) 5La. +9

PAD WALK (—+ OE *weal-can*) 5La.12, 6Y.12, 12St.3

PAD WAY (—+ OE *weg*) 21Nf.11, 29Ess.10

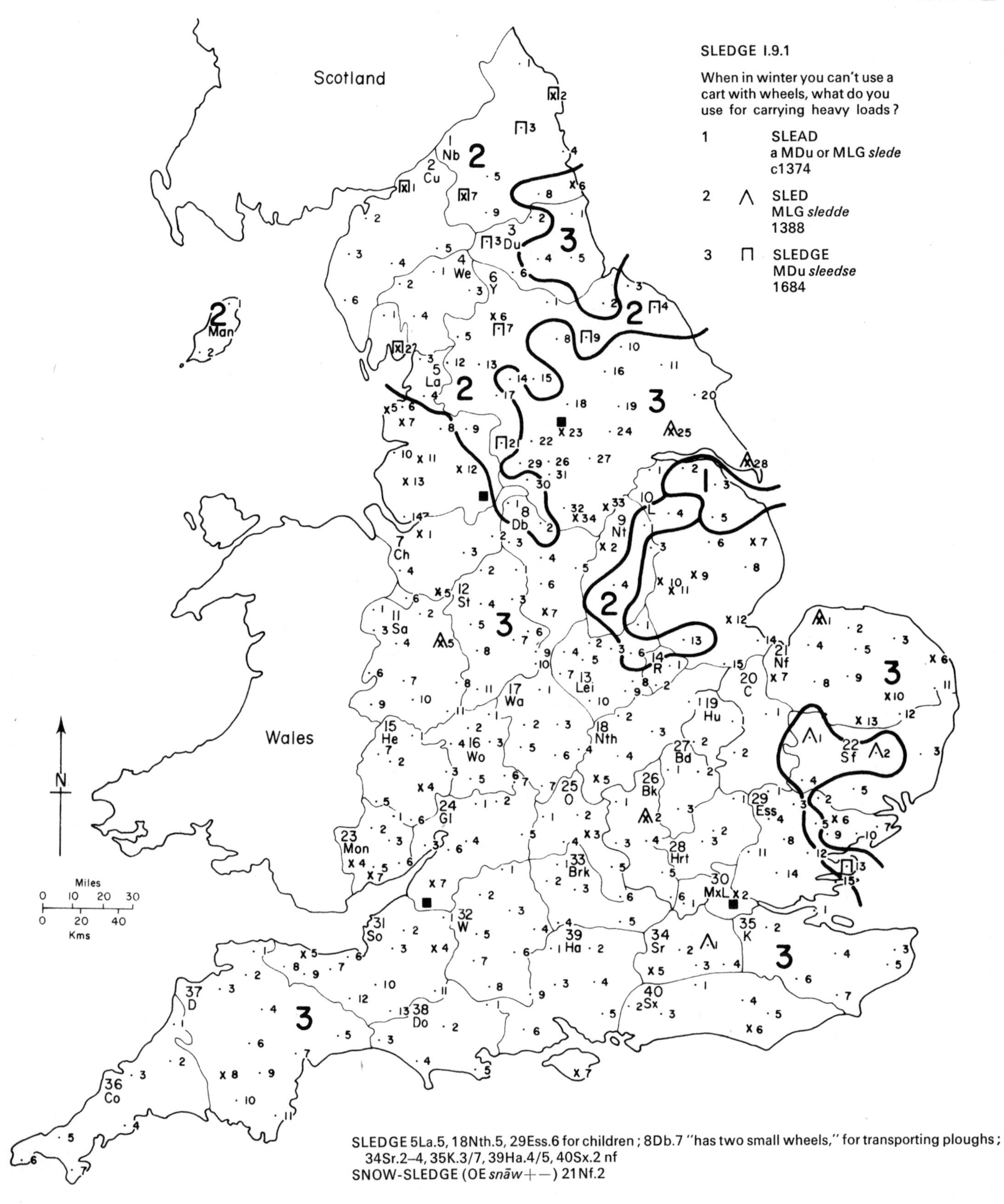

SLEDGE 5La.5, 18Nth.5, 29Ess.6 for children; 8Db.7 "has two small wheels," for transporting ploughs; 34Sr.2–4, 35K.3/7, 39Ha.4/5, 40Sx.2 nf
SNOW-SLEDGE (OE *snāw*+—) 21Nf.2

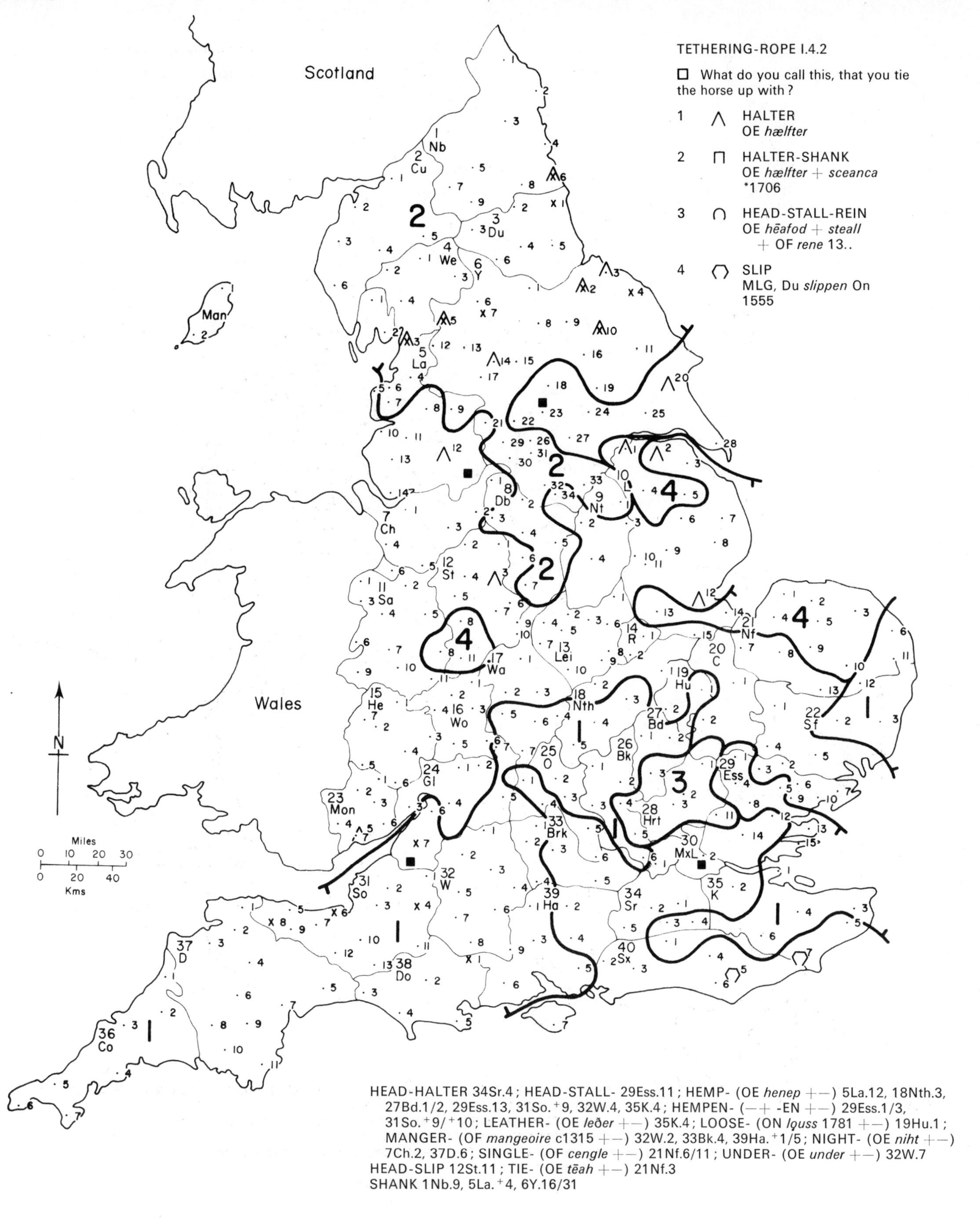

HEAD-HALTER 34Sr.4 ; HEAD-STALL- 29Ess.11 ; HEMP- (OE *henep* +—) 5La.12, 18Nth.3, 27Bd.1/2, 29Ess.13, 31So.$^{+}$9, 32W.4, 35K.4 ; HEMPEN- (—+ -EN +—) 29Ess.1/3, 31So.$^{+}$9/$^{+}$10 ; LEATHER- (OE *leðer* +—) 35K.4 ; LOOSE- (ON *lǫuss* 1781 +—) 19Hu.1 ; MANGER- (OF *mangeoire* c1315 +—) 32W.2, 33Bk.4, 39Ha.$^{+}$1/5 ; NIGHT- (OE *niht* +—) 7Ch.2, 37D.6 ; SINGLE- (OF *cengle* +—) 21Nf.6/11 ; UNDER- (OE *under* +—) 32W.7
HEAD-SLIP 12St.11 ; TIE- (OE *tēah* +—) 21Nf.3
SHANK 1Nb.9, 5La.$^{+}$4, 6Y.16/31

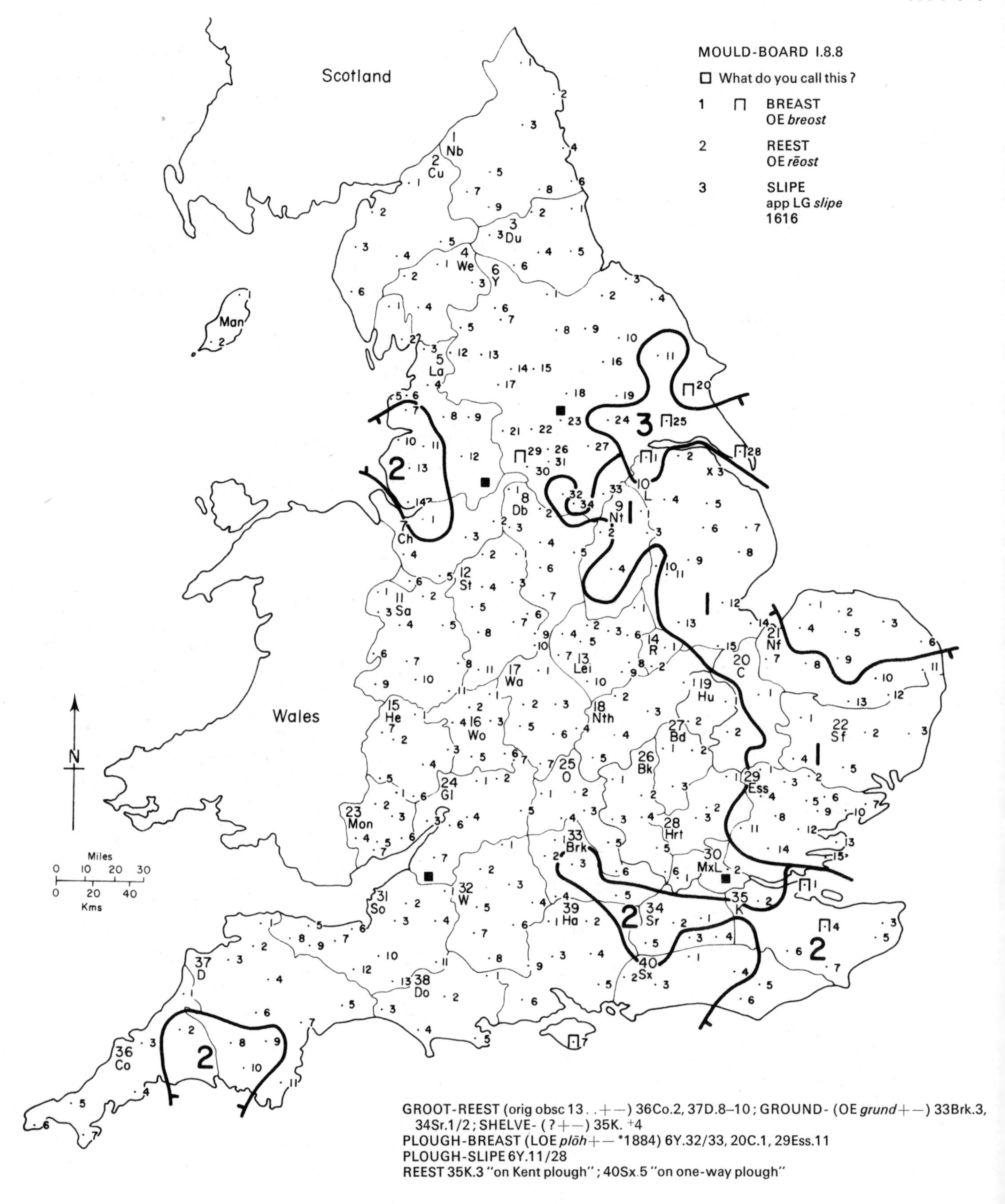
MOULD-BOARD I.8.8
What do you call this?
1 BREAST OE *breost*
2 REEST OE *rēost*
3 SLIPE app LG *slipe* 1616
Scotland
Wales
Man
N
Miles 0 10 20 30
0 20 40 Kms
GROOT-REEST (orig obsc 13 . . +—) 36Co.2, 37D.8–10; GROUND- (OE *grund*+—) 33Brk.3, 34Sr.1/2; SHELVE- (?+—) 35K. +4
PLOUGH-BREAST (LOE *plōh*+— *1884) 6Y.32/33, 20C.1, 29Ess.11
PLOUGH-SLIPE 6Y.11/28
REEST 35K.3 "on Kent plough"; 40Sx.5 "on one-way plough"

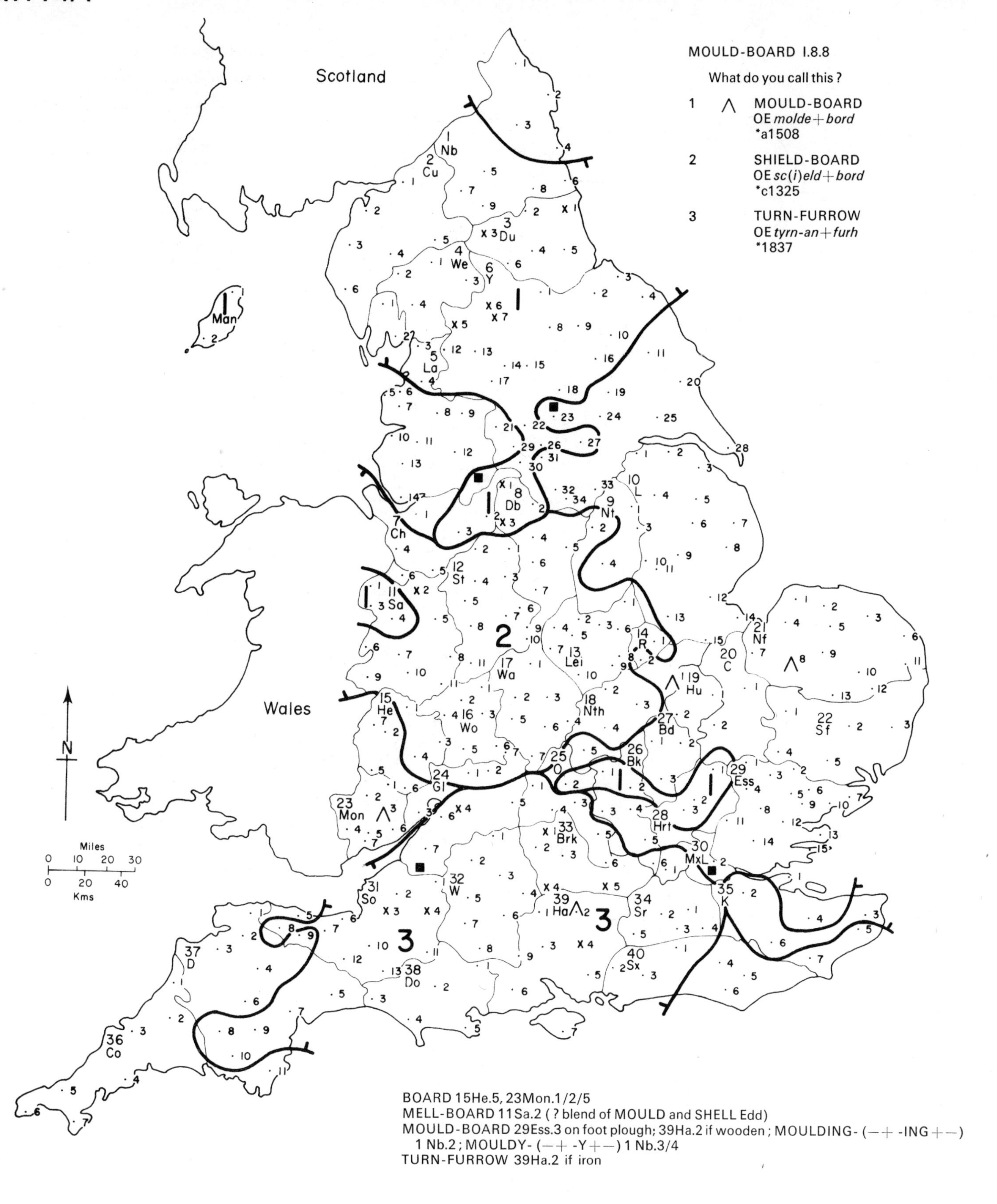

BOARD 15He.5, 23Mon.1/2/5
MELL-BOARD 11Sa.2 (? blend of MOULD and SHELL Edd)
MOULD-BOARD 29Ess.3 on foot plough; 39Ha.2 if wooden ; MOULDING- (—+ -ING+—) 1 Nb.2 ; MOULDY- (—+ -Y+—) 1 Nb.3/4
TURN-FURROW 39Ha.2 if iron

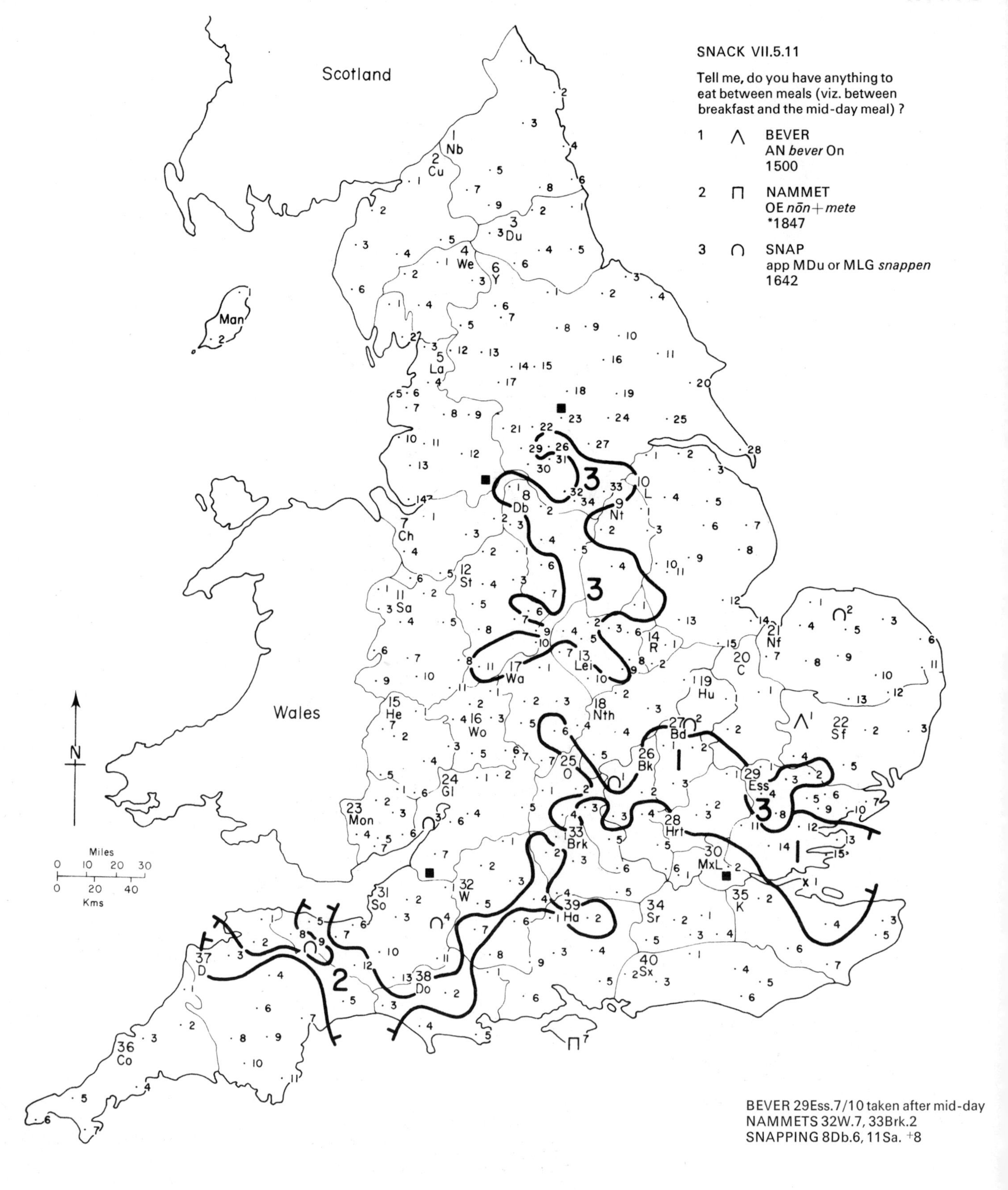
SNACK VII.5.11
Tell me, do you have anything to eat between meals (viz. between breakfast and the mid-day meal) ?
1 Λ BEVER
AN *bever* On
1500
2 ⊓ NAMMET
OE *nōn*+*mete*
*1847
3 ∩ SNAP
app MDu or MLG *snappen*
1642
Scotland
Wales
Man
N
Miles
0 10 20 30
0 20 40
Kms
BEVER 29Ess.7/10 taken after mid-day
NAMMETS 32W.7, 33Brk.2
SNAPPING 8Db.6, 11Sa. +8

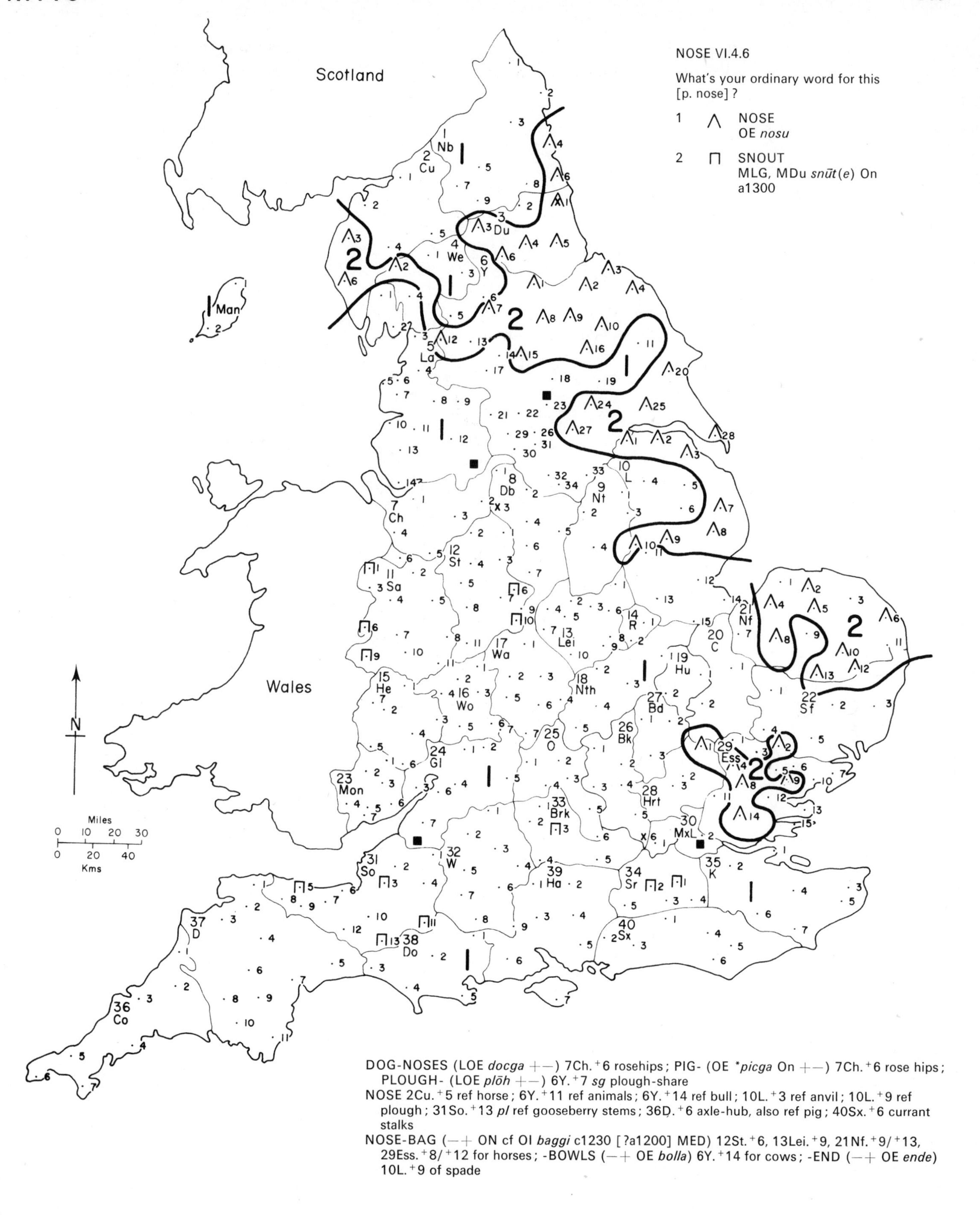

DOG-NOSES (LOE *docga* +—) 7Ch.+6 rosehips; PIG- (OE **picga* On +—) 7Ch.+6 rose hips; PLOUGH- (LOE *plōh* +—) 6Y.+7 *sg* plough-share

NOSE 2Cu.+5 ref horse; 6Y.+11 ref animals; 6Y.+14 ref bull; 10L.+3 ref anvil; 10L.+9 ref plough; 31So.+13 *pl* ref gooseberry stems; 36D.+6 axle-hub, also ref pig; 40Sx.+6 currant stalks

NOSE-BAG (—+ ON cf OI *baggi* c1230 [?a1200] MED) 12St.+6, 13Lei.+9, 21Nf.+9/+13, 29Ess.+8/+12 for horses; -BOWLS (—+ OE *bolla*) 6Y.+14 for cows; -END (—+ OE *ende*) 10L.+9 of spade

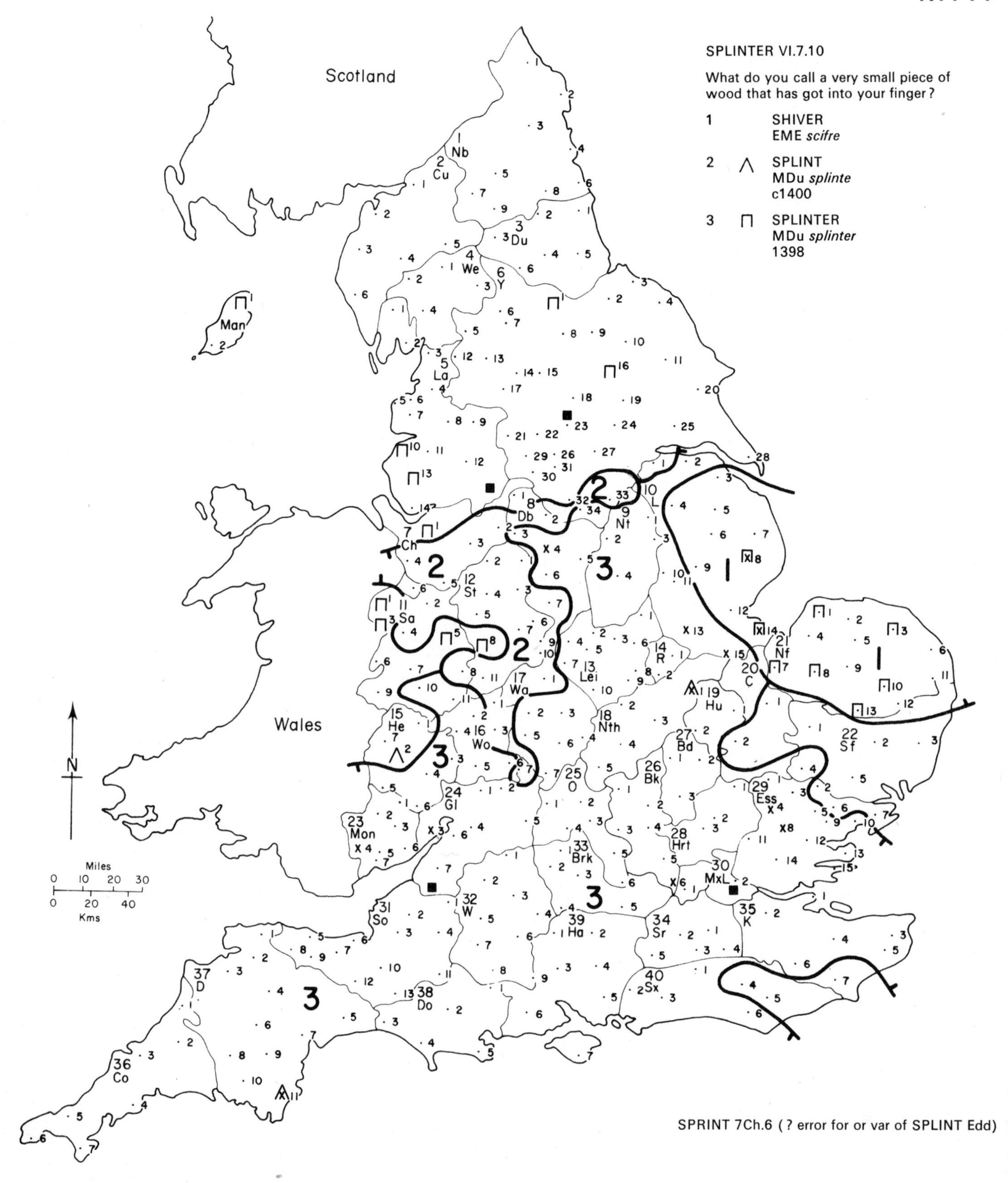
SPLINTER VI.7.10
What do you call a very small piece of wood that has got into your finger?
1 SHIVER
EME *scifre*
2 ⋀ SPLINT
MDu *splinte*
c1400
3 ⊓ SPLINTER
MDu *splinter*
1398
Scotland
Wales
Man
N
Miles
0 10 20 30
0 20 40
Kms
SPRINT 7Ch.6 (? error for or var of SPLINT Edd)

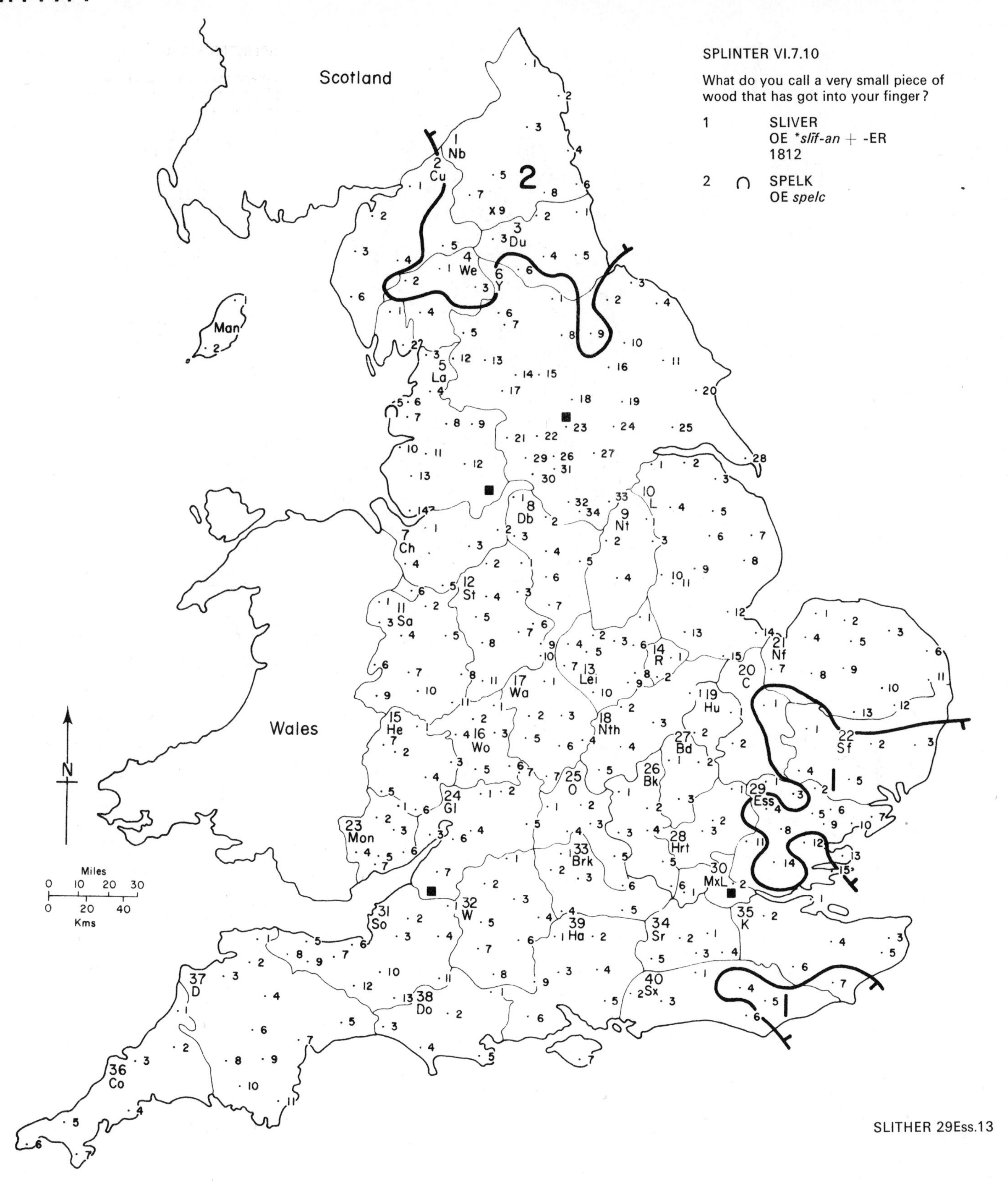
SPLINTER VI.7.10
What do you call a very small piece of wood that has got into your finger?
1 SLIVER
OE *slīf-an + -ER
1812
2 ∩ SPELK
OE spelc
Scotland
Wales
Man
Miles
0 10 20 30
0 20 40
Kms
N
SLITHER 29Ess.13

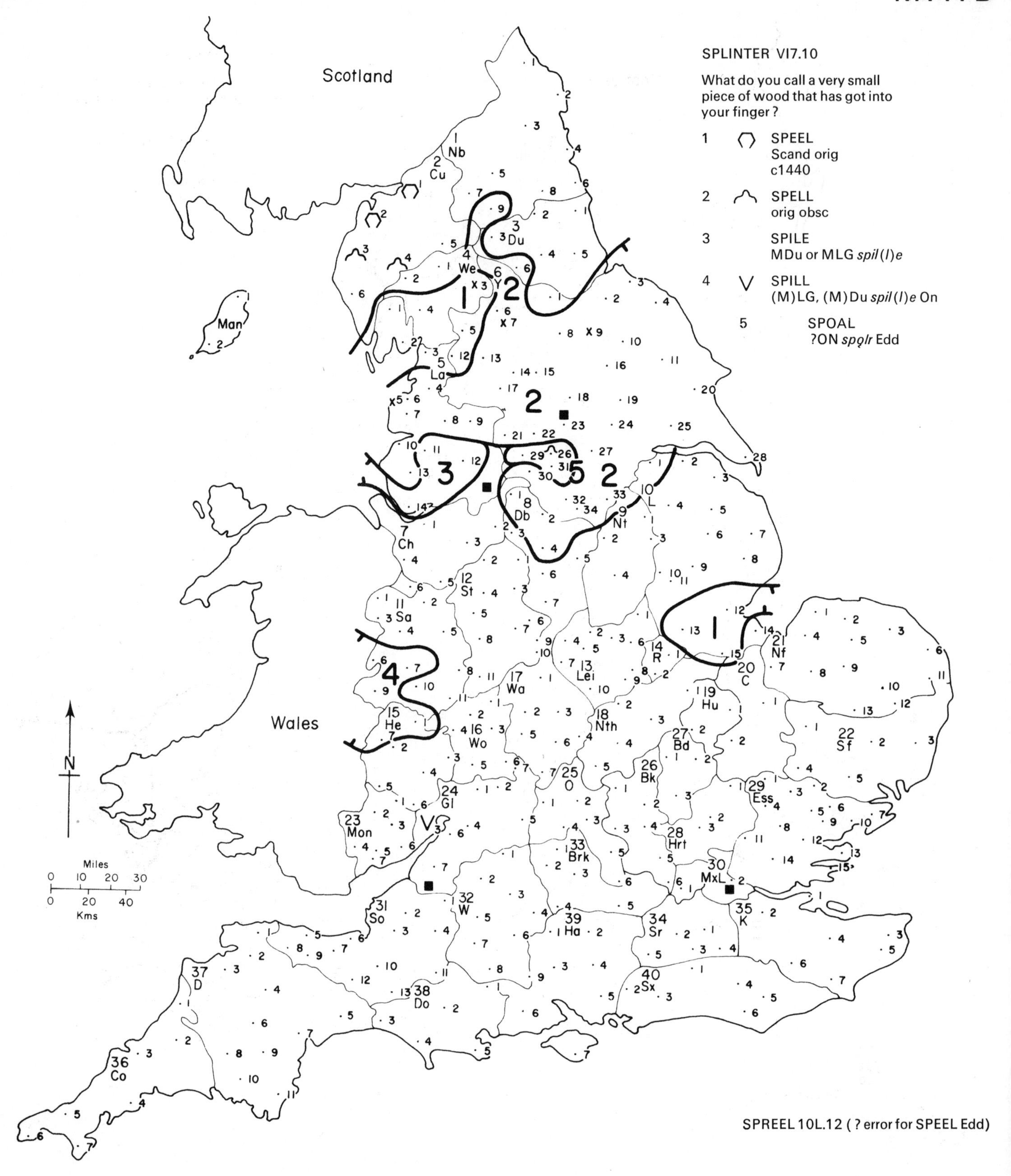
Scotland
Wales
Man
SPLINTER VI7.10
What do you call a very small piece of wood that has got into your finger?
1 SPEEL Scand orig c1440
2 SPELL orig obsc
3 SPILE MDu or MLG spil(l)e
4 V SPILL (M)LG, (M)Du spil(l)e On
5 SPOAL ?ON spǫlr Edd
Miles 0 10 20 30
0 20 40 Kms
SPREEL 10L.12 (? error for SPEEL Edd)

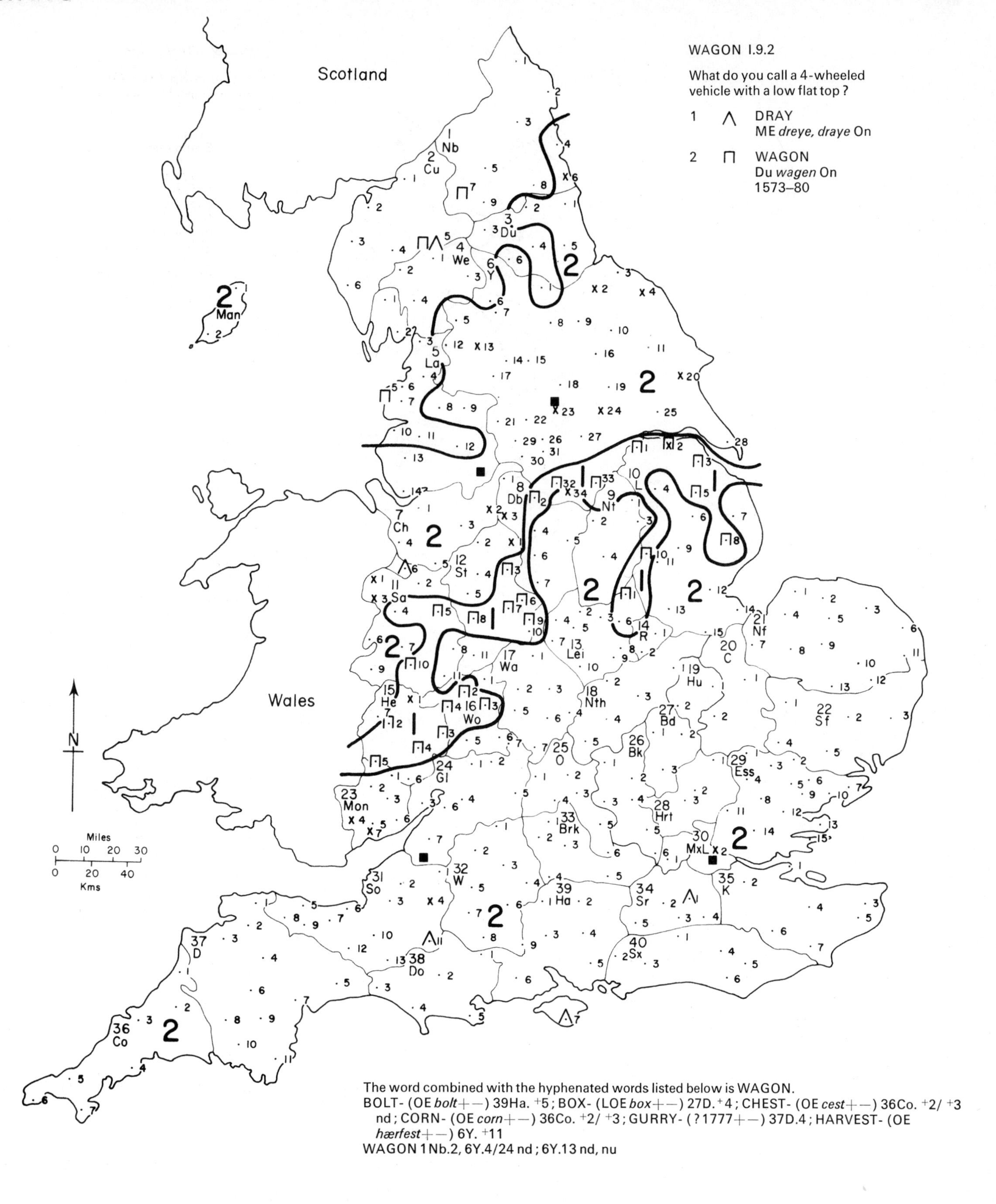

The word combined with the hyphenated words listed below is WAGON.

BOLT- (OE *bolt*+—) 39Ha. $^{+}$5; BOX- (LOE *box*+—) 27D. $^{+}$4; CHEST- (OE *cest*+—) 36Co. $^{+}$2/ $^{+}$3 nd; CORN- (OE *corn*+—) 36Co. $^{+}$2/ $^{+}$3; GURRY- (?1777+—) 37D.4; HARVEST- (OE *hærfest*+—) 6Y. $^{+}$11

WAGON 1Nb.2, 6Y.4/24 nd; 6Y.13 nd, nu

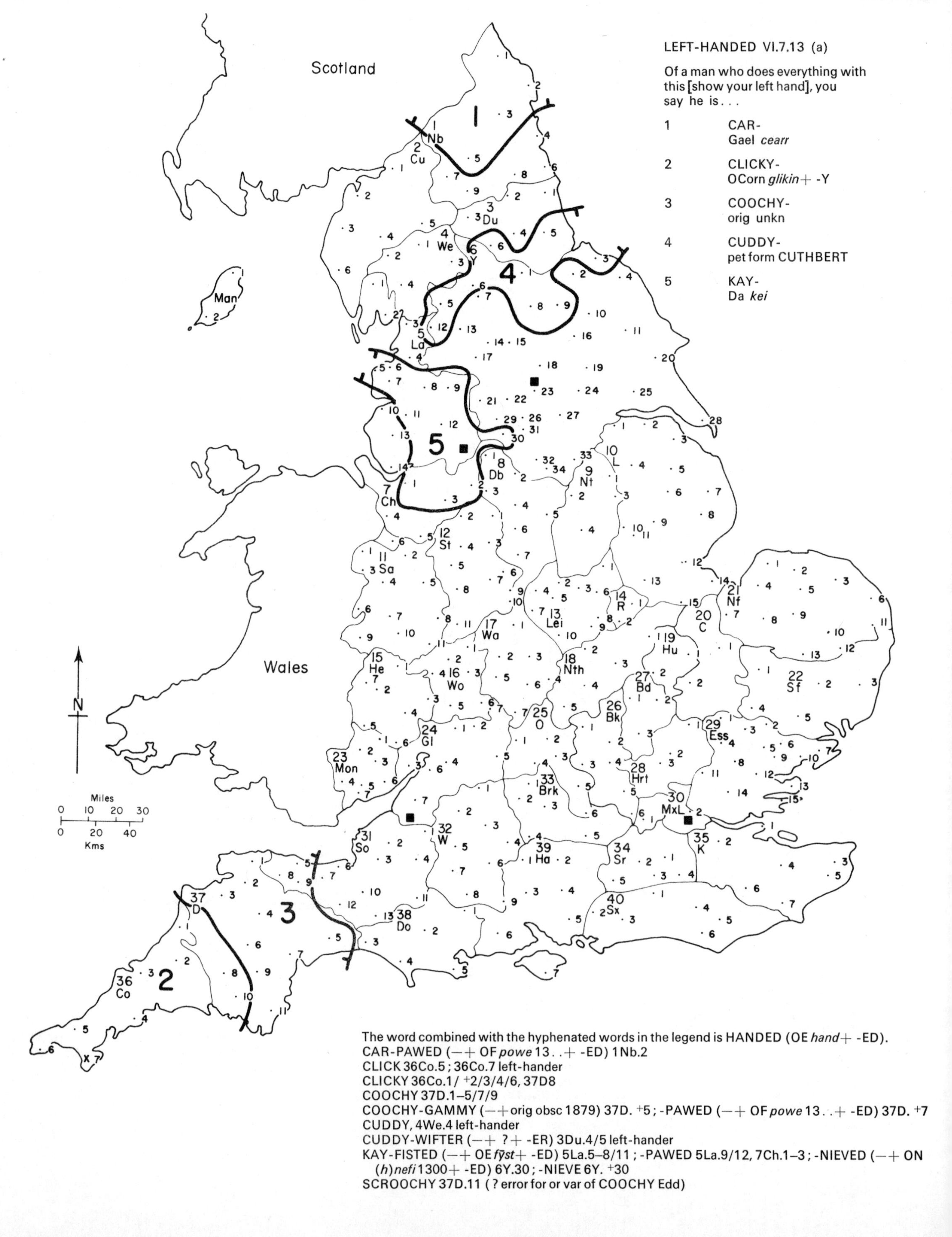
LEFT-HANDED VI.7.13 (a)
Of a man who does everything with this [show your left hand], you say he is . . .
1 CAR- Gael *cearr*
2 CLICKY- OCorn *glikin* + -Y
3 COOCHY- orig unkn
4 CUDDY- pet form CUTHBERT
5 KAY- Da *kei*
Scotland
Wales
Man
N
Miles 0 10 20 30
0 20 40 Kms
The word combined with the hyphenated words in the legend is HANDED (OE *hand* + -ED).
CAR-PAWED (— + OF *powe* 13. . + -ED) 1Nb.2
CLICK 36Co.5 ; 36Co.7 left-hander
CLICKY 36Co.1/ +2/3/4/6, 37D8
COOCHY 37D.1–5/7/9
COOCHY-GAMMY (— + orig obsc 1879) 37D. +5 ; -PAWED (— + OF *powe* 13. . + -ED) 37D. +7
CUDDY, 4We.4 left-hander
CUDDY-WIFTER (— + ? + -ER) 3Du.4/5 left-hander
KAY-FISTED (— + OE *fȳst* + -ED) 5La.5–8/11 ; -PAWED 5La.9/12, 7Ch.1–3 ; -NIEVED (— + ON (*h*)*nefi* 1300 + -ED) 6Y.30 ; -NIEVE 6Y. +30
SCROOCHY 37D.11 (? error for or var of COOCHY Edd)

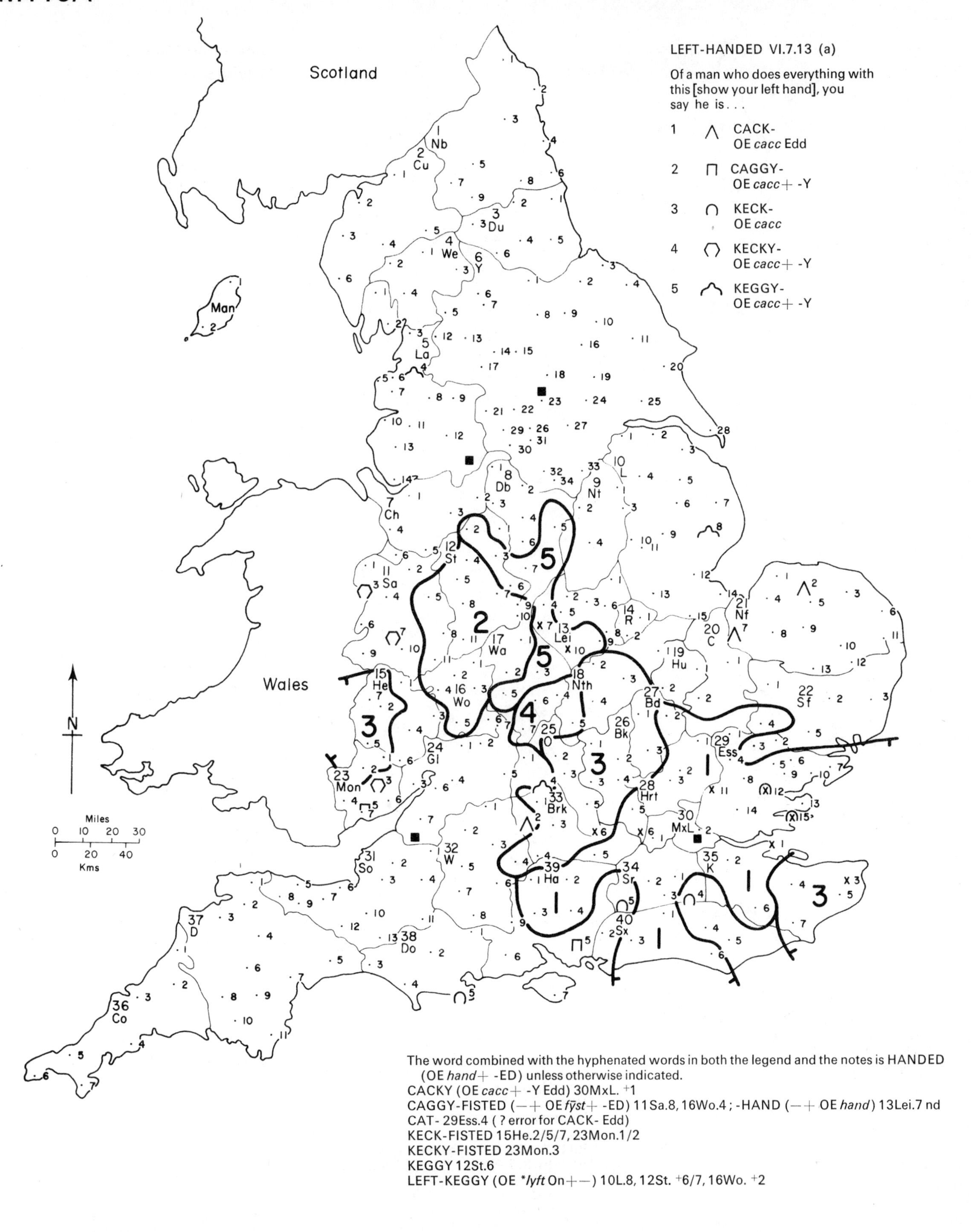

The word combined with the hyphenated words in both the legend and the notes is HANDED (OE *hand*+ -ED) unless otherwise indicated.
CACKY (OE *cacc*+ -Y Edd) 30MxL. +1
CAGGY-FISTED (—+ OE *fȳst*+ -ED) 11Sa.8, 16Wo.4; -HAND (—+ OE *hand*) 13Lei.7 nd
CAT- 29Ess.4 (? error for CACK- Edd)
KECK-FISTED 15He.2/5/7, 23Mon.1/2
KECKY-FISTED 23Mon.3
KEGGY 12St.6
LEFT-KEGGY (OE **lyft* On+—) 10L.8, 12St. +6/7, 16Wo. +2

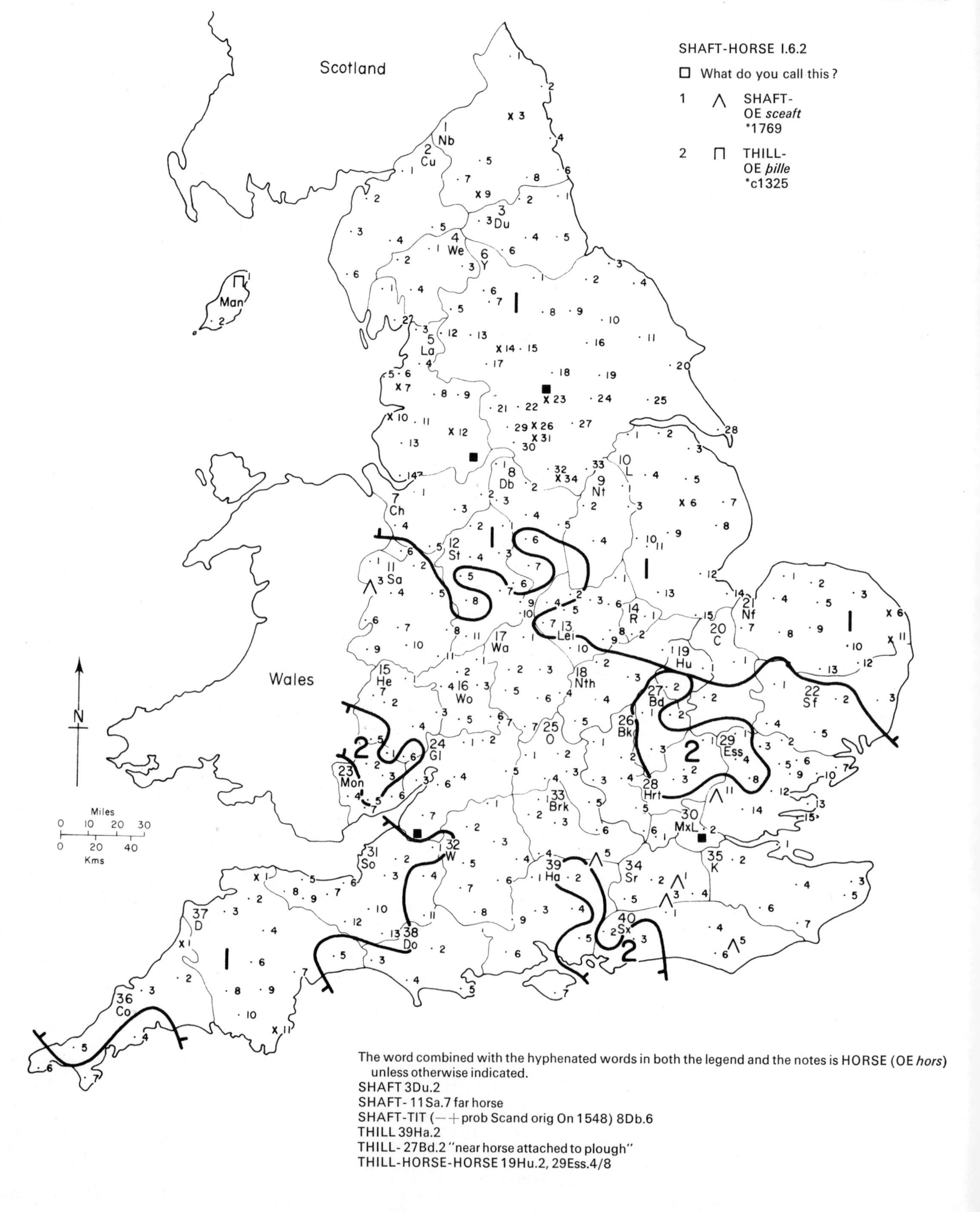

The word combined with the hyphenated words in both the legend and the notes is HORSE (OE *hors*) unless otherwise indicated.
SHAFT 3Du.2
SHAFT- 11Sa.7 far horse
SHAFT-TIT (—+prob Scand orig On 1548) 8Db.6
THILL 39Ha.2
THILL- 27Bd.2 "near horse attached to plough"
THILL-HORSE-HORSE 19Hu.2, 29Ess.4/8

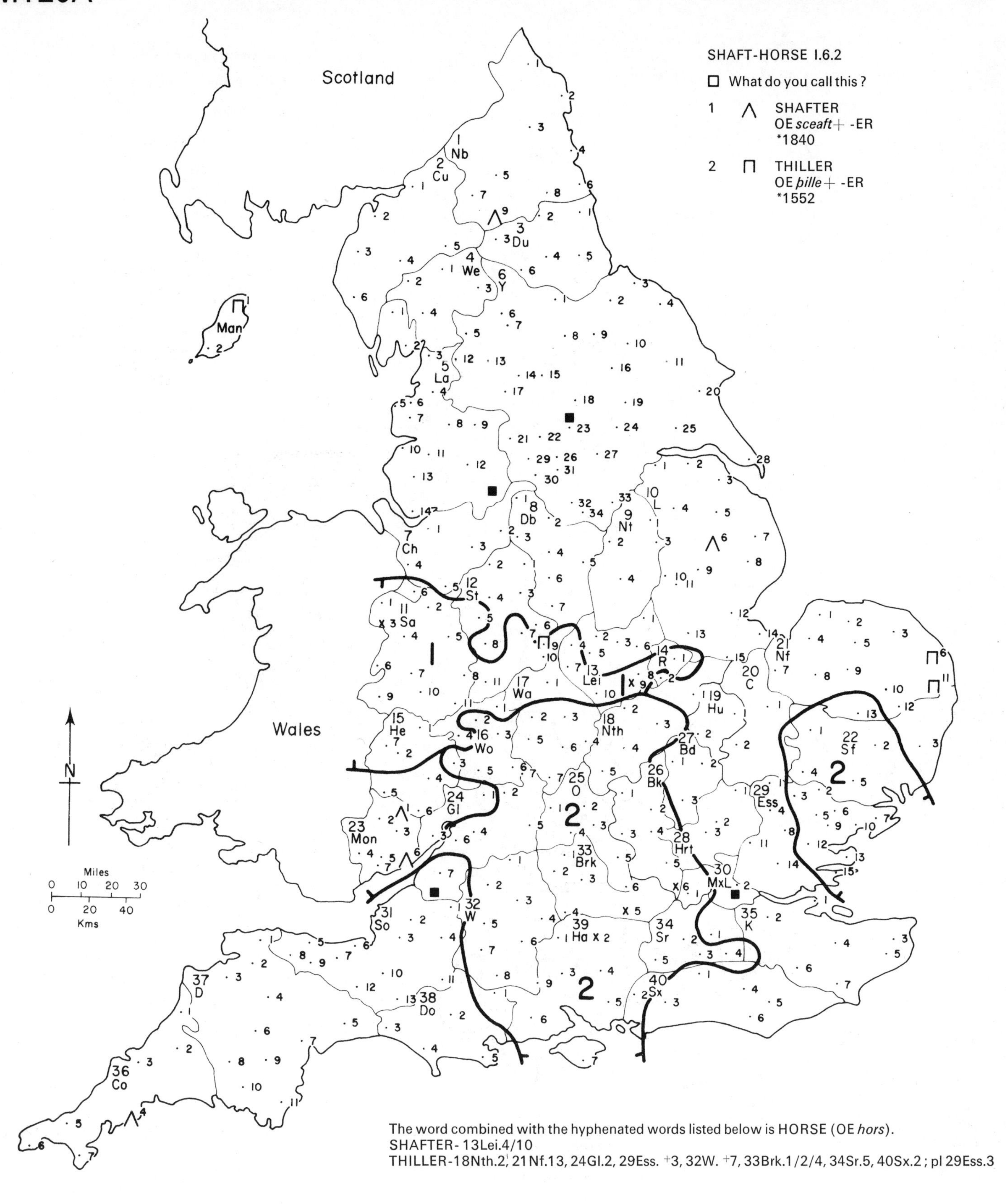

The word combined with the hyphenated words listed below is HORSE (OE *hors*).
SHAFTER- 13Lei.4/10
THILLER-18Nth.2, 21Nf.13, 24Gl.2, 29Ess. +3, 32W. +7, 33Brk.1/2/4, 34Sr.5, 40Sx.2 ; pl 29Ess.3

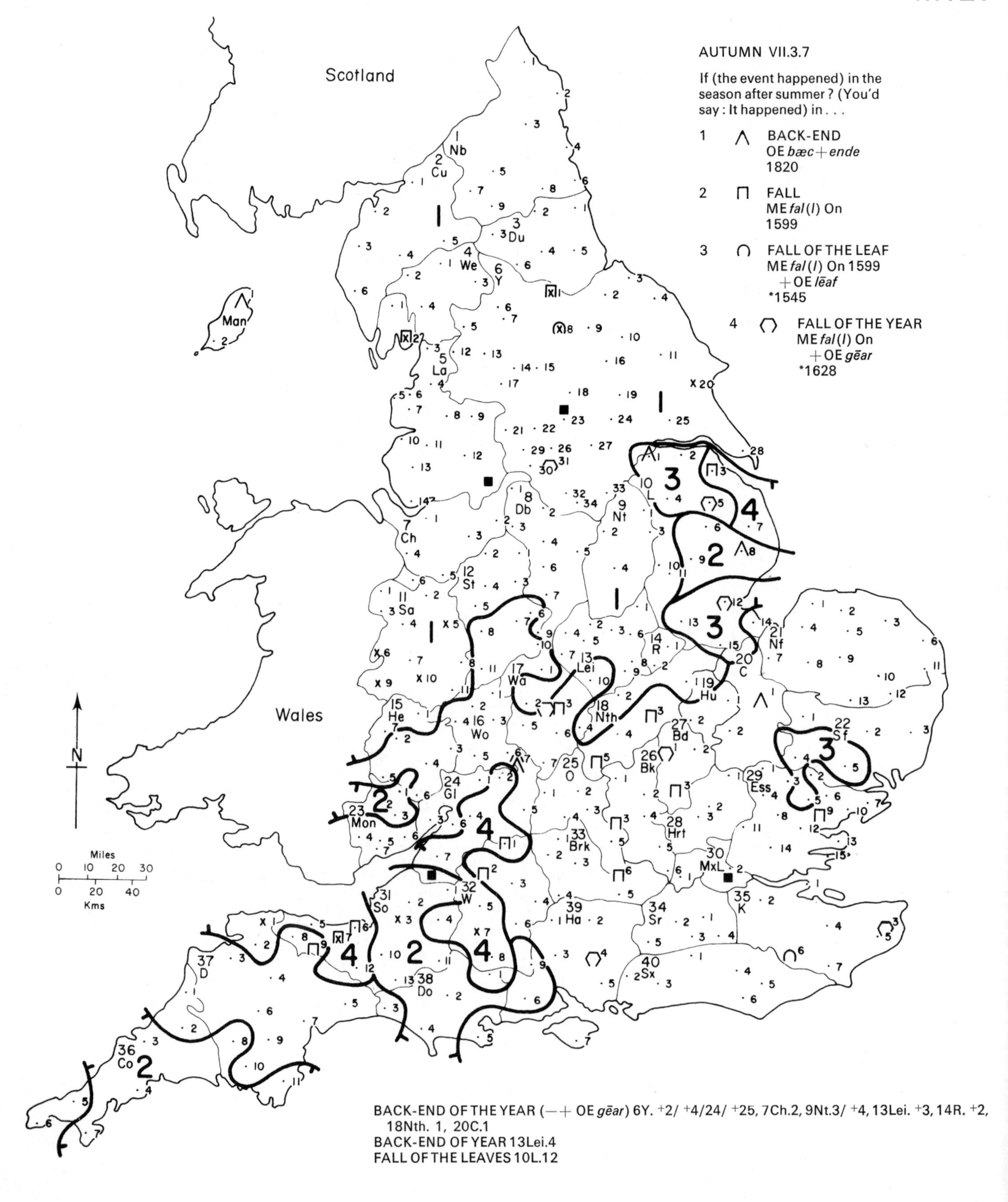
AUTUMN VII.3.7
If (the event happened) in the season after summer? (You'd say: It happened) in . . .
1 BACK-END OE bæc+ende 1820
2 FALL ME fal(l) On 1599
3 FALL OF THE LEAF ME fal(l) On 1599 +OE lēaf *1545
4 FALL OF THE YEAR ME fal(l) On +OE gēar *1628
Scotland
Wales
N
Miles 0 10 20 30
0 20 40 Kms
BACK-END OF THE YEAR (—+ OE gēar) 6Y. +2/ +4/24/ +25, 7Ch.2, 9Nt.3/ +4, 13Lei. +3, 14R. +2, 18Nth. 1, 20C.1
BACK-END OF YEAR 13Lei.4
FALL OF THE LEAVES 10L.12

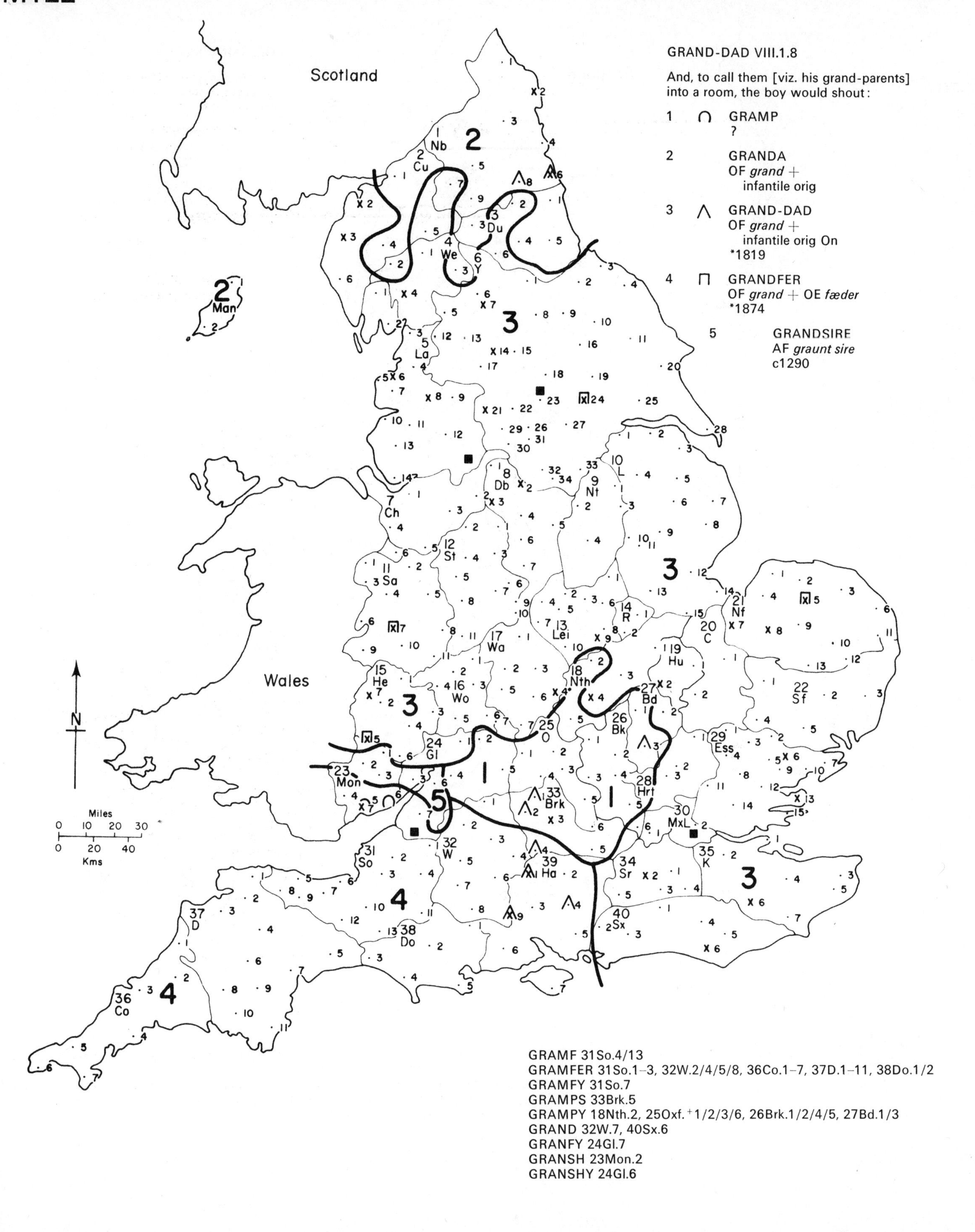

GRAND-DAD VIII.1.8
And, to call them [viz. his grand-parents] into a room, the boy would shout:
1 ∩ GRAMP
?
2 GRANDA
OF *grand* + infantile orig
3 ∧ GRAND-DAD
OF *grand* + infantile orig On *1819
4 ⊓ GRANDFER
OF *grand* + OE *fæder* *1874
5 GRANDSIRE
AF *graunt sire* c1290
Scotland
Wales
Miles
Kms
GRAMF 31So.4/13
GRAMFER 31So.1–3, 32W.2/4/5/8, 36Co.1–7, 37D.1–11, 38Do.1/2
GRAMFY 31So.7
GRAMPS 33Brk.5
GRAMPY 18Nth.2, 25Oxf.+1/2/3/6, 26Brk.1/2/4/5, 27Bd.1/3
GRAND 32W.7, 40Sx.6
GRANFY 24Gl.7
GRANSH 23Mon.2
GRANSHY 24Gl.6

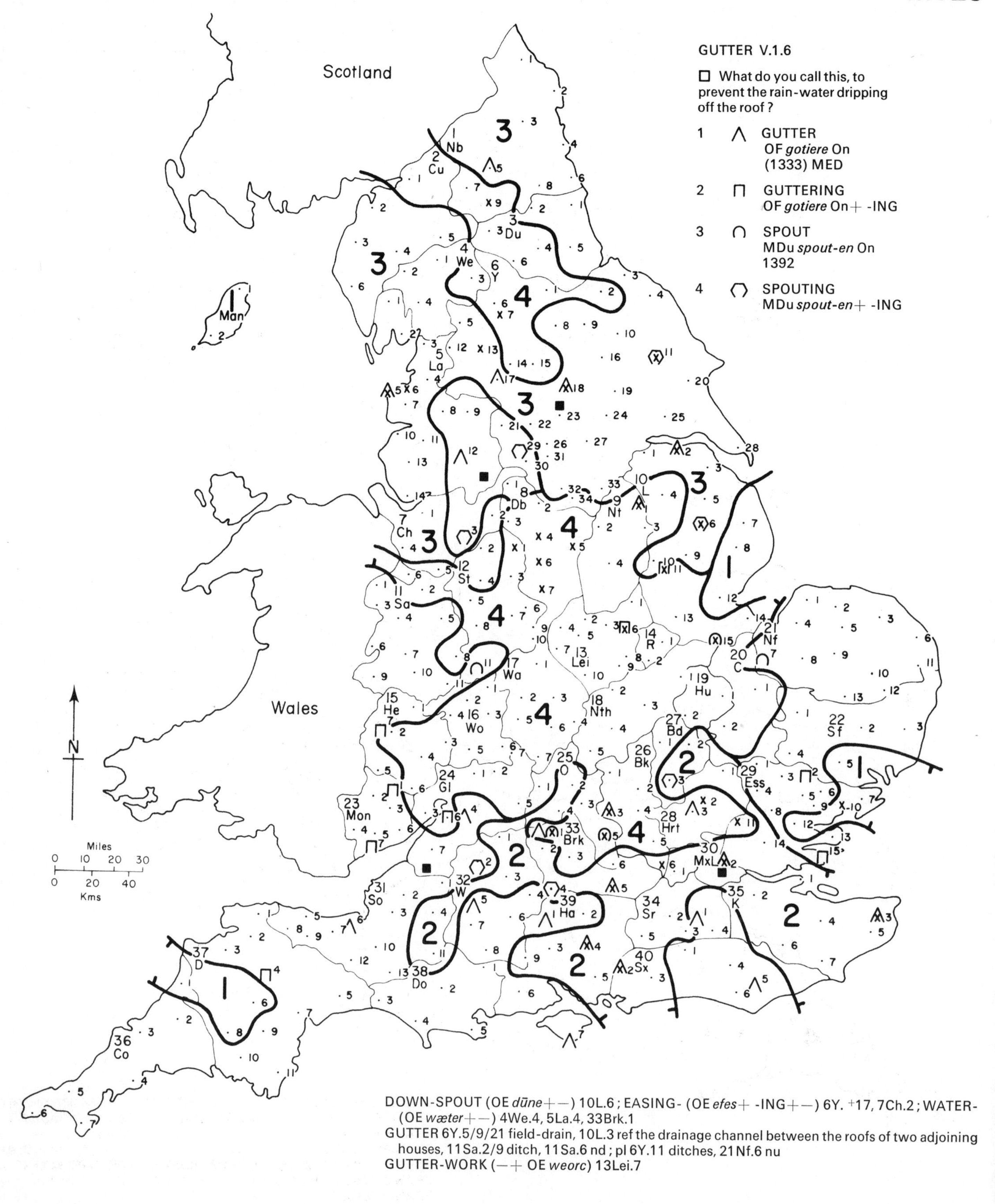

DOWN-SPOUT (OE *dūne*+—) 10L.6; EASING- (OE *efes*+ -ING+—) 6Y. +17, 7Ch.2; WATER- (OE *wæter*+—) 4We.4, 5La.4, 33Brk.1

GUTTER 6Y.5/9/21 field-drain, 10L.3 ref the drainage channel between the roofs of two adjoining houses, 11Sa.2/9 ditch, 11Sa.6 nd; pl 6Y.11 ditches, 21Nf.6 nu

GUTTER-WORK (—+ OE *weorc*) 13Lei.7

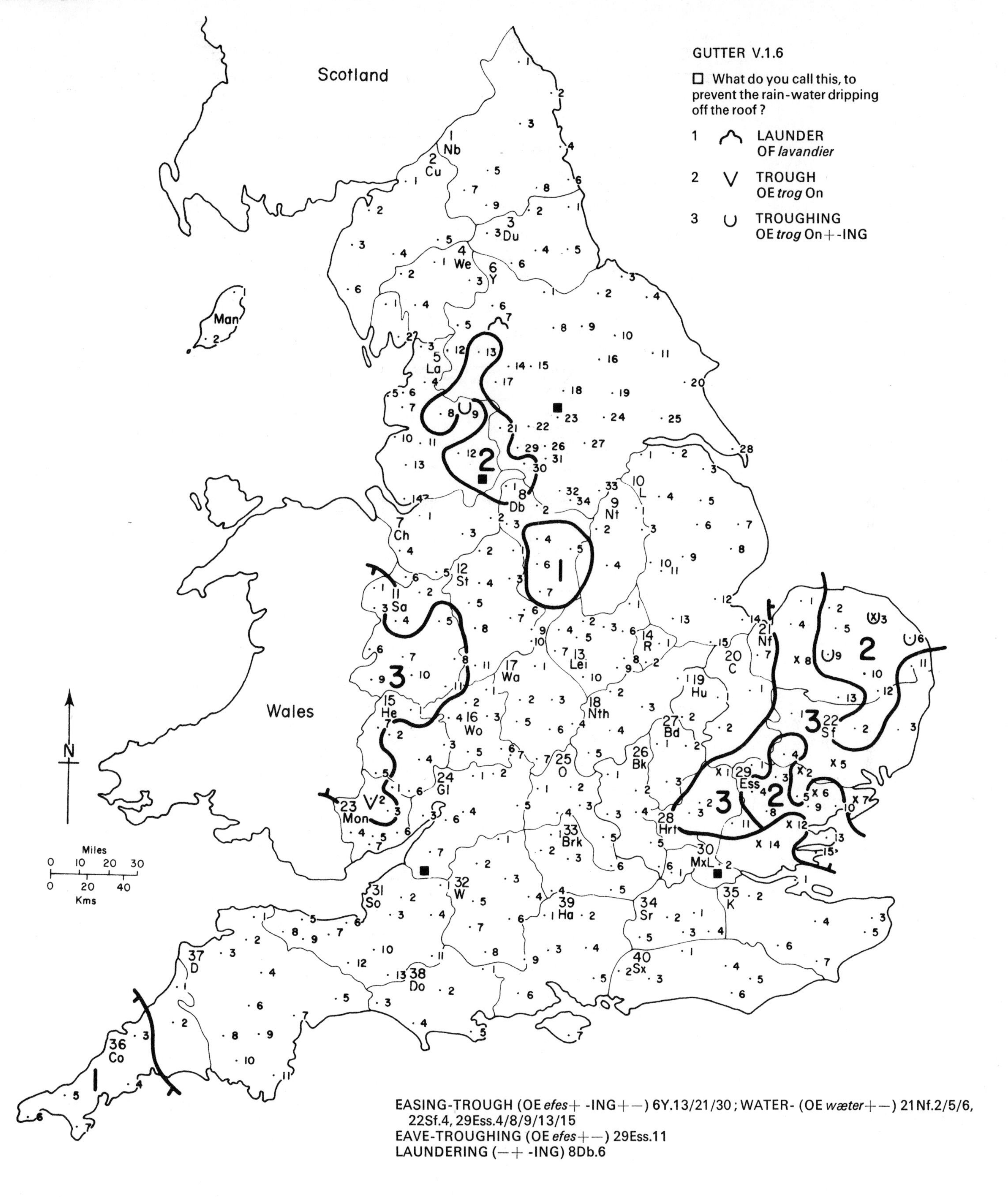

EASING-TROUGH (OE *efes*+ -ING+—) 6Y.13/21/30; WATER- (OE *wæter*+—) 21Nf.2/5/6, 22Sf.4, 29Ess.4/8/9/13/15
EAVE-TROUGHING (OE *efes*+—) 29Ess.11
LAUNDERING (—+ -ING) 8Db.6

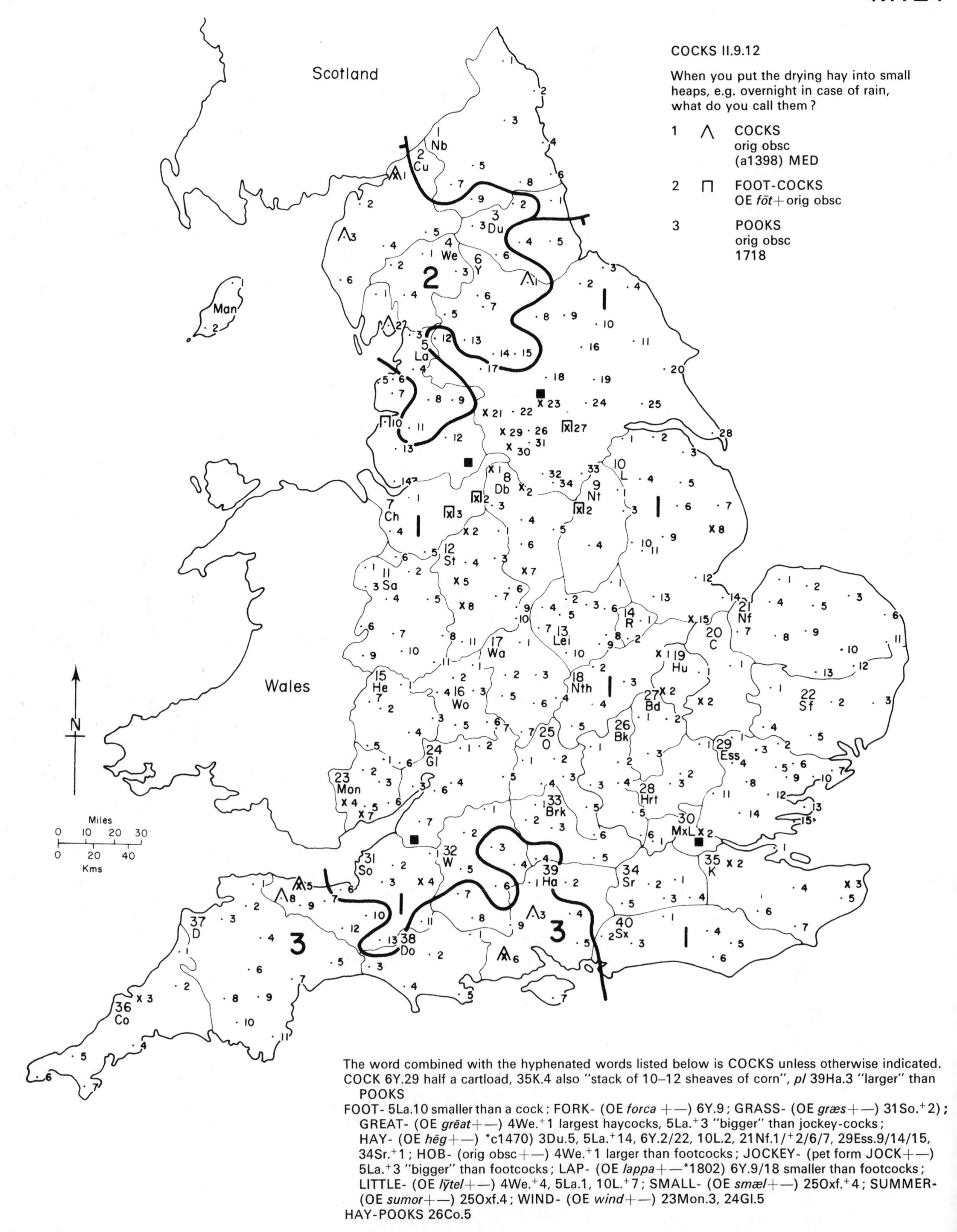

COCKS II.9.12

When you put the drying hay into small heaps, e.g. overnight in case of rain, what do you call them?

1 Λ COCKS
orig obsc
(a1398) MED

2 ⊓ FOOT-COCKS
OE *fōt*+orig obsc

3 POOKS
orig obsc
1718

The word combined with the hyphenated words listed below is COCKS unless otherwise indicated.

COCK 6Y.29 half a cartload, 35K.4 also "stack of 10–12 sheaves of corn", *pl* 39Ha.3 "larger" than POOKS

FOOT- 5La.10 smaller than a cock; FORK- (OE *forca* +—) 6Y.9; GRASS- (OE *græs*+—) 31So.$^{+}$2); GREAT- (OE *grēat*+—) 4We.$^{+}$1 largest haycocks, 5La.$^{+}$3 "bigger" than jockey-cocks; HAY- (OE *hēg*+—) *c1470) 3Du.5, 5La.$^{+}$14, 6Y.2/22, 10L.2, 21Nf.1/$^{+}$2/6/7, 29Ess.9/14/15, 34Sr.$^{+}$1; HOB- (orig obsc+—) 4We.$^{+}$1 larger than footcocks; JOCKEY- (pet form JOCK+—) 5La.$^{+}$3 "bigger" than footcocks; LAP- (OE *lappa*+—*1802) 6Y.9/18 smaller than footcocks; LITTLE- (OE *lȳtel*+—) 4We.$^{+}$4, 5La.1, 10L.$^{+}$7; SMALL- (OE *smæl*+—) 25Oxf.$^{+}$4; SUMMER- (OE *sumor*+—) 25Oxf.4; WIND- (OE *wind*+—) 23Mon.3, 24Gl.5

HAY-POOKS 26Co.5

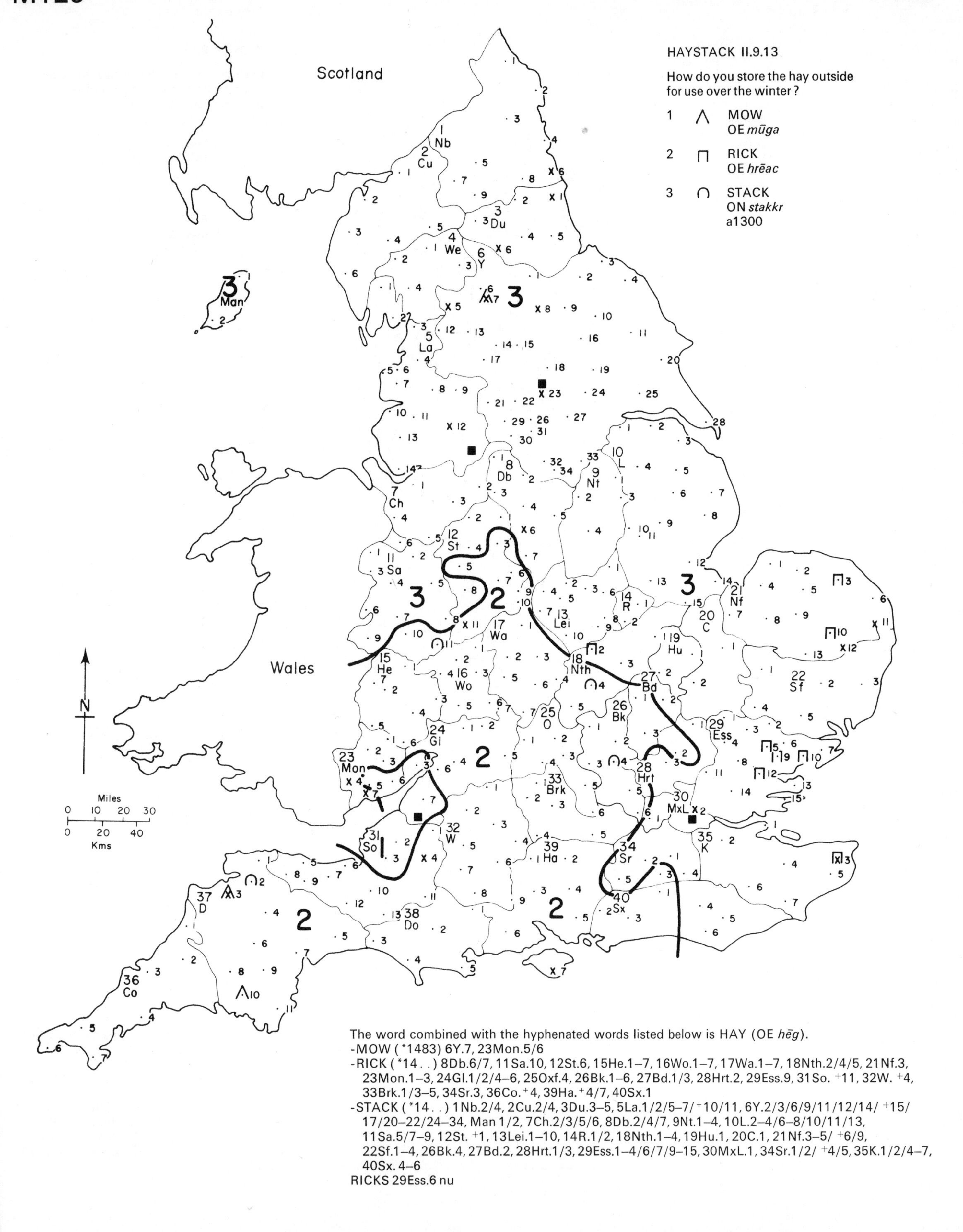

The word combined with the hyphenated words listed below is HAY (OE *hēg*).

-MOW (*1483) 6Y.7, 23Mon.5/6

-RICK (*14. .) 8Db.6/7, 11Sa.10, 12St.6, 15He.1–7, 16Wo.1–7, 17Wa.1–7, 18Nth.2/4/5, 21Nf.3, 23Mon.1–3, 24Gl.1/2/4–6, 25Oxf.4, 26Bk.1–6, 27Bd.1/3, 28Hrt.2, 29Ess.9, 31So. +11, 32W. +4, 33Brk.1/3–5, 34Sr.3, 36Co. +4, 39Ha. +4/7, 40Sx.1

-STACK (*14. .) 1Nb.2/4, 2Cu.2/4, 3Du.3–5, 5La.1/2/5–7/+10/11, 6Y.2/3/6/9/11/12/14/+15/17/20–22/24–34, Man 1/2, 7Ch.2/3/5/6, 8Db.2/4/7, 9Nt.1–4, 10L.2–4/6–8/10/11/13, 11Sa.5/7–9, 12St. +1, 13Lei.1–10, 14R.1/2, 18Nth.1–4, 19Hu.1, 20C.1, 21Nf.3–5/+6/9, 22Sf.1–4, 26Bk.4, 27Bd.2, 28Hrt.1/3, 29Ess.1–4/6/7/9–15, 30MxL.1, 34Sr.1/2/+4/5, 35K.1/2/4–7, 40Sx. 4–6

RICKS 29Ess.6 nu

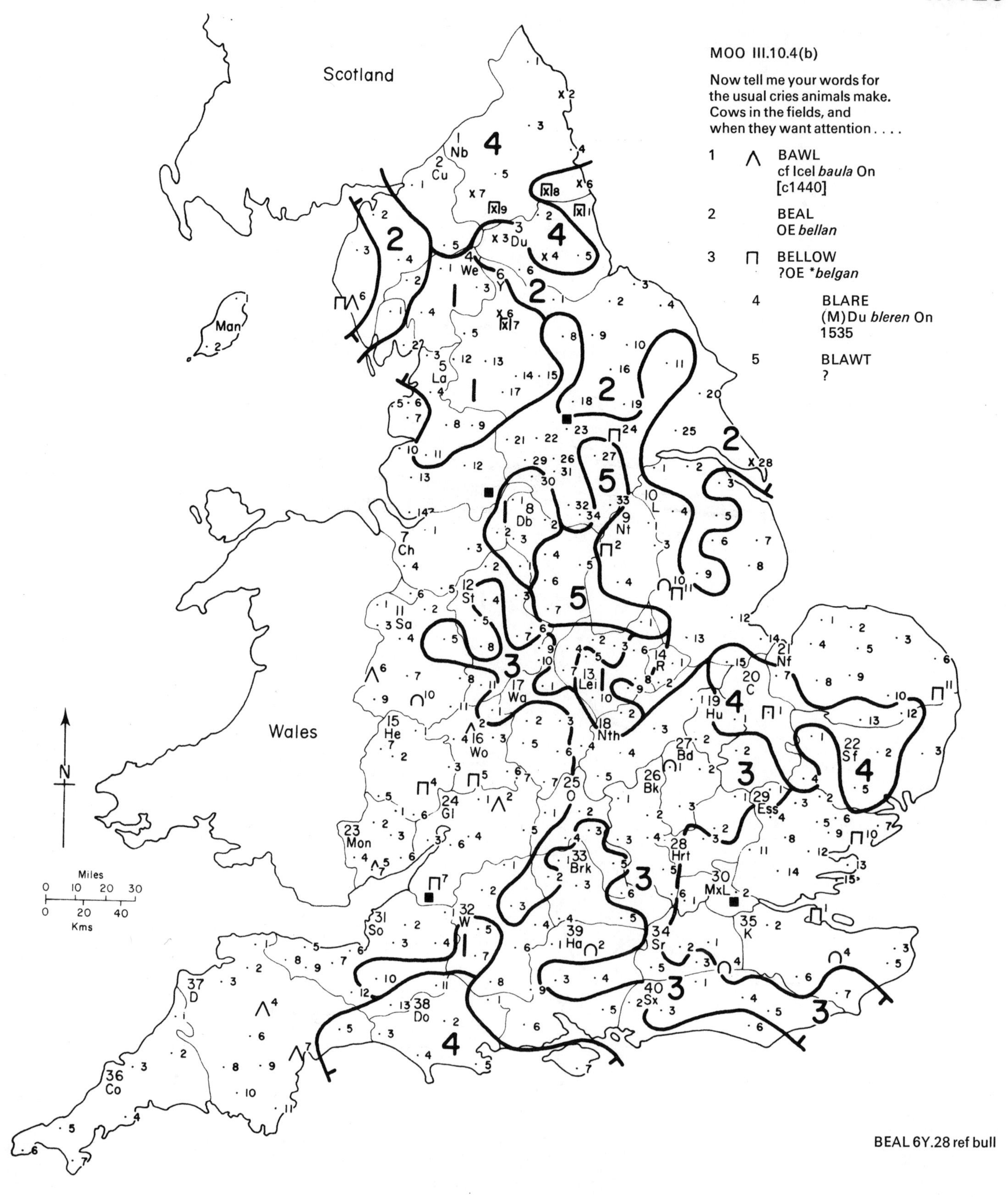

Scotland
Wales
Man
MOO III.10.4(b)
Now tell me your words for the usual cries animals make. Cows in the fields, and when they want attention . . . .
1 BAWL cf Icel *baula* On [c1440]
2 BEAL OE *bellan*
3 BELLOW ?OE *belgan
4 BLARE (M)Du *bleren* On 1535
5 BLAWT ?
Miles 0 10 20 30
0 20 40 Kms
BEAL 6Y.28 ref bull

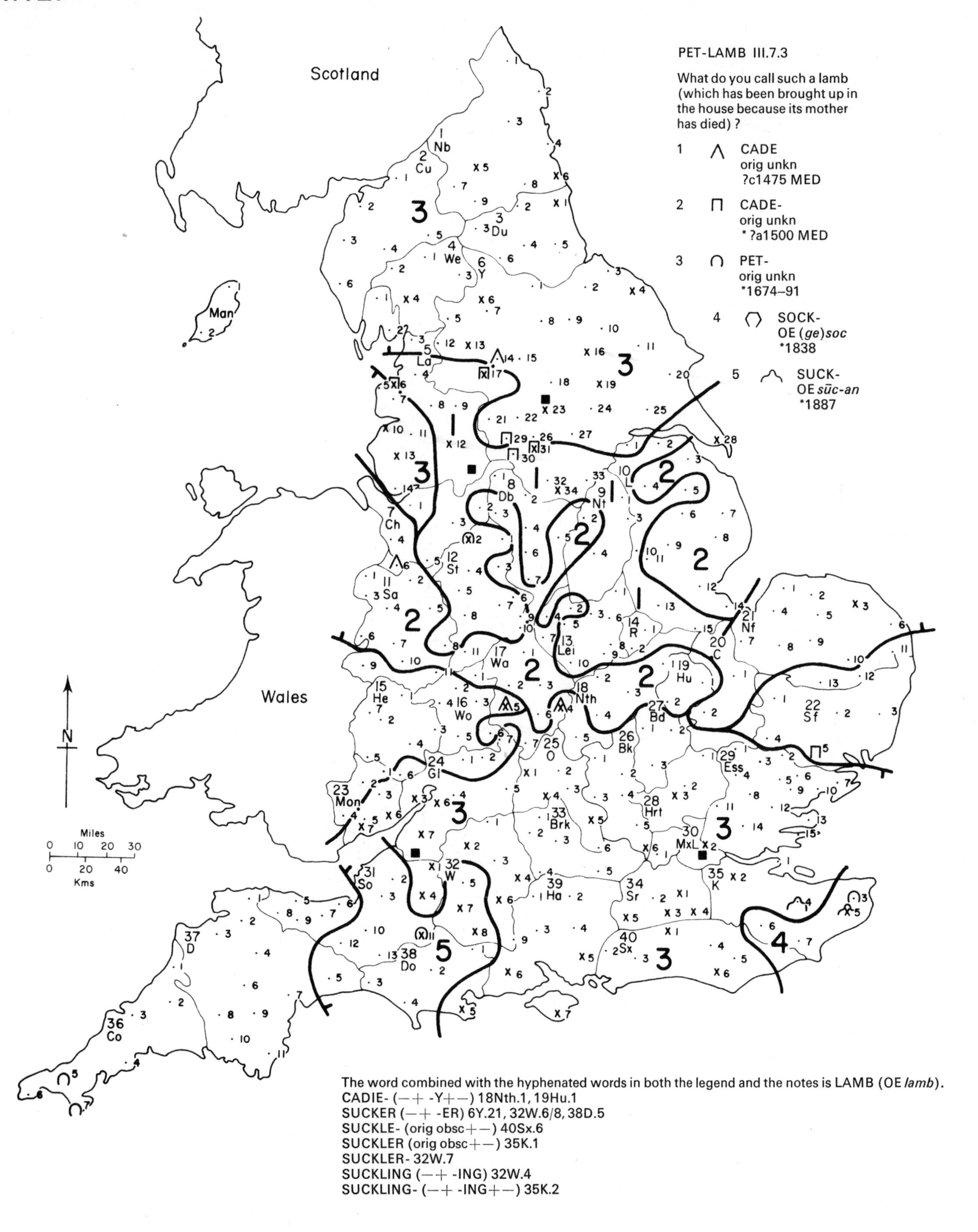
PET-LAMB III.7.3
What do you call such a lamb (which has been brought up in the house because its mother has died) ?
1 CADE orig unkn ?c1475 MED
2 CADE- orig unkn * ?a1500 MED
3 PET- orig unkn *1674–91
4 SOCK- OE (ge)soc *1838
5 SUCK- OE sūc-an *1887
Scotland
Wales
Man
Nb
Cu
Du
We
Y
La
Ch
Db
Nt
L
St
Sa
Lei
R
Nf
C
Wa
Hu
He
Wo
Nth
Bd
Sf
Gl
O
Bk
Ess
Mon
Hrt
Brk
MxL
So
W
Ha
Sr
K
D
Do
Sx
Co
Miles
0 10 20 30
0 20 40
Kms
N
The word combined with the hyphenated words in both the legend and the notes is LAMB (OE lamb).
CADIE- (—+ -Y+—) 18Nth.1, 19Hu.1
SUCKER (—+ -ER) 6Y.21, 32W.6/8, 38D.5
SUCKLE- (orig obsc+—) 40Sx.6
SUCKLER (orig obsc+—) 35K.1
SUCKLER- 32W.7
SUCKLING (—+ -ING) 32W.4
SUCKLING- (—+ -ING+—) 35K.2

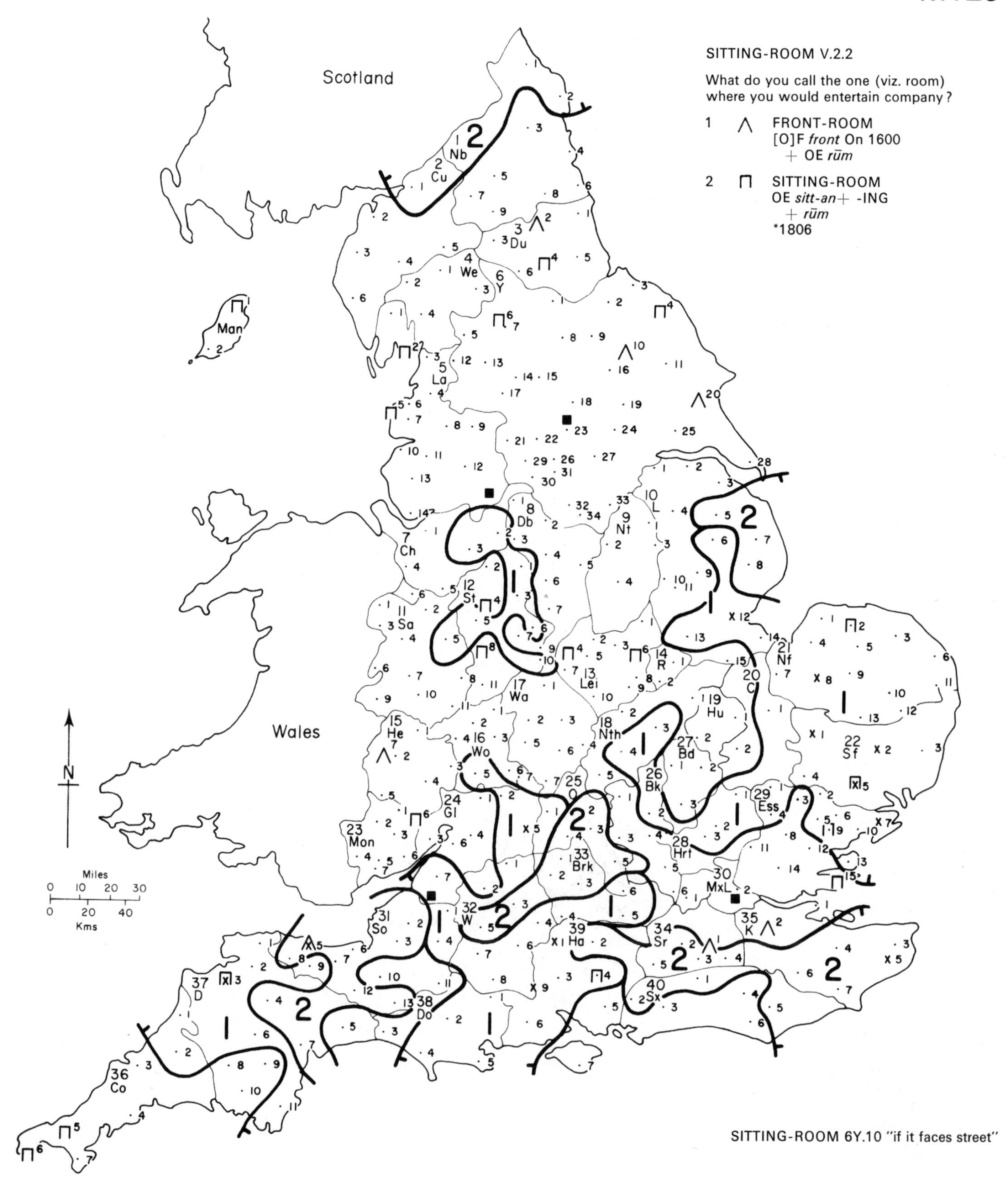
SITTING-ROOM V.2.2
What do you call the one (viz. room) where you would entertain company?
1 ⋀ FRONT-ROOM
[O]F *front* On 1600
+ OE *rūm*
2 ⊓ SITTING-ROOM
OE *sitt-an*+ -ING
+ *rūm*
*1806
Scotland
Wales
Man
N
Miles
0 10 20 30
0 20 40
Kms
SITTING-ROOM 6Y.10 "if it faces street"

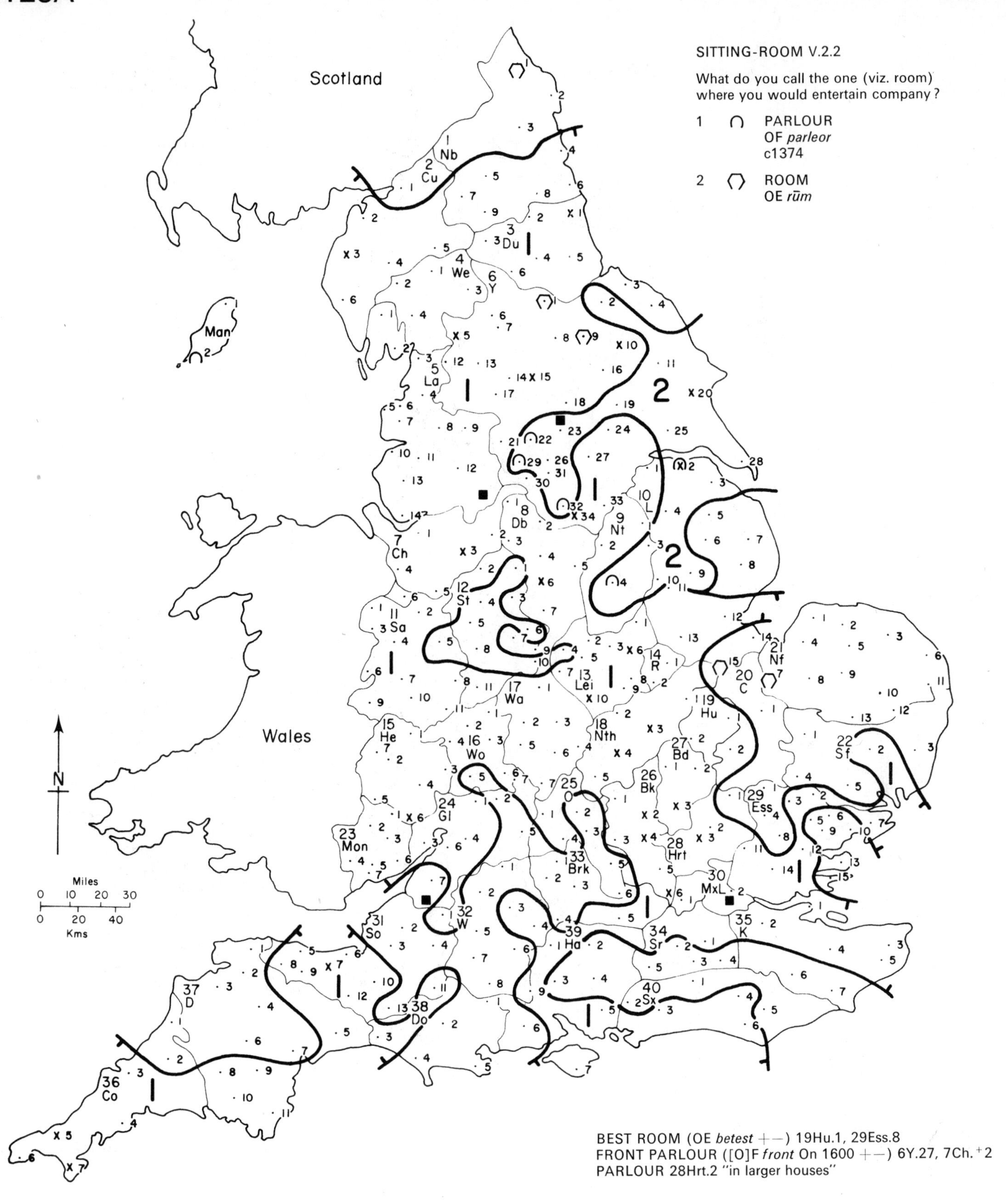
SITTING-ROOM V.2.2
What do you call the one (viz. room) where you would entertain company?
1 PARLOUR
OF *parleor*
c1374
2 ROOM
OE *rūm*
Scotland
Wales
Man
Miles
0 10 20 30
0 20 40
Kms
N
BEST ROOM (OE *betest* +—) 19Hu.1, 29Ess.8
FRONT PARLOUR ([O]F *front* On 1600 +—) 6Y.27, 7Ch.+2
PARLOUR 28Hrt.2 "in larger houses"

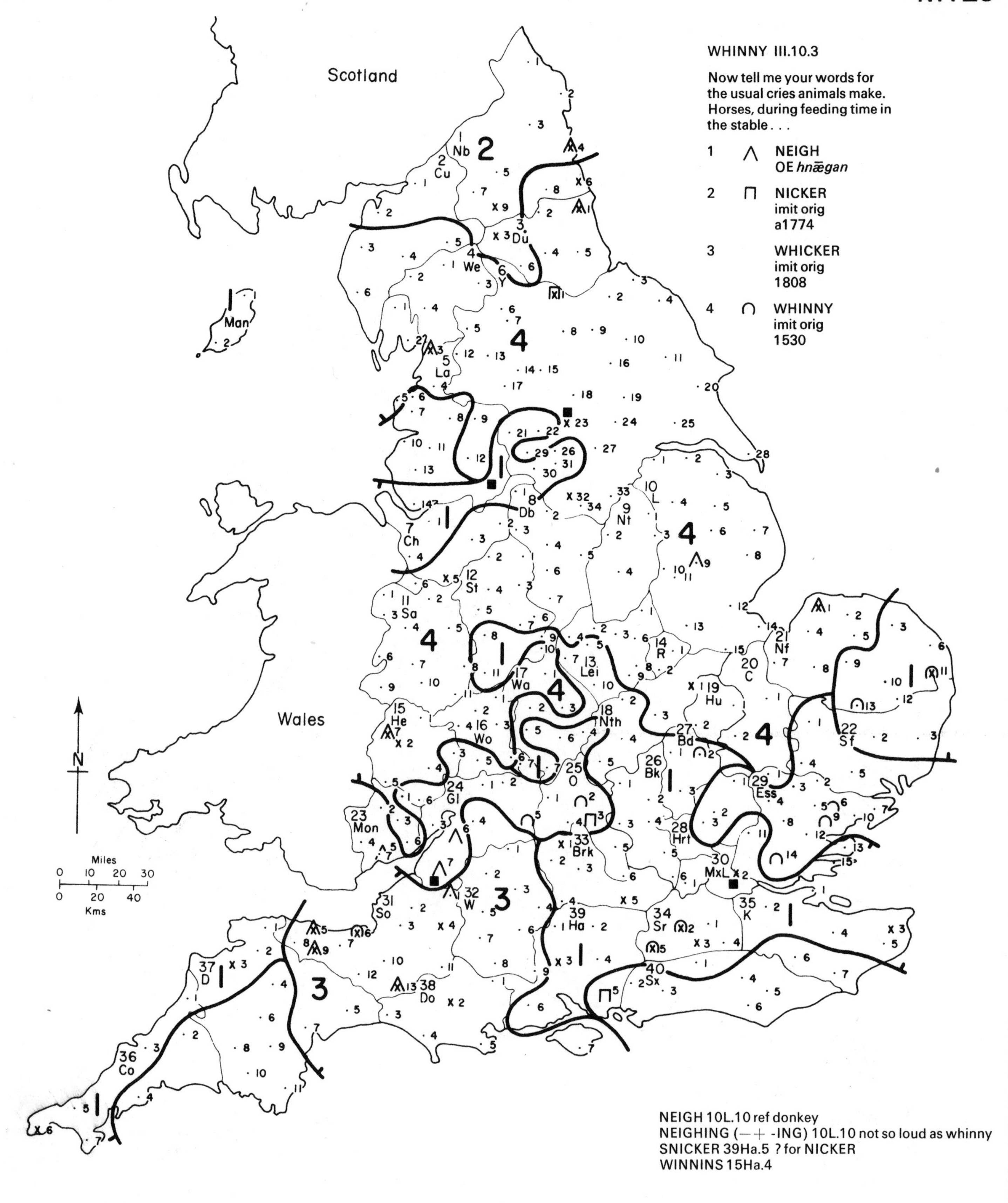
WHINNY III.10.3
Now tell me your words for the usual cries animals make. Horses, during feeding time in the stable . . .
1 ⋀ NEIGH OE *hnǣgan*
2 ⊓ NICKER imit orig a1774
3 WHICKER imit orig 1808
4 ∩ WHINNY imit orig 1530
Scotland
Wales
Man
N
Miles 0 10 20 30
0 20 40 Kms
NEIGH 10L.10 ref donkey
NEIGHING (— + -ING) 10L.10 not so loud as whinny
SNICKER 39Ha.5 ? for NICKER
WINNINS 15Ha.4

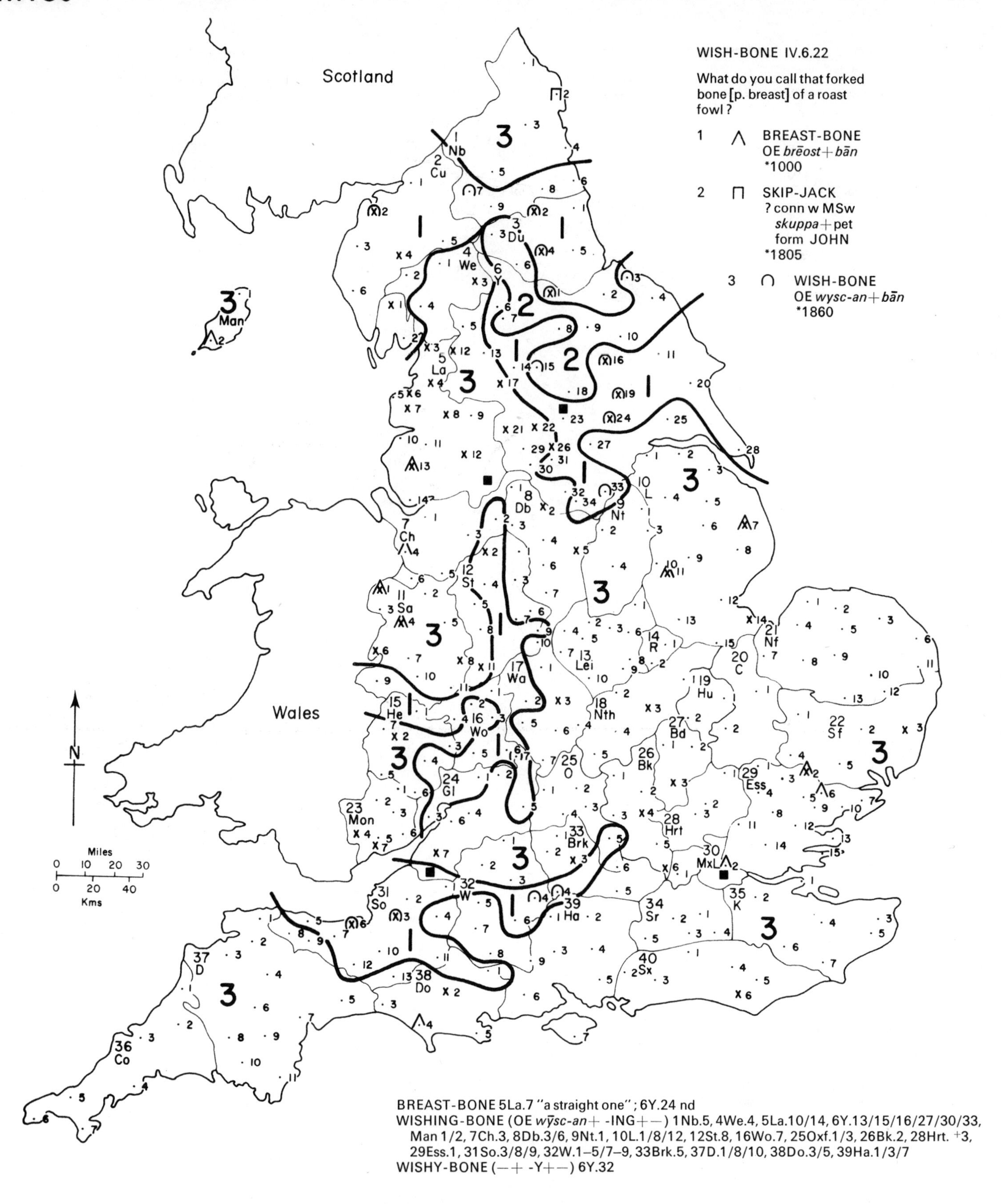

BREAST-BONE 5La.7 "a straight one"; 6Y.24 nd

WISHING-BONE (OE *wȳsc-an* + -ING + —) 1Nb.5, 4We.4, 5La.10/14, 6Y.13/15/16/27/30/33, Man 1/2, 7Ch.3, 8Db.3/6, 9Nt.1, 10L.1/8/12, 12St.8, 16Wo.7, 25Oxf.1/3, 26Bk.2, 28Hrt. +3, 29Ess.1, 31So.3/8/9, 32W.1–5/7–9, 33Brk.5, 37D.1/8/10, 38Do.3/5, 39Ha.1/3/7

WISHY-BONE (— + -Y + —) 6Y.32

To ACHE VI.13.3

But what do you say your belly does?

1 ⋀ ACHES f OE *ac-an*

2 WARKS f OE *wærc-an*

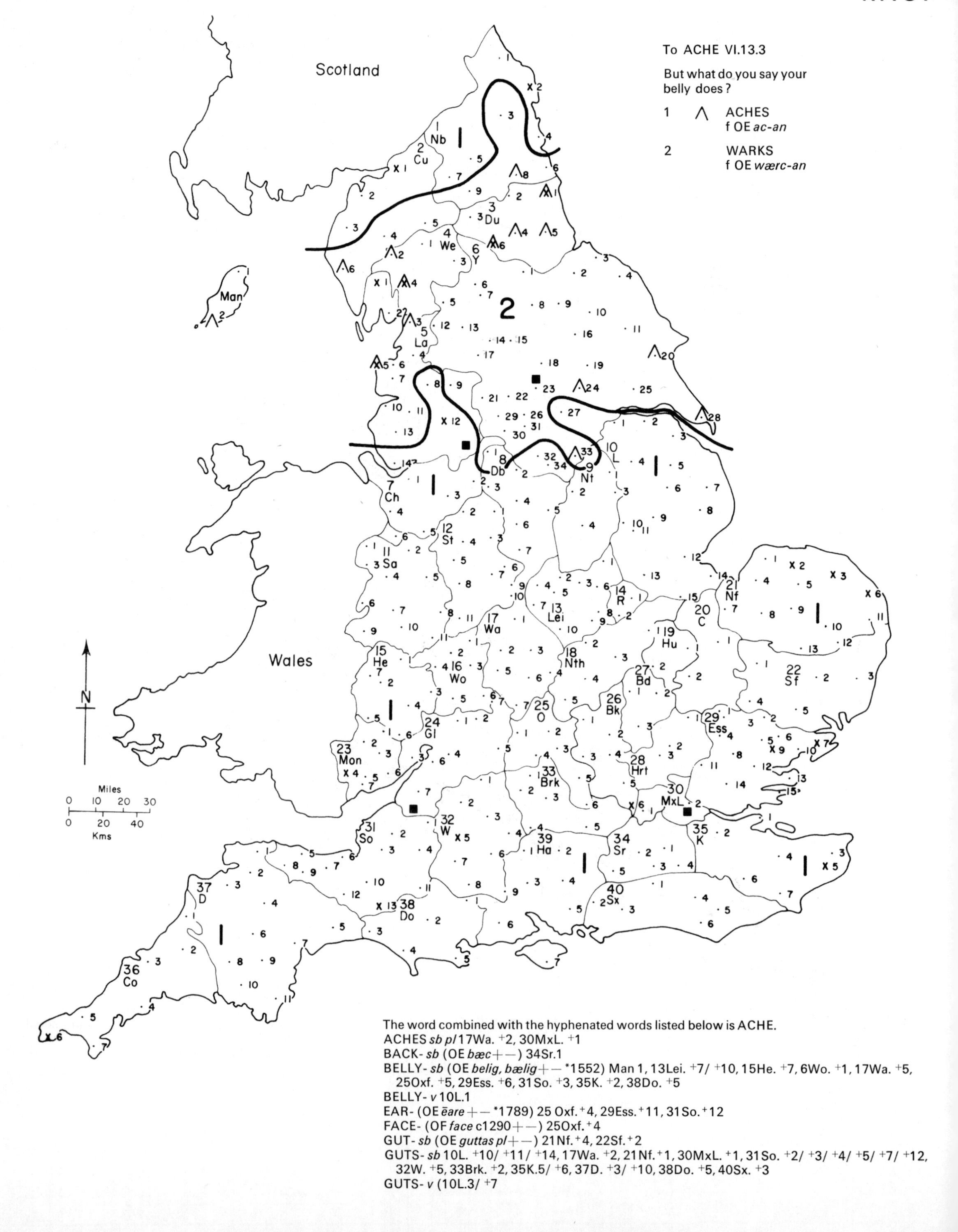

The word combined with the hyphenated words listed below is ACHE.
ACHES *sb pl* 17Wa. +2, 30MxL. +1
BACK- *sb* (OE *bæc* +—) 34Sr.1
BELLY- *sb* (OE *belig, bælig* +— *1552) Man 1, 13Lei. +7/ +10, 15He. +7, 6Wo. +1, 17Wa. +5, 25Oxf. +5, 29Ess. +6, 31So. +3, 35K. +2, 38Do. +5
BELLY- *v* 10L.1
EAR- (OE *ēare* +— *1789) 25 Oxf. +4, 29Ess. +11, 31So. +12
FACE- (OF *face* c1290 +—) 25Oxf. +4
GUT- *sb* (OE *guttas pl* +—) 21Nf. +4, 22Sf. +2
GUTS- *sb* 10L. +10/ +11/ +14, 17Wa. +2, 21Nf. +1, 30MxL. +1, 31So. +2/ +3/ +4/ +5/ +7/ +12, 32W. +5, 33Brk. +2, 35K.5/ +6, 37D. +3/ +10, 38Do. +5, 40Sx. +3
GUTS- *v* (10L.3/ +7

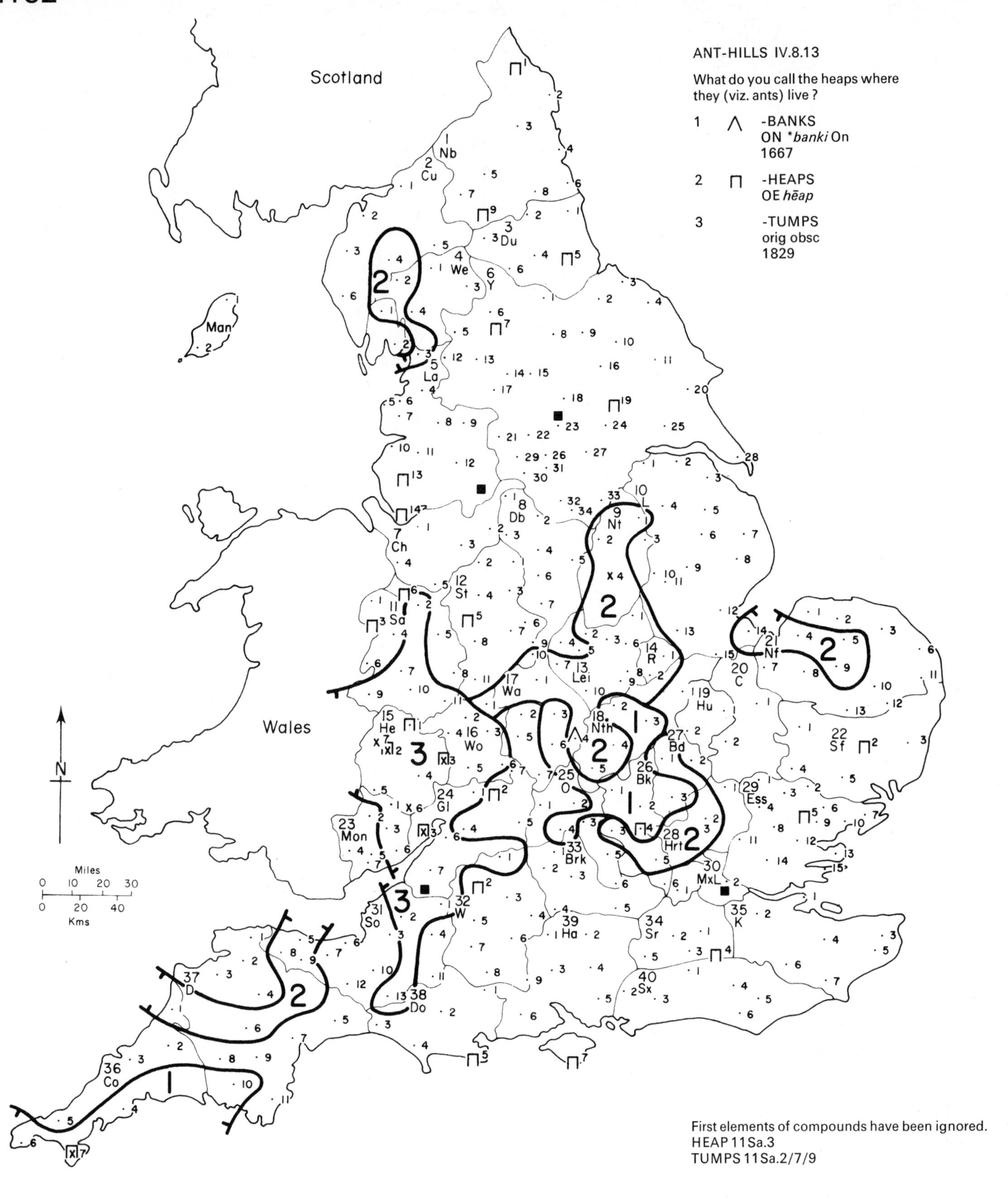
ANT-HILLS IV.8.13
What do you call the heaps where they (viz. ants) live?
1 -BANKS ON *banki On 1667
2 -HEAPS OE hēap
3 -TUMPS orig obsc 1829
Scotland
Wales
Man
Miles 0 10 20 30
0 20 40 Kms
N
First elements of compounds have been ignored.
HEAP 11Sa.3
TUMPS 11Sa.2/7/9

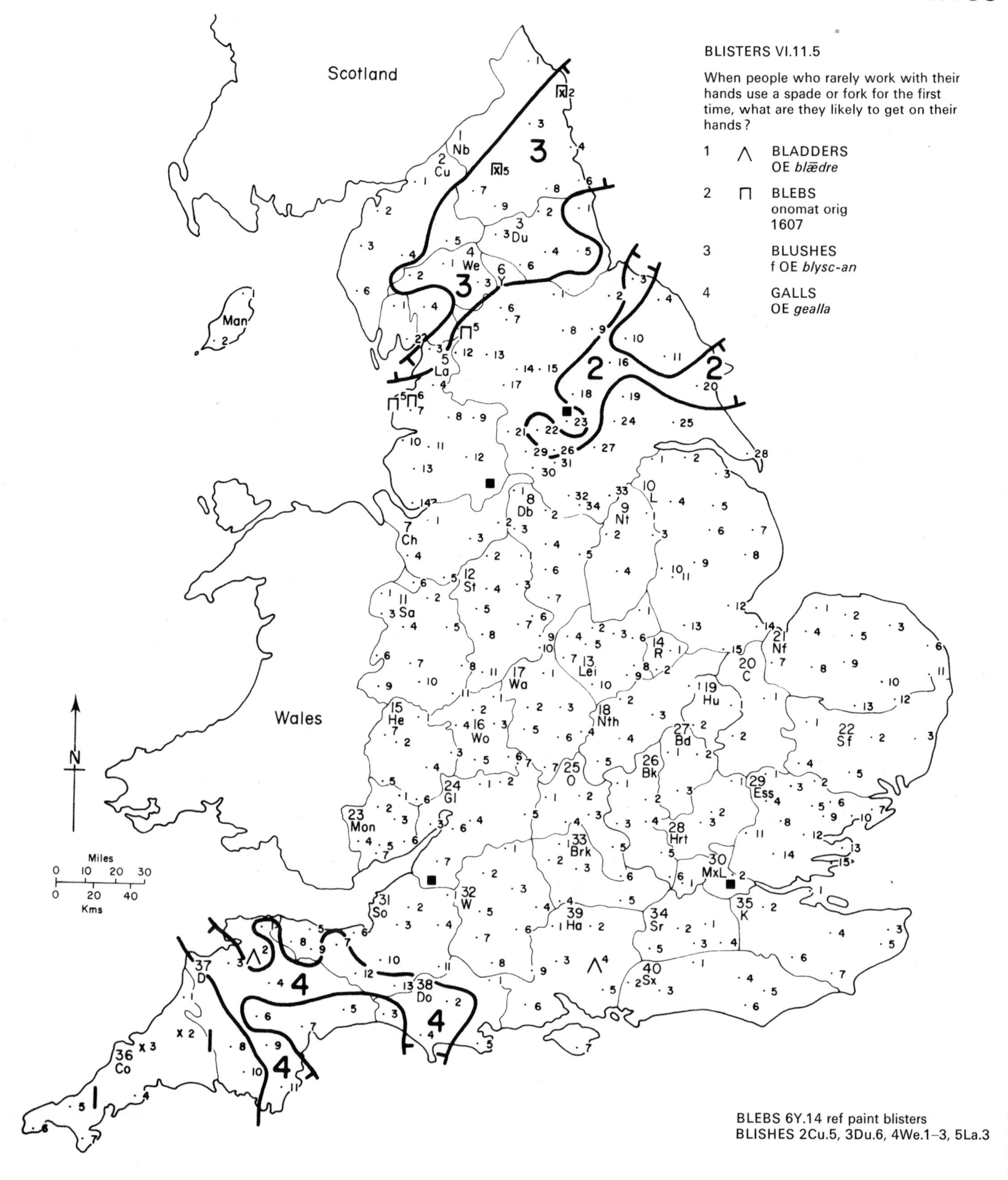
BLISTERS VI.11.5
When people who rarely work with their hands use a spade or fork for the first time, what are they likely to get on their hands?
1 Λ BLADDERS OE blǣdre
2 ⊓ BLEBS onomat orig 1607
3 BLUSHES f OE blysc-an
4 GALLS OE gealla
Scotland
Wales
Man
N
Miles
0 10 20 30
0 20 40
Kms
Nb
Cu
Du
We
Y
La
L
Db
Nt
Ch
St
Sa
R
Lei
Nf
C
Wa
Hu
He
Wo
Nth
Bd
Sf
Gl
O
Bk
Ess
Mon
Brk
Hrt
W
MxL
So
Ha
Sr
K
D
Do
Sx
Co
BLEBS 6Y.14 ref paint blisters
BLISHES 2Cu.5, 3Du.6, 4We.1–3, 5La.3

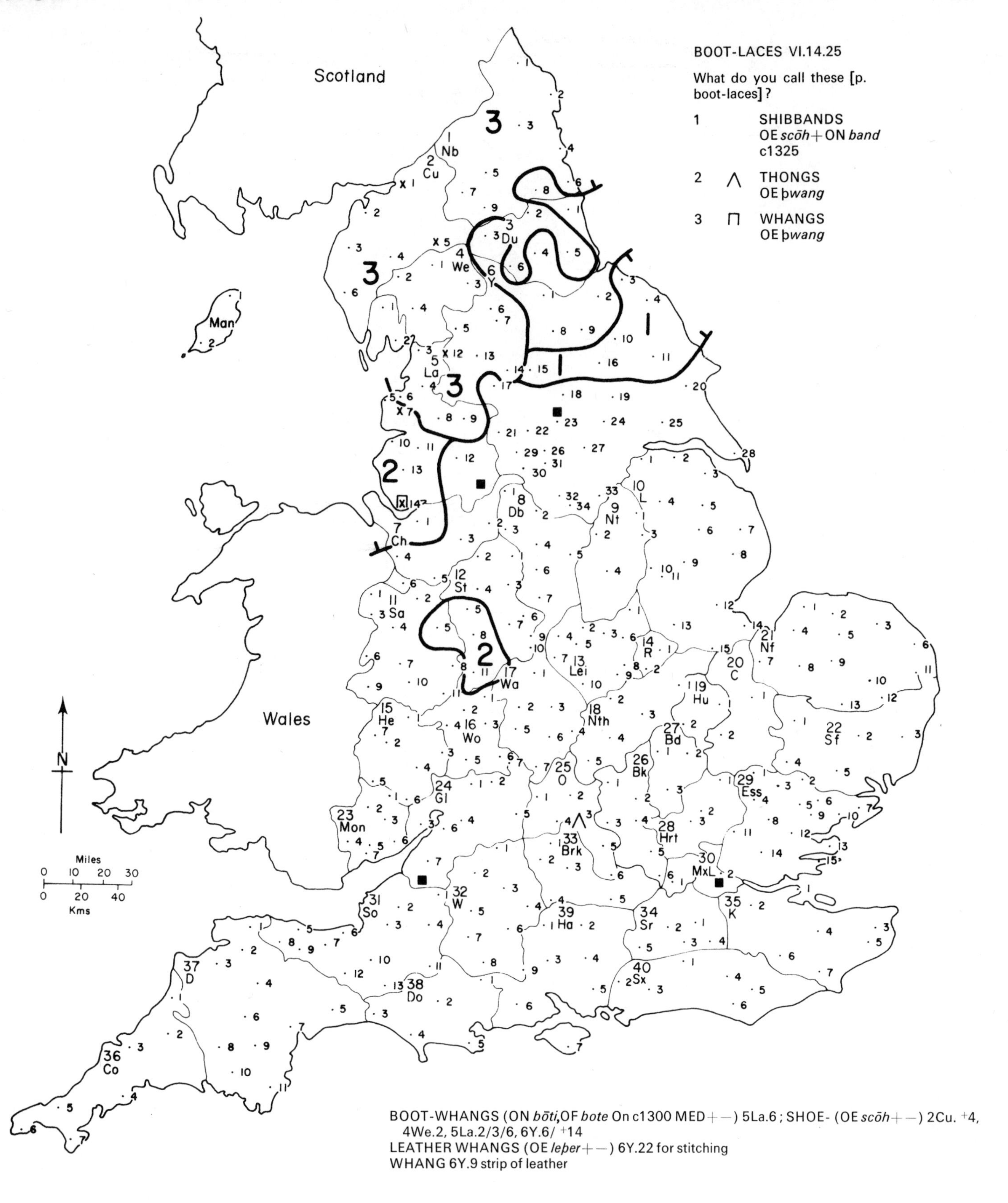

BOOT-WHANGS (ON bōti, OF bote On c1300 MED + —) 5La.6; SHOE- (OE scōh + —) 2Cu. +4, 4We.2, 5La.2/3/6, 6Y.6/ +14
LEATHER WHANGS (OE leþer + —) 6Y.22 for stitching
WHANG 6Y.9 strip of leather

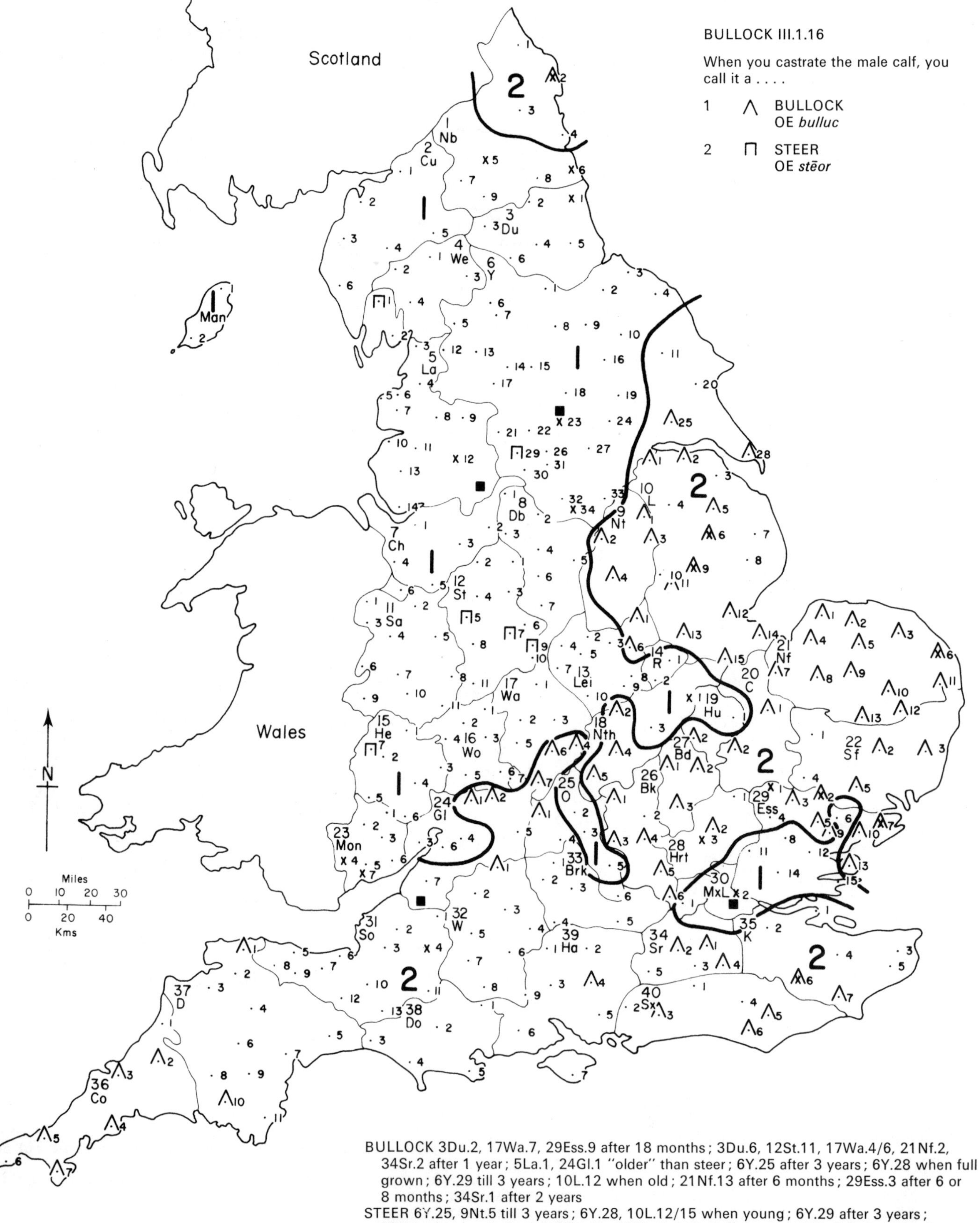

BULLOCK 3Du.2, 17Wa.7, 29Ess.9 after 18 months; 3Du.6, 12St.11, 17Wa.4/6, 21Nf.2, 34Sr.2 after 1 year; 5La.1, 24Gl.1 "older" than steer; 6Y.25 after 3 years; 6Y.28 when full grown; 6Y.29 till 3 years; 10L.12 when old; 21Nf.13 after 6 months; 29Ess.3 after 6 or 8 months; 34Sr.1 after 2 years

STEER 6Y.25, 9Nt.5 till 3 years; 6Y.28, 10L.12/15 when young; 6Y.29 after 3 years; 9Nt.4 ref young bullocks; 12St.11, 17Wa.4, 34Sr.2 till 1 year; 15He.7 "when little"; 17Wa.7, 21Nf.1/9/11, 22Sf.5, 29Ess.9 till 18 months; 19Hu.2 till 6 to 8 months; 24Gl.1 when 2 years; 24Gl.2 when "older"; 26Bk.1 at 1 year; 28Hrt.2 till 2 or 3 years; 34Sr.1 till 2 years

STEER-CALF (— + OE *cælf* On) 15He.⁺7, 18Nth.⁺2, 21Nf.4, 31So.⁺3

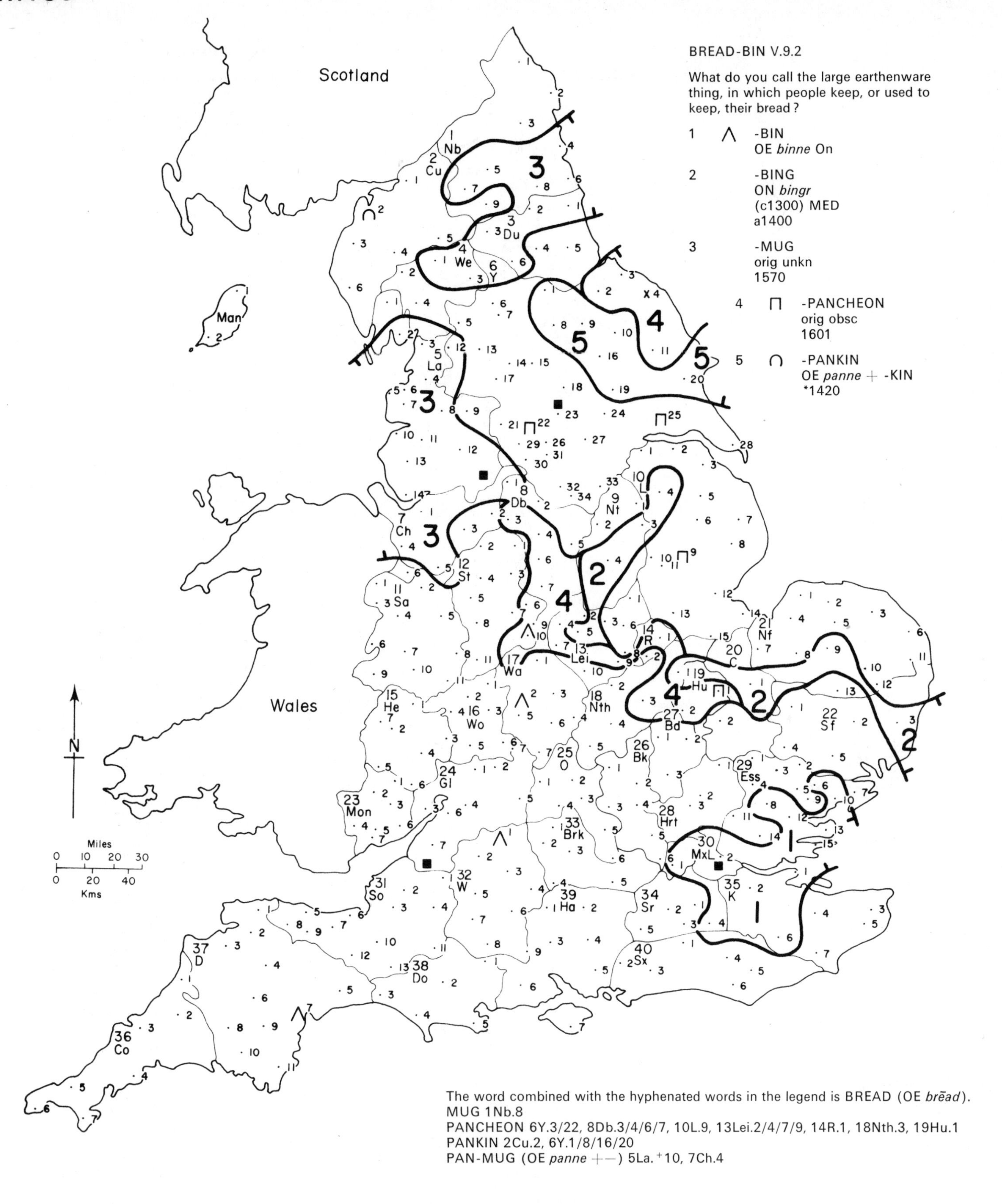

The word combined with the hyphenated words in the legend is BREAD (OE *brēad*).
MUG 1Nb.8
PANCHEON 6Y.3/22, 8Db.3/4/6/7, 10L.9, 13Lei.2/4/7/9, 14R.1, 18Nth.3, 19Hu.1
PANKIN 2Cu.2, 6Y.1/8/16/20
PAN-MUG (OE *panne* +—) 5La.+10, 7Ch.4

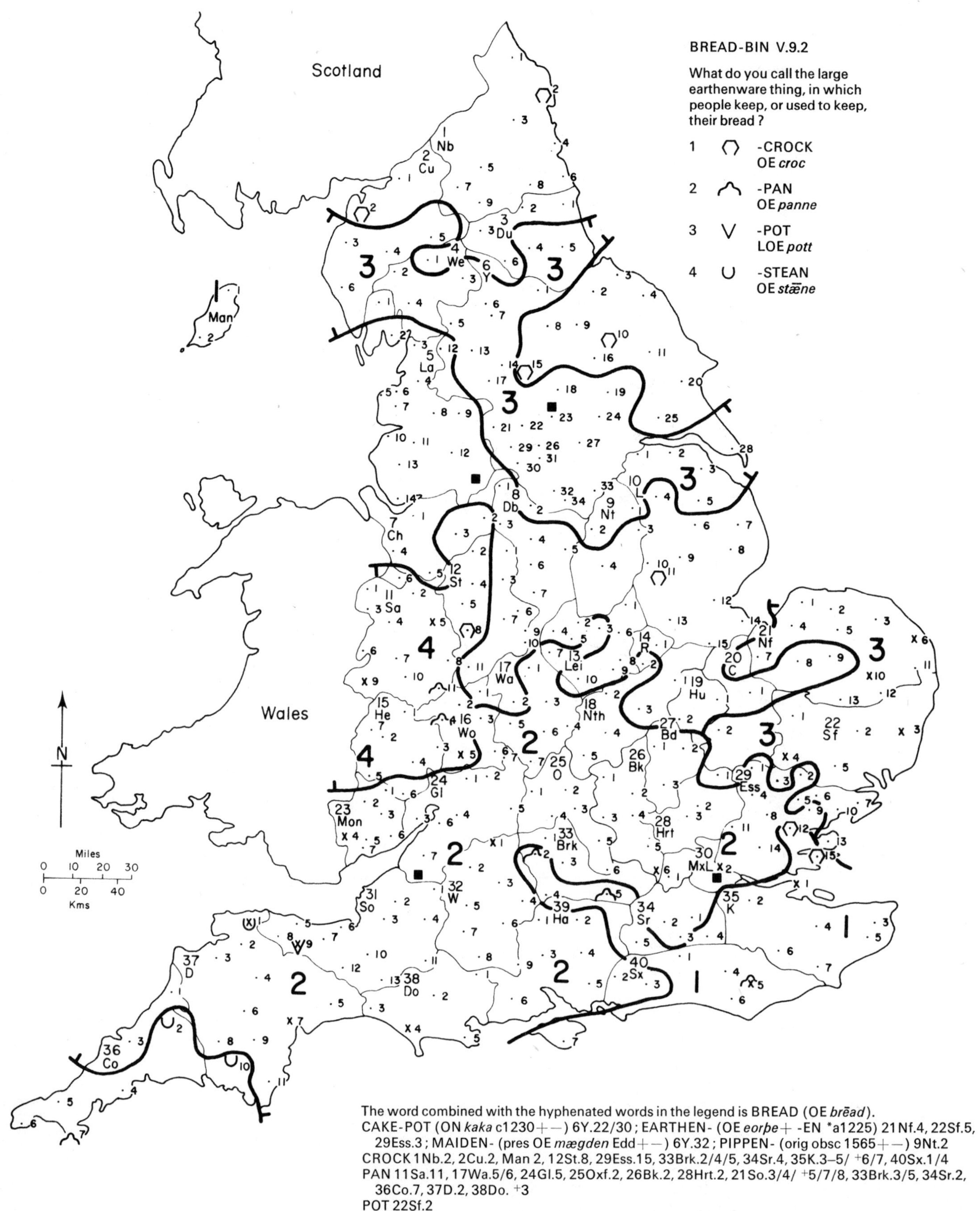

The word combined with the hyphenated words in the legend is BREAD (OE *brēad*).
CAKE-POT (ON *kaka* c1230+—) 6Y.22/30; EARTHEN- (OE *eorþe*+ -EN *a1225) 21Nf.4, 22Sf.5, 29Ess.3; MAIDEN- (pres OE *mægden* Edd+—) 6Y.32; PIPPEN- (orig obsc 1565+—) 9Nt.2
CROCK 1Nb.2, 2Cu.2, Man 2, 12St.8, 29Ess.15, 33Brk.2/4/5, 34Sr.4, 35K.3–5/ +6/7, 40Sx.1/4
PAN 11Sa.11, 17Wa.5/6, 24Gl.5, 25Oxf.2, 26Bk.2, 28Hrt.2, 21So.3/4/ +5/7/8, 33Brk.3/5, 34Sr.2, 36Co.7, 37D.2, 38Do. +3
POT 22Sf.2
STEAN 7Ch.3/6, 11Sa.2–4/6, 12St.2/4/5/8, 15 He.1–3/7, 16Wo.2/4, 37D.8 earthenware pan for salting meat in, 37D.9 for butter, 37D. +10

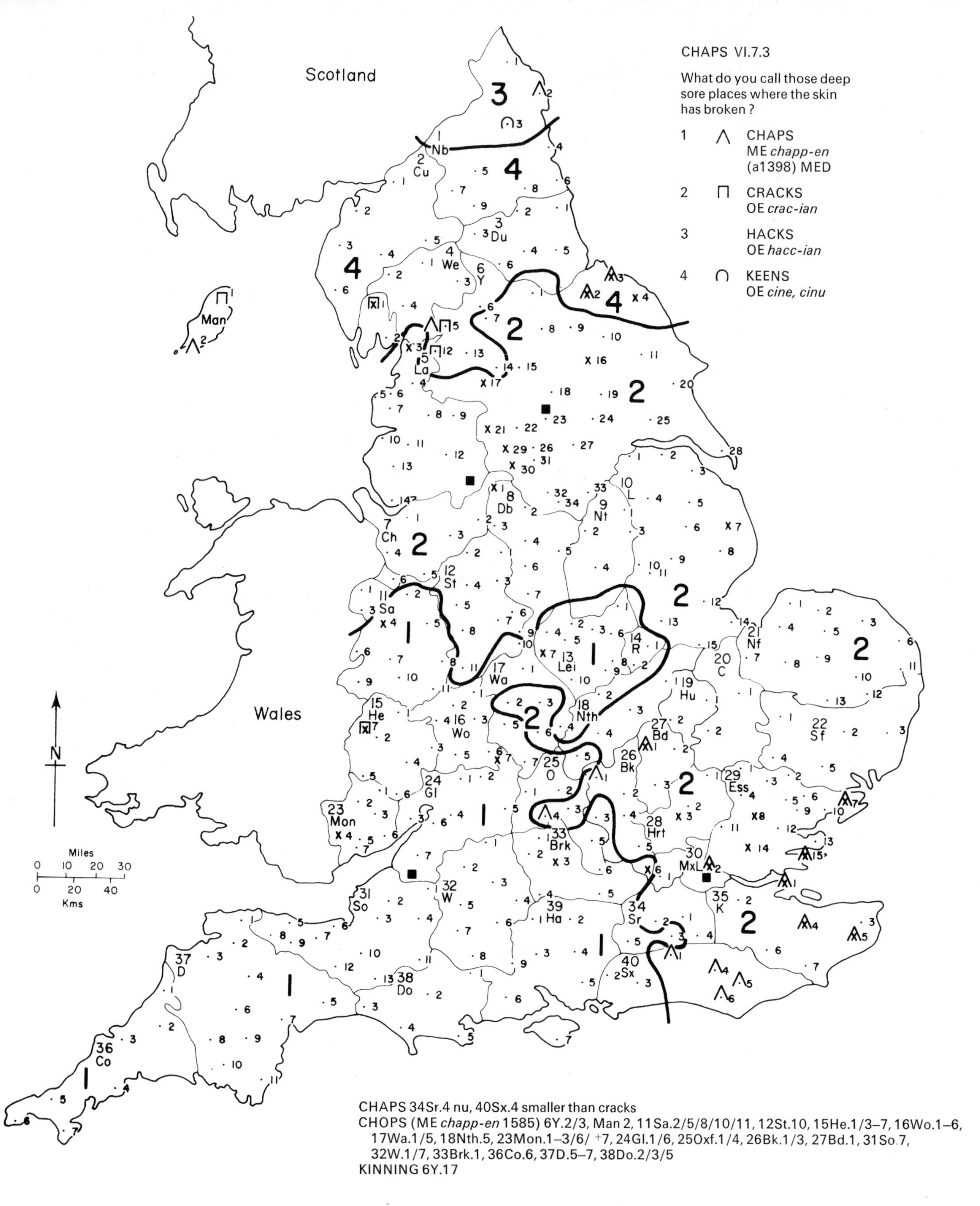

CHAPS 34Sr.4 nu, 40Sx.4 smaller than cracks
CHOPS (ME *chapp-en* 1585) 6Y.2/3, Man 2, 11Sa.2/5/8/10/11, 12St.10, 15He.1/3–7, 16Wo.1–6, 17Wa.1/5, 18Nth.5, 23Mon.1–3/6/ +7, 24Gl.1/6, 25Oxf.1/4, 26Bk.1/3, 27Bd.1, 31So.7, 32W.1/7, 33Brk.1, 36Co.6, 37D.5–7, 38Do.2/3/5
KINNING 6Y.17

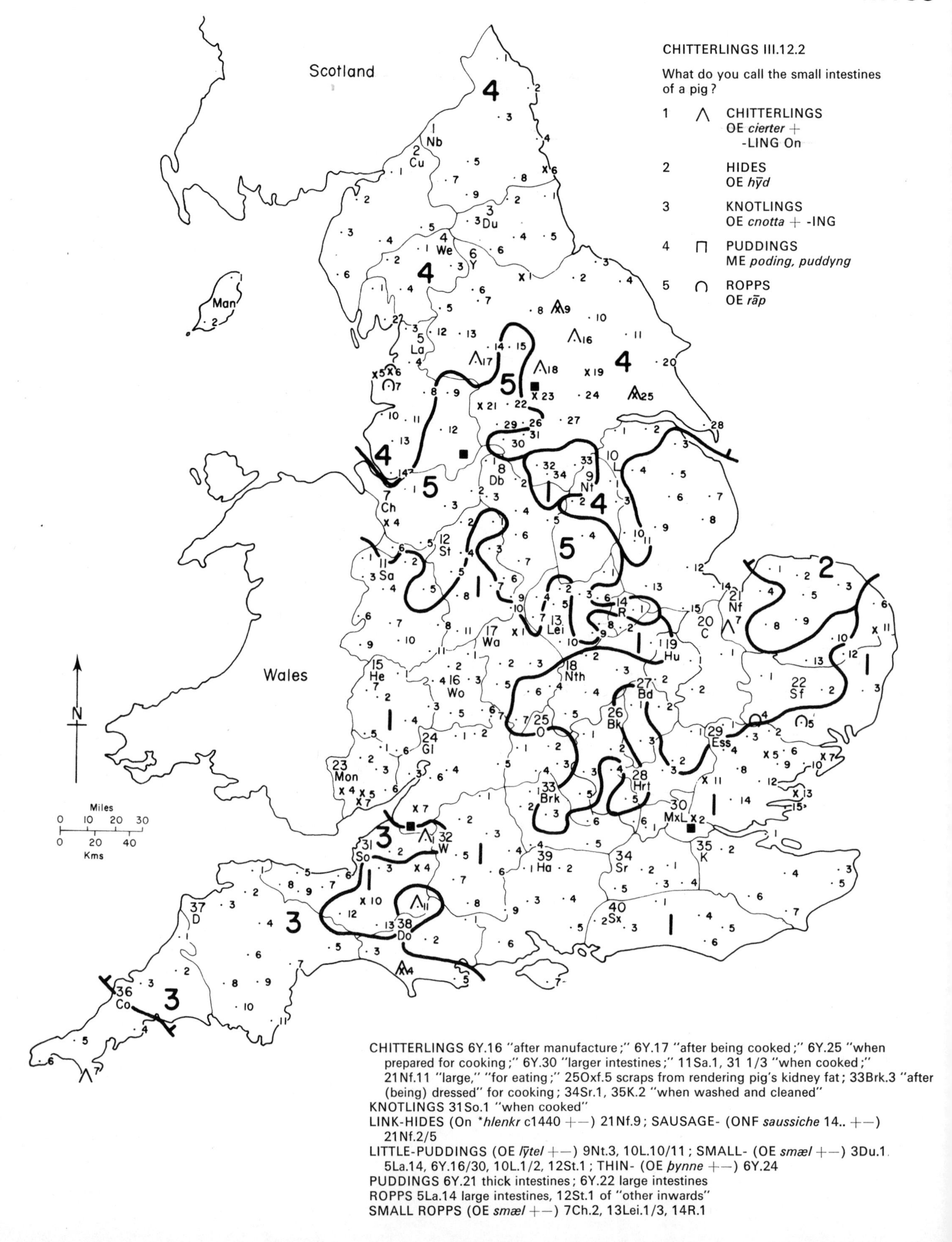
CHITTERLINGS III.12.2
What do you call the small intestines of a pig?
1 Λ CHITTERLINGS OE *cierter* + -LING On
2 HIDES OE *hȳd*
3 KNOTLINGS OE *cnotta* + -ING
4 ⊓ PUDDINGS ME *poding, puddyng*
5 ∩ ROPPS OE *rāp*
Scotland
Wales
Man
N
Miles 0 10 20 30
0 20 40 Kms
CHITTERLINGS 6Y.16 "after manufacture;" 6Y.17 "after being cooked;" 6Y.25 "when prepared for cooking;" 6Y.30 "larger intestines;" 11Sa.1, 31 1/3 "when cooked;" 21Nf.11 "large," "for eating;" 25Oxf.5 scraps from rendering pig's kidney fat; 33Brk.3 "after (being) dressed" for cooking; 34Sr.1, 35K.2 "when washed and cleaned"
KNOTLINGS 31So.1 "when cooked"
LINK-HIDES (On *hlenkr c1440 +—) 21Nf.9; SAUSAGE- (ONF *saussiche* 14.. +—) 21Nf.2/5
LITTLE-PUDDINGS (OE *lȳtel* +—) 9Nt.3, 10L.10/11; SMALL- (OE *smæl* +—) 3Du.1, 5La.14, 6Y.16/30, 10L.1/2, 12St.1; THIN- (OE *þynne* +—) 6Y.24
PUDDINGS 6Y.21 thick intestines; 6Y.22 large intestines
ROPPS 5La.14 large intestines, 12St.1 of "other inwards"
SMALL ROPPS (OE *smæl* +—) 7Ch.2, 13Lei.1/3, 14R.1

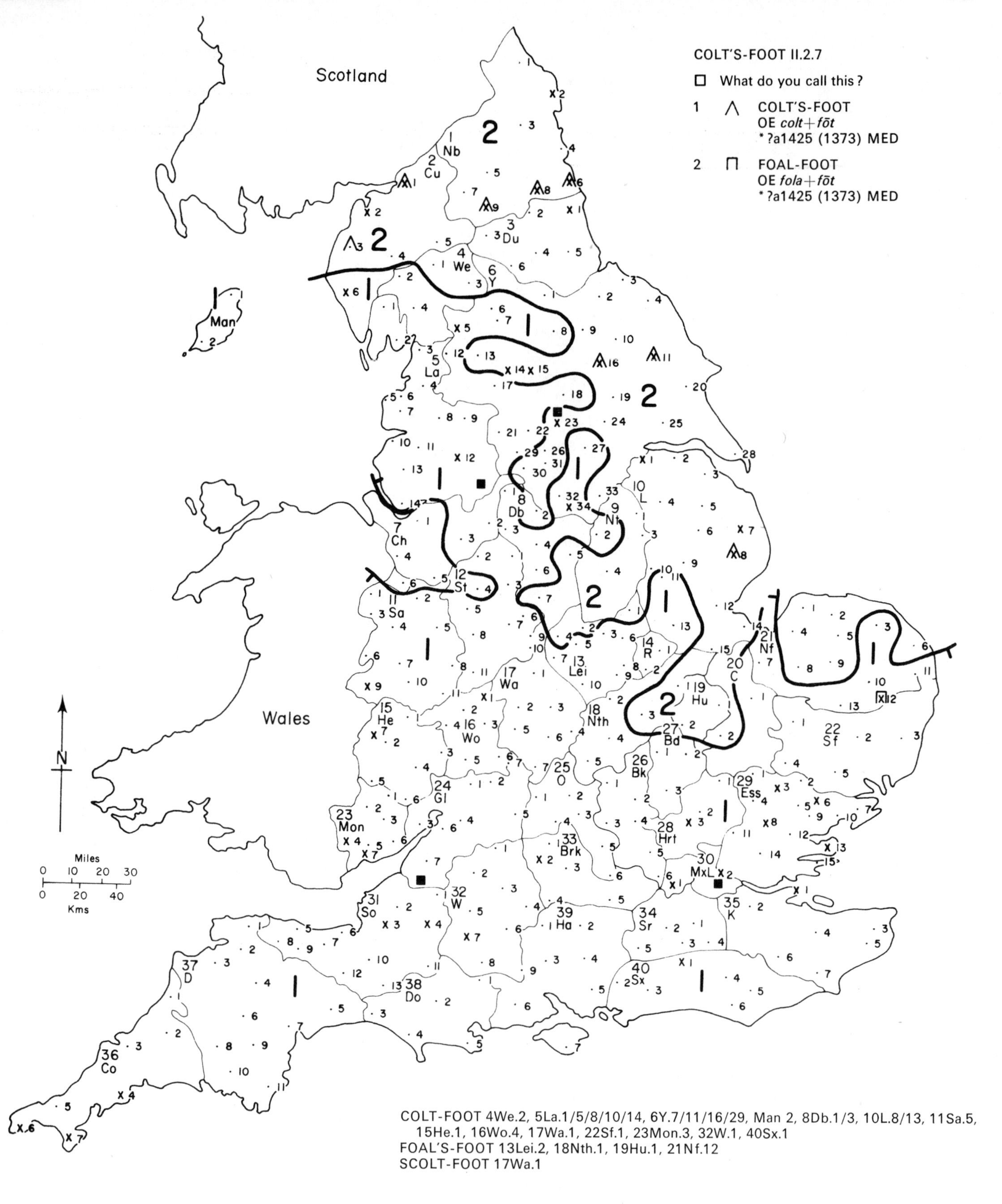

COLT-FOOT 4We.2, 5La.1/5/8/10/14, 6Y.7/11/16/29, Man 2, 8Db.1/3, 10L.8/13, 11Sa.5, 15He.1, 16Wo.4, 17Wa.1, 22Sf.1, 23Mon.3, 32W.1, 40Sx.1
FOAL'S-FOOT 13Lei.2, 18Nth.1, 19Hu.1, 21Nf.12
SCOLT-FOOT 17Wa.1

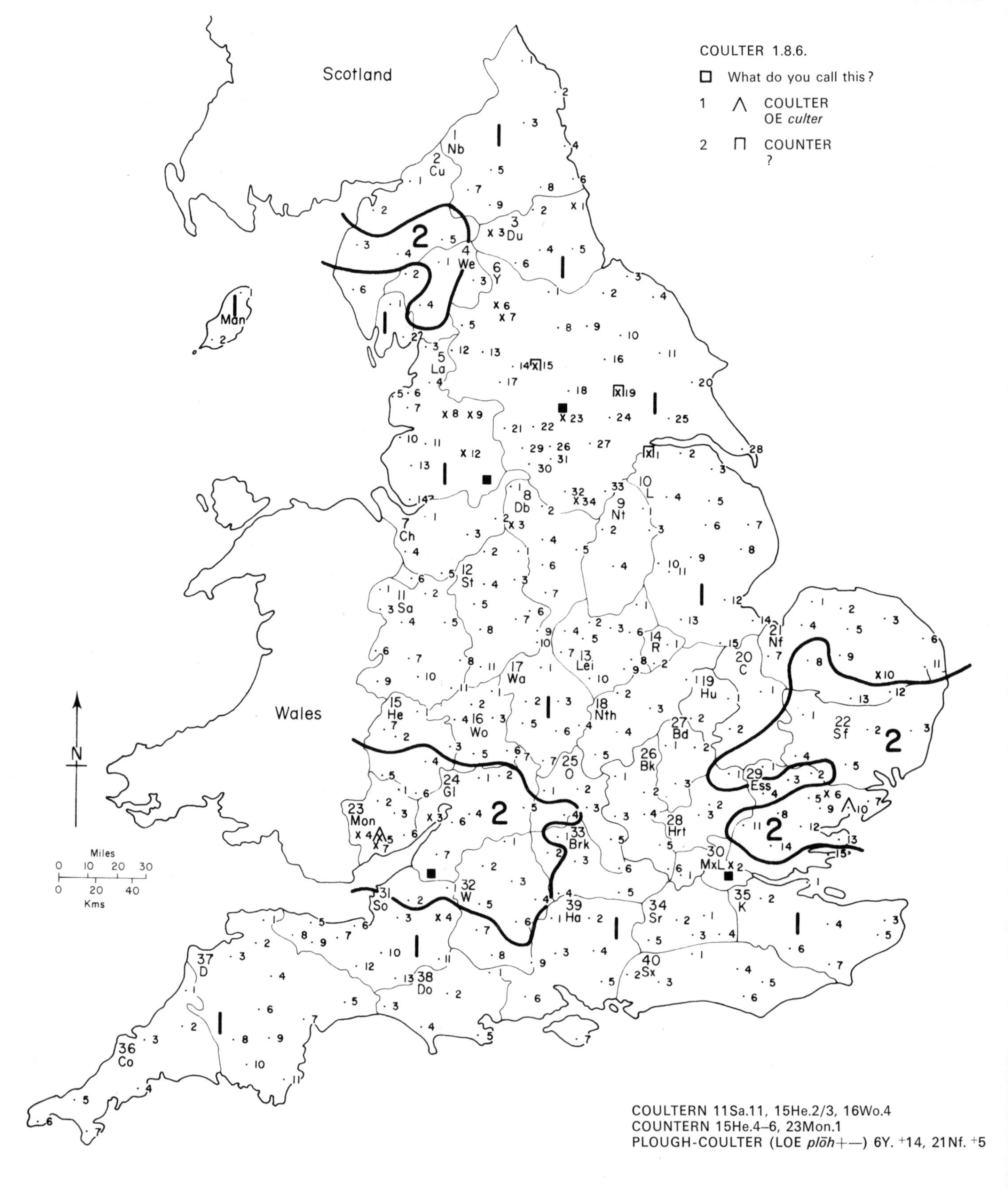
COULTER 1.8.6.
☐ What do you call this?
1 ⋀ COULTER
OE *culter*
2 ⊓ COUNTER
?
Scotland
Wales
N
Miles
0 10 20 30
0 20 40
Kms
COULTERN 11Sa.11, 15He.2/3, 16Wo.4
COUNTERN 15He.4–6, 23Mon.1
PLOUGH-COULTER (LOE *plōh*+—) 6Y. +14, 21Nf. +5

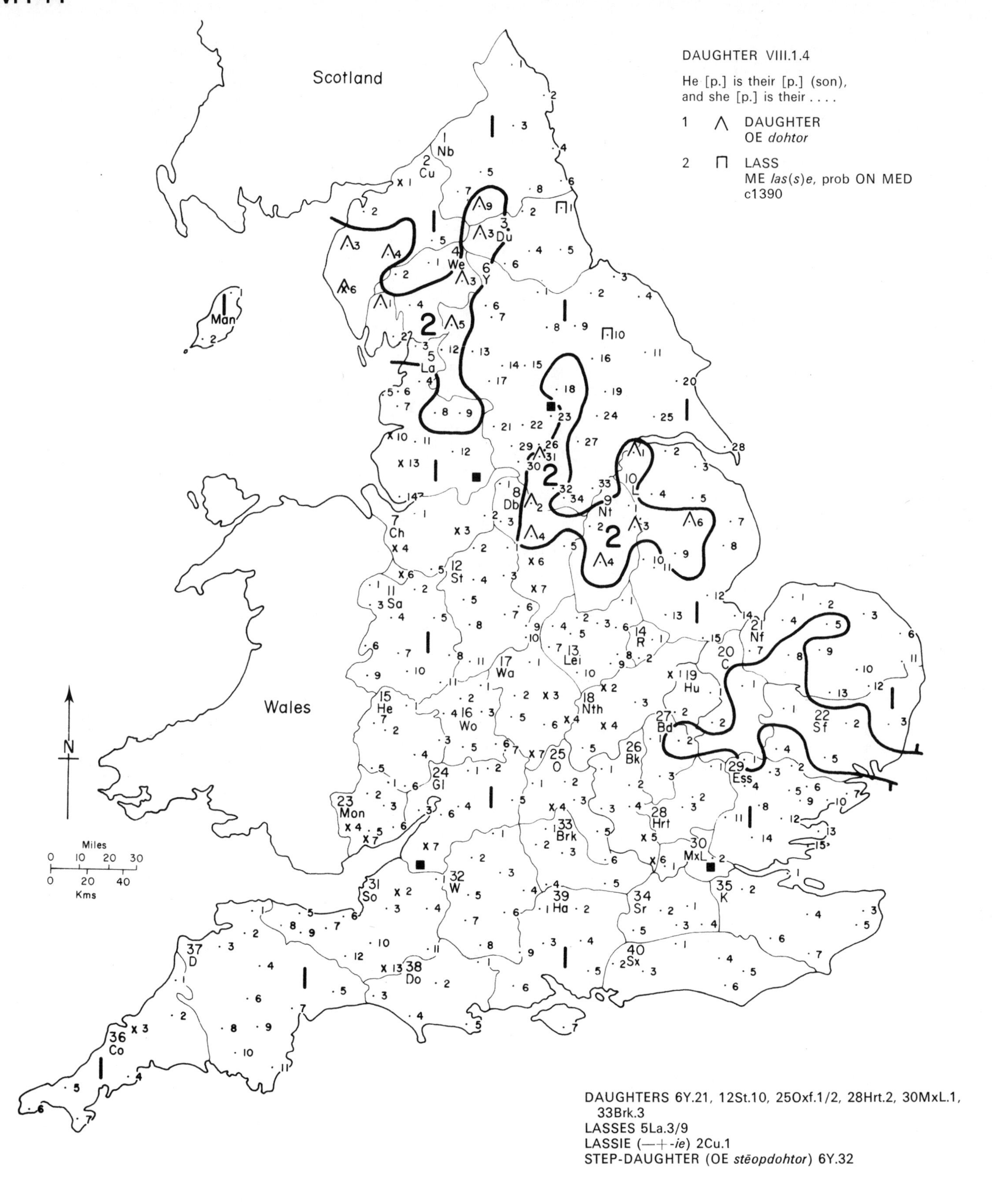

DAUGHTER VIII.1.4
He [p.] is their [p.] (son), and she [p.] is their . . . .
1 ⋀ DAUGHTER
OE dohtor
2 ⊓ LASS
ME las(s)e, prob ON MED c1390
Scotland
Wales
Man
N
Miles
0 10 20 30
0 20 40
Kms
Nb
Cu
Du
We
Y
La
Ch
Db
Nt
L
St
Sa
Lei
R
Nf
C
Hu
Wa
He
Wo
Nth
Bd
Sf
Bk
O
Gl
Ess
Mon
Brk
Hrt
MxL
So
W
Ha
Sr
K
D
Do
Sx
Co
DAUGHTERS 6Y.21, 12St.10, 25Oxf.1/2, 28Hrt.2, 30MxL.1, 33Brk.3
LASSES 5La.3/9
LASSIE (— + -ie) 2Cu.1
STEP-DAUGHTER (OE stēopdohtor) 6Y.32

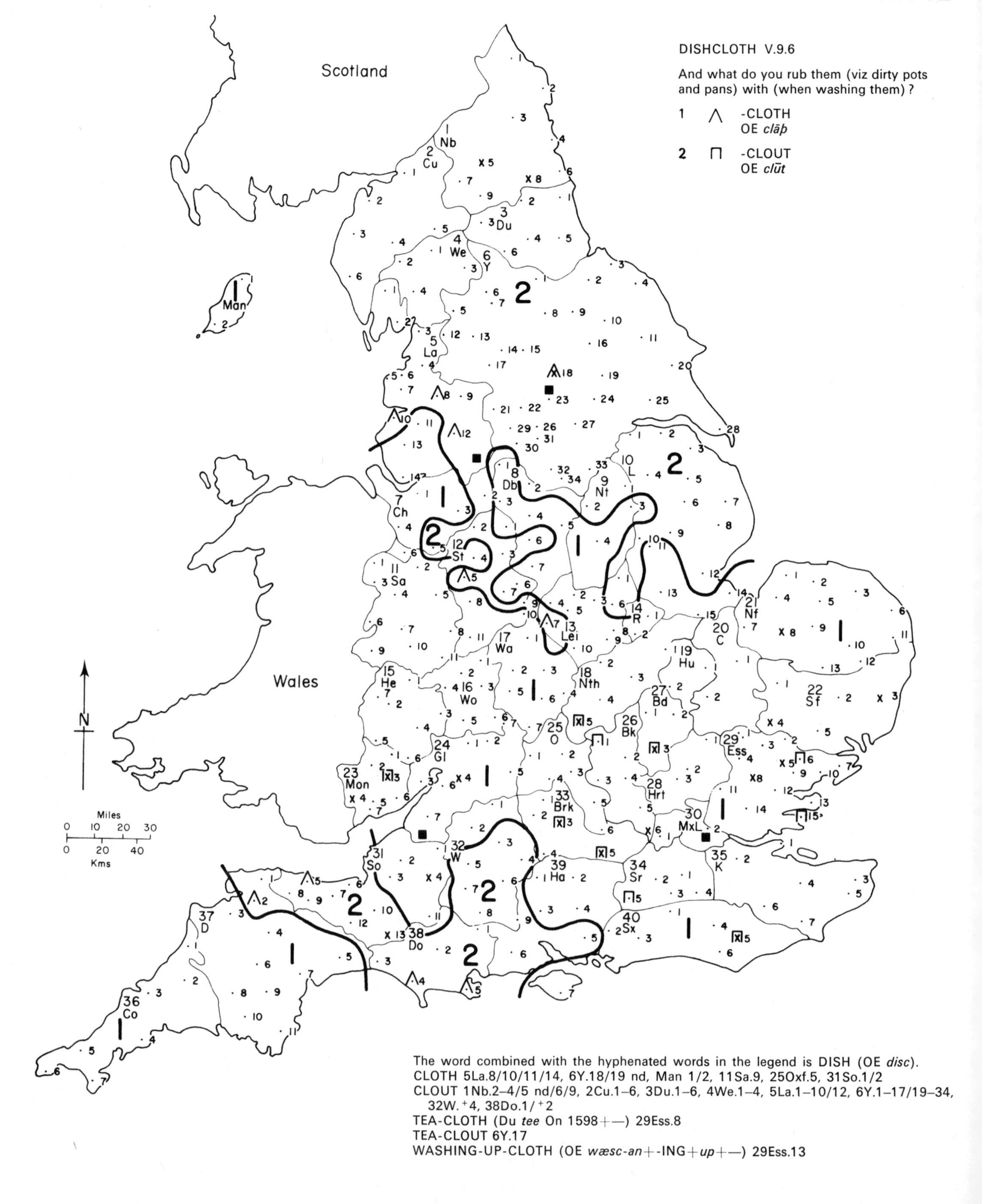

DISHCLOTH V.9.6

And what do you rub them (viz dirty pots and pans) with (when washing them)?

1 ⋀ -CLOTH OE *clāþ*

2 ⊓ -CLOUT OE *clūt*

The word combined with the hyphenated words in the legend is DISH (OE *disc*).
CLOTH 5La.8/10/11/14, 6Y.18/19 nd, Man 1/2, 11Sa.9, 25Oxf.5, 31So.1/2
CLOUT 1Nb.2–4/5 nd/6/9, 2Cu.1–6, 3Du.1–6, 4We.1–4, 5La.1–10/12, 6Y.1–17/19–34, 32W.$^{+}$4, 38Do.1/$^{+}$2
TEA-CLOTH (Du *tee* On 1598+—) 29Ess.8
TEA-CLOUT 6Y.17
WASHING-UP-CLOTH (OE *wæsc-an*+-ING+*up*+—) 29Ess.13

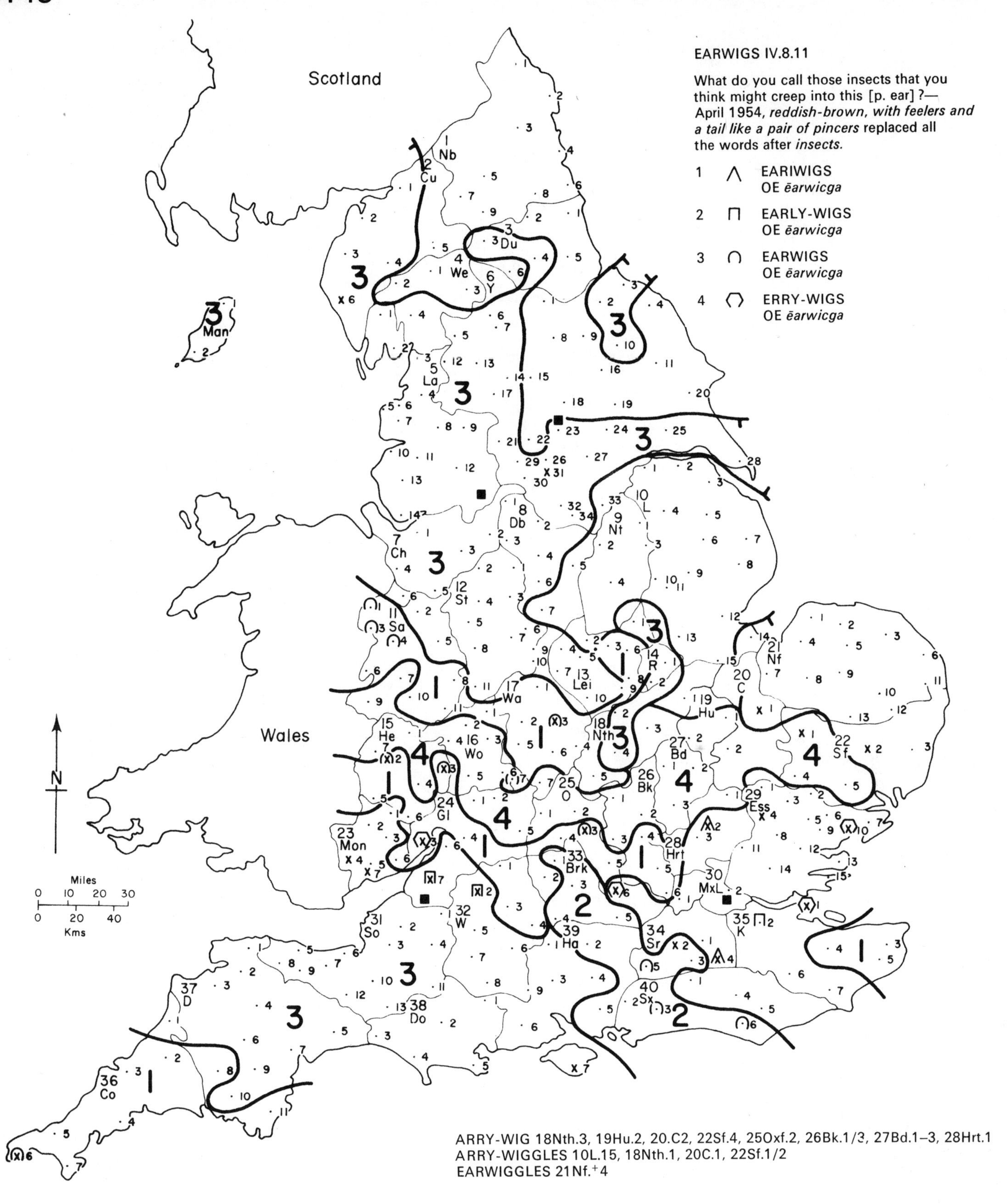

EARWIGS IV.8.11
What do you call those insects that you think might creep into this [p. ear] ?— April 1954, *reddish-brown, with feelers and a tail like a pair of pincers* replaced all the words after *insects.*
1 EARIWIGS OE *ēarwicga*
2 EARLY-WIGS OE *ēarwicga*
3 EARWIGS OE *ēarwicga*
4 ERRY-WIGS OE *ēarwicga*
Scotland
Wales
Miles
0 10 20 30
0 20 40
Kms
ARRY-WIG 18Nth.3, 19Hu.2, 20.C2, 22Sf.4, 25Oxf.2, 26Bk.1/3, 27Bd.1–3, 28Hrt.1
ARRY-WIGGLES 10L.15, 18Nth.1, 20C.1, 22Sf.1/2
EARWIGGLES 21Nf.+4

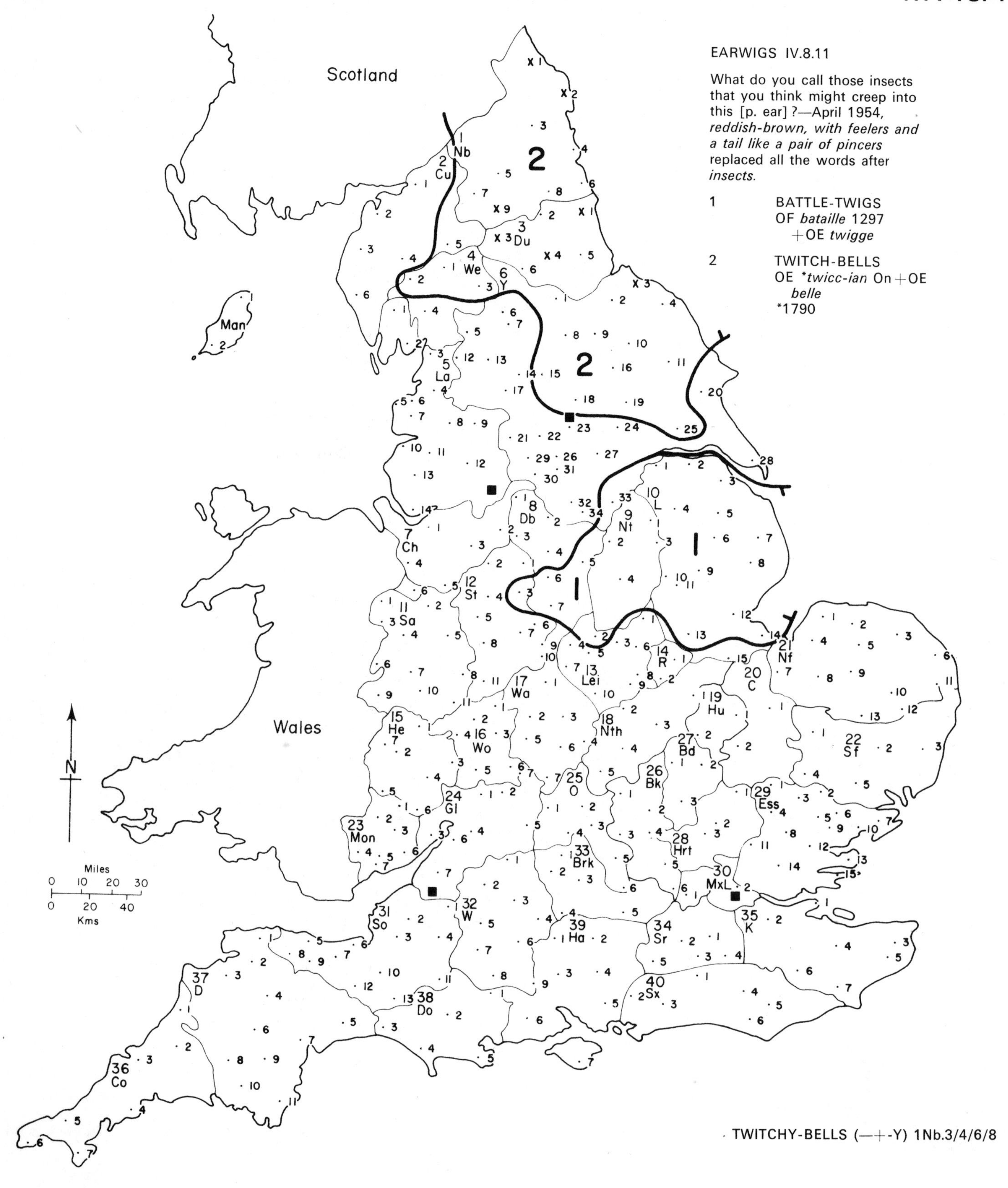
EARWIGS IV.8.11
What do you call those insects that you think might creep into this [p. ear] ?—April 1954, *reddish-brown, with feelers and a tail like a pair of pincers* replaced all the words after *insects.*
1 BATTLE-TWIGS
OF *bataille* 1297 +OE *twigge*
2 TWITCH-BELLS
OE **twicc-ian* On+OE *belle*
*1790
Scotland
Wales
Man
Miles
0 10 20 30
0 20 40
Kms
N
· TWITCHY-BELLS (—+-Y) 1Nb.3/4/6/8

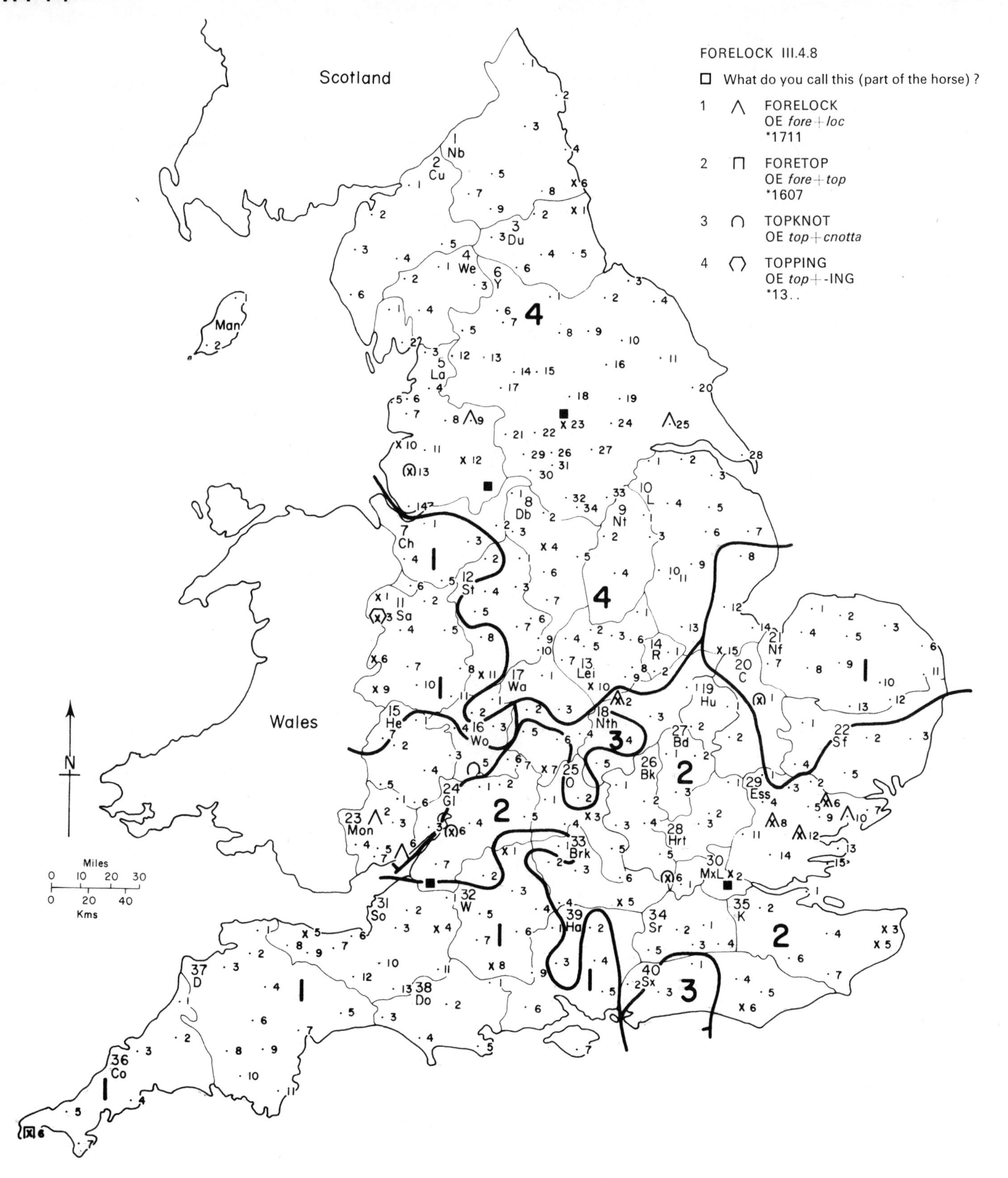
FORELOCK III.4.8
☐ What do you call this (part of the horse) ?
1 FORELOCK OE fore+loc *1711
2 FORETOP OE fore+top *1607
3 TOPKNOT OE top+cnotta
4 TOPPING OE top+-ING *13..
Scotland
Wales
Man
N
Miles 0 10 20 30
0 20 40 Kms

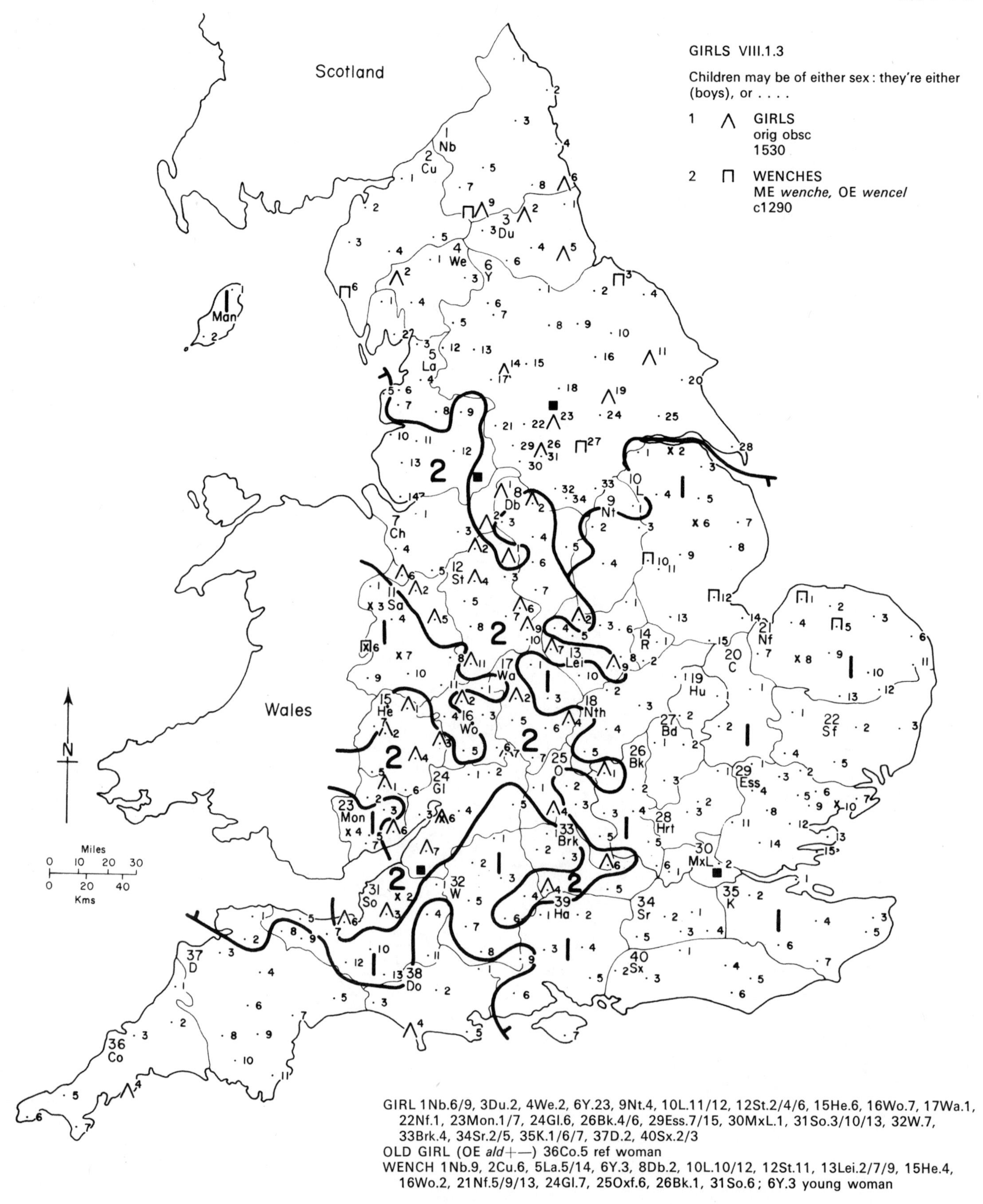

GIRL 1Nb.6/9, 3Du.2, 4We.2, 6Y.23, 9Nt.4, 10L.11/12, 12St.2/4/6, 15He.6, 16Wo.7, 17Wa.1, 22Nf.1, 23Mon.1/7, 24Gl.6, 26Bk.4/6, 29Ess.7/15, 30MxL.1, 31So.3/10/13, 32W.7, 33Brk.4, 34Sr.2/5, 35K.1/6/7, 37D.2, 40Sx.2/3
OLD GIRL (OE *ald*+—) 36Co.5 ref woman
WENCH 1Nb.9, 2Cu.6, 5La.5/14, 6Y.3, 8Db.2, 10L.10/12, 12St.11, 13Lei.2/7/9, 15He.4, 16Wo.2, 21Nf.5/9/13, 24Gl.7, 25Oxf.6, 26Bk.1, 31So.6; 6Y.3 young woman

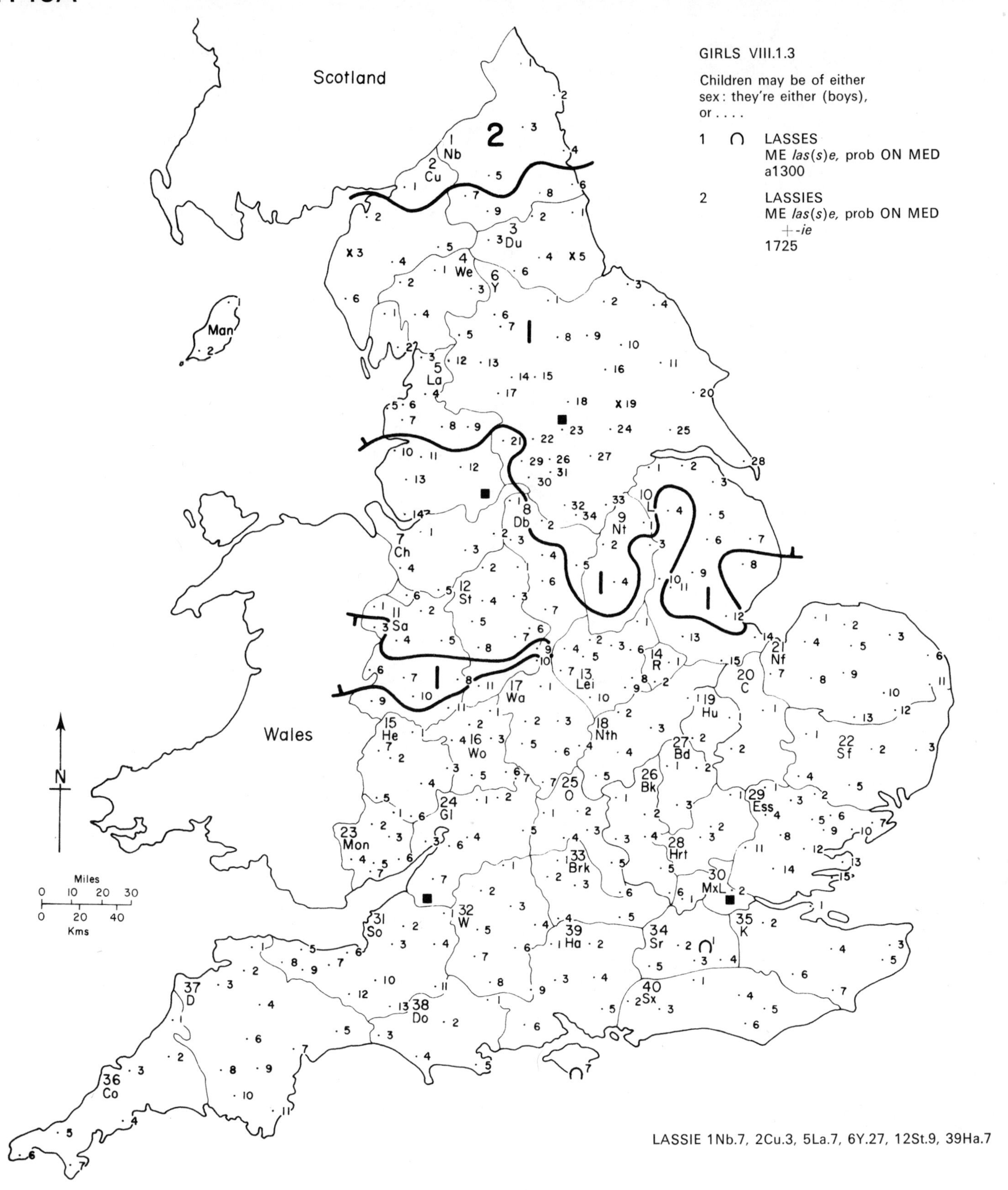
GIRLS VIII.1.3
Children may be of either sex: they're either (boys), or . . . .
1 ∩ LASSES
ME *las(s)e*, prob ON MED
a1300
2 LASSIES
ME *las(s)e*, prob ON MED
+ *-ie*
1725
Scotland
Wales
Man
N
Miles
0 10 20 30
0 20 40
Kms
LASSIE 1Nb.7, 2Cu.3, 5La.7, 6Y.27, 12St.9, 39Ha.7

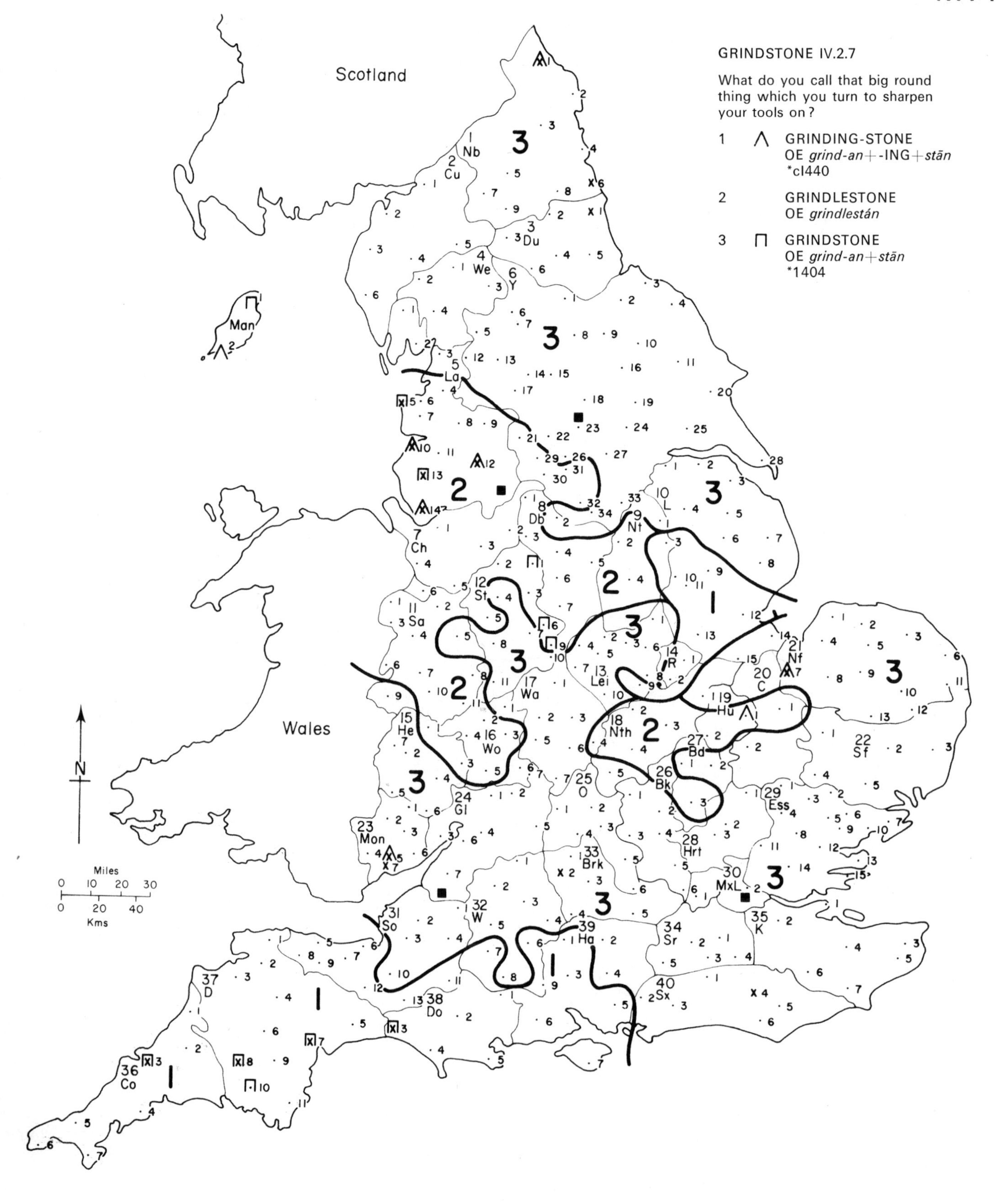
GRINDSTONE IV.2.7
What do you call that big round thing which you turn to sharpen your tools on?
1 GRINDING-STONE
OE *grind-an*+-ING+*stān*
*cl440
2 GRINDLESTONE
OE *grindlestán*
3 GRINDSTONE
OE *grind-an*+*stān*
*1404
Scotland
Wales
Man
N
Miles
0 10 20 30
0 20 40
Kms
Nb
Cu
Du
We
Y
La
L
Ch
Db
Nt
St
Sa
R
Lei
Nf
Wa
C
Hu
He
Wo
Nth
Bd
Sf
Bk
O
Gl
Ess
Mon
Brk
Hrt
MxL
So
W
K
Ha
Sr
D
Do
Sx
Co

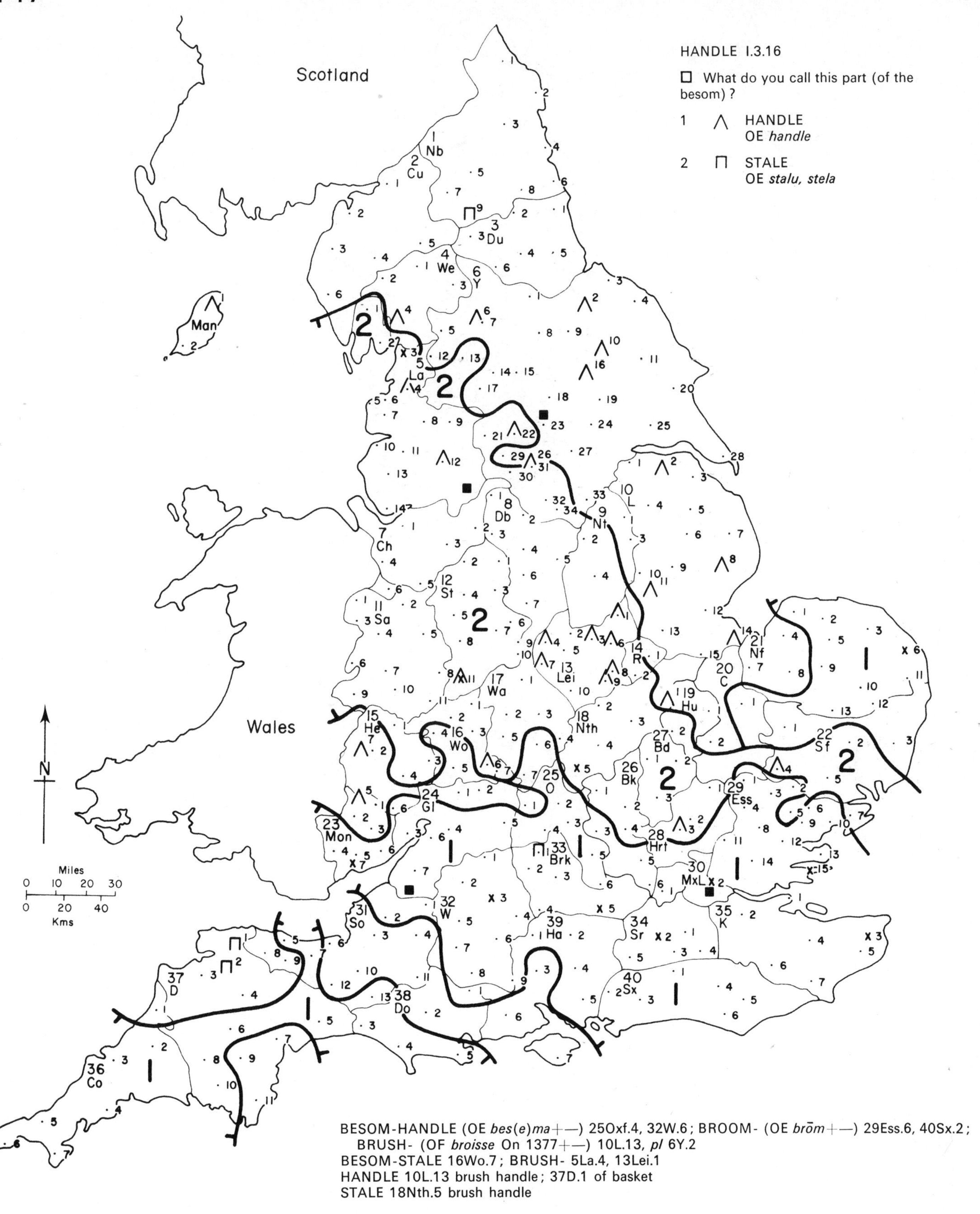

BESOM-HANDLE (OE *bes(e)ma*+—) 25Oxf.4, 32W.6; BROOM- (OE *brōm*+—) 29Ess.6, 40Sx.2; BRUSH- (OF *broisse* On 1377+—) 10L.13, *pl* 6Y.2
BESOM-STALE 16Wo.7; BRUSH- 5La.4, 13Lei.1
HANDLE 10L.13 brush handle; 37D.1 of basket
STALE 18Nth.5 brush handle

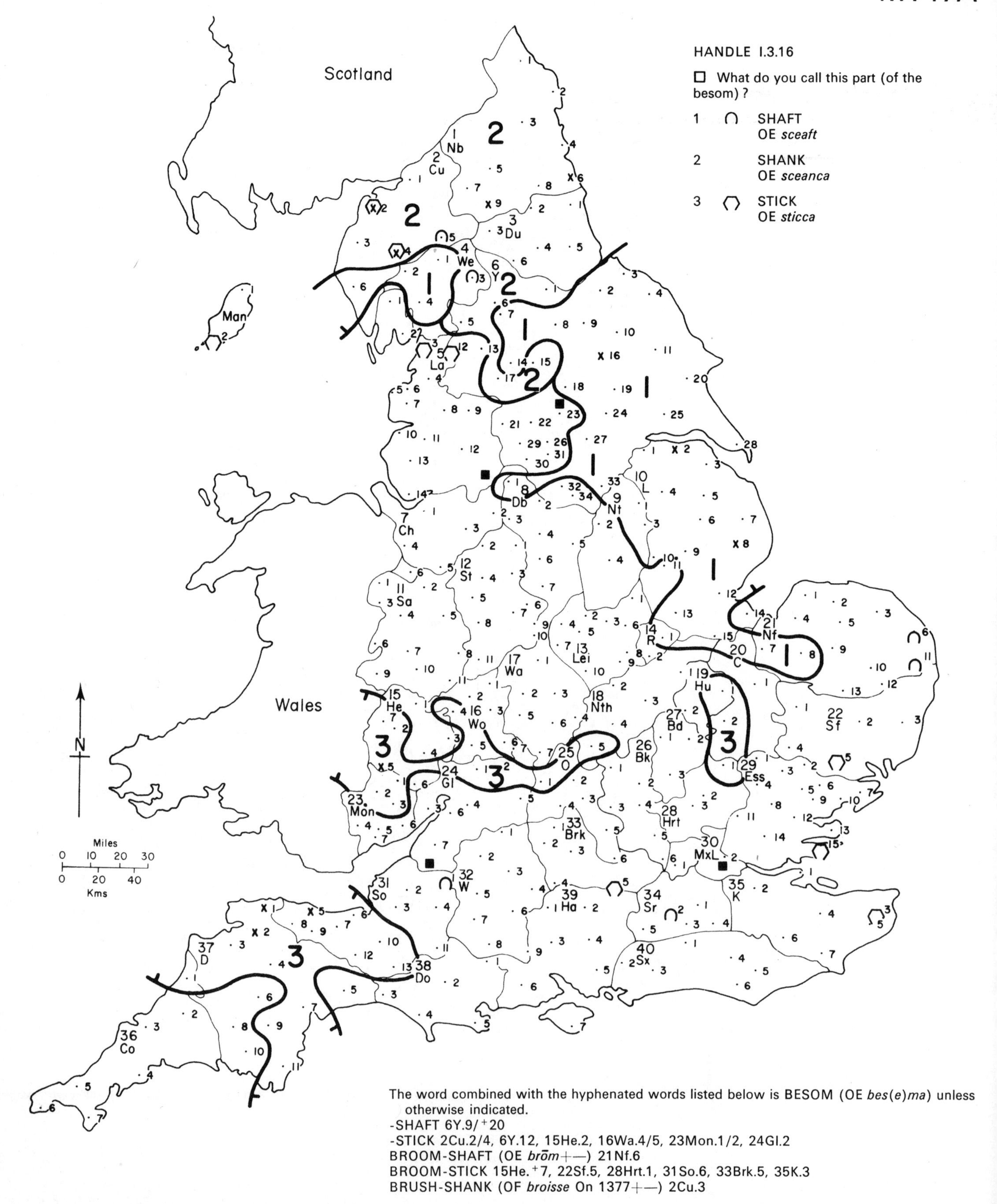

The word combined with the hyphenated words listed below is BESOM (OE *bes(e)ma*) unless otherwise indicated.
-SHAFT 6Y.9/⁺20
-STICK 2Cu.2/4, 6Y.12, 15He.2, 16Wa.4/5, 23Mon.1/2, 24Gl.2
BROOM-SHAFT (OE *brōm*+—) 21Nf.6
BROOM-STICK 15He.⁺7, 22Sf.5, 28Hrt.1, 31So.6, 33Brk.5, 35K.3
BRUSH-SHANK (OF *broisse* On 1377+—) 2Cu.3

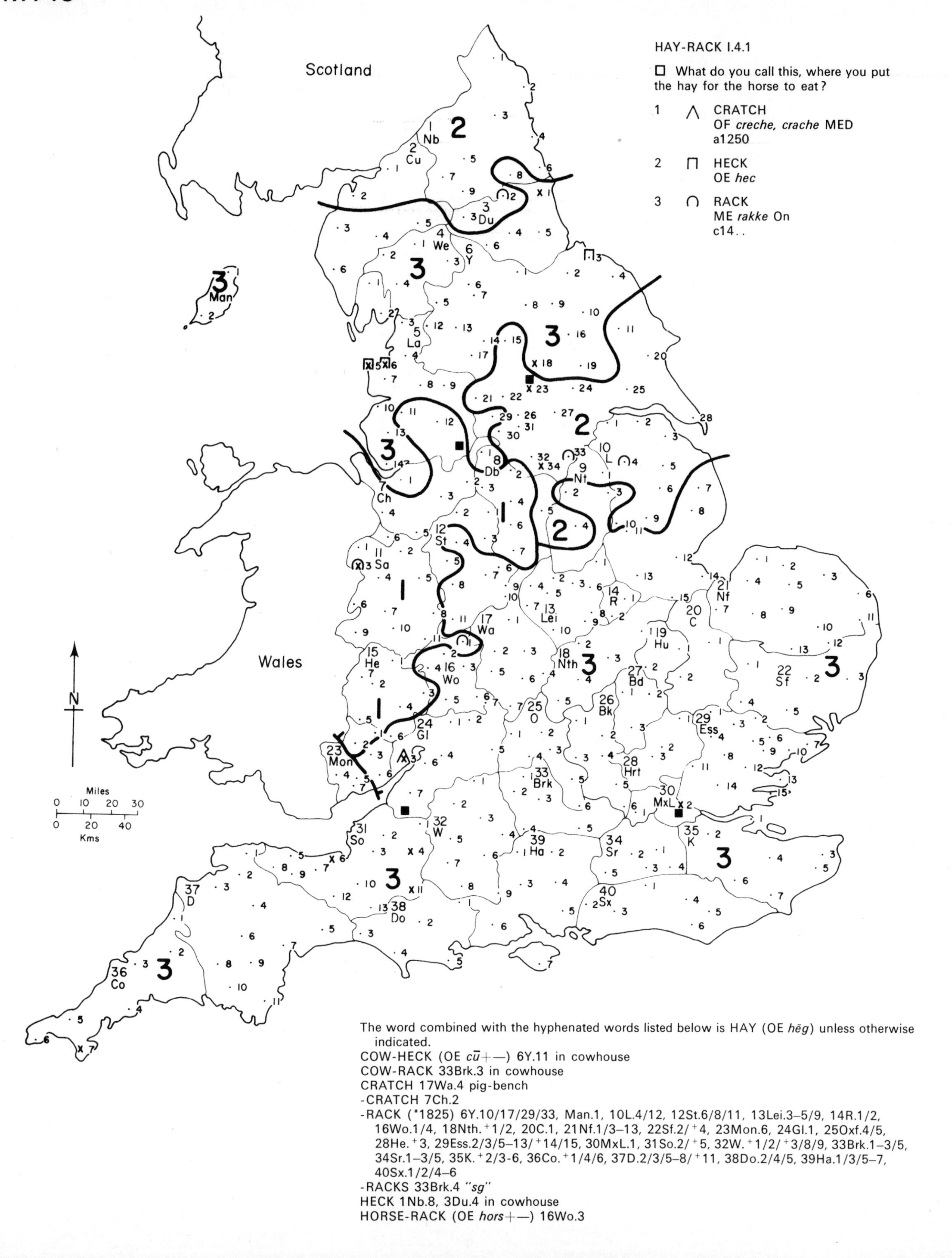

The word combined with the hyphenated words listed below is HAY (OE *hēg*) unless otherwise indicated.
COW-HECK (OE *cū*+—) 6Y.11 in cowhouse
COW-RACK 33Brk.3 in cowhouse
CRATCH 17Wa.4 pig-bench
-CRATCH 7Ch.2
-RACK (*1825) 6Y.10/17/29/33, Man.1, 10L.4/12, 12St.6/8/11, 13Lei.3–5/9, 14R.1/2, 16Wo.1/4, 18Nth.$^{+}$1/2, 20C.1, 21Nf.1/3–13, 22Sf.2/$^{+}$4, 23Mon.6, 24Gl.1, 25Oxf.4/5, 28He.$^{+}$3, 29Ess.2/3/5–13/$^{+}$14/15, 30MxL.1, 31So.2/$^{+}$5, 32W.$^{+}$1/2/$^{+}$3/8/9, 33Brk.1–3/5, 34Sr.1–3/5, 35K.$^{+}$2/3-6, 36Co.$^{+}$1/4/6, 37D.2/3/5–8/$^{+}$11, 38Do.2/4/5, 39Ha.1/3/5–7, 40Sx.1/2/4–6
-RACKS 33Brk.4 *"sg"*
HECK 1Nb.8, 3Du.4 in cowhouse
HORSE-RACK (OE *hors*+—) 16Wo.3

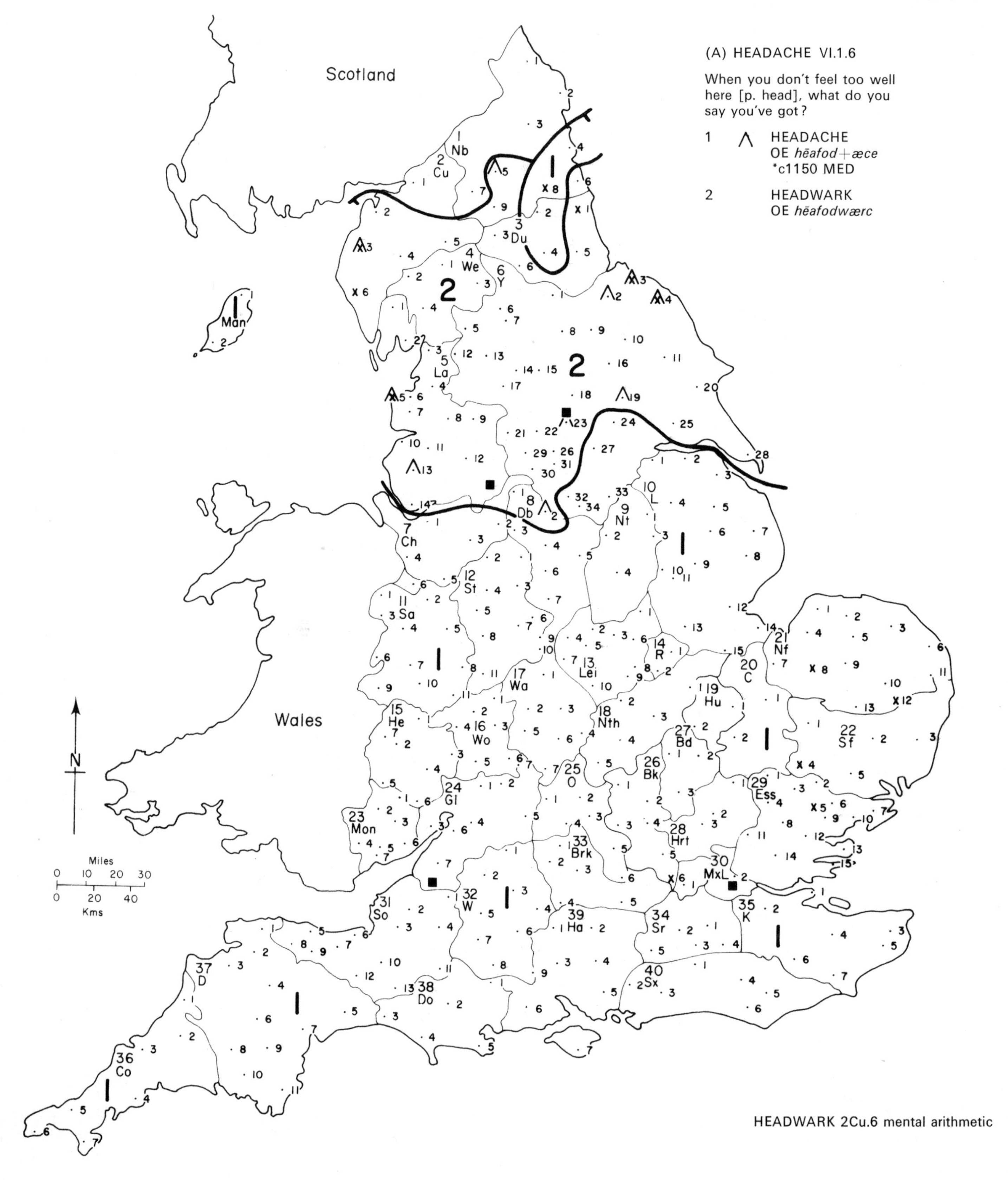

HEADWARK 2Cu.6 mental arithmetic

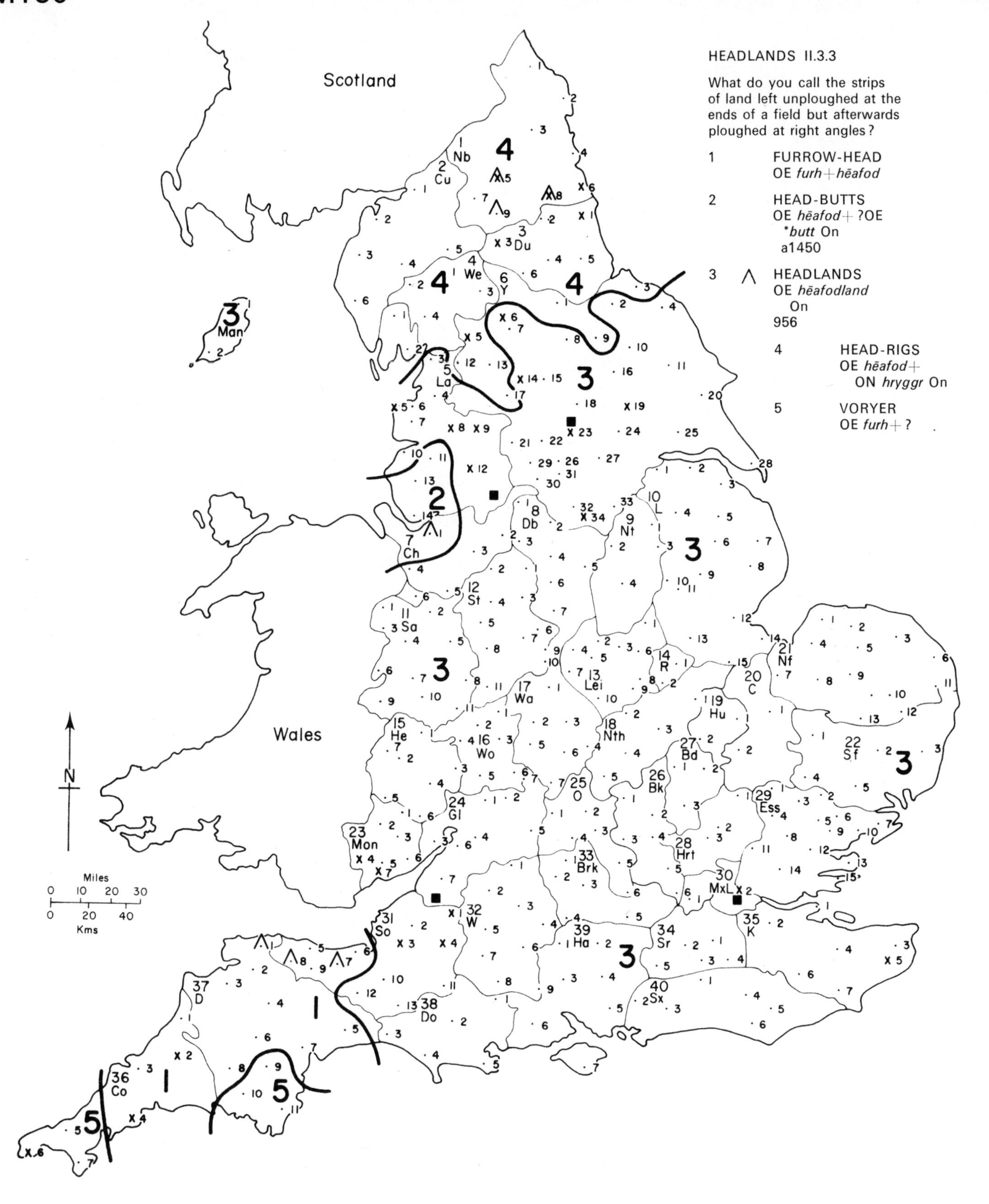
Scotland
Wales
HEADLANDS II.3.3
What do you call the strips of land left unploughed at the ends of a field but afterwards ploughed at right angles?
1 FURROW-HEAD
OE furh+hēafod
2 HEAD-BUTTS
OE hēafod+?OE *butt On a1450
3 Λ HEADLANDS
OE hēafodland On 956
4 HEAD-RIGS
OE hēafod+ ON hryggr On
5 VORYER
OE furh+?
Miles
0 10 20 30
0 20 40
Kms
N

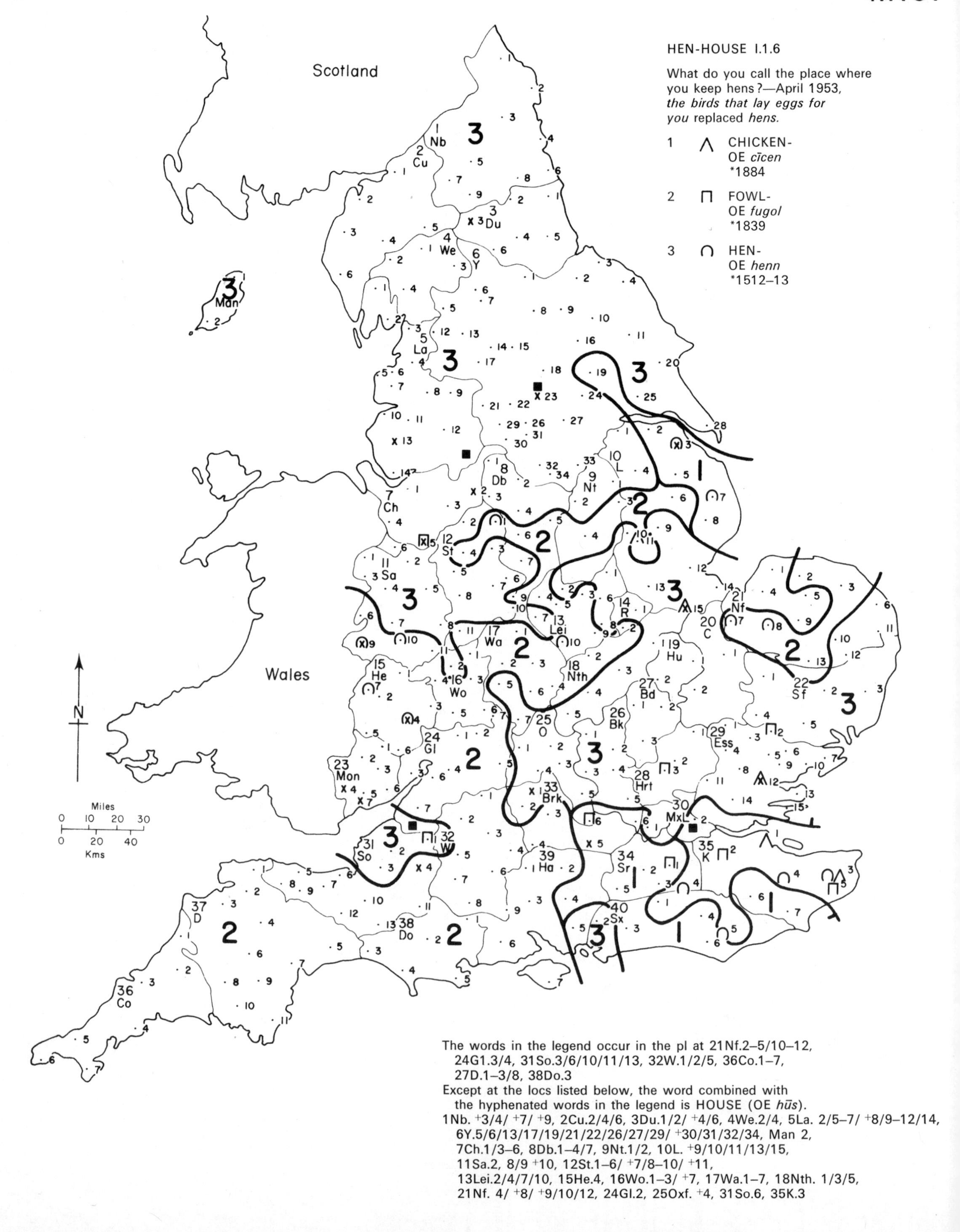

The words in the legend occur in the pl at 21Nf.2–5/10–12, 24Gl.3/4, 31So.3/6/10/11/13, 32W.1/2/5, 36Co.1–7, 27D.1–3/8, 38Do.3

Except at the locs listed below, the word combined with the hyphenated words in the legend is HOUSE (OE *hūs*).

1Nb. +3/4/ +7/ +9, 2Cu.2/4/6, 3Du.1/2/ +4/6, 4We.2/4, 5La. 2/5–7/ +8/9–12/14, 6Y.5/6/13/17/19/21/22/26/27/29/ +30/31/32/34, Man 2, 7Ch.1/3–6, 8Db.1–4/7, 9Nt.1/2, 10L. +9/10/11/13/15, 11Sa.2, 8/9 +10, 12St.1–6/ +7/8–10/ +11, 13Lei.2/4/7/10, 15He.4, 16Wo.1–3/ +7, 17Wa.1–7, 18Nth. 1/3/5, 21Nf. 4/ +8/ +9/10/12, 24Gl.2, 25Oxf. +4, 31So.6, 35K.3

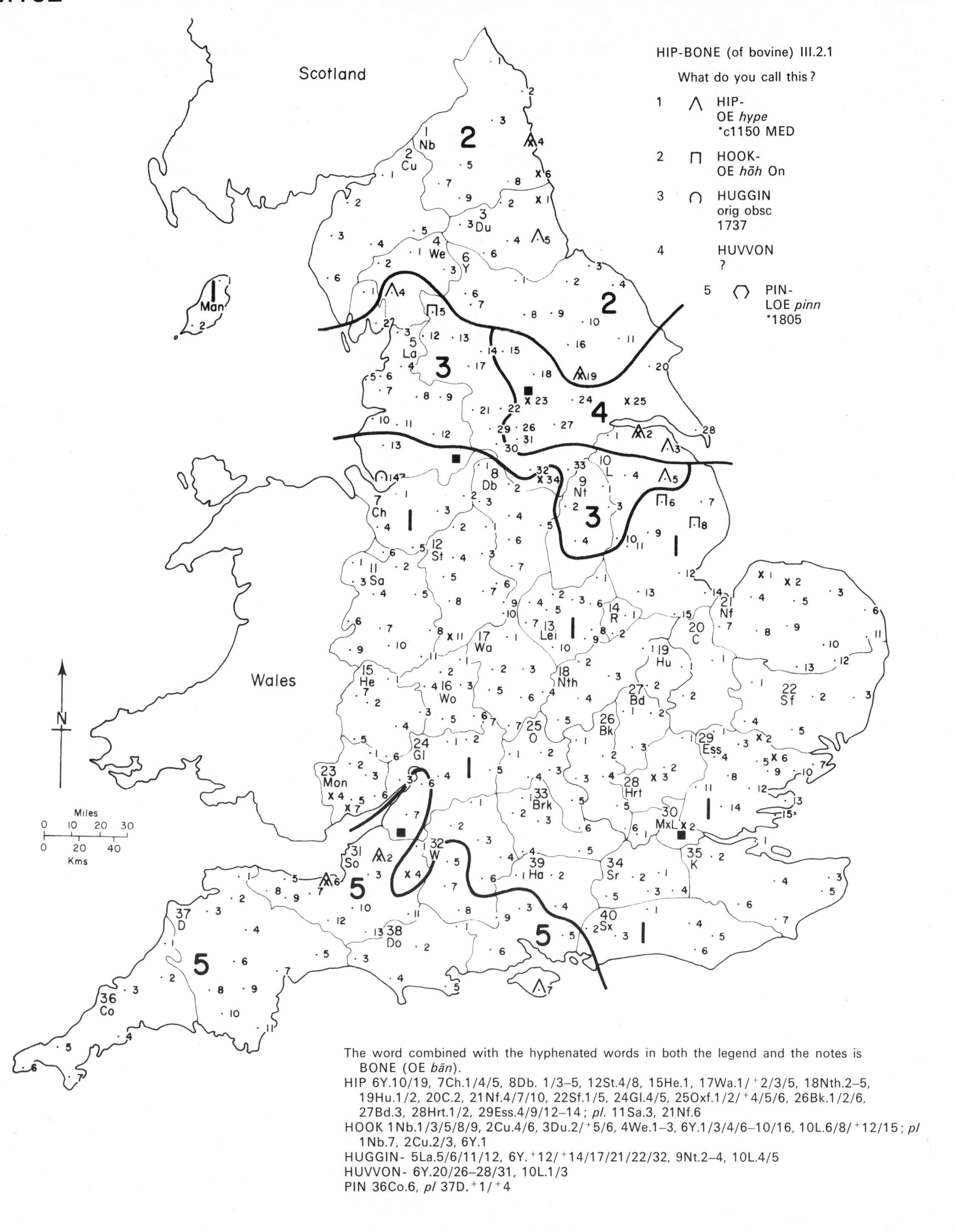

The word combined with the hyphenated words in both the legend and the notes is BONE (OE *bān*).

HIP 6Y.10/19, 7Ch.1/4/5, 8Db. 1/3–5, 12St.4/8, 15He.1, 17Wa.1/ ⁺2/3/5, 18Nth.2–5, 19Hu.1/2, 20C.2, 21Nf.4/7/10, 22Sf.1/5, 24Gl.4/5, 25Oxf.1/2/ ⁺4/5/6, 26Bk.1/2/6, 27Bd.3, 28Hrt.1/2, 29Ess.4/9/12–14; *pl.* 11Sa.3, 21Nf.6

HOOK 1Nb.1/3/5/8/9, 2Cu.4/6, 3Du.2/ ⁺5/6, 4We.1–3, 6Y.1/3/4/6–10/16, 10L.6/8/ ⁺12/15; *pl* 1Nb.7, 2Cu.2/3, 6Y.1

HUGGIN- 5La.5/6/11/12, 6Y. ⁺12/ ⁺14/17/21/22/32, 9Nt.2–4, 10L.4/5

HUVVON- 6Y.20/26–28/31, 10L.1/3

PIN 36Co.6, *pl* 37D. ⁺1/ ⁺4

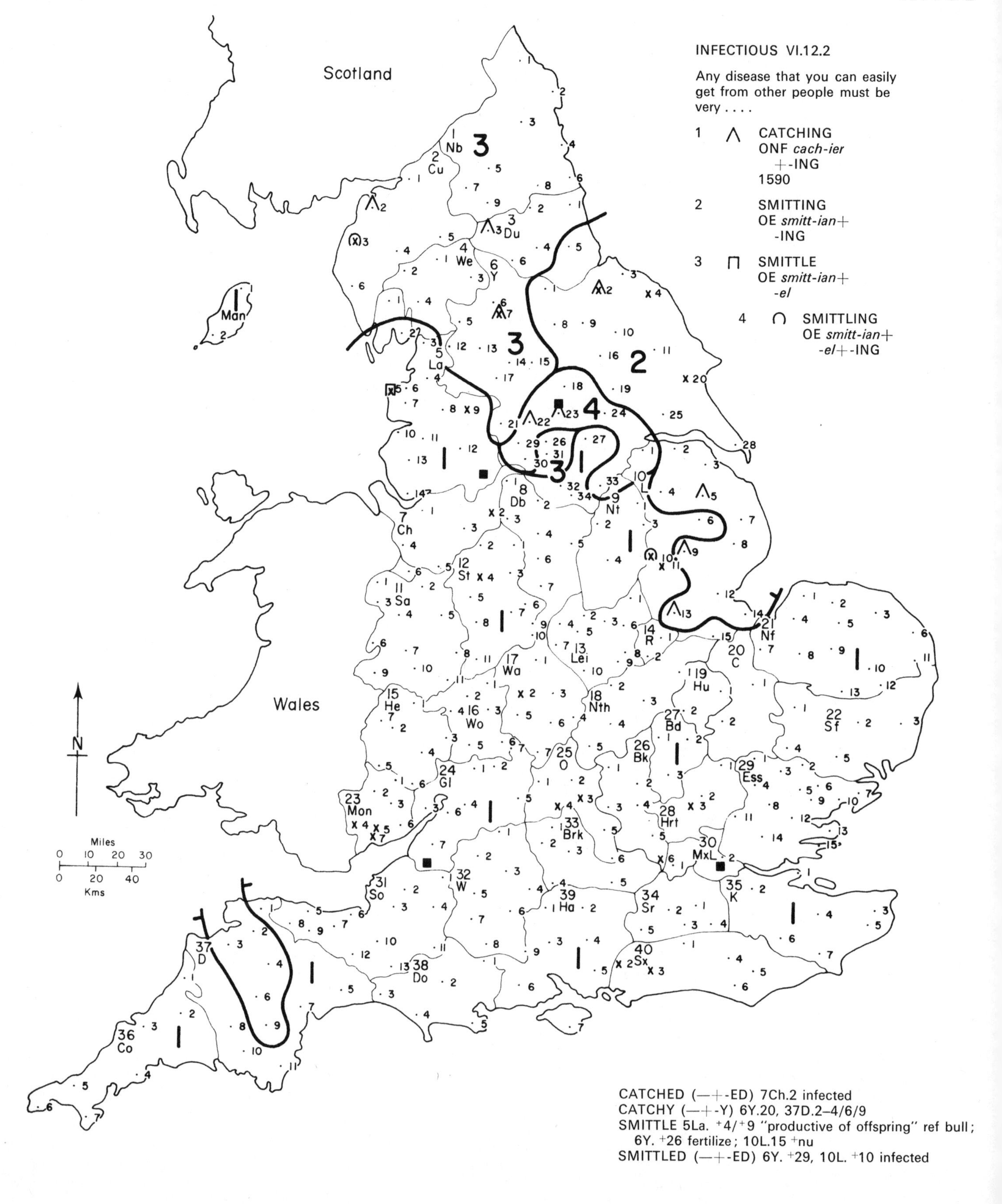
INFECTIOUS VI.12.2
Any disease that you can easily get from other people must be very . . . .
1 Λ CATCHING ONF *cach-ier* +-ING 1590
2 SMITTING OE *smitt-ian*+ -ING
3 ⊓ SMITTLE OE *smitt-ian*+ -*el*
4 ∩ SMITTLING OE *smitt-ian*+ -*el*+-ING
Scotland
Wales
Man
Nb
Cu
Du
We
Y
La
Ch
Db
Nt
L
St
Sa
Lei
R
Nf
Wa
He
Wo
Nth
Hu
C
Sf
Bd
Bk
O
Gl
Mon
Ess
Hrt
Brk
MxL
So
W
Ha
Sr
K
D
Do
Sx
Co
N
Miles
0 10 20 30
0 20 40
Kms
CATCHED (—+-ED) 7Ch.2 infected
CATCHY (—+-Y) 6Y.20, 37D.2–4/6/9
SMITTLE 5La. +4/+9 "productive of offspring" ref bull; 6Y. +26 fertilize; 10L.15 +nu
SMITTLED (—+-ED) 6Y. +29, 10L. +10 infected

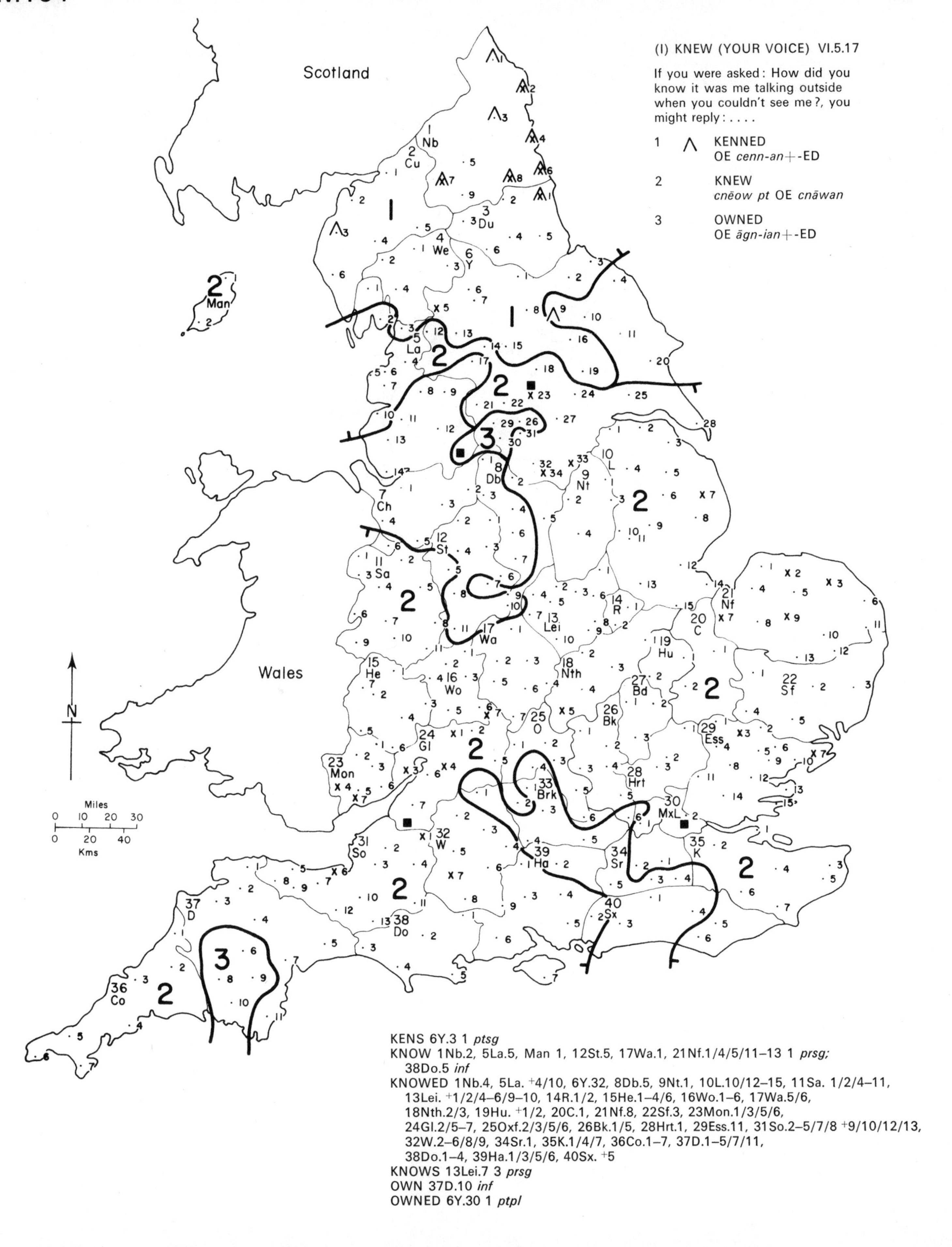
(I) KNEW (YOUR VOICE) VI.5.17
If you were asked: How did you know it was me talking outside when you couldn't see me?, you might reply: . . . .
1 Λ KENNED
OE cenn-an+-ED
2 KNEW
cnēow pt OE cnāwan
3 OWNED
OE āgn-ian+-ED
Scotland
Wales
Man
Miles
Kms
N
KENS 6Y.3 1 ptsg
KNOW 1Nb.2, 5La.5, Man 1, 12St.5, 17Wa.1, 21Nf.1/4/5/11–13 1 prsg; 38Do.5 inf
KNOWED 1Nb.4, 5La. +4/10, 6Y.32, 8Db.5, 9Nt.1, 10L.10/12–15, 11Sa. 1/2/4–11, 13Lei. +1/2/4–6/9–10, 14R.1/2, 15He.1–4/6, 16Wo.1–6, 17Wa.5/6, 18Nth.2/3, 19Hu. +1/2, 20C.1, 21Nf.8, 22Sf.3, 23Mon.1/3/5/6, 24Gl.2/5–7, 25Oxf.2/3/5/6, 26Bk.1/5, 28Hrt.1, 29Ess.11, 31So.2–5/7/8 +9/10/12/13, 32W.2–6/8/9, 34Sr.1, 35K.1/4/7, 36Co.1–7, 37D.1–5/7/11, 38Do.1–4, 39Ha.1/3/5/6, 40Sx. +5
KNOWS 13Lei.7 3 prsg
OWN 37D.10 inf
OWNED 6Y.30 1 ptpl

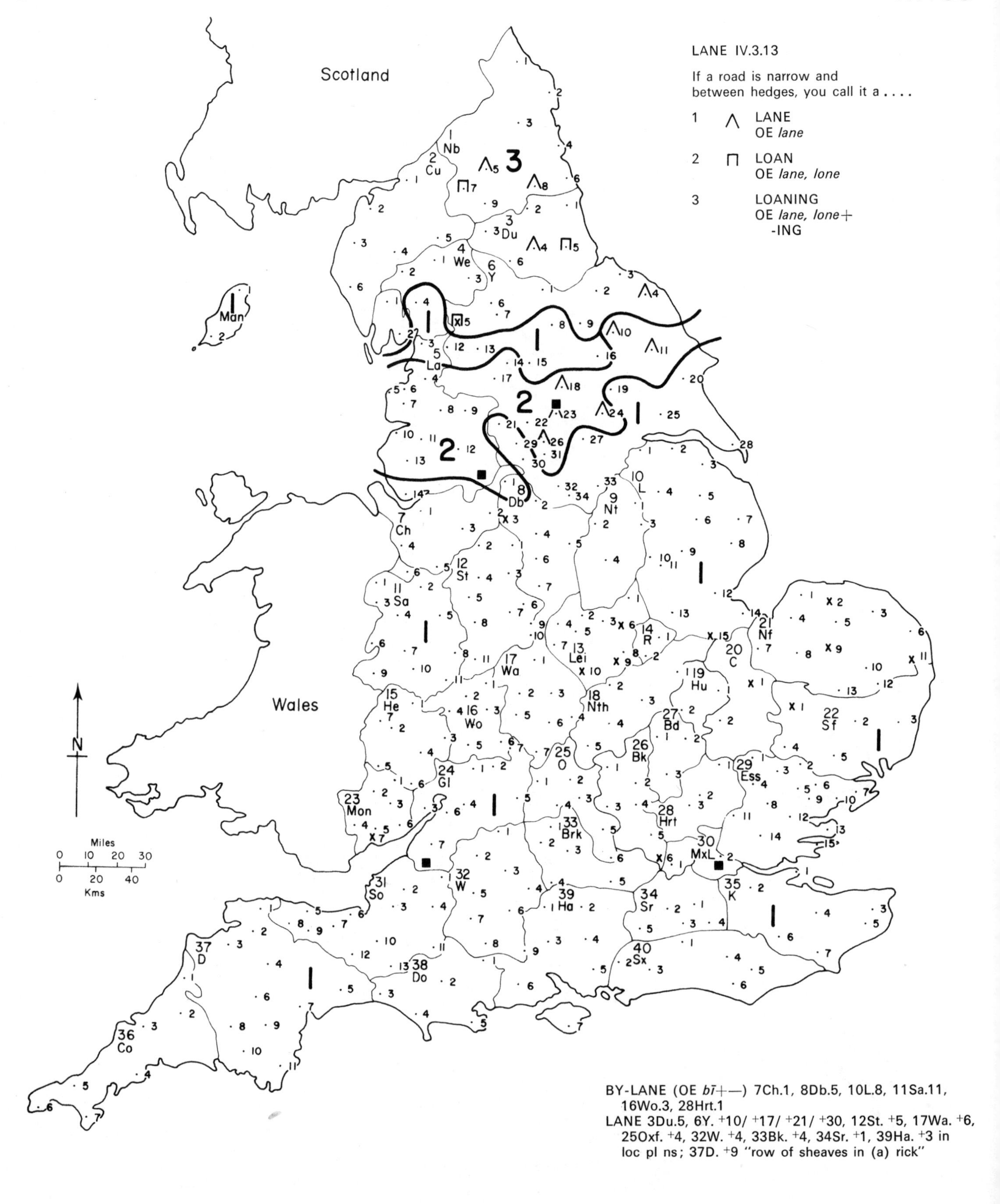
Scotland
Wales
LANE IV.3.13
If a road is narrow and between hedges, you call it a . . . .
1 LANE OE *lane*
2 LOAN OE *lane, lone*
3 LOANING OE *lane, lone*+ -ING
Miles 0 10 20 30
0 20 40 Kms
N
BY-LANE (OE *bī*+—) 7Ch.1, 8Db.5, 10L.8, 11Sa.11, 16Wo.3, 28Hrt.1
LANE 3Du.5, 6Y. +10/ +17/ +21/ +30, 12St. +5, 17Wa. +6, 25Oxf. +4, 32W. +4, 33Bk. +4, 34Sr. +1, 39Ha. +3 in loc pl ns; 37D. +9 "row of sheaves in (a) rick"

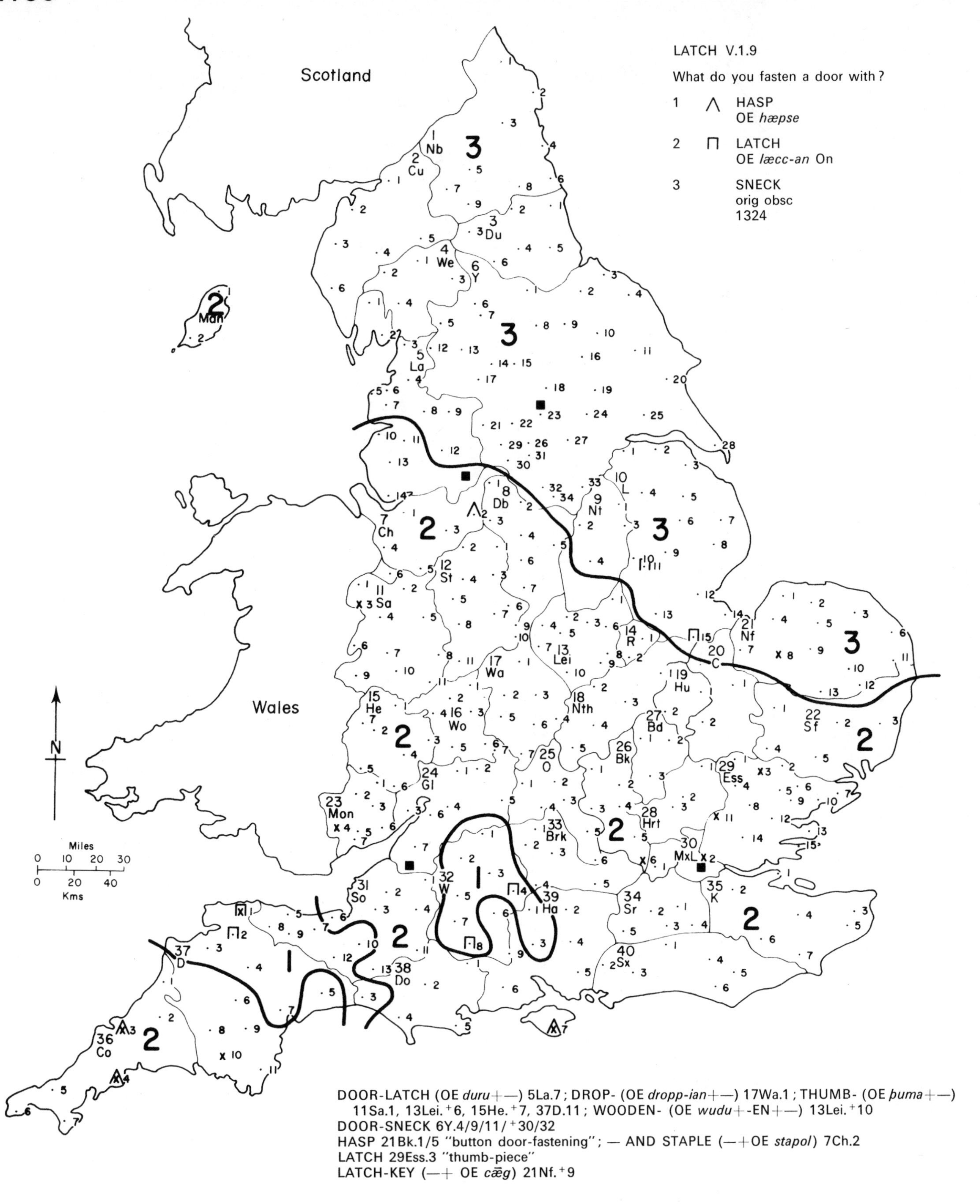
LATCH V.1.9
What do you fasten a door with?
1 ∧ HASP
OE *hæpse*
2 ⊓ LATCH
OE *læcc-an* On
3 SNECK
orig obsc
1324
Scotland
Wales
N
Miles
0 10 20 30
0 20 40
Kms
DOOR-LATCH (OE *duru*+—) 5La.7; DROP- (OE *dropp-ian*+—) 17Wa.1; THUMB- (OE *þuma*+—) 11Sa.1, 13Lei.+6, 15He.+7, 37D.11; WOODEN- (OE *wudu*+-EN+—) 13Lei.+10
DOOR-SNECK 6Y.4/9/11/+30/32
HASP 21Bk.1/5 "button door-fastening"; — AND STAPLE (—+OE *stapol*) 7Ch.2
LATCH 29Ess.3 "thumb-piece"
LATCH-KEY (—+ OE *cæg*) 21Nf.+9

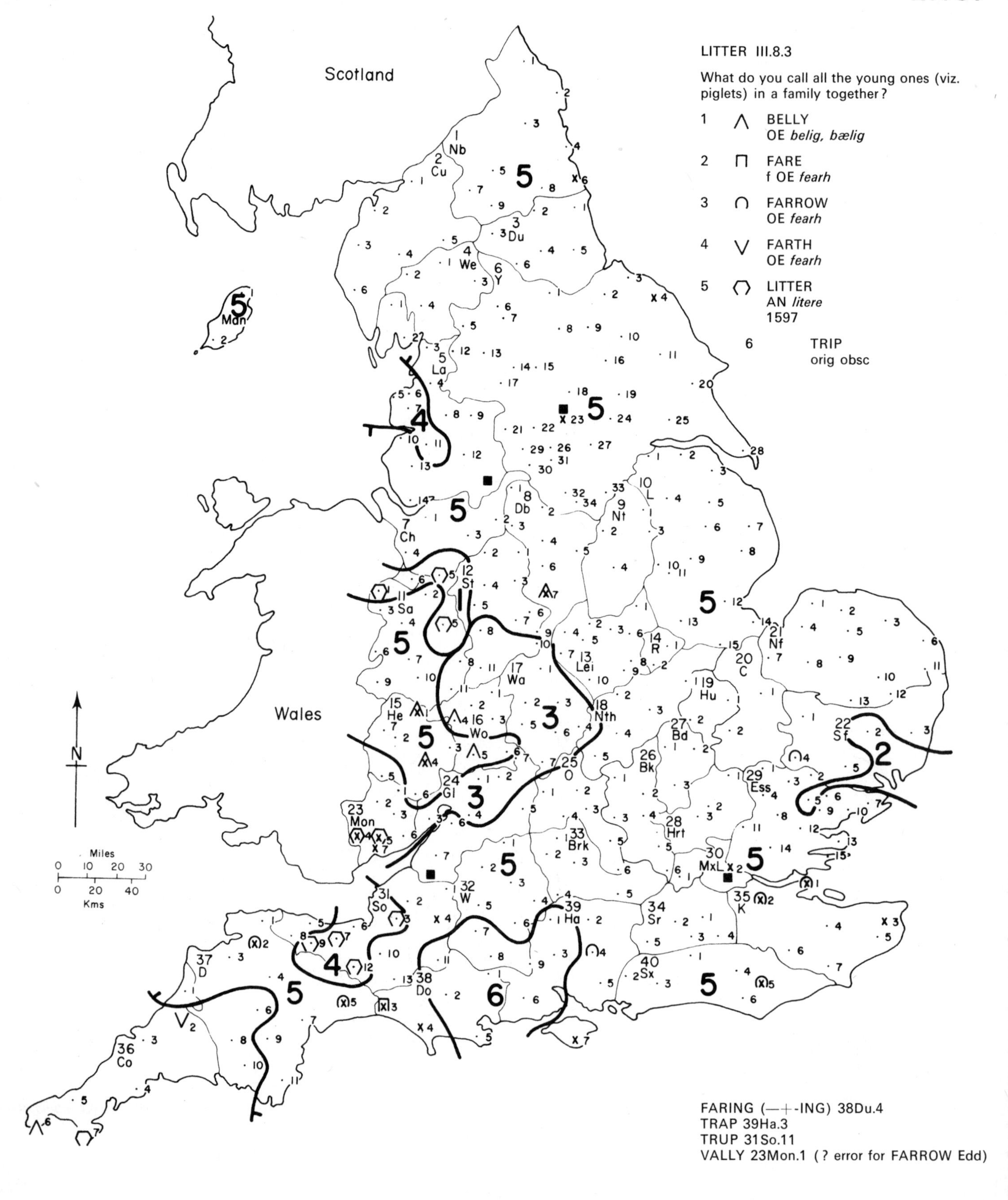
Scotland
Wales
LITTER III.8.3
What do you call all the young ones (viz. piglets) in a family together?
1 BELLY OE belig, bælig
2 FARE f OE fearh
3 FARROW OE fearh
4 FARTH OE fearh
5 LITTER AN litere 1597
6 TRIP orig obsc
Miles 0 10 20 30
0 20 40 Kms
N
FARING (—+-ING) 38Du.4
TRAP 39Ha.3
TRUP 31So.11
VALLY 23Mon.1 (? error for FARROW Edd)

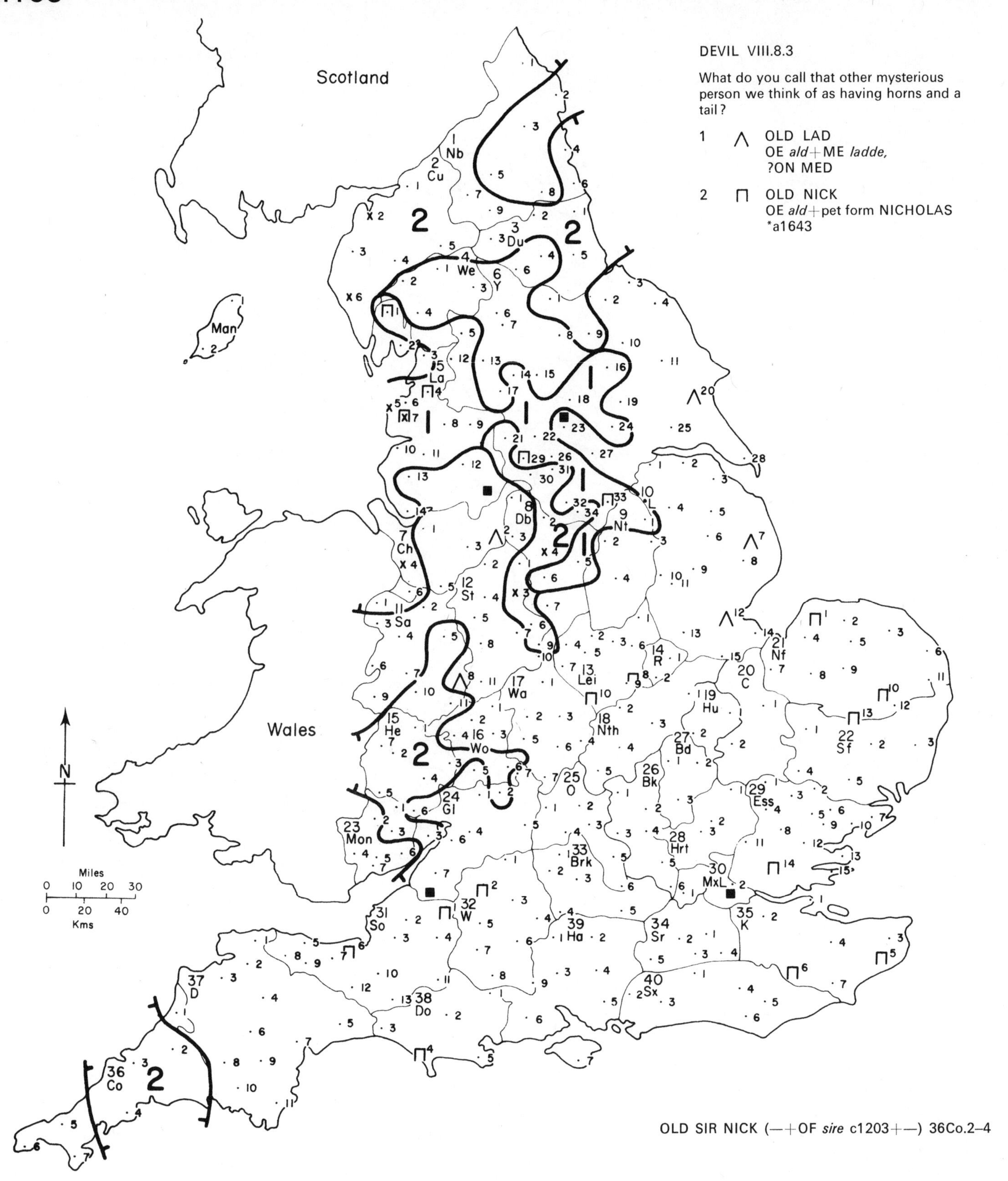
DEVIL VIII.8.3
What do you call that other mysterious person we think of as having horns and a tail?
1 Λ OLD LAD
OE *ald*+ME *ladde*,
?ON MED
2 ⊓ OLD NICK
OE *ald*+pet form NICHOLAS
*a1643
Scotland
Wales
Man
Nb
Cu
Du
We
Y
La
Ch
Db
Nt
L
St
Sa
Lei
R
Nf
C
Hu
Wa
He
Wo
Nth
Sf
Bd
Gl
O
Bk
Ess
Mon
Hrt
Brk
MxL
So
W
Ha
Sr
K
D
Do
Sx
Co
Miles
0 10 20 30
0 20 40
Kms
N
OLD SIR NICK (—+OF *sire* c1203+—) 36Co.2–4

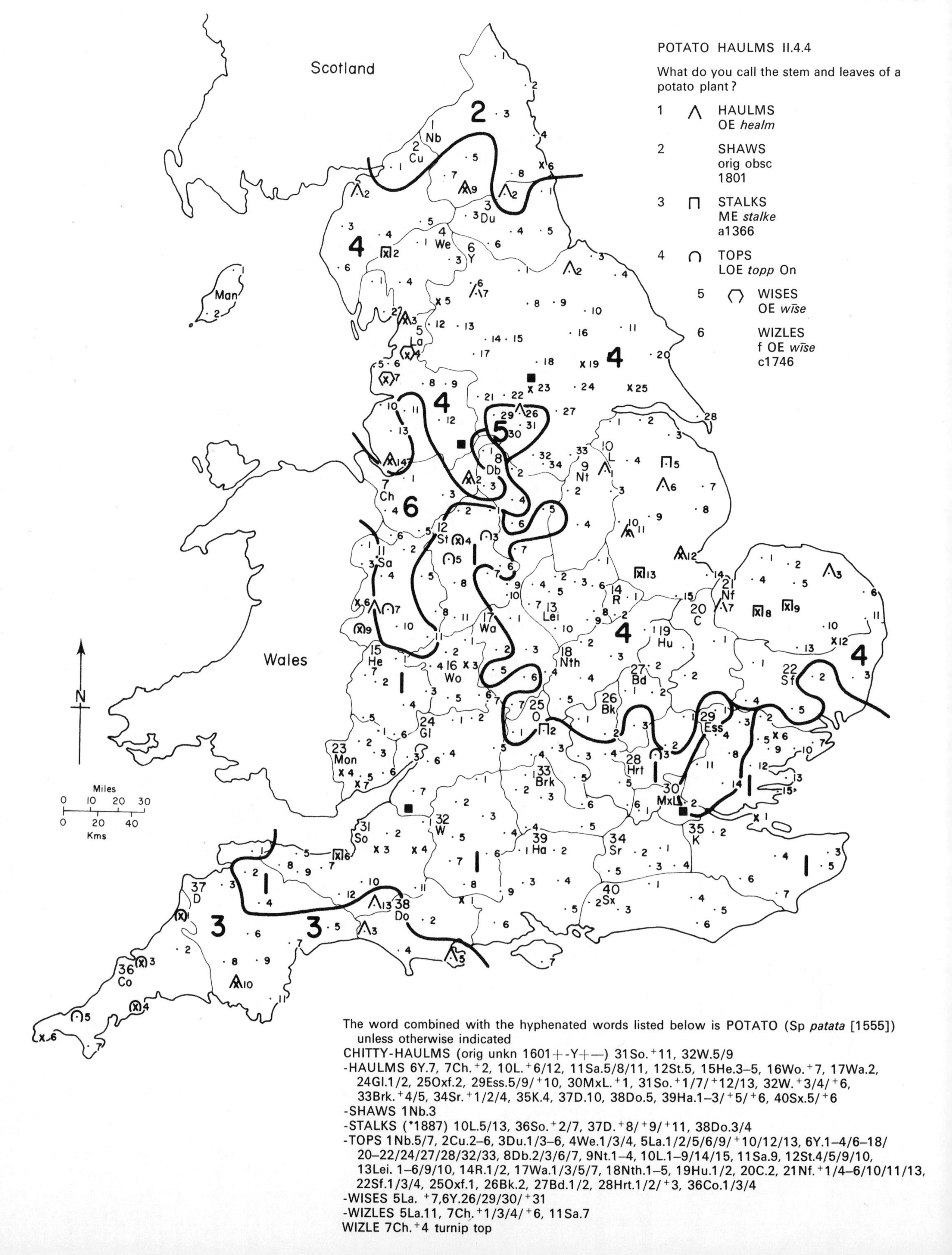

POTATO HAULMS II.4.4

What do you call the stem and leaves of a potato plant?

1 Λ HAULMS
OE *healm*

2 SHAWS
orig obsc
1801

3 ⊓ STALKS
ME *stalke*
a1366

4 ∩ TOPS
LOE *topp* On

5 WISES
OE *wīse*

6 WIZLES
f OE *wīse*
c1746

The word combined with the hyphenated words listed below is POTATO (Sp *patata* [1555]) unless otherwise indicated

CHITTY-HAULMS (orig unkn 1601+-Y+—) 31So.+11, 32W.5/9

-HAULMS 6Y.7, 7Ch.+2, 10L.+6/12, 11Sa.5/8/11, 12St.5, 15He.3–5, 16Wo.+7, 17Wa.2, 24Gl.1/2, 25Oxf.2, 29Ess.5/9/+10, 30MxL.+1, 31So.+1/7/+12/13, 32W.+3/4/+6, 33Brk.+4/5, 34Sr.+1/2/4, 35K.4, 37D.10, 38Do.5, 39Ha.1–3/+5/+6, 40Sx.5/+6

-SHAWS 1Nb.3

-STALKS (*1887) 10L.5/13, 36So.+2/7, 37D.+8/+9/+11, 38Do.3/4

-TOPS 1Nb.5/7, 2Cu.2–6, 3Du.1/3–6, 4We.1/3/4, 5La.1/2/5/6/9/+10/12/13, 6Y.1–4/6–18/20–22/24/27/28/32/33, 8Db.2/3/6/7, 9Nt.1–4, 10L.1–9/14/15, 11Sa.9, 12St.4/5/9/10, 13Lei. 1–6/9/10, 14R.1/2, 17Wa.1/3/5/7, 18Nth.1–5, 19Hu.1/2, 20C.2, 21Nf.+1/4–6/10/11/13, 22Sf.1/3/4, 25Oxf.1, 26Bk.2, 27Bd.1/2, 28Hrt.1/2/+3, 36Co.1/3/4

-WISES 5La. +7,6Y.26/29/30/+31

-WIZLES 5La.11, 7Ch.+1/3/4/+6, 11Sa.7

WIZLE 7Ch.+4 turnip top

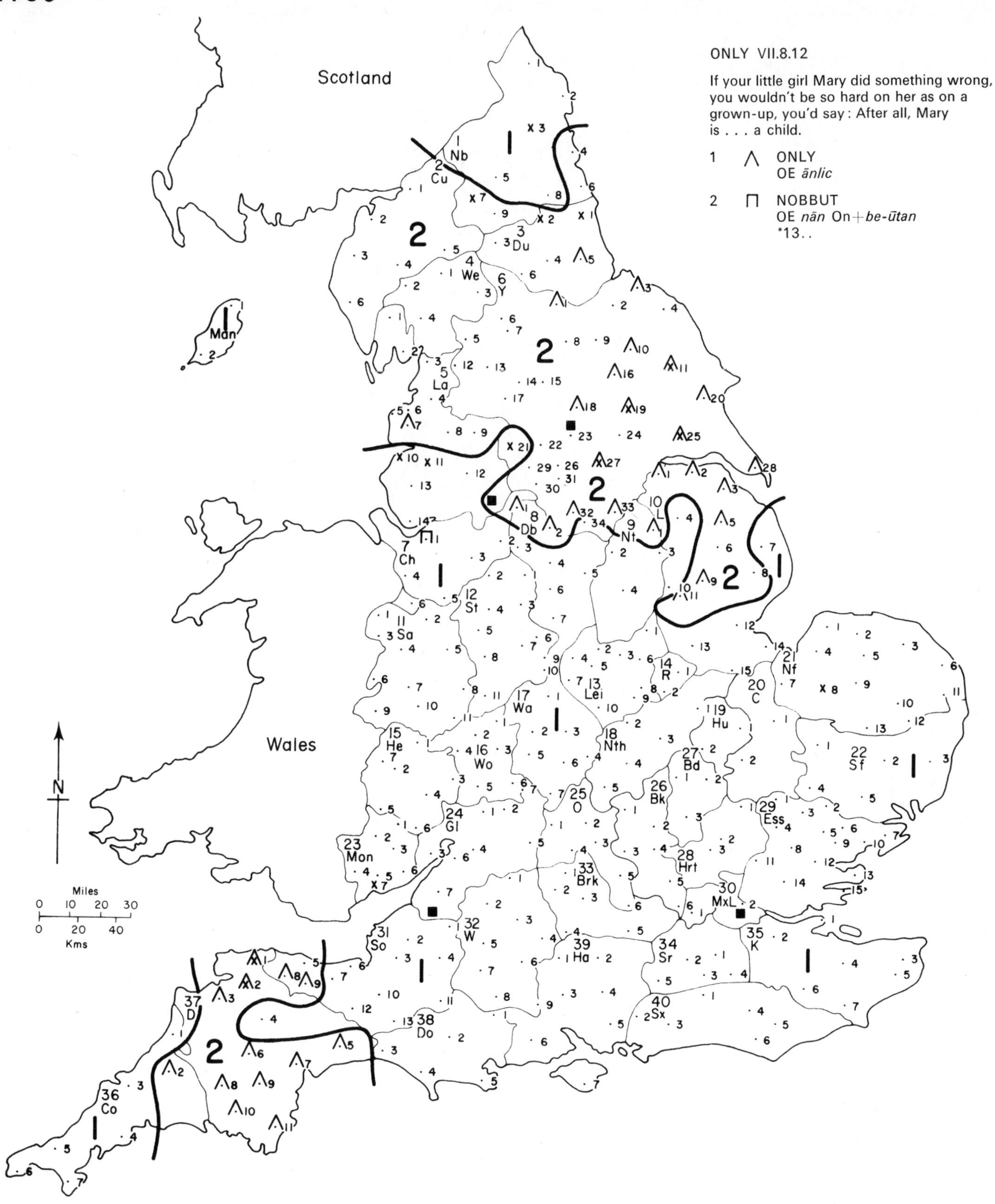
ONLY VII.8.12
If your little girl Mary did something wrong, you wouldn't be so hard on her as on a grown-up, you'd say: After all, Mary is . . . a child.
1 ONLY
OE ānlic
2 NOBBUT
OE nān On+be-ūtan
*13..
Scotland
Wales
Man
Nb
Cu
Du
We
Y
La
Ch
Db
Nt
L
St
Sa
Lei
R
Nf
C
Hu
Wa
He
Wo
Nth
Bd
Sf
O
Bk
Gl
Mon
Ess
Hrt
Brk
MxL
So
W
Ha
Sr
K
D
Do
Sx
Co
N
Miles
0 10 20 30
0 20 40
Kms

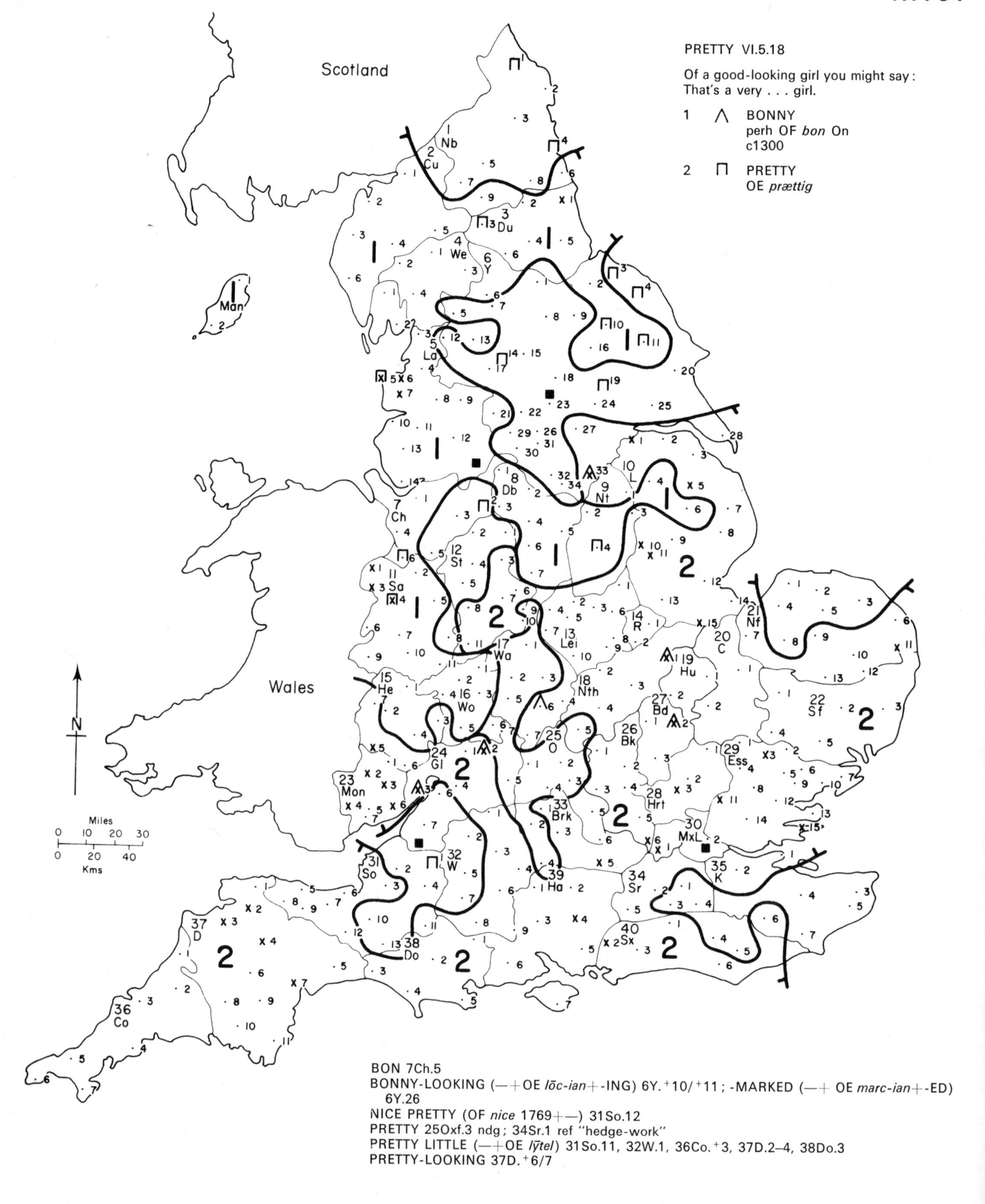

BON 7Ch.5
BONNY-LOOKING (—+OE *lōc-ian*+-ING) 6Y.+10/+11; -MARKED (—+ OE *marc-ian*+-ED) 6Y.26
NICE PRETTY (OF *nice* 1769+—) 31So.12
PRETTY 25Oxf.3 ndg; 34Sr.1 ref "hedge-work"
PRETTY LITTLE (—+OE *lȳtel*) 31So.11, 32W.1, 36Co.+3, 37D.2–4, 38Do.3
PRETTY-LOOKING 37D.+6/7

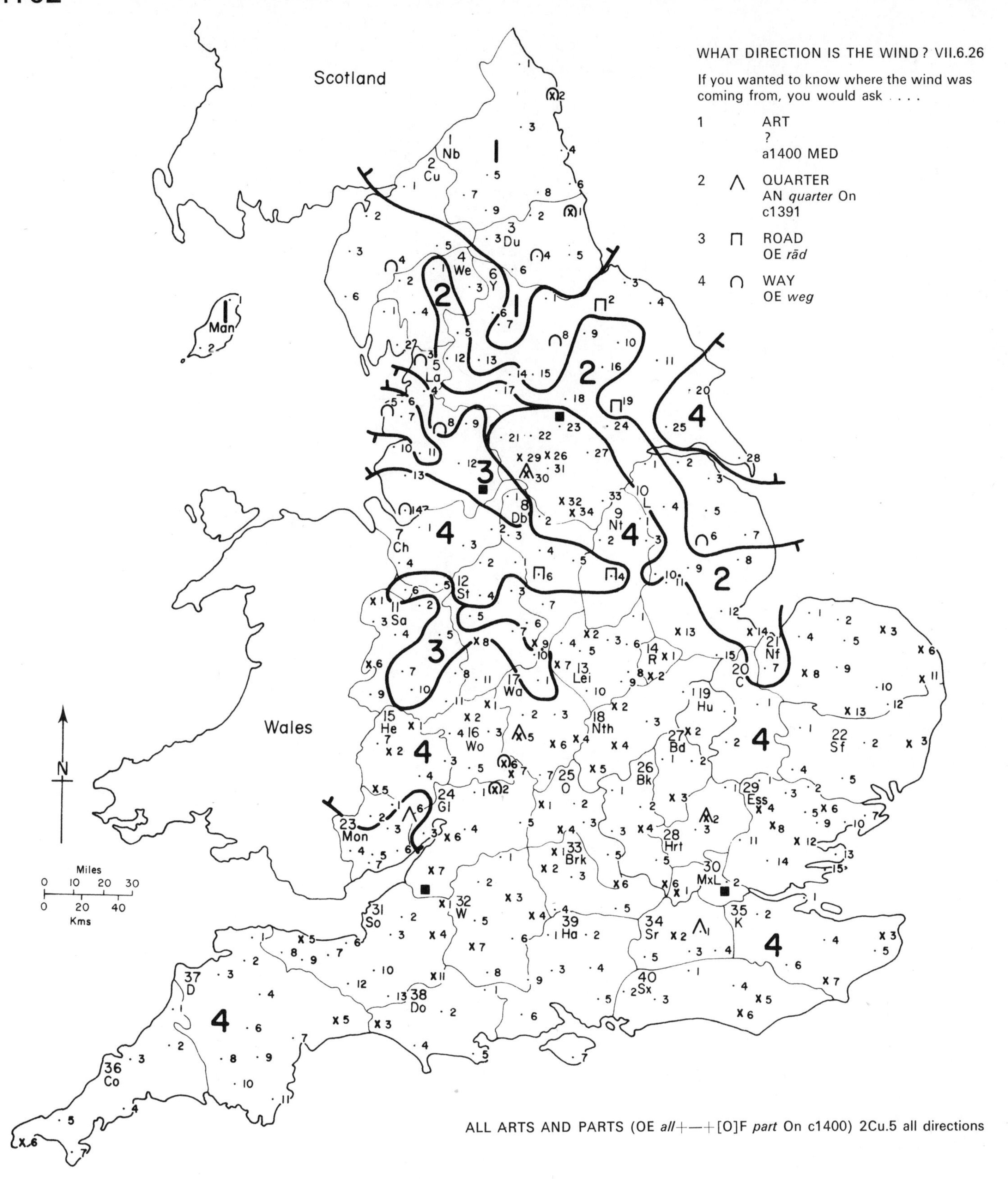
WHAT DIRECTION IS THE WIND? VII.6.26
If you wanted to know where the wind was coming from, you would ask . . . .
1 ART
?
a1400 MED
2 Λ QUARTER
AN *quarter* On
c1391
3 Π ROAD
OE *rād*
4 ∩ WAY
OE *weg*
Scotland
Wales
Man
N
Miles
0 10 20 30
0 20 40
Kms
ALL ARTS AND PARTS (OE *all*+—+[O]F *part* On c1400) 2Cu.5 all directions

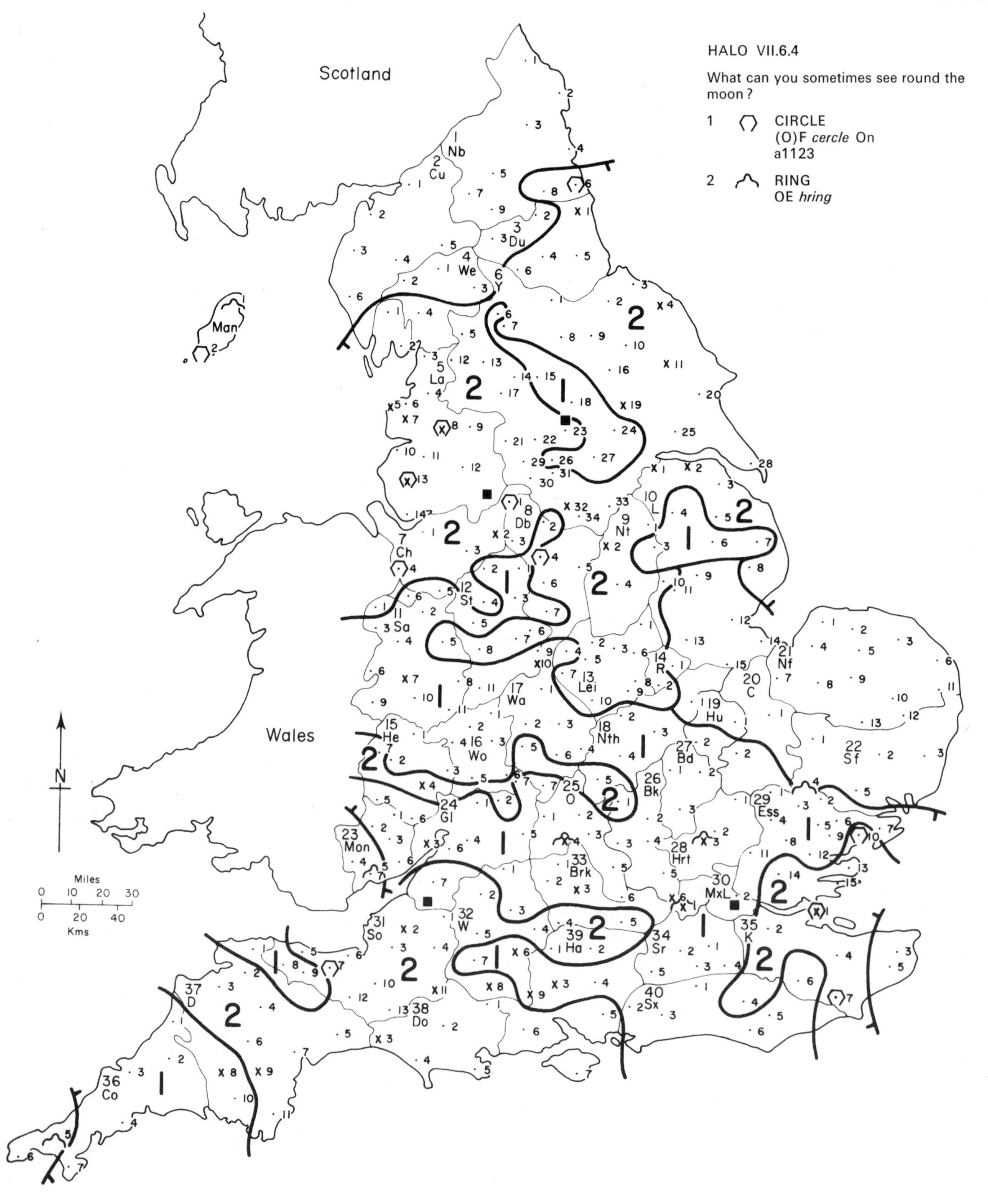
HALO VII.6.4
What can you sometimes see round the moon?
1 CIRCLE
(O)F *cercle* On
a1123
2 RING
OE *hring*
Scotland
Wales
Man
N
Miles
0 10 20 30
0 20 40
Kms

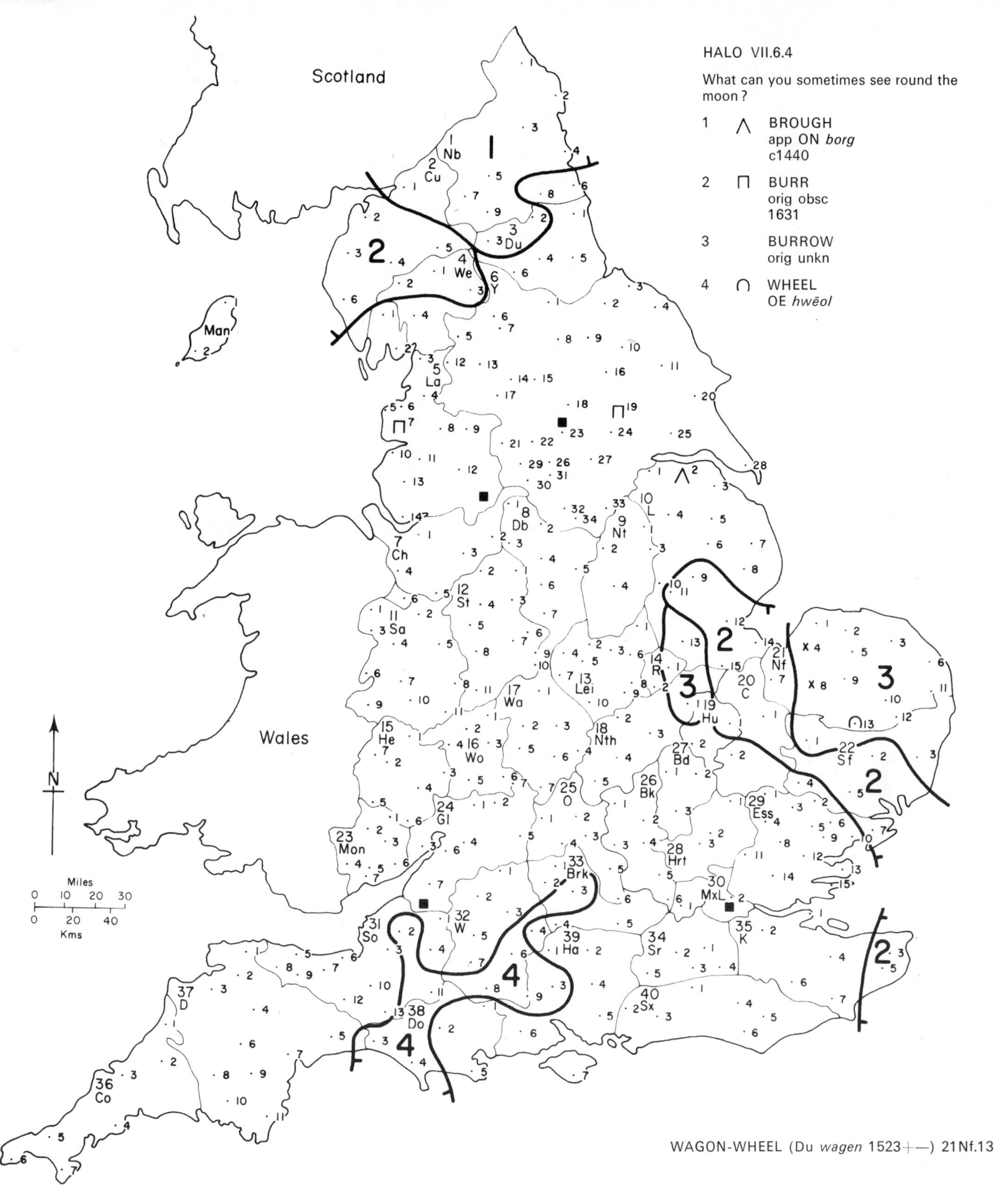

WAGON-WHEEL (Du *wagen* 1523+—) 21Nf.13

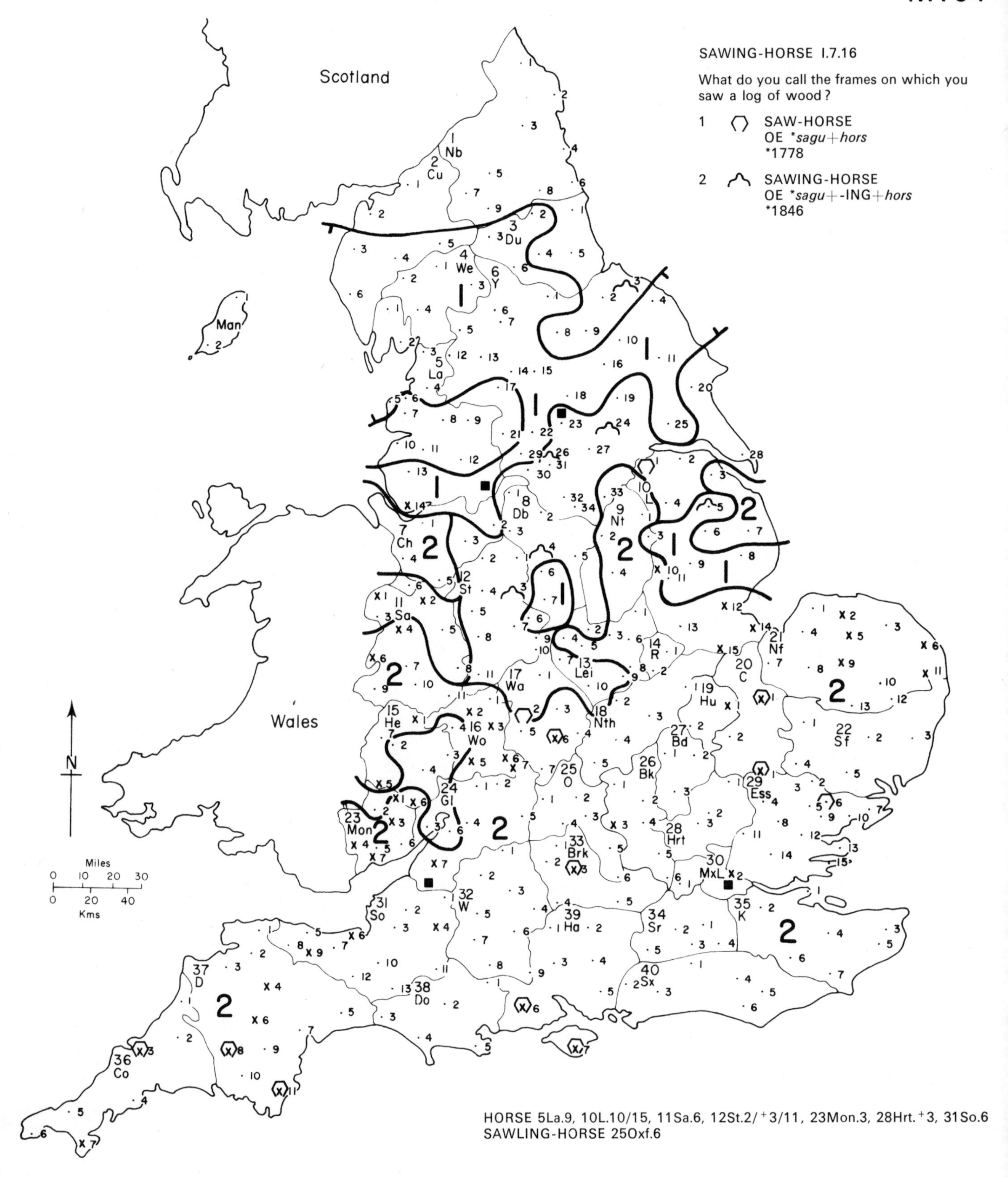

HORSE 5La.9, 10L.10/15, 11Sa.6, 12St.2/+3/11, 23Mon.3, 28Hrt.+3, 31So.6
SAWLING-HORSE 25Oxf.6

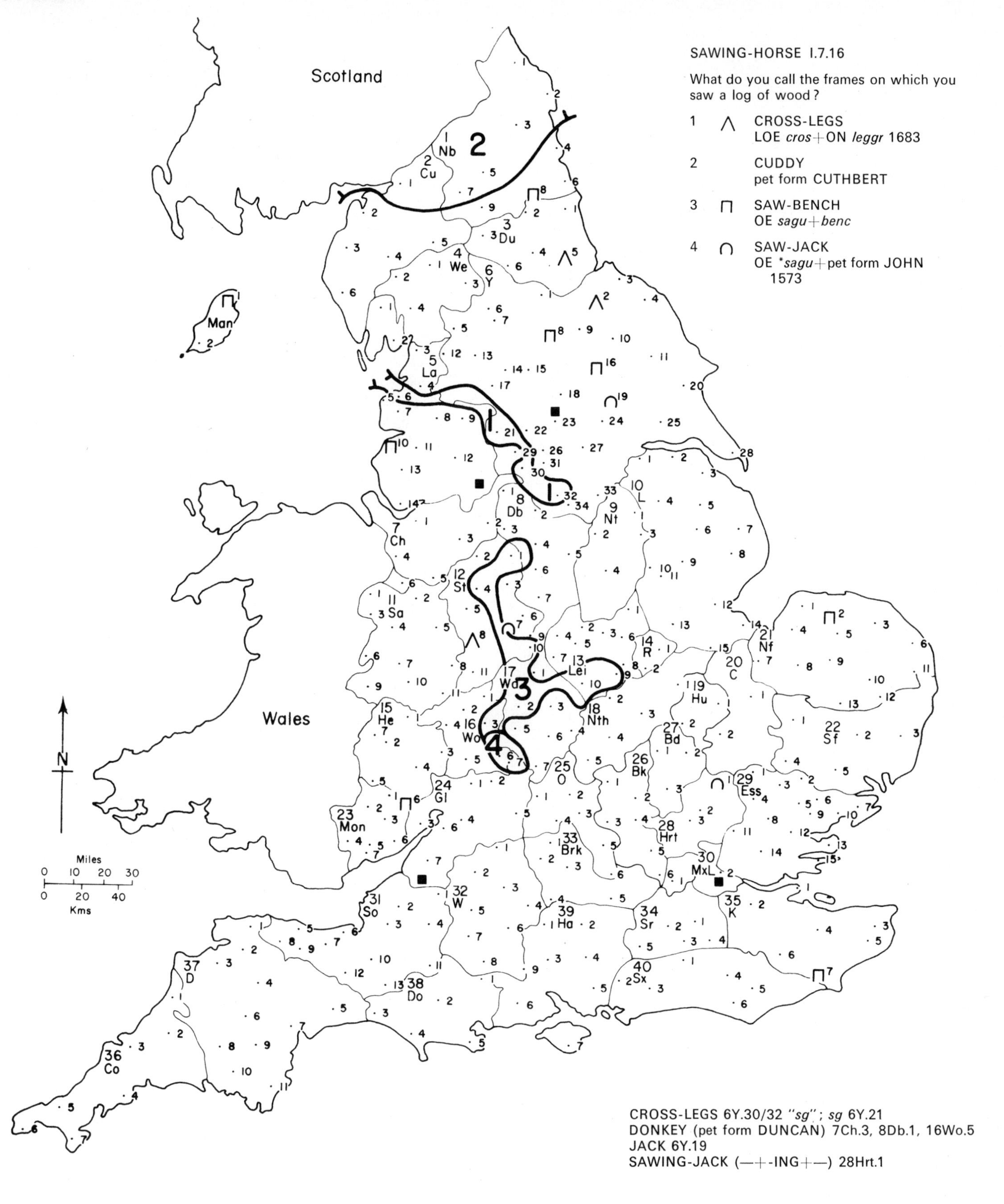
SAWING-HORSE I.7.16
What do you call the frames on which you saw a log of wood?
1 ⋀ CROSS-LEGS
LOE cros+ON leggr 1683
2 CUDDY
pet form CUTHBERT
3 ⊓ SAW-BENCH
OE sagu+benc
4 ∩ SAW-JACK
OE *sagu+pet form JOHN 1573
Scotland
Wales
Man
Miles
0 10 20 30
0 20 40
Kms
N
CROSS-LEGS 6Y.30/32 "sg"; sg 6Y.21
DONKEY (pet form DUNCAN) 7Ch.3, 8Db.1, 16Wo.5
JACK 6Y.19
SAWING-JACK (—+-ING+—) 28Hrt.1

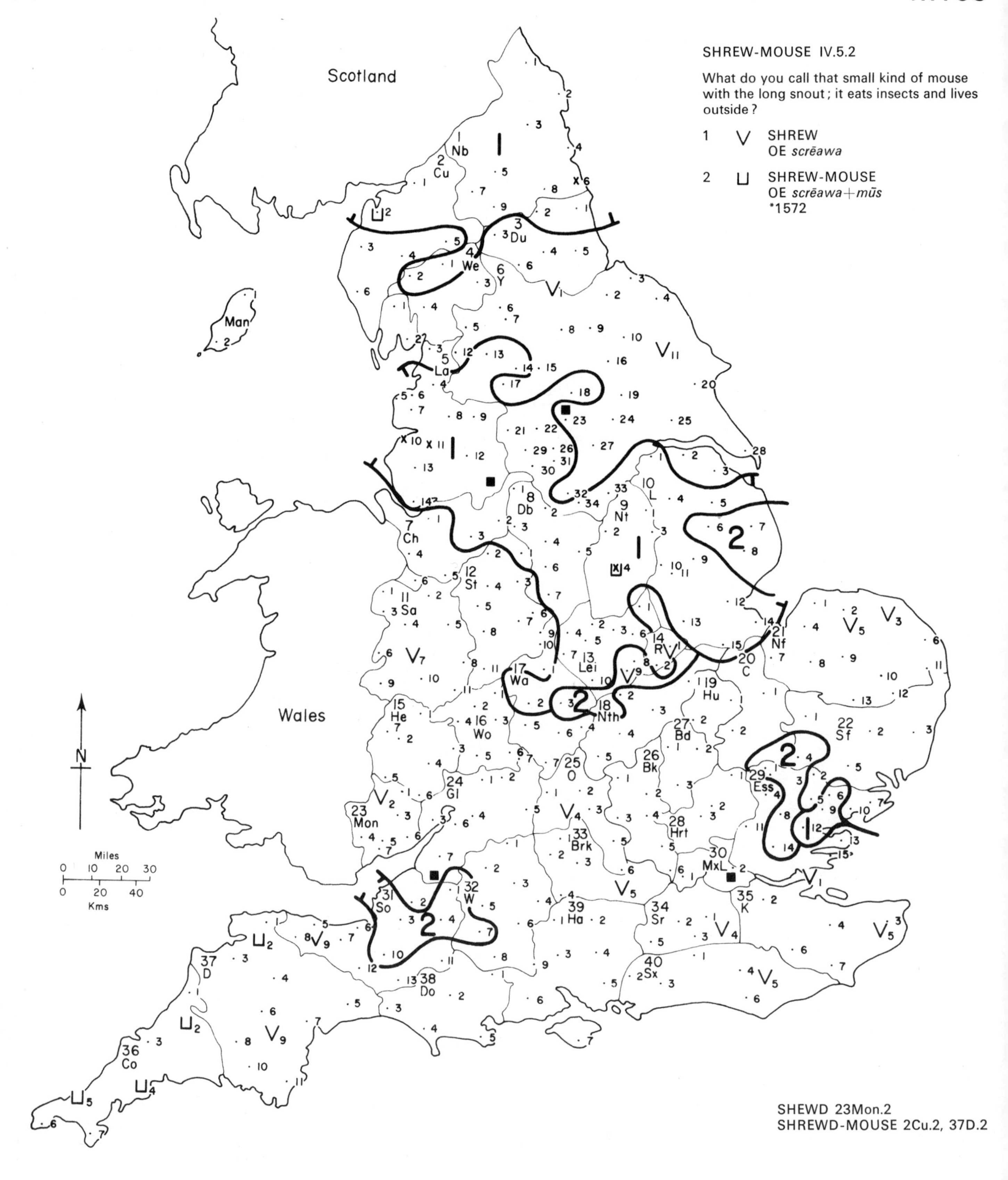
SHREW-MOUSE IV.5.2
What do you call that small kind of mouse with the long snout; it eats insects and lives outside?
1 V SHREW
OE *scrēawa*
2 ⊔ SHREW-MOUSE
OE *scrēawa*+*mūs*
*1572
Scotland
Wales
Man
N
Miles
0 10 20 30
0 20 40
Kms
Nb
Cu
Du
We
Y
La
Ch
Db
Nt
L
St
Sa
Lei
R
Nf
Wa
Nth
Hu
C
He
Wo
Bd
Sf
O
Bk
Ess
Gl
Mon
Brk
Hrt
MxL
So
W
K
Ha
Sr
D
Do
Sx
Co
SHEWD 23Mon.2
SHREWD-MOUSE 2Cu.2, 37D.2

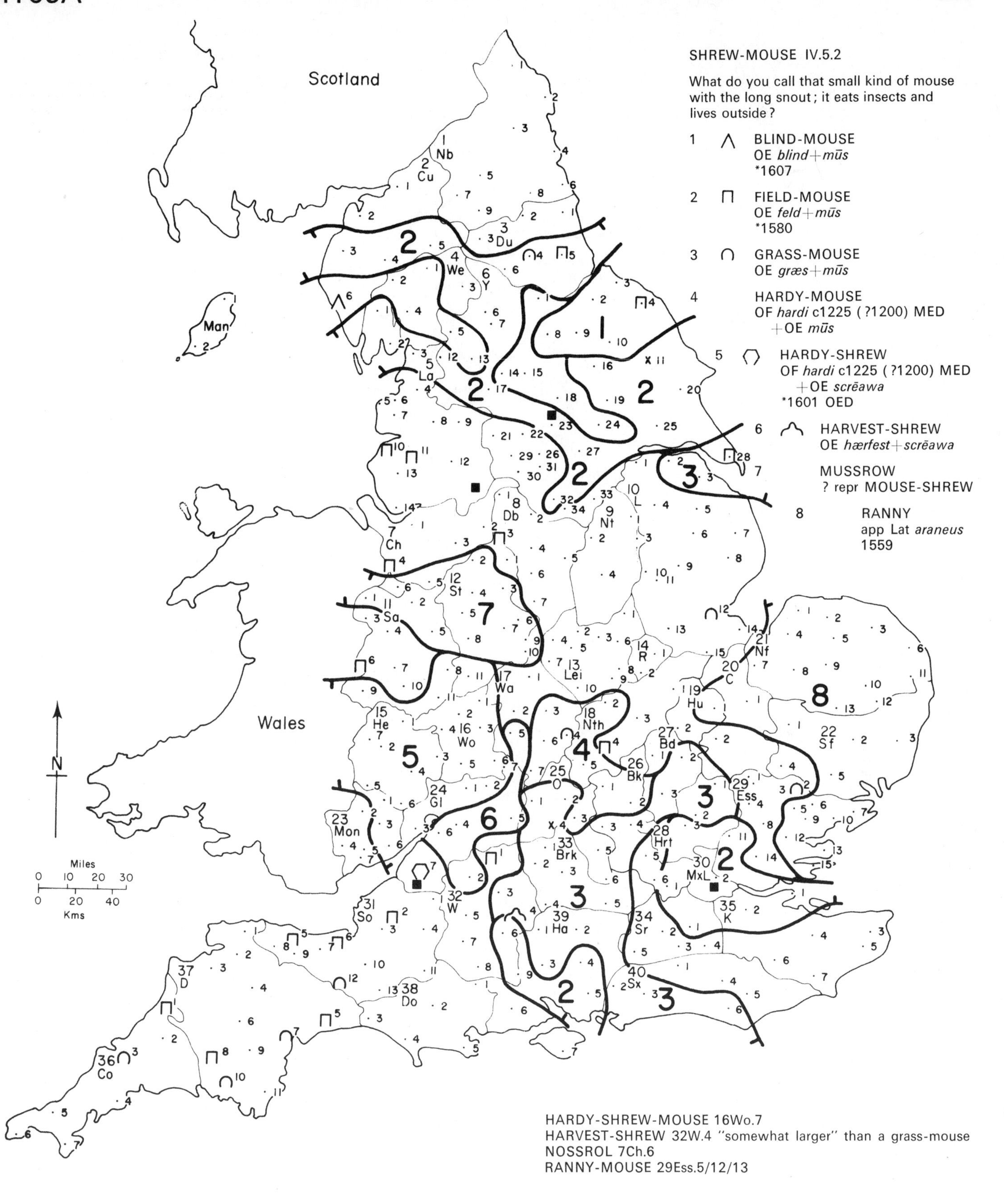

SHREW-MOUSE IV.5.2
What do you call that small kind of mouse with the long snout; it eats insects and lives outside?
1 BLIND-MOUSE
OE blind+mūs
*1607
2 FIELD-MOUSE
OE feld+mūs
*1580
3 GRASS-MOUSE
OE græs+mūs
4 HARDY-MOUSE
OF hardi c1225 (?1200) MED
+OE mūs
5 HARDY-SHREW
OF hardi c1225 (?1200) MED
+OE scrēawa
*1601 OED
6 HARVEST-SHREW
OE hærfest+scrēawa
7 MUSSROW
? repr MOUSE-SHREW
8 RANNY
app Lat araneus
1559
Scotland
Wales
Man
Miles
Kms
HARDY-SHREW-MOUSE 16Wo.7
HARVEST-SHREW 32W.4 "somewhat larger" than a grass-mouse
NOSSROL 7Ch.6
RANNY-MOUSE 29Ess.5/12/13

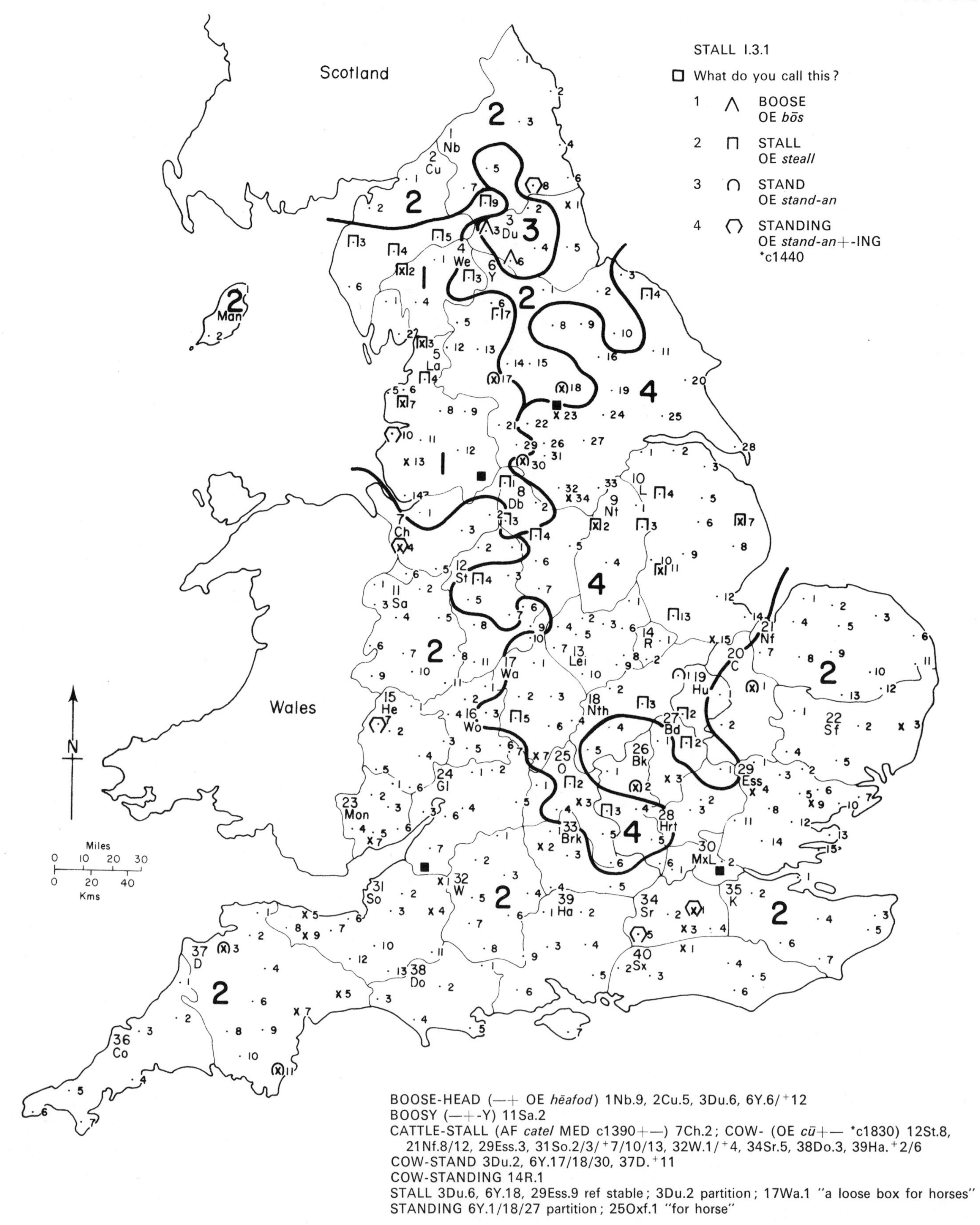

BOOSE-HEAD (—+ OE *hēafod*) 1Nb.9, 2Cu.5, 3Du.6, 6Y.6/+12
BOOSY (—+-Y) 11Sa.2
CATTLE-STALL (AF *catel* MED c1390+—) 7Ch.2; COW- (OE *cū*+— *c1830) 12St.8, 21Nf.8/12, 29Ess.3, 31So.2/3/+7/10/13, 32W.1/+4, 34Sr.5, 38Do.3, 39Ha.+2/6
COW-STAND 3Du.2, 6Y.17/18/30, 37D.+11
COW-STANDING 14R.1
STALL 3Du.6, 6Y.18, 29Ess.9 ref stable; 3Du.2 partition; 17Wa.1 "a loose box for horses"
STANDING 6Y.1/18/27 partition; 25Oxf.1 "for horse"

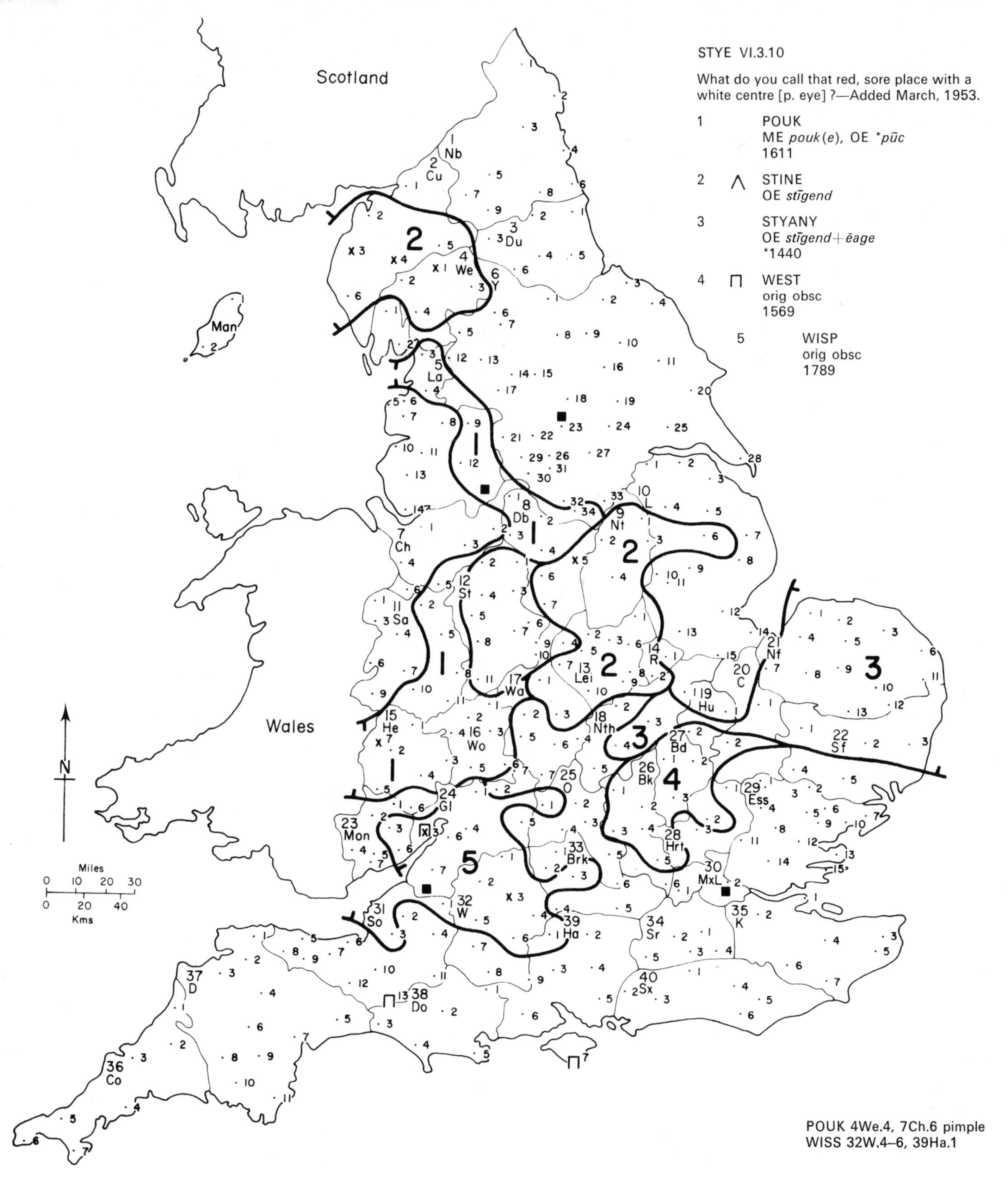
STYE VI.3.10
What do you call that red, sore place with a white centre [p. eye] ?—Added March, 1953.
1 POUK
ME pouk(e), OE *pūc
1611
2 Λ STINE
OE stīgend
3 STYANY
OE stīgend + ēage
*1440
4 ⊓ WEST
orig obsc
1569
5 WISP
orig obsc
1789
Scotland
Wales
Man
Miles
0 10 20 30
0 20 40
Kms
N
POUK 4We.4, 7Ch.6 pimple
WISS 32W.4–6, 39Ha.1

(OLDER) THAN VIII.1.21

Talking of people's ages: most husbands are not younger but . . . their wives.

1 ⋀ NOR
orig obsc
c1400

2 ⊓ THAN
OE *þanne*

3 TILL
OE *til* a ON *til*

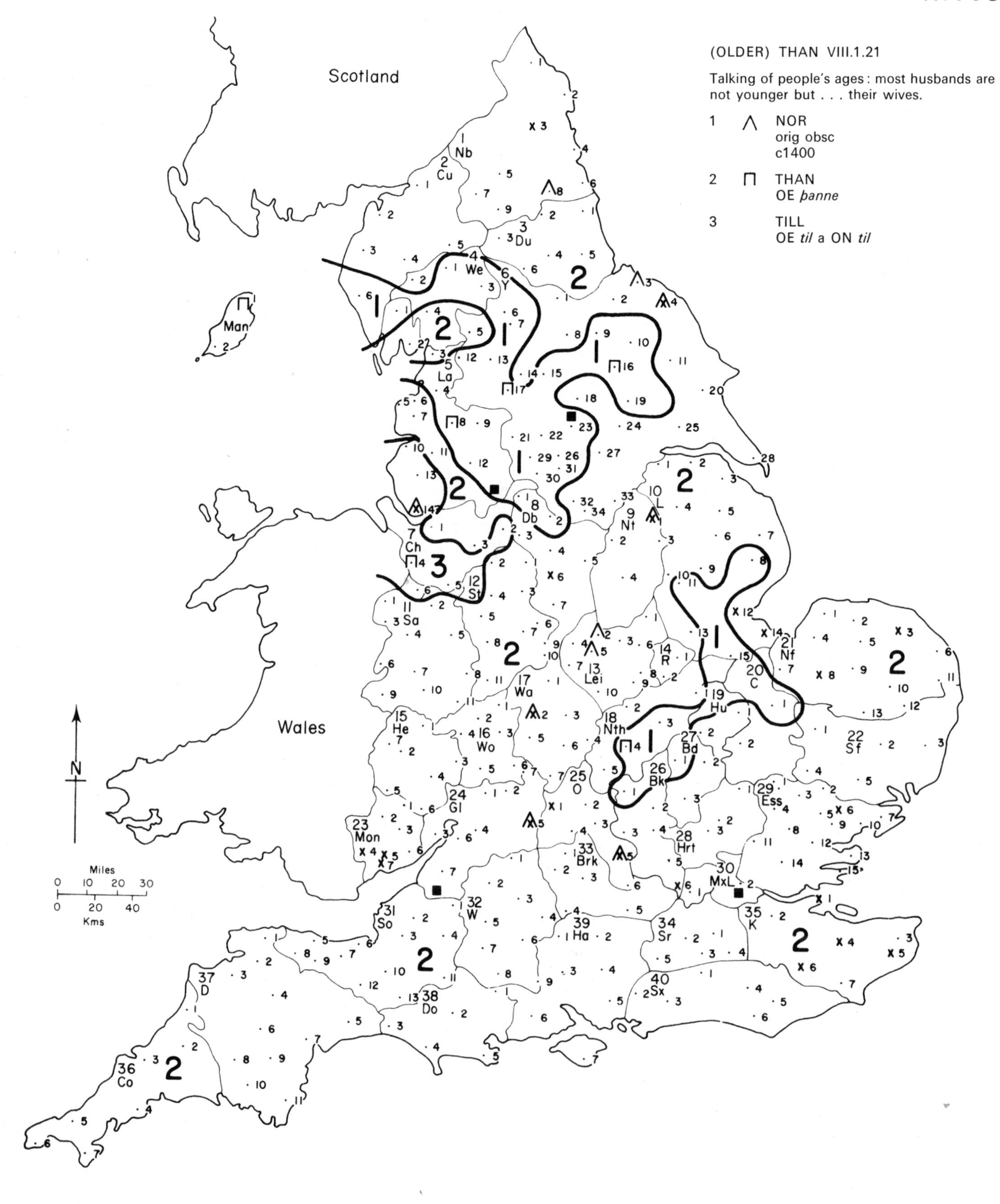

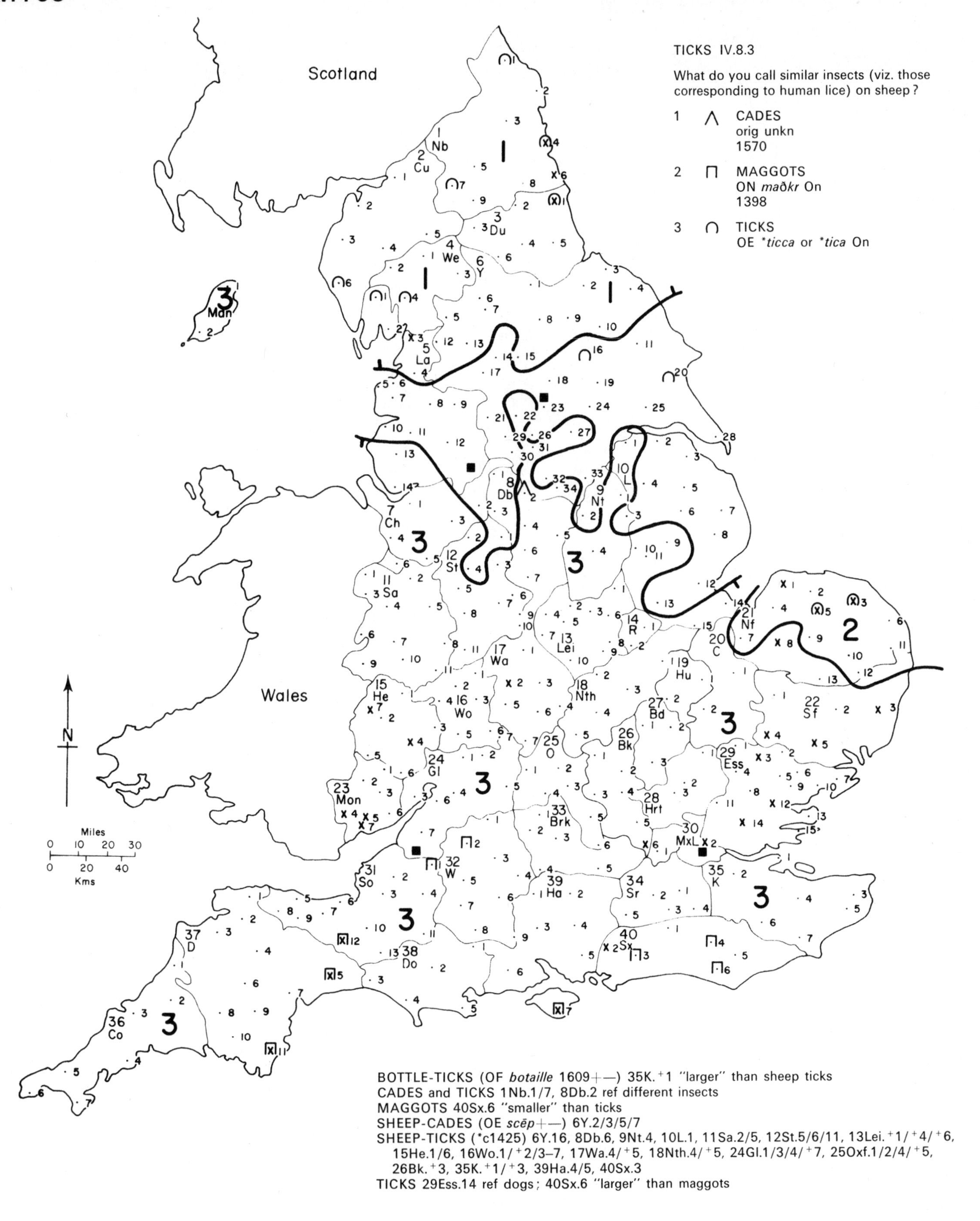
TICKS IV.8.3
What do you call similar insects (viz. those corresponding to human lice) on sheep?
1 ⋀ CADES
orig unkn
1570
2 ⊓ MAGGOTS
ON *maðkr* On
1398
3 ∩ TICKS
OE *ticca or *tica On
Scotland
Wales
Man
N
Miles
0 10 20 30
0 20 40
Kms
BOTTLE-TICKS (OF *botaille* 1609+—) 35K.⁺1 "larger" than sheep ticks
CADES and TICKS 1Nb.1/7, 8Db.2 ref different insects
MAGGOTS 40Sx.6 "smaller" than ticks
SHEEP-CADES (OE *scēp*+—) 6Y.2/3/5/7
SHEEP-TICKS (*c1425) 6Y.16, 8Db.6, 9Nt.4, 10L.1, 11Sa.2/5, 12St.5/6/11, 13Lei.⁺1/⁺4/⁺6, 15He.1/6, 16Wo.1/⁺2/3–7, 17Wa.4/⁺5, 18Nth.4/⁺5, 24Gl.1/3/4/⁺7, 25Oxf.1/2/4/⁺5, 26Bk.⁺3, 35K.⁺1/⁺3, 39Ha.4/5, 40Sx.3
TICKS 29Ess.14 ref dogs; 40Sx.6 "larger" than maggots

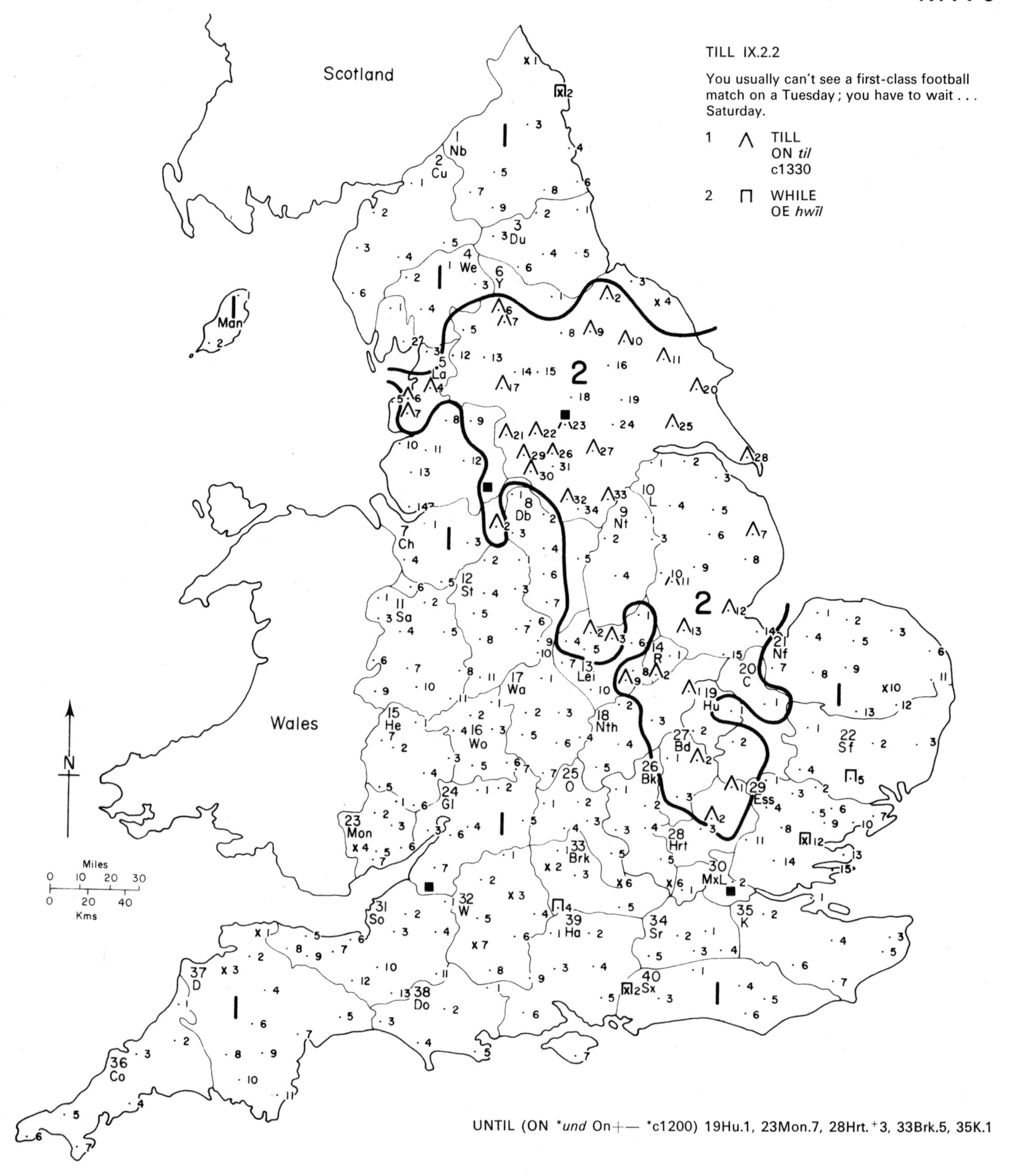

TILL IX.2.2

You usually can't see a first-class football match on a Tuesday; you have to wait . . . Saturday.

1 Λ TILL ON *til* c1330

2 ⊓ WHILE OE *hwīl*

UNTIL (ON **und* On+— *c1200) 19Hu.1, 23Mon.7, 28Hrt.+3, 33Brk.5, 35K.1

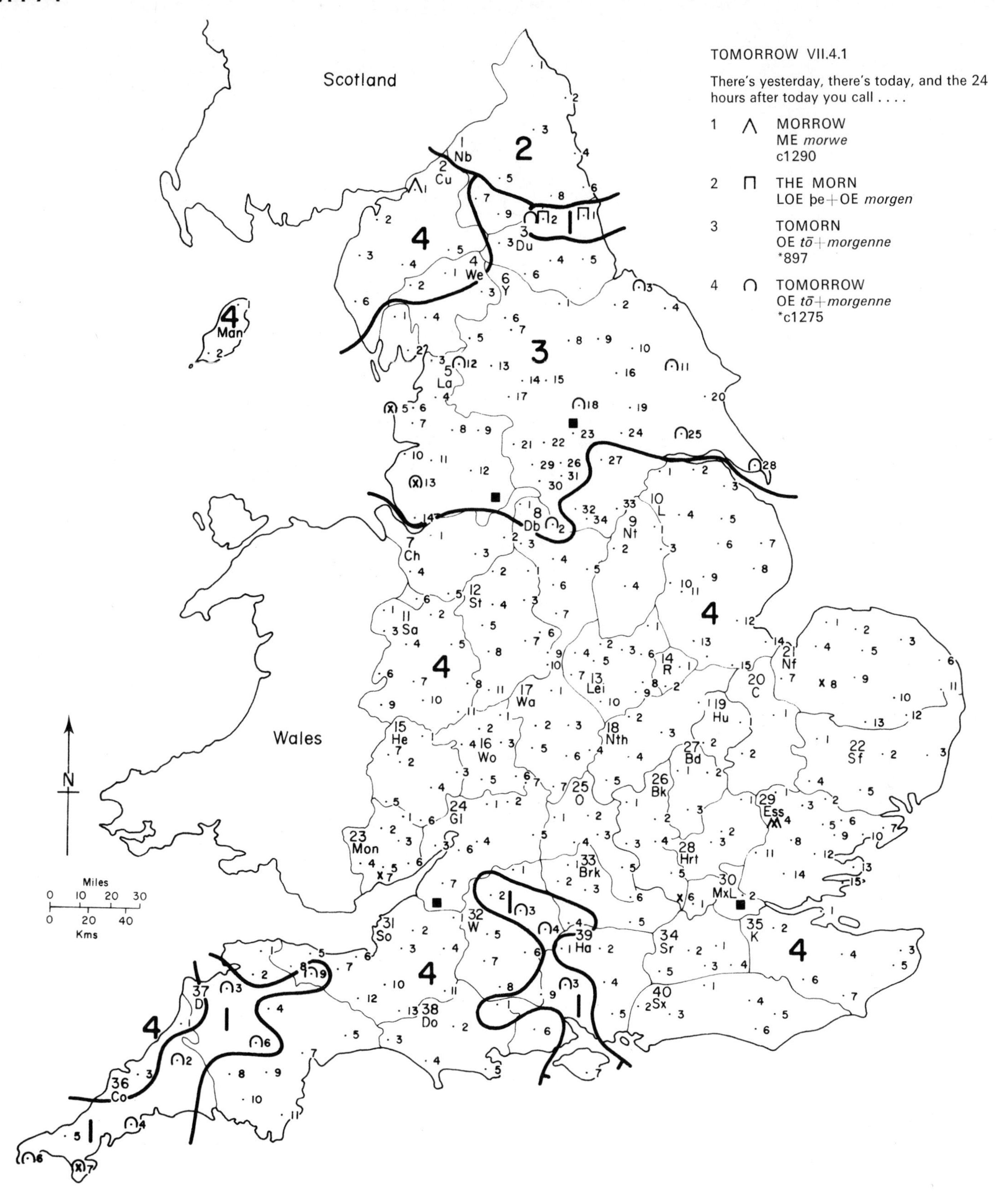
TOMORROW VII.4.1
There's yesterday, there's today, and the 24 hours after today you call . . . .
1 MORROW ME *morwe* c1290
2 THE MORN LOE þe+OE *morgen*
3 TOMORN OE *tō*+*morgenne* *897
4 TOMORROW OE *tō*+*morgenne* *c1275
Scotland
Wales
Man
Nb
Cu
Du
We
Y
La
Ch
Db
Nt
L
St
Sa
R
Lei
Wa
Nf
C
Hu
He
Wo
Nth
Bd
Sf
Gl
O
Bk
Ess
Mon
Hrt
Brk
MxL
So
W
Ha
Sr
K
D
Do
Sx
Co
N
Miles
0 10 20 30
0 20 40
Kms

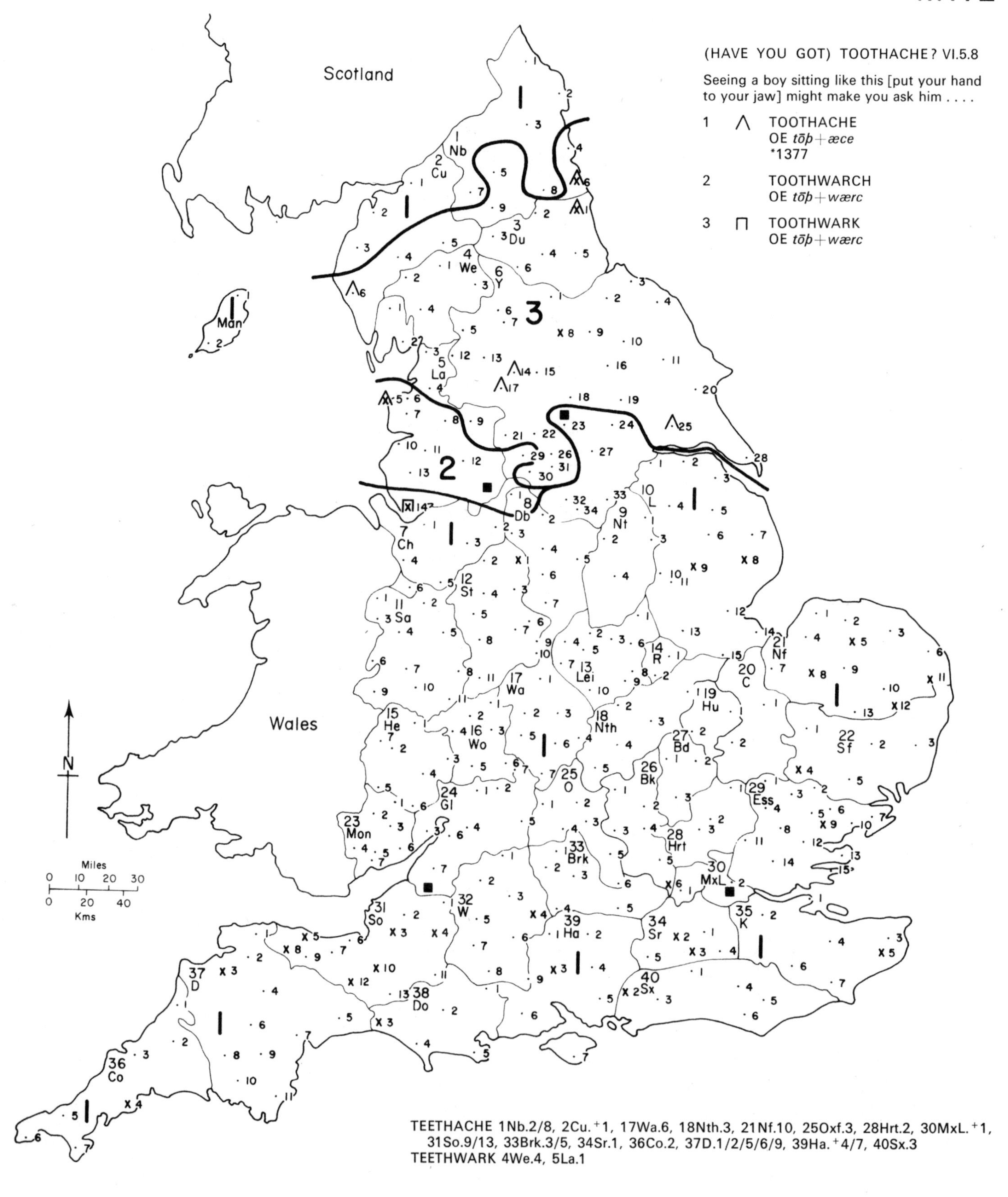
(HAVE YOU GOT) TOOTHACHE? VI.5.8
Seeing a boy sitting like this [put your hand to your jaw] might make you ask him . . . .
1 TOOTHACHE
OE *tōþ*+*æce*
*1377
2 TOOTHWARCH
OE *tōþ*+*wærc*
3 TOOTHWARK
OE *tōþ*+*wærc*
Scotland
Wales
N
Miles
0 10 20 30
0 20 40
Kms
TEETHACHE 1Nb.2/8, 2Cu.+1, 17Wa.6, 18Nth.3, 21Nf.10, 25Oxf.3, 28Hrt.2, 30MxL.+1, 31So.9/13, 33Brk.3/5, 34Sr.1, 36Co.2, 37D.1/2/5/6/9, 39Ha.+4/7, 40Sx.3
TEETHWARK 4We.4, 5La.1

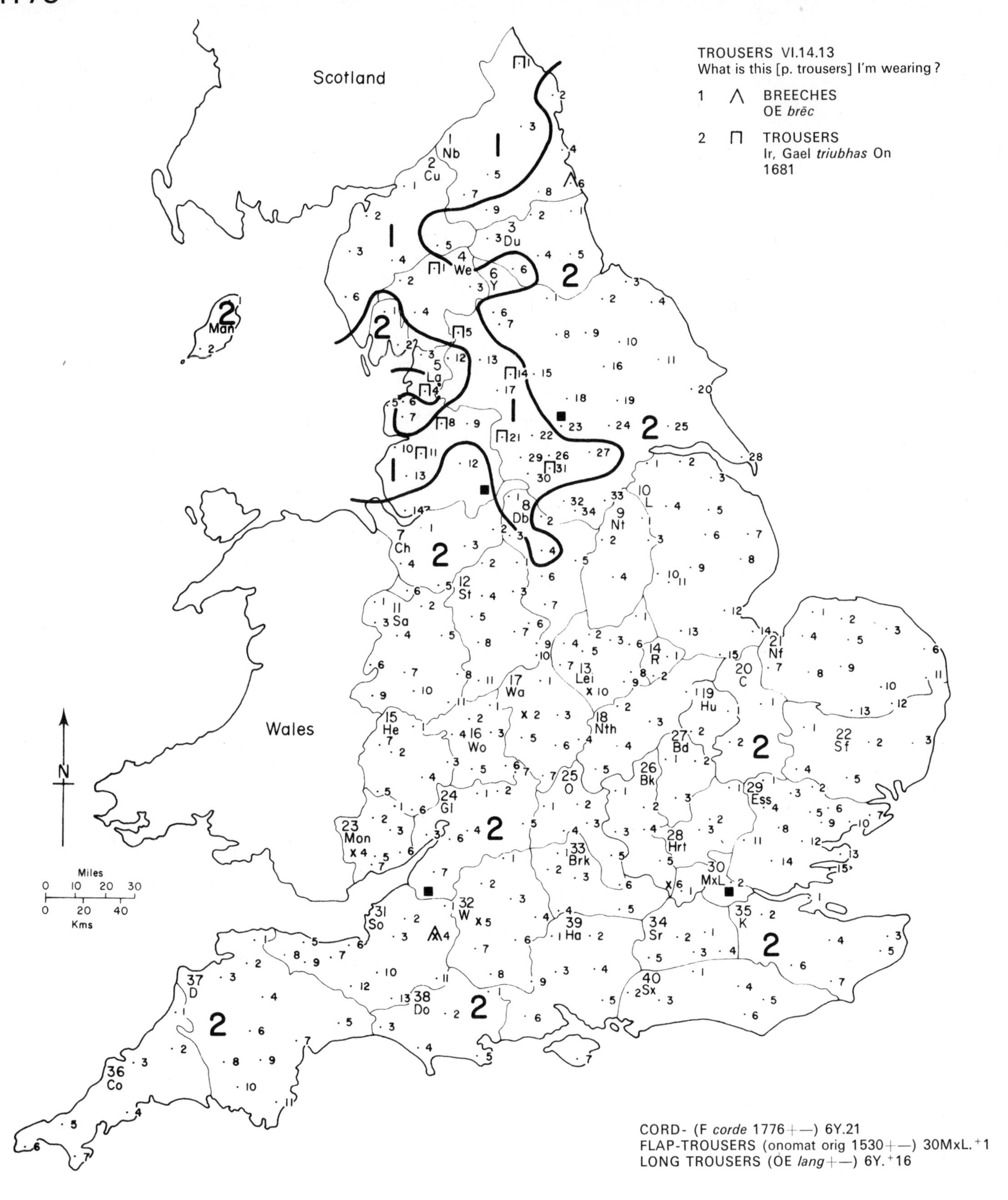

CORD- (F *corde* 1776+—) 6Y.21
FLAP-TROUSERS (onomat orig 1530+—) 30MxL.+1
LONG TROUSERS (OE *lang*+—) 6Y.+16

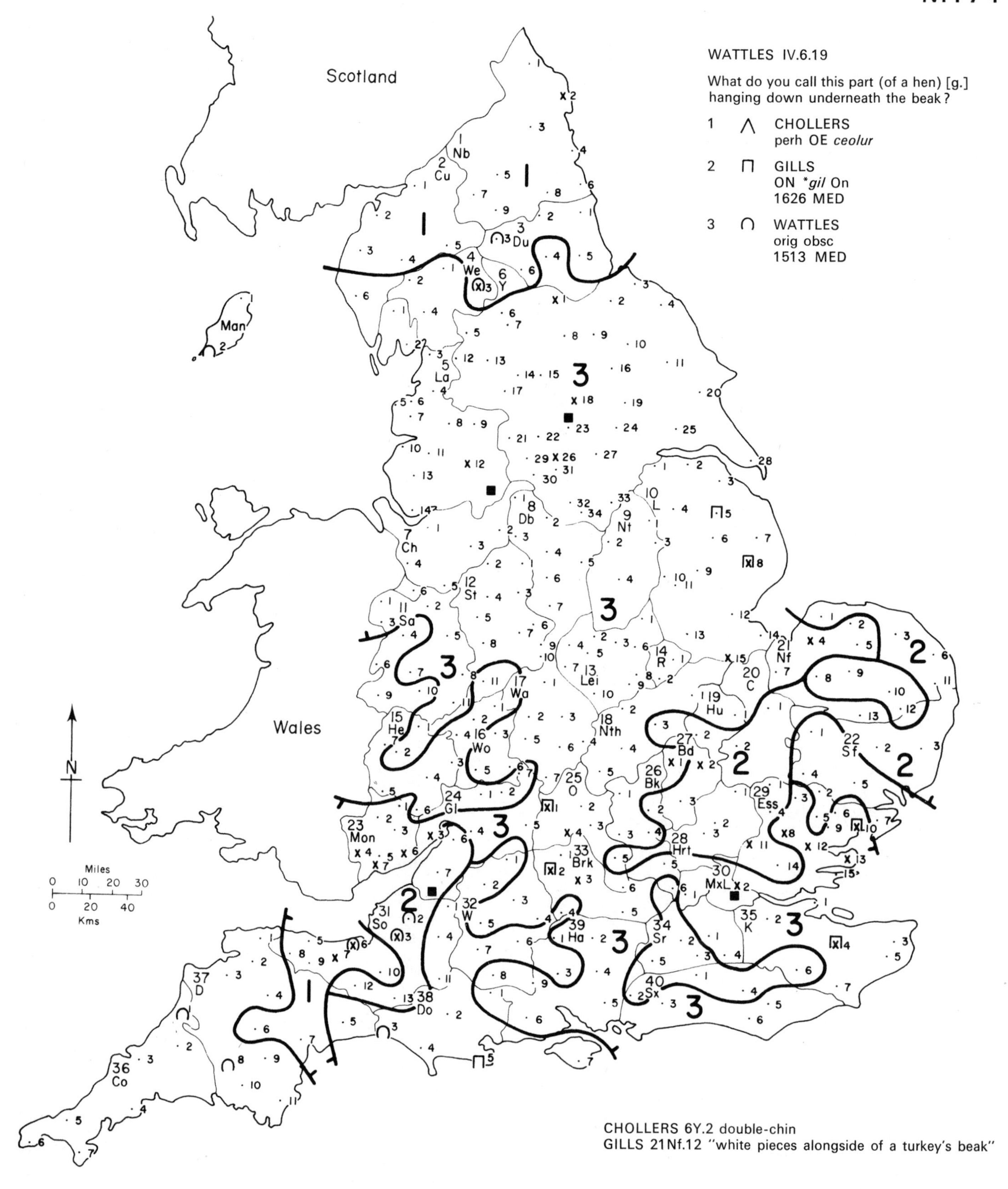

WATTLES IV.6.19
What do you call this part (of a hen) [g.] hanging down underneath the beak?
1 Λ CHOLLERS
perh OE *ceolur*
2 ⊓ GILLS
ON *gil On
1626 MED
3 ∩ WATTLES
orig obsc
1513 MED
Scotland
Wales
Man
N
Miles
0 10 20 30
0 20 40
Kms
CHOLLERS 6Y.2 double-chin
GILLS 21Nf.12 "white pieces alongside of a turkey's beak"

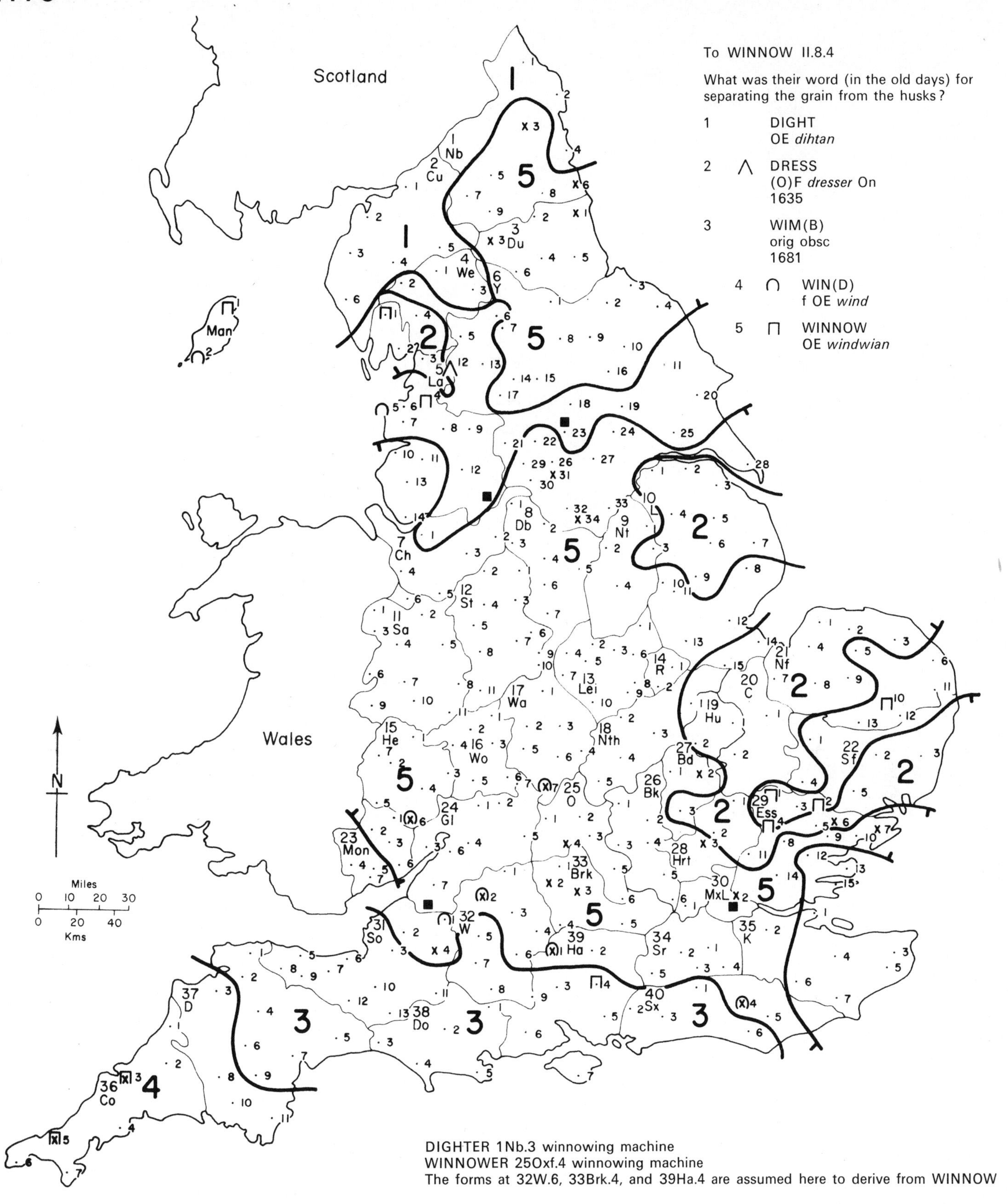

DIGHTER 1Nb.3 winnowing machine
WINNOWER 25Oxf.4 winnowing machine
The forms at 32W.6, 33Brk.4, and 39Ha.4 are assumed here to derive from WINNOW

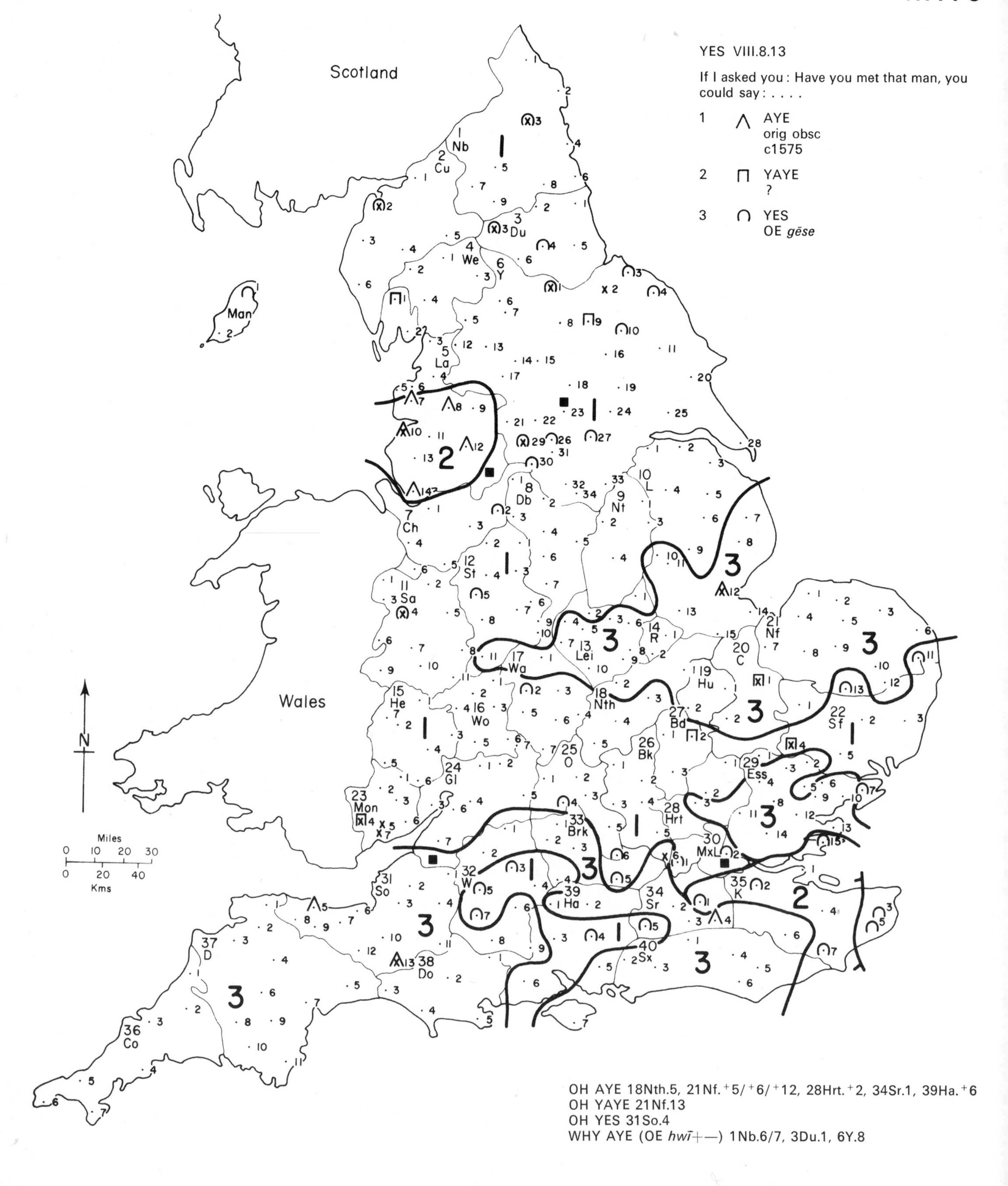
YES VIII.8.13
If I asked you: Have you met that man, you could say: . . . .
1 ∧ AYE orig obsc c1575
2 ⊓ YAYE ?
3 ∩ YES OE *gēse*
Scotland
Wales
Man
Miles 0 10 20 30
0 20 40 Kms
N
OH AYE 18Nth.5, 21Nf.+5/+6/+12, 28Hrt.+2, 34Sr.1, 39Ha.+6
OH YAYE 21Nf.13
OH YES 31So.4
WHY AYE (OE *hwī*+—) 1Nb.6/7, 3Du.1, 6Y.8

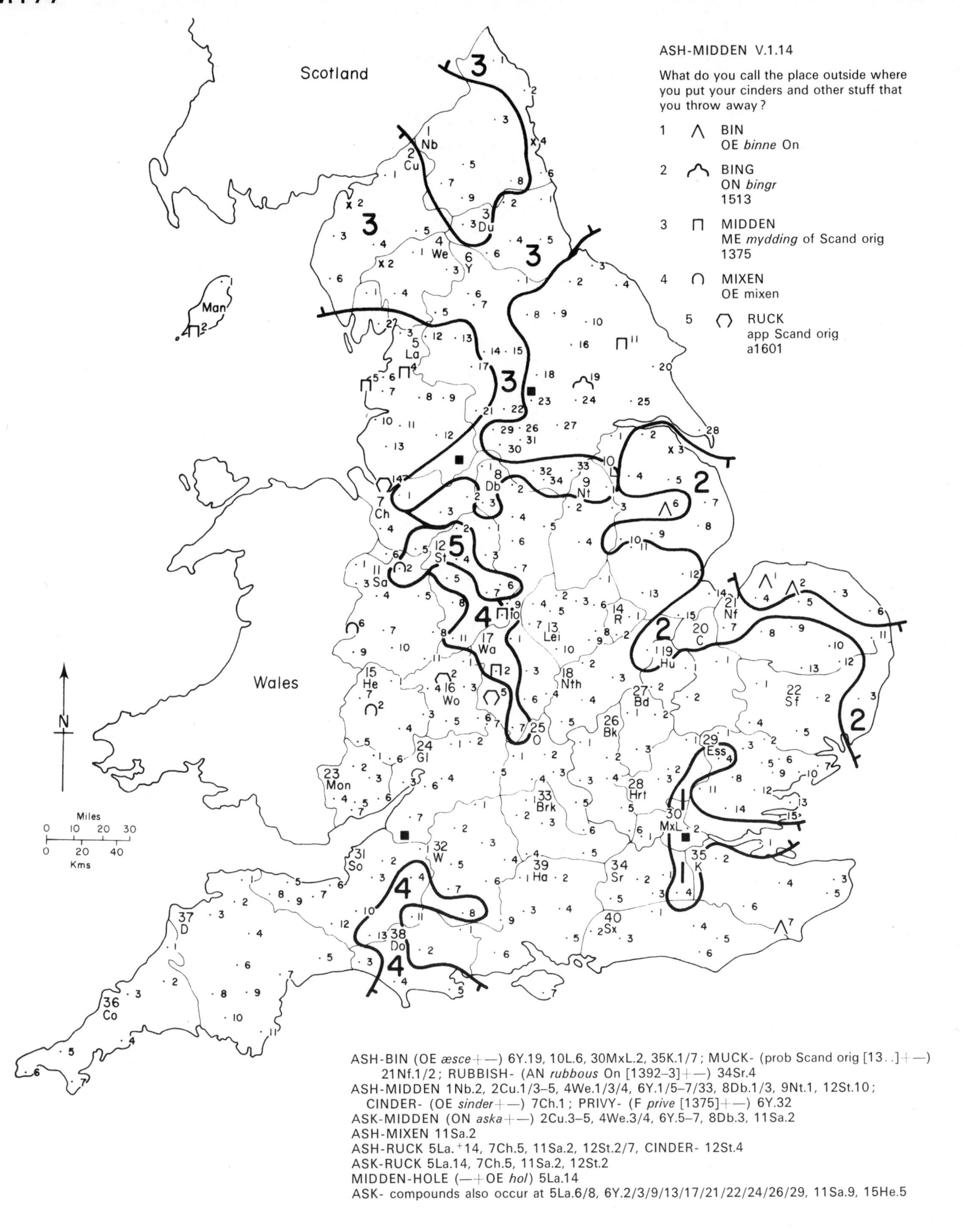

ASH-BIN (OE *æsce*+—) 6Y.19, 10L.6, 30MxL.2, 35K.1/7; MUCK- (prob Scand orig [13..]+—) 21Nf.1/2; RUBBISH- (AN *rubbous* On [1392–3]+—) 34Sr.4

ASH-MIDDEN 1Nb.2, 2Cu.1/3–5, 4We.1/3/4, 6Y.1/5–7/33, 8Db.1/3, 9Nt.1, 12St.10; CINDER- (OE *sinder*+—) 7Ch.1; PRIVY- (F *prive* [1375]+—) 6Y.32

ASK-MIDDEN (ON *aska*+—) 2Cu.3–5, 4We.3/4, 6Y.5–7, 8Db.3, 11Sa.2

ASH-MIXEN 11Sa.2

ASH-RUCK 5La.+14, 7Ch.5, 11Sa.2, 12St.2/7, CINDER- 12St.4

ASK-RUCK 5La.14, 7Ch.5, 11Sa.2, 12St.2

MIDDEN-HOLE (—+OE *hol*) 5La.14

ASK- compounds also occur at 5La.6/8, 6Y.2/3/9/13/17/21/22/24/26/29, 11Sa.9, 15He.5

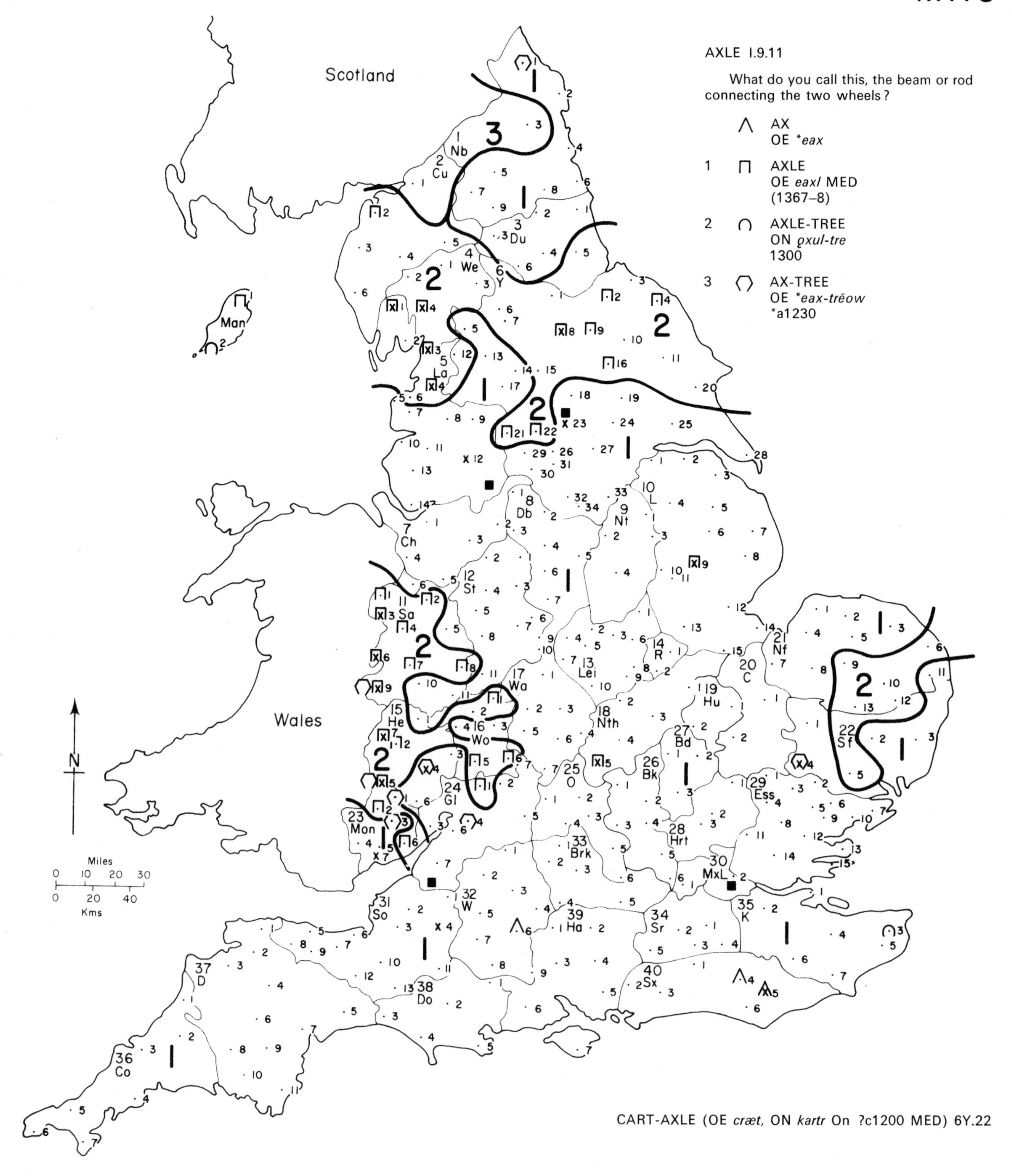
AXLE I.9.11
What do you call this, the beam or rod connecting the two wheels?
Λ AX
OE *eax
1 ⊓ AXLE
OE eaxl MED (1367–8)
2 ∩ AXLE-TREE
ON ǫxul-tre 1300
3 ⬡ AX-TREE
OE *eax-trēow *a1230
Scotland
Wales
Man
Nb
Cu
Du
We
Y
La
Ch
Db
Nt
L
St
Sa
Lei
R
Nf
Wa
He
Wo
Nth
Hu
C
Sf
Gl
O
Bk
Bd
Ess
Mon
Hrt
Brk
MxL
So
W
Ha
Sr
K
D
Do
Sx
Co
Miles
0 10 20 30
0 20 40
Kms
N
CART-AXLE (OE cræt, ON kartr On ?c1200 MED) 6Y.22

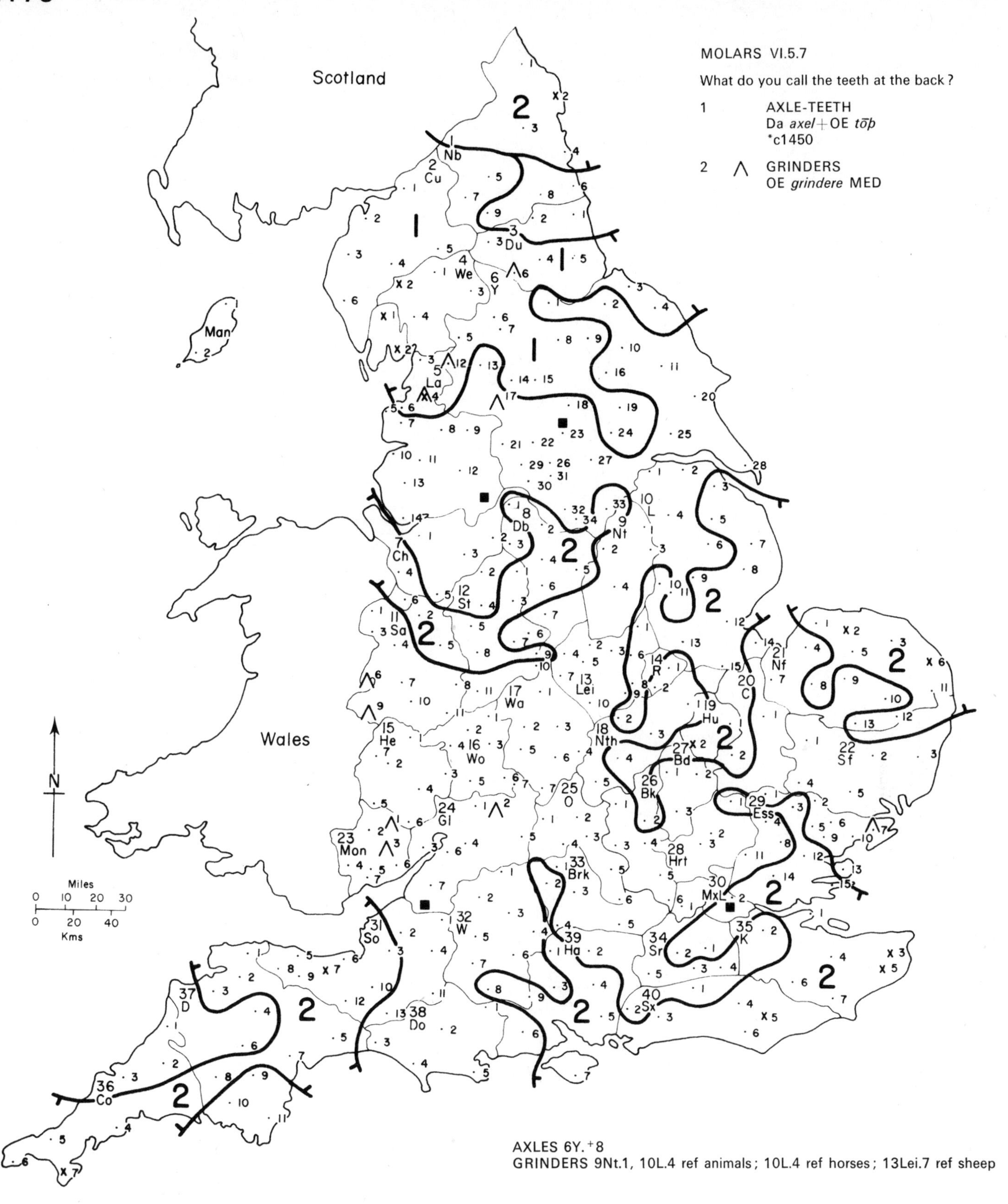
MOLARS VI.5.7
What do you call the teeth at the back?
1 AXLE-TEETH
Da *axel* + OE *tōþ*
*c1450
2 ⋀ GRINDERS
OE *grindere* MED
Scotland
Wales
Man
N
Miles
0 10 20 30
0 20 40
Kms
AXLES 6Y.+8
GRINDERS 9Nt.1, 10L.4 ref animals; 10L.4 ref horses; 13Lei.7 ref sheep

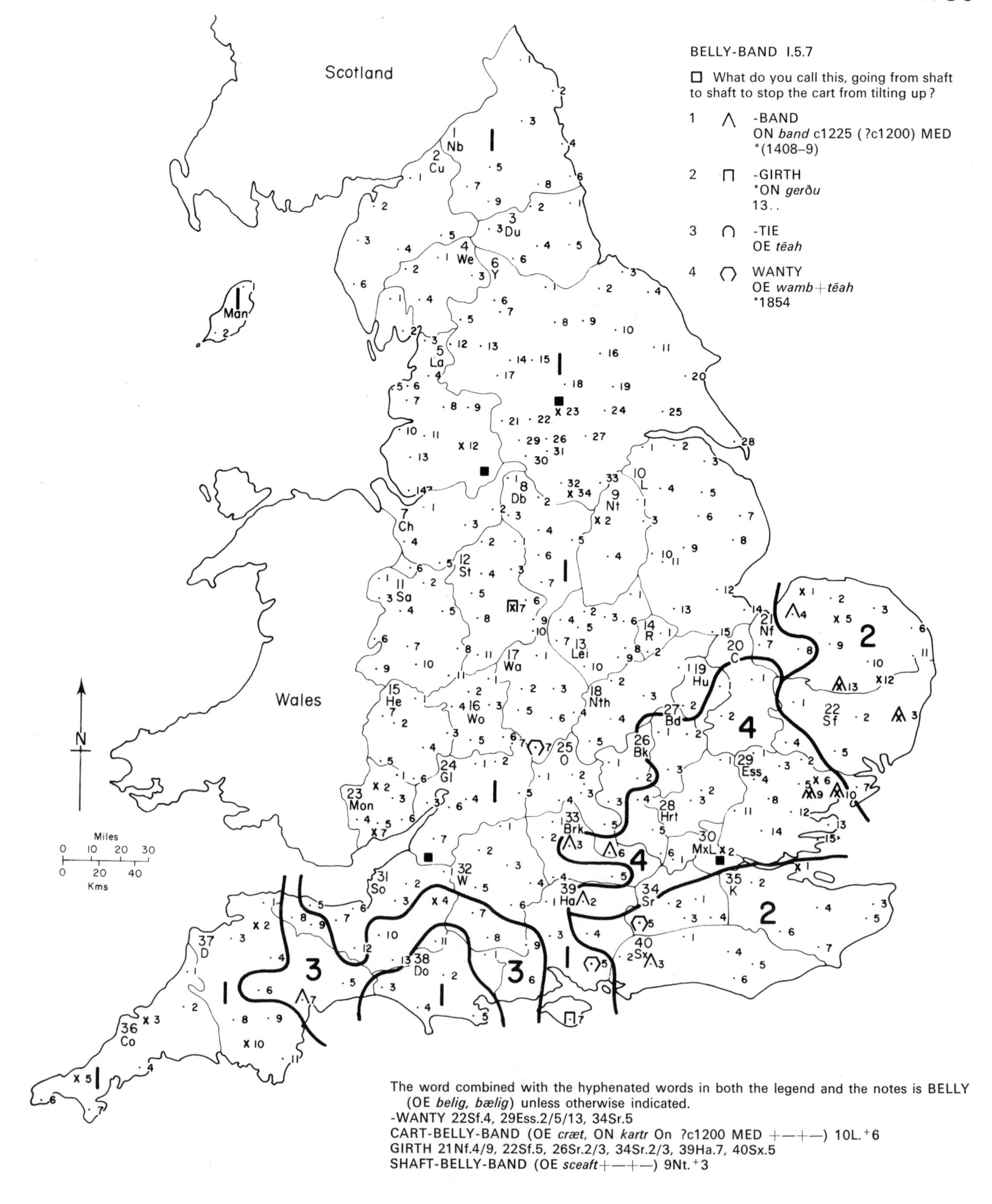

The word combined with the hyphenated words in both the legend and the notes is BELLY (OE *belig, bælig*) unless otherwise indicated.

-WANTY 22Sf.4, 29Ess.2/5/13, 34Sr.5

CART-BELLY-BAND (OE *cræt*, ON *kartr* On ?c1200 MED +—+—) 10L.+6

GIRTH 21Nf.4/9, 22Sf.5, 26Sr.2/3, 34Sr.2/3, 39Ha.7, 40Sx.5

SHAFT-BELLY-BAND (OE *sceaft*+—+—) 9Nt.+3

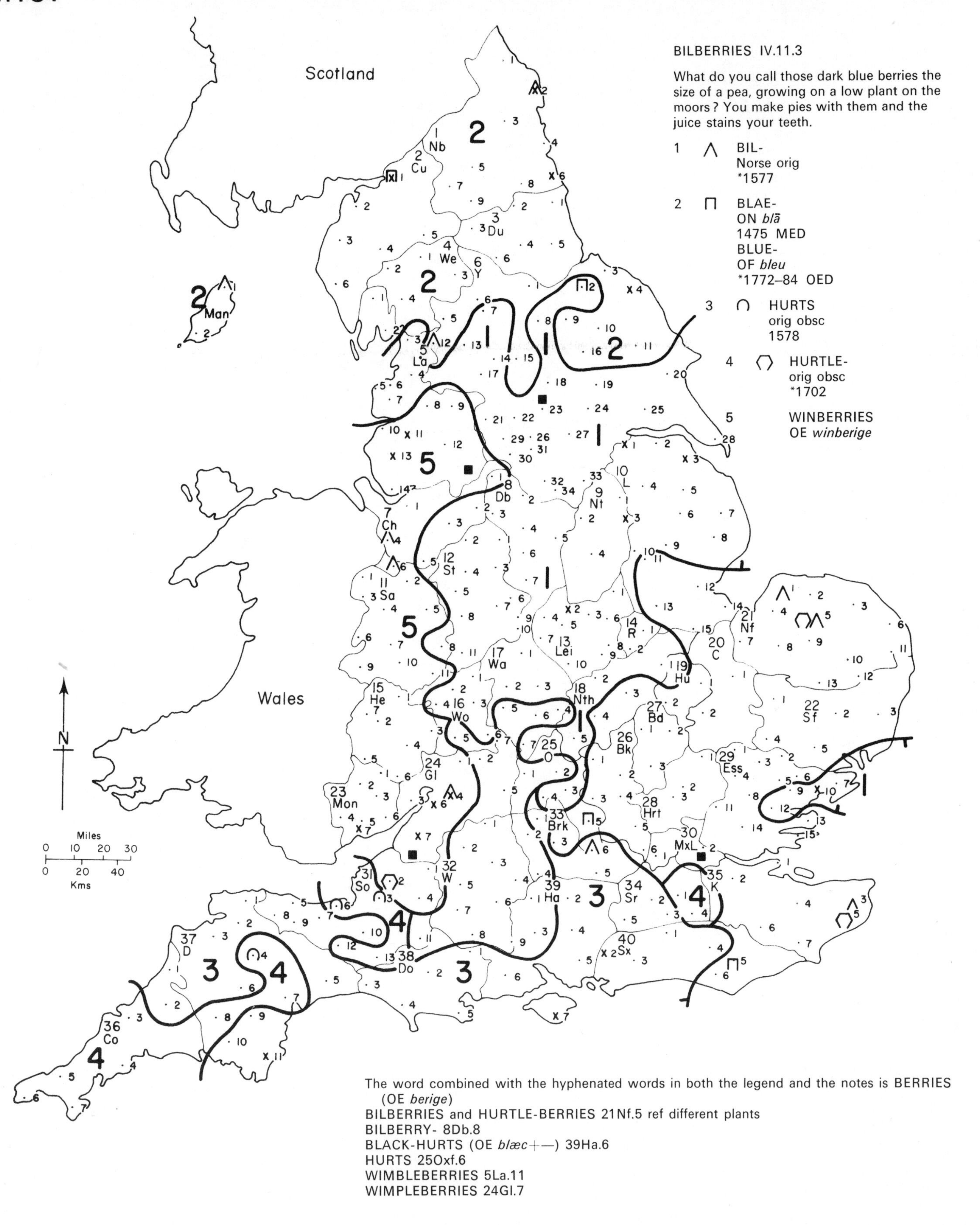
BILBERRIES IV.11.3
What do you call those dark blue berries the size of a pea, growing on a low plant on the moors? You make pies with them and the juice stains your teeth.
1 BIL- Norse orig *1577
2 BLAE- ON *blā* 1475 MED
BLUE- OF *bleu* *1772–84 OED
3 HURTS orig obsc 1578
4 HURTLE- orig obsc *1702
5 WINBERRIES OE *winberige*
Scotland
Wales
Man
Miles
0 10 20 30
0 20 40
Kms
N
The word combined with the hyphenated words in both the legend and the notes is BERRIES (OE *berige*)
BILBERRIES and HURTLE-BERRIES 21Nf.5 ref different plants
BILBERRY- 8Db.8
BLACK-HURTS (OE *blæc*+—) 39Ha.6
HURTS 25Oxf.6
WIMBLEBERRIES 5La.11
WIMPLEBERRIES 24Gl.7

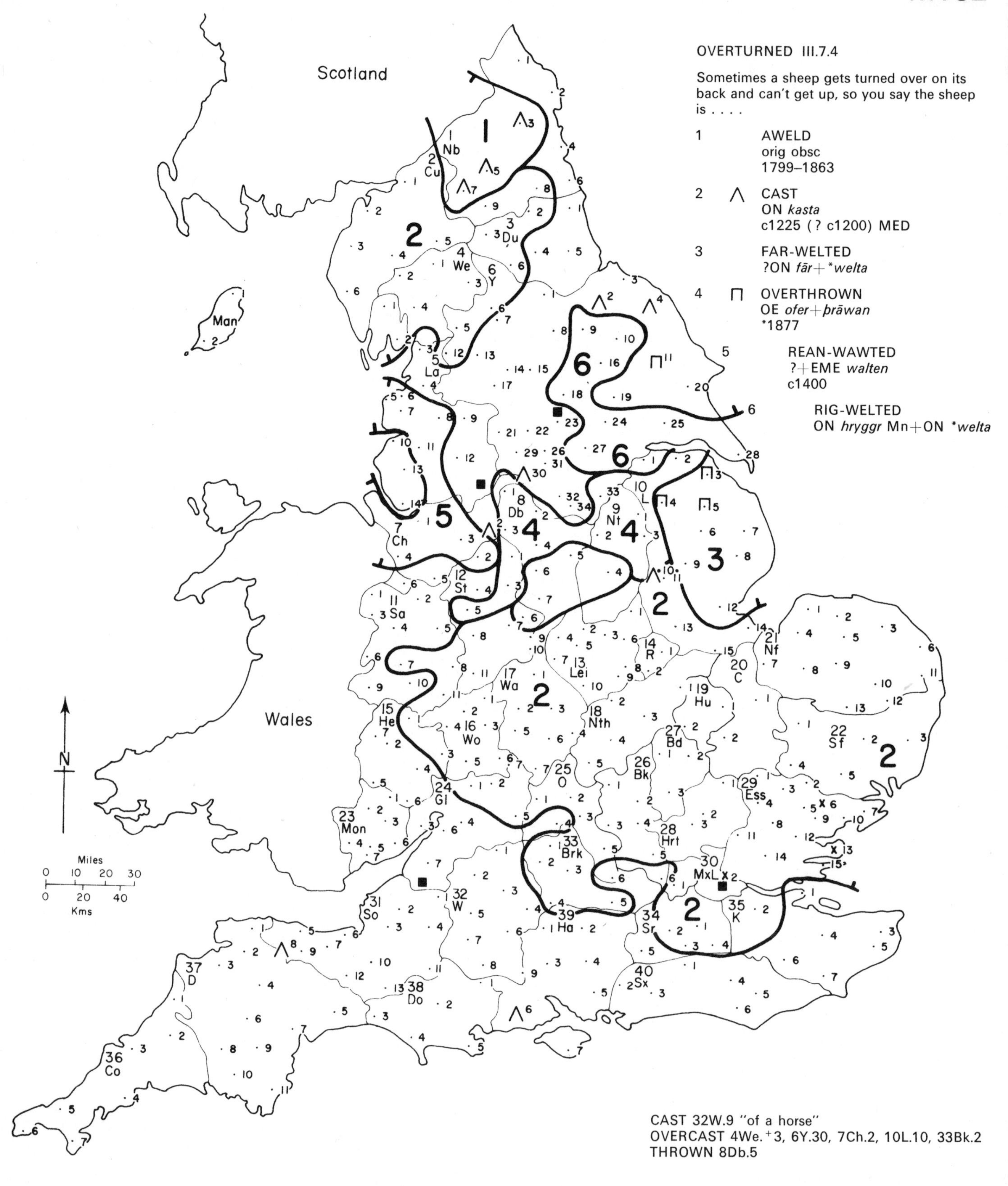
OVERTURNED III.7.4
Sometimes a sheep gets turned over on its back and can't get up, so you say the sheep is . . . .
1 AWELD
orig obsc
1799–1863
2 Λ CAST
ON *kasta*
c1225 (? c1200) MED
3 FAR-WELTED
?ON *fār*+**welta*
4 Π OVERTHROWN
OE *ofer*+*þrāwan*
*1877
5 REAN-WAWTED
?+EME *walten*
c1400
6 RIG-WELTED
ON *hryggr* Mn+ON **welta*
Scotland
Wales
Man
N
Miles
0 10 20 30
0 20 40
Kms
CAST 32W.9 "of a horse"
OVERCAST 4We.+3, 6Y.30, 7Ch.2, 10L.10, 33Bk.2
THROWN 8Db.5

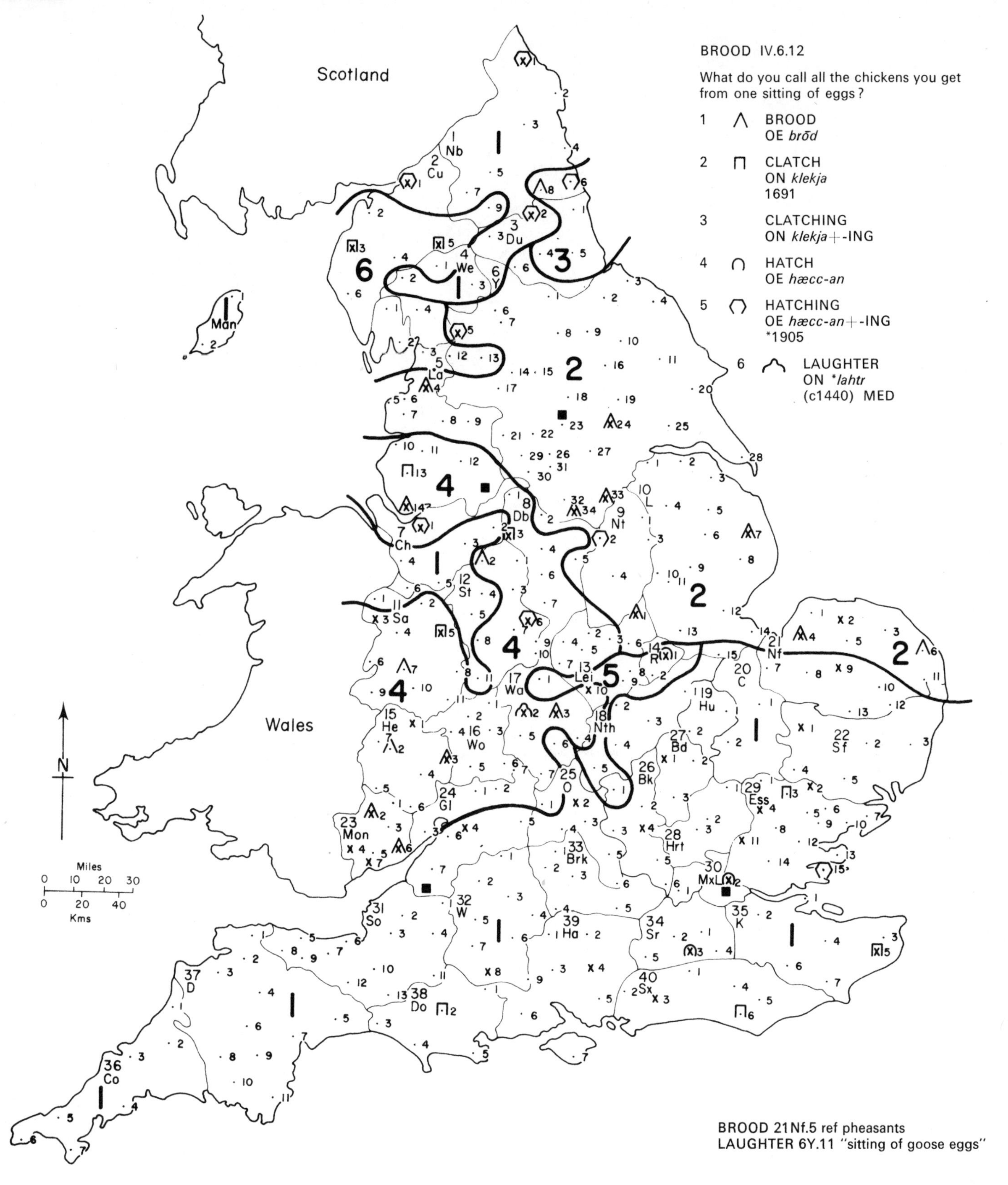
BROOD IV.6.12
What do you call all the chickens you get from one sitting of eggs?
1 BROOD OE *brōd*
2 CLATCH ON *klekja* 1691
3 CLATCHING ON *klekja*+-ING
4 HATCH OE *hæcc-an*
5 HATCHING OE *hæcc-an*+-ING *1905
6 LAUGHTER ON *lahtr (c1440) MED
Scotland
Wales
Man
Miles 0 10 20 30
0 20 40 Kms
N
BROOD 21Nf.5 ref pheasants
LAUGHTER 6Y.11 "sitting of goose eggs"

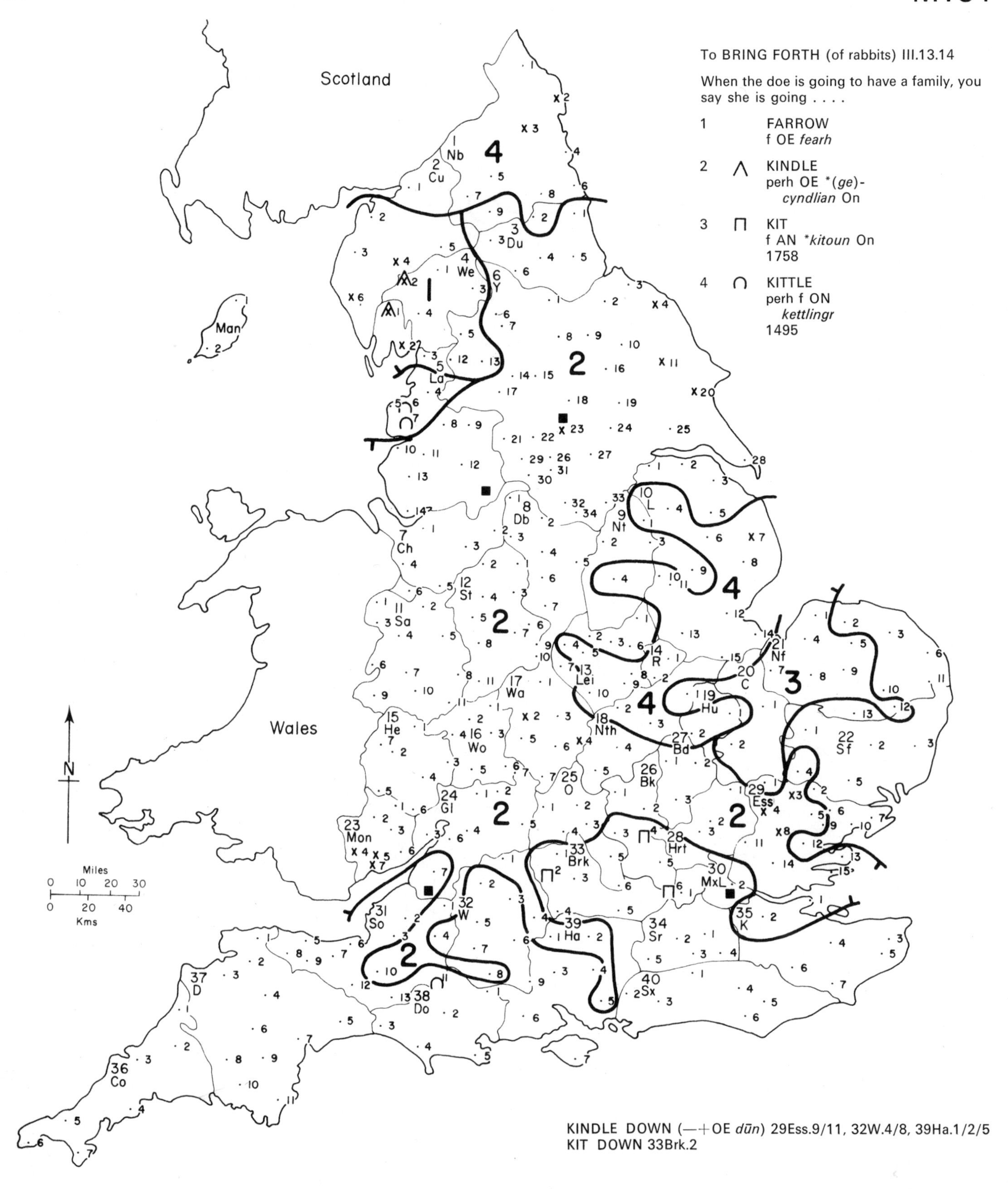
To BRING FORTH (of rabbits) III.13.14
When the doe is going to have a family, you say she is going . . . .
1 FARROW
f OE *fearh*
2 ∧ KINDLE
perh OE *(*ge*)-cyndlian* On
3 ⊓ KIT
f AN **kitoun* On
1758
4 ∩ KITTLE
perh f ON *kettlingr*
1495
Scotland
Wales
Man
N
Miles
0 10 20 30
0 20 40
Kms
Nb
Cu
Du
We
Y
La
L
Nt
Db
Ch
St
Sa
Lei
R
Nf
C
Hu
Wa
He
Wo
Nth
Bd
Sf
O
Bk
Gl
Ess
Mon
Hrt
Brk
MxL
So
W
K
Ha
Sr
D
Do
Sx
Co
KINDLE DOWN (—+OE *dūn*) 29Ess.9/11, 32W.4/8, 39Ha.1/2/5
KIT DOWN 33Brk.2

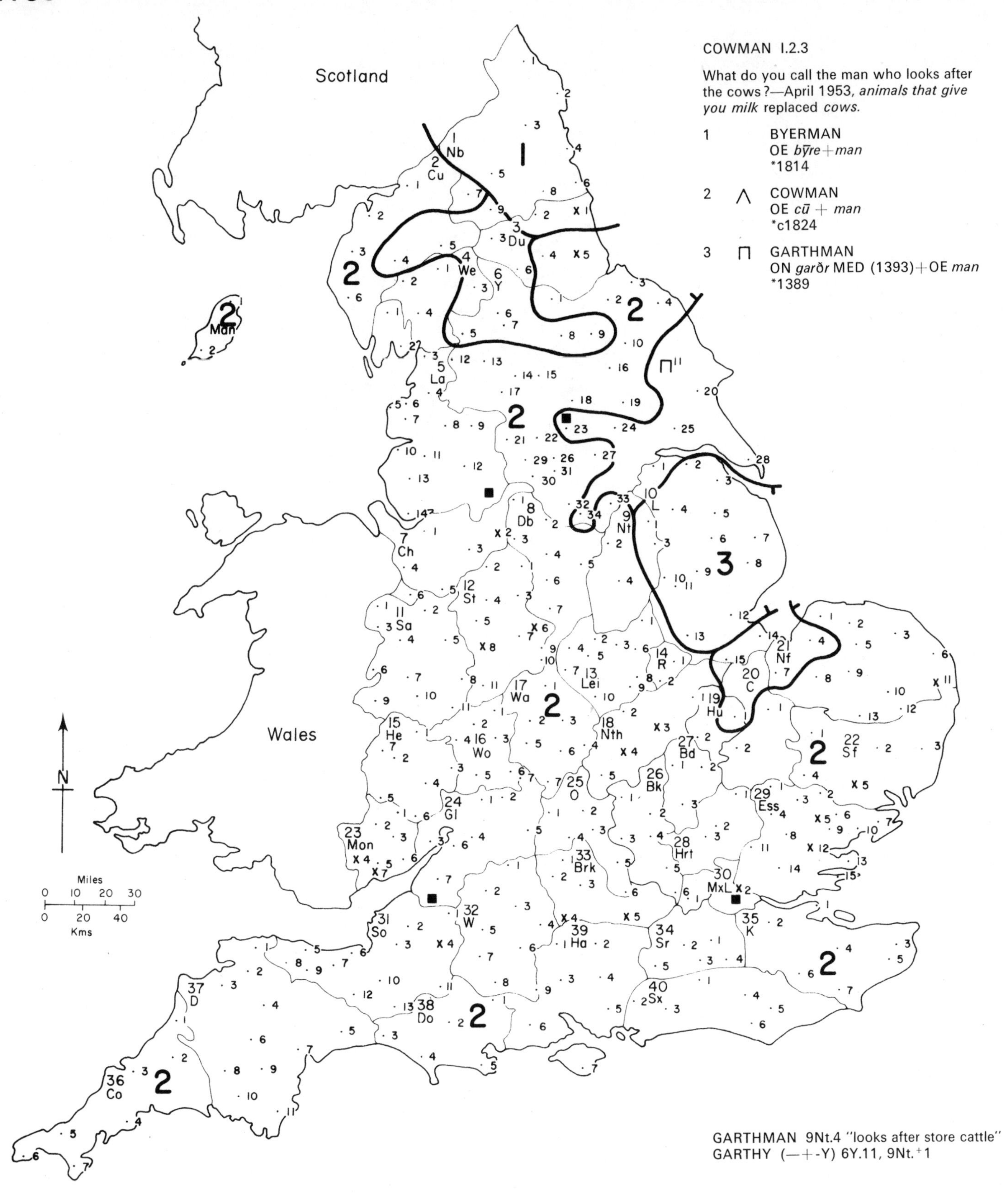
COWMAN I.2.3
What do you call the man who looks after the cows?—April 1953, *animals that give you milk* replaced *cows*.
1 BYERMAN
OE *bȳre*+*man*
*1814
2 Λ COWMAN
OE *cū* + *man*
*c1824
3 ⊓ GARTHMAN
ON *garðr* MED (1393)+OE *man*
*1389
Scotland
Wales
Miles 0 10 20 30
0 20 40 Kms
N
GARTHMAN 9Nt.4 "looks after store cattle"
GARTHY (—+-Y) 6Y.11, 9Nt.+1

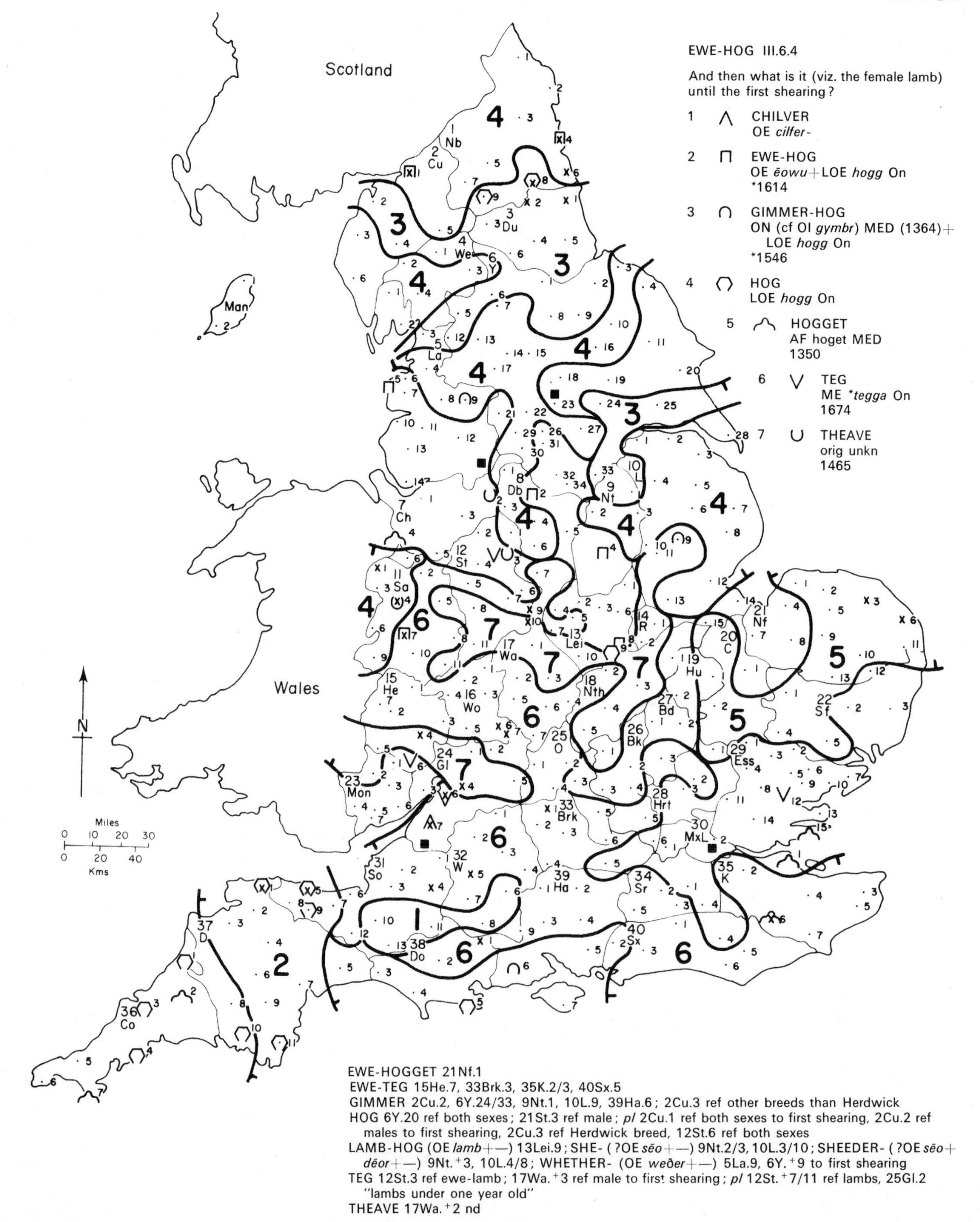

EWE-HOGGET 21Nf.1
EWE-TEG 15He.7, 33Brk.3, 35K.2/3, 40Sx.5
GIMMER 2Cu.2, 6Y.24/33, 9Nt.1, 10L.9, 39Ha.6; 2Cu.3 ref other breeds than Herdwick
HOG 6Y.20 ref both sexes; 21St.3 ref male; *pl* 2Cu.1 ref both sexes to first shearing, 2Cu.2 ref males to first shearing, 2Cu.3 ref Herdwick breed, 12St.6 ref both sexes
LAMB-HOG (OE *lamb*+—) 13Lei.9; SHE- (?OE *sēo*+—) 9Nt.2/3, 10L.3/10; SHEEDER- (?OE *sēo*+ *dēor*+—) 9Nt.+3, 10L.4/8; WHETHER- (OE *weðer*+—) 5La.9, 6Y.+9 to first shearing
TEG 12St.3 ref ewe-lamb; 17Wa.+3 ref male to first shearing; *pl* 12St.+7/11 ref lambs, 25Gl.2 "lambs under one year old"
THEAVE 17Wa.+2 nd

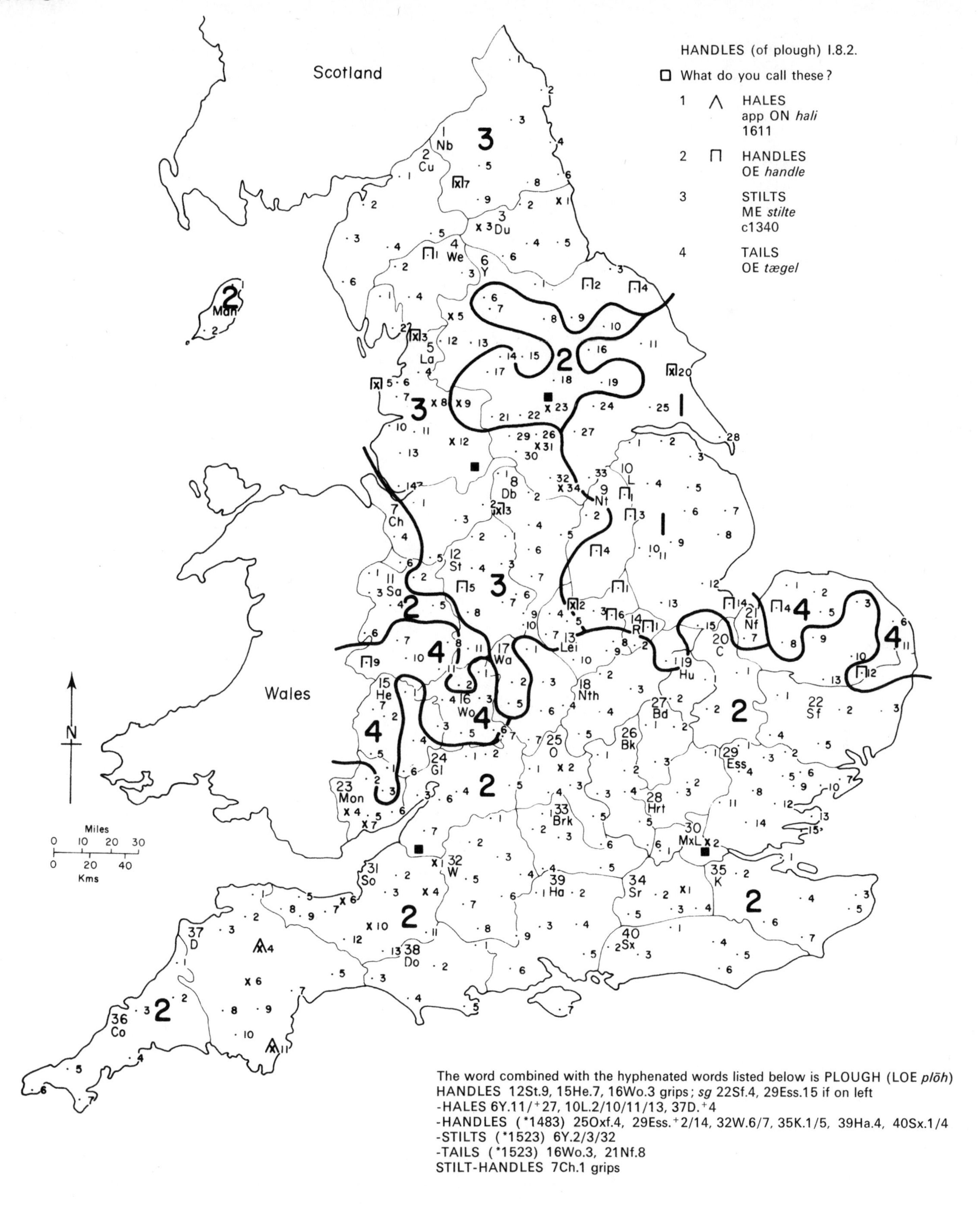

The word combined with the hyphenated words listed below is PLOUGH (LOE *plōh*)
HANDLES 12St.9, 15He.7, 16Wo.3 grips; *sg* 22Sf.4, 29Ess.15 if on left
-HALES 6Y.11/+27, 10L.2/10/11/13, 37D.+4
-HANDLES (*1483) 25Oxf.4, 29Ess.+2/14, 32W.6/7, 35K.1/5, 39Ha.4, 40Sx.1/4
-STILTS (*1523) 6Y.2/3/32
-TAILS (*1523) 16Wo.3, 21Nf.8
STILT-HANDLES 7Ch.1 grips

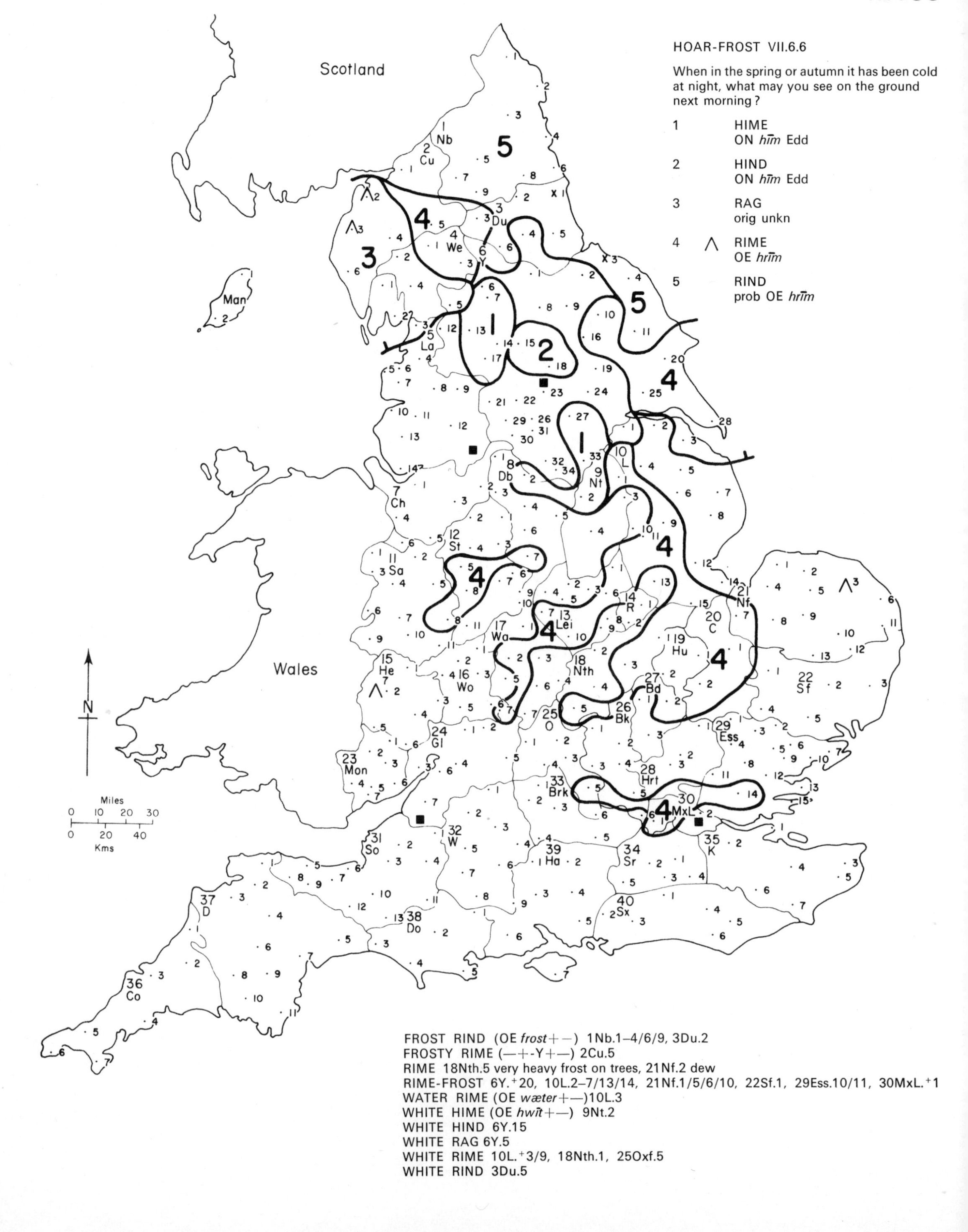
Scotland
Wales
Man
HOAR-FROST VII.6.6
When in the spring or autumn it has been cold at night, what may you see on the ground next morning?
1 HIME
ON *hīm* Edd
2 HIND
ON *hīm* Edd
3 RAG
orig unkn
4 ⋀ RIME
OE *hrīm*
5 RIND
prob OE *hrīm*
Miles 0 10 20 30
0 20 40 Kms
N
FROST RIND (OE *frost*+–) 1Nb.1–4/6/9, 3Du.2
FROSTY RIME (—+-Y+—) 2Cu.5
RIME 18Nth.5 very heavy frost on trees, 21Nf.2 dew
RIME-FROST 6Y.+20, 10L.2–7/13/14, 21Nf.1/5/6/10, 22Sf.1, 29Ess.10/11, 30MxL.+1
WATER RIME (OE *wæter*+—)10L.3
WHITE HIME (OE *hwīt*+—) 9Nt.2
WHITE HIND 6Y.15
WHITE RAG 6Y.5
WHITE RIME 10L.+3/9, 18Nth.1, 25Oxf.5
WHITE RIND 3Du.5

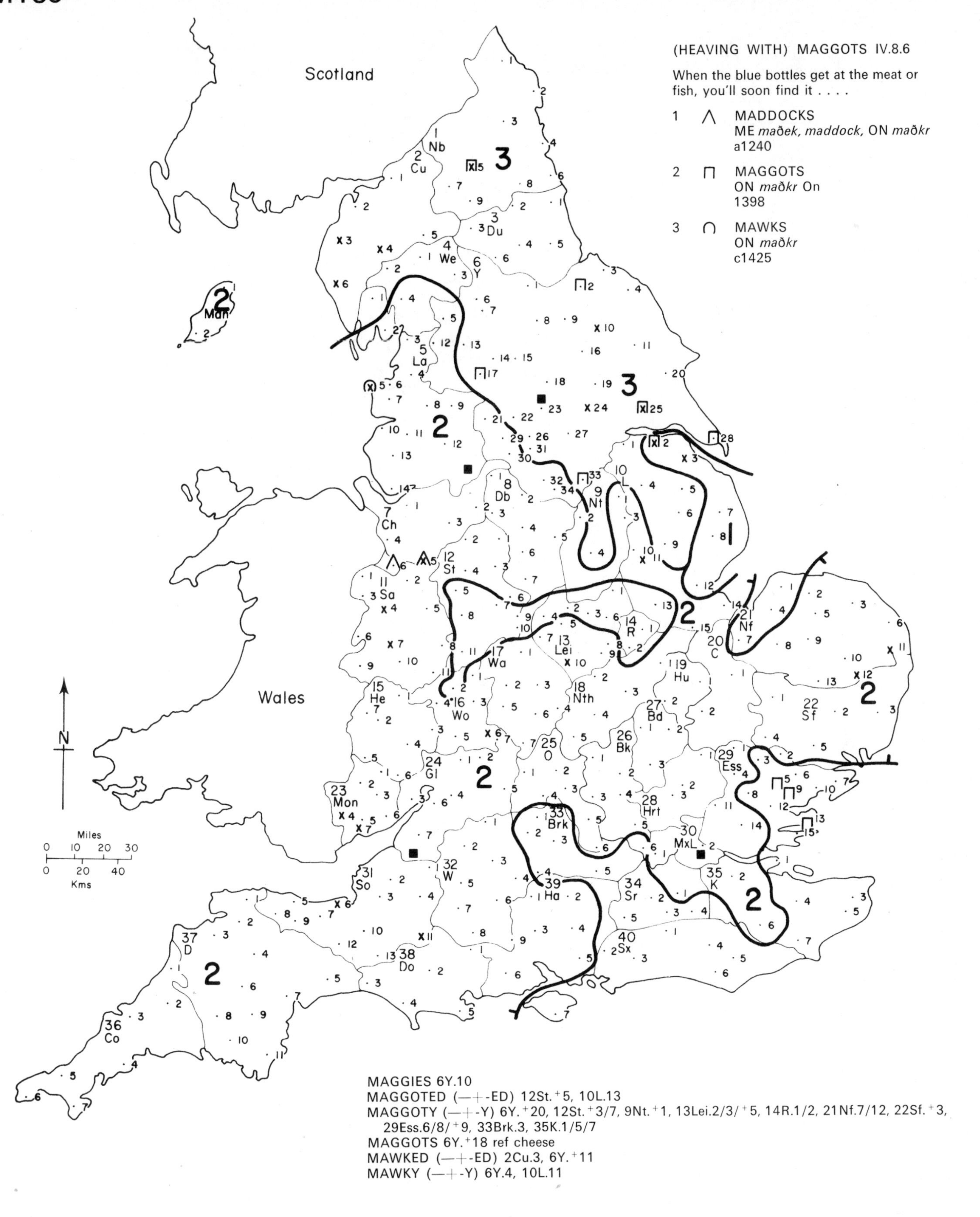
(HEAVING WITH) MAGGOTS IV.8.6
When the blue bottles get at the meat or fish, you'll soon find it . . . .
1 MADDOCKS
ME *maðek, maddock,* ON *maðkr*
a1240
2 MAGGOTS
ON *maðkr* On
1398
3 MAWKS
ON *maðkr*
c1425
Scotland
Wales
Man
Miles 0 10 20 30
Kms 0 20 40
N
MAGGIES 6Y.10
MAGGOTED (—+-ED) 12St.+5, 10L.13
MAGGOTY (—+-Y) 6Y.+20, 12St.+3/7, 9Nt.+1, 13Lei.2/3/+5, 14R.1/2, 21Nf.7/12, 22Sf.+3, 29Ess.6/8/+9, 33Brk.3, 35K.1/5/7
MAGGOTS 6Y.+18 ref cheese
MAWKED (—+-ED) 2Cu.3, 6Y.+11
MAWKY (—+-Y) 6Y.4, 10L.11

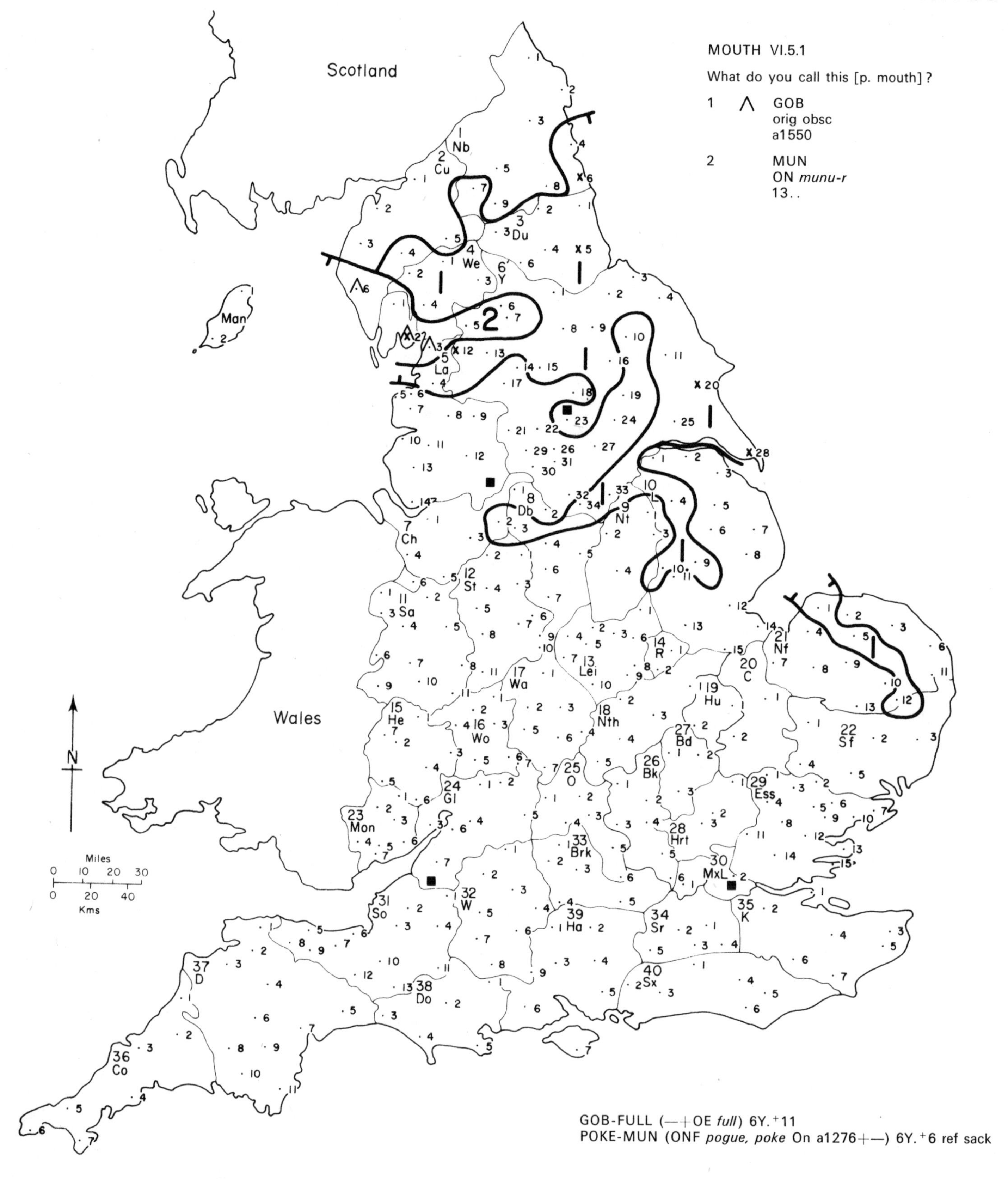
MOUTH VI.5.1
What do you call this [p. mouth]?
1 Λ GOB
orig obsc
a1550
2 MUN
ON munu-r
13..
Scotland
Wales
Man
N
Miles
0 10 20 30
0 20 40
Kms
Nb
Cu
Du
We
Y
La
Ch
Db
Nt
L
St
Sa
Lei
R
Nf
C
Hu
Wa
He
Wo
Nth
Bd
Sf
Gl
O
Bk
Ess
Mon
Brk
Hrt
MxL
So
W
Ha
Sr
K
D
Do
Sx
Co
GOB-FULL (—+OE full) 6Y.+11
POKE-MUN (ONF pogue, poke On a1276+—) 6Y.+6 ref sack

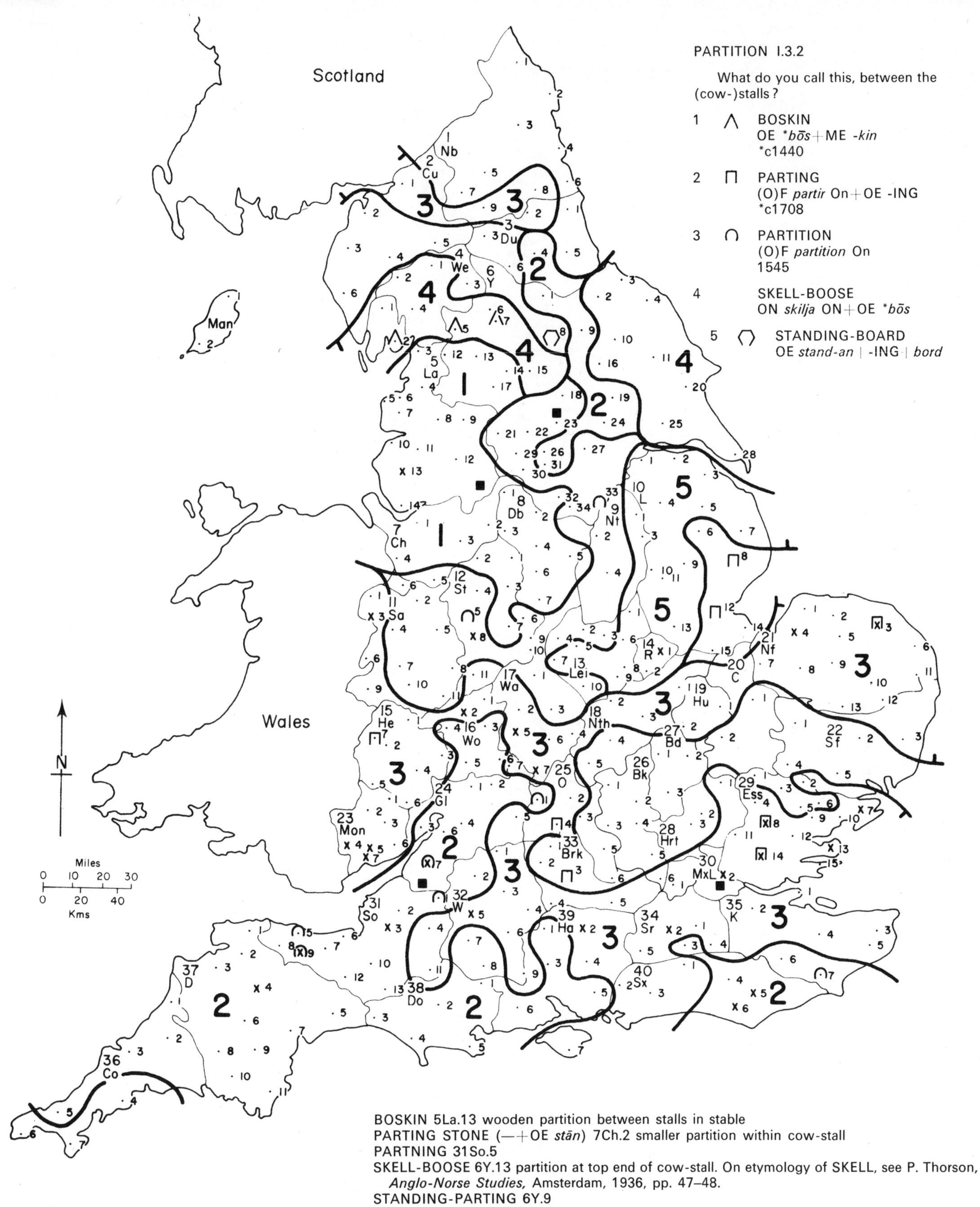

BOSKIN 5La.13 wooden partition between stalls in stable
PARTING STONE (—+OE *stān*) 7Ch.2 smaller partition within cow-stall
PARTNING 31So.5
SKELL-BOOSE 6Y.13 partition at top end of cow-stall. On etymology of SKELL, see P. Thorson, *Anglo-Norse Studies*, Amsterdam, 1936, pp. 47–48.
STANDING-PARTING 6Y.9

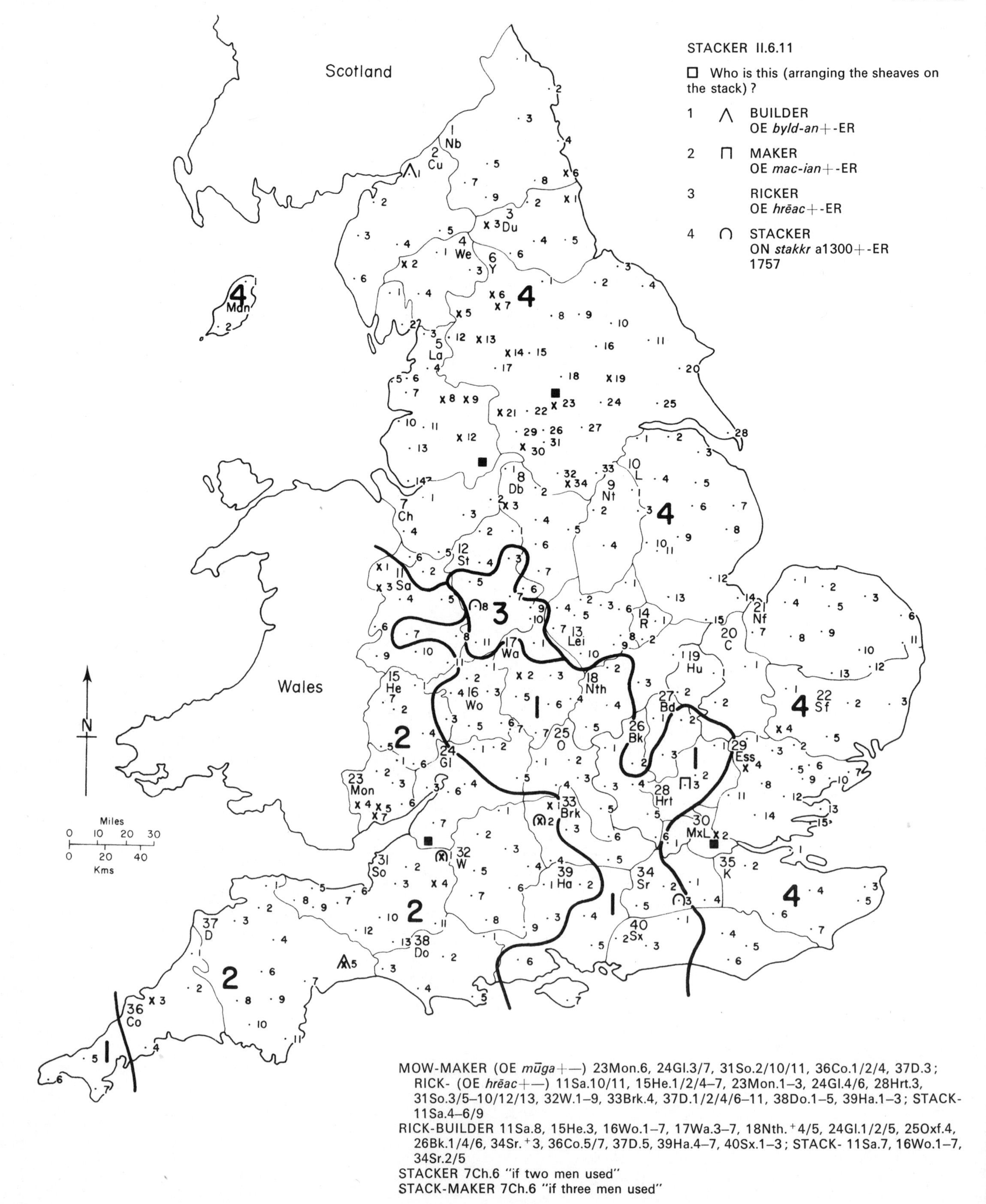

MOW-MAKER (OE *mūga*+—) 23Mon.6, 24Gl.3/7, 31So.2/10/11, 36Co.1/2/4, 37D.3; RICK- (OE *hrēac*+—) 11Sa.10/11, 15He.1/2/4–7, 23Mon.1–3, 24Gl.4/6, 28Hrt.3, 31So.3/5–10/12/13, 32W.1–9, 33Brk.4, 37D.1/2/4/6–11, 38Do.1–5, 39Ha.1–3; STACK- 11Sa.4–6/9

RICK-BUILDER 11Sa.8, 15He.3, 16Wo.1–7, 17Wa.3–7, 18Nth.+4/5, 24Gl.1/2/5, 25Oxf.4, 26Bk.1/4/6, 34Sr.+3, 36Co.5/7, 37D.5, 39Ha.4–7, 40Sx.1–3; STACK- 11Sa.7, 16Wo.1–7, 34Sr.2/5

STACKER 7Ch.6 "if two men used"

STACK-MAKER 7Ch.6 "if three men used"

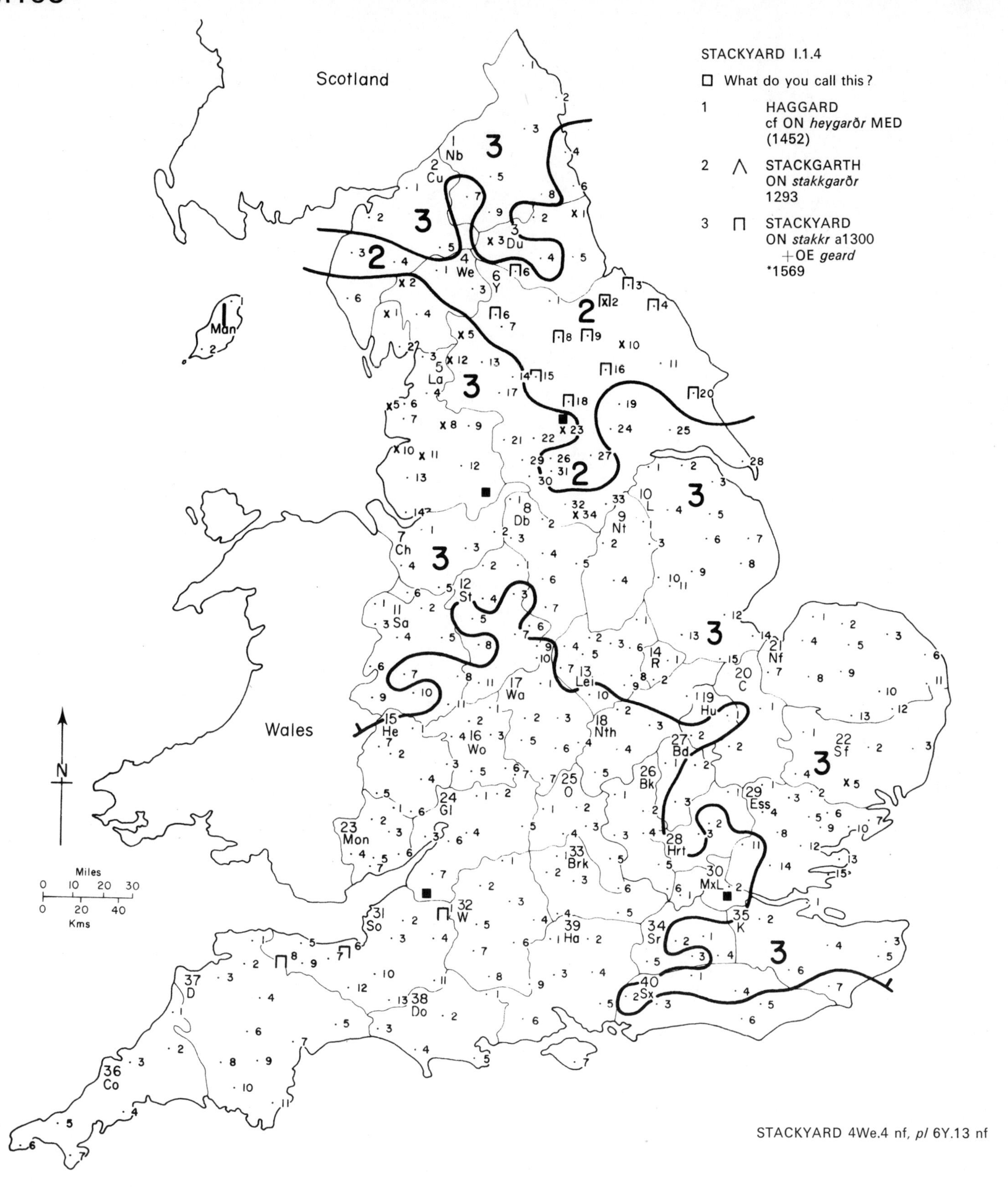

STACKYARD I.1.4
☐ What do you call this?
1 HAGGARD cf ON *heygarðr* MED (1452)
2 ⋀ STACKGARTH ON *stakkgarðr* 1293
3 ⊓ STACKYARD ON *stakkr* a1300 +OE *geard* *1569
Scotland
Wales
Man
N
Miles 0 10 20 30
0 20 40 Kms
STACKYARD 4We.4 nf, *pl* 6Y.13 nf

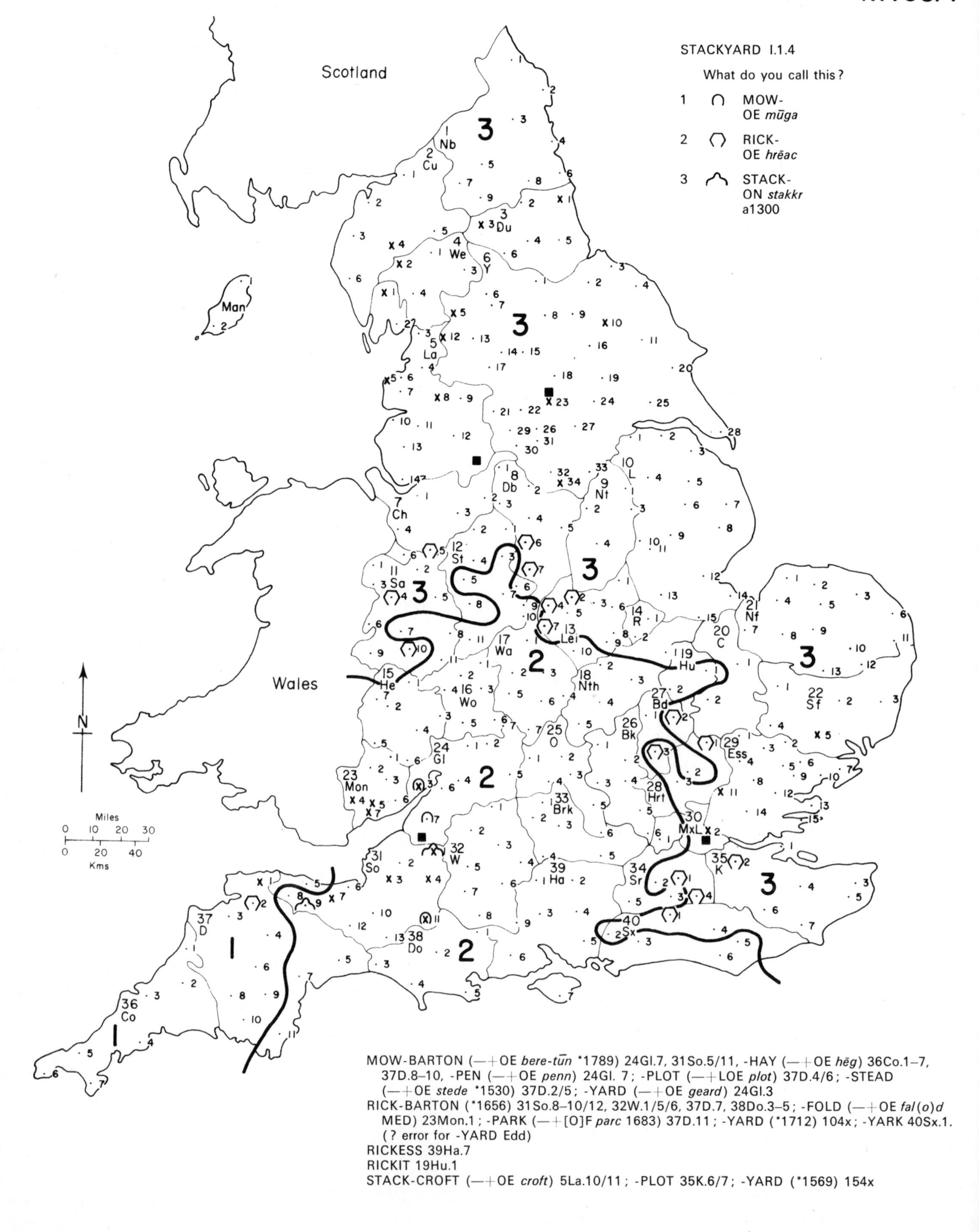

MOW-BARTON (—+OE *bere-tūn* *1789) 24Gl.7, 31So.5/11, -HAY (—+OE *hēg*) 36Co.1–7, 37D.8–10, -PEN (—+OE *penn*) 24Gl. 7; -PLOT (—+LOE *plot*) 37D.4/6; -STEAD (—+OE *stede* *1530) 37D.2/5; -YARD (—+OE *geard*) 24Gl.3

RICK-BARTON (*1656) 31So.8–10/12, 32W.1/5/6, 37D.7, 38Do.3–5; -FOLD (—+OE *fal(o)d* MED) 23Mon.1; -PARK (—+[O]F *parc* 1683) 37D.11; -YARD (*1712) 104x; -YARK 40Sx.1. (? error for -YARD Edd)

RICKESS 39Ha.7

RICKIT 19Hu.1

STACK-CROFT (—+OE *croft*) 5La.10/11; -PLOT 35K.6/7; -YARD (*1569) 154x

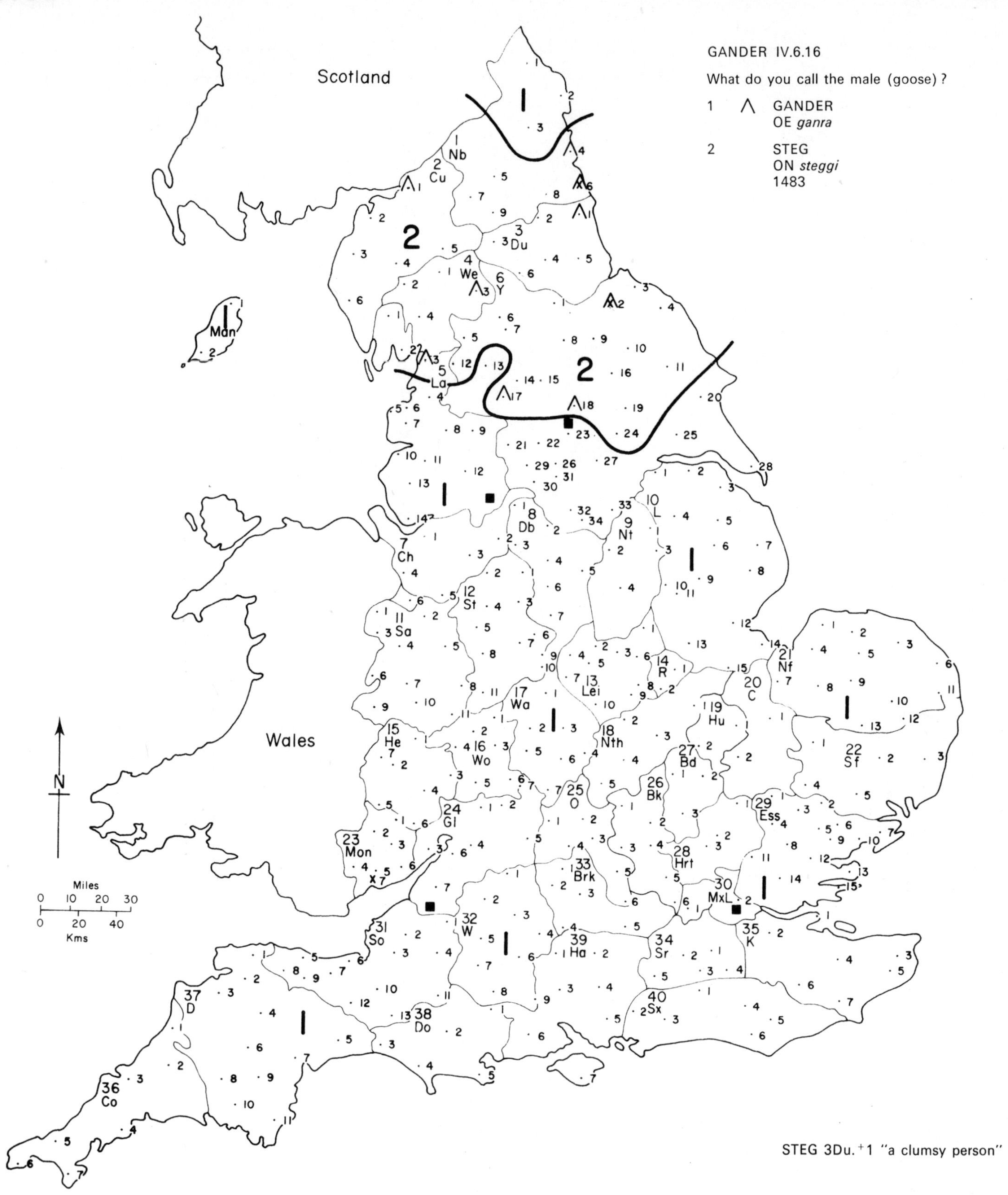
GANDER IV.6.16
What do you call the male (goose) ?
1 ⋀ GANDER
OE *ganra*
2 STEG
ON *steggi*
1483
Scotland
Wales
N
Miles
0 10 20 30
0 20 40
Kms
Nb
Cu
Du
We
Y
Man
La
Ch
Db
Nt
L
St
Sa
R
Lei
Nf
C
Hu
Wa
He
Wo
Nth
Bd
Sf
Bk
O
Gl
Mon
Ess
Hrt
Brk
MxL
W
So
Ha
Sr
K
D
Do
Sx
Co
STEG 3Du. +1 "a clumsy person"

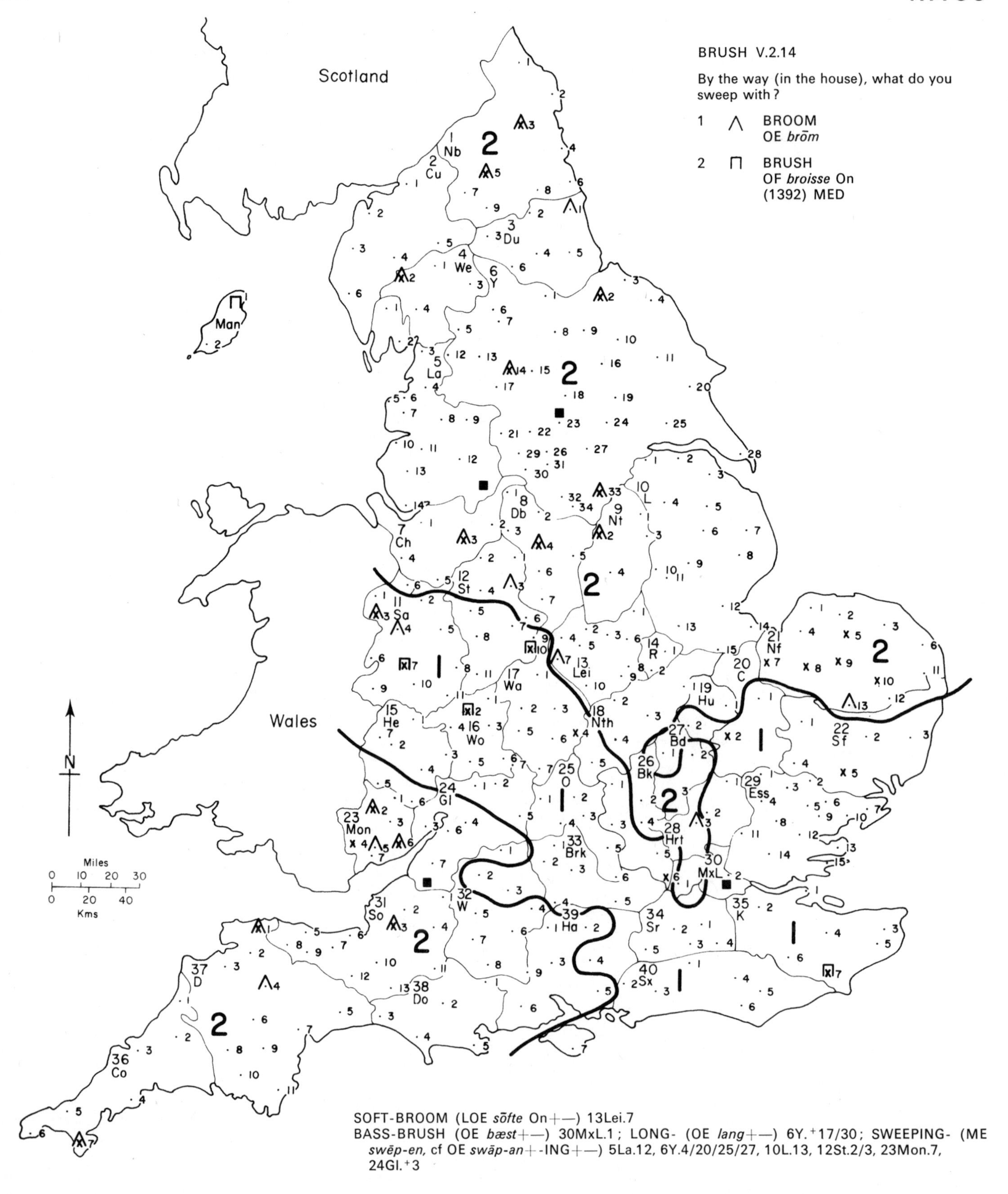

SOFT-BROOM (LOE *sōfte* On+—) 13Lei.7
BASS-BRUSH (OE *bæst*+—) 30MxL.1; LONG- (OE *lang*+—) 6Y.+17/30; SWEEPING- (ME *swēp-en,* cf OE *swāp-an*+-ING+—) 5La.12, 6Y.4/20/25/27, 10L.13, 12St.2/3, 23Mon.7, 24Gl.+3

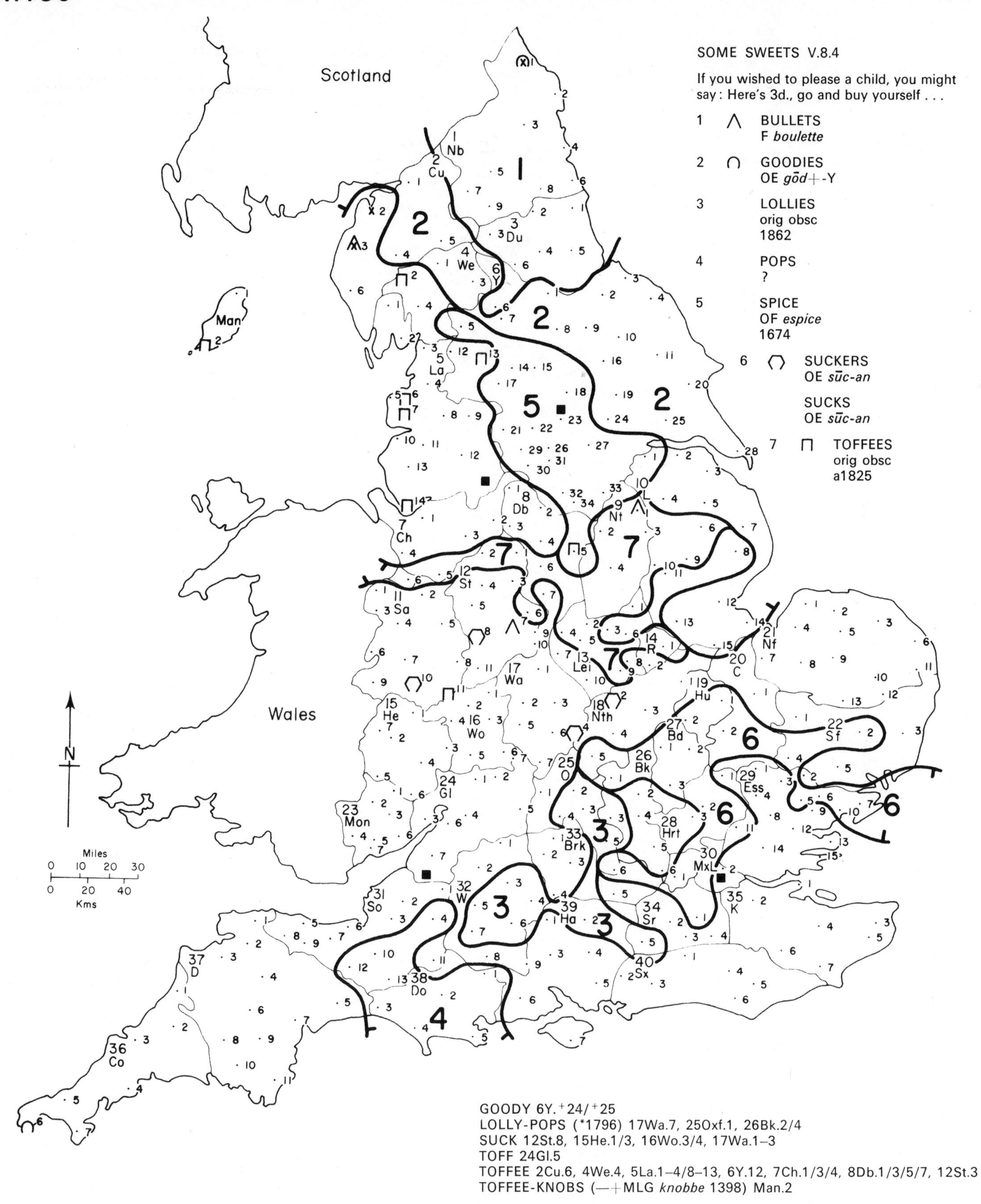

SOME SWEETS V.8.4
If you wished to please a child, you might say: Here's 3d., go and buy yourself . . .
1 BULLETS F *boulette*
2 GOODIES OE *gōd*+-Y
3 LOLLIES orig obsc 1862
4 POPS ?
5 SPICE OF *espice* 1674
6 SUCKERS OE *sūc-an*
SUCKS OE *sūc-an*
7 TOFFEES orig obsc a1825
Scotland
Wales
Man
N
Miles 0 10 20 30
0 20 40 Kms
GOODY 6Y.+24/+25
LOLLY-POPS (*1796) 17Wa.7, 25Oxf.1, 26Bk.2/4
SUCK 12St.8, 15He.1/3, 16Wo.3/4, 17Wa.1–3
TOFF 24Gl.5
TOFFEE 2Cu.6, 4We.4, 5La.1–4/8–13, 6Y.12, 7Ch.1/3/4, 8Db.1/3/5/7, 12St.3
TOFFEE-KNOBS (—+MLG *knobbe* 1398) Man.2

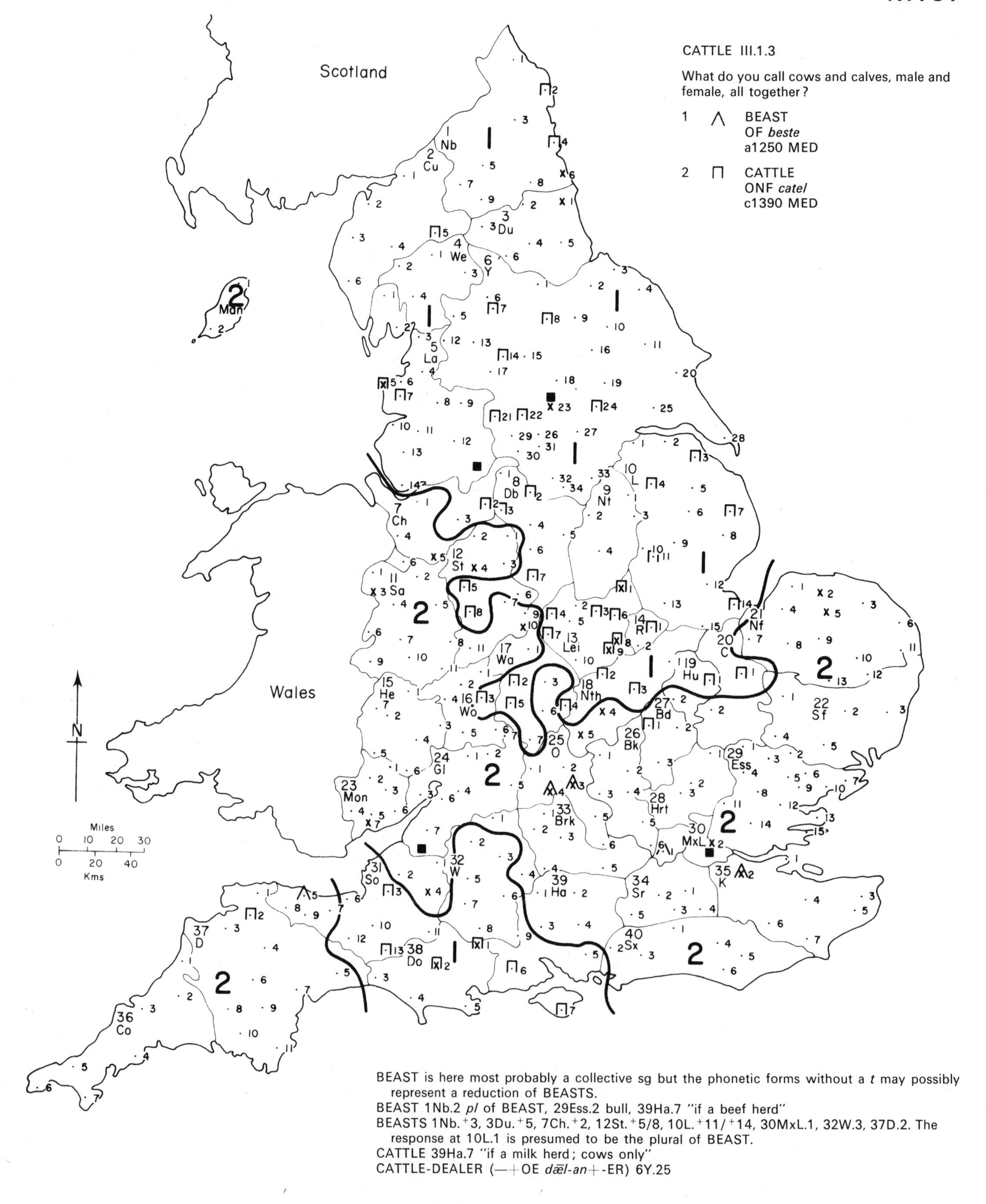

BEAST is here most probably a collective sg but the phonetic forms without a *t* may possibly represent a reduction of BEASTS.
BEAST 1Nb.2 *pl* of BEAST, 29Ess.2 bull, 39Ha.7 "if a beef herd"
BEASTS 1Nb.+3, 3Du.+5, 7Ch.+2, 12St.+5/8, 10L.+11/+14, 30MxL.1, 32W.3, 37D.2. The response at 10L.1 is presumed to be the plural of BEAST.
CATTLE 39Ha.7 "if a milk herd; cows only"
CATTLE-DEALER (—+OE *dǣl-an*+-ER) 6Y.25

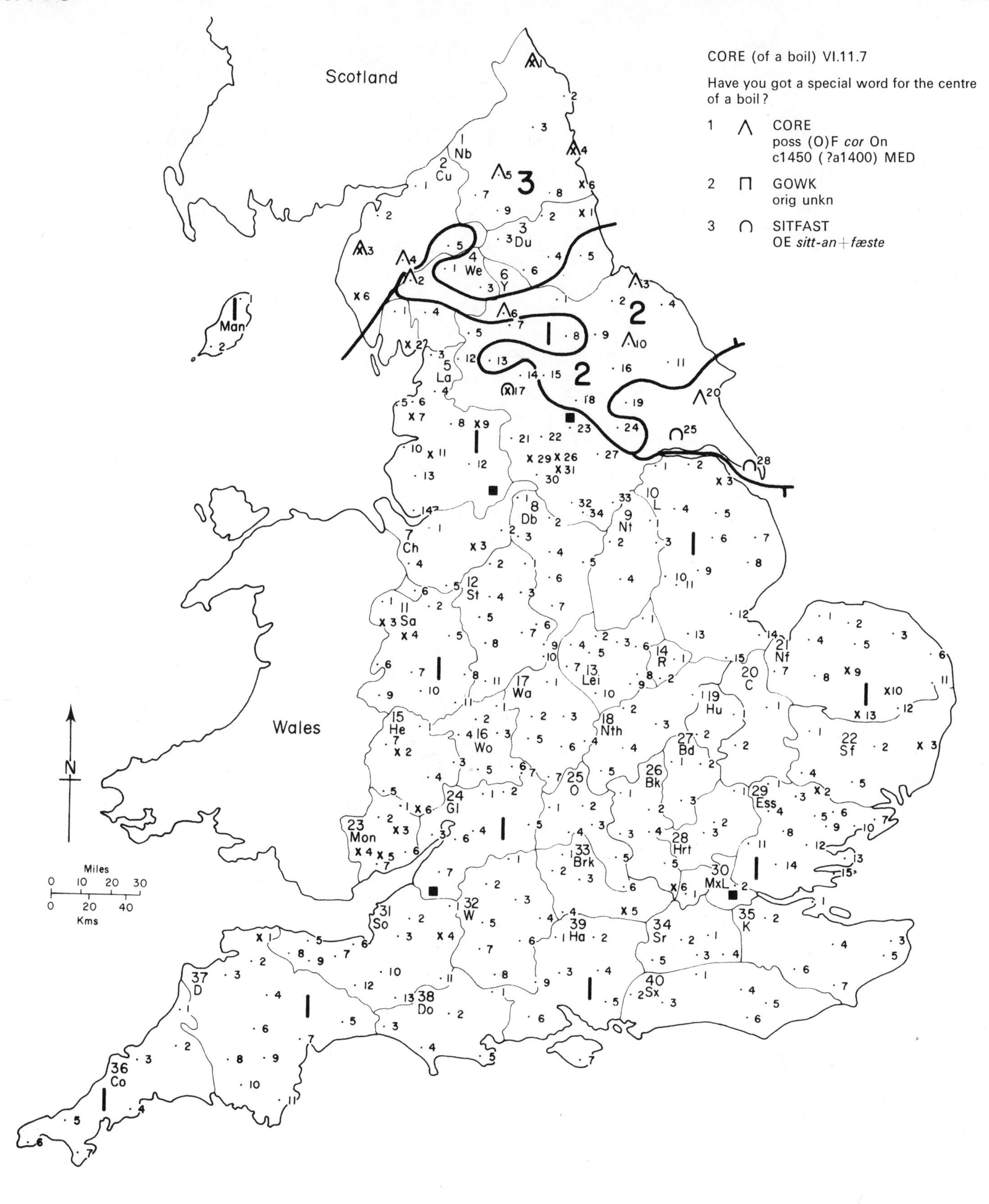
CORE (of a boil) VI.11.7
Have you got a special word for the centre of a boil?
1 CORE
poss (O)F *cor* On
c1450 (?a1400) MED
2 GOWK
orig unkn
3 SITFAST
OE *sitt-an*+*fæste*
Scotland
Wales
Man
N
Miles
0 10 20 30
0 20 40
Kms

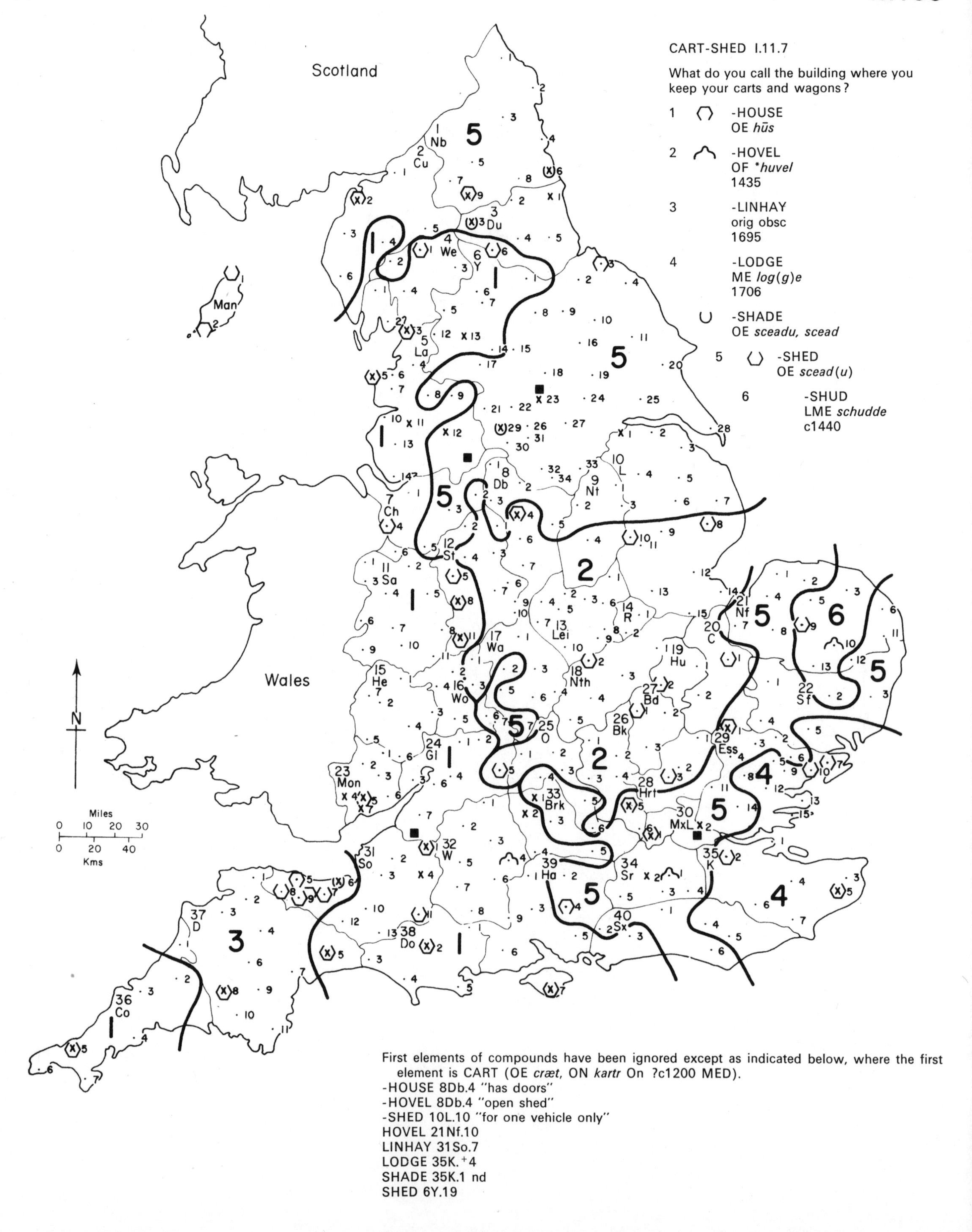

First elements of compounds have been ignored except as indicated below, where the first element is CART (OE *cræt*, ON *kartr* On ?c1200 MED).

-HOUSE 8Db.4 "has doors"
-HOVEL 8Db.4 "open shed"
-SHED 10L.10 "for one vehicle only"
HOVEL 21Nf.10
LINHAY 31So.7
LODGE 35K.+4
SHADE 35K.1 nd
SHED 6Y.19

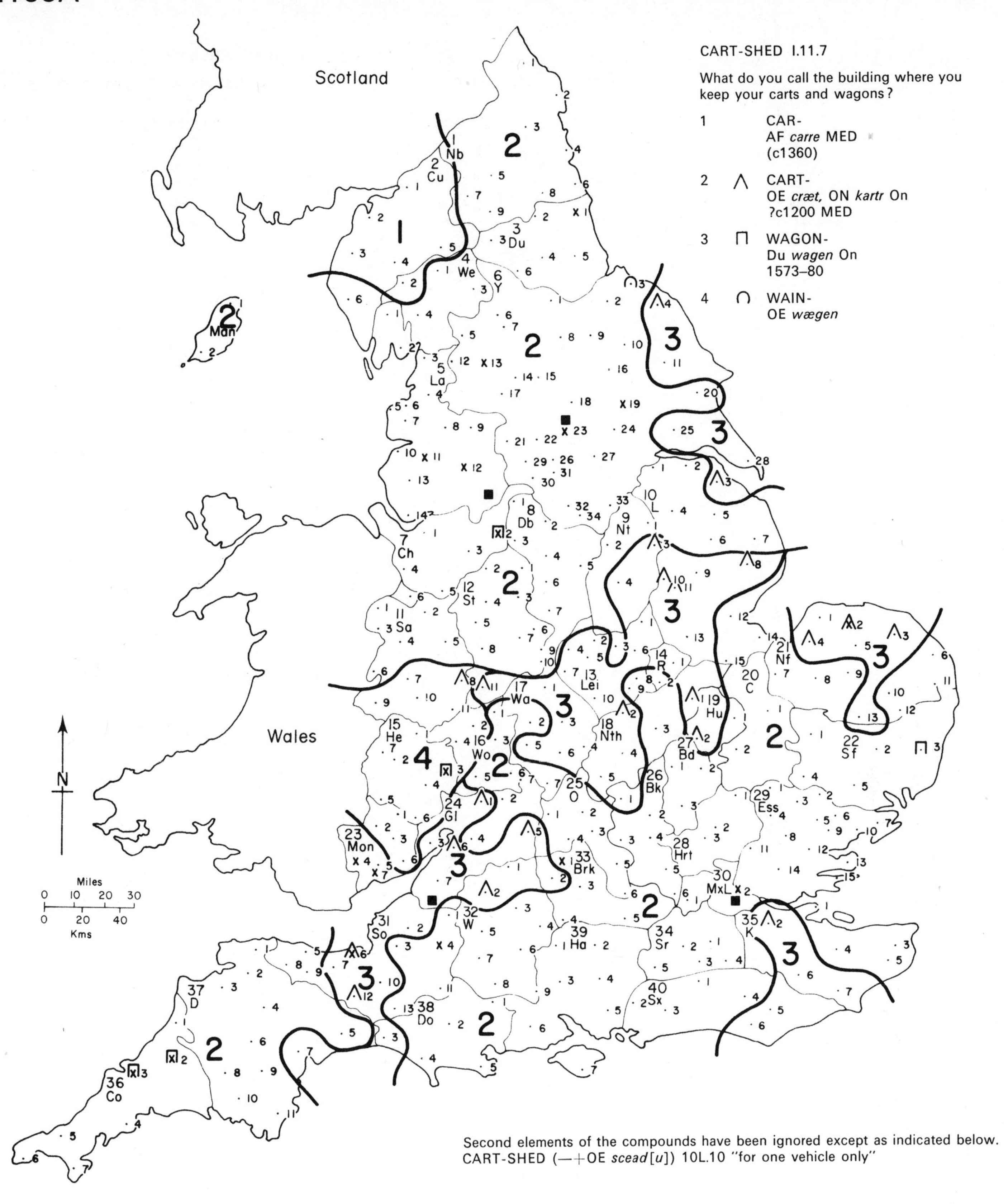

Second elements of the compounds have been ignored except as indicated below.
CART-SHED (—+OE *scead[u]*) 10L.10 "for one vehicle only"

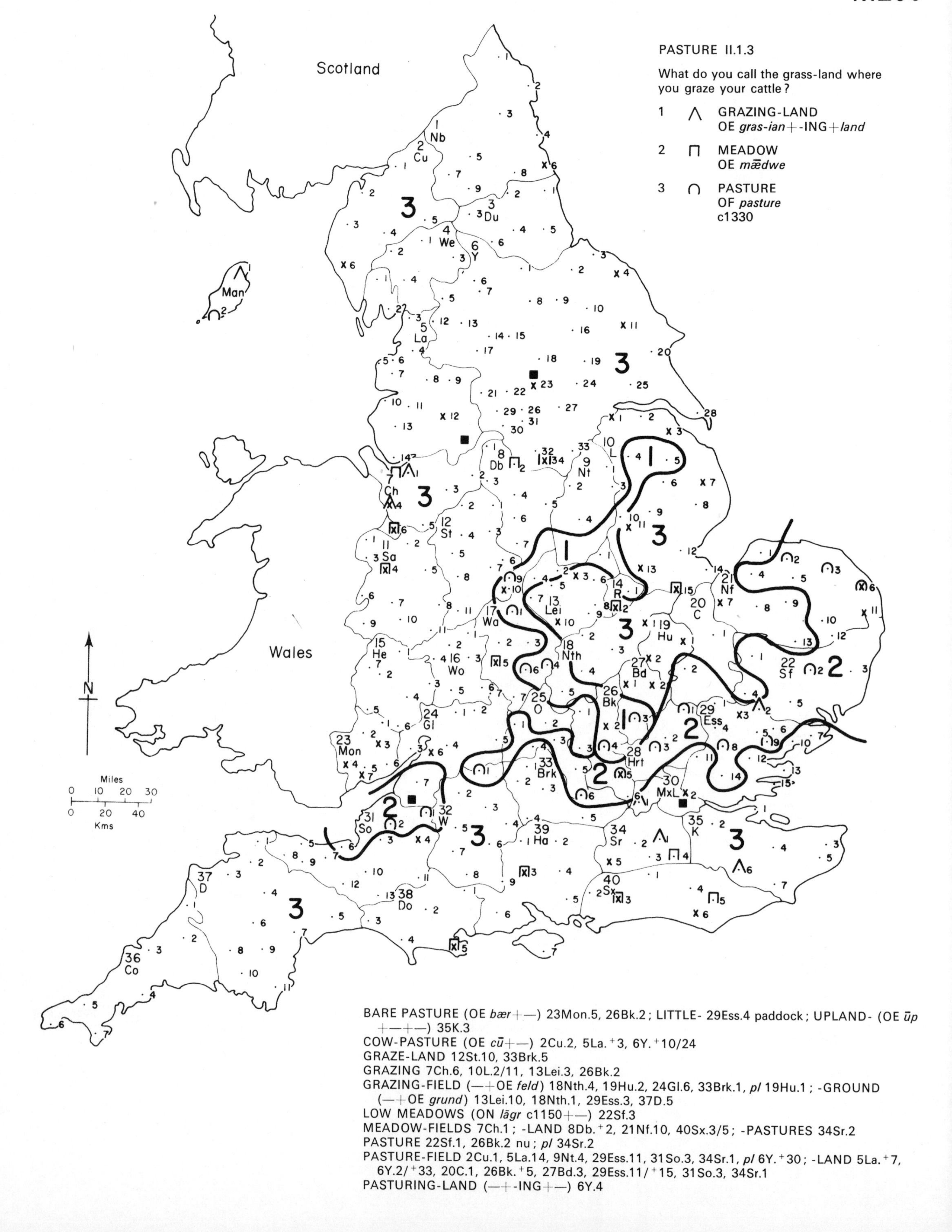

BARE PASTURE (OE *bær* + —) 23Mon.5, 26Bk.2; LITTLE- 29Ess.4 paddock; UPLAND- (OE *ūp* + — + —) 35K.3

COW-PASTURE (OE *cū* + —) 2Cu.2, 5La.+3, 6Y.+10/24

GRAZE-LAND 12St.10, 33Brk.5

GRAZING 7Ch.6, 10L.2/11, 13Lei.3, 26Bk.2

GRAZING-FIELD (— + OE *feld*) 18Nth.4, 19Hu.2, 24Gl.6, 33Brk.1, *pl* 19Hu.1; -GROUND (— + OE *grund*) 13Lei.10, 18Nth.1, 29Ess.3, 37D.5

LOW MEADOWS (ON *lāgr* c1150 + —) 22Sf.3

MEADOW-FIELDS 7Ch.1; -LAND 8Db.+2, 21Nf.10, 40Sx.3/5; -PASTURES 34Sr.2

PASTURE 22Sf.1, 26Bk.2 nu; *pl* 34Sr.2

PASTURE-FIELD 2Cu.1, 5La.14, 9Nt.4, 29Ess.11, 31So.3, 34Sr.1, *pl* 6Y.+30; -LAND 5La.+7, 6Y.2/+33, 20C.1, 26Bk.+5, 27Bd.3, 29Ess.11/+15, 31So.3, 34Sr.1

PASTURING-LAND (— + -ING + —) 6Y.4

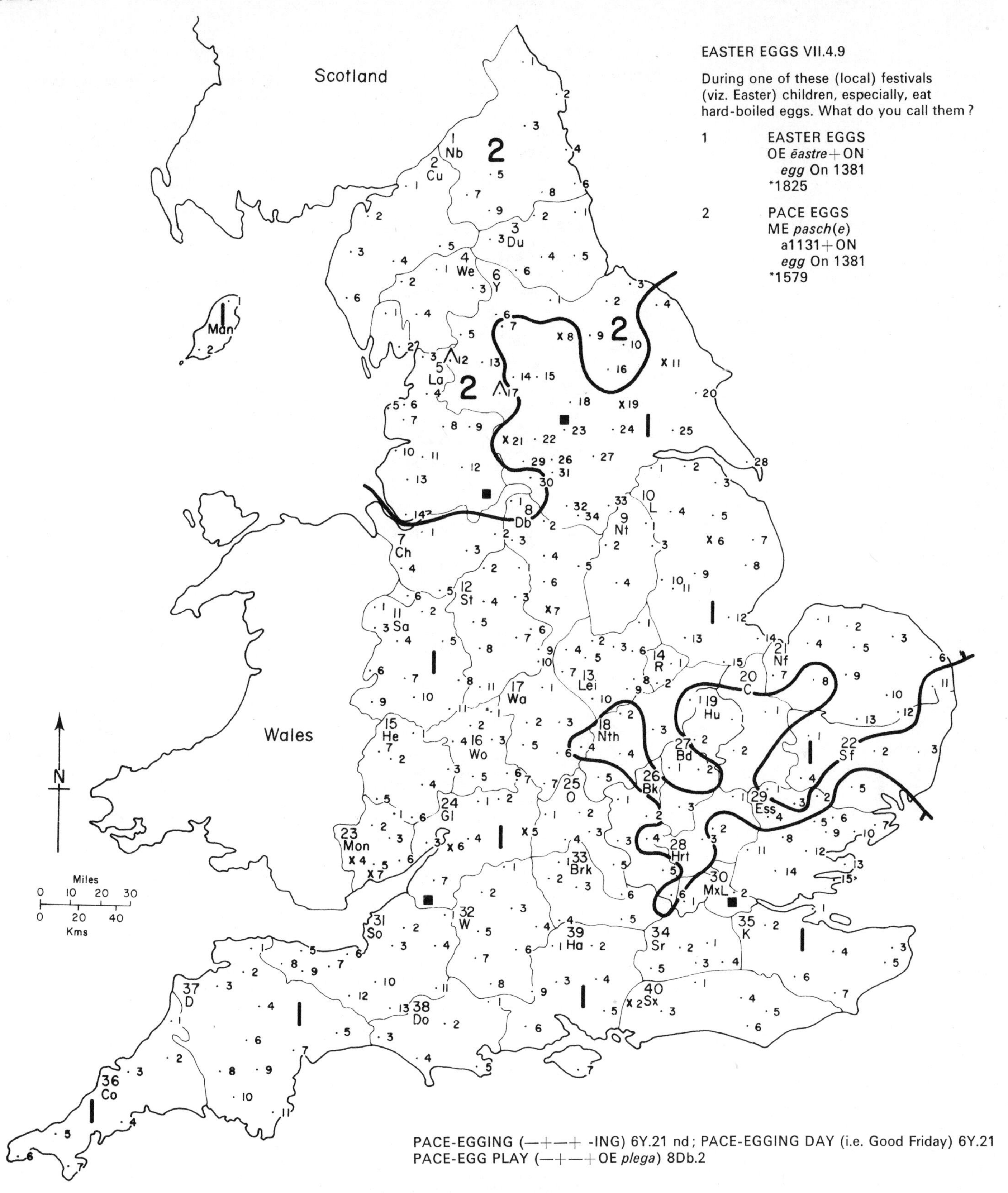
EASTER EGGS VII.4.9
During one of these (local) festivals (viz. Easter) children, especially, eat hard-boiled eggs. What do you call them?
1 EASTER EGGS
OE *ēastre*+ON *egg* On 1381
*1825
2 PACE EGGS
ME *pasch(e)* a1131+ON *egg* On 1381
*1579
Scotland
Wales
N
Miles
0 10 20 30
0 20 40
Kms
PACE-EGGING (—+—+ -ING) 6Y.21 nd; PACE-EGGING DAY (i.e. Good Friday) 6Y.21
PACE-EGG PLAY (—+—+OE *plega*) 8Db.2

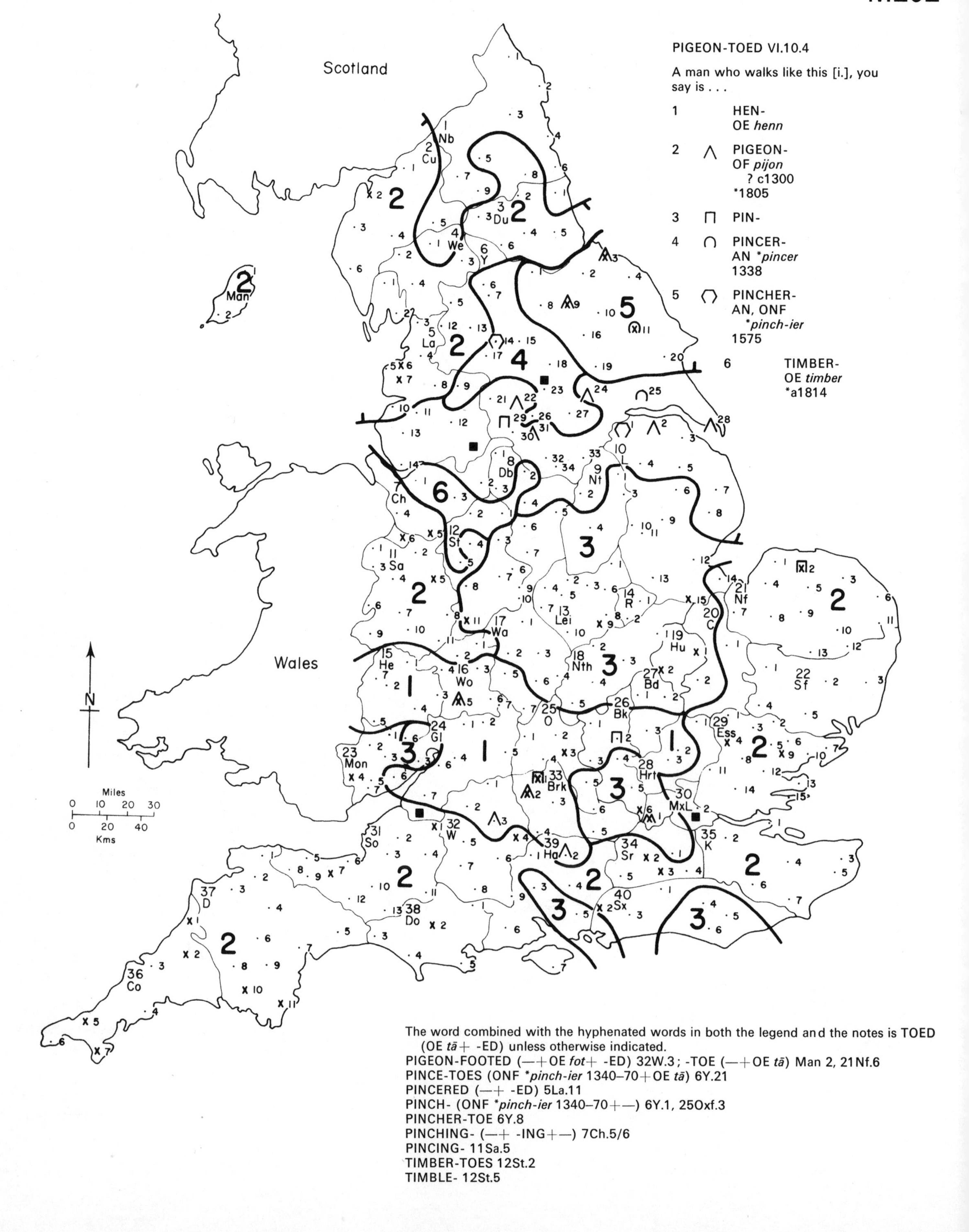

The word combined with the hyphenated words in both the legend and the notes is TOED (OE *tā*+ -ED) unless otherwise indicated.

PIGEON-FOOTED (—+OE *fot*+ -ED) 32W.3; -TOE (—+OE *tā*) Man 2, 21Nf.6

PINCE-TOES (ONF **pinch-ier* 1340–70+OE *tā*) 6Y.21

PINCERED (—+ -ED) 5La.11

PINCH- (ONF **pinch-ier* 1340–70+—) 6Y.1, 25Oxf.3

PINCHER-TOE 6Y.8

PINCHING- (—+ -ING+—) 7Ch.5/6

PINCING- 11Sa.5

TIMBER-TOES 12St.2

TIMBLE- 12St.5

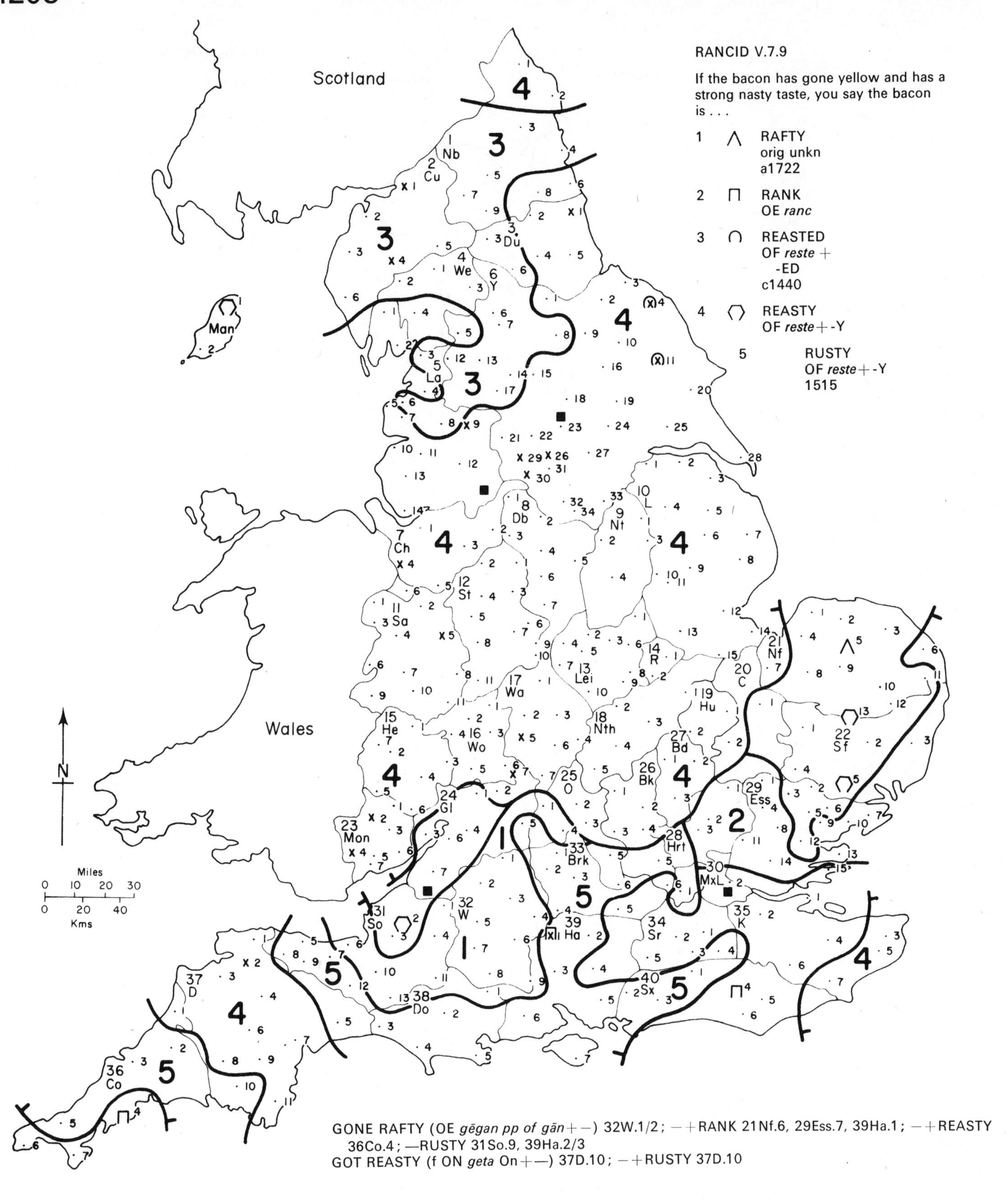
RANCID V.7.9
If the bacon has gone yellow and has a strong nasty taste, you say the bacon is . . .
1 RAFTY orig unkn a1722
2 RANK OE *ranc*
3 REASTED OF *reste* + -ED c1440
4 REASTY OF *reste* + -Y
5 RUSTY OF *reste* + -Y 1515
Scotland
Wales
Man
Nb
Cu
Du
We
Y
La
Ch
Db
Nt
L
St
Sa
Lei
R
Nf
C
Hu
Wa
He
Wo
Nth
Bd
Sf
Bk
O
Gl
Mon
Ess
Hrt
Brk
MxL
So
W
Ha
Sr
K
Sx
Do
D
Co
Miles
0 10 20 30
0 20 40
Kms
N
GONE RAFTY (OE *gēgan pp of gān* + —) 32W.1/2; — + RANK 21Nf.6, 29Ess.7, 39Ha.1; — + REASTY 36Co.4; —RUSTY 31So.9, 39Ha.2/3
GOT REASTY (f ON *geta* On + —) 37D.10; — + RUSTY 37D.10

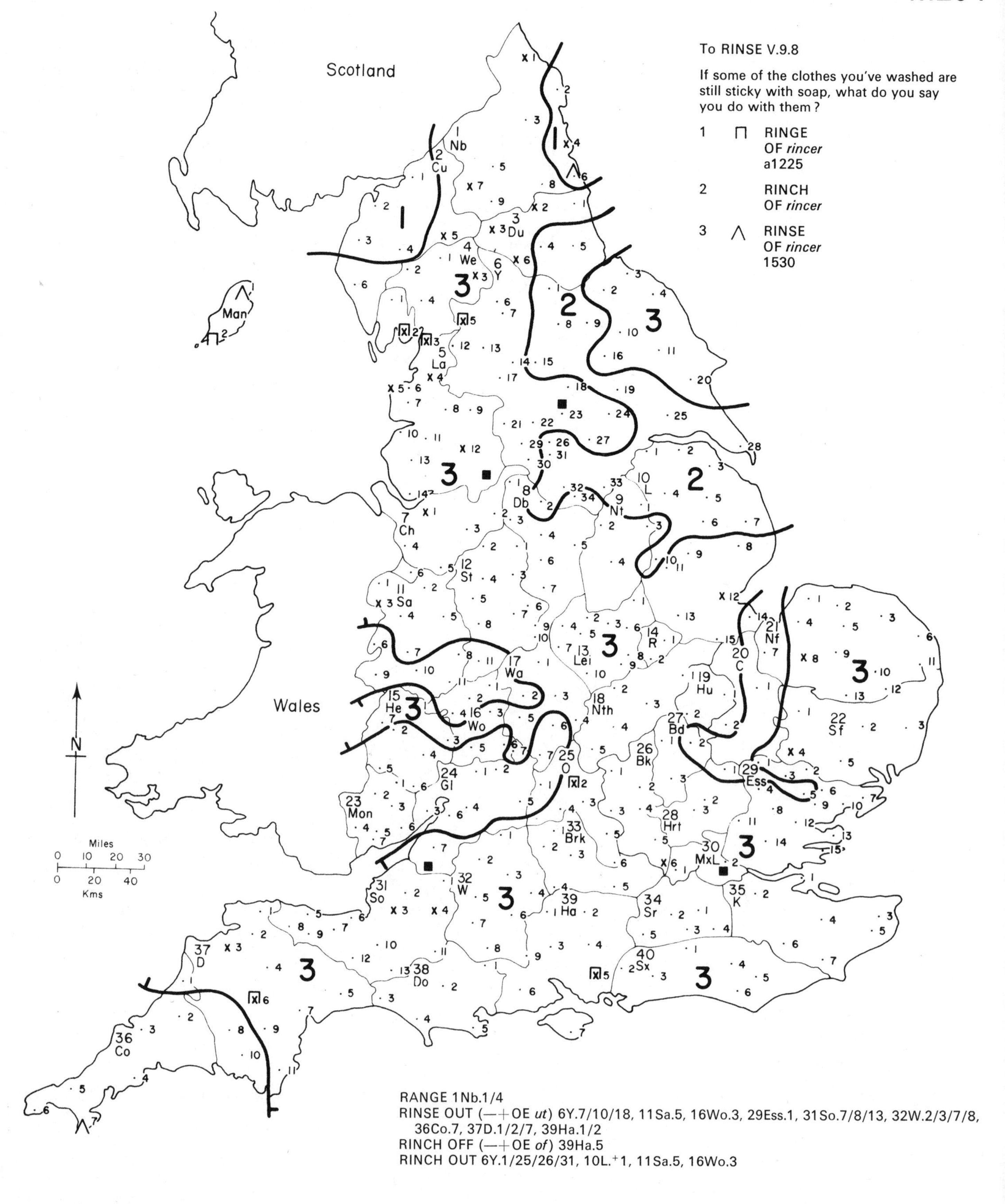

RANGE 1Nb.1/4

RINSE OUT (—+OE *ut*) 6Y.7/10/18, 11Sa.5, 16Wo.3, 29Ess.1, 31So.7/8/13, 32W.2/3/7/8, 36Co.7, 37D.1/2/7, 39Ha.1/2

RINCH OFF (—+OE *of*) 39Ha.5

RINCH OUT 6Y.1/25/26/31, 10L.+1, 11Sa.5, 16Wo.3

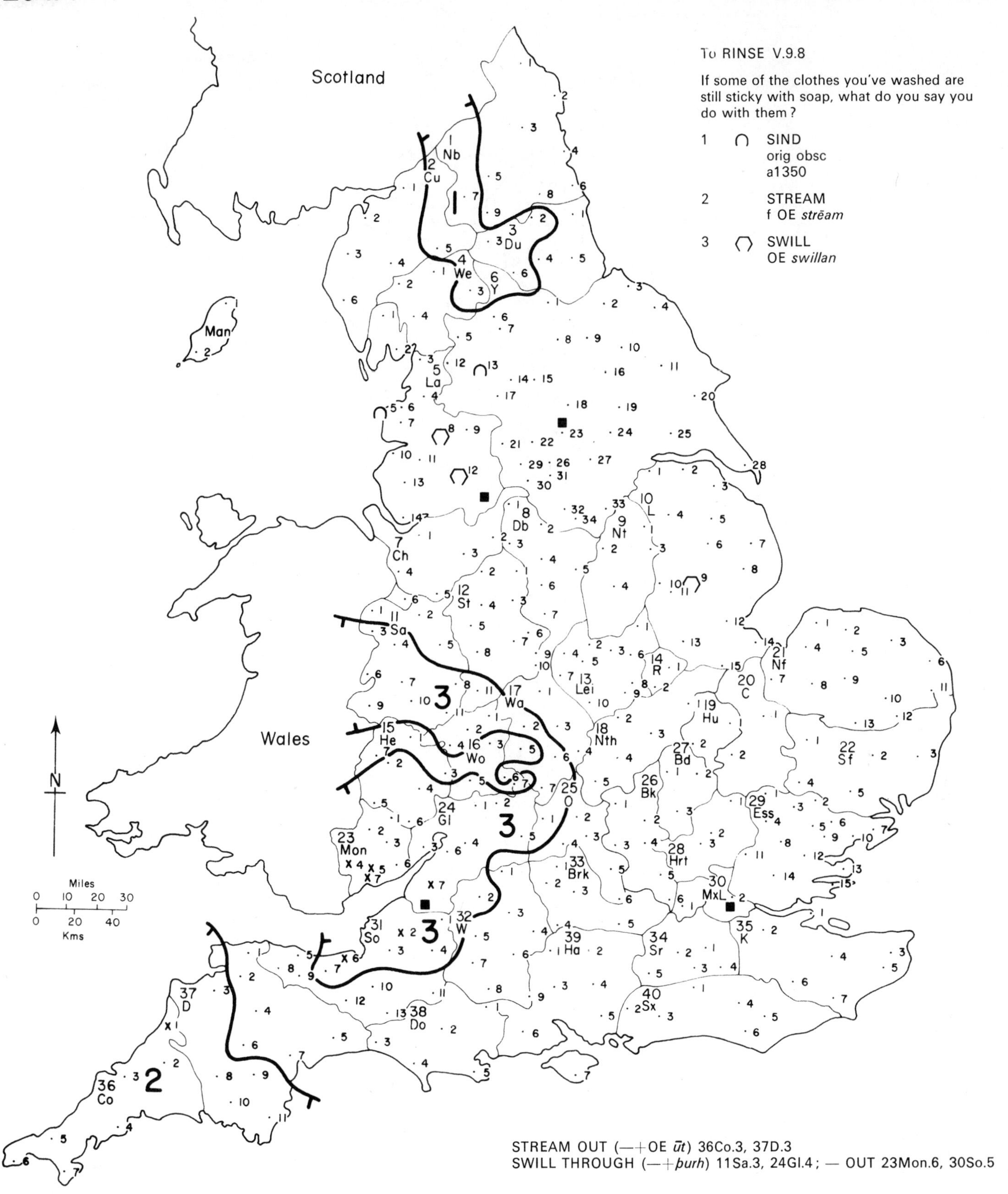
To RINSE V.9.8
If some of the clothes you've washed are still sticky with soap, what do you say you do with them?
1 SIND orig obsc a1350
2 STREAM f OE strēam
3 SWILL OE swillan
Scotland
Wales
Man
N
Miles 0 10 20 30
0 20 40 Kms
STREAM OUT (—+OE ūt) 36Co.3, 37D.3
SWILL THROUGH (—+þurh) 11Sa.3, 24Gl.4; — OUT 23Mon.6, 30So.5

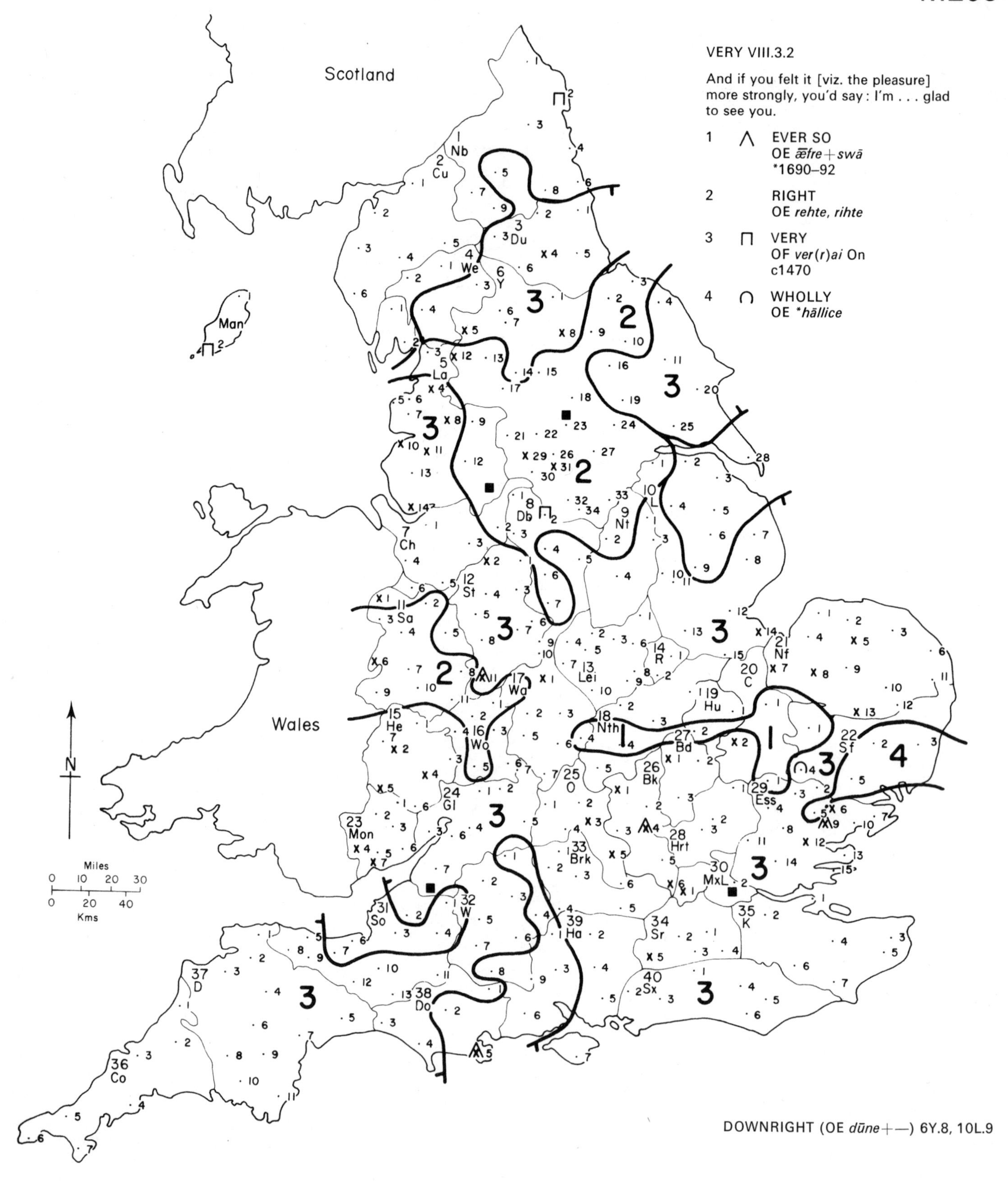
VERY VIII.3.2
And if you felt it [viz. the pleasure] more strongly, you'd say: I'm . . . glad to see you.
1 Λ EVER SO
OE ǣfre+swā
*1690–92
2 RIGHT
OE rehte, rihte
3 ⊓ VERY
OF ver(r)ai On
c1470
4 ∩ WHOLLY
OE *hāllice
Scotland
Wales
Man
N
Miles
0 10 20 30
0 20 40
Kms
DOWNRIGHT (OE dūne+—) 6Y.8, 10L.9

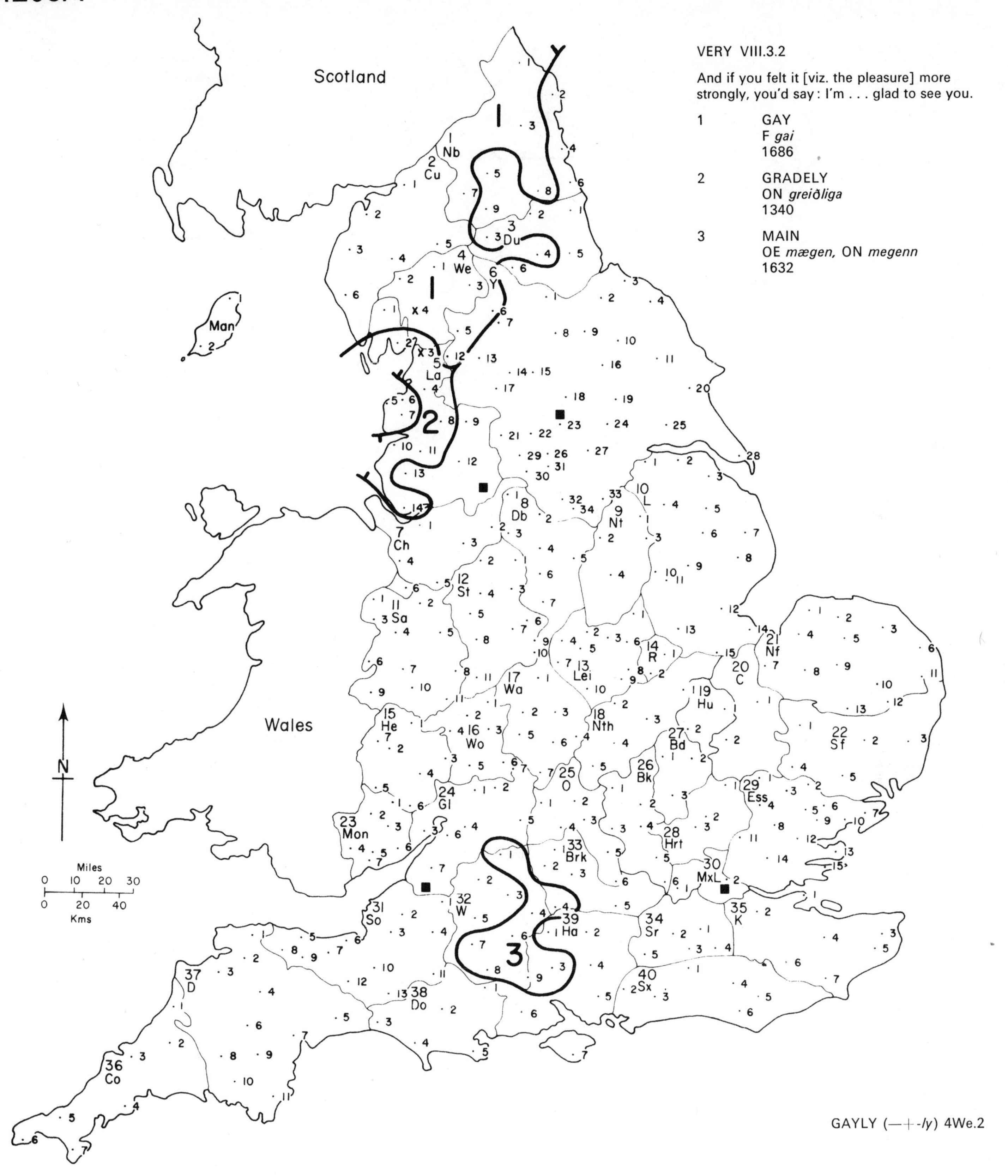
VERY VIII.3.2
And if you felt it [viz. the pleasure] more strongly, you'd say: I'm . . . glad to see you.
1 GAY
F *gai*
1686
2 GRADELY
ON *greiðliga*
1340
3 MAIN
OE *mægen,* ON *megenn*
1632
Scotland
Wales
Man
N
Miles
0 10 20 30
0 20 40
Kms
GAYLY (—+-*ly*) 4We.2

WEAKLING III.8.4

What do you call the smallest and weakest pig of the litter?

1 CAD
F *cadet*

2 CRUT
cf Welsh *crut*
1808–25

3 Λ DILLING
orig obsc
1890

4 NESTLE-TRIPE and variants
OE *nestl-ian* + (O)F *tripe* On

5 NISGAL and variants
orig obsc

6 PETMAN and variants
orig obsc

7 ⊓ RECKLING and variants
orig obsc
1781

CRIT 1Nb.1/2
DIDDLING 25Oxf.6, 30MxL.1
NESTLE 31So.3
NESTLE-BIRD 36Co.3/4, 37D.10/11; -DRAF 36Co.1, 37D.1–4/6; -DRISH 36Co.2, 37D.8
NISKRAL 23Mon.1
NISKWAL 15He.5/6, 23Mon.3
PEPMAN 21Nf.6; PIPMAN 21Nf.3/10–13, 22Sf.1–3; PITMAN 21Sf.8
RACK 20C.1/2
RACKLING 18Nth.1; RATLING 11Sa.1/3–10, 19Hu.1
RECKLIEN 6Y.2
RETLING 9Nt.+2
RICK 6Y.+19
RIDLING 5La.5/10
RINKLIN 12St.5; RINKLING 1Nb.8, 12St.5, 13Lei.1/6
RINNICK 23Mon.6, 24Gl.3/6/7, 32W.1/2
RIT 5La.4, 7Ch.1/3–6, 12St.2
RITLING 5La.10/13, 7Ch.2, 8Db.1–3/5–7, 11Sa.2, 12St.1/3/4/8
RUNTLING 13Lei.2
RUT 12St.6
RUTLING 8Db.7, 13Lei.4/5/7

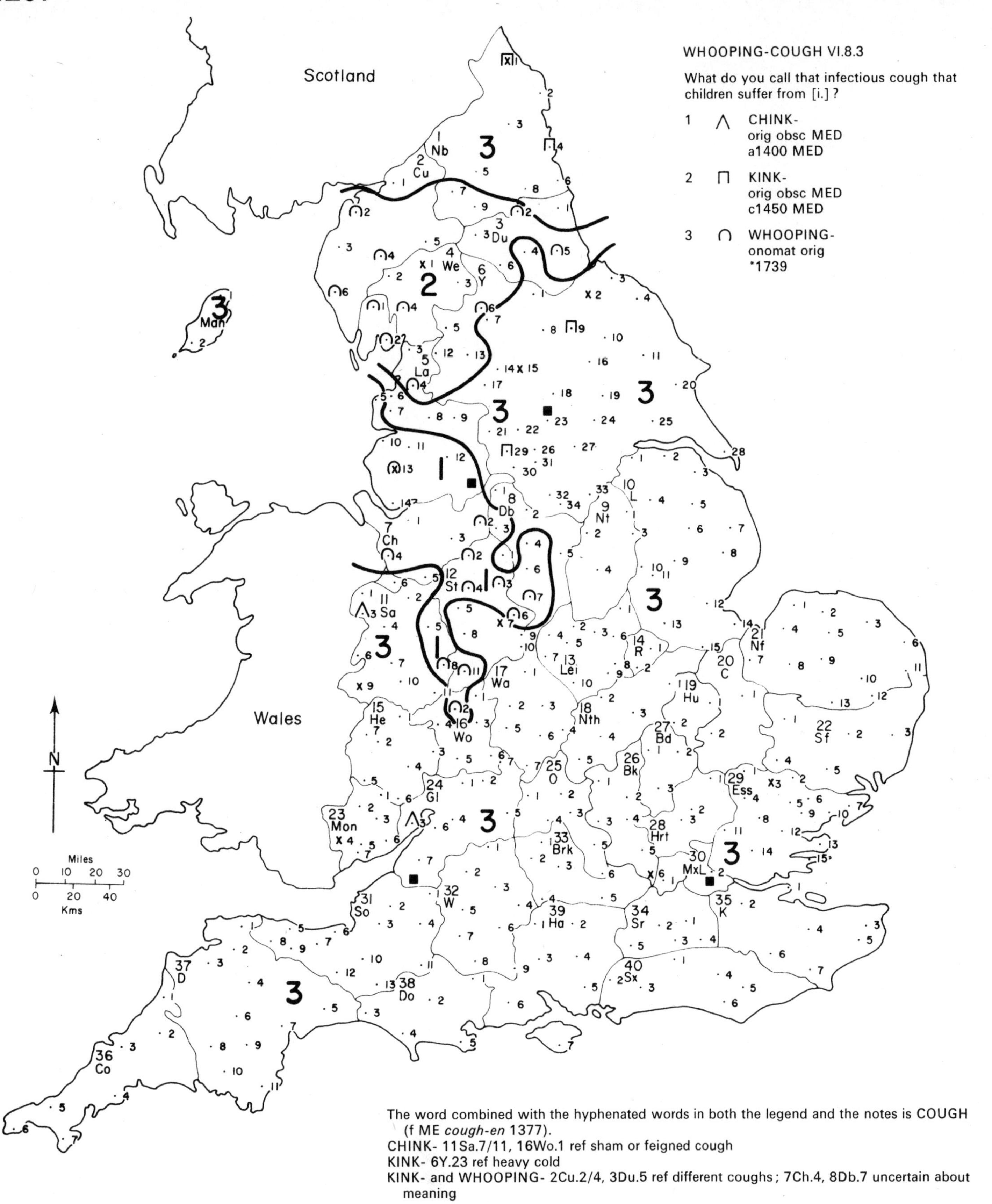

The word combined with the hyphenated words in both the legend and the notes is COUGH (f ME *cough-en* 1377).

CHINK- 11Sa.7/11, 16Wo.1 ref sham or feigned cough

KINK- 6Y.23 ref heavy cold

KINK- and WHOOPING- 2Cu.2/4, 3Du.5 ref different coughs; 7Ch.4, 8Db.7 uncertain about meaning

INDEX

In this index the numbers not preceded by M refer to pages in the Introduction. The numbers preceded by M refer to the word maps.

1. Notions Mapped

2. Responses and Words from the Incidental Material

D